LIBERTY AND UNION

LIBERTY AND UNION
THE CIVIL WAR ERA
AND AMERICAN
CONSTITUTIONALISM

TIMOTHY S. HUEBNER

UNIVERSITY PRESS OF KANSAS

Published by the University Press of Kansas (Lawrence, Kansas 66045), which was
organized by the Kansas Board of Regents and is operated and funded by Emporia
State University, Fort Hays State University, Kansas State University, Pittsburg State
University, the University of Kansas, and Wichita State University

Library of Congress Cataloging-in-Publication Data

Names: Huebner, Timothy S., 1966– author.
Title: Liberty and union : the Civil War era and American constitutionalism /
    Timothy S. Huebner.
Description: Lawrence, Kansas : University Press of Kansas, 2016. | Includes
    bibliographical references and index.
Identifiers: LCCN 2016004959 |
ISBN 978-0-7006-2269-6 (hardback)
ISBN 978-0-7006-2486-7 (paperback)
ISBN 978-0-7006-2270-2 (ebook)
Subjects: LCSH: Constitutional history—United States. | United States—Politics
and government—1861–1865. | BISAC: HISTORY / United States / Civil War
Period (1850–1877). | LAW / Constitutional. | SOCIAL SCIENCE / Ethnic
    Studies / African American Studies.
Classification: LCC KF4541 .H84 2016 | DDC 342.7302/9—dc23
LC record available at http://lccn.loc.gov/2016004959.

British Library Cataloguing in Publication Data is available.

Printed in the United States of America

10 9 8 7 6 5 4 3 2

The paper used in this publication is recycled and contains 30 percent
postconsumer waste. It is acid free and meets the minimum requirements of the
American National Standard for Permanence of Paper for Printed Library
Materials Z39.48-1992.

To Mom and Dad

I know of no soil better adapted to the growth of reform than American soil. I know of no country where the conditions for affecting great changes in the settled order of things, for the development of right ideas of liberty and humanity, are more favorable than here in these United States. The very groundwork of this government is a good repository of Christian civilization. The Constitution, as well as the Declaration of Independence, and the sentiments of the founders of the Republic give us a platform broad enough, and strong enough, to support the most comprehensive plans for the freedom and elevation of all the people of this country, without regard to color, class, or clime.

—*Frederick Douglass, 1857*

CONTENTS

PREFACE

This book is about the relationship between the Civil War generation and the founding generation. That is, it examines how Americans of the mid-nineteenth century understood the founders' handiwork, the Declaration of Independence of 1776, and the Constitution of 1787. When the last of the living signers of the Constitution, James Madison, passed away in 1836, Abraham Lincoln, Jefferson Davis, and their contemporaries were well into their adult lives, and their generation possessed a keen sense of the legacy they had inherited. Whether political leaders or plain folk, Northerners or Southerners, black or white, most free Americans of the mid-nineteenth century believed in the efficacy of the American heritage of liberty and constitutional government, and this belief consistently animated the nation's political debates. Social, economic, and cultural factors also shaped political development, and although the interests of the South and North diverged, a common commitment to constitutionalism remained.

War unleashed revolutionary changes—changes that were inspired, defined, and limited by Americans' understanding of their founding texts. To some, the Declaration of Independence and its promise that "all men are created equal" represented the guiding principle of American political development, while for others, the Constitution—with its sharp demarcation of national and state authority—represented the ultimate expression of republican government. As Americans debated and fought over the meaning of these two great documents and how they related to one another, the war ultimately produced two significant outcomes: slavery ended and secession failed. In the years after the war, some hoped to bring about even more far-reaching changes—such as granting to African Americans all of the same rights as whites or establishing the unquestioned supremacy of the national government. But Americans' commitment to the preservation of state power and persistent strains of white supremacy acted as countervailing forces, which ultimately contained and controlled the scope of change. Most Americans—more precisely, most white

Americans—came to believe that the end of slavery and the defeat of secession were revolutionary enough. Given that slavery had existed in North America for nearly two and a half centuries and that the shadow of secession had long loomed over the nation's political landscape, these were surely revolutionary developments. However incomplete these changes might appear from an early twenty-first-century vantage point, for those who lived through these momentous events, the question during and after the war was never whether a revolution was occurring. Rather, it was always how far that revolution would go.

A narrative history of the era of the American Civil War, this study flows into and out of three historiographical streams: Civil War history, US constitutional history, and African American history. Over the past several decades, historical writing on the Civil War has taken a number of turns. At one time, historians and popular writers conceived of the war almost entirely as a military and political conflict, as a brothers' war—a white man's war—largely devoid of ideological content but rich in examples of honor and heroism. During the past three or four decades, though, professional historians, in addition to adding new layers to our understanding of military events and political debates, have investigated the social and cultural history of the conflict—the lives of common soldiers, the influence of guerilla warfare, the effects of the war on women and gender relations. If the notion of heroism once lay behind most interpretations of the war, a disillusionment fed by American involvement in Vietnam and other post-Vietnam entanglements underlay many of these new interpretations. Emphasizing the horrors of violence, death, and social destruction, recent studies have served as a sobering corrective to earlier writing. Some historians, however, have taken this antiwar theme too far, describing the Civil War as "America's greatest failure" and lamenting that it "watered the seeds of an American-led Christian imperialism."[1] Despite whatever contemporary unease we may feel about the blending of patriotism, religion, and violence, the fact remains the hard hand of war merged with nationalistic and Christian impulses to bring about the abolition of slavery—the greatest reform in American history and one of the central events in the history of the Western world. Rather than viewing the conflict through the lens of contemporary disenchantment, this book aims to understand the war on its own terms, in the context of its own time. The book does not intend to glorify war, but it does attempt to tell a more authentic story, one that acknowledges that, given the economic interests and ideological commitments of white Southerners, only war could have brought about American emancipation. It thus portrays the human cost in a realistic manner while also recapturing some of the heroic character of the conflict.

The second historiographical stream is the study of American constitutionalism. While for decades constitutional history seemed almost synonymous with the study of Supreme Court opinions, recent scholars have stretched well beyond examining appellate decisions. In particular, the notion of "popular constitutionalism"—the idea that "the people themselves" give meaning to the constitutional text—has dominated scholarship in the field. Many champions of popular constitutionalism are present-minded legal scholars, whose eagerness to find historical support for a popular understanding of the Constitution stems from their desire to counter contemporary decisions of the Supreme Court with which they disagree.[2] This book takes a different, more purely historical, approach. It treats nineteenth-century Americans' attachment to the founding texts not as a vehicle for mounting a democratic challenge to an unelected judiciary but as an expression of a larger nineteenth-century culture of constitutionalism. The existence of a constitutional culture was clearly evident in the newspapers, speeches, letters, and diary entries of those who lived through the war. To any scholar investigating the era, the words and ideas associated with the nation's founding principles practically jump off the page. When white Southerners seceded from the Union, they cited their property rights in slaves and the right to revolt implicit in the Declaration of Independence. When military officers and enlisted men went off to fight, whether Union or Confederate, they frequently referred to their devotion to their country, their desire to protect their liberties, or the need to preserve the American experiment in constitutional government. And, of course, when presidents and members of Congress debated the best course for reconstructing the nation, they always did so by appealing to the dictates of the Declaration of Independence and the provisions of the Constitution. Quite simply, the founders and their handiwork hovered over the Civil War era. To be sure, other ideas were often at work as well—notions of race, beliefs about religion, and concepts of honor and courage—but constitutionalism served as a constant common language among Americans, both North and South. At times, this sentimental nineteenth-century language, laced with patriotism and principle as it was, sounds insincere or even silly to twenty-first-century ears. But as historian James McPherson once noted, if it is hard for us to fathom the deeply held ideals of nineteenth-century Americans, that is "more our problem than theirs."[3] At bottom, the Civil War was a war of principle, fought on constitutional terrain.

The book's connection to the third historiographical stream, African American history, speaks to both the heroic and constitutional character of the war. Civil War historians of late have increasingly turned their attention to the African American dimensions of the conflict, while historians of the African

American experience have discovered in the mid-nineteenth-century struggle the crucible of black activism. These are significant scholarly developments. If the black experience proved critical to the war and if it demonstrated the deep desire for black liberty, then historians can never again tell the story of the war as simply a family quarrel between whites.[4] Such a conception of the war is no longer tenable, given what we know about the African American experience. If four million enslaved people could have only secured their freedom through the tumult and violence of a civil war, an assumption borne out by the rest of American history, then the war and the accompanying triumph of black freedom was heroic indeed. Drawing upon this research, this study weaves the voices of African Americans into the traditional political narrative. Almost from the founding of America, black leaders claimed the words of the Declaration of Independence and used them to promote the rights of African Americans. Throughout the Civil War era, black people assembled in conventions, made speeches, drafted resolutions, walked off plantations, enlisted to fight for their country, and issued petitions—all in support of the advance of liberty. While historians have described black abolitionism, black self-emancipation, and black politics, they have missed what bound all these phenomena together—African Americans' deep belief in the idea that "all men are created equal," the idea that black people deserved an equal share of the American heritage of liberty. This theme of "black constitutionalism" runs throughout the book. To be clear, nineteenth-century African Americans—particularly those coming out of slavery—could have advanced a different agenda. They could have advocated and engaged in a race war, taking vengeance on their former masters, as many white Southerners at the time feared. They could have argued for racial separation within the United States, as many whites at the time, Northerners and Southerners, surely would have favored. They could have organized to leave the country in massive numbers, making the journey back to the continent of their ancestors, a position that a sizable minority of whites—even Lincoln— supported until early in the war. Instead, the dominant position within the black community was to claim all that they thought they deserved as Americans, clinging to the promise of human dignity inherent in their Christian beliefs and implied in Jefferson's Declaration of Independence. While there is a great deal of truth to the arguments of early twenty-first-century commentators that American liberty was inherently flawed, born of and dependent on black bondage and oppression, nineteenth-century African Americans had a different, more idealistic perspective. They saw instead an America that, despite its flaws, possessed the potential to live up to its promises, and they were determined to make sure that it did so.

In engaging these historiographical debates, this study takes a long view, examining the Civil War through a wide-angle lens. Ambitious in scope, the book surveys the antebellum era, the war, and the period of reconstruction in a single volume that devotes equal attention to the Union and Confederate sides of the conflict. It attempts to integrate political, military, and social developments into a readable narrative, with the thread of constitutionalism woven throughout.

While this book traverses a great deal of familiar territory, drawing on the vast body of scholarship on the war, it also delves into the published primary sources of the period—things well known and lesser known: congressional statutes, political speeches, and the official military records, of course, but also the decisions of state supreme courts, the proceedings of black conventions, and contemporary newspapers and pamphlets. While I hope I have contributed a new synthesis that engages and challenges historians in these three fields, I will be even more satisfied if I have produced an accessible narrative that speaks to an audience beyond the academy.

Finally, in the pages to follow, I hope that I have conveyed that the American founding planted the seeds of its own flowering, its own growth and expansiveness. Even if Jefferson had not intended to do so and even if the drafters of the Constitution were equally unconscious of their achievement, the founding generation produced a pair of remarkable texts that, over time, inspired millions to fulfill the promise of freedom and individual rights. In part because of the work of the nation's black founding fathers—men such as Absalom Jones, David Walker, Frederick Douglass, as well as the 200,000 black soldiers and sailors who fought valiantly for the Union—the Civil War generation helped expand the definition of American liberty. The changes that resulted, I hope to show, were truly revolutionary and profoundly significant— and thus worth the price paid in blood and treasure. By the time it was over, the Union had become more perfect, and the Constitution had come closer to being a Constitution for all Americans.

Part I
SLAVERY AND SOVEREIGNTY

Prologue
SLAVERY, SOVEREIGNTY, AND AMERICAN CONSTITUTIONALISM

On March 4, 1845, James Knox Polk, the surprise victor in a close election four months earlier, outlined in his inaugural address the principles that would guide his presidency. A former speaker of the US House of Representatives, the forty-nine-year-old Democrat from Tennessee had become the eleventh president of the United States and the youngest man yet to assume the office. Humbled by his victory, Polk struck a cautious tone, invoking the aid of the Almighty and announcing a dutiful adherence to the law of the land. "The Constitution itself, plainly written as it is," he stated, "the safeguard of our federative compact, the offspring of concession and compromise, binding together in the bonds of peace and union this great and increasing family of free and independent States, will be the chart by which I shall be directed."[1]

At numerous points, Polk praised and quoted the Constitution of 1787. He lauded it as "the most admirable and wisest system of well-regulated self-government among men ever devised," and he cited its provisions as he described the relationship between the federal government and the states, the power of Congress to tax, and the nature of executive authority.[2] Avoiding partisan rhetoric, Polk presented himself as a careful constitutionalist, bound by his presidential oath to uphold a sacred text. Although concerned about "sectional jealousies," the new president expressed a deep faith in Americans' ability to resolve amicably their disputes. "If our laws be just and the Government be practically administered strictly within the limits of power prescribed to it," he confidently stated, "we may discard all apprehensions for the safety of the Union."[3] Polk's constitutionalism reflected a national commitment to honoring the handiwork of the American founders, as well as a deep belief that doing so would prevent partisan factionalism or sectional strife from undermining the republic. Yet by the time that Polk took the oath of office, the country had long been divided over issues that the founders had neglected to resolve.

THE FOUNDERS' CONSTITUTION

The Constitution that Polk claimed could prevent dangerous divisions was itself the product of competing and often conflicting ideals. Launched during the late eighteenth century, at a time when Enlightenment thinkers emphasized human reason and progress and in a place where goods and ideas traveled in and out of busy Atlantic seaports, the Constitution grew out of intense political discussion and debate. Pamphlets, newspapers, handbills, speeches, and sermons all served as vehicles for expressing Americans' dynamic and diverse beliefs about such concepts as liberty, property, taxation, rights, and the nature of government.

At least three ideological strains informed the thinking of the American founders. One mode of thought emphasized government by consent, private rights, and the right of revolution. Owing to the late-seventeenth-century British political theorist John Locke, this position stressed that people entered into civil society and formed governments in order to protect the fruits of their labor. Locke's claims bolstered an evolving tradition that emphasized "the rights of Englishmen," the idea that all Englishmen possessed certain fundamental liberties, including, for example, the right of trial by jury. If government became destructive of these ends, Locke believed, the governed possessed the right to change or reconstitute the governing authorities. Lockean thought particularly permeated Thomas Jefferson's Declaration of Independence. In addition to being framed as a list of abuses carried out by the English monarch at the expense of the rights of colonists, Jefferson argued that "all men were created equal" and "were endowed by their Creator with certain unalienable rights," including, borrowing from Locke, "life, liberty, and the pursuit of happiness." Jefferson insisted in the Declaration that the American colonists possessed a right to separate themselves from England because English governance of the colonies had become destructive of the ends for which it had been established. A second, older way of thinking emphasized virtue and the common good. Drawing from classical political thought, many eighteenth-century British and American thinkers emphasized public virtue, or republicanism. Viewing the individual primarily as a citizen of the republic, this strain of thought warned against self-interest and emphasized the need for wise, virtuous representatives to look out for the good of the whole. The emphasis on morality tapped into Americans' growing religiosity coming out of the Great Awakening, and many of the most fervent republicans held strong religious-based communitarian views. In a political sense, the ideal of civic virtue served as a sort of middle way between the excesses of liberty and the threat of concentrated power, two forces that republicans believed always existed in tension with each other. Only in a republic, wherein virtuous citizens elected virtuous leaders, could liberty survive. A third way of thinking emphasized national glory, greatness, and power. Hoping to emulate the best in the British experience, some of the founders saw the chance to build a great American nation and empire. Alexander Hamilton in particular worked to ensure that the American people observed the "principle of strength and stability in the organization of our government, and vigor in its operations."[4] Like-minded nationalists, including George Washington, looked to the imperial rather than the republican tradition in ancient history, focusing on "the moral, heroic, and self-realizing dimensions of the exercise and use of power."[5] Usually well-traveled and cosmopolitan in outlook, these nationalists often drew on their own experience of having waged a nearly eight-year-long struggle against one of the most powerful nations on earth. Aware that the American colonies lay on the periphery of the Atlantic world and that the British viewed them with condescension, nationalists sought to prove that America could survive—even thrive—on the international stage. The Constitution reflected in some measure all of these strains of thought.

In the most basic sense, by 1787 the founders clearly desired to increase national power. Although the thirteen American colonies had declared their independence from Great Britain in 1776, not until five years later, in the midst of the war for independence, did they ratify their first constitution, the Articles of Confederation. The Articles had definitively preserved the sovereignty of the states and granted few powers to a central government. Dependent on the states for revenue and hampered by a provision that required nine of the thirteen states to approve any significant legislation, the government under the Articles proved weak and ineffective, for it functioned more as a treaty among the states than as a blueprint for governing a nation. These shortcomings prompted a convention in May 1787, in Philadelphia, where all the delegates agreed that a stronger central government was necessary for the survival of their new country.

Still, they disagreed about exactly how much power to grant to the new government. While nationalists championed a vigorous government with an energetic executive, many at the convention, based on a republican reading of history and the experience of the British colonies, sought to disperse power in order to prevent its abuse. After months of debate and a series of compromises, the new constitution provided for three branches of government, each of which possessed specific responsibilities and powers. Article I provided for a two-house legislature, the Congress, to perform the lawmaking function. States would have a variable number of members in the House of Representatives, based on population in a decennial census, while each state, regardless of population, would choose two members to serve in the Senate. Article I, Section 8 of the Constitution outlined the powers of Congress, including the power to declare war, to tax, to make rules regarding new territories, and to regulate interstate commerce. Article II provided for a chief executive with ambiguous but potentially far-reaching authority. The Constitution conferred upon the president the power to veto acts of Congress (although Congress could override the veto with a two-thirds vote in both houses), made him the "Commander in Chief of the Army and Navy of the United States," and gave him the power to make treaties with other nations. Article III created a federal judiciary, with the Supreme Court at its head, with authority to hear cases and controversies arising under the Constitution, federal laws, and treaties. The new government, in short, possessed numerous powers that had not existed under the Articles of Confederation. Nevertheless, the framers carefully attempted to delineate and separate power so that no one branch dominated the others. Such a scheme decreased the likelihood that power would be abused and necessitated deliberation and compromise in lawmaking.

To protect the private rights of individuals, meanwhile, many delegates argued for specific guarantees regarding property and other liberties. Framers with a liberal orientation, for example, sought to prevent reckless state legislatures from interfering with private contracts and property rights. Viewing government in Lockean terms as a neutral arbiter among competing interests, James Madison and others believed that one of the primary aims of the new government was to "establish justice," meaning to prevent the passage of state laws reflecting a popular "rage for paper money, for an abolition of debts, for an equal division of property."[6] This view found its way into the Constitution's preamble ("establish justice"), as well as the Article I, Section 10 prohibition on state laws "impairing the obligation of contracts." Those with republican sympathies, who believed that the national government posed the greatest threat to individual liberty, argued that the Constitution should contain an actual list of rights that would be protected from encroachment by the new government. After considerable debate, in 1791 Congress and the states adopted a bill of rights in the form of a series of amendments to the Constitution. The last of these amendments, the Tenth, declared that "the powers not delegated to the United States by the Constitution, nor prohibited by it to the States, are reserved to the States respectively, or to the people."

Nationalism, liberalism, and republicanism, in other words, all influenced the writing of the Constitution. The dividing lines among these ideologies were not always clear, and what resulted from the discussions and debate was the product of a series of compromises. The founders were both traditionalists and innovators in that they derived many of their ideas from well-established political philosophies while they also attempted to apply these lessons in the American setting. The Constitution thus privileged no one ideological perspective. Rather, the founders created a constitutional order that protected liberal self-interest by preserving property rights while at the same time attempting to preserve republican virtue by dividing and separating powers. Although they established a stronger central authority than had existed before, the founders remained divided over the precise relationship between the central government and the states. Paradoxically, the document they created provided for popular participation in politics at the same time that it served as a fundamental law placed above politics.

THE PROBLEM OF SLAVERY

Slavery emerged as the great unresolved issue of the founding era. As early as the drafting of the Declaration of Independence in 1776, slavery had divided those who sought to create an American nation. Jefferson's original draft of the Declaration had included harsh criticism of the slave trade. Referring to King George III, Jefferson wrote, "He has waged cruel war against human nature itself, violating its most sacred rights of life & liberty in the persons of a distant people who never offended him, captivating & carrying them into slavery in another hemisphere, or to incur miserable death in their transportation thither." Perhaps more important to Jefferson and his fellow Americans was the fact that the king was, in Jefferson's words, "exciting those very people to rise in arms among us, and to purchase that liberty of which he has deprived them, by murdering the people upon whom he also obtruded them."[7] This passage referred to Lord Dunmore's Proclamation of 1775, which promised freedom to American slaves who sided with the British. At the urging of delegates from South Carolina and Georgia, the Continental Congress nixed Jefferson's criticism of the slave trade, and the final version of the passage—"He has excited domestic insurrections amongst us"—highlighted only the threat of rebellion.

The Constitution ultimately contained three clauses that pertained directly to the institution of slavery. First, Article I provided that three-fifths of the total number of slaves in a state be counted when calculating a state's population for purposes of taxation and representation in Congress. Known as the Three-Fifths Clause, this provision resulted from a compromise about whether to count slaves when calculating a state's population. The three-fifths ratio itself originated in a proposed amendment to the Articles of Confederation that had pertained to how much revenue each state would contribute, based on its population, to the Confederation government. In 1787, Madison reintroduced the three-fifths ratio, or "federal ratio" as it was sometimes called, as a means of resolving a dispute between free and slave states under the new constitution. On the one hand, because slavery was rapidly disappearing from the North, few Northerners favored counting slaves at all for purposes of representation. On the other hand, Southerners maintained that accounting for slaves in this way reflected Southerners' greater share of national wealth and ensured that this economic interest could not be ignored. The fact that the sides agreed on the three-fifths ratio reflected perhaps the founders' ambiguity about whether population or wealth was being represented in the House of Representatives. Although Northerners reluctantly agreed to the three-fifths ratio, the practical effect of counting a portion of the slave population in addition to the free population was to increase the influence of the slave-holding states in Congress, to provide Southerners with a sort of bonus when it came to representation.[8]

Second, the Slave Trade Clause, also in Article I, stated that Congress could not prohibit the importation of slaves until the year 1808, twenty years after the ratification of the Constitution. This provision represented a compromise. Many Northern delegates at the Convention who opposed the slave trade as immoral sought its outright abolition, while representatives from Georgia and South Carolina saw no reason to place any limits on the practice. The possibility of a ban two decades in the future represented the moderate position between these positions. Moreover, the clause constituted a compromise on the larger issues of commerce and taxation. Most Northern delegates favored an unlimited power to regulate commerce with foreign nations and among the states, including the power to impose a tax on exports, while Southerners sought to limit congressional power over the slave trade and prevent any possibility of an export tax on Southern agricultural commodities. In essence, the Slave Trade Clause constituted an exception to Congress's overall power to regulate commerce with foreign nations. The slave states, meanwhile, succeeded in writing a ban on export taxes into the Constitution.

Third, the Fugitive Slave Clause—by far the most contentious of the slavery clauses in subsequent decades—generated virtually no debate at the Philadelphia Convention. Located in Article IV, this clause required that a runaway slave be "delivered up" upon the claim of a master. Introduced near the end of the Convention's deliberations, the clause ensured that enslaved persons could not simply gain their freedom by crossing from a slave state into a free state. An obviously important provision for slaveholders, the Fugitive Slave Clause ensured that the newly added free territories north of the Ohio River would not become a haven for runaway slaves, and it seemed to imply that slaveholders possessed an affirmative property right to hold slaves that could not be interfered with by states. Other clauses also appeared to ease the minds of slaveholders who feared slave revolts, for Congress possessed the power under Article I, Section 8 to "suppress insurrections" and Article IV provided that the US government could protect states from "domestic violence."

Taken together, all of these provisions of the Constitution put slaveholders in a much stronger position than they had been under the Articles of Confederation. Some Southerners said so. Charles Cotesworth Pinckney of South Carolina seemed especially confident. "We have a security that the general government may never emancipate [slaves], for no such authority is granted; and it is admitted, on all hands, that the general government has no powers but what are expressly granted by the Constitution, and that all rights not expressed were reserved by the several states," he reasoned. "We have obtained a right to recover our slaves in whatever part of America they may take refuge," he correctly continued, "which is a right we had not before."[9]

Yet slaveholders had not won a complete victory at the Philadelphia convention. In at least two significant and related respects, the Constitution failed to protect the interests of slaveholders. First, neither the word "slavery" nor "slave" actually appeared in the text. Although delegates to the Philadelphia Convention routinely referred to "blacks," "Negroes," and "slaves" in the course of debate, the framers excluded such terms from the nation's founding document. Instead, the Constitution referred to a fugitive slave as a "person held in service or labour," while the Three-Fifths Clause referred to slaves simply as "other persons." Some Northern delegates, who undoubtedly hoped that slavery would eventually wither away and did not want to write it into the Constitution in an overt way, favored such ambiguous language. These delegates assured themselves that the abolition of slavery in the Northern states during the 1770s and 1780s and Congress's prohibition of slavery from the territory north of the Ohio River in the Northwest Ordinance of 1787 had placed the United States on an abolitionist trajectory. The slave trade, they figured, would probably come to a halt in twenty years, and they imagined that the institution of slavery in the Southern states would eventually end as well. In 1808, without controversy, Congress did in fact pass legislation banning the importation of African slaves. Certainly many of the Northern delegates believed that they, by neglecting to mention it by name, had in an important way left slavery out of the Constitution. Second, and perhaps more important, Southern delegates failed to gain explicit recognition of their slaves as property. Despite his apparent satisfaction with the outcome of the convention, the South Carolinian Pinckney had actually sought specific language recognizing property in slaves, thus keeping it safe from the reach of federal power to emancipate. After debating the wording of the Slave Trade Clause, Madison declared in the convention that it would be "wrong to admit in the Constitution the idea that there could be property in men," and his position won the day despite Pinckney's repeated efforts to the contrary.[10] Thus, although the Constitution implied that slaves were property, the document never explicitly said so, and the Fugitive Slave Clause even seemed to make slaves sound more like indentured servants, as "a person held to service or labour." Enough ambiguity existed, in short, to allow for the development of sharply divergent opinions.

Within a few years of the Constitution's ratification, a massive slave revolt in the French colony of Saint Domingue put white Southerners on edge. Beginning in 1791, the revolution just to the south of the United States convulsed the island in bloody conflict for several years. French, British, and Spanish forces all attempted unsuccessfully to put down the uprising, but eventually the revolutionaries proclaimed the creation of the Haitian Republic of 1804, the second independent nation in the western hemisphere. When some Northerners expressed sympathy for the black revolutionaries, white Southerners concentrated all the more on the guarantees they believed the Constitution provided with respect to slavery.

THE ISSUE OF SOVEREIGNTY

Slavery was not the only matter left unresolved by the founding generation. The ambiguous relationship between the central government and the states in the Constitution raised the critical issue of sovereignty. Republican political theory held that sovereignty—the supreme authority in any government—could not be divided. There could be only one sovereign, one ultimate authority. In England, after the Glorious Revolution of 1688, Parliament possessed supremacy. But the US Constitution appeared to break with this tradition by creating a federal system, one in which a central government and individual state governments overlapped and coexisted, each with specific powers. The establishment of a federal structure complicated the question of where authority under the Constitution actually lay. More than a matter of abstract theory, the answer to this question had implications for how the new government would function.

The founders and the Constitution offered at least three possible answers to the problem of sovereignty. One answer was that the whole people of the United States—"We the People," as the preamble put it—were sovereign. According to this nationalistic interpretation, the people of the United States acted in their collective capacity both in creating and ratifying the Constitution. In marked contrast to the Articles of Confederation, which explicitly affirmed the sovereignty of the states and mentioned the name of each state in its opening section, the preamble of the US Constitution began by asserting the sovereignty of the people without mentioning the states. Therefore, this way of thinking went, the Constitution established a "national government" that possessed the power to act directly upon the whole people. This theory offered justification for a vigorous central government at the expense of state power. Nationalists at the Constitutional Convention, led by Hamilton and James Madison, in some respects succeeded in advocating this position. In addition to creating new powers for the central government, the Constitution included the Supremacy Clause, which stated that the Constitution, federal law, and treaties, "shall be the supreme law of the land; and the judges in every state shall be bound thereby, anything in the constitution or laws of any state to the contrary notwithstanding." The ratification process, moreover, seemed to lend credence to the belief that the founders had created a truly national government that issued directly from the American people. Article VII provided that popular "conventions" held in each state—rather than the existing state legislatures—would determine whether or not to adopt the new constitution.

A second, more moderate interpretation was that the Constitution had created a system of dual sovereignty in which both the people and the separate states retained authority. Under this formulation, which Madison ultimately accepted and later articulated in *Federalist* 39, the Constitution's authority derived from the people, "not as individuals composing one entire nation, but as composing the distinct and independent states to which they respectively belong."[11] The new government, therefore, was "partly national; partly federal," as Oliver Ellsworth of Connecticut described it.[12] The founders had divided sovereignty in the sense that the House of Representatives, based on population and popularly elected, represented the sovereignty of the people, while the Senate, where each state had two senators sent by their respective legislatures, embodied the sovereignty of the states. Although the nationalists did not succeed in creating a congressional veto over the states, they did place limits on what state governments could do. Article I, Section 10 provided that states could not, for example, enter into treaties with foreign nations, coin money, or pass any law "impairing the obligation of contracts." Still, while the central government had extensive powers, it could not properly be called "national," Madison claimed, "since its jurisdiction extends to certain enumerated objects only, and leaves to the several States a residuary and inviolable sovereignty over all other objects."[13] Under this theory of dual sovereignty, buttressed by the Tenth Amendment, states retained power over such matters as navigation, commerce, and taxation, so long as no explicit federal constitutional prohibition existed.

A third answer was that the states retained their sovereignty under the new constitution. Despite attempts to augment the powers of the general government and circumscribe state power, after all, the founders never considered abolishing the states. Jefferson's Declaration of Independence had established the idea that the "United Colonies are, and of Right ought to be, Free and Independent States," meaning "free and independent" of England but also "free and independent" of each other. Rejecting the idea that the language of the preamble had in any way diminished the sovereignty of states, this theory held that it had been the states, as states, that had come together in a compact to form a union and write the Constitution, just as they had in writing the Articles of Confederation. As parties to the compact, states retained their sovereignty and granted to the central government a set of specific and limited powers enumerated in the Constitution. Once the new government actually started to enact legislation, critics in the states found this theory particularly useful as a means of challenging federal power. In the late 1790s, extreme versions of the theory—advocated by Jefferson and even Madison (who in this instance believed that Congress had exceeded its powers)—held that state governments could interpose themselves between the federal government and the people of a state to protect the liberties of their people, or even nullify federal laws that states believed were unconstitutional. If this theory held sway—if states could nullify federal laws—then the argument that states could withdraw from the compact altogether would not be far behind. Given the range of possible answers to the question of sovereignty, the Constitution possessed more ambiguity than clarity on the issue. For this reason, finding the proper balance between the central government and the states would prove one of the central dilemmas of the fledgling nation.

Because the Constitution resolved neither the sovereignty issue nor the slavery problem, the union of the states remained a fragile one. Freed from British control for a brief time, only since the conclusion of the American Revolutionary War in 1783, the inhabitants of the thirteen states looked to an uncertain future. Although they had joined together to win their independence, most had not surrendered their emotional loyalties to a new central government. The Union seemed more idea than reality, the Constitution a mere hopeful experiment. The latter's fate, for all the founders knew, could very well end up the same as that of the short-lived Articles of Confederation. True, a succession of compromises at the Philadelphia Convention had eliminated many of the problems of the Articles and smoothed over some of the differences that divided Americans. But the actual operation of the federal system remained to be determined, and the founders' divergent assumptions regarding the future of slavery held the potential for continued division. While many other matters also remained unresolved at the founding—the distinction between direct and indirect taxes, the definition of citizenship, the meaning of treason, for example—none shook the political system as profoundly and consistently as the issues of slavery and sovereignty.

POLITICAL CRISES

Decades after the founding, in 1819–1820, a controversy over Missouri statehood first brought the issue of slavery to the forefront of American politics. In 1803, President Thomas Jefferson had led the United States to purchase the Louisiana Territory from France, thereby doubling the size of the country. Roughly defined by the Missouri and Mississippi river watersheds, these vast lands welcomed tens of thousands of settlers over the next several years, and many of these newcomers held slaves. In 1804, a minor controversy over proposed limits on slavery in Orleans Territory was settled in favor of proslavery interests, and in 1812 Congress admitted Louisiana to the Union as a slave state. As slavery spread, some Northerners in Congress grew concerned that this development ran counter to the designs of the founders, and just as many worried that the admission of new slave states eventually meant increased Southern influence in the halls of Congress, which would in turn lead to more slave states. During the War of 1812, a group of New Englanders, dissatisfied with the fact that the United States had entered a second war with Britain, protested what they viewed as the South's unwarranted power over the direction of the country. All but one US president at that point had been a Virginian, Southerners retained key positions in Congress, and these very Southern leaders had championed a military conflict with a nation that most New Englanders saw as a trusted trading partner. The discontented New Englanders organized the Hartford Convention in 1814, where they argued for a host of reforms to reduce Southern influence, including a proposal to abolish the Three-Fifths Clause. This clause, they believed, unduly augmented

Southern power in Congress and the presidential election process. Though their proposed reforms had little influence beyond the convention hall, the question of the power of slaveholding interests in the national government lingered.

When Missouri Territory applied for statehood in 1819, it seemed a foregone conclusion that it would become a slave state. At that time, some ten thousand slaves already lived there, constituting about 16 percent of the total population. In February 1819, Representative James Tallmadge of New York raised the issue that nearly everyone believed was already settled. Hoping to restrict the growth of slavery and Southern power, the New Yorker proposed prohibiting the further introduction of slavery into Missouri and gradually freeing all slave children born after the date of admission when they reached the age of twenty-five. Because it did not affect slaves already living in Missouri, the Tallmadge amendment would have extended the process of abolition over a half century. A few years before, Tallmadge had helped his home state enact a gradual emancipation law, and the Missouri proposal was even more limited. The proposed law would have allowed blacks to be sold "down the river" into slavery before their emancipation dates, just as had happened in New York. It was hardly a radical proposal. Despite the limited nature of Tallmadge's plan, Southern members of Congress reacted with alarm. Although the Tallmadge proposal passed in the House of Representatives (with the voting along sectional lines), the amendment failed in the Senate.

After months of stalemate, in the spring of 1820, Jesse B. Thomas, a Maryland-born senator from Illinois, proposed a compromise. Congress consented to the admission of Missouri without any restrictions on slavery and preserved the existing balance of slave states and free states by adding Maine (which had previously been part of Massachusetts) to the Union. Further, Congress enacted legislation providing that, in the rest of the Louisiana Purchase, slavery would be restricted to the region below Missouri's southern border, the latitude line at 36 degrees, 30 minutes. Despite the passage of the so-called Missouri Compromise, members of Congress voted again almost wholly along sectional lines. On the critical question of admitting Missouri without any restrictions on slavery, every single member of Congress from the slaveholding states voted in favor, while most Northerners voted against. This aspect of the compromise, in other words, rested in the hands of a small group of Northerners who joined Southerners in admitting Missouri as a slave state. Southerners seemed perfectly willing to ban the institution of slavery in the lands to the north and west of Missouri, which they believed to be ill suited for slavery and plantation agriculture anyway. From the start, in other words, the crisis had been about possible emancipation in Missouri, and the matter of slavery's extension into the rest of the Louisiana Purchase engendered little debate.

By the time the Missouri crisis had subsided, one thing remained clear: sectional loyalties within the United States had begun to emerge. During the crisis, Northerners for the most part came together in their opposition to admitting a new slave state, while Southerners united in support of extending slavery into new territory. In particular, the crisis signaled the rise of a Southern political consciousness centered on the protection of the rights and interests of slaveholders. During the first three decades of the country's history, Southerners had held the presidency for all but four years, held considerable power in Congress, and felt no threat from the North. During the Missouri crisis, in contrast, for the first time Southerners in Congress employed the rhetoric of disunion, looked with suspicion on national power, and took a firm stance in support of the rights of slaveholders. Confronted with the prospect of gradual emancipation in Missouri, Southerners took a hard line in support of the permanence of their peculiar institution.

Less than a decade after the Missouri crisis, a debate over sovereignty brought the state of South Carolina to the brink of secession. An increase in the federal tariff—the tax placed on foreign imports to the United States—triggered the four-year-long controversy. When Congress raised the tariff in 1828, many Southerners, particularly those with a stake in the cotton-export economy, expressed alarm. With a thriving plantation belt, South Carolina was particularly vulnerable to fluctuations in the price of cotton. The state's planter class spearheaded the opposition to what some took to calling the Tariff of Abominations. Economic opposition to the tariff arose for two reasons. First, many Southerners believed that Congress had increased the tariff not simply to raise revenue but also to protect the manufacturing economy of the Northeast. A higher tariff, by taxing goods imported from other countries, assisted developing industries in the United States by effectively eliminating foreign competition. This meant that Northern manufacturers could increase output and sell their finished products at a higher price than otherwise. Southern agriculturalists, who reaped no benefits from this policy, viewed the higher tariff as pure favoritism. Second, the tariff hurt the South's export-based economy. By reducing the volume of European sales to the United States, a higher tariff would eventually reduce the amount of plantation staples that Europeans could afford to buy. In the minds of Southern agriculturalists, the imposition of protective measures by the United States, moreover, could lead to the rise of similar trade barriers in Europe, which would further interfere with free trade. Southern states thus passed a number of resolutions against the tariff. For South Carolina, coming out of an economic slump in the late 1820s and facing increasing competition for cotton from newer states to the south and west, any possibility of economic harm seemed foreboding.

In the hands of South Carolina's John C. Calhoun, this dispute became the vehicle for articulating a comprehensive theory of state power. In 1828 Vice President Calhoun, writing anonymously, penned the "South Carolina Exposition and Protest," in which he laid out the compact theory of government and the doctrine of nullification. The Constitution, he argued, was a compact or a contract among several equal, sovereign states. The states established the federal government, and in doing so, they did not in any way surrender their own sovereignty. The government they established, moreover, possessed only those powers specifically enumerated in the Constitution. When the federal government exceeded its constitutional authority, a state possessed the power to nullify an act of Congress—to declare the operation of the law void in that state. If a state did nullify a law, Congress either had to yield to the state and refrain from enforcing the law, or take the much more difficult route of amending the Constitution so as to give Congress the specific power in question. Nullification, Calhoun reasoned, was necessary in order to prevent a consolidated national government from threatening the liberties of the people. Nowhere in the Constitution, Calhoun argued, did Congress possess the authority to enact a tariff specifically designed to favor one section of the country or one set of interests over another. Congress's taxing power existed only to raise revenue and to provide for "the general welfare." The so-called Tariff of Abominations, therefore, failed the test. Significantly, nullification also gave South Carolina, which by this time was composed of more black slaves than free whites, a constitutional justification for opposing any federal legislative attempt to interfere with slavery.

In making the argument for nullification, Calhoun joined the vigorous debate over sovereignty that had existed from the founding of the republic. Although earlier in his career Calhoun had taken a nationalist position, increases in the tariff, as well as internal politics in South Carolina, had driven him increasingly toward an extreme state sovereignty position. Calhoun drew from Jefferson's and Madison's Virginia and Kentucky resolutions of 1798–1799 and argued that sovereign states could assert their power as a bulwark against overarching federal authority. In doing so, he challenged a line of nationalists from Alexander Hamilton to Chief Justice John Marshall, the early nineteenth-century Supreme Court chief justice whose judicial decisions energetically championed popular sovereignty and national supremacy. Inveighing against the Marshall Court's attempts to establish a stronger national government, Calhoun described judicial review as the "fatal project of giving to the General Government the sole and final right of interpreting the Constitution—thereby reversing the whole system, making that instrument the creature of its will."[14] Calhoun's forceful assertion of the compact theory spawned national discussion. In the US Senate, the controversy over the tariff, as well as other issues, manifested itself in a famous debate over the nature of the Union that lasted for several days in 1830. Daniel Webster of Massachusetts and Robert Hayne of South Carolina delivered lengthy speeches that articulated the opposing positions. While Hayne asserted the Calhounian notion of state sovereignty, Webster eloquently echoed the nationalistic claims of Hamilton and Marshall—that the Constitution was "not a league, compact, or confederacy, but *a fundamental law.*"[15] Thus, Calhoun's much-debated theory of nullification cut to the heart of the sovereignty debate—whether the United States was a union of several sovereign states or a single united people under the authority of a national government.

South Carolina officially adopted Calhoun's position, which prompted a showdown between Calhoun and President Andrew Jackson. Although generally a champion of strong states, Jackson took a firm stance against a state's power to nullify. When Calhoun's authorship of the "South Carolina Exposition" became apparent, a rift developed between the two that resulted in Jackson selecting a new vice presidential candidate when he sought a second term in 1832. Calhoun eventually resigned his position. Even though Congress had enacted and President Jackson had signed a somewhat lower tariff in 1832, the supporters of nullification in South Carolina pressed their agenda. In fact, even before Calhoun's resignation, nullifiers had won control of the South Carolina legislature and called for a state convention to address the matter. Gathering in November 1832, the convention passed a resolution declaring the tariff acts "unauthorized by the Constitution of the United States" and "null, void and no law, nor binding upon this State, its officers, or citizens."[16] The convention went further. Enforcing the tariff laws in South Carolina would constitute a violation of state law, and all officials of the state had to swear their loyalty to the nullification ordinance. If the federal government attempted to force South Carolina to adhere to the law, the convention declared, the state would sever its relationship with the other states in the Union. Furious, Jackson privately stated that he would personally lead an army into South Carolina and threatened to hang Calhoun and his fellow traitors. The fact that no other Southern state went so far as to join South Carolina in its protest made it easier for Jackson to stand his ground. Confronted with a state in constitutional rebellion, Jackson issued a proclamation against South Carolina's actions. Jackson made much of the phrase "to form a more perfect Union" in the preamble of the Constitution. Not mincing words, Jackson declared nullification "incompatible with the existence of the Union, contradicted expressly by the letter of the Constitution, unauthorized by its spirit, inconsistent with every principle on which it was founded, and destructive of the great object for which it was formed."[17]

The resolution of the crisis came when Congress passed two pieces of legislation, collectively known as the Compromise of 1833. The first authorized the president to use force to collect tariff revenue in South Carolina and keep the state in the Union, and the second gradually reduced tariff levels over a ten-year period. Although few in Congress supported both pieces of legislation, the passage of both measures effectively ended the crisis. Like any compromise, the legislative enactments that ended the controversy over nullification fully satisfied no one yet still allowed both sides to claim victory. Jackson kept the Union together and his pride intact, while South Carolinians congratulated themselves on achieving lower tariff rates. As the tariff issue faded, talk of disunion subsided. Still, Calhoun's elaborate constitutional justification for state power and secession was the most significant legacy of the four-year-long dispute. While compromise had settled the short-term matter of tariff rates, it had not resolved the fundamental issue of sovereignty.

AMERICAN CONSTITUTIONALISM

Despite these political crises, Americans remained united in their commitment to a unique experiment in constitutional governance. From the start, constitutionalism wove itself deeply into the fabric of American thought. The notion of a written constitution as a supreme law that transcended politics figured prominently in the thinking of the founding generation. In 1791, Thomas Paine explained that a constitution was "a thing *antecedent* to a government" that "a government is only the creature of a constitution."[18] This idea, the founders realized, distinguished American from English constitutional development. In England, the government, acts of Parliament, and the "constitution" were all the same thing. Acts of Parliament—because they were acts of Parliament—were inherently constitutional. But in America, the dividing line between the political and the constitutional, and even the "legal" and the "constitutional," was critical. Just because a law had been enacted in accordance with proper procedure did not mean that it conformed to the principles of rights and justice. Because it supposedly embodied these higher principles, the Constitution became a sacred public text. This supreme law, moreover, was to be enforced by government officials' adherence to established processes and procedures, further held in check by the courts of justice and even by the people themselves. Constitutionalism, the belief in adhering to and governing under a constitution, became a central feature of American life and thought.

Popular reverence for the Constitution developed through the widespread dissemination of books and manuals written with a didactic purpose. When Supreme Court justice and Harvard professor of law Joseph Story completed his three-volume *Commentaries on the Constitution* in 1833, he declared that the goal of the work was "to fix in the minds of American youth a more devout enthusiasm for the constitution of their country," and he later published two different abridged versions written specifically for use in high schools and colleges.[19] Others followed suit in attempting to educate the public. William Hickey's *The Constitution of the United States of America, with an Alphabetical Analysis* first appeared in 1846 and went through multiple printings. The US Senate purchased tens of thousands of copies of Hickey's work, perhaps the first official dissemination of information about the Constitution on a wide scale. One such edition included in the front matter an endorsement from George M. Dallas, the vice president of the United States under Polk. The text of the Constitution, Dallas wrote, "should be found wherever there is a capacity to read: not alone in legislative halls, judicial councils, libraries, and colleges, but also in the cabins and steerages of our mariners, at every common-school, log-hut, factory, or fireside."[20]

Popular veneration for the founders' Constitution contributed to the development of American nationalism. The memory and history of the creation of the republic formed the basis of a nascent national identity that bound Americans to one another. Biographies of the founders began to appear, beginning with John Marshall's five-volume *Life of Washington* published during the early 1800s and followed by a host of history and law books during the 1820s that exalted the work of the authors of the Declaration of Independence and the Constitution. Gradually, partly as a result of the efforts of the aging founders themselves and their descendants, America developed its own pantheon of statesmen and heroes, including Washington and Jefferson, Adams and Madison. Just as the nation's capital city on the banks of the Potomac River began to take shape—including a massive monument to its namesake begun during the 1840s—the American founders emerged in the popular imagination as models of courage and virtue. President Polk's appeal to constitutionalism in his inaugural address reflected, by that time, the close relationship between founding principles and nationalistic ideals.

But sectional forces also resulted from the founding. The Declaration's soaring language proclaiming that "all men are created equal" by the early nineteenth century drove a wedge between those who questioned the morality of slavery and those who reaped the profits of slave labor. The Declaration thus began to serve as a political touchstone, as its words lent support to those, black and white, who challenged slavery while putting on the defensive those who supported it. Competing interpretations of the Constitution also contributed to sectionalism. Conflicts over tariffs and territories, sovereignty and slavery plagued the United States throughout the first six decades of its history, and each political crisis threatened to undo the work of the founders. By raising the question of whether slavery would continue unchecked, the Missouri Crisis, if only temporarily, created rival sectional camps, each of which clung tenaciously to its ideas about what the founders intended and what the Constitution provided. The Nullification Controversy, in raising the even more enigmatic issue of sovereignty, supplied advocates of state power a well-developed, ready-made theory of nullification and secession, to be employed at any future date when minority interests seemed particularly threatened by the federal government.

At the time of his inaugural address, President Polk surely knew the threat posed by sectionalism. Noting that Congress had just approved the annexation of Texas, an independent republic since 1836, the new president warned "foreign powers" against interfering with America's intention to incorporate the former Mexican territory into the Union.[21] In 1846, after Mexico refused an offer from the US government to purchase extensive territory bordering the western portion of the United States, Polk asked for and Congress granted a formal declaration of war. Perhaps Polk believed that a policy of aggressive territorial expansion to the south would serve as much as a unifying force for the fragile republic as its constitution. To be sure, Polk's war against Mexico prompted a surge of patriotic sentiment, but American nationalism at the time achieved "an ominous fulfillment."[22] The United States' military victory and its resulting acquisition of more than a half million square miles raised the sectionally divisive and constitutionally ambiguous issue of slavery in new territories. From the time of the founding, slavery had represented the single greatest difference between the societies, economies, and cultures of the Northern and Southern states. The Mexican-American War, by laying bare that essential distinction, abruptly ended nationalism's march. Perhaps not even Polk's antidote for national unity—an adherence to the Constitution "plainly written as it is"—would prove sufficient.

1
SLAVERY, THE SOUTH, AND THE NORTH

On September 6, 1848, an assembly of free African Americans from the Northern states met in the courthouse building in Cleveland, Ohio, to promote black freedom. With the Wilmot Proviso proposing to establish all new territories gained from Mexico as free soil, the Colored National Convention, as it was called, affirmed its full support for the growing political movement to prevent the spread of slavery into federal territories. The convention, however, pressed a much more ambitious agenda. "Slavery is the greatest curse ever inflicted on man, being of hellish origin, the legitimate offspring of the Devil," the delegates wrote, "and we therefore pledge ourselves, individually, to use all justifiable means for its speedy and immediate overthrow." Other resolutions called on blacks to petition free state legislatures to repeal laws "militating against the interests of colored people" and to provide political support only for those candidates and parties that advocated "the establishment of equal rights and privileges, without distinction of color, clime, or condition." Describing the fate of free and enslaved black people as inextricably linked—"we are as a people chained together," they affirmed—the delegates' bold proclamations on behalf of liberty and equality blended Christian theology with constitutional principles, thus capturing the spirit of the early nineteenth-century black freedom movement.[1]

In announcing these resolutions, the delegates in Cleveland attempted to strike a blow at an institution that had existed on North American soil for more than two and a quarter centuries. Slavery not only affected the everyday lives of those held in bondage but it also in a larger sense shaped the development of antebellum Southern society and culture, while its absence influenced the formation of Northern society and culture. Largely because of slavery, the South remained as much of America had been in the mid-eighteenth century: agricultural in terms of its economy, hierarchical in its social organization, and homogenous in its culture. Beginning in the early nineteenth century, though, a portion of the North began to follow a different path of development, because it had established an economy based on free labor rather than slave labor. Over time, the Northeast—and, as time passed, those areas to its west along the rivers, canals, and overland trade routes—took on a more socially dynamic, economically diverse character. The advent of a transportation revolution and an increase in immigration fueled the growth of urban areas and the rise of manufacturing, all of which gradually transformed society. While Americans in the South and the North still had a great deal in common, their respective societies were headed in different directions. Thus, in calling for the abolition of slavery, the black delegates to the Colored National Convention not only attempted to work for the liberation of their fellow African Americans, whether consciously or not, but also leveled an attack on a system that lay at the heart of sectional differences.

THE ORIGINS OF AMERICAN SLAVERY

In 1619, a Dutch captain unloaded a cargo of twenty blacks in Virginia, and over the next few decades, small numbers of Africans continued to be brought into the colony. Although the legal status of these first Africans in North America was unclear, the growth of tobacco as a cash crop created an increasing demand for labor, and for the next few decades, white European servants almost exclusively met this need. Indentured servants worked a term of four to seven years—an indenture—in order to pay the cost of their passage, and once they completed this term, they received their freedom. Then, hiring out their labor for a time, former servants usually gained enough cash to purchase land of their own. The perpetuation of this cycle rested on a steady stream of servants to fulfill the colony's labor needs, the availability of cheap land for those who had completed their indentures, and the maintenance of stable prices for tobacco. Eventually, an oversupply of servants, conflicts with Native Americans, and the depletion of the soil prevented white Virginians from satisfying their hunger for land, and when tobacco overproduction and imperial regulations led to a decline in tobacco prices in the 1660s, many young Virginians found themselves lacking land and hope. As word reached Europe of the dire situation in Virginia, and as opportunities for wage workers in England improved, the supply of servants gradually slowed.

Decreased availability of white servants coincided with increased access to black slaves. In 1672, the founding of the Royal African Company marked England's direct involvement in the slave trade, and in 1674 the company began to ship Africans to the North American mainland. Like the Dutch and

Portuguese before them, English slave traders operated from a series of forts along the West African coast. They typically brought weapons, rum, and other manufactured goods, which they exchanged with African rulers and merchants for slaves. Slavery had existed in Africa and elsewhere for centuries, and the enslavement of Africans could come about as a punishment for indebtedness or as a result of kidnapping. The vast majority of slaves, though, were prisoners of wars among rival African peoples. In African culture, slaves could expect that they or their children would eventually gain acceptance or freedom in the society in which they had been enslaved. Africans in America faced a very different future, for slavery in America proved to be a system of hereditary bondage based on race. Deeply ingrained negative attitudes on the part of the English toward blacks meant that enslavement of Africans was as much a cultural as an economic phenomenon. Centuries of literary and cultural tradition, including much of Christian theology, imparted negative connotations to blackness and darkness, perhaps unconsciously influencing the English view of Africans as a servile and semihuman race.

During the first century of its existence in North America, slavery took distinct forms in different regions. In the area around the Chesapeake Bay, in the colonies of Virginia and Maryland, Africans began arriving steadily by the end of the seventeenth century, until they gradually replaced indentured servants as the primary source of labor. By 1700, black slaves made up more than half of the agricultural workforce in Virginia. Over the next century, as the colony became more settled, the slave population increased naturally as high disease rates and low fertility gave way to lower mortality rates and higher fertility. While white indentured servants continued to arrive in the Chesapeake along with African slaves throughout the eighteenth century, by midcentury an American-born slave population emerged. In the colonies further to the south, the situation proved very different. The advent of rice as a cash crop led to huge increases in the number of Africans brought to South Carolina. With expertise in rice growing in West Africa, slaves supplied knowledge as well as labor, and large groups of enslaved laborers worked the rice plantations that developed throughout the region. By 1730, slaves outnumbered whites by nearly two to one in South Carolina, and the continued infusion of Africans into the colony helped the Carolina low country become the most Africanized part of the South. In 1739, the first slave rebellion on American soil occurred when a group of South Carolina blacks unsuccessfully attempted a mass escape to Spanish Florida, where they hoped to attain their freedom. The suppression of the rebellion and the harsh slave code that ensued showed how significant racial slavery had become in South Carolina.

The late eighteenth century witnessed the entrenchment of the slave system in the South. Initially it appeared that natural rights ideology coming out of the Enlightenment and the American Revolution would serve as an ameliorating force with regard to race relations. In 1782, Virginia passed legislation allowing masters to free their slaves by deed or will, and within a decade, Maryland, Delaware, and Kentucky had enacted similar measures. Despite these developments in the Upper South and border states, the momentum was moving in the other direction in the rest of the slaveholding states—that is, in support of a deeper commitment to slavery as a labor system. Advances in cotton ginning technology particularly strengthened white Southerners' interest in acquiring more slaves. With a simplified process of separating seeds from fibers, cotton became instantly profitable. The fact that cotton could be grown in much of the South meant that future fortunes would rest on acquiring new lands for clearing, settlement, and cultivation. Eventually, by 1860, the American South produced two-thirds of all the cotton grown in the world.

SOUTHERN SLAVERY AND THE BLACK COMMUNITY

Throughout the antebellum period, enslaved people accounted for about a third of the total population of the American South. About four in ten slaves lived in the Upper South and border states, where small farms predominated. The majority of the enslaved, though, lived in the states of the Deep South, where the cotton economy reigned supreme. Over time, the slave population gradually moved further west and south, as planters sought new lands and as plantations attempted to keep up with the increasing demand for the crop. The demographics of slavery thus varied greatly. Old eastern seaboard states such as Virginia, Maryland, and Delaware gradually lost slaves during the first half of the nineteenth century as slaveholders there sold thousands of slaves to masters in the bourgeoning cotton lands of Alabama, Mississippi, and Louisiana. In some of the most important plantation districts—in the Mississippi Delta region and the Alabama Black Belt, for example—slaves constituted more than 75 percent of the population. In one county, Issaquena County in Mississippi, in 1860 slaves constituted 92.5 percent of the total populace. In other areas—the mountains of East Tennessee, for example—the institution of slavery was practically nonexistent. By 1860, largely because of natural increases in the population, nearly four million slaves lived in the South.

Because it cost a slaveholder far less to feed, clothe, and house a slave per year than the master made from the crops produced by slave labor, slavery proved profitable. This was particularly true in more recently settled parts of

This map from the period shows the distribution of the enslaved population in the Southern states. The darker areas denote the highest concentrations of slaves and plantations. Image from NOAA's Office of Coast Survey Historical Map & Chart Collection (http://historical charts.noaa.gov)

the South, where the soil had not been exhausted and crop yields remained high. The fact that Congress ended the importation of African slaves in 1808 meant that the supply of slaves remained limited, thereby keeping the price high. In fact, slave prices steadily increased throughout the antebellum era, and masters who purchased slaves and sold them later thus invested wisely. A lucrative internal slave trade developed during the antebellum era as slaves were bought, transported, and sold to meet the shifting regional and local demands of production. As the South's cash-crop economy continued to expand, in order to meet rising demand for cotton and other crops both in the North and in England, slavery became the engine of the region's growth and prosperity.

About 75 percent of the enslaved population worked the land, and close to half of all slaves labored on plantations. Large, self-sufficient farms, plantations usually produced the South's major cash crops—cotton, tobacco, sugar, and rice—as well as a host of other minor crops. On plantations, slaves generally worked in groups known as gangs, and the nature and extent of their labor varied according to the season. High fertility rates in the Old South meant that slave women spent considerable time pregnant, nursing, or tending to children. Still, during the peak seasons of the agricultural cycle, plantations usually practiced little in the way of differentiation of labor. Male or female, young or old, nearly all hands worked in the fields to bring in the crop. On small plantations, where the master owned twenty to fifty slaves, planters typically directed the slaves' labor, perhaps with the help of a black slave driver who acted as foreman. The organization of larger plantations was more complex. White overseers, often aided by black slave drivers, usually supervised the labor force. On the largest plantations, some with hundreds of slaves, a typical slave might never know or come in contact with the master, who relied on a management team of overseers and slave drivers. Overseers had to attempt to maximize crop yields and plantation profits on behalf of the master while maintaining peace and enforcing discipline. Slave drivers occupied an even more perilous middle ground. As the handpicked agent of the master, a slave driver enjoyed rights and privileges far beyond those of the typical field hand. As slaves, though, they possessed limited opportunities, and as symbols of the master's authority, they often incurred the resentment of their fellow slaves. On small farms, in contrast to plantations, masters owned few slaves and usually worked alongside their laborers.

About 25 percent of slaves provided some form of nonagricultural labor. Those who lived and worked within the master's household usually served as cooks, butlers, or nurses, or they worked in other positions that brought them into close contact with the master's family. Field hands often resented these, who, like slave drivers, lived far better than their counterparts. At the same time, house slaves experienced a much greater degree of supervision and scrutiny than common slaves. Another elite within the slave community consisted of craftsmen or artisans—carpenters, blacksmiths, wheelwrights, masons, and others who performed skilled tasks. Because the master valued their abilities, these slaves typically lived far better than most others. Finally, the small number employed in industry had vastly different lives from those who worked on plantations and farms. As the South began to industrialize somewhat during the late 1850s, slaves began to work in cotton mills in states such as Georgia and South Carolina, the iron and tobacco industries in Virginia, and on steamboats and wharves in river towns such as New Orleans, Louisville, and Memphis. Although their numbers grew in the years before the Civil War, those employed in industry accounted for only about 5 percent of all enslaved people. Because most slaves employed in nonagricultural trades lived in cities, they typically enjoyed more freedoms than their rural and agricultural counterparts.

Slave owners used a variety of incentives and punishments to ensure control and promote productivity. On the one hand, incentives included granting holidays, allowing travel to nearby plantations or towns, permitting the cultivation of vegetable gardens, allowing for the ownership of property, and permitting slaves to hire themselves out for wages at certain times of the year. Masters allowed certain trusted slaves to take on roles of great responsibility as slave drivers, messengers, and emissaries, and slaves working with masters in urban areas or those whose work revolved around steamboats or railroads frequently possessed considerable freedom of movement. On the other hand, punishments could be severe; some of the most common included whipping, branding, and confinement. Punishments on large plantations usually involved public humiliation, thus allowing masters to make examples of disobedient slaves in order to maintain discipline. Excessive physical harm, however, clearly did not serve the interest of slaveholders, particularly small slaveholders, who tended to view their slave property as a costly investment to be kept healthy and productive. The condemnation of the community, as well as the conscience of the master, moreover, usually helped prevent acts of extraordinary cruelty or barbarism, and when masters violated the established norms embodied in the law, they could find themselves in court.

While the law at times afforded slaves protections, the vast majority of enslaved people never saw the inside of a courtroom. Particularly for those who lived on large plantations, the master was the law, and resistance provided the only hope of relief. In a sense, slavery on most plantations was a daily battle between owners and the enslaved. Masters continually attempted to maximize the labor of their bondspersons, while slaves attempted to resist in both subtle and overt ways. Resistance in its mildest form manifested itself in slowing down the pace of work, breaking the master's tools, and feigning illness to avoid labor. Women slaves more often succeeded at using sickness as an excuse. Young slave women were frequently pregnant, and they used this fact to their advantage whether they were pregnant or not. More overt forms of resistance included attempting to run away to freedom or simply going into hiding for a few days. Both practices involved great risks, and few women—mainly because of their role in bearing and caring for children—numbered among the runaway population. Advertisements describing and seeking the return of runaways filled Southern newspapers, with owners offering physical descriptions and monetary rewards for their escaped property. A small proportion of slaves resisted their bondage by attempting to inflict physical harm on their masters through such acts as arson, poisoning, or battery.

Organized conspiracies and rebellions occurred infrequently in the Old South, particularly compared to the Caribbean. The combination of a high ratio of whites to blacks, the relatively small size and dispersed nature of slaveholding, and a politically stable environment in which most masters remained fairly vigilant made slave rebellions nearly impossible in the American South. Nevertheless, the massive uprising in the French colony of Saint-Domingue during the 1790s, led by Toussaint L'Ouverture and culminating in the proclamation of the republic of Haiti, provided inspiration to black Americans held in bondage. Slaves living in or near coastal towns or along river routes certainly heard of these events, which soon became part of the oral tradition that spread throughout the community. In 1800, an enslaved blacksmith named Gabriel, who hired himself out around Richmond, planned a large-scale insurrection involving slaves in three cities. A literate man with a remarkable political consciousness, Gabriel looked specifically to the Haitian revolution as an example and viewed violence as the only means of attaining black liberty. When a black informer revealed the plan, white authorities mobilized quickly before any violence occurred, and thirty-five alleged rebels, including Gabriel, were eventually hanged. A much larger revolt occurred in 1811 in the parishes surrounding New Orleans. Involving perhaps as many as 500 slaves, the German Coast slave uprising also reflected the influence of the Haitian revolt. Two whites died as more and more slaves, some wielding axes and shovels, burned plantations over two days before local militia companies quashed the rebellion. In confrontations with whites and in executions afterward, ninety-five African Americans lost their lives.[2] The bloodiest slave revolt in American history occurred two decades later, in 1831, when Nat Turner led a band of slaves against whites in Southampton County, Virginia. Having had frequent dreams and visions, Turner believed God had chosen him for a special task. During two days of mayhem, Turner and his followers went on a rampage across the countryside, killing fifty-five white people. An equal number of slaves died in the white community's attempt to suppress the rebellion, and after offering an extended confession, Turner met the same fate as the other rebels.

Whether or not they resulted in actual rebellions, insurrectionary scares prompted whites to strengthen existing laws controlling the enslaved population. Virginia had passed the first Southern slave code in 1705, and by the early nineteenth century, all of the Southern states had well-developed legal codes governing slavery and the lives of slaves. These laws typically forbade slaves from playing drums or horns, owning guns or dogs, and gambling or trading with others, and they prohibited slaves from testifying against whites, suing, or being sued. In addition, nearly every Southern state outlawed teaching enslaved people to read and write. Still, the passage and enforcement of slave codes proved uneven. During periods of relative calm, when whites had little fear of black resistance, legislators typically loosened restrictions, and some proved willing to carve out a limited set of legal rights for black slaves. When white fears rose, lawmakers again tightened regulations. During periods of heightened tension, the slave patrol played a particularly significant role in Southern society. Composed of both slaveholders and nonslaveholders, the patrol regularly engaged in searching slave quarters for evidence of conspiracy, dispersing slave gatherings, and guarding areas surrounding plantations or within towns by monitoring slave behavior. When patrollers did discover evidence of a conspiracy, they moved swiftly against the suspects and worked closely with courts or local justices of the peace to discover the extent of the cabal.

In the midst of bondage and its attendant hardships, enslaved people attempted to maintain family and community life. Especially on large plantations, where the number of blacks far outnumbered whites, slaves spent most of their time with each other. Whether laboring alongside each other in work gangs or spending time after hours in the slave quarters, African Americans carved out lives and identities beyond the gazes of their masters. Even on smaller plantations and farms, enslaved people formed bonds of community with those with whom they lived or worked, including other slaves living in the vicinity. Families stood at the center of the community. Unlike in Latin America, where unbalanced gender ratios prevented the natural increase of the population and the growth of families, monogamous relationships between enslaved men and women constituted an important aspect of slavery in the American South. Although marriage was legally forbidden and children belonged to masters rather than parents, slaveholders often encouraged traditional family arrangements. Many slaveholders held simple marriage ceremonies for their slaves, and enslaved people lived in family units, usually in housing provided by the master. Parents exercised considerable authority over the raising of their children, especially if the children were too young to work. Families, of course, lived constantly under the threat of sale and separation, particularly if they lived in the Upper South states that increasingly supplied slave labor to the expanding plantation districts of the Deep South. Still, the family served as the primary mechanism for survival and the main source of identity within the community, as family members provided love, support, and self-esteem to one another. Beyond their relatives, slaves typically developed strong relationships with the other slaves on a given farm or plantation, as well as those who lived in the vicinity.

Religion unified enslaved people and served as the foundation of slave culture. As evangelical Christianity swept across the South during the Second Great Awakening of the early nineteenth century, many masters attempted to convert their slaves and provide them with religious instruction. Such masters regularly brought their slaves to worship services. Here they heard sermons from white ministers, who habitually admonished them to obey their masters and to labor faithfully, "as unto the Lord." Slaves implicitly rejected this message by initiating their own religious gatherings, usually at nighttime, in the slave quarters or the "brush arbor"—anywhere apart from the master's watchful eye. With enthusiastic shouts and songs, slaves worshipped God in their own way and preached their own messages. The vast majority of American slaves embraced a form of Christianity, although they infused it with their own ideas and practices, some of which originated in Africa. Slaves often adhered to a theology of deliverance that identified the black experience with the biblical exodus of the Hebrew people out of bondage and promised hope for freedom in both this life and the next.

In addition to nearly four million enslaved people, the South also possessed a substantial population of free blacks. On the eve of the Civil War, about 262,000 free blacks resided in the South, accounting for roughly 6 percent of the region's black population. The number of free blacks and the conditions under which they lived differed markedly between the Upper South and Deep South. The overwhelming majority lived in the Upper South states, with over half of the South's free black population concentrated in Virginia and Maryland, where most traced their freedom back to private manumissions of the post-Revolutionary era. In contrast, free blacks in the Deep South were a rarity (only 0.2 percent of the black population in Mississippi, for example, was free in 1860), and most lived in urban centers. Because they were often the mulatto offspring of wealthy whites who took a special interest in their progeny, free blacks in the Deep South tended to be better educated, more skilled, and more closely connected with whites than their counterparts in the Upper South. Apart from such blood relationships, free blacks in Deep South cities at times forged important connections with whites. In general, though, free blacks lived and worked on the margins of the Southern society and economy. The unskilled worked as domestics, factory hands, gardeners, laborers, and waiters, while skilled free people served in a variety of roles, such as bakers, blacksmiths, bricklayers, carpenters, printers, tailors, and wheelwrights. A very small number of the most elite blacks—almost all of them mulattoes—owned slaves, who were sometimes family members purchased from white slaveholders. Still, the number of free blacks who entered the Southern elite proved exceedingly small, and most free African Americans found themselves on a perilous middle ground between freedom and slavery. Rarely recognized as the equals of whites and yet not sharing the status of the enslaved, free blacks lived within the boundaries established by Southern whites. As time passed, those boundaries mostly became more restrictive.

ANTEBELLUM SOUTHERN SOCIETY AND CULTURE

The institution of slavery shaped both the structure and culture of the white South. Although land and livestock were important indicators of wealth, the ownership of slaves came to be the most important and visible sign of both wealth and status among whites. While the absolute numbers of slaveholders grew substantially during the early decades of the nineteenth century, the white population of the South grew at an even faster rate. Thus, the percentage of slaveholding families within the overall population declined over time: 36 percent owned slaves in 1830, 31 percent in 1850, and 26 percent by 1860. Nevertheless, because the institution of slavery had such a pervasive effect on society and culture, slave ownership proved to be the defining feature of the white South's three-tiered social order.

Planters stood at the top of Southern society. Defined by most historians as those who owned at least twenty slaves and at least one plantation, planters accounted for only about 3 percent of all white Southerners in 1860. They owned and managed large-scale agricultural enterprises that produced cash crops, usually for export. Throughout the Deep South, cotton plantations were the norm, but tobacco plantations existed in Virginia and North Carolina, rice plantations thrived in coastal South Carolina and Georgia, and sugar plantations dominated in eastern Louisiana. All plantations also grew food crops in some measure, with corn, wheat, sweet potatoes, and peas among the most common. Differences in attitudes and behavior within the planter class reflected the hybrid nature of the antebellum plantation. That is, plantations exhibited characteristics of both a premodern social order and a modern capitalistic system. On the one hand, plantations seemed to reinforce patriarchal social values, deeply rooted in history and custom, whereby masters—like feudal lords—possessed the responsibility to govern and protect their social inferiors. Some planters, living on grand estates and conceiving of themselves as benevolent paternalists, viewed their slaves as part of the master's family and household. On the other hand, because they produced crops for export, plantations represented key components of a modern, international market economy. In the Mississippi Delta, for example, planters shipped cotton grown on plantations via steamboat to New Orleans or Memphis, where agents, known as factors, arranged for shipment and sale to financial and manufacturing centers in the Northeast, Great Britain, or continental Europe. In this sense, planters acted as capitalists who exploited the slave labor force for the sake of maximizing profits. The behavior of planters varied widely, as they played the parts of traditional patriarchs and modern businessmen at different times and to varying degrees.

The second tier of society included those who held slaves in smaller numbers. Most of these small slaveholders engaged in agricultural pursuits. Depending on how many slaves they owned, their farms either resembled plantations on a smaller scale, or in the case of those who owned only one or two slaves, their farmsteads functioned primarily to grow food crops for subsistence, perhaps with some cash crops grown on the side. The values of these producers ranged from those who associated with and resided near plantations—who aspired to the planter lifestyle or who expected to inherit large numbers of slaves—to those whose backgrounds and orientations placed them more within the world of nonslaveholding whites. Typically, small slaveholding farmers knew their slaves on a more personal level than planters did, and as a general rule, the fewer slaves one owned, the more likely the master himself worked alongside them. As a group, small slaveholding farmers tended to lack education and sophistication. Instead, they relied on the richness of the soil, the bonds of kinship and community, the labor of slaves, as well as their own ambition, to rise within society.

Professionals, also part of this group of small slaveholders, played a vital role in the South's economy and society. Merchants, factors, bankers, teachers, editors, physicians, lawyers, and ministers typically owned small numbers of slaves, who assisted in household tasks rather than field work. Although economic and social relationships invariably connected them to slaveholding planters and farmers, many professionals argued that the South's future lay in expanding its base of wealth beyond that generated by plantation agriculture. For the most part, these professionals lived in urban areas. The South's leading cities, situated along the coastline, dated back to the settlement of the region during the seventeenth and eighteenth centuries. Baltimore, Charleston, Savannah, and New Orleans long served as important nodes in the Atlantic economy, while other cities, such as Richmond, Louisville, St. Louis, and Memphis, grew up later along rivers and trade routes. In addition, although for the most part the plantation economy promoted scattered settlement, country stores, courthouses, and churches everywhere became key points of interaction that eventually led to the development of hundreds of small towns and villages. In these places, farmers, laborers, and businessmen met and made deals, lawyers looked for litigants whose agreements had gone awry, and ministers and physicians provided care and comfort to both the affluent and the afflicted. In urban areas, moreover, Southerners formed literary societies, debating clubs, and temperance groups, all of which contributed to the region's intellectual and cultural life. The professional class, in short, although small in number, played no small part in shaping Southern life.

The third tier of Southern society—the vast majority of whites—did not own slaves at all. These nonslaveholders, who constituted 74 percent of the white population in 1860, were overwhelmingly yeoman farmers who owned their own land, which they cultivated primarily for subsistence. Yeomen families grew food crops such as corn, peas, and sweet potatoes, raised hogs and chickens, and hunted small game. On their small farmsteads, they maintained a household economy, meaning that they produced all that they needed to live. They milked cows, churned butter, and made candles, and they often planted enough cotton to make their own clothing and still have a little left over to sell. They joined with extended family and neighbors to build homes and barns, clear land, shuck corn, and hold quilting bees. For the most part, the yeomanry lived simple lives marked by hard work and neighborly cooperation. Unlike planters and professionals, yeoman families were spread throughout the South, from its hilly regions to its fertile lowlands. Because of their land ownership, economic self-sufficiency, and basic literacy, the yeomanry in many respects represented the backbone of Southern society. Beneath the yeomanry on the social scale were the very poorest whites, who lived in the region's most wretched and remote places: the swamps of Louisiana and Florida, the pine barrens of southern Georgia, and the most isolated parts of Appalachia. Southern society thus exhibited great disparities of wealth and status.

Despite these social distinctions, white Southerners shared a set of cultural values and assumptions, including a white racial identity and the ethic of honor. No matter where they stood in the region's social hierarchy, whites shared the notion of "herrenvolk democracy," the idea of themselves as a master race. Racial power and privilege went hand in hand with honor. From the time of the first white settlement in North America, this ancient masculine concept helped to shape Southern ethics and behavior. Put simply, honor was the idea that one's inner sense of self-worth was intimately connected to the perceptions of the community. This sensitivity to reputation dictated that men could not back down from a challenge. Because a white man's sense of himself was closely connected to his standing among his peers, the slightest insult required a response. Planter aristocrats maintained their reputations by dueling with their opponents (typically with pistols), while nonslaveholding whites protected their pride by engaging in bare-knuckle brawling or no-holds-barred fighting. Regardless of what form it took, honor served as an unwritten, nearly universal code among white men. No matter his class or status, every white man felt compelled to protect his own good name, as well as the reputation of his wife, family members, and extended kin or clan. Such values reflected the crudeness, harshness, and insecurity of frontier life, as well as Southerners' reverence for traditional notions of authority and duty. The code of honor, moreover, reinforced the institution of slavery, for in the eyes of whites, slaves lacked all honor. Indeed, by definition, in the minds of white Southerners, men of honor were those who refused to be insulted—refused to be treated as slaves—by others. Honor, in short, rested on white male prerogative and patriarchy, raw power and physical prowess. It sustained women's subordination to men, supported white men's domination of black slaves, and spawned a pervasive culture of extralegal violence.

Evangelical Christianity, another powerful element in Southern culture, eventually softened some of honor's rough edges. For at least a century after the South's initial settlement, religious devotion played a relatively minor role in Southern life. Evangelistic preachers first appeared during the Great Awakening of the mid-eighteenth century. The revival emphasized individual commitment, which, combined with the American founders' devotion to religious liberty, began to produce both religious fervor and greater religious diversity. When another series of revivals broke out in the South during the early nineteenth century—the Second Great Awakening—evangelical Christianity became a hallmark of Southern life. The defining characteristic of evangelicals was the emphasis they placed on the need for a personal conversion experience. When men and women acknowledged their sinfulness and received forgiveness through faith in Jesus Christ, evangelicals believed, they became transformed and empowered to live holy lives. Conversion required believers to spread this gospel, or good news, to all who would hear it. The Bible, the source of this good news, assumed a central position in evangelical theology. Not only did it contain the message of salvation, but its inspirational teaching exhorted believers to live godly lives. Only if men and women read, learned, and understood the Scripture's teachings would the Christian message be realized in the world. The missionary impulse inherent in evangelicalism lay behind the explosive growth of churches and other religiously oriented voluntary societies in the South. With zealous preachers and enthusiastic laypeople, the Methodist, Baptist, and Presbyterian denominations welcomed thousands of new members to their ranks during the first half of the nineteenth century. In addition, Bible and tract societies printed and distributed countless copies of the scriptures, as well as sermons and other forms of Christian literature. Fervent faith soon spread across the Southern landscape.

Over time, evangelicalism existed in tension with the ethic of honor. The Christian emphasis on loving and forgiving one's neighbor bluntly contrasted with the almost uncontrolled exercise of masculine prerogative associated with honor, and evangelicals emerged as staunch opponents of such behaviors as dueling, fighting, cockfighting, and drinking. Clergymen and laypeople, particularly women, formed scores of antidueling associations, temperance organizations, and charitable societies in the South. Over time, however, as more men embraced evangelicalism, piety in some respects merged with honor to produce the ideal of the Christian gentlemen, whose genteel, upper-class brand of honor emphasized generosity and conviviality rather than vengeance and power. Many Southern colleges and fraternal organizations, regardless of whether they had religious roots, eventually advanced this seamless blending of honor and Christian ethics.

THE PROSLAVERY ARGUMENT AND SOUTHERN CONSTITUTIONALISM

The white South was slow to mount a vigorous defense of the institution of slavery. In fact, in the late eighteenth century, a number of prominent Southerners expressed public doubts about and even moderate criticism of the region's "peculiar institution." In addition to the critique of the slave trade in his original draft of the Declaration of Independence, Thomas Jefferson later wrote in his *Notes on the State of Virginia* in the 1780s of the negative effects of slavery on white masters, each of whom learned at an early age what it meant to be a petty tyrant exercising absolute authority over the slave. Slavery, Jefferson even implied, violated fundamental liberties that came from God. "Indeed I tremble for my country when I reflect that God is just; that his justice cannot sleep forever; that considering numbers, nature, and natural means only, a revolution of the wheel of fortune is among possible events; an exchange of situation, that it may become probable by supernatural interference," he wrote.[3] Although he expressed the deepest fears of slaveholders, Jefferson nevertheless hoped that emancipation would eventually ensue by the voluntary actions of masters rather than the violent actions of slaves.

Other Southerners in Jefferson's day joined in criticizing slavery. St. George Tucker, a leading Virginia jurist, in 1796 published a comprehensive proposal for abolition that included the manumission of female slaves and their offspring, compensation for masters, and the removal of freed slaves to the West. The young Maryland lawyers Francis Scott Key, author of the "Star Spangled Banner," and Roger B. Taney, later the chief justice of the United States, also championed gradual emancipation. In arguing a legal case on behalf of an abolitionist minister in 1819, the young Taney went so far as to describe slavery as "a blot on our national character" that violated the spirit of Jefferson's Declaration of Independence.[4] Hundreds of other prominent men and women, particularly in the Upper South and border states, advocated liberating and colonizing African Americans, usually in Africa or the Caribbean. Although motivated by a mixture of humanitarianism and racism, colonization advocates cast a critical eye on the institution of slavery and argued that continuing to hold African Americans in bondage in the United States was contrary to the nation's interests and ideals. Racism and economic considerations, of course, proved nearly insurmountable barriers when it came to actually putting any of these emancipation plans, domestic or foreign, into practice. Jefferson proved unable to bring himself to liberate more than a handful of his own slaves, and his writings—while laced with the high-sounding rhetoric of liberty—also revealed his deep belief in black inferiority.

The turn toward a proslavery argument came during the 1830s. After Nat Turner's uprising in 1831, the Virginia legislature engaged in a searching debate over the future of slavery, and the state's consideration (and ultimate rejection) of gradual emancipation proved to be the last gasp of the antislavery movement in the South. In the years to follow, the rise of an organized abolitionist effort in the North snuffed out whatever remained of antislavery sentiment in the South. A massive mail campaign in 1835, in which the American Anti-Slavery Society sent more than 20,000 pieces of antislavery literature into the slaveholding states, provoked the ire of Southerners, who raided post offices and burned the incendiary newspapers, books, and pamphlets.

The tide had turned. If late eighteenth- and early nineteenth-century critics of slavery had characterized slavery as a necessary evil—an institution the South would have to live with until it could come up with a means of emancipation—post-1831 Southern polemicists began to cast slavery as a benevolent institution. In an 1837 speech on the floor of the Senate, John C. Calhoun made no apologies for slavery: "I hold that in the present state of civilization, where two races of different origin, and distinguished by color, and other physical differences, as well as intellectual, are brought together, the relation now existing in the slaveholding states between the two, is, instead of an evil, a good—a positive good." Calhoun claimed that Africans had arrived in the United States in a "low, degraded, and savage condition" but that "under the fostering care of our institutions" had attained a state of relative civilization.[5] In characterizing slavery as beneficial to both races, white Southerners responded to the fear of slave rebellion and the rise of the Northern abolitionist movement while proving their increasing addiction to black labor and the profits that it produced. The rise of this new orthodoxy in thought led to the imposition of restrictions on free speech and drove remaining antislavery critics out of the South. A pair of sisters from a large slaveholding family in South Carolina, Angelina and Sarah Grimke, became important advocates of antislavery and women's rights in Philadelphia, while slaveholder turned abolitionist James Birney of Kentucky moved to Ohio, where he began operating an antislavery newspaper. The increasingly closed-minded South had no room for such dissenters.

Evangelicals, initially some of the harshest critics of slavery, followed the same path toward the "positive good" position and even influenced church doctrine on a national scale. When founded in the United States in 1784, the Methodist Episcopal Church, for example, had held to explicitly antislavery teachings. Methodism had begun in England under the leadership of John Wesley, a passionate preacher and advocate for justice among the poor, and for decades, British Methodists stood alongside Quakers at the vanguard of the movement to abolish the slave trade in the British empire during the late eighteenth century. Eventually, however, the success of American Methodists and other evangelicals in gaining adherents whose livelihoods were intertwined with the slave economy brought about changes in church doctrine in the United States. In 1836, the Methodists' General Conference explicitly rejected the claims of "modern abolitionism" and announced that the church had no "right, wish, or intention to interfere in the civil and political relations between master and slave, as it exists in the slave-holding states in this union."[6] At around the same time, Southern evangelicals began to argue that the scriptures offered clear support for the institution of slavery. From the story of the sons of Noah in Genesis to the account of the last judgment in Revelation, they claimed, the Bible depicted masters and slaves as part of the natural order of society. The New Testament letters of the apostle Paul, moreover, appeared to provide unambiguous evidence of a grand, divinely ordained social hierarchy, which required the submission of women, children, and slaves to benevolent Christian masters. Southern clergymen placed special emphasis on such passages—for example, from Ephesians: "Slaves, be obedient to those who are your earthly masters, with fear and trembling, in singleness of heart, as to Christ." Routinely citing such verses, Southern evangelicals wrote books and tracts and delivered speeches and sermons in support of slavery. In short, Southern evangelicals' reading of scripture and tradition convinced them that owning slaves was in no way immoral. To the contrary, they believed that the institution of slavery served as a means of "civilizing" Africans and ordering society in accordance with God's will.

Southerners' white racial identity, their ethic of honor, and their religious defense of slavery combined to produce a deep commitment to the protection of Southern liberties. Beginning in the 1830s, a new style of politics contributed to this developing Southern interpretation of constitutional liberty. Fueled by the gradual decline of property qualifications for voting and an attendant increase in white political activity, politicians began catering to the desires of voters by attempting to appear humble in origins and antiaristocratic in manner. Mass voting led to a sharpened style of political rhetoric, as candidates frequently charged each other with representing corruption and concentrated power. Echoing the republican themes of the founding era, those seeking political office often spoke in terms of upending an entrenched establishment that had formed a tyrannical government harmful to the people's interests. Articulating the desire to avoid enslavement and dishonor at all costs, Southern politicians focused relentlessly on protecting and preserving white liberty. White Southerners' sense of liberty, of course, encompassed the freedom to hold slaves, and whether Whigs or Democrats, Southerners vying for political office engaged in political one-upmanship on the issue as each attempted to outdo his opponent in his commitment to protecting the right of slaveholding. Racial solidarity, the code of honor, and evangelical religion all lent support to Southerners' deeply held sense of liberty. Racism restricted political participation to whites, honor promoted chest-thumping speeches by politicians, and evangelicalism underlay the moral certitude that increasingly marked the Southern worldview.

Despite the fact that a minority of white Southerners actually owned slaves, the preservation of white liberty and the commitment to black slavery increasingly defined Southern constitutionalism. In the aftermath of the 1835 mail campaign, Southern-state legislatures passed resolutions calling for the suppression of abolitionist societies in the North. In doing so, they articulated their belief not only in the sovereign power of their own states to control the institution of slavery but also the idea that the federal Union served as a means of mutual defense among the states for the protection of their rights. In 1837, Calhoun took these ideas further, when he introduced a set of resolutions that articulated Southerners' rights as slaveholders and asserted that the federal government possessed a constitutional obligation to protect those rights. As whites increasingly saw their sense of liberty bound up with the right to hold slaves, the Southern worldview became increasingly intolerant of the rights of free blacks. It was no coincidence that during the mid-1830s—as the emphasis on white liberty merged with the hardening of proslavery thought—the two Southern states that had previously allowed free blacks to vote, North Carolina and Tennessee, changed their constitutions to end the practice.

ANTEBELLUM NORTHERN SOCIETY AND CULTURE

Northern society and culture developed differently than in the South, primarily because of the relative insignificance and eventual absence of slavery. While slavery did exist in the Northern colonies, the institution was never as strong there as in the Chesapeake and Southern colonies. During the late eighteenth century, most states north of the Mason-Dixon Line took some action to emancipate slaves through constitutional revision, statutory enactment, or judicial decision. Although the slave trade had served as an important component of the commercial economy and enriched Northern urban merchants for at least a century, a combination of natural rights principles and religious sentiments advanced the cause of abolition. Advocates of emancipation, both white and black, made appeals to the incompatibility of slavery with the American Revolution, while egalitarian-minded Quakers played a significant role in some antislavery organizations, particularly in Pennsylvania. Vermont became the first to abolish slavery, which it did by constitutional amendment in 1777, while New York and New Jersey, the last to do so, ended slavery by enacting gradual emancipation laws in 1799 and 1804, respectively. By 1840, only 1,139 black people remained in bondage in the Northern states, the majority of them in New Jersey. Because the numbers of slaves had never been high in the North, and because the Northern states with the largest slave populations—New York and New Jersey—ended slavery over a period of many years, whites in the region displayed none of the anguish over the consequences of emancipation that marked the South's experience.

By the time of the writing of the Constitution, freedom had increasingly become a feature of Northern society. As the Northern population expanded westward, freedom spread with it. During the years after the American Revolution, thousands of white settlers migrated from the Northeast and Mid-Atlantic to the area to the north of the Ohio River. In 1787, Congress (still operating under the Articles of Confederation) passed the Northwest Ordinance, which established the boundaries of several new western territories, including what later became Ohio, Indiana, Illinois, Michigan, and Wisconsin. Because the ordinance also prohibited slavery from these areas, all of these new territories eventually joined the Union as free states. With a booming population, Ohio first achieved statehood in 1803, and within the next decade and a half, Indiana and Illinois also became states. Michigan joined the Union in 1836, followed by Iowa and Wisconsin during the 1840s. By 1848, when the acquisition of new territory from Mexico precipitated a national political crisis, fifteen free states in the North counterbalanced the fifteen slave states of the South. Freedom made a difference. On farms large and small, most Northerners continued to make their living off the land, and the states of the Old Northwest became huge producers of wheat and corn. But the absence of slavery fostered economic enterprises beyond agriculture. With wealth held in a variety of forms, the free states quickly evolved into a more dynamic society than the slave states. And the North grew more quickly. Between 1840 and 1860, the free white population of the North increased by 95 percent, while the free white population of the South increased by 75 percent. During the first few decades of the nineteenth century, the North witnessed an array of social and economic transformations that slowly began to distinguish it from the South.

The earliest and most important of these changes was the growth of a transportation network. Turnpikes, financed by states and the national government, appeared first in New England, New York, and Pennsylvania. Mostly completed in the first years of the nineteenth century, these roads made it much easier for farmers to transport their goods to market. Canals had a greater effect. The Erie Canal epitomized the willingness of some Northern states to initiate massive projects for the benefit of the public. Built between 1817 and 1825, the Erie Canal stretched 364 miles, from Albany on the Hudson River to Buffalo on Lake Erie. Within a few years of its opening, the canal paid enormous dividends for the state's economy. New commerce and new towns—including Syracuse and Rochester—sprang up along the route almost overnight, creating thousands of jobs in commerce, manufacturing, and steamboat navigation. Railroads proved even more transformative. Beginning in the 1840s, the North witnessed a boom in railroad building that tightly bound

Table 1.1. Population of the Ten Largest US Cities, 1860

Rank	Place	Population
1	New York City, NY[a]	1,080,330
2	Philadelphia, PA	565,529
3	Baltimore, MD	212,418
4	Boston, MA	177,840
5	New Orleans, LA	168,675
6	Cincinnati, OH	161,044
7	St. Louis, MO	160,773
8	Chicago, IL	112,172
9	Buffalo, NY	81,129
10	Newark, NJ	71,941

[a]Some census information lists New York City and Brooklyn as separate entities, with New York City's population at 813,669 and Brooklyn's population at 266,661. Here the two are combined.

Source: US Bureau of the Census (https://www.census.gov/population/www/documentation/twps0027/tab09.txt).

the Northeast to the Great Lakes and made possible the rapid movement of goods and persons. Although the South also built railroads, by 1860 the North contained nearly two and a half times the railroad track mileage as the South. The growth of canals and railroads precipitated harbor improvements in the Great Lakes region, which in turn spurred further advances in the movement and trade of goods. In short, within a generation, the Northern states constructed a modern system of transportation and infrastructure that replaced the simple paths and rutted trails that had barely cut through the forests and set the stage for the region's rapid economic expansion.

Advances in transportation, which facilitated the movement of agricultural commodities and raw materials, fueled the growth of cities. In 1820 only 6.1 percent of Americans lived in cities, but by 1860 nearly 20 percent did. The northeastern states urbanized most rapidly. By 1860, 36 percent of the population of the Northeast resided in cities, compared to 14 percent of the population in the states of the recently settled Old Northwest and 10 percent in the South. The western outposts of Cincinnati, Chicago, and Buffalo rose to among the top ten largest cities in the country, and because of their proximity to transportation routes, all three originated as commercial centers. Cincinnati lay along the Ohio River, Chicago emerged as a railway hub linking the eastern states to the West, and Buffalo owed its rise to the Erie Canal. Of course, the vast majority of Northerners remained on family farms. The free states as a whole continued to produce large amounts of wheat and corn, far more than the slave states. Nevertheless, by 1860 a rapidly increasing segment of the population resided in one of the North's booming cities.

Immigration contributed significantly to urban growth. Again, the numbers provide a glimpse of the dramatic nature of the change. In 1820, immigration to the United States proceeded at a trickle, as a little more than 8,000 immigrants arrived that year. But in 1840, more than 84,000 foreigners landed on American shores, and between 1850 and 1860 an average of about 260,000 immigrants arrived per year. The poorest and most numerous came from Ireland. Desperate to start over in a new land, over the next decade or so, hundreds of thousands of Irish fled famine in their country to come to American cities on the East Coast. Germans also came in impressive numbers, but for a variety of economic, religious, and political reasons. Between 1820 and 1860, more than a million and a half Germans settled in the United States. Most worked as skilled craftsmen, laborers, and domestic servants in Eastern cities, while others established farmsteads in states such as Illinois, Michigan, Wisconsin, and Iowa. In addition to the Irish and Germans, residents of Great Britain continued to arrive, and a fair number of Scandinavians also came to the United States. Roughly nine out of ten of these immigrants established themselves in the free states, mostly in cities. Remarkably, in 1860, nearly half of the population in the cities of New York, Cincinnati, St. Louis, Chicago, and Milwaukee was foreign born.

The growth of manufacturing complemented the extensive commercial activity that took place in urban areas. Before about 1820, most production occurred in the household, carried out by skilled artisans or craftsmen. Thereafter, however, factories gradually replaced residences as the primary sites of production. Originating with the large merchant grist mills of the eighteenth century, the modern factory concentrated workers and materials in one place and organized production for market sale. Cloth manufacturers were the most common. Supplied by Southern cotton planters and powered by water, textile mills spun, wove, bleached, and dyed cloth. By 1860, New England—the center of textile production—had 472 cotton mills situated along rivers and streams throughout the region, including the most famous complex of mills in Lowell, Massachusetts. Lowell contained nearly six miles of canals, which powered thousands of spindles and looms operated by young women in several mill buildings. Although dwarfed by the textile industry, Northern factories also produced other products: boots and shoes, lumber, iron, carriages and wagons, and leather goods. By 1860, the free states accounted for approximately 90 percent of the capital invested in manufacturing in the United States.

A dynamic economy and a booming population did not necessarily translate into unlimited opportunity, however. In the rural North, the distribution of land was more equal than in the South, but significant pockets of poverty and inequality persisted throughout the prewar period. Northern cities, crowded with laborers, quickly came to resemble their European counterparts, with plenty of crime, vice, and filth. Poverty emerged as a serious problem, especially among the working class, and as the number of wage laborers grew, opportunities for social mobility shrank and wealth came to be concentrated in fewer hands. Despite a diversified economy that incorporated both a tremendous amount of agricultural production and ever-increasing industrial output, life in the Northern states, most historians agree, offered only a modest amount of social mobility.

SOCIAL REFORM, ABOLITIONISM, AND NORTHERN POLITICAL CULTURE

If freedom contributed to the economic growth of the Northern states, it also affected Northerners' outlook on their society. In general, Northern values and culture emphasized possibilities and progress, individual accomplishment, and social improvement. Rooted in a religious vision stretching back to Puritanism, and coated with a layer of enthusiasm growing out of the religious revivals of the eighteenth and early nineteenth centuries, most Northerners believed in their ability to live out God's will in their daily work and in their larger communities. This busy, optimistic spirit—evident in the rapid growth and change taking place all around them—manifested itself in a faith in economic progress and a growing commitment to reform.

Even though rapid social mobility often proved to be more myth than reality, most Northerners held a hopeful attitude with regard to their economic futures. Middle-class Protestants in particular extolled the dignity of labor and glorified the work of the producing classes. Hard work and commitment to one's calling, in their view, would enable wage earners to attain their economic independence by becoming individual landowners or proprietors, while those who already had independence would achieve increased prosperity and status through their own efforts. Master craftsmen and factory owners shared this belief in progress, for it reinforced their efforts to promote harmony among apprentices, laborers, and all who engaged in a particular productive enterprise or industry. Shaped by the centuries-old Protestant work ethic, the absence of feudalism and aristocratic privilege, and the rapid pace of change occurring in their society, Northerners celebrated economic growth, opportunity, and entrepreneurship. Despite the rise of a dependent wage-earning working class, in general Northerners saw little cause for alarm. For the most part, they viewed wage labor as a temporary status and concluded that westward migration and land ownership would solve the problem of urban poverty. Most Northerners believed that their system of free labor—in which men worked hard and climbed the social ladder—created economic prosperity and the good society. Despite signs of ethnic tension and class conflict in the North's largest cities, the optimism of free society was contagious.

The religion of middle-class Northerners especially embodied a spirit of hopefulness. As in the South, the series of religious revivals that hit the country in the first few decades of the nineteenth century proved particularly significant in shaping public values. In New England, where Lyman Beecher emerged as the leading evangelical voice, the weight of Puritan theology, which had emphasized predestination, gave way to a more emotional and individualistic brand of Protestantism. From the pulpits of the prominent churches that he served in Connecticut and Massachusetts, Beecher preached powerful sermons and published a newspaper that popularized Protestant theological ideas and brought thousands to embrace the gospel. Evangelicals also won new converts further west. In 1831 in Rochester, New York, the evangelist Charles G. Finney presided over a six-month-long revival that particularly attracted middle-class professionals and resulted in a doubling of the city's church membership. Calling his listeners to repentance, Finney invented the use of the "anxious bench," where those wrestling with their sins came to sit in the front of the congregation before rising to make a public profession of faith. Despite coming from all points on the economic and cultural spectrum, evangelicals united in their belief that individuals were free moral agents, who needed to turn from sin and accept God's forgiveness. Confident that God would bless their efforts, evangelicals formed Bible societies to distribute the scriptures, as well as tract societies and Sunday Schools to instruct others in the faith.

Many middle-class evangelicals also set out to fight sin in their midst, and social reform emerged as an important manifestation of Northern religious culture. Spurred by their belief that remaking society to conform to God's wishes would help speed the return of Christ to earth, pious men and women worked across denominational lines to form a variety of benevolent associations. These organizations opposed excessive drinking and supported the urban poor. They championed the building of hospitals to heal the sick, schools to educate children, and prisons to rehabilitate criminals, while some went so far as to advocate varieties of pacifism and utopianism. Women's rights also emerged during the period, spurred by the activism of women in all of these other areas of reform. In addition to exemplifying the religious zeal of their members, voluntary organizations also served an important societal function, for in joining reform organizations, urban evangelicals in particular defined themselves as part of the rising middle class. In a city such as New York, for example, where the shifting circumstances of life and the marketplace could change one's fortunes in an instant, participation in a reform organization lent an air of respectability to ambitious men, while it affirmed women's role as the moral guardians of the republic. Although some reformers had little respect for the cultures or lifestyles of those whom they sought to assist, for the most part reformers were more humanitarian than controlling.

The movement to abolish slavery eventually became the most important—and controversial—reform of the age. During the late eighteenth century, Quaker antislavery societies had emphasized the equality of all people before God and had exerted considerable influence in the passage of Pennsylvania's gradual emancipation act. But by the early nineteenth century, with slavery for the most part eliminated from the North, abolitionist efforts there lost momentum. Not until the 1830s did a full-blown egalitarian, abolitionist movement develop. Most significant in furthering this cause was William Lloyd Garrison, a zealous Baptist from Massachusetts. In 1831, Garrison founded *The Liberator* and, recanting previous support for gradualism, cited the Declaration of Independence and its proclamation that "all men are created equal" in support of immediate abolition. Garrison gathered a coterie of like-minded reformers around him, including a number of women, whose rights Garrison also supported. The Garrisonians believed in moral suasion, meaning that they hoped to convince their audiences with emotional appeals and accounts of slavery's brutality, and they forsook involvement in politics and parties, which they viewed as corrupt and compromising. In an 1845 letter, Garrison referred to the dominant party of the day, the Democratic Party, in scathing terms—as having "a cannibal appetite for human flesh and blood, which seems to grow rapacious in proportion to the number of its victims." "Dead to shame, its conscience seared as with a hot iron, and possessed of a legion of devils," Garrison wrote, "it is desperately bent on perpetrating every crime that can inflame heaven, or curse the earth."[7] Garrison, moreover, frequently denounced the Constitution as a "covenant with death" and "an agreement with hell."[8] Garrisonians won few friends in the North, as most recoiled at the extremism that Garrison and his allies appeared to represent.

Equally pious, though more restrained, was a faction of abolitionists that grew up around brothers Arthur and Lewis Tappan. Successful New York businessmen, the Tappans took part in a number of reforms that reflected their evangelical faith, including attempts to rescue prostitutes, as well as a petition campaign to close all of New York's public facilities on Sundays. But the abolitionist cause eventually grabbed their attention. In 1831, Arthur Tappan helped fund the start of Garrison's *Liberator*, and a few years later the Tappans, Garrison, and others came together to launch the American Anti-Slavery Society. Bringing their business acumen to the movement, the Tappans raised countless dollars from churchgoers and engineered a massive campaign to mail abolitionist materials to churches throughout the country. In contrast to the Garrisonians, the Tappans and their allies worked through the established political system. In 1839, they helped to form the Liberty Party, an antislavery political party that nominated the former Kentucky slaveholder turned abolitionist James G. Birney for president in both 1840 and 1844. They also used the courts. In 1841, the Tappans successfully freed a group of imprisoned Africans who had mutinied on the Spanish slave ship *Amistad*, and whose case came before the US Supreme Court. The Tappan brothers believed that consistent recruitment and fund-raising, as well as concrete legal victories, were the keys to ending slavery.

Regardless of the differences among them, evangelical abolitionists shared a belief that human bondage violated eternal moral precepts. Slavery, they held, stood opposed to Christ's commands to love one's neighbor as oneself and violated the Golden Rule, "whatsoever would that men should do to you, do ye even so to them." These deeply held convictions and abolitionists' fervent desire to eradicate the sin of slavery from the land placed them in the forefront of Northern reform. To be sure, these morally motivated abolitionists constituted a small portion of the Northern population. During the 1830s and 1840s, their views stood outside the mainstream of opinion, and their actions occurred generally outside the operation of the political system. In most areas of the North, their critique of slavery won few friends. In 1837, in Alton, Illinois, an angry mob, after repeatedly destroying his printing presses, murdered the minister and editor Elijah Lovejoy for his frequent and overt expression of his abolitionist opinions. Although Lovejoy soon became a martyr of the abolitionist cause, the vast majority of Northerners during his time would just as well leave Southerners and their slaves alone.

The dynamism and diversity of Northern society and opinion manifested itself in intense competition between political parties, as Democrats and Whigs battled over the proper relationship between liberty and power. In contrast to the slaveholding states, where Democrats dominated, the parties engaged on a level playing field in the free states. Northern Whigs emphasized the use of government power to promote the economic, social, and moral progress of the nation. Increasingly influenced by the reform impulse, Whigs represented middle-class Protestantism and desired to use government to harness the nation's entrepreneurial energies and to assist in economic development. They advocated higher tariffs and excise taxes in order to build turnpikes, canals, and railroads, which they believed would bind together the Union through commercial prosperity. They also believed that the power of government should be used to promote moral progress. Whigs generally supported temperance and prohibition regulations, and they also promoted state legislative efforts to enforce Sabbath keeping as well as to establish penitentiaries, hospitals, and asylums. Both economic development and moral reform legislation, they believed, fit within the republican tradition of promoting the public good while at the same time creating an energetic American state. Northern Democrats, in contrast, stressed the Jeffersonian values of individual liberty, limited government, and freedom of conscience. A diverse coalition of workingmen, agriculturalists, small entrepreneurs, and freethinkers, Democrats emphasized government's role in breaking monopolies, as well as protecting economic opportunity and minority rights. The Democratic Party particularly served as a political home for the region's burgeoning population of Irish Catholic immigrants, who feared that zealous Protestant Whigs would use government power to ban the consumption of alcohol or otherwise institute anti-Catholic policies. By instructing these newcomers in America's heritage of constitutional liberty, the Democratic Party saw itself as teaching valuable lessons in what it meant to be American. As more Whigs became sympathetic to antislavery principles, moreover, Democrats emphasized the political threat posed by an organized antislavery movement, as well as the economic threat that emancipated black laborers would pose to the region's workingmen. Because Whigs and Democrats in the Northern states were evenly matched, each party did all that it could to increase party loyalty and voting, and each contended that its interpretation of the relationship between liberty and power reflected America's true constitutional heritage.

NORTHERN FREEDOM AND BLACK CONSTITUTIONALISM

If the absence of slavery shaped the development of Northern society as a whole, it profoundly affected the Northern black community. Emancipation in the Northern states created a climate of freedom that nurtured and sustained black activism. A free North enabled a steady stream of black fugitive slaves to escape from bondage in the South in hopes of establishing new lives in the free states, and ex-slaves emerged as powerful firsthand witnesses against the institution. There they joined others who had been born free. In 1800, the free black community of Philadelphia, an emerging center of black protest, submitted a petition to Congress. Led by Absalom Jones, a remarkable former slave from Delaware who had purchased his freedom and become the first priest of the first black Episcopal congregation in the United States, the Philadelphia black community called for the end of the African slave trade and criticized the federal Fugitive Slave Act of 1793, which laid out the means by which fugitive slaves were to be returned to their masters. The petitioners noted that neither the Constitution nor the Fugitive Slave Act mentioned black people or slaves. For this reason, they continued, "We beseech that as we are men, we may be admitted to partake of the Liberties and unalienable Rights therein held forth—firmly believing that the extending of Justice and equity to all Classes, would be a means of drawing down the blessings of Heaven upon this Land."[9] Although Congress ignored the petition, black activism had made an auspicious debut on the national stage.

Black leaders soon incorporated the language of the founding texts into a distinctive vision of equality. One of the signers of the Philadelphia petition, James Forten, a successful businessman, emerged as a particularly powerful voice within the Northern black community. In his *Series of Letters by a Man of Color*, written in 1813 in response to proposed restrictions on the rights of blacks in Pennsylvania, Forten appealed to the state's Quaker heritage as well as to Jefferson's Declaration of Independence. "We hold this truth to be self-evident, that God created all men equal," Forten wrote, "is one of the most prominent features of the Declaration of Independence, and in that glorious fabric of collected wisdom, our noble Constitution." Appropriating the language and symbolism of both the Declaration and the Constitution, Forten set out an inclusive vision of equality: "This idea embraces the Indian and the European, the savage and the Saint, the Peruvian and the Laplander, the white man and the African, and whatever measures are adopted subversive of this estimable privilege, are in direct violation of the letter and spirit of our Constitution."[10] Within a few years, some African American voices called for American blacks to migrate to Africa. These leaders joined the American Colonization Society at its founding in 1816 and supported the establishment and subsequent settlement of the nation of Liberia in Africa. Still, most African American activists joined Forten both in claiming the American constitutional heritage as their own and in aiming to improve the lot of blacks in the United States.

During the first decades of the nineteenth century, African Americans in the North possessed limited political rights and economic opportunities. Only in five New England states (where few blacks actually lived) did free African Americans possess the right to vote, and between 1818 and 1820 Connecticut and New Jersey amended their constitutions to end black voting. At around the same time, New York imposed property qualifications for black voters. Although most free blacks had initially lived in cities along the eastern seaboard, eventually the overwhelming majority of blacks were concentrated in the Mid-Atlantic and Midwest, particularly in Pennsylvania, New York, New Jersey, and Ohio. While their situations varied, most Northern free blacks worked in some service capacity or performed menial labor, particularly in cities. Men worked as laborers, servants, waiters, barbers, coachmen, boot-blacks, and porters, while women worked most often as domestics, washer-women, seamstresses, and cooks. Although some African Americans in the North could be found in skilled trades and professions, white laborers feared the competition and loss of status associated with blacks working in the same positions, and white workers usually did all they could to prevent black advancement. During the 1840s, the arrival of Irish immigrant laborers, more-over, depressed wages in many service occupations while costing blacks jobs in others. Black–Irish economic rivalry in Northern cities provoked decades of tension between the two groups. Despite the grim realities of second-class status, free blacks in the North lived far better than their free counterparts in the South, with the presumption of freedom constituting a key difference.

Freedom fueled further black protest. In 1827, two African Americans named Samuel Cornish and John Brown Russwurm began publishing the nation's first black newspaper, *Freedom's Journal,* in New York City. The paper emphasized American and Christian ideals, promoted moral uplift among the black population, and hoped to advance the cause of freedom by helping African Americans earn the respect of whites. David Walker took a harsher tack. Born a free black man in North Carolina, Walker learned to read and write, joined the Methodist Church, and eventually moved to Boston, where he became a prominent voice within the black community. In 1829, Walker published in four parts his *Appeal to the Coloured Citizens of the World,* in which he sharply criticized the nation's treatment of its black population. An admirer of the American Revolution and an advocate of Christian morality, Walker attacked slavery and white domination. "I ask the candid and unprej-udiced of the whole world, to search the pages of historians diligently, and see if the Antideluvians—the Sodomites—the Egyptians—the Babylonians—the Ninevites—the Carthagenians—the Persians—the Macedonians—the Greeks—the Romans—the Mahometans—the Jews—or devils, ever treated a set of human beings, as the white Christians of America do us, the blacks, or Africans," Walker wrote.[11] In particular, Walker echoed Forten in using the Declaration of Independence as the standard against which to measure the nation's treatment of its black population. "See your Declaration Ameri-

06

WALKER'S

A P P E A L,

With a Brief Sketch of his Life.

BY

HENRY HIGHLAND GARNET.

AND ALSO

GARNET'S ADDRESS

TO THE SLAVES OF THE UNITED STATES OF AMERICA.

———

NEW-YORK:
Printed by J. H. Tobitt, 9 Spruce-st.
1848.

David Walker's Appeal, *published in 1829, relied on the Declaration of Independence to highlight white hypocrisy and assert blacks' claim to equal rights in the United States. Courtesy of the Library of Congress, LC-USZ62-105530*

cans!!!" Walker implored his readers. "Do you understand your own language? Hear your language, proclaimed to the world, July 4th, 1776—'We hold these truths to be self evident—that ALL MEN ARE CREATED EQUAL!! that they are endowed by their Creator with certain unalienable rights; that among these are life, liberty, and the pursuit of happiness!!'" Walker went on: "Compare your own language above, extracted from your Declaration of Independence, with your cruelties and murders inflicted by your cruel and unmerciful fathers and yourselves on our fathers and on us—men who have never given your fathers or you the least provocation!!!!!!"[12] Walker's scathing critique of white oppression and hypocrisy nudged Northern white abolitionists, struck fear in the hearts of white slaveholding Southerners, and surely inspired those free blacks and slaves who read or heard of his stirring words.

In 1830, the year after the appearance of Walker's *Appeal,* a small group of African American leaders held the first national convention devoted to black advancement. At the urging of Hezekiah Grice, a young Baltimore activist, forty delegates from Delaware, Maryland, Massachusetts, Pennsylvania, and New York gathered at Bethel Church in Philadelphia. Primarily they met to discuss emigration to Canada, an issue that had arisen among Northern blacks after tensions over job competition between blacks and whites in Cincinnati had erupted in violence and prompted the migration of hundreds of African Americans to Canada. The venerable Bishop Richard Allen, a former slave who had purchased his freedom and had become the founding bishop of the African Methodist Episcopal Church, presided over the meeting, which ended up passing a resolution recommending emigration.[13] More important than the substance of the discussion at the convention was the precedent that it set. Belief in emigration waned, but the mode of assembling in convention, rooted in the history of the founding of America, proved an enduring model of black activism. Motivated by protest pamphlets and newspapers, and connected through a network of black churches and Masonic lodges, African Americans embraced this overtly political and constitutional model of protest. That is, assembling as a body of delegates, discussing issues, voting on resolutions, and announcing those resolutions to the public both revealed the American identity of those who assembled and set a course for the next four decades of black activism in the United States. In fact, for the next five years in a row, national conventions of free African American delegates met, usually in Philadelphia, to discuss a broad range of issues, while a host of state and local conventions also began to meet regularly.

National conventions continued during the 1840s, although not on an annual basis, and the leaders who emerged from those meetings figured prominently for decades to come. Henry Highland Garnett, a former Maryland slave, became a minister in New York who championed a militant form of political abolitionism. Martin R. Delaney, born free in Virginia, moved to Pennsylvania and became a prominent physician and activist. Most famous of all the leaders who emerged from the convention movement was Frederick Douglass. Born into bondage in Maryland, Douglass proved a powerful first-hand witness against the horrors of slavery. In his lectures and writings, Douglass related his travails as a slave before his daring escape to freedom in 1838. His autobiographical *Narrative of the Life of Frederick Douglass,* published in 1845, proved one of the most successful pieces of antislavery protest literature of the nineteenth century, as it compellingly related the story of his life in bondage, his attempts to resist dehumanization, and his struggles to become literate and free. The book became an immediate sensation in both the United States and Europe. Although he initially joined the group of abolitionists that coalesced around Garrison, Douglass eventually parted ways with the Garrisonians on a number of issues. Douglass favored direct involvement in politics rather than moral suasion, and he came to believe that the Constitution could be used as a tool in the antislavery arsenal rather than as a foil. Equally important perhaps were personality conflicts, for Douglass chafed under the Garrisonians' attempts to stage-manage his appearances, his message, and even his dialect. With a powerful physical presence and tremendous oratorical skills, Douglass gave hundreds of speeches in the North, toured Great Britain after the publication of his autobiography, and turned into a celebrity of the abolition movement. Douglass exerted a powerful influence over the black freedom movement of the 1840s. In 1843, when Garnett sought to publish his controversial "Address to the Slaves of the United States of America," in which he urged Southern slaves to forcibly resist their oppression, Douglass succeeded in convincing delegates to oppose its immediate publication. With a keen sense of tact and timing, Douglass built a power base within the black community, forged alliances with white abolitionists, and in 1847 began publishing his own newspaper, the *North Star.*

The black convention movement, as well as the leaders and ideals that it spawned, wrought a slow transformation in the legal treatment of Northern blacks. Beginning in the early 1840s, the legal status of Northern African Americans gradually began to improve. State judges began freeing slaves who were traveling in the North, while many Northern states began to enact personal liberty laws to protect fugitive slaves who had escaped from the South. Over the next two decades, Northern blacks made concrete gains under the law. In 1841, New York enacted legislation that guaranteed public education to all children in the state, regardless of their race. In 1849, the Ohio legislature repealed its repressive "black laws," thereby allowing unrestricted black immigration, providing some public education for African Americans, and permitting blacks to testify in court against whites. And in 1855, Massachusetts enacted legislation providing public education to students on a racially integrated basis. While certainly not a racial utopia, the free states became increasingly hospitable to African Americans, and the growth rate of the Northern free black population—nearly fivefold between 1800 and 1860—outpaced that of the enslaved or free black populations of the South during the same period.

Black conventions not only helped develop a movement that made concrete legal advances for Northern blacks but also embodied the spirit of black constitutionalism. If white Americans in both the North and the South expressed deep admiration and reverence for their Constitution, African Americans offered their own distinct interpretation of the nation's founding. The same ideals that inspired the Declaration of Independence—equality, inalienable rights, and liberty—prompted the first wave of emancipation, resulting in the liberation of slaves in the Northern states and some in the border and Upper South states. Free blacks in the Northern states held tightly to these principles. From Revolutionary-era free black petitioners such as Absalom Jones to midcentury abolitionists such as Frederick Douglass, African American activists forged their own understanding of the American founding and American freedom. Uniformly idealist in their orientation, they combined the principle of equality inherent in the Declaration of Independence, the notion that the Constitution referred to slaves as persons, rather than property, and the ideal of Christian brotherhood under the fatherhood of God into a powerful, comprehensive critique of both slavery and white supremacy.[14] In contrast to white abolitionists who narrowly attacked Southern slavery, black constitutionalists took aim at the entire apparatus of white supremacy in both the North and the South. While white abolitionists mostly avoided questions about what rights blacks should possess in a postemancipation republic, black constitutionalists claimed all the rights they believed their essential dignity as human beings afforded them. Through newspapers, pamphlets, books, and speeches, through organizing in local churches, Masonic lodges, and national conventions, black activists consistently advocated this distinctive brand of American constitutionalism.

While freedom spurred the development of black activism in the North, slavery suffocated black advancement in the South. By the time the delegates to the Colored National Convention gathered in Cleveland in 1848, most Southern slaves saw little hope for change on the horizon. Slavery reinforced the economic and political power and privilege of the planter elite at the same time that it created an illusion of equality among whites. Reaping enormous profits from their slaves, slaveholders had few reasons to reform their society or to look beyond the next cotton crop, while nonslaveholders had little power and little motivation to change a society that ensured their superiority over blacks and held out at least some promise of social mobility. Because nearly all white Southerners believed they held a stake in the system of racial slavery, they embraced the proslavery argument as an article of faith. The old ways persisted, religion reinforced the status quo, and tradition reigned. In much of the North, by contrast, the pace of change was frenetic. Freed from the social and economic shackles associated with slavery, a more dynamic society emerged, one that little resembled the North of the late eighteenth century. The free states had created a more economically enterprising, socially fluid, and intellectually open society than existed in the slave states. Rather than reinforcing the old order, religious impulses in the North pushed the limits, making possible a white abolitionist movement that complemented the black struggle for freedom. Although emigration and violence remained outlets of black assertiveness and protest, black constitutionalism in many respects served as a more potent weapon against the system of slavery. By using the nation's own founding documents and principles in the cause of freedom, Northern black activists and abolitionists—whose words filtered into the Southern slave community—helped to prepare the ground for freedom in the South. Only a deep crisis in the nation's political system could change slaves' grim expectations for the future and allow African Americans' unique interpretation of the nation's founding documents to come to the forefront of national debate.

2

POLITICS AND THE PROSLAVERY CONSTITUTIONAL ORDER, 1846–1857

On April 6, 1846, just a few months before President Polk initiated war with Mexico, a middle-aged enslaved African American filed suit in the Missouri circuit court at St. Louis. Alleging that his travels in free territory with his deceased former master, army surgeon John Emerson, made him a free man, the slave, Dred Scott, sued his new owner, the widow Irene Emerson. Aided by the children of his former owners, Scott made his mark with an "X" on court documents that initiated his suit. Under existing Missouri law, Scott was likely to be successful in securing his freedom. He needed only prove that he had resided in the state of Illinois and in Wisconsin Territory, both of which prohibited slavery, for Missouri law at the time held that "slave sojourners" who lived on free soil and returned to the state were free. Legal technicalities postponed the case for a time, and in 1850 the circuit court granted Scott his freedom. Mrs. Emerson promptly appealed to the Missouri supreme court, which in 1852 reversed a string of state legal precedents and held that Scott remained enslaved. Over the next several years, Scott's journey through the justice system continued until the United States Supreme Court, in March 1857, agreed with the Missouri high court and ruled that Scott's travels had indeed not changed his legal status. The US Supreme Court also decided, more significantly, that the Constitution guaranteed the right of slaveholders to take their slaves into new territories.

Between the time when Scott filed the initial lawsuit and the US Supreme Court rendered its decision in his case, the nation experienced more than a decade of turmoil over questions related to slavery. In the mid-1840s, if Americans thought at all about the constitutional status of slavery, the overwhelming majority—including most Northerners—believed that the Constitution not only permitted the existence of slavery but also generally protected masters' property rights as slaveholders. Over time, white Southerners would become rigidly committed to an extreme version of this position, arguing that the Constitution guaranteed them an unqualified right both to recapture fugitives in the North and take their slaves into new territories in the West. Meanwhile, many Northerners would drift toward wanting to place limits on slaveholders' rights, particularly the right to take slaves into territories. Although national political parties had always succeeded in muting sectional tensions and promoting compromise, American political parties proved unable to contain the conflict between these increasingly polarized positions. By the time of the *Dred Scott* decision, many Northerners warned that a "Slave Power" had assumed control of the national government, while many Southerners convinced themselves that abolitionists had gained the upper hand in the North. Reality fully justified neither perception, but the Supreme Court's decision sought to end the sectional crisis once and for all. By ruling in favor of the Southern argument—that the Constitution was unambiguously proslavery—the Court attempted to clarify the question of slavery's constitutional status and conclude eleven years of rancorous political debate on the subject. In actuality, the Supreme Court's definitive decision in *Dred Scott* all but eliminated the possibility of future compromise.

THE CONSTITUTIONAL POLITICS OF SLAVERY

When Dred Scott first filed suit for his freedom, most white Americans seemed satisfied that the Constitution protected the rights of slaveholders where slavery already existed. Leaders in every branch of government apparently agreed, for recent American history contained not a single instance or episode that indicated a threat to slavery in the South. Not since 1808, when Congress passed legislation ending the importation of African slaves, had the federal government taken any action aimed at limiting slavery. When confronted with the admission of Missouri in 1820, Congress had debated only whether gradually to eliminate slavery in Missouri. At the time, no one had proposed banning slavery outright in all of the Louisiana territory (of which Missouri was a part) or even enacting immediate abolition in Missouri. In its few decisions involving slavery prior to the 1840s, moreover, the Supreme Court had not attempted in the least to interfere with the South's peculiar institution, which the justices seemed to agree existed as a state institution subject only to state laws. No American president, the majority of whom had been slaveholders, had ever made any public statement in opposition to slavery. By the mid-1840s, a general indifference to the slavery question, perhaps even a vague proslavery consensus, existed among most white Americans and their leaders.

Abolitionists knew this, of course, for they had experienced firsthand the wrath of a Northern public that largely regarded them as radicals and rabble-rousers. Some abolitionists did nothing to dispel this image, and even reveled in the disapproval. Viewing slavery as a strictly moral question, they railed against any and all institutions that they saw as complicit with sinful Southern slaveholders, including the Constitution, the national government, and political parties. After the 1840 publication of James Madison's *Notes* from the Constitutional Convention, William Lloyd Garrison and his followers believed they had plenty of evidence that the founders had repeatedly compromised to preserve slavery in order to form a union. Rejecting the framers' flawed handiwork, they abhorred voting, parties, and any involvement in politics. In 1844, Garrisonians indirectly called for secession from the Union by proclaiming "no union with slaveholders."

Anti-Garrisonian abolitionists, unwilling to concede that the nation's founding buttressed the claims of their opponents, joined black abolitionists in seeing the Constitution as a potential weapon in the antislavery arsenal. In 1844, the white abolitionist Gerrit Smith published a pamphlet in which he made much of the absence of the word "slavery" from the constitutional text and argued that, from its preamble to its amendments, the Constitution "present[ed] itself as a noble and beautiful Temple of Liberty."[1] The following year, Massachusetts lawyer Lysander Spooner authored a more influential pamphlet, *The Unconstitutionality of Slavery,* which attempted to prove more systematically that the Constitution provided no support for slavery. A careful legal theorist, Spooner defined true law as "*natural,* unalterable, universal principles," and through a close analysis of state constitutions, the Declaration of Independence, and the Constitution, he concluded that the entire American constitutional tradition promoted the ideals of liberty and citizenship for all of the people in the United States. Unwilling to grant that local practice or majority will constituted true law, Spooner offered a sophisticated—if at times complicated—reading of the founding texts.

Ohio abolitionist and attorney Salmon P. Chase made the greatest contribution to the development of an antislavery constitutional argument. In contrast to the claims of Spooner and black constitutionalists, who relied heavily on the Declaration of Independence, Chase followed Smith's lead in attempting to argue that the Constitution was itself an antislavery document. Noting the absence of the word "slavery," Chase claimed that the founders had held antislavery beliefs and that the national government could neither control slavery nor protect it. Slavery existed, Chase argued, as an entirely local institution. On this point, he relied on a late eighteenth-century English legal precedent. In the case of *Somerset v. Stewart* (1772), the English jurist Lord Mansfield had declared free an African-born slave, who had been purchased in Virginia by an Englishman and taken to live in Britain. Although Mansfield did not question the authority of contracts regarding slave property, his attempt to prevent American law from dictating the status of black people in England resulted in a compelling legal critique of slavery. "The state of slavery is of such a nature," Mansfield wrote, "that it is incapable of being introduced on any reasons, moral or political. . . . It's so odious, that nothing can be suffered to support it but positive law."[2] While the decision itself was ambiguous in some ways, such stirring words proved powerful in the hands of Chase and others, who took Mansfield to mean that slavery could not exist in the absence of local statutory law establishing it. So, Chase reasoned, when a slave passed beyond the jurisdiction of a slave state, the enslaved person immediately became free.

The fact that the Constitution never referred to slaves and always instead to "persons," moreover, prompted Chase to argue that as persons, slaves retained the protections of the Bill of Rights. The Fifth Amendment in particular protected persons against Congress depriving them of "life, liberty, or property" without due process of law. Chase interpreted this to mean that enslaved persons could not be deprived of their liberty—held as slaves—in any areas subject to the exclusive jurisdiction of the national government. According to Chase, this meant that slavery in the District of Columbia, the federal territories, or on the high seas violated the US Constitution. As for the Constitution's Fugitive Slave Clause, which required that "persons held in service or labour" escaping to freedom be "delivered up" to their masters, Chase offered a strict reading of the text. Because this power to return fugitive slaves was not included among the enumerated powers of Congress listed in Article I, Section 8, Chase asserted that the clause represented a compact among the states rather than an affirmative grant of power to Congress. Federal legislation on fugitive slaves, therefore, was unconstitutional. As for the states, he argued, each "must judge for itself as to the character of the compact, and the extent of the obligation created by it."[3] Chase put forth these arguments in a number of legal cases on behalf of those who had escaped to freedom, thereby earning the nickname "the attorney general for fugitive slaves." A skillful strategist who understood that the Northern public disdained abolitionist agitation, Chase did more than anyone else to move the antislavery argument out of the purely moral sphere and into the realm of political discussion. There the slavery issue presented itself as two distinct questions, each pertaining to the constitutional rights of slaveholders.

THE FUGITIVE SLAVE ISSUE

During the early 1840s, the primary debate was over the right of slaveholders to reclaim fugitives who had escaped into the North. In 1793, in order to deal with slaves who escaped to the free states, Congress had enacted the first federal fugitive slave law. Over time, Southern slaveholders found fault with the act, particularly because it established a minimal federal role in the process of returning fugitive slaves to their masters. In order to return a fugitive, a slave owner or his agent first had to, on his own, find and seize the runaway. At times this proved to be no easy task, particularly if the slave catcher encountered local resistance. Next, the slave owner or his representative had to bring the fugitive before a federal judge, state judge, or "any magistrate of a county, city or town corporate" where the fugitive had been seized and offer proof, either oral or by affidavit, "that the person so seized or arrested, doth, under the laws of the State or Territory from which he or she fled, owe service or labor to the person claiming him or her."[4] Upon seeing satisfactory proof, the magistrate thereupon issued a certificate that allowed the slave catcher to return the fugitive to slavery. Beginning in the 1820s, some Northern states enacted personal liberty laws. Rooted in the presumption of freedom, these laws attempted to protect Northern free blacks from being kidnapped by unscrupulous slave catchers and sold into slavery. They provided basic guarantees—the right to trial by jury, for example—for those accused of running away from slavery, but in the process they denied the right of recaption (the right to recapture a fugitive without going to court) that slaveholders claimed under the Fugitive Slave Law of 1793. As a consequence, questions of comity (the right of a state to respect the laws of another) and federalism began to arise.

Controversy over the Fugitive Slave Act of 1793 and Northern personal liberty laws culminated in *Prigg v. Pennsylvania* (1842), a United States Supreme Court case. For many years, the easy passage of fugitive slaves from Maryland into Pennsylvania and the efforts of professional slave catchers to track them down had been a source of contention between the two states, particularly after the passage of an 1826 Pennsylvania personal liberty law. The case of Margaret Morgan, a runaway slave living in Pennsylvania, provided a test of the law. After obtaining an arrest warrant from a Pennsylvania justice of the peace, professional slave catcher Edward Prigg found Morgan and seized her. When Prigg brought Morgan and her children before a justice of the peace, the justice refused to participate further in the case, a right he possessed under the Pennsylvania statute. Prigg then forced Morgan and her children back to Maryland, even though he lacked the necessary certificate from a judge. A county court thus brought kidnapping charges against the slave catcher, and Maryland extradited him to stand trial. After being convicted, Prigg appealed to the US Supreme Court.

In its 8–1 decision, the Court reversed Prigg's conviction, and in the process for the first time spoke on the fugitive slave issue. Writing the majority opinion, Justice Joseph Story of Massachusetts held, in sweeping language, that the Constitution's Fugitive Slave Clause guaranteed to slaveholders "the complete right and title of ownership in their slaves, as property, in every State in the Union into which they might escape from the State where they were held in servitude."[5] Under the clause, masters or slave catchers could remove fugitives from free states without any judicial oversight, so long as these actions were carried out "without any breach of the peace, or any illegal violence."[6] The Court's broad reading of the Fugitive Slave Clause included the idea that Congress possessed exclusive power over the rendition of runaway slaves. It made no sense, according to Story, that slaveholding states would leave to nonslaveholding states the power to regulate fugitives within their own borders. Doing so would practically destroy the rights of slave owners and create chaos in the rendition process. Only Congress, the Court held, could enact legislation regulating the return of fugitives.

The decision in *Prigg* held a number of implications. First, the exclusive nature of congressional power, coupled with the fact that the Fugitive Slave Clause included no reference to state enforcement, meant that states could in no way be required to aid in the return of fugitives. Second, Story's ruling attempted to put to rest doubts—raised by antislavery lawyers—about the constitutionality of the 1793 statute. Employing a loose construction of the Constitution, Story argued that congressional authority could not be confined to the powers listed in Article I, Section 8. Rather, the authority of Congress on this matter fell within its obligation "to provide for the ordinary exigencies of the national government, in cases where rights are intended to be absolutely secured, and duties are positively enjoined by the Constitution."[7] Third, the Court deemed the Pennsylvania personal liberty law unconstitutional. That law, Story held, "purports to punish as a public offense against that state, the very act of seizing and removing a slave by his master, which the Constitution of the United States was designed to justify and uphold."[8] *Prigg v. Pennsylvania* thus put the national government squarely on the side of slaveholders' rights.

Still, the Court's decision generated a degree of confusion. Abolitionists began to argue that the *Prigg* decision meant that states were prohibited from participating at all in the rendition of fugitive slaves, and over the next five years, six free states explicitly forbade state officials from assisting with the return process. Other antislavery activists, meanwhile, continued to doubt the constitutionality of the Fugitive Slave Act of 1793. In part to clear up some of the confusion, the Court took up the matter again in *Jones v. Van Zandt* (1847), a case involving an Ohio abolitionist, John Van Zandt, who had harbored in his covered wagon nine fugitives fleeing from Kentucky. Faced with a civil action in federal court alleging that he had violated the Fugitive Slave Act, Van Zandt acquired the services of antislavery lawyers Chase and William H. Seward of New York, who attempted to use the case again to argue against the constitutionality of the 1793 law. Drawing from the Declaration of Independence, the Bill of Rights, and natural law, the two drafted lengthy legal briefs, which they circulated in abolitionist circles both in the United States and abroad, that attacked the constitutionality of the statute. In making these arguments, Chase and Seward echoed the emphasis of black constitutionalists, who had initially formulated an argument for racial equality under the law based on the Declaration of Independence and the Constitution. The justices were not receptive. Dismissing such "theoretical opinions" regarding slavery, a unanimous Supreme Court reaffirmed its stance in *Prigg* as it upheld the Fugitive Slave Act as well as the conviction of the Ohioan.

Despite the Court's supposedly definitive decision, the fugitive slave issue continued to fester. As long as African Americans fled bondage in the South and sought freedom in the North, the issue remained alive, and the Constitution's Fugitive Slave Clause and the federal Fugitive Slave Act, rather than settling the matter, simply raised the stakes. In the minds of Southerners, particularly slaveholders, the return of fugitives involved the protection of both their constitutional rights and economic interests. Increasing numbers of Northerners, meanwhile, began to see personal liberty laws as more than just a way to prevent the kidnapping of free blacks. For some, stories of enslaved people risking life and limb to escape to liberty raised doubts about the supposed humanity of slavery, of which the South's proslavery apologists so frequently spoke. Thus, controversy over fugitives would not soon disappear.

THE TERRITORIAL QUESTION

While the Constitution had specifically addressed the rights of slaveholders to reclaim fugitives, the Constitution said nothing about the rights of slaveholders to take slaves into federal territories. Lawmakers generally assumed that Congress possessed the power to legislate on the matter under the Constitution's Territories Clause, which gave Congress authority to "make all needful Rules and Regulations respecting the Territory or other Property belonging to the United States." Congress had done just that when, in 1820, it enacted the Missouri Compromise, which allowed slavery in Missouri while banning it from all other portions of Louisiana Territory north of Missouri's southern border. But the South's growing commitment to slaveholders' rights during the 1830s and the acquisition of new territories from Mexico during the 1840s promised to bring this controversial question back to the forefront of American life. Because the two political parties were national parties—that is, because they included voters from both the free and slaveholding states—Whigs and Democrats alike feared the potentially disruptive effects of the slavery issue.

When the debate over slaveholders' rights in the territories began in the halls of Congress, three venerable titans continued to hold sway. John C. Calhoun of South Carolina, the instigator of the nullification movement, stood out as the most prominent spokesman for the slaveholding states. At age sixty-four in 1846, Calhoun had spent his career in Congress, as vice president, and in the Cabinet. Now in the Senate, Calhoun looked upon abolitionism as a dangerous doctrine and grew increasingly restive about the future of the South in the Union. A former Jacksonian Democrat, Calhoun at this point in his career felt loyal to neither political party. Instead, he longed for the creation of a Southern party that would preserve the constitutional rights and economic interests of his home region within the Union. Five years older than Calhoun, Henry Clay had also spent decades in Congress. A Kentucky-born Whig, Clay earned a reputation as the "Great Compromiser" for his role in brokering agreements in the midst of the Missouri controversy and the Nullification Crisis. Over the course of his career, he had run unsuccessfully for president three times. After an unexpected defeat at the hands of James K. Polk in 1844, Clay stepped out of the national spotlight, but after a brief retirement he returned in 1849 to the Senate, where his career had originally begun. Daniel Webster of Massachusetts, equally renowned, had served in Washington nearly as long as Calhoun and Clay. Known for both his oratorical and legal skills, he had first won election to the House of Representatives in 1823, served as secretary of state, and argued a number of cases before the Supreme Court. An opponent of the war with Mexico, Webster feared the effects of slavery's extension on the Union he so revered. All three men would play out the final dramatic chapters in their lives in the controversy over the place of slavery in new territories.

The Wilmot Proviso sparked the great debate. On August 12, 1846, Representative David Wilmot of Pennsylvania introduced an amendment to an appropriations bill requested by President James K. Polk. "As an express and fundamental condition to the acquisition of any territory from the Republic of Mexico by the United States, by virtue of any treaty which may be negotiated between them," it read, "neither slavery nor involuntary servitude shall ever exist in any part of said territory."[9] The Wilmot Proviso mirrored the language of the Northwest Ordinance of 1787, which had prohibited slavery in the territories north of the Ohio River.

Northern Democrats who pushed the proviso did so for an assortment of reasons. In part, internal party politics were at work. Frustrated at Democratic president Polk's willingness to annex all of Texas while simultaneously negotiating a treaty with Great Britain for only half of Oregon Territory, Northern Democrats suspected that Polk and his Southern allies controlled the party and sought only to further the interests of slaveholders. These Democrats supported the proviso as a way to undermine the growth of this special interest within the party, what they termed the Slave Power. Northern public opinion, more importantly, lent growing support to the nonextension principle. Many Northerners opposed the spread of slavery on economic grounds, believing that the introduction of slave labor would hinder economic growth in new territories and provide unfair competition with free white laborers there. Some opposed the extension of slavery to the West for racial reasons—in other words, because they did not want African Americans settling in new lands. Wilmot himself fell into this category. Denying that he was an abolitionist, Wilmot made clear that he possessed "no squeamish sensitiveness on the subject of slavery, no morbid sympathy for the slave." To Wilmot, free soil served the interests of free whites. "I plead the cause and rights of white freemen," he announced. "I would preserve to free white labor a fair country, a rich inheritance, where the sons of toil, of my own race and own color, can live without the disgrace which association with negro slavery brings upon free labor."[10] Some in the North worried that the addition of new slave states would augment Southern power in Congress, which would in turn decrease the likelihood that Congress would enact policies such as high tariffs and internal improvements. Finally, a small segment of the Northern population opposed the spread of slavery for moral reasons. Because they believed in abolishing slavery where it already existed, abolitionists thought it unconscionable that human bondage should take root in new lands. By focusing on the extension of slavery in territories potentially gained from Mexico, Wilmot's short and simple proviso thus served to unify Northerners who held a wide range of political beliefs on the issues of slavery and race.

To white Southerners, what mattered was that Northerners thought they could actually impose such a free soil policy. In Southerners' mind, halting the spread of slavery violated their constitutional rights, ran counter to their economic interests, and seemed an affront to their honor. By this time, the vast majority of Southerners believed that their rights to hold and take slaves where they wished rested on a solid constitutional foundation. Although the Constitution did not specifically address the matter of slavery in new territories, the Fugitive Slave Clause required the return of those who escaped to freedom, which Southerners understood as a clear affirmation of slaveholders' rights as property owners. If Northerners believed they could prevent slaveholders from exercising these rights in federal territories, did they also believe that they could interfere with slaveholders' rights in the South, where slavery already existed? Apart from the constitutional aspects of the question, any restriction on the expansion of slavery threatened to decrease the demand for slaves, thereby lowering slave prices and devaluing masters' economic investments. Northern advocacy of the nonextension principle, moreover, offended white Southerners. By attempting to prohibit slavery from new lands, Northerners appeared to want to dictate the terms.

The Wilmot Proviso failed to pass in 1846, but the political effects of its introduction were immediate. Significantly, voting on the proviso in both houses of Congress emerged along sectional lines, with all Southerners opposing the measure and nearly all Northerners supporting it. As distinct from the sectional voting pattern that had emerged during the Missouri crisis, when political parties were still in the developing stage, the clear sectional alignment that emerged during the controversy over the proviso occurred in an age of strict party discipline, a fact that made the alignment all the more striking.[11] Suddenly sectional loyalties seemed to matter more than party affiliation. Over the next two years, as US soldiers ground down the Mexican army 2,000 miles to the south, debate continued to rage in Congress over the fate of whatever territories might result from an American victory. During subsequent congressional sessions, Wilmot's Northern Democratic colleagues continued to reintroduce the proviso, while others put forth competing proposals.

Three alternatives to the Wilmont Proviso eventually emerged. First, Senator Calhoun, representing the Southern extremist position, argued that the Constitution protected slaveholders' rights, thus allowing masters to take their slaves into any new territory without restriction. Arguing that federal territories were the "common property" of the American people, Calhoun claimed that all of the Constitution's guarantees—including the protection of slave property—applied there. Second, some political leaders, including President Polk, supported the idea of simply extending the Missouri Compromise line all the way to the Pacific Ocean. Such a plan would thus permanently divide the continent into two halves, slave and free. Third, others, notably Democratic senator Lewis Cass of Michigan, promoted the notion of what came to be known as "popular sovereignty" or "squatter sovereignty"—the idea that settlers themselves, rather than Congress, should have the power to decide whether new territories would allow slavery. American military victory over Mexico and the signing of the Treaty of Guadalupe Hidalgo in February 1848 meant that the fierce, and increasingly complicated, debate over slavery in the territories would soon need to be resolved.

THE ELECTION OF 1848

In this highly charged atmosphere, the two major political parties nominated candidates for president. Attempting to maintain party unity, both the Democrats and Whigs aimed to tamp down sectional division within their ranks over the slavery question. Focused more on finding an electable nominee than on defining a clear position on the issues before the nation, the Democrats selected a candidate before ever drafting a platform. Content with having served a single successful term, President Polk chose to retire after four years in office, and Senator Lewis Cass emerged as the Democratic nominee. Once written, the party's platform evaded the territorial question, criticized abolitionists, and simply held that "the principles and compromises of the Constitution" were "broad enough and strong enough to embrace and uphold the Union as it was, the Union as it is, and the Union as it shall be."[12] The Whig Party too attempted to obfuscate its position on the slavery question. Nominating General Zachary Taylor of Louisiana, who had never before voted, much less held office, the Whig Party avoided drafting a platform at its convention. The party did later pass a brief set of resolutions, which, in their vagueness, exceeded even the Democratic platform. Describing Taylor as the candidate of "Peace, Prosperity, and Union," the resolutions suggested that Taylor's "position as a Southwestern man" was key. "Reared on the banks of the great stream whose tributaries, natural and artificial, embrace the whole Union," the resolutions assured readers, Taylor would put the interests of the Union first, as his "various duties in past life have been rendered, not on the soil or under the flag of any State or section, but over the wide frontier, and under the broad banner of the Nation."[13]

Determined proponents of the Wilmot Proviso, unsatisfied with the mushiness of the major parties, formed their own organization. In their minds, by nominating Cass, a leading champion of popular sovereignty, the Democrats had embraced that compromise solution for the future of the territories. Moreover, because Taylor owned more than a hundred slaves on plantations in Mississippi and Louisiana, Free Soilers—as those opposed to the extension of slavery now called themselves—distrusted his yet-to-be-declared intentions. The new Free Soil Party united the remnants of the Liberty Party of 1844,

Northern Democrats who favored the proviso, and antislavery Whigs who could not stomach the nomination of Taylor. Although strong personalities and old loyalties made the joining of these forces a difficult undertaking, together they nominated presidential candidate Martin Van Buren, the Democratic ex-president from New York.

While national party platforms and statements by the candidates scrupulously avoided the most pressing issues regarding slavery, the campaign between Taylor and Cass demonstrated the level of polarization that had already taken place. Surrogates essentially ran two different campaigns for their candidates—one each in the North and the South. In addition to issuing two different campaign biographies for Cass, the Democratic Party emphasized distinct themes in the two sections. In the North, the party claimed that because few believed that slavery would ever take root in the arid Southwest, popular sovereignty was unlikely to produce anything but freedom in new territories. In the South, meanwhile, party officials focused relentlessly on Cass's pledge to veto the Wilmot Proviso, if it ever passed. Whigs used a similar strategy. In the North, surrogates focused on Taylor's apparent pledge not to veto congressional legislation unless it explicitly violated the Constitution. This meant, they believed, that Taylor would sign the Wilmot Proviso if it passed. In the South, though, Whigs emphasized Taylor's credentials as a Southerner and slaveholder—whom few imagined would ever sign the hated proviso. By 1848, in other words, sectional pressures had already shaped the two national parties.

Taylor and his running mate, New Yorker Millard Fillmore, won the election by a margin of 163 to 127 electoral votes. Taylor claimed victory in fifteen of thirty states, including the two biggest electoral prizes, New York and Pennsylvania. Southern Democratic defections to Taylor, as well as a weak overall Democratic turnout, also helped Taylor win eight slave states, three more than Whig Henry Clay had won four years before. For his part, the Free Soiler Van Buren won more than 291,000 votes, nearly five times what the abolitionist Birney had won in 1844. Although he did not win any states, Van Buren garnered more votes than Cass in Massachusetts, New York, and Ver-

Table 2.1. Presidential Election of 1848

Candidate	Party	Electoral Votes	Percent of Popular Vote
Zachary Taylor	Whig	163	47.3
Lewis Cass	Democratic	127	42.4
Martin Van Buren	Free Soil	—	10.1

mont, a fact that signaled the Northern electorate's willingness to support the Free Soil position even against an established political party. Given the president-elect's silence, it was unclear what Taylor's victory meant for the immediate future of slavery in the territories.

CRISIS AND THE COMPROMISE OF 1850

In March 1849, Zachary Taylor took the oath of office as the twelfth president of the United States. One observer on meeting him for the first time described him as "old, outrageously ugly, uncultivated [and] uninformed," a "mere military chieftain" who knew nothing of politics or affairs of state.[14] With little in his bearing to inspire the nation's confidence, Taylor's inaugural address offered no hint of how he would approach the issue at hand, for he noted simply that he "would be devoted to the welfare of the whole country, and not to the support of any particular section or merely local interest."[15] In the meantime, the establishment of civil government in the lands gained from Mexico the year before became increasingly urgent. In the aftermath of American military victory, the army remained in charge, but California's sudden population boom dramatized the need to establish order. In early 1848, gold had been discovered at Sutter's Mill near San Francisco, prompting the famous gold rush of 1849. Almost overnight, San Francisco became a boom town as tens of thousands of fortune seekers converged on the area. California's status was therefore of immediate concern. What to do with the other lands of the West proved less critical but still problematic. New Mexico—encompassing a portion of the territory to the east of California and to the west of Texas—was still undefined, as its border with Texas remained disputed. (New Mexico primarily consisted of a population of settlers clustered in the settlement of Santa Fe, on the east bank of the Rio Grande.) Meanwhile, Mormons who had settled in the region around the Great Salt Lake made a competing claim. They petitioned to form a new territory they named Deseret, which included nearly all of the new lands gained from Mexico, with the notable exception of the portion of California populated by the gold rush.

During his first few months in office, Taylor decided that both California and New Mexico could skip the territorial stage and gain immediate admission to the Union as free states. Although he issued no public statements in this regard, he sent emissaries to the West to convey this message to residents. Taylor's actions provoked outrage from Southerners, shocked that a slaveholder had betrayed them. A few months later, as Congress convened and the level of sectional invective continued to rise, Taylor directly confronted his critics. In a January 1850 special message to Congress, the president argued that his proposal to admit both areas immediately as states, rather than territories, would avoid a lengthy, polarizing debate in Congress over the status of slavery there. Such a policy, moreover, would respect the wishes of the people of California, who had already drafted a constitution to submit to Congress for admission to statehood. (Settled mostly by Northerners obsessed with gold, Californians wanted theirs to be a free state.) Taylor claimed that New Mexico as well would soon be ready to submit a proposed state constitution, presumably banning slavery. Although he appealed to love of the Union, the president's stance provoked anything but goodwill from Southern members of Congress, who feared that new free states would upset the sectional balance of power in the Senate and lead to Northern interference with slavery in the South. Many Southerners hoped that Texas, whose western boundary remained undefined, would be broken up into several slave states, while others began to talk of secession.

In keeping with his reputation as a voice of moderation, Henry Clay hoped to craft a compromise. In two major speeches in early 1850, the aging Kentuckian offered a number of proposals: that California be admitted to the Union as a free state, that New Mexico and Deseret form territorial governments without any restrictions on slavery, that Texas' boundary be settled and its remaining debts paid by the US government, that the slave trade (the public buying and selling of slaves) be abolished in Washington, DC, and that a new, more effective fugitive slave law be enacted. During the weeks to follow, Clay's fellow senators debated the measures, and both Northerners and Southerners at the extreme ends of the spectrum clung rigidly to their positions. Calhoun opposed Clay's compromise, for he believed that only a preservation of the equilibrium between the free and slave states could save the Union. The previous fall, Mississippians had issued a call for a Southern convention to be held in the summer of 1850, where delegates from the slaveholding states could discuss their common concerns. As debate continued into the spring, several Southern states, urged on by an ailing Calhoun, sent delegates to just such a meeting in June. At the same time, Texas prepared to invade New Mexico in order to prevent its establishment as a free state, and several Southern governors expressed their support for such action. Meanwhile, one of the North's most committed abolitionists in Congress, freshman senator William H. Seward of New York, delivered a remarkable speech in the course of debate, in which he denied that lawmakers need adhere only to the Constitution as they considered the fate of slavery in the West. Using some of the most controversial rhetoric of the decade, Seward claimed that "there is a higher law than the Constitution, which regulates our authority over the domain, and devotes it to the same noble purposes."[16] As stewards of God's creation, in other words, Americans possessed an obligation to extend the blessings of freedom to these new lands. President Taylor, meanwhile, held fast to his own plans for California and New Mexico, and he reportedly vowed to blockade Southern harbors and to send troops both to defend New Mexico and put down a Southern secessionist movement. Despite earnest pleas and eloquent speeches from compromise supporters such as Daniel Webster, neither side appeared willing to budge.

With Clay's compromise stalled and the Union on the brink of collapse, President Taylor suddenly died. On the Fourth of July, 1850, the president had spent hours in the hot sun listening to speeches at the Washington Monument construction site and afterward had consumed large amounts of cherries and milk, which Washington's residents had been warned to avoid out of fear of the spread of an Asiatic cholera epidemic. The next day Taylor had taken ill, and he died on July 9. With the key opponent of Clay's compromise bill now deceased, Millard Fillmore, the new president and a native of New York, took steps that contributed to an accommodation between the sections. First, Fillmore appointed an entirely new Cabinet, which included Webster, a strong advocate of compromise, as secretary of state. Second, the president attempted to resolve the New Mexico situation. He informed Congress of the details of the threat from Texas, promised military support to settlers in Santa Fe if invaded, and asked lawmakers to fix a boundary between Texas and New Mexico to resolve the dispute. Congress's success in drawing an acceptable boundary between the two appeared to end the long stalemate. Senator Stephen Douglas of Illinois, who had taken over management of the Compromise after Clay took ill and left Washington, then broke Clay's omnibus compromise bill into several component parts and adroitly consolidated separate majorities for each one. As Douglas's five bills individually passed, President Fillmore signed each into law.

In the end, the so-called Compromise of 1850 closely resembled Clay's original omnibus bill. The Compromise established the boundary of Texas and mandated federal payment of Texas's outstanding debts, admitted California as a free state, abolished the public sale of slaves in the District of Columbia (a mostly symbolic issue), established the territorial boundaries and governments of New Mexico and Utah (a much smaller version of the original Deseret), and enacted a new fugitive slave law. Some in Congress congratulated themselves on coming up with a deal that seemed to offer something to all sides, while President Fillmore optimistically referred to the measures as a "final settlement" of the disagreements over slavery that had plagued the nation for the past four years.[17]

At best the Compromise of 1850 produced a fragile peace. Because of Douglas's tactic of separating the bills—each of which appealed specifically to either the North or South—nothing like an overall consensus in support of compromise ever existed. In the months after the passage of the agreement, activists at both ends of the spectrum continued their agitation. In Georgia, Mississippi, and South Carolina, anger over the admission of California prompted Southern proslavery "fire-eaters" to attempt to whip up public support for secession, while in Northern hotbeds of abolitionism, outrage over the new fugitive law generated meetings, resolutions, and protests. National political leaders, moreover, greatly exaggerated the extent to which the Compromise actually resolved the issues of the day. Although the agreement settled the questions of California's status and the boundary between Texas and New Mexico, the larger question of the future of slavery in all areas except California remained unresolved. The laws that established the territories of New Mexico and Utah stated only that "when admitted as a State, the said Territory, or any portion of the same, shall be received into the Union, with or without slavery, as their constitution may prescribe at the time of their admission."[18] This popular sovereignty language clearly took the matter out of the hands of Congress, but lawmakers held conflicting views about whether it meant that territorial legislatures could actually exclude slavery.

Most contentious was the new fugitive slave law. While it passed by relatively wide margins and appeared to reflect a traditional American commitment to protecting property rights and to enforcing the Fugitive Slave Clause, the law held the potential to be even more provocative than the Wilmot Proviso. It denied a fugitive's right of jury trial, instead allowing for a hearing before a court-appointed commissioner whose fees depended on the outcome of the case. If the commissioner granted a certificate authorizing a claimant to take an alleged fugitive, the claimant paid the commissioner $10, but where the evidence did not warrant seizure of the fugitive, the claimant paid the commissioner $5. Most strikingly, the law potentially enlisted even the most unwilling of Northerners to participate in the capture of fugitives, for it provided that "all good citizens are hereby commanded to aid and assist in the prompt execution of this law."[19]

African Americans vehemently protested the measure. In mass meetings throughout the free states, they issued resolutions and proclamations affirming black liberty and pledging themselves to resist the law, by force if necessary. After a meeting at an African Methodist Episcopal Church in Philadelphia, a committee of black leaders there issued a set of resolutions charging that the act violated the Declaration of Independence, the privilege of the writ of habeas corpus (the idea that one could not be detained without

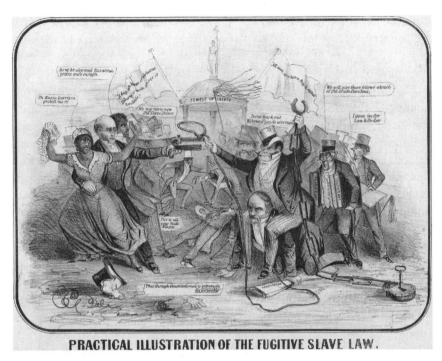

PRACTICAL ILLUSTRATION OF THE FUGITIVE SLAVE LAW.

This 1851 drawing captures the political controversy over the Fugitive Slave Law. The sketch depicts abolitionist William Lloyd Garrison, on the left, attempting to prevent a slave catcher, riding on the back of Secretary of State Daniel Webster, from returning a fleeing slave woman to her owner. The enforcement of the law, more than any other legislative enactment, demonstrated the extent to which the national government protected the rights of slaveholders during the 1850s. Courtesy of the Library of Congress, LC-USZC4-4660

cause), and the constitutional guarantee of due process of law. Describing the law as "utterly at variance with the principles of the Constitution," the Philadelphia blacks pledged "to resist this law at any cost and at all hazards."[20] Within months, in nearby Christiana, Pennsylvania, blacks led a band of local resisters to the recapture of a fugitive slave, resulting in a violent skirmish and the mortal wounding of a Maryland planter. In Boston, African Americans emphasized their heritage of liberty in the birthplace of Crispus Attucks, the black martyr of the Boston Massacre, and vowed to fight the return of fugitives through a revitalized Boston Vigilance Committee. In Albany, the New York State Convention of Colored People summed up its opposition to the law in three concise resolutions: "Resolved: That the fugitive slave law is the law of tyrants. Resolved: That disobedience to tyrants is obedience to God.

Resolved: That we will obey God." Other Northern blacks decided to leave the country. Out of fear of what the new Fugitive Slave Act might mean to them, thousands of African Americans in the North—both free and fugitives—emigrated to Canada.[21]

Most Northern whites saw the law as a necessary, if at times distasteful, solution to the problem of preserving slaveholders' rights to recapture fugitive slaves. Acknowledging the necessity of upholding the Constitution's Fugitive Slave Clause, some Northerners reacted with alarm to the requirement that citizens collaborate with authorities in enforcing the measure. Between June 1851 and April 1852, Harriet Beecher Stowe, the daughter of prominent clergyman Lyman Beecher, published in serial form *Uncle Tom's Cabin*. With its sympathetic portrayal of slave families, grotesque characterization of a slave trader, and heartfelt account of an enslaved mother and child escaping to freedom, the antislavery novel profoundly affected the perceptions of the Northern public. In the first year after its publication as a book, *Uncle Tom's Cabin* sold 300,000 copies and began to lend an air of respectability not only to opposition to the fugitive slave law but also to abolitionism itself. Despite such controversy, the Compromise alleviated in the short term some of the tensions that had nearly dissolved the Union. Both major political parties committed themselves to the settlement in the 1852 presidential election, and two moderate candidates emerged. The Democratic Party nominated Franklin Pierce of New Hampshire, a relatively unknown former congressman and US senator, while the Whig Party nominated General Winfield Scott, a military hero who pledged his support for the Compromise. Scott's stance alienated a group of Northern Whigs, who bolted the party and nominated Senator John P. Hale of New Hampshire on the Free Soil ticket. Despite this drama, in general, sectional tensions remained muted in the election. Hale received only about half the number of votes as the Free Soil candidate in 1848, and with the Whigs in disarray, the Democrat Pierce won twenty-seven of thirty-one states. Despite lingering anger among extremists in both sections of the country, most Americans seemed satisfied with the Compromise. Pierce came into office stating that "the laws of 1850, commonly called the 'compromise measures,' are strictly constitutional and to be unhesitatingly carried into effect." In his 1853 inaugural address, Pierce appealed to the history of the young republic and issued an eloquent plea for continued peace between the sections: "Standing, as I do, almost within view of the green slopes of Monticello, and, as it were, within reach of the tomb of Washington . . . I can express no better hope for my country than that the kind Providence which smiled upon our fathers may enable their children to preserve the blessings they have inherited."[22] But Pierce was neither a Jefferson nor a Washington.

A man of limited political abilities, the new president proved unable to handle the storms that lay ahead.

KANSAS, NEBRASKA, BOSTON, AND THE REPUBLICANS

The major political crisis of the Pierce administration arose from a proposal that initially had nothing to do with slavery. Senator Stephen Douglas, stretching back to his days as a member of the House of Representatives in the mid-1840s, had long championed a transcontinental railroad linking Chicago to the Pacific coast. With its position on the Great Lakes, as well as its proximity to the Mississippi River, Chicago seemed a likely hub for a railroad connecting the populous East to the frontier West. Like others who dreamed of this extraordinary technological achievement, Douglas saw the extension of the railroad as a way to fulfill the promise of westward expansion, promote economic opportunities, and bind the country together. A leader within the so-called Young America movement, a political culture that emphasized democratic government and national progress, Douglas believed that Manifest Destiny, economic development, and popular rule were the keys to national glory and greatness. (The Illinois senator also stood to profit from such a venture, for he had invested heavily in Chicago real estate.) In order to build a rail line, the large territory to the north and west of Missouri and Iowa would have to be organized. Railroad workers would need to be housed, land would need to be distributed, and disputes would need to be resolved. All would require the existence of a territorial government. Organization of the territory also stood to benefit farmers migrating from the free states of the Midwest, who could not make land claims in the area until a government existed. Neither railroad interests nor land-hungry farmers wanted slavery in the new territory, and Douglas's initial draft of a bill organizing the region simply ignored the slavery question. In 1850, Douglas had described the Compromise, which he had played a large part in passing, as a final solution to the issue of slavery in the territories. Privately reluctant to raise the question again, Douglas knew that doing so would cause, in his words, "a hell of a storm."[23]

Under pressure from key Southern members of Congress, Douglas agreed to the idea of taking the popular sovereignty language from the Compromise of 1850—the laws organizing New Mexico and Utah Territories—and inserting it into the new bill. In January 1854, Douglas introduced a revised version that established two new territories, Nebraska and Kansas. According to the bill, both territories, when admitted as states, "shall be received into the

Senator Stephen A. Douglas of Illinois, who advocated popular sovereignty as a way of dealing with the slavery issue in new territories, adhered to Democratic Party orthodoxy that the government created by the American founders was a white man's government. Courtesy of the Library of Congress, LC-DIG-cwpbh-00881

Union with or without slavery, as their constitution may prescribe at the time of their admission."[24] Popular sovereignty, Douglas hoped, would peacefully resolve the slavery question, and many historians believe that Douglas fully expected popular sovereignty to yield antislavery results there. The Kansas–Nebraska bill declared the Missouri Compromise line, which in 1820 had banned slavery from these areas, to be "inoperative and void." Trumpeting the popular sovereignty solution, moreover, the bill itself noted that the purpose of the proposed law was "not to legislate slavery into any Territory or State, nor to exclude it therefrom, but to leave the people thereof perfectly free to form and regulate their domestic institutions in their own way, subject only to the Constitution of the United States."[25] Douglas thought that linking the slavery question to the deeply American ideals of democracy and self-government offered the best chance to end sectional squabbling over the issue.

An ambitious politician who hoped to curry favor with the South, unify his party, and provide economic opportunities for his Illinois constituents, Douglas perhaps underestimated the reaction to his bill.

Antislavery leaders excoriated the proposed legislation. A group of six Northern members of Congress, including Senator Chase of Ohio (elected in 1850) and Senator Charles Sumner of Massachusetts, composed the "Appeal of the Independent Democrats," which denounced the proposed measure. "We arraign this bill as a gross violation of a sacred pledge," the appeal stated, "as a criminal betrayal of precious rights; as part and parcel of an atrocious plot to exclude from a vast unoccupied region, immigrants from the Old World and free laborers from our own States, and convert it into a dreary region of despotism, inhabited by masters and slaves." Reviewing the history of the passage of the Missouri Compromise, the appeal described the 1820 law as a "solemn compact," agreed to by Northerners and Southerners alike, that had prohibited slavery from the area.[26] Offended by the harsh response, Douglas staunchly defended the proposal. After five months of bitter debate, he managed to assemble a slim majority in Congress—composed of prorailroad Northerners and proslavery Southerners—to pass the bill. President Pierce quickly added his signature on May 30, 1854, and the bill became law. Despite success, the political costs to Douglas were enormous. The passage of the Kansas-Nebraska Act greatly damaged his standing, as well as that of his party, in the eyes of the Northern public. Later, he famously remarked that when making his way home to Illinois at the end of the congressional session, "I could travel from Boston to Chicago by the light of my own effigy."[27] Ironically, in spite of Douglas's persistent efforts, the following year his bill authorizing a transcontinental railroad failed, and it would be another seven years—after Douglas had died—before Congress would pass such an act.

At the same time that members of Congress passed legislation regarding the future of slavery in Kansas and Nebraska, residents of Boston found themselves confronting slavery in their midst. The leading city in New England and in many ways the center of American abolitionism, Boston suddenly felt itself—like Kansas and Nebraska—subject to the whims of the Slave Power. In March 1854, the enslaved man Anthony Burns had escaped from Virginia and made his way to the city, where he began working in a clothing store owned by Lewis Hayden, himself a former slave who had escaped before establishing himself as a successful businessman. In late May, just as the Kansas-Nebraska Act was passed, Burns's master attempted to reclaim him under the Fugitive Slave Act. Organizing quickly to rescue Burns, on May 26 local black and white abolitionists led by Hayden stormed the courthouse jail that held Burns. In the melee that ensued between Boston abolitionists and US marshals, thirteen people sustained injuries and one marshal died of a gunshot wound. Black Bostonians had made good on their vow of resistance. The following day, with the tense city filled with both federal troops and abolitionist protesters, the US commissioner tried Burns's case under the terms of the Fugitive Slave Act. Confirming Burns's identity and his master's title to ownership, the commissioner ruled in favor of Burns's owner, and less than a week later, a phalanx of federal troops escorted Burns to a ship in Boston Harbor, which he boarded to return to slavery.

In 1854, the two elements of the slavery controversy—the territorial question and the fugitive issue—converged. Southerners saw their rights at stake in both situations. In Kansas and Nebraska, popular sovereignty seemed to offer adequate protection of the rights of those slaveholders who wished to settle in the territories, so long as they constituted a majority and could codify those rights into law. In Boston, Southerners claimed that all they wanted was for the Constitution and the law to be enforced. But in both instances, the Northern reaction was strong and swift. The public outcry over the seizure of a fugitive in Boston, the very city where Crispus Attucks had died in the Boston Massacre, prompted the state legislature to enact a far-reaching personal liberty law. The act explicitly guaranteed extensive due process rights for fugitives and put insuperable barriers in the way of all who would attempt to assist the federal government in the rendition process. Offended that the passage of the Kansas-Nebraska Act and the arrest of Burns indicated the growth of an aggressive Slave Power, Massachusetts residents—and many other sympathizers throughout the North—believed that they needed to recommit themselves to the idea of establishing the Northern states as truly free territory, in defiance of the federal fugitive slave law. On the heels of the passage of the Kansas-Nebraska Act, the events in Boston produced a backlash that bolstered the Northern antislavery cause.

The events of 1854 produced a seismic shift in American politics. With the publication of the "Appeal of the Independent Democrats" and the rendition of Anthony Burns, increasing numbers of Northern voters became convinced that the Democratic Party was a mere tool of an aggressive Slave Power. Reality soon caught up with perception. In the elections of 1854–1855, the Democrats lost sixty-six of their ninety-one seats in Congress in the free states, and the scale of their defeat in the Northern states converted the party into a Southern-dominated organization. While the Democratic Party's base of support had always been in the South, the flap over the Kansas-Nebraska Act transformed the political landscape. Only Southerners or "Northern men with Southern principles," such as Pierce and Douglas, could hope to receive Democratic support. After 1854, the Democrats were rapidly becoming a pro-

This 1855 print portrays scenes from the life of Anthony Burns, the fugitive slave whose arrest and trial stoked antislavery sentiment in Boston and throughout the North. The controversy over the rendition of Burns and other fugitive slaves brought to the forefront for the first time the question of the rights of African Americans. Courtesy of the Library of Congress, LC-DIG-pga-04268

Southern party, a party that promoted a brand of racial nationalism that caricatured African Americans, exonerated Southern slaveholders, and promoted sectional compromise in the face of political tension over slavery.

The Whig Party, meanwhile, disintegrated. A fragile coalition and a minority party from the start, the Whigs had won few presidential elections during their brief history, and in 1852, Pierce's resounding defeat of the Whig candidate, Winfield Scott, had thrown the party into disarray. Essentially, the Whigs proved unable to survive the sectional split within their ranks. As Northern Whigs grew increasingly hostile to the extension of slavery, cooperation with Southern Whigs became more difficult. In the 1852 election, Whig support in the Lower South had completely evaporated as many Southern Whigs migrated to the Democratic Party. Afterward, a despondent contingent of party loyalists in the Upper South and North clung to fading hopes that Whiggery could survive.

At the same time, powerful anti-immigrant sentiment also hurt the Whigs' position. The American Party, also known as the Know-Nothing Party, arose during the mid-1850s as a significant political force, especially in the Northern states. (They earned the nickname because when initially formed as a secret society, its members claimed to "know nothing" when asked about their organization.) These native-born Protestants expressed dismay at the huge influx of mostly Irish Catholic immigrants who seemed to be invading northeastern cities and by now had emerged as a key Democratic constituency. In some places xenophobia proved stronger than opposition to the Slave Power. In fact, to some degree the nativist movement and the antislavery movement competed for the same voters, for both found their basis of support among Northern evangelical Protestants. For this reason, the Know-Nothings siphoned off a sizable bloc of former Whig voters in the North and thus contributed to the demise of the Whigs. Where Whig candidates did win in the North in 1854–1855, it was usually because they had Know-Nothing support.

More significant as an outlet for antislavery Whigs, though, was the newly formed Republican Party. As the debate over the Kansas-Nebraska Act unfolded in early 1854, a broad opposition coalition began to emerge. By early summer, within a few weeks of the passage of the act, a variety of new antislavery political organizations had formed under various names in several Northern states. Among the many names proposed, "Republican" eventually stuck. The party began as a loose political alliance among a variety of factions. The party included radical elements, primarily New Englanders, who vehemently opposed slavery on moral grounds. It incorporated remnants of the Free Soilers, who firmly opposed the spread of slavery into the West often for racial rather than humanitarian reasons. It included Northern former Democrats, disillusioned by the Southerners' apparent takeover of their party. And its foundation lay in Northern Whigs—some moderate, some conservative—who held a deep devotion to the preservation of the Union and a strong belief that the spread of slavery would work to the economic and moral detriment of the nation's future development. This new Republican Party soon ran candidates for office throughout the North on a platform opposing the extension of slavery. Significant numbers of Know-Nothings also joined the Republicans, and in certain states, Republicans consciously made nativist appeals in order to attract Know-Nothing support. Still, the new Republican Party coalesced mostly around its opposition to the South and the Slave Power. Although one historian has described them as a "polyglot coalition," arising more because of a common enemy than from mutual attachments, the cry of "Free soil, free labor, free men, free speech" reflected their foundational principles.[28] In short, Republicans saw themselves as opponents of the Southern "slavocracy" that seemed to hold the Democratic Party in its grasp.

PROSLAVERY IDEOLOGY AND SLAVEHOLDERS' RIGHTS

Meanwhile, the Republicans' common enemy, the South, displayed an increasing commitment to slavery and white supremacy. By the 1850s, the Southern defense of its peculiar institution encompassed a variety of social, economic, religious, and scientific arguments. Socially, white Southerners claimed that slavery served as "an indispensable police institution," in the words of proslavery writer George Fitzhugh, which prevented crime, poverty, and chaos from enveloping society.[29] Economically, white Southerners convinced themselves that because plantations proved to be both productive and profitable, the slave laborers who served as the "mud sill" of Southern society—the lowest social class—benefited both from the paternalistic outlook and the material abundance of their masters. One of the most frequent claims was that the South's social and economic order proved far superior to the heartless, industrial form of capitalism that had taken root in Northern cities. "Your whole hireling class of manual laborers and 'operatives,' as you call them, are essentially slaves," the South Carolina planter and senator James Henry Hammond proclaimed to the North. "The difference between us is, that our slaves are hired for life and well compensated. . . . Yours are hired by the day, not cared for, and scantily compensated."[30] Religiously, the region's evangelicals viewed the enslavement and conversion of the South's slave population as a glorious achievement. "The spectacle of three hundred thousand barbarians, emerging, under the mild and humane treatment of their owners, into near four millions of civilized Christians, is not only without a parallel in the history of the African race, but of the whole world," enthused Georgia chief justice Joseph H. Lumpkin, a prominent Presbyterian layman who in his earlier career had been critical of slavery.[31] Evangelical slaveholders routinely trumpeted the paternalistic idea that masters had a responsibility to take care of their slaves in the same way that they took care of their children, thus accusing abolitionists of un-Christian irresponsibility toward blacks. Of course, this paternalistic understanding rested on a biblical foundation, of which evangelicals were so confident that Baptist minister Thornton Stringfellow of Virginia could state, "Slavery was instituted by Jehovah himself."[32] Finally, scientists such as Dr. Samuel A. Cartwright of Louisiana argued that physiological differences justified slavery. "It is this defective hematosis or atmospherization of the blood, conjoined with a deficiency of cerebral matter in the cranium, . . . that is the true cause of that debasement of mind, which has rendered the people of Africa unable to take care of themselves," Cartwright wrote in 1851 with scientific certainty.[33] While the defense of slavery encompassed a set of deeply intertwined and widely held beliefs, all of these justifications for slavery— social, economic, religious, and scientific—rested on the foundational tenets of white supremacy and black inferiority. Racism preceded and undergirded all of the other reasons that white Southerners gave for their peculiar institution.

Because slavery rested on white supremacy, white Southern lawmakers became increasingly restive about the notion of free black people living in a slave society. Laws regulating the movement and behavior of free blacks grew more restrictive during this time, and theological ideas regarding alleged racial inferiority found their way into the law. Georgia's Judge Lumpkin took his cues from the Genesis story of Noah and his sons when he declared in an 1853 case that free blacks, like their slave counterparts, lived under a divine curse. "The act of manumission confers no other rights but that of freedom from the dominion of the master and the limited liberty of locomotion," Lumpkin asserted. "It does not and cannot confer citizenship, nor any of the powers, civil or political, incident to citizenship; that the social and civil degradation, resulting from the taint of blood, adheres to the descendants of Ham in this country."[34] Such declarations presaged a more public debate by the late 1850s in some Southern states about whether free blacks should be reenslaved. The solidifying of the connection between white racism and black slavery deepened all white Southerners' commitment to slavery and the society it had created. "Color alone is here the badge of distinction," exclaimed proslavery theorist Thomas Dew of Virginia, "and all who are white are equal in spite of the variety of occupations."[35]

Notions of the supposed equality of all white Southerners, despite huge differences in wealth in Southern society, lay behind the developing notion of slaveholders' rights. If all white Southerners were potential slave owners, then all white Southerners possessed the right to own slave property, the right to reclaim escaped fugitives, and the right to settle new territories. Northern Republicans never questioned the right of Southerners to hold slaves where slavery already existed, and they certainly never challenged the notion of white supremacy. But to white Southerners, these were distinctions without a difference. Because Republicans seemed to want to limit the right to recapture fugitives, and because they strongly opposed slaveholders' rights in the territories, white Southerners looked with alarm at their rapid ascent. By the mid-1850s, white supremacy, proslavery, and Southern rights became one ideology, three cords bound tightly together in the Southern mind. Witnessing the rise of an exclusively sectional party in the North, many Southerners feared that Republican success would mean nonenforcement of the fugitive slave law, the halt of the spread of slavery into new territories, and eventually the end of slavery in the South. Racial integration, black equality, and interracial marriage would soon follow. Struck by fear of a nightmare scenario, horrified white Southerners took to derisively calling the new political party the "Black Republicans."

THE ANTISLAVERY MOVEMENT AND THE CONSTITUTION

If white Southerners increasingly coalesced around a set of common assumptions, abolitionists began moving toward the political brand of antislavery that allowed them to join in the Republican coalition. Diversity and debate had always marked the internal dynamics of the Northern antislavery movement. During the early nineteenth century, those advocating black emigration to Canada or colonization in Africa squared off against those who favored remaining in America. Later, some wanted to broaden the movement to include women's rights or pacifism, while others preferred to confine the battle to the struggle against slavery. More significant than these divisions, though, was the ongoing conflict over involvement in politics and allegiance to the Constitution. Because Garrison and his followers took an uncompromising position in support of immediate abolition, they disdained involvement in politics. Garrisonians viewed the entire structure—politics, government, and the Constitution—as fundamentally corrupt, tarnished with the sin of slavery.

In 1852, Frederick Douglass publicly broke with Garrisonian orthodoxy,

Frederick Douglass, the foremost champion of the rights of African Americans during the nineteenth century, attempted to keep the nation's founding principles at the forefront of the abolition movement. Courtesy of the Library of Congress, LC-USZ62-15887

a development that helped lay the groundwork for the Free Soil–Republican coalition. Douglass echoed earlier black constitutionalists in criticizing the United States for failing to live up to the principles articulated at its founding. His most famous oration, "What to the Slave Is the Fourth of July," a trenchant analysis of enslaved people's relationship to the United States, emphasized American hypocrisy. Delivered in Rochester, New York, in 1852, the speech praised the founders of the country as brave, heroic men who had been willing to sacrifice their lives for the sake of liberty. Douglass urged his audience to honor the founders, the Declaration of Independence, and the date on which it was signed: "The 4th of July is the first great fact in your nation's history—the very ring-bolt in the chain of your yet undeveloped destiny."[36] But Douglass lamented that the ideals that it enunciated did not apply to those of his race, a fact that made a celebration of the nation's birth little more than a charade. "What, to the American slave, is your 4th of July? I answer: a day that reveals to him, more than all other days in the year, the gross injustice and cruelty to which he is the constant victim. To him, your celebration is a sham; your boasted liberty, an unholy license; . . . your shouts

*William Lloyd Garrison,
one of the leading
abolitionists of the
antebellum era, took a
hard line against the
Constitution, which he
viewed as a proslavery
compact. Courtesy of the
Library of Congress, LC-
USZ62-10320*

of liberty and equality, hollow mockery."[37] Douglass criticized Americans for failing to live up to their own principles, in the process exalting and venerating both the Declaration of Independence and the Constitution, the latter of which he now described as "a glorious liberty document." Offering a critique of Garrisonianism and an undoubtedly more palatable message to his Northern audience, Douglass characterized the Constitution in favorable terms, thus echoing the arguments of Smith, Spooner, and Chase. "Read its preamble, consider its purposes. Is slavery among them? Is it at the gateway? Or is it in the temple? It is neither."[38] To Douglass, both the Declaration of Independence and the Constitution served as foundational texts and sources of inspiration for the antislavery movement.

In response, Garrison adopted an even more vitriolic, anti-Constitution tone. In 1854, in his own Fourth of July speech at Framingham's Grove in Massachusetts, Garrison proved himself without peer as a moralist and agitator. He began his speech in a familiar vein, by celebrating the language of the

Declaration of Independence and condemning American hypocrisy. But then he began burning documents—first the federal fugitive slave law, then a copy of a recent federal court decision sending the fugitive slave Burns back to the South. Building toward the climax of his speech, with a keen sense of the theatrical, Garrison then denounced the Constitution as "the source and parent of all the other atrocities," again labeling it "a covenant with death" and "an agreement with hell" before setting it afire as well. As a copy of the Constitution dissolved into ashes on the stage, Garrison added, "So perish all compromise with tyranny!"[39] At the end of the ceremonies that day, Garrison blatantly advocated secession from the slaveholding states.

The contrast between the two Fourth of July speeches captured the crossroads at which the antislavery movement found itself by the mid-1850s. Douglass's antislavery position drew on the black constitutional tradition and conformed to Chase's legal arguments, which contributed to a growing political antislavery coalition in the Northern states. Douglass and other black abolitionists would soon find a home in the Republican Party. Having staked out an absolute position in opposition to constitutional politics, Garrison and his followers were left to ponder the future of their own narrower version of antislavery.

BLEEDING KANSAS, BLEEDING SUMNER, AND THE ELECTION OF BUCHANAN

Events in Kansas further contributed to the growth of Republicanism. After the passage of the Kansas-Nebraska Act, most assumed that Nebraska would be a free state. Kansas was another story. Situated just to the west of slaveholding Missouri, where an aggressively proslavery governor and US senator held office, Kansas emerged almost immediately as the next battleground over slavery. The first sign of conflict came early in 1854 when the Massachusetts Emigrant Aid Company proposed to assist free-state advocates in settling the territory. Missourians promptly responded by forming their own organizations in order to remove those whom they viewed as meddlers. As new settlers streamed in, a federally appointed territorial governor arrived and ordered an election for the legislature. In March 1855, massive numbers of Missourians, many of them heavily armed, promptly moved across the border into Kansas to vote in the elections, for the law allowed "residents" to take part in the balloting. (Most of these "border ruffians" immediately returned to Missouri, thus proving that their residency lasted no longer than the election.) Casting their own votes as well as hundreds of other fraudulent ballots, the proslavery forces, not surprisingly, won a huge victory. While a territorial census had shown only 2,905 eligible voters, 6,307 votes were cast. Only about a quarter of the total votes were probably legal. When the proslavery legislature later assembled, it immediately enacted a host of laws intended to harass and expel free-state advocates from the territory. Although proslavery forces would have carried the day without stuffing the ballot boxes (at the time, their numbers were greater), the overt fraud in the Kansas elections added fuel to Republican claims about the sinister nature of the Slave Power.

The situation in Kansas deteriorated rapidly. Soon a rival free-state government formed, which the Pierce administration summarily denounced. With pro- and antislavery governments arrayed against each other, violence erupted. Two incidents within days of each other in May 1856 attracted national attention. First, on May 21, a group of hundreds of armed proslavery Missourians rode into the town of Lawrence, where they destroyed two printing presses owned by free-state forces and burned a few buildings, including the Free State Hotel. Although no one was killed in the attack, the Republican press immediately dubbed the episode "the sack of Lawrence," an act of treachery that supposedly demonstrated the ruthlessness of the Slave Power. A more serious—and indeed bloody—event occurred on May 24, when the white abolitionist John Brown and his sons murdered five Southern settlers along Pottawatomie Creek. Although they held no slaves, the five victims had all sided with proslavery forces in the territory, and one served in the territorial legislature. These two violent incidents caused the mobilization of virtual armies on both sides, who for the next several months marched against, threatened, and shot at each other. By the time violence subsided in 1859, nearly five dozen people had died. Deemed "Bleeding Kansas" by New York newspaper editor Horace Greeley, the situation in the territory proved beyond the control of the Pierce administration. Ironically, most of the settlers in Kansas cared more about obtaining land titles than becoming caught up in the national dispute over slavery. In fact, no more than 200 slaves ever actually lived in Kansas. Nevertheless, the formation of rival parties and governments soon led to a polarization of political opinion that forced individuals to choose sides and left little room for moderation or indifference.

If the bloodshed in Kansas helped Republicans' political fortunes, so did a horrible incident on the floor of the United States Senate. Just as Kansas was about to devolve into civil war, Senator Charles Sumner delivered a speech that provoked a violent response. A Massachusetts abolitionist who had won election in 1851 and had helped draft "The Appeal of the Independent Democrats," Sumner titled his oration "The Crime against Kansas." A portion of his two-day speech took aim at Senator Andrew P. Butler of South

Carolina and Stephen Douglas, cosponsors of the Kansas-Nebraska Act. Sumner especially criticized Butler. In the most provocative section of the speech, the Massachusetts senator compared Butler's love of slavery to devotion to a prostitute. "The senator from South Carolina has read many books of chivalry, and believes himself a chivalrous knight with sentiments of honor and courage," Sumner began, poking fun at his Southern colleague. "Of course he has chosen a mistress to whom he has made his vows, and who, though ugly to others, is always lovely to him; though polluted in the sight of the world, is chaste in his sight—I mean the harlot, slavery. For her his tongue is always profuse in words. Let her be impeached in character, or any proposition made to shut her out from the extension of her wantonness, and no extravagance of manner or hardihood of assertion is then too great for this senator."[40] Although Douglas sat nearby as Sumner spoke, Butler was absent from the chamber.

Butler's young cousin, Congressman Preston Brooks, also of South Carolina, did hear the speech. Reading the published version a few days later and seething with anger, Brooks resolved to defend the honor of his kinsman and home state by punishing Sumner for the insult. Viewing Sumner as his social inferior, Brooks proceeded according to the Southern code of honor: he would attack him with his cane. On May 22, Brooks strode onto the Senate floor, and while Sumner sat hunched over his desk, Brooks approached, muttered a few sentences about having read the speech, and then began thrashing the Massachusetts senator over the head. Over the next minute or so, Brooks hit his foe approximately thirty times with his gutta-percha cane, which broke in two. When the blows stopped, Sumner lay senseless near his desk, his clothes drenched in his own blood. Doctors later discovered, in addition to multiple serious bruises on his hands, arms, and shoulders, two major injuries to his head—both severe lacerations, cut to the bone. It would take Sumner three years to recover and fully resume his Senate duties.

The political effects of Brooks's assault on Sumner were immediate. Nothing could have better dramatized the Slave Power's opposition to free speech than the brutal attack, especially since it took place on the Senate floor, a supposedly safe site for unrestricted debate. Sumner received an outpouring of sympathy in the North, and as the press dramatized the viciousness of the assault, Northern support for the Republicans soared. Happening as it did on the same day as the sack of Lawrence, the two events seemed a stark display of the malevolence of the Slave Power. In the South, the Brooks–Sumner affair had the opposite effect. Previously a little-known congressman, Brooks became a hero throughout the region and received innumerable messages of congratulation—and plenty of new canes. Although Brooks was eventually fined for his behavior, a motion to expel him from the House failed to receive the requisite two-thirds majority. Every Southern congressman but one voted against it.

In the midst of these dramatic events, the parties nominated candidates for the 1856 presidential election. The Democrats chose the dull and experienced James Buchanan. At age sixty-five, Buchanan had served in both houses of Congress, as secretary of state under Polk, and most recently as minister to Great Britain in the Pierce administration. He benefitted politically from having been out of the country during the explosive Kansas–Nebraska debate, but as a signatory to the Ostend Manifesto, an 1854 proclamation favoring the annexation of Cuba as a slave territory, he nevertheless possessed pro-Southern credentials. A native of Pennsylvania, Buchanan stood to gain enough Northern support to make him a strong Democratic nominee. The Republican Party, meanwhile, nominated as its first candidate for president the explorer John C. Fremont. Young and impulsive, Fremont had neither political experience nor savvy, but reports of his expeditions into the West had brought him a fair degree of fame. Finally, former president Millard Fillmore received the nomination of what remained of the Whig Party, as well as the endorsement of the Southern wing of the Know-Nothing Party. Both the Democratic and Whig platforms offered vague support for popular sovereignty, while the Republican Party endorsed the Free Soil position, thus rejecting the Compromise of 1850 and Kansas-Nebraska Act. The only national candidate in the race, Buchanan essentially ran against Fremont in the North and against Fillmore in the South. Buchanan defeated Fillmore easily in the slave states, where the former president won only Maryland's eight electoral votes. But in the North, Buchanan suffered defeat at the hands of his inexperienced opponent. Somewhat surprisingly, Fremont carried the entire Northeast and four states in the Midwest, for a total of eleven free states to Buchanan's five—quite a show of strength for the loose, recently formed anti–Kansas-Nebraska Act coalition known as the Republican Party. Even the antipolitical Garrison accorded the Republicans a measure of respect that he had never conceded to other antislavery political organizations, and the votes of some abolitionists no doubt contributed to Fremont's impressive showing in the free states. The political ground in the North was shifting. Buchanan won a total of 174 electoral votes to Fremont's 114. But Republicans figured that if they could pry away the remaining free states from the Democratic candidate in the next election, they could capture the presidency.

THE *DRED SCOTT* DECISION AND THE PROSLAVERY CONSTITUTIONAL ORDER

In early 1856, after winding its way through the courts for a decade, Dred Scott's case finally made it to the US Supreme Court. At a time when the slavery issue dominated the political landscape, the appeal of the Missouri slave sojourner seeking his freedom initially drew little attention. Most observers undoubtedly thought the justices would reject Scott's claim to freedom on narrow grounds and establish no new precedent. But as both sides made their arguments, one particular contention immediately changed the tenor of the case. Lawyers for Sanford, Scott's owner, claimed that Scott had not become free during his stay in federal territory because the law that had forbidden slavery there at the time, the Missouri Compromise, was unconstitutional. At the height of sectional tension over the future of slavery in Kansas, this argument had the potential to augment the significance of the litigation by raising the issue of slavery in the territories. Although the Kansas-Nebraska Act had by this time overturned the Missouri Compromise, the Republicans accepted the legitimacy of neither the Kansas-Nebraska Act nor the Compromise of 1850. In this charged political atmosphere, the justices postponed making a decision and ordered reargument at the end of the year, after the presidential election.

At the time it heard the *Dred Scott* case, the Supreme Court remained overwhelmingly Southern and Democratic. Still bearing the stamp of Andrew Jackson, who had appointed four of its nine members two decades before, the justices had issued a string of moderately proslavery decisions during the 1840s and early 1850s. In *Prigg v. Pennsylvania* (1842), the Court had upheld the Fugitive Slave Act of 1793 and invalidated a state personal liberty law, a decision that the Court subsequently reaffirmed in *Jones v. Van Zandt* (1847). Four years after *Van Zandt*, in *Strader v. Graham* (1851), Chief Justice Taney and his colleagues upheld the power of Southern states to protect slavery by dismissing a suit for damages involving a group of slaves who had been taken briefly into Ohio and later fled from Kentucky into Canada. When the owner of the slaves sued a group of men who had allegedly aided their escape, defense counsel argued that the Northwest Ordinance, which had banned slavery in the Old Northwest in 1787, freed the slaves upon their stepping foot on Ohio soil. Writing for a unanimous Court, Taney dismissed the case for lack of jurisdiction by claiming that the laws of Kentucky superseded the Northwest Ordinance. None of these decisions proved particularly controversial, but they all pointed toward a proslavery way of thinking that gave deference to the rights of slaveholders.

The political climate had changed considerably by 1857, and the introduction of the question of the constitutionality of the Missouri Compromise undoubtedly raised the stakes. Once the lawyers had presented their cases a second time, deep divisions began to appear among the justices about whether to confine themselves to narrow issues or deliver a sweeping opinion on the extension of slavery. The movement of Scott's case from the Missouri state court into a lower federal court, moreover, had injected the citizenship question into the suit because attorneys for John Sanford, Mrs. Emerson's brother and the administrator of her late husband's estate, claimed that Scott did not have standing as a citizen to sue in federal court. Justice Samuel Nelson of New York favored a limited ruling that would focus only on Scott's status rather than on broader questions. Most of the Southern justices, in contrast, sought a decision that would deny black citizenship as well as grant authority to slaveholders to take their human property into the territories. In addressing the citizenship question, proslavery Southern justices tackled the race issue as well as the slavery question. That is, a ruling undermining the notion of black citizenship would resolve the problematic status of free blacks in the South's slave society. After some discussion, on February 14, 1857, the majority agreed to issue a narrow decision that would follow the existing precedent, *Strader v. Graham*, and simply rule that Scott's case was governed by Missouri state law and was not properly before the federal courts. Justice Nelson received the assignment to write the opinion. But within a few days, the Court changed its position. Because two of the Court's four Northern justices indicated that they planned to dissent and declare Scott free under the terms of the Missouri Compromise, the majority felt a need to respond to their arguments on the controversial question of slavery in the territories.

Some on the Court undoubtedly believed that the justices had a duty, once and for all, to resolve in a far-reaching opinion the political issue of slavery in the territories that had vexed the nation for at least the past decade. Many moderates, in both the North and South, pressed for just such a judicial solution to the problem. An 1856 article in the respected *American Law Register* expressed this hope. "In such a crisis, it is the duty of all honest thinking men to join in an endeavor to remove all those causes of controversy which are rankling and festering in the heart of the nation, by submitting them to the peaceful arbitration of the Supreme Court."[41] With Congress unlikely to reach another compromise on the slavery question, the Court seemed the logical body to resolve the matter, for at the time the Taney Court possessed a reputation for dispassionate and reasoned decision making. Although controversial at his nomination for the chief justice position in 1836, during his tenure Taney had employed a nondoctrinaire approach to constitutional law that not only helped him to win over all of his major critics but also enjoyed broad public support. George Van Santvoord's *Sketches of the Lives and Judicial Services of the Chief Justices* captured the public mood when it described Taney in 1854 as possessing "a reputation beyond reproach or the breath of calumny, a purity of life that no man can assail."[42]

President-elect Buchanan too hoped that the Court would issue a definitive decision in order to take the issue out of national politics. That winter, Justice John Catron of Tennessee, who had somewhat of a reputation for meddling in political matters, corresponded regularly with the president-elect. Catron particularly urged Buchanan to lean on Justice Robert C. Grier, who, like the incoming president, hailed from Pennsylvania. Buchanan and Catron believed that the broadest possible decision delivered by the greatest number of justices would have the most potent effect in resolving the issue of slavery in the territories. Grier notified Buchanan that he planned to concur with the lengthy opinion that Chief Justice Taney had begun writing, which would address the issues of black citizenship and slavery in the territories. In his inaugural address on March 4, 1857, Buchanan—who knew full well what the Court was about to decide—coyly stated that he would "cheerfully submit" to the Court's opinion in the case, "whatever this may be."[43]

Two days later, on March 6, 1857, Chief Justice Taney and his colleagues filed into the courtroom in the basement of the Senate chamber to render the Court's decision in *Dred Scott v. Sandford*. (John Sanford's name was misspelled in the official court records.) A packed room watched and listened as the seventy-nine-year-old Taney read his decision with trembling hands and fading voice. Although each of the nine justices wrote a separate opinion in the case, evidence of both the complexity and significance of the issues involved, the opinion of Chief Justice Taney immediately became the most important and has often been deemed the opinion of the Court. Taney devoted most of the first half of the opinion to the question of Scott's citizenship status. Addressing the matter from the perspective of the original intent of the founders, the chief justice held that neither slaves nor free blacks could claim citizenship under the Constitution. "The legislation and histories of the times, and the language used in the Declaration of Independence," Taney wrote, "show, that neither the class of persons who had been imported as slaves, nor their descendants, whether they had become free or not, were then acknowledged as a part of the people, nor intended to be included in the general words used in that memorable instrument." In contrast to antislavery activists, black and white, who for decades had used the Declaration of Independence's claim that "all men were created equal" as a means to challenge the nation to live up to its founding ideals, Taney turned this argument on its head. The chief justice

Chief Justice Roger B. Taney attempted to resolve the question of the rights of slaveholders, as well as the issue of the rights of black people, in his controversial decision in the case of Dred Scott v. Sandford. *Taney's proslavery ruling practically eliminated the possibility of political compromise on the constitutional issues surrounding slavery. Courtesy of the Library of Congress, LC-USZ62-107588*

claimed instead that the founders' use of such high-sounding rhetoric surely meant that because many of the founders owned slaves, they could not possibly have intended to include blacks as members of the nation's political community. The contradiction was too obvious for them to have intended such.

Taney continued, claiming in the most infamous lines in Supreme Court history, that they "had no rights which the white man was bound to respect."[44] Two clauses of the Constitution, he argued, specifically singled out the black race as a separate category excluded from citizenship: the Slave Trade Clause, which referred "unquestionably," in Taney's words, to "persons of the race of which we are speaking," and the Fugitive Slave Clause. "Certainly these two clauses were not intended to confer on [slaves] or their posterity the blessings of liberty, or any of the personal rights so carefully provided for the citizen," the chief justice asserted.[45] Taney rested his views on black citizenship on what he believed to be the intentions of the framers. Because the founders had deemed blacks inferior to whites, blacks—whether slave or free— had no legitimate claims to citizenship, he concluded. Taney thus lumped all

Americans of African descent together, conveniently sidestepping the distinction that the Constitution's other slavery clause, the Three-Fifths Clause, had made between them as "free persons" and "other persons." The citizenship portion of Taney's opinion, although deeply offensive to abolitionists, remained within the mainstream of American constitutional thought at the time. Although black constitutionalists had appealed to the notion of citizenship in a host of antebellum conventions and resolutions, during the two decades before the *Dred Scott* case, many state courts in both the North and South had issued similar decisions limiting or excluding African Americans from citizenship.[46]

More significant within the context of the political and constitutional debate of the time was Taney's other holding: that Congress possessed no power to restrict slavery in federal territories. This conclusion rested, first, on a narrow view of congressional power under the Territories Clause. On the basis of this clause, Congress had enacted a series of measures pertaining to slavery in territories, including the Missouri Compromise and the Kansas-Nebraska Act. Taney put forth an unorthodox and dubious interpretation of the clause, arguing that it applied only to those territories that were part of the United States at the time of the drafting of the Constitution. In doing so, Taney limited congressional power over more recent territorial acquisitions such as the Louisiana Purchase and the lands gained in the Mexican-American War.

Having restricted congressional power, Taney held that slaveholding in federal territories was a constitutional right. In order to make this point, Taney claimed that the Fifth Amendment's Due Process Clause prohibited Congress from interfering with slavery in the territories, because to do so violated the property rights of slaveholders who settled there. The amendment states that no person could "be deprived of life, liberty, or property, without due process of law." An act of Congress that attempted to restrict this right, he asserted, "could hardly be dignified with the name of due process of law."[47] By making this argument, Taney not only relied on the Fifth Amendment but also seemed to inject higher law principles into the Constitution—in effect, holding that certain fundamental rights lay beyond the reach of congressional regulation. Slaves were no different than any other form of property, Taney concluded, and the rights of such property holders required constitutional protection.

Taney also relied on both the Slave Trade Clause and the Fugitive Slave Clause for support. The former established that "the right to traffic in [slave property], like an ordinary article of merchandise and property, was guarantied [*sic*] to the citizens of the United States in every State that might desire it for twenty years."[48] The latter also affirmed slaveholders' rights. "The government in express terms is pledged to protect [slave property] in all future time if the slave escapes from his owner," Taney wrote. "And no word can be found in the Constitution which gives Congress a greater power over slave property, or which entitles property of that kind to less protection than property of any other description."[49] In Taney's estimation, Congress could do nothing to interfere with the rights of slaveholders in federal territories, and because slaveholding was constitutionally protected, neither could a territorial legislature. In mentioning territorial legislatures, in an almost offhanded way, Taney took a swipe at popular sovereignty, the foundation of both the Compromise of 1850 and the Kansas-Nebraska Act. One line of the opinion succinctly captured Taney's view: "The right of property in a slave is distinctly and expressly affirmed in the Constitution."[50]

Taney's opinion was a proslavery tour de force. Dismissing the long-standing arguments of black constitutionalists and other advocates of antislavery constitutionalism, Taney held that blacks lacked citizenship and possessed "no rights." At the same time, Taney affirmed Calhoun's idea that slaveholders had a right to take their slave property into the territories. Taney's opinion was thus as definitive as it was all-encompassing: no rights for blacks, whether slave or free, and absolute rights for white slaveholders in the territories. It is worth noting that in its nearly seventy-year history to that point, the Supreme Court had never struck down a federal law as violating a constitutional right. The *Dred Scott* case was the first time that it did so—in order to protect the property rights of slaveholders.

In the ongoing dispute over the extension of slavery, Taney's opinion constituted a clear victory for the South. Although one scholar has shown that a variety of deep doctrinal disputes among the justices, some of which had nothing to do with slavery, helped to produce the decision, the end result remained the same: the Court stood unabashedly with slaveholders, and given the politics of the late 1850s, this was what mattered.[51] In some respects, the decision diverged from the Court's previous, more moderate proslavery record, and it represented a significant change in Taney's own opinions on the subject. As a young lawyer in Maryland nearly four decades before, Taney had expressed antislavery sentiments, opposed a proslavery resolution in the state senate during the Missouri crisis, and liberated nearly all of his own slaves. But by 1857, Taney's view had changed significantly. He accepted the argument of Southern proslavery paternalists that enslavement benefited African Americans, and he believed that emancipation would bring disaster. Holding great faith in the power of his court to solve the great dispute of the age, Taney hoped to resolve the sectional crisis by forever putting to rest the antislavery interpretation of the Constitution. Six other justices, although they differed in some respects in their reasoning, generally agreed with Taney's conclusions. One justice, the firebrand Virginian Peter V. Daniel, went farther than Taney, even arguing that "the property of the master in his slave" held an exalted position, as "the only private property which the Constitution has specifically recognized."[52]

Justices John McLean and Benjamin Curtis, the two antislavery Northerners on the Court, wrote dissenting opinions. Both argued for the constitutionality of the Missouri Compromise and attacked Taney's rejection of black citizenship. McLean emphasized the need for local, positive law in order for slavery to be sustained. A prominent Methodist layman, McLean also emphasized slaves as "persons" under the Constitution and as human beings made in the image of God. "A slave is not a mere chattel," McLean wrote. "He bears the impress of his Maker, and is amenable to the laws of God and man; and he is destined to an endless existence."[53] Curtis authored a more thorough legal opinion, the longest of all of the opinions of the justices in the case. His dissent made the compelling point that before the adoption of the Constitution, five states recognized blacks as citizens and even granted them the right of suffrage. Curtis used this evidence to contradict directly Taney's claim that blacks could not be counted as members of the political community at the time of the founding. Curtis's dissent went so far as to state that the majority opinion lacked judicial force, as he asserted that the chief justice's denial of Scott's citizenship meant that the Court lacked jurisdiction over the case. Curtis's incisive legal arguments and evidence made his opinion an important document of the antislavery cause and a campaign tract for the Republicans. A disagreement between Taney and Curtis over the timing of the release of the dissent prompted Curtis to resign from the bench soon after the announcement of the decision. It was a bitter postscript to a deeply polarizing legal dispute, both for the country and for the Court.

African Americans felt most keenly the sting of the decision. A few months later, in a Fourth of July address to the Massachusetts Anti-Slavery Society, Charles Lenox Remond, a free black activist, took the Court to task. "Shame on Judge Taney! Shame on the United States Supreme Court! . . . My God and Creator has given me rights which you are as much bound to respect as those of the whitest man among you, if I make the exhibitions of a man," he stated. "And black men did make the exhibition of manhood at Bunker Hill, and Lexington, and Concord, as I can well testify." The following year, at the Convention of the Colored Citizens of Massachusetts, the free black delegates argued forcefully that the dissents of justices Curtis and McLean captured the true interpretation of the Constitution, and they described the majority decision as "in palpable violation of the 1st section of Article 4 of the Constitution of the United States, which expressly declares—'The citizens of each State shall be entitled to all the privileges and immunities of citizens in the several states.'" Affirming their historic status as citizens and identity as Americans, the delegates resolved to reject emigration and remain in the United States "in defiance of Judge Taney." A year later, the New England Colored Citizens Convention described the *Dred Scott* decision as possessing "a brutality of spirit, a daring disregard of all historical verity, a defiant contempt for state sovereignty, a wanton perversion of the Constitution of the United States in regard to the rights of American citizens, [and] an audacious denial of all the principles of justice and humanity."[54]

The *Dred Scott* decision was a landmark in American constitutional history. It claimed to settle, once and for all, the question that had bedeviled the republic from its inception. From the beginning, black constitutionalists had attempted to use both the Declaration of Independence and the Constitution in support of their quest for freedom and equality under the law. While for a long time most white Americans seemed either indifferent or generally willing to acknowledge the rights of slaveholders under the Constitution, the Mexican-American War and controversy over the return of fugitive slaves stirred the passions of the nation. With vast new territory within their grasp, Northerners and Southerners debated the constitutional status of the peculiar institution. Southern proslavery voices asserted that the Constitution shielded the right to own property in slaves, just as it protected any other form of property. Those who owned slaves in the Southern states, they insisted, ought to be able to carry them to the territories. Northern antislavery constitutionalists, in contrast, claimed that slavery could only exist if established by local positive law and that the Constitution recognized enslaved African Americans as persons rather than property. A series of political developments gradually pushed Northern public opinion toward the Free Soil position, despite a heavy overlay of racism. Just at this moment—with Northern opinion crystallizing against the extension of slavery—the Supreme Court issued its decision in *Dred Scott.*

The Court's ruling shattered whatever hopes might have existed for political reconciliation between the sections. Taney's opinion struck at the heart of the Republican Party, for it declared the principle on which the party had been founded—the nonextension of slavery—to be unconstitutional. But rather than killing the nascent party, the decision strengthened it. The ruling stoked Northern fears of the Slave Power, which had the effect of aiding the Republican cause in the free states. In essentially adopting Calhoun's extreme proslavery position that the Constitution guaranteed slaveholders' property rights, moreover, the ruling seemed to discredit the notion of popular sovereignty, held dear by so many compromise-minded Northern Democrats. With the Northern compromise position weakened, Southern Democrats became emboldened and even more outspoken in support of the rights of slaveholders. Democratic unity, long a force for national unity and compromise, lay in tatters. Far from resolving the issue of slavery in the territories, the Court's attempt to secure the proslavery constitutional order generated renewed distrust between the North and the South.

3

THE PATH TO SECESSION AND THE OUTBREAK OF WAR, 1858–1861

Nearly four years to the day after the *Dred Scott* decision, on March 4, 1861, president-elect Abraham Lincoln rose from his seat on a wooden platform in front of the portico of the US Capitol to take the oath of office. A previously obscure former congressman from Illinois, Lincoln had in recent years gained national fame as the most thoughtful and outspoken critic of the *Dred Scott* opinion. Now he would take the constitutionally required oath from the author of the proslavery ruling, the aged chief justice Roger B. Taney. It was a dramatic moment. Surely the chief justice knew that by swearing in the first Republican president, he was in effect witnessing the demise of the Court's supposedly definitive decision on slavery in the territories. In a series of Senate campaign debates with Stephen Douglas in 1858, Lincoln had sharply criticized the Court's holding that the Constitution prohibited Congress from banning slavery in the territories, and in 1860 the platform of Lincoln's Republican Party had denounced *Dred Scott* as "a dangerous political heresy."[1] In effect, the inauguration of President Lincoln signaled the unraveling of the proslavery constitutional order that Chief Justice Taney had attempted to hold together.

In the four years between *Dred Scott* and the inauguration, the position of the South in the federal Union had considerably deteriorated. Initially buoyed by the decision, Southern spokesmen had at the time boasted that their constitutional rights had been protected and their way of life vindicated. "The *nation* has achieved a triumph, *sectionalism* has been rebuked, and abolitionism has been staggered and stunned," the *Richmond Enquirer* had confidently opined.[2] But a subsequent constitutional struggle in Kansas and the great debate between Lincoln and Douglas in Illinois demonstrated that the Court's decision had merely widened the fault lines dividing the nation. Southerners became adamant in protecting what they viewed as their constitutional right to hold slaves, while Northerners became fearful of the nationalization of slavery. In 1860, Lincoln's election confirmed what Southerners knew and what John C. Calhoun had predicted years before—that the sheer population of the North made the South a permanent electoral minority within the nation, regardless of whose side the Supreme Court took. With a Republican president in office who had not won a single slave state and a new Republican majority in the House of Representatives, the South feared the consequences and eventually turned to secession. Southerners, who had for years grown accustomed to setting the national agenda, found themselves abandoning the Union of their forefathers.

BUCHANAN, LECOMPTON, AND THE DEFEAT OF SLAVERY IN KANSAS

When the Supreme Court announced its decision in *Dred Scott* on the third day of his presidency, James Buchanan truly believed that the sectional conflict had come to an end. The new president seemed confident that the Court's ruling would silence and demoralize the upstart Republicans, whose stance against the expansion of slavery had been declared unconstitutional. At the same time, Buchanan reasoned, by ruling that slaveholding in the territories was a constitutionally protected right, *Dred Scott* had laid the theory of popular sovereignty to rest. In an effort to bring peace to Kansas, Buchanan determined to admit the territory as a slave state as quickly as possible. Doing so would protect the rights of slaveholders there and even the number of slave and free states at sixteen. A new slave state of Kansas seemed to him a solution to the problem of sectional division. The new president appointed as territorial governor former US senator from Mississippi Robert J. Walker, a loyal Democrat and slaveholder. While at first glance a proslavery pick, the ambitious Walker was aware that Kansas had wrecked the careers of previous governors, and he convinced Buchanan to promise that any state constitution be submitted in its entirety for a vote by all true residents. Walker desired a fair solution to the Kansas dilemma.

It was unclear what the *Dred Scott* decision actually meant for the state of affairs in Kansas. At the time of the new governor's arrival in May 1857, the territory remained a turbulent place. Two rival legislatures existed, neither of which recognized the legitimacy of the other, and the proslavery legislature had already called for a constitutional convention that fall. Upon arriving, Governor Walker immediately angered proslavery forces by declaring that he believed Kansas climatically unsuited to slavery, and he urged the more numerous free-state population to participate in the election of delegates for the convention. Convinced, however, that proslavery forces would fix the outcome, free staters refused to take part, and proslavery forces won a huge victory. Members of the new constitutional convention assembled that September, but they soon decided to adjourn in anticipation of the election of a new territorial legislature. For their part, free-state advocates staked their hopes on this legislative election.

As they had before, massive numbers of proslavery Missourians crossed the border and perpetrated fraud. In a few places in particular, the vote tallies simply did not add up. The most egregious case came in the results from the village of Oxford, located in the northeastern part of the state. Oxford had only six houses and a handful of voters. Yet the results noted that 1,628 votes had been cast there for proslavery legislators.[3] Presented with such an obvious example of fraud, Governor Walker threw out the results from the disputed districts, which then gave free-state forces the majority in the legislature. At this point, Kansas thus had a proslavery constitutional convention and an antislavery legislature.

Undeterred by Governor Walker's actions, the convention assembled in Lecompton and proceeded to draft a constitution. The first section of the constitutional article devoted to slavery undoubtedly reflected the influence of *Dred Scott.* "The right of property is before and higher than any constitutional sanction," it read, "and the right of the owner of a slave to such slave and its increase is the same and as inviolable as the right of the owner of any property whatever."[4] The document forbade the emancipation of any slave in Kansas by the legislature, provided for strict enforcement of the federal fugitive slave law, and excluded free blacks from the state. A referendum on the constitution was scheduled for December 1857. Although touted as offering a choice between the "constitution with slavery" and the "constitution without slavery," the referendum would not offer voters a chance to approve or reject the Lecompton Constitution per se. Instead, the referendum actually only offered a choice about whether to allow the further introduction of slaves into Kansas. About 200 enslaved persons already lived there, and both they and their progeny would remain in bondage no matter which way the vote went. The constitution, moreover, stipulated that it could not be amended for seven years, time enough for slavery to become more deeply rooted. Despite such problems, Buchanan heartily endorsed the proposed proslavery constitution. Undercut by the very president who had appointed him, Governor Walker left Kansas that fall and never returned.

Even overwhelming evidence that the Lecompton Constitution lacked popular support in Kansas did not seem to faze the pro-Southern president. Free-state forces boycotted the December referendum, which left approximately 6,000 Kansans who voted in favor of the constitution. The free-state legislature then initiated a second referendum, which gave residents a chance to vote on the entire constitution. In this vote, with the slave-state advocates now boycotting, more than 10,000 residents rejected the Lecompton Constitution outright. These numbers clearly indicated that the proposed constitution did not reflect the will of the majority. Although aware of the results of both referenda, Buchanan stubbornly pushed his agenda. Denouncing the free-state forces in Kansas, in February 1858 Buchanan reiterated the proslavery ruling of the Supreme Court and urged Congress to adopt the Lecompton Constitution. "It has been solemnly adjudged by the highest judicial tribunal known to our laws that slavery exists in Kansas by virtue of the Constitution of the United States," he argued in a message to Congress. "Kansas is therefore at this moment as much a slave State as Georgia or South Carolina."[5] Like the contentious Kansas–Nebraska showdown in 1854, when the Northern Democrat Pierce had supported the pro-Southern position, Buchanan staked his presidency on the outcome of the debate.

Significantly, Stephen Douglas, the architect of the Kansas-Nebraska Act, broke with the Buchanan administration on the Lecompton issue. In contrast to his fellow Democrat in the White House, Douglas saw the Lecompton Constitution as a fraud, a clear violation of the principle of popular sovereignty that he so cherished. Douglas supported *Dred Scott*, but he perceived no conflict between the ruling and the principles of popular sovereignty, which he still viewed as the ultimate solution to the slavery problem. Although Douglas fought hard against it, he could not prevent the statehood bill from passing in the Senate. Still, a bloc of about twenty anti-Lecompton Northern Democrats did join with Republicans to defeat the bill in the House of Representatives. The House's action mirrored public opinion in the North, which stood firmly opposed to making Kansas a slave state.

With the pro-Southern administration and the Senate on one side and Northern public opinion and the House on the other, a compromise Senate–House conference bill resolved the stalemate. The bill provided for another referendum in Kansas to occur in August 1858. In this vote, residents of the territory rejected the Lecompton Constitution by a wide margin, 11,300 to 1,788, although again proslavery forces boycotted the vote. With the refusal of both Congress and the residents of Kansas to ratify the proslavery charter, the Lecompton Constitution died. After four years of sporadic violence and contentious debate, Kansas would not become a slave state.

THE RISE OF ABRAHAM LINCOLN

In the midst of the tempest over *Dred Scott* and Lecompton, Abraham Lincoln emerged as a national figure in Republican politics. Born in 1809 in the wilds of central Kentucky, the young Lincoln moved with his family from one rough patch of land to the next, first to southern Indiana and then Illinois. Abe, as he was known, hated the laborious life of a frontier farmer, and the young man got hold of whatever books were available in order to educate himself. With his formidable physical size and strength, he emerged as a natural leader in the male-dominated culture of the frontier, and his talents for talking and storytelling served him well. Tragedy also marked his youth. He lost his mother and sister to sickness, and he acquired a deep sense of fatalism that remained with him for the rest of his life. He worked a variety of jobs and served briefly in the state militia, but not until his early twenties did Lincoln gain any sense of direction in his life.

Fiercely ambitious, Lincoln ran for political office before ever beginning his study of the law, the opposite career course of most lawyer-politicians. In 1832, he lost his bid for a seat in the state legislature, but he won election two years later, the same year that he began his self-education as a lawyer. Again unlike most in the profession, Lincoln never studied with another attorney but instead devoted himself to careful study of the leading legal treatises of the day. As a politician, he worked just as hard. A Whig who deeply admired Henry Clay, Lincoln won reelection three times to his legislative seat and served as floor leader of the Illinois Whigs before retiring in 1841 to pursue his legal practice in Springfield. He served a single term in the US House of Representatives, during which time he opposed the war with Mexico and voted for the Wilmot Proviso. After his term expired, he returned home from Congress (an informal rotation system among Whigs in his home county prevented him from seeking reelection), and, somewhat disillusioned with politics, he again turned his attention to the law.

Subsequent events—the Kansas-Nebraska Act, *Dred Scott*, and Lecompton—fueled both Lincoln's outrage and his ambition. The Kansas-Nebraska Act, by potentially opening up new territories to slavery, motivated Lincoln to again seek elective office. "I object to it because it assumes that there can be moral right in the enslaving of one man by another," Lincoln noted in a speech in October 1854. In his view, the founders had rejected such a notion. Outlining the Constitution's few provisions with regard to slavery, Lincoln echoed Salmon Chase in arguing that the founders had viewed slavery as a temporary necessity, which they intended to limit and ultimately abolish. In doing so, Lincoln ridiculed white Southerners' increasing emphasis on their supposed rights. "The plain and unmistakable spirit of [the founding] age, toward slavery," said Lincoln, "was hostility to the principle, and toleration, only by necessity. But now it is to be transformed into a 'sacred right.'"[6] Although he lost a bid for the US Senate in 1855, Lincoln remained in public view, and over the next few years he continued to make speeches that focused on his opposition to the extension of slavery.

In June 1858, Lincoln delivered his most famous speech yet, and one of the most important of his career, when he again sought a seat in the US Senate. The Republican Party of Illinois, in an unprecedented move, nominated Lincoln as its candidate for the position occupied by Douglas. In an age when Senate campaigns often consisted of no more than candidates writing letters to members of a state legislature (who elected US senators at the time), this official endorsement drew popular attention to Lincoln's candidacy. Accepting his party's nomination at the state Republican convention, Lincoln sought to distinguish himself from Douglas who, after all, had joined with Republicans to oppose the Lecompton Constitution. To do this, the Republican standard-bearer attempted to exploit Douglas's support of Taney's decision in *Dred Scott*. Sharpening the distinction was important for Lincoln, for some power brokers, including *New York Tribune* editor Horace Greeley, hoped to recruit Douglas to run for president as a Republican in 1860.

Borrowing a well-known biblical metaphor, Lincoln spoke passionately about the threat the *Dred Scott* decision posed to nationalize the institution of slavery. "A house divided against itself cannot stand," Lincoln emphatically stated. "I believe this government cannot endure, permanently half slave and half free. I do not expect the Union to be dissolved—I do not expect the house to fall—but I do expect it will cease to be divided. It will become all one thing, or all the other." Lincoln's stark language and ominous tone provided Illinoisans with two distinct visions of the future. "Either the *opponents* of slavery, will arrest the further spread of it, and place it where the public mind shall rest in the belief that it is in course of ultimate extinction; or its *advocates* will push it forward, till it shall become alike lawful in *all* the States, *old* as well as *new*—*North* as well as *South*."[7] Douglas's endorsement of *Dred Scott*, Lincoln continued, put him in the company of a rogues' gallery of proslavery conspirators. Lincoln cleverly asserted that "Stephen, Franklin, Roger, and James all understood one another from the beginning and all worked upon a common plan or draft drawn up before the first lick was struck."[8] Lincoln had no evidence that Douglas's popular sovereignty doctrine, Pierce's support of the Kansas-Nebraska bill, Taney's decision, and Buchanan's Kansas policy had all been worked out in advance to spread slavery. But in the midst of the Lecompton controversy, his argument certainly held great popular appeal in the North. Lincoln's "House Divided" speech electrified Illinois Republicans and at once catapulted him onto the national stage.

LINCOLN AND DOUGLAS DEBATE *DRED SCOTT*

In the summer and fall of 1858, Douglas would have a chance to respond to Lincoln's charges, as the two agreed to meet each other in a series of open-air debates across the state of Illinois. Like the nation as a whole, Illinois was sharply divided—the north solidly antislavery and Republican, the south pro-Southern and Democratic, and the middle of the state split. Thousands attended each of the three-hour, open-air sessions to witness Lincoln debate Douglas, the most important Democratic politician in the country other than Buchanan and an almost certain contender for the presidency in 1860. Technology made Lincoln's and Douglas's words available to the nation. Stenographers recorded the debates in shorthand, and runners converted the shorthand into text while riding the train to Chicago. Once they arrived, a complete text was ready to send out by telegraph to newspapers across the country.

Throughout the debates, Lincoln harshly criticized the idea of popular sovereignty. Lincoln spoke repeatedly and eloquently of his commitment to the Declaration of Independence—to Jefferson's idea that "all men are created equal and endowed by their Creator with certain unalienable rights." In Lincoln's mind, this did not mean the same thing that it meant to black constitutionalists—that all racial distinctions should be removed from the law. What it did mean to Lincoln was that all people had a right to live in liberty and to enjoy the fruits of their own toil. Slavery, Lincoln believed, was "a moral, social, and political wrong."[9] Douglas's notion of popular sovereignty represented, in contrast, moral neutrality on the issue of slavery. What mattered to Douglas, it seemed, was not the outcome of a popular referendum but the referendum itself. To Lincoln, the results of such a vote mattered a great deal, for he believed that slavery needed to be restricted in order to be put "in course of ultimate extinction."[10]

Lincoln also hit Douglas hard for his support of *Dred Scott*. In the second debate, in Freeport, Lincoln pointed out the apparent contradiction between Taney's decision protecting the right of slaveholding and Douglas's continued advocacy of popular sovereignty. In light of the Court's ruling, Lincoln asked his opponent, could a territorial legislature exclude slavery from the limits of the territory? Lincoln, more importantly, warned of a "second *Dred Scott* decision," a case in which the justices might soon decide that not even a state legislature could ban slavery within its limits, thus nationalizing the institution.[11] In short, Lincoln reiterated the themes from his "House Divided" speech, arguing that only he, a Republican, could be trusted to check the growth of slavery.

Douglas responded by emphasizing white superiority and advocating popular sovereignty. Picking up on Taney's claim in *Dred Scott* that the founders had never intended to include African Americans in the body politic, Douglas argued that the United States was a white man's republic, and he assailed Lincoln's attempt to portray the founders as opponents of slavery. Instead, Douglas argued, the founders envisioned that the nation would be divided between free states and slave states, based on the attitudes and circumstances of white residents who decided whether or not they wanted slavery. Douglas, moreover, charged that Lincoln and other "Black Republicans" advocated equality between the races, an extremely unpopular idea in a state that ten years earlier had enacted legislation banning free blacks. Finally, in response to Lincoln's query at Freeport about the apparent contradiction between popular sovereignty and *Dred Scott*, Douglas held firmly to his position. Slavery could not live a day unless supported by local legislation, he argued, and if a territorial legislature simply refused to enact such legislation, slavery would not exist regardless of what the Supreme Court had ruled. (This idea became known as the Freeport Doctrine.) Thus, Douglas argued, no real contradiction existed between *Dred Scott* and popular sovereignty.

That fall, because the Democrats retained a majority of legislative seats in Illinois, Douglas won another term in the Senate. In the course of their debates, both candidates had negotiated treacherous terrain. Lincoln's emphasis on the Declaration of Independence and the notion of equality forced him to explain to his audiences whether he still believed in white superiority. In the fourth debate, in Charleston, Illinois, Lincoln conceded, "I am not, nor ever have been, in favor of bringing about in any way the social and political equality of the white and black races."[12] Still, his eloquently stated antislavery position won him wide acclaim in the North, and he instantly became a viable candidate for his party's nomination for president in 1860. Douglas's admission that slavery could not exist without local legislation offended most Southerners, thus setting up a showdown with the Democratic Party's powerful Southern wing two years down the road. In effect, Douglas won the Senate election, but Lincoln positioned himself better to win his party's nomination for president.

In a broader sense, the Lincoln–Douglas debates showed how the political ground was shifting. While the territorial issue had dominated national politics since the introduction of the Wilmot Proviso in 1846, Lincoln's attempts to connect opposition to the extension of slavery with the idea of putting it on a path toward extinction showed that the Republican Party—and Northern sentiment—was moving toward a more hard-line antislavery position, in opposition to the rights claimed by slaveholders under *Dred Scott.* In October 1858, New York senator William Seward reiterated Lincoln's ideas about the nation not being able to survive "half slave and half free" when he spoke of an "irrepressible conflict" between slave society and free society. "I know and you know that a Revolution has begun," the New Yorker asserted. "I know, and all the world knows, that revolutions never go backwards." Seward's speech concluded with a rousing call to his fellow countrymen "to confound and overthrow, by one decisive blow, the betrayers of the Constitution and freedom forever."[13] Although such rhetoric troubled many Northerners, Seward's words nevertheless reflected the Republicans' unabashed willingness by 1858 to push the limit on the issue of slavery.

THE SOUTH REACTS TO THE LECOMPTON DEFEAT

If *Dred Scott* represented a victory for slaveholders' rights, then the demise of the Lecompton Constitution was a defeat of nearly equal magnitude. Ever since the passage of the Kansas-Nebraska Act, Southerners had pinned their hopes on Kansas. Now that those plans lay in ruins, Southerners felt both betrayed and stunned—betrayed by Northern Democrats Buchanan and Douglas, on whom they had relied to defend their interests, and stunned that, in the wake of a favorable Supreme Court decision, they had lost at all. But if *Dred Scott* had not established slavery in Kansas, it surely bolstered Southerners' confidence in the rightness of their cause. In the aftermath of the Lecompton controversy, radical leaders within the South pushed an extreme proslavery agenda.

Part of this program included efforts to acquire new territory for slavery. While Southerners had for years hoped to expand into the Caribbean and Central America, defeat in Kansas made adding more slave states an urgent matter. Not since 1845, with the admission of Texas and Florida, had a slave state entered the Union, while a parade of free states—Iowa (1846), Wisconsin (1848), California (1850), and Minnesota (1858)—had done so. Yet another free state, Oregon, would follow in early 1859, putting the total of free states at eighteen, compared to fifteen slave states. Since the end of the Mexican-American War, negotiation with foreign nations had yielded little in the way of any potential new territory for slavery. The Pierce administration's half-hearted attempts to acquire Cuba proved to expansionists that official diplomacy was unlikely to be effective. Only through the efforts of the so-called filibusterers, swashbuckling soldiers of fortune, would an American empire rise to the south. With, and then without, official support, Mississippi's John Quitman attempted to acquire Cuba through invasion in 1854–1855, for example, while William Walker of Tennessee landed in Nicaragua and during his brief "rule" in 1856–1857 legalized slavery there. These audacious attempts to acquire territory ran into strong opposition in most slaveholding states. Concerned about incorporating disparate and mixed-blood races into the Union, as well as about draining slaves from the Upper South, most Southerners ultimately did not back such reckless schemes.

Somewhat more popular were Southern efforts to reopen the African slave trade, which Congress had banned in 1808. At that time, most Americans considered the seizing and shipment of Africans to the western hemisphere to be immoral and inhumane. But by the late 1850s, the logic of the proslavery argument had caught up with white Southerners. If slavery really did benefit society, as proslavery propagandists claimed, if it really did assist in "civilizing" and Christianizing heathen savages, as so many Southern evangelicals believed, why should the ban on imported Africans continue? An infusion of new slaves, advocates of the trade reasoned, would lower slave prices, increase agricultural production, and broaden the population of slaveholders. At a time when Southern leaders worried about shrinking slave populations in the Upper South and border states, additional slaves promised to strengthen the South's economy. Still, although three states—South Carolina, Georgia, and Louisiana—did come close to overturning their state laws prohibiting the trade, most Southerners never supported the movement. In particular, opponents of reopening the trade expressed alarm about incorporating large numbers of Africans into the South, a development that would require renewed application of harsh discipline to what white masters believed was a paternalistic slave system that they had nearly perfected. Those in the Upper South who benefited from the high price of slaves also opposed reopening the trade, so in the end, support for reactivating the slave trade made little headway.

At the same time, several Southern states seriously debated reenslaving free African Americans. In South Carolina, nonslaveholding whites pushed the reenslavement agenda but failed to bring about any change in the state's laws. Instead, stricter enforcement of existing laws regulating free blacks led to a decline in the state's free black population. Unable or unwilling to produce the necessary papers proving their manumission, about a thousand free blacks in 1858–1859 fled Charleston for the North. In Maryland, meanwhile, the debate over reenslavement pitted rival factions of planters against each other.

With its shrinking slave population, by the late 1850s the state possessed a roughly equal number of enslaved blacks and free blacks. Alarmed at slavery's deteriorating position, one faction of the plantation aristocracy pushed to require free blacks to either leave Maryland or enter slavery. Other planters, distressed that so many productive laborers might actually depart, railed against the proposal. In the end, reenslavement also failed in Maryland, as it did in every state where it was proposed. In each of these campaigns—Caribbean expansion, reopening the slave trade, reenslaving free blacks—extremists attempted to rally support among white Southerners to formulate a pure Southern orthodoxy on the slavery question. The *Dred Scott* decision, by convincing Southerners that the law stood on their side, helped to foster this radical agenda.

The most extreme reaction to Lecompton was to embrace the idea of secession. Southern fire-eaters who had championed disunion in 1850 reemerged while the dispute over Kansas raged. William Lowndes Yancey of Alabama, Robert Barnwell Rhett of South Carolina, and Edmund Ruffin of Virginia—the three most famous of these advocates of Southern independence—believed that only secession would ensure protection of the region's way of life. Gathering in Montgomery, Alabama, in May 1858, ostensibly to attend a commercial convention, over 700 like-minded partisans from all over the South heard speeches and rallied for the cause of Southern separatism. A *New York Times* correspondent captured the tone of the gathering when he reported at the outset, "A strong disunion sentiment pervades the Convention."[14] Yancey took center stage. A former two-term congressman, he had abandoned political office years before to focus on drumming up support for the Southern cause through a variety of state and local organizations. In a three-day-long oration before the delegates, Yancey railed against the federal prohibition on the importation of African slaves and argued that the South should no longer submit to degradation at the hands of the North. "The time was coming," Yancey proclaimed, "which would nerve every Southern arm, and strengthen every Southern heart to strike the blow for Southern independence."[15]

ANTISLAVERY RESISTANCE AND FEDERAL ENFORCEMENT

Despite the fire-eaters' rhetoric and the South's defeat in Kansas, by the late 1850s, the proslavery constitutional order remained a formidable force in American life. Throughout the decade, the national government, when necessary, had gone to extraordinary lengths to enforce the federal fugitive slave law. According to one study, out of 191 known cases, federal tribunals successfully remanded and delivered to the states from which they had fled 157 fugitive slaves—a rate of more than 82 percent. In another 141 instances for which records exist, fugitives were returned to their owners or the agents of the owners with little difficulty and without any involvement by a federal tribunal. In the handful of cases where opposition to rendition did arise, the government often went to great expense to see that the rights of slaveholders were protected. The total cost to the federal government for the military-enforced rendition of Anthony Burns in Boston, for example, was $14,165.78. Despite a handful of famous cases where local opposition to the fugitive slave law generated national attention, popular resistance and Northern state personal liberty laws never posed a significant threat to federal enforcement efforts.[16] Two significant events in 1859 showed that even if opposition to slavery was on the upswing in the North, the Constitution and the weight of federal power remained on the side of slaveholders.

The case of *Ableman v. Booth* arose from a dispute over an attempt by a St. Louis slave owner to recover in 1854 a fugitive, Joshua Glover, who had escaped to the town of Racine, Wisconsin, where he had quietly worked in a local saw mill for two years. Glover evoked the sympathy and support of many Wisconsin residents, and the ensuing showdown over his status pitted anti-slavery public opinion in a Northern state against the proslavery constitutional order. Under the Fugitive Slave Act of 1850, the pursuing slave owner filed the appropriate complaint before the US commissioner in Milwaukee, who issued a warrant for Glover's arrest. Acting on this authority, a deputy marshal forced his way into Glover's home, bound him, and carried him off to the Milwaukee jail. Spurred on by the abolitionist editor Sherman Booth, a large public rally denounced the seizure and vowed to liberate the escaped slave. Booth, meanwhile, secured from a sympathetic local judge a writ of habeas corpus, which provided for Glover's release. When the federal marshal, Stephen Ableman, denied that the state habeas corpus proceeding had any legal authority over the federal prisoner, the crowd broke into the jail and freed Glover, who was spirited off to Canada.

A month later, with abolitionist sentiment in Wisconsin at a fever pitch, an antislavery convention urged defiance of the Fugitive Slave Act and even claimed the state possessed power to nullify the federal law. Following the example of Jefferson and Madison in the late 1790s and South Carolina during the 1830s, Northern antislavery activists exulted in their newfound devotion to state sovereignty. In the midst of the debate, Benjamin Wade, a Republican senator from Ohio, declared, "I am no advocate for Nullification, but in the nature of things, according to the true interpretation of our institutions, a State, in the last resort, crowded to the wall by the General Gov-

ernment seeking by the strong arm of its power to take away the rights of the
State, is to judge of whether she shall stand on her reserved rights."[17] Meanwhile, federal authorities arrested Booth and charged him with violating the
Fugitive Slave Act. Booth promptly appealed to the Wisconsin supreme court
for a writ of habeas corpus, and the court ordered his release on the grounds
that the Fugitive Slave Act violated the Constitution. In order to keep Booth
in jail, Ableman then appealed to the US Supreme Court. In a clash between
the state and federal judicial power, the Wisconsin supreme court asserted that
it would not carry out a judicial order of the US Supreme Court.

In a unanimous decision, the US Supreme Court ruled in *Ableman v. Booth*
(1859) that the Wisconsin supreme court had no grounds to defy federal
authority. Chief Justice Taney, after affirming the constitutionality of the Fugitive Slave Act, flatly denied that a state court possessed any power to challenge
the nation's highest court. Taney cited the Supremacy Clause of the Constitution and maintained that federal judicial supremacy constituted an essential
element of the supremacy of the national government. No state court could,
he argued, refuse to abide by or interfere with a federal judicial decision. "No
power is more clearly conferred by the Constitution and laws of the United
States, than the power of this court to decide, ultimately and finally, all cases
arising under such Constitution and laws," Taney wrote.[18] In one of the most
nationalistic rulings in Supreme Court history, the justices came down wholly
on the side of federal judicial authority. The effect of the ruling was that neither Booth nor the Wisconsin supreme court could interfere with the enforcement of the fugitive slave law. (Booth served several months in prison,
although President Buchanan pardoned him during his last days in office.)
Like *Dred Scott*, *Booth* was a resounding victory for the rights of slaveholders.

In October, 1859, six months after the *Booth* decision, white abolitionist
John Brown's attempt to initiate an armed slave rebellion in Virginia met swift
federal resistance. Believing that God called him to wage war against slavery
and cognizant of the black tradition of rebellion in Haiti, Brown was unafraid
to use violence to advance abolitionism. After murdering five Southern settlers in Kansas Territory, he returned east to plot his next move. Eluding the
authorities and denying he had killed anyone in Kansas, Brown took on the
air of a mythical figure among abolitionists and delivered clandestine fund-
raising speeches to antislavery groups throughout the North. In early 1858,
he spent nearly a month at the home of his friend Frederick Douglass, at
which time Brown wrote a provisional constitution for the revolutionary state
that he dreamed of creating. With its provisions for confiscating slave owners' property, imposing martial law, and governing an extended territory in
the mountains of Virginia, Brown must have envisioned a widespread slave

revolution to overthrow the established order. Bankrolled by a group of wealthy abolitionists known as the Secret Six, Brown and a band of loyal followers determined to strike at slavery in Virginia. Unconvinced, Douglass thought the plan was suicidal.

On the night of October 16, 1859, Brown and a small force of twenty-one—sixteen whites and five blacks—marched through the countryside to Harper's Ferry, a village located at the confluence of the Potomac and Shenandoah rivers, just south of the Maryland border. The town was the home of a federal arsenal, as well as a rifle works that produced weapons for the federal government. Brown and his small band easily secured these points, but afterward his immediate plans seemed not to make much sense. Having seized a cache of weapons and a few hostages, Brown hunkered down inside the arsenal. As the news spread by word of mouth and telegraph, the militia arrived. Upon orders from President Buchanan, the following night, federal forces under the command of Lieutenant Colonel Robert E. Lee surrounded the area, and on the morning of October 18, marines stormed the armory, wounding and capturing Brown. Within ten days, the fierce antislavery prophet stood trial in a state courtroom for treason, murder, and inciting a slave rebellion. On December 2, 1859, a month after his conviction and a mere forty-seven days after the seizure of the arsenal, Brown was executed. Justice proved swift.

In the minds of Southerners, the shock of John Brown's attempt to incite a slave revolt outweighed whatever reassurance they might have taken from his immediate capture, trial, and execution. Brown's raid met with a variety of responses in the North, which reflected the range of opinion on the slavery issue. To like-minded abolitionists, black and white, Brown became a martyr, while to Democrats his violent actions represented the worst form of extremism. Republicans, caught in the middle, admired Brown's principles yet abhorred his tactics. Mostly they worried that Brown's holy war against slavery would cost them votes in the coming election. But in the South, the incident solidified white opinion that Northerners held little respect for the rights of slaveholders. Confronted with armed aggression against slavery on Southern soil—with the prospect of a crazed Northern abolitionist commanding a multitude of rebellious slaves—white Southerners shuddered simultaneously with fear and outrage. In the wake of Brown's raid, rumors of rebellions raced across the South and created a climate of frightful vigilance. To Southerners, more clearly than ever before, slavery represented law, order, and stability, while abolitionism connoted lawlessness, chaos, and violence. Unable to make distinctions among the variety of Northern opinions, white Southerners became convinced that "John Brownism," abolitionism, and

Republicanism were one and the same. The minority of Southerners who actually owned slaves experienced particular paranoia. In the face of the 1857 publication of Hinton Rowan Helper's *The Impending Crisis of the South*—a treatise that argued that slavery and the slavocracy worked to the detriment of non-slaveholders—masters imagined a "triple threat" of homegrown white abolitionists, rebellious slaves, and Yankee militants in their midst.[19] Clearly, federal enforcement of the right of slaveholding in the South and the right of fugitive recapture in the North remained secure. At the same time, in the minds of white Southerners, the threat to slavery and Southerners' rights had never seemed greater.

THE ELECTION OF 1860 AND THE SECESSION WINTER

With the Democratic Party more divided than ever and Republicans ascendant in the populous North, a Republican victory seemed likely in the 1860 presidential election. Initially, Seward was the favorite to win both his party's nomination and the presidency. Nationally known for more than a decade, the New York senator possessed strong antislavery credentials, particularly in light of his "higher law" and "irrepressible conflict" speeches. These very comments, though, hurt Seward in the traditionally Democratic states of the Lower North—Illinois, Indiana, and Pennsylvania—as they made him appear more radical in his convictions than was actually the case. Shrewd Republican operatives knew they would need all the states that had gone for Fremont in 1856, plus these three, to win the presidency. "The country is not Anti-Slavery," Republican editor Horace Greeley admitted in 1860. "It will only swallow a little Anti-slavery in a great deal of sweetening. An Anti-Slavery Man per se cannot be elected; but a Tariff, River and Harbor, Pacific Railroad, Free Homestead man may succeed although he is Anti-Slavery."[20] After a series of well-received speeches in the Northeast in 1859, Lincoln emerged as the more electable alternative. The Illinois lawyer made his reputation by arguing that Republicans embodied the true spirit of the founders, particularly the ideals of Jefferson, the supposed intellectual progenitor of the Democrats. "The Jefferson party," Lincoln wrote in 1859, "were formed upon its supposed superior devotion to the personal rights of men, holding the rights of property to be secondary only, and greatly inferior. . . . The Democracy of today hold the liberty of one man to be absolutely nothing, when in conflict with another man's right of property."[21] Lincoln's notable oration at Cooper Union in New York City in early 1860 dazzled the sophisticated crowd by presenting an incisive critique of the Democrats' popular sovereignty position, based on the words and voting records of the founders. Nominated on the third ballot, having beaten out the better-known Seward, Lincoln represented a united party that eagerly anticipated winning its first presidential election. The Republican Party rounded out the ticket by nominating the more radical Hannibal Hamlin, a former Democrat from Maine, as its vice presidential candidate.

Democrats lacked both the enthusiasm and the unity of Republicans. Douglas remained the dominant figure in the party, but by this time he had alienated nearly all of his Southern allies. The South's latest demand—that Congress pass a federal slave code to protect slave property carried into federal territories—became the dividing line at the party convention in April. Although a total of only forty-six slaves resided in all of the territories, according to the 1860 census, the issue nevertheless highlighted the difference between Southerners committed to *Dred Scott* and Northerners still clinging to popular sovereignty. Southerners saw the enactment of a federal slave code as a way to overcome their Lecompton defeat by ensuring that any territory containing slaves (including Kansas) would eventually become a slave state. When the Douglas forces defeated a federal slave code provision in the drafting of the platform, a group of delegates from nine Southern states marched out of the convention, and the rest of the delegates adjourned without nominating a candidate. Ultimately, two more Democratic conventions assembled that summer in Baltimore—one that nominated Douglas and another that chose John C. Breckinridge of Kentucky, Buchanan's vice president. The Democratic Party, long a bisectional force for accommodation in American politics, had split in two.

Finally, another group composed of the conservative remnants of the Whig and American parties gathered that summer, in hopes that a new coalition could prevent the dissolution of the Union. Delegates dubbed themselves the Constitutional Union Party and nominated former senator John Bell of Tennessee, a slaveholder who had opposed both the Kansas-Nebraska Act and Lecompton. Their meager platform—just 211 words—consisted of an unswerving devotion to "the Constitution of the Country, the Union of the States, and the Enforcement of the Laws."[22] Of course, such vague verbiage avoided the central issue that still plagued the republic—the constitutional status of slavery, both in the territories and the states.

Ultimately, the presidential election of 1860 funneled all of the conflict of the past decade and a half into three distinct positions: the Republican Lincoln opposed *Dred Scott* and the extension of slavery in the territories, in order to put it "in course of ultimate extinction"; the Southern Democrat Breckinridge, who in accordance with *Dred Scott* believed slaveholding to be a constitutional right, supported federal protection of slavery in the territories; the

Abraham Lincoln, shown in this photograph by Matthew Brady, rose rapidly to earn the Republican Party's nomination for president in 1860. Brady took this picture at the time of Lincoln's address at Cooper Union in New York City. Courtesy of the Library of Congress, LC-BH8277-242

Northern Democrat Douglas believed that local democratic majorities should determine the future of slavery. The candidates' arguments pertained not only to existing territories but also to the possible addition of new territories or to a future Supreme Court decision on a state's power to prohibit slavery. The acquisition of Cuba remained a possibility—both the Northern and Southern Democratic platforms endorsed it—and expansion into the rest of the Caribbean or Central America also seemed plausible.

The other chief campaign issue was the future of the Union. Hoping to avoid the subject, Lincoln and his surrogates dismissed talk of Southern secession as bluster, while Breckinridge somewhat disingenuously denied that his candidacy represented the cause of disunion. (Clearly, while all Breckinridge voters were not secessionists, all secessionists were Breckinridge voters.) Douglas and Bell, in contrast, presented themselves as moderate voices of conciliation and compromise. Douglas, the only one of the four to wage a campaign in the modern sense, traveled around the country—particularly the South—in an attempt both to promote his candidacy and to save the Union. Indeed, in the final days before the vote, Douglas talked more about the Union than about himself. Realizing that Lincoln's election loomed over the horizon, Douglas attempted to convince Southerners not to break the bonds of union. Speaking in Montgomery, Alabama, in response to a question about a possible Lincoln victory, Douglas boldly announced that "the election of any man on earth by the American people, according to the Constitution, is no justification for breaking up this government."[23] While Douglas presented himself as the only truly national candidate, in the end, the country seemed to hold two distinct presidential elections that year. For the most part, Northern voters decided between Lincoln and Douglas, while Southerners chose between Breckinridge and Bell. In nine slaveholding states, in fact, Lincoln's name did not even appear on the ballot.

On November 6, 1860, with 71 percent of eligible voters nationwide casting ballots, Lincoln won the presidency with 180 electoral votes, 28 more than needed. He won every free state except New Jersey (where he still took 4 of the state's 7 electoral votes), and his margin of victory in fifteen of the seventeen states he won was large enough that even the combined votes of his opponents would not have defeated him. At the same time, he won fewer than 40 percent of the popular votes cast nationally, making him president with one of the smallest percentages of the popular vote in American history, and he won two states (California and Oregon) with only about one-third of the votes cast in those states. Breckinridge swept all of the slaveholding states except for Tennessee, Virginia, and Kentucky, which went for Bell. Douglas, although he received nearly 30 percent of the popular vote nation-

Table 3.1. Presidential Election of 1860

Candidate	Party	Electoral Votes	Percent of Popular Vote
Abraham Lincoln	Republican	180	39.8
Stephen Douglas	Democratic (Northern)	12	29.5
John C. Breckinridge	Democratic (Southern)	72	18.1
John Bell	Constitutional-Union	39	12.6

ally, won only New Jersey and Missouri. Although a purely sectional candidate, Lincoln would soon take the oath as the sixteenth president of the United States.

In the weeks after the election, from his home in Springfield, the incoming president reached out to Southern friends. "Do the people of the South really entertain fear that a Republican administration would, *directly or indirectly*, interfere with their slaves, or with them, about their slaves?" he wrote to his former Whig colleague in Congress, Alexander Stephens of Georgia. "If they do, I wish to assure you, as once a friend, and still, I hope, not an enemy, that there is no cause for such fears. The South would be in no more danger in this respect, than it was in the days of Washington."[24] Meanwhile, black Southerners had a different reading of the situation. Enslaved African Americans had watched the election of 1860 with great anticipation and had repeatedly heard their white masters vilify the "Black Republicans." Slaves sensed that Lincoln's victory and the subsequent Southern response portended great change, particularly for them. Despite Lincoln's attempts to soothe white Southerners' anxieties about his election, African Americans clearly viewed the new president and his party as allies.

Lincoln's election spurred a vigorous public debate in the Southern states over whether to remain in the Union. From the founding, the relationship between the states and the federal government had been imprecise, thus subject to varying interpretations. The early nineteenth-century Supreme Court under John Marshall had championed the notion of national supremacy, while the Court under Roger Taney had leaned toward the idea of dual sovereignty. Southern secessionists represented neither one of these mainstream positions. Instead, they embodied a more extreme tradition, evident in the periodic threats of disunion that arose in the early nineteenth century. Of course, the most momentous of these threats came in the late 1820s in the Nullification Crisis, and Southern advocates of secession drew heavily on South Carolinian John C. Calhoun's notion of state sovereignty, as well as Locke's notion of the right of revolution. Thus, secessionists believed that the states had created both the federal government and the Constitution and, if the government became destructive to the ends for which it had been created, states possessed the right to withdraw from the compact.

Fire-eaters led the charge for Southern secession. Their rigid ideals and scorching rhetoric drew on a potent mix of constitutional principles, honorific ideals, evangelical self-righteousness, raw economic interest, and deep-seated racism. Widespread in the Lower South states, where slavery remained stronger than ever, secessionism played on white Southern fears that Lincoln and his fellow "Black Republicans" would interfere with slavery—perhaps initially by ending federal enforcement of the fugitive slave law, banning slavery in Washington, DC, forbidding the acquisition of any new territory for slavery, and eventually abolishing the institution in the South. At a minimum, as president, Lincoln would undoubtedly fill countless federal patronage positions with antislavery Republicans. Deep South slaveholders had a hard time imagining how Lincoln's election could lead to anything but a steady onslaught of legislative and political activity against slavery. Completely distrustful of any statements by Lincoln to the contrary, secessionists convinced themselves that emancipation was the inevitable consequence of Republican rule. Any move against slavery they interpreted as a violation of their constitutional rights and an insult to their honor. Convinced of the benefits that slavery bestowed on both blacks and whites, secessionists imagined a nightmare scenario of Northern Republican domination, in which rebellion, race war, and racial amalgamation would bring about the destruction of Southern civilization as they knew it.

Still, in the weeks immediately following Lincoln's election, substantial Unionist sentiment existed in the slaveholding states, particularly the Upper South and border states, where slavery's grip was less secure and the African American population less numerous. "Cooperationists" across the South advocated an approach based on Southern unity. Wanting all of the slaveholding states to work together to present a united front, they hoped to achieve a compromise that would protect the interests of Southern slaveholders. Other moderates hoped to take a wait-and-see approach toward the new president, who had, at least some Southerners noticed, repeatedly pledged not to interfere with slavery where it already existed. Southern Unionists also pointed to the fact that although Lincoln had won the White House and Republicans constituted a majority in the House of Representatives, Democrats still controlled the Senate. Any legislation would have to be passed by the Senate before it could become law. Moreover, they observed, even if the Republicans did enact antislavery measures, the Supreme Court—a Democratic, pro-Southern stronghold—would surely invalidate them. The Unionists claimed, in other words, that the best way to protect slavery was actually to remain in the Union, to rely on the existing constitutional system that had protected Southern rights and interests since the founding. Above all, Unionists stressed, because of their love and devotion to the Constitution and Union of their fathers, they were unwilling to take rash action without clear provocation. "Let us, therefore, reason together," pleaded Georgia's Alexander Stephens, in the midst of that state's secession debate. "The constitutional election of no man is sufficient cause to break up the Union," he argued. Outlining an alternative course of action to extremism, Stephens concluded, "I am for exhausting all that patriotism demands before taking the last step" of secession.[25]

Despite such pleas, during the winter months after Lincoln's election, secessionists won the day in the Deep South. South Carolina, the cradle of nullification, took the lead. Soon after Election Day, Robert Barnwell Rhett urged quick and decisive action. In a letter appearing in the *Charleston Mercury* on November 10, 1860, Rhett opposed any delay—for waiting, he believed, stood to benefit the Unionists. "Why do we pause in so vital a cause when all are, or ought to be, ready to resent our injuries & daily insults, saying nothing of our increasing risks of internal domestic discontent, which the North will be heaping upon us, by hordes of emissaries pouring in & no law to prevent their ingress."[26] With its legislature already in session to cast the state's electoral votes for president, lawmakers heeded Rhett's words. That night, the legislature provided for an election of members to a constitutional convention to take up secession the following month.

Such Deep South secessionists unhesitatingly rejected the Constitution and the Union. "Has that sacred instrument [the Constitution] protected us from the jealousy and aggressions of the Northern people, which commenced forty years ago, and which ended in the Missouri Compromise?" South Carolina secessionist David F. Jamison asked. "Has it saved us from abolition petitions, intended to annoy and insult us, on the very floors of Congress? Has not that instrument been trodden under their very feet by every Northern State, by placing on their books statutes nullifying the laws for the recovery of fugitive slaves?"[27] Acting on the belief that as a sovereign state, South Carolina possessed the power to withdraw from the constitutional compact, on December 17, the popularly elected convention voted to depart from the Union, thus ending the relationship with the Union that it had begun seventy-two years before. "The union now subsisting between South Carolina and the other States under the name of the United States of America," the secession ordinance stated, "is hereby dissolved."[28] Unlike in 1832, when South Carolina had attempted to nullify the federal tariff only to see no other Southern states follow suit, this time Southern unity gradually emerged. On January 9, Mississippi seceded, and over the next three and a half weeks, Florida, Alabama,

Georgia, Louisiana, and Texas all followed, in that order. By February 1, 1861, still a month before Lincoln's inauguration, seven of the fifteen slaveholding states had abandoned the Union.

Clearly, the leaders of these Deep South states seceded primarily to protect the institution of slavery and slaveholders' rights. The "Declaration of Causes Which Induced the Secession of South Carolina," after laying out the theory of state sovereignty justifying the action, plainly stated the threat that South Carolinians believed they faced. "A geographical line has been drawn across the Union, and all the States north of that line have united in the election of a man to the high office of President of the United States whose opinions and purposes are hostile to Slavery."[29] In greater detail, the "Mississippi Resolutions on Secession" outlined a litany of outrages, in the style of the American Declaration of Independence, that had been committed by the North against the South. All of these involved slavery. "That the institution of slavery existed prior to the formation of the Federal Constitution, and is recognized by its letter, and all efforts to impair its value or lessen its duration by Congress, or any of the free states, is a violation of the compact of Union," it solemnly resolved. The resolution went on to cite interference with the return of fugitive slaves, abolitionists' distribution of "incendiary publications," and "a hostile invasion of a southern state to excite insurrection" as among the state's many reasons for seceding.[30]

Secession commissioners, moreover, sent out as emissaries from the initially seceding states to other slaveholding states, focused relentlessly on the need both to protect slavery and to prevent the imposition of racial equality. "Our fathers made this a government for the white man," argued William L. Harris, a secession commissioner from Mississippi, while speaking in Georgia, "rejecting the negro, as an ignorant, inferior, barbarian race, incapable of self-government, and not, therefore, entitled to be associated with the white man upon terms of civil, political, or social equality."[31] Using vivid language in a letter to the governor of Kentucky, another secession commissioner, Stephen F. Hale of Alabama, presented a dire scenario: "The triumph of this new [Republican] theory of government destroys the property of the South, lays waste her fields, and inaugurates all the horrors of a Santo Domingo servile insurrection, consigning her citizens to assassinations and her wives and daughters to pollution and violation to gratify the lust of half-civilized Africans."[32] Such rhetoric, which played on whites' racial fears, left little doubt that Deep South secessionists left the Union to defend slavery and preserve white supremacy. In fact, attempts to unite all Southern whites under a banner of racism became a key component of the secessionist strategy to appeal to slaveholders and nonslaveholders alike.

Southern religion and Southern honor fueled secessionist sentiment and rhetoric, thus further marginalizing Deep South Unionists. Ever since the 1830s, Southern evangelical clergymen had substantially contributed to the development of the proslavery argument. Through tracts, denominational newspapers, and sermons, most Southern clergymen had asserted that because of the moral and biblical nature of the slavery issue, religious leaders had a special obligation to ensure that their voices entered the public sphere. When the possibility of disunion arose, Southern clergy continued their vocal participation in the nation's political debates and proved especially unified in their devotion to secession. Portraying the Union and the North that had come to dominate it as corrupt and degenerate, clergyman argued that only secession could allow the South to become a true Christian republic. While ministers cast the conflict in moral terms, many Southern political leaders viewed secession as a matter of honor. In fiery speeches, secessionists not only railed against their Yankee foes but also portrayed Southern cooperationists and moderates as cowardly "submissionists," who seemed too quick to surrender the sacred traditions, economic interests, and constitutional liberties of their Southern homeland. The political crisis of the moment demanded, secessionists felt, a manly defense of the Southern way of life. In other words, Southern culture, long intolerant of dissent and dispassion, worked against Unionists' calls for patience and sober reflection.

THE PEACE CONFERENCE AND PROPOSED AMENDMENTS

Even after seven states had already seceded, some American political leaders still believed the Union could be salvaged. The most promising proposal came from Senator John J. Crittenden, an aging Kentuckian who held Henry Clay's old seat and hoped to live up to his forebear's reputation as the Great Compromiser. Crittenden's plan revived the idea of extending the Missouri Compromise line to the Pacific. It thus forever banned slavery north of the latitude line at 36 degrees, 30 minutes while it recognized and maintained the institution in all territory south of the line. With hope for national reconciliation and a concrete proposal as a basis for discussion, on January 19, Virginia, the most populous and most important slaveholding state, extended an invitation to all states, including those that had seceded, to attend a peace conference on February 4, to be presided over by former president John Tyler.

The sitting president, meanwhile, seemed unwilling to take any action. A pathetic figure by his last year in office, President Buchanan displayed a curious mixture of pro-Southern and antisecession sentiment. "I wish Massachusetts would secede," he reportedly said in private during the fall of 1860. "She is practically already out of the Union by her action in the fugitive-slave matter."[33] The president's public statements were more measured. In a series of pronouncements between the time of Lincoln's election and inauguration, the lame-duck leader expressed his opposition to secession, along with his belief that he could do nothing to stop it. "In all its various bearings, therefore, I commend the question to Congress," he noted in a January 8 message, "as the only human tribunal under Providence possessing the power to meet the existing emergency."[34]

While Buchanan insisted on his own powerlessness, Republicans in Congress flexed their muscles. With the Lower South states out of the Union and out of Congress, a new Republican majority speeded consideration of a Kansas statehood bill, which passed on January 29, 1861. Kansas thus became the nineteenth free state in the Union, which would give the free states thirty-eight US senators, compared to the remaining slave states' sixteen. The Republicans also moved to increase the federal tariff. A source of contention between the sections stretching back to the Nullification Crisis, the tariff became an important issue again in the late 1850s, in the midst of the Panic of 1857. In May 1860, the House had voted in favor of increasing the tariff, but not until March 1861, when Republicans suddenly found themselves ascendant, did senators join their counterparts in the House. Drafted by Senator Justin Morrill of Vermont, the new tariff legislation imposed moderate rate increases and specifically protected iron, coal, and wool producers, as well as other industries. This unabashedly protective tariff, which favored Northern manufacturers, did nothing to win the favor of Upper South moderates.

Within this climate, the peace conference appeared destined to fail. Only twenty-one of the thirty-three states sent delegates, with the seven seceded states of the Deep South, the strongly Republican states of Michigan, Wisconsin, and Minnesota, and the far-flung states of California and Oregon not represented. Northern states in attendance outnumbered slave states fourteen to seven, and many members of Northern delegations were Republicans who wanted to control the outcome of the meeting. Still, although at times acrimonious, by the time it ended, the conference put forth a moderate proposal. Delegates recommended a constitutional amendment that extended the Missouri Compromise line, limited the possibility of future territorial expansion, protected slavery in the Southern states, prohibited personal liberty laws, forever banned the slave trade, and authorized financial compensation for owners of fugitive slaves. Although comprehensive in scope and based for the most part on good intentions, the proposed amendment had no chance of resolving the secession crisis. The fire-eaters had already driven the Deep South out of the Union, while most Republicans, excited about their victory in the presidential election, saw little reason to compromise. The incoming president seemed to agree that certain matters were not on the table. Although he offered no public statements of any kind for the three months after his election, Lincoln knew where he stood on the questions being debated in the nation's capital. "Let there be no compromise on the question of *extending* slavery," Lincoln wrote confidentially to fellow Illinois Republican and political associate Lyman Trumbull.[35] The House refused even to consider the proposed amendment, while the Senate rejected it by a wide margin. Other measures discussed in Congress met a similar fate.

By the time of Lincoln's inauguration, only one prospective constitutional amendment remained. Originally advocated by Senator Seward (the incoming secretary of state under Lincoln), compared to the seven-point proposal that had come out of the peace conference, this amendment was simple: "No amendment shall be made to the Constitution which will authorize or give to Congress the power to abolish or interfere, within any State, with the domestic institutions thereof, including that of persons held to labor or service by the laws of said State."[36] Known as the Corwin Amendment, after its chief sponsor in the House of Representatives, Ohio representative Thomas Corwin, the proposed thirteenth amendment to the Constitution thus reiterated what Lincoln had already said many times and would soon say again—that he had no power to interfere with slavery where it already existed. Approved by the House on February 28, the amendment won Senate approval early on the morning of March 4, Inauguration Day.

THE FOUNDING OF THE CONFEDERACY

Meanwhile, the seceded states went about the business of creating a new nation. Six of the seven sent delegates to a convention in Montgomery, Alabama, where on February 4, 1861—the same day that the peace conference assembled—they met to form a confederacy. (Texas's delegates arrived later and did not participate in this initial meeting.) The delegates moved swiftly. Within days, the convention, presided over by Georgia's Howell Cobb, drafted a provisional Constitution of the Confederate States of America and agreed to elect a provisional president and vice president. Within weeks, a committee of the convention drafted and approved a permanent constitution. Throughout this process, the seceding Southerners kept nearly the entire US Constitution intact, for they changed only those specific provisions about which they had quarreled with the North.

The preamble came in for considerable revision. A source of some controversy since the early nineteenth century, when Chief Justice Marshall had used the Constitution's opening declamation, "We the People," as a way to assert the sovereignty of the whole people and the supremacy of the national government, the Confederates' preamble now began by asserting the sovereignty of the states. "We the people of the Confederate States, each state acting in its sovereign and independent character," it read. Noticeably absent from the Confederate preamble, moreover, was any reference to the Union, to which Northerners—in the midst of the secession crisis—now ascribed an almost sacred quality. Thus, "in order to form a more perfect Union" in the US Constitution—which carried almost metaphysical connotations—became the much more utilitarian "in order to form a permanent federal government" in the Confederate Constitution. Most strikingly, the Confederate preamble invoked "the favor and guidance of Almighty God."[37] By including such language, the Confederate Constitution reflected the view of many Southern evangelicals that the southland represented a new Zion, a chosen people with a unique divine mission. Over the years, many evangelical leaders had criticized the American founders for writing a constitution that had never mentioned the Almighty. By explicitly invoking God's favor, Southern constitution makers sought to correct this supposed error by establishing a theistic—if not an overtly evangelical—republic.

Confederates embraced other innovations. These included a line-item veto as well as a single six-year term for the president. In the realm of economic policy, they wrote two key changes into their constitution. First, showing their long-standing opposition to a protective tariff, Southerners included a provision stating, "Nor shall any duties or taxes on importations from foreign nations be laid to promote or foster any branch of industry." Clearly content to remain an almost purely agricultural people, Southerners forbade any effort to keep out cheap foreign goods in order to protect industry. Second, the Confederate Constitution, although it included a clause granting the Congress power to regulate interstate commerce, made clear that this clause, nor any other, "be construed to delegate the power to Congress to appropriate money for any internal improvement intended to facilitate commerce."[38] Again, this provision built on the South's long-standing opposition to using federal funds to pay for internal improvement projects—the construction of roads, bridges, railroads, and the like. Responsibilities for such improvements, in the minds of most Southerners, rested with state governments.

Most important, the Confederate Constitution resolved any doubt about where the new nation stood with regard to slavery. The US Constitution, of course, had never mentioned the word "slavery," a fact that underlay much of the decades-long sectional crisis and fueled the growth of antislavery constitutionalism. Confederate founders sought to remedy this problem, for their constitution used the word "slavery" or "slaves" a total of six times. Most notably, Article I, Section 9, a list of limitations on the states (much like Article I, Section 10 of the US Constitution), explicitly forbade any state from passing a "law denying or impairing the right of property in negro slaves." Article IV, moreover, demonstrated that the Confederate founders envisioned an expanding slaveholding republic. This article included a fugitive slave provision relating to slaves escaping into Confederate territories and held that in all territory, "the institution of negro slavery, as it now exists in the Confederate States, shall be recognized and protected by Congress and by the Territorial government." These provisions demonstrated the impact of the *Dred Scott* decision, for the Confederate founders wrote the notion of slaveholding as a constitutional right into their founding charter. Finally, the use of the phrase "negro slavery," significantly, gave slavery in the Confederacy an overtly racial cast.[39] No mention of any race or racial classification existed in the US Constitution.

Before the final ratification of the constitution, delegates at the Montgomery convention, voting by state delegation, elected Jefferson Davis of Mississippi as provisional president of the Southern nation. Fire-eaters such as Rhett and Yancey might have had a claim to lead the Confederacy, and they certainly had their supporters. But Davis was a more moderate, sensible choice. Born in Kentucky near the Ohio River—not too far from the birthplace of Lincoln—Davis had spent more than a decade in national politics and was probably the best known of the South's leaders. Elected to the US Senate as a Democrat in 1847, he forcefully advocated slaveholders' rights during his early years in Washington. After his service as secretary of war under Franklin Pierce and a trip to New England in 1858, he became more of a moderate on the questions that divided the country. Still a strong proponent of Southern rights, including federal protection of the right to hold slaves in the territories, Davis did not advocate secession upon news of Lincoln's election. Although he counseled against disunion, when his state seceded, he reluctantly followed and delivered a graceful farewell speech to his colleagues on the floor of the Senate. Southerners viewed Davis, with his reputation for intelligence, eloquence, and gentility, as a much superior man to the supposedly coarse and unsophisticated Lincoln. Delegates believed, moreover, that with all his charm and talent, as well as his reputation for moderation, Davis could convince the Upper South states to join the Confederacy and persuade European powers to support it. (Virginia had rejected secession in early February, and other slaveholding states at the time expressed little support for disunion.) For similar reasons, the convention chose Georgian Alexander Stephens, a former Whig with a reputation for states-manship, as provisional vice president. A formal election for both positions would take place in fall 1861, but in the meantime, both men enjoyed support across the Southern political spectrum. The fire-eater Edmund Ruffin praised Davis and Stephens as men "who for intellectual ability and moral worth are superior to any President and Vice-President elected together . . . since Madison's Administration."[40]

On February 9, 1861, while at home at his Mississippi plantation, Davis received word of his election, and two days later, he began a five-day trip to Montgomery, the national capital of the Confederacy, for his inauguration. Traveling by rail from Mississippi through Tennessee and Georgia before arriving in Montgomery, Davis spoke to warm and enthusiastic crowds at every stop. One reporter characterized the tour as "one continuous ovation."[41] On Inauguration Day, February 18, thousands of cheering admirers gathered to celebrate their new leaders, as Davis and Stephens paraded through the streets in an elegant barouche drawn by six gray horses. In his inaugural address, delivered from the steps of the state capitol, the new president drew on Jefferson's Declaration of Independence in arguing that the US government had become destructive to the ends for which it had been established. Secession, Davis proclaimed, echoing the republican rhetoric of America's founding, was "sanctified by its justice and sustained by a virtuous people."[42]

THE INAUGURATION OF LINCOLN

Two weeks later, and 700 miles to the northeast, another presidential inauguration took place. In contrast to the festive atmosphere in Montgomery, the air in Washington, DC, on March 4 was thick with tension. Because of rumors that the president-elect would be assassinated or kidnapped in Baltimore, Lincoln had been smuggled into the nation's capital in disguise. On Inauguration Day, when he rode down Pennsylvania Avenue in a carriage with Buchanan, a heavy guard walked alongside the two leaders while sharpshooters stood positioned throughout the route. Security remained tight on the steps of the still unfinished Capitol, where Lincoln stood to deliver his own speech. Removing his new stovepipe hat and fumbling with it awkwardly, Lincoln glanced around for a place to set it. The new president's old nemesis, Stephen Douglas, who sat nearby, politely offered to assist. "Permit me," he reportedly said, and promptly took hold of Lincoln's hat.[43] Douglas's humble gesture seemed to signal his unwavering support for the nation's new leader in this moment of crisis.

This photograph, taken at the first inauguration of President Abraham Lincoln in March 1861, shows the Capitol dome still unfinished. Courtesy of the Library of Congress, LC-DIG-ppmsca-35445

Lincoln then delivered an inaugural address that included mostly clear language on the issues pertaining to the future of slavery. On slavery in the Southern states, Lincoln quoted his own previous speeches, as well as the Republican Party platform, in order to reiterate his pledge not to interfere with slavery where it already existed. He even endorsed Seward's constitutional amendment, which had passed both houses of Congress just hours before. On the matter of fugitive slaves, Lincoln quoted the Constitution's language on the subject and pleaded for enforcing the law while establishing safeguards to prevent the kidnapping of free people. In fact, the new president narrowed the source of sectional division to a single issue—the extension of slavery into the territories. "One section of the country believes slavery is right and ought to be extended, while the other believes it is wrong and ought not to be extended," he argued. "This is the only substantial dispute." Because the *Dred Scott* decision had affirmed the right to take slave property into the territories, Lincoln criticized the Supreme Court, arguing that if such important questions of policy were left to unelected judges, "the people will have ceased to be their own rulers." But even then, with Chief Justice Taney seated on the platform, Lincoln admitted, "It is a duty from which they may not shrink to decide cases properly brought before them."[44] Even though he wanted to offer forceful criticism of the Court for its *Dred Scott* decision, the new president could not quite bring himself to do it. All in all, Lincoln attempted to allay Southern fears with regard to slavery.

More important, in the midst of a secession crisis, Lincoln made known his unwavering devotion to the Union. "I hold that in contemplation of universal law and of the Constitution, the Union of these States is perpetual," he announced, after which a cheer went up from the crowd. In preparation for the speech, Lincoln had spent a good deal of time studying the words of previous leaders, including President Andrew Jackson's proclamation during the Nullification Crisis, as well as Henry Clay's oration during the debates over the Compromise of 1850. While the notions of state sovereignty and secession had been a part of the nation's constitutional history from the start, the idea of an enduring, perpetual Union was, by comparison, relatively new and fairly undeveloped. Still, Lincoln believed that the Constitution's claim to create "a more perfect Union" implied that a union had existed before the constitutional convention of 1787. Lincoln thus concluded that "the Union is much older than the Constitution" and dated back to the first united efforts among the colonies. Pronouncing secession ordinances as illegal and describing the notion of secession as "the essence of anarchy," he pledged to hold all federal property and enforce the laws of the Union in all of the states.[45]

The major themes of the speech were constitutionalism and conciliation. Lincoln mentioned the US Constitution thirty-eight times. By comparison, his immediate predecessors had referred to the document far fewer times in their inaugural addresses, despite the critical circumstances during which they too had assumed office: Buchanan made seventeen references to the nation's founding charter, Franklin Pierce eleven, and Zachary Taylor—in the midst of Southern secession threats in 1849—just five. The essence of Lincoln's constitutionalism in early 1861 appeared to boil down to this: the Constitution protected some slaveholders' rights (to reclaim fugitives) and established a perpetual Union among the states. Perhaps Lincoln believed that an explicit acknowledgment of slaveholders' rights—those stated in the constitutional text—would cause Southerners to give up their dream of a slaveholding republic, for conciliation proved to be the other undercurrent of the speech. Lincoln's closing sentences, at the urging of Seward, struck a peaceful note. "I am loath to close. We are not enemies, but friends," Lincoln implored. "The mystic chords of memory, stretching from every battlefield and patriot grave to every living heart and hearthstone all over this broad land, will yet swell the chorus of the Union, when again touched, as surely they will be, by the better angels of our nature."[46] Despite its eloquent conclusion, Lincoln's inaugural address proved ineffective in bringing about constitutional conciliation. Partisans, North and South, saw in the speech what they wanted to see—Northerners, a firm commitment to the Union; Southerners, a clear justification for secession and war.

Some African Americans, meanwhile, viewed the inauguration of a Northern Republican president as a portent of changing times. For months, African Americans had heard Southern politicians railing against Lincoln and the "Black Republicans," who were supposedly intent on abolishing slavery and establishing social equality, and for much of 1860, Southerners had feared a massive, violent slave insurrection in anticipation of Republican victory. Actual resistance came in a different form. A week after Lincoln took the oath of office, a young fugitive male slave made the perilous journey in a canoe across miles of open water from Charleston to Fort Sumter, which remained a US military outpost, where he sought protection from his abusive master. The next day, eight more slaves boldly took the initiative to claim their freedom by making their way to the Union garrison at Fort Pickens in Pensacola, Florida. The federal commander there reported to his superiors that the runaways "came to the fort entertaining the idea that we were placed here to protect them and grant them their freedom," but he quickly returned the men to their masters, as had occurred at Fort Sumter.[47] Because it remained the policy of the US government to enforce the Fugitive Slave Act—Lincoln had said so in his speech—these slaves were clearly mistaken in their interpretation of the new president's inauguration. Only a war could change the administration's policy.

FORT SUMTER AND THE FIRST SHOT

Apart from the question of fugitives, Lincoln inherited a precarious situation with regard to Union-held forts in the seceded states. During the waning weeks of the Buchanan administration, a series of federal military sites had fallen into the hands of Confederates, until by the time of Lincoln's inauguration, only a handful remained under Union control. Fort Pickens, as well as two forts near Key West, still lay in Union hands. But the most important federal possession was Fort Sumter, located just off the coast of Charleston and within sight of Confederate cannon. The nation had nearly come to war over Sumter in January, when the *Star of the West*, a Union vessel attempting to provide reinforcements and supplies to the fort, had come under fire from batteries along the coast. The ship returned to port, but the eighty soldiers garrisoned at Sumter would eventually need more food. On March 5, his second day in office, Lincoln learned from the commander at Sumter, Major Robert Anderson, that he might be able to stretch his supplies out for six more weeks before having to surrender. The situation at Sumter would force Lincoln to clarify his announced intention to "hold, occupy, and possess the property, and places belonging to the Government."[48]

After nearly a month of deliberation, Lincoln decided to send food supplies to Fort Sumter. He did so on the recommendation of a nearly unanimous Cabinet, for only Seward dissented. But there was a reason for Seward's hesitancy. For weeks, he had been negotiating behind the scenes—without Lincoln's knowledge—and had already promised to Confederates, through intermediaries, that Sumter would be abandoned. From Seward's perspective, such a strategy would take the wind out of the sails of the secessionist movement and allow Southern Unionists to step forward and help negotiate a settlement. Now, with Lincoln poised to supply Sumter, Seward wrote a memo to the president, in which he proposed an alternative policy. In his April 1 letter, the secretary of state urged that Lincoln respond vigorously to recent moves by Spain to annex Santo Domingo in order to provoke a foreign policy crisis—possibly war—with Spain or its ally, France. Such an event, Seward believed, would draw the seceded states back into the Union. Moreover, Seward urged Lincoln to abandon Sumter and instead attempt to hold Fort Pickens. Finally, Seward observed that "it must be somebody's business to pursue and direct [the policy] incessantly." Either the president should do it— if he wished to spend all of his time on the matter—or "devolve it on some member of his Cabinet."[49] Seward volunteered for the task. Showing a glimpse of the tremendous tact he would later display during wartime, Lincoln responded without offending Seward by ignoring the suggestion to provoke a foreign crisis and declaring that the president himself must lead the nation. Forging ahead, on April 6, Lincoln informed South Carolina's governor that he planned a relief expedition, and within four days, three ships loaded with food supplies set sail for Sumter. Viewed in context, Lincoln's orders constituted bold action and an expansive view of the powers of the

This print portrays the bombardment of Fort Sumter from an artillery battery in Charleston in April 1861, the start of the American Civil War. Courtesy of the Library of Congress, LC-DIG-ppmsca-35361

presidency. Buchanan, on whose watch seven states had claimed to have left the Union, believed he possessed constitutional power neither to hold federal property in the South nor to take any military action to oppose the newly formed Confederacy. Lincoln took a very different position. Inspired by his belief that his presidential oath to "preserve, protect, and defend the Constitution" empowered the executive to suppress a rebellion, Lincoln acted.

In the meantime, Confederates were ready for war. For months, South Carolinians had seen the American flag flying atop the fort as an affront. As the diplomatic crisis between the Union and Confederacy dragged on, Southern volunteers had converged on Charleston, eager to take shots at the Yankees occupying the fort. When informed of Lincoln's decision to send supplies, President Davis demanded the immediate surrender of Fort Sumter. When Anderson refused, early on the morning of April 12, 1861, Confederate forces under the command of Brigadier General Pierre Gustave Toutant (P. G. T.) Beauregard attacked. Reportedly given the honor of firing the first shot was Edmund Ruffin, the sixty-seven-year-old fire-eater who had long dreamed of Southern independence. "Of course, I was highly gratified by the compliment," Ruffin wrote in his diary, "and delighted to perform the service."[50] With long hair and a short temper, the hot-headed Virginian fired the first cannon shot from the Iron Battery on Morris Island. Just as the battle began, the provision-laden ships sent by Lincoln arrived in the harbor, but their crews—unarmed—could only watch helplessly as the bombardment got under way. No one died or was wounded on either side, but after thirty-four hours of cannon fire and extensive damage to the fort, Major Anderson surrendered. The only casualty that day was the Union.

THE SECESSION SPRING

The pace of events soon quickened. Within a few days, on April 15, Lincoln issued a proclamation under his authority as commander in chief, calling for 75,000 troops to be supplied by the militias of the several states. While Northerners responded enthusiastically to Lincoln's call to serve, the Upper South states expressed indignation. "I can be no party to this wicked violation of the laws of the country, and to this war upon the liberties of a free people. You can get no troops from North Carolina," Governor John Ellis wrote to Lincoln.[51] Such sentiment, it soon became apparent, was common throughout the Upper South states. Lincoln had miscalculated, for he had hoped, along with Seward, that at some point Southern Unionists would stand up and be counted, thereby restraining fellow Southerners and preventing the Confederacy from ever getting off the ground. Instead, Sumter and the call for troops created momentum for secession.

Virginia's response to Lincoln proved particularly significant. In the days and weeks after Lincoln's election, tension between moderates and secessionists in the state had reached a boiling point. Fears of a slave insurrection gripped Virginia slaveholders (concentrated in the Tidewater region), while moderate, mostly nonslaveholding forces concentrated in the northwestern part of the state pleaded with their fellow citizens to remember the state's historic ties to the Union. A special convention to consider the secession question had assembled in mid-February 1861, but Unionist forces dominated the meeting for several weeks as many Virginians hoped that the peace conference would provide a way out of the crisis. The oldest, most populous, and arguably most significant slaveholding state—home to many of the American founders and the birthplace of four out of the first five US presidents— Virginia seemed an unlikely candidate to abandon the Union. Even some of the most proslavery delegates argued that preserving the historic Union offered the best protection for slavery and slaveholders.

Nevertheless, the course of events swiftly altered the political dynamics in the Old Dominion. Many moderates heard little in Lincoln's inaugural address that gave them hope for a compromise, and when a Virginia delegation met with Lincoln to urge him not to attempt to hold Fort Sumter, the new president's firm policy on the matter prompted nothing but dismay. Quite simply, the outbreak of war and call for troops dealt a death blow to moderate forces in the state. On April 15, the same day as the president's proclamation, crowds assembled in Richmond clamoring for secession and raising a Confederate banner over the state capitol. Formal action ensued. Inspired by the brazen announcement by former governor Henry Wise, as he brandished a horse pistol, that his supporters were planning to seize federal installations in the state, on April 17, the convention approved an ordinance of secession. (The sitting governor, John Letcher, apparently intimidated by his predecessor, had allowed Wise to raise his own militia.) Former president John Tyler, writing to his wife, concluded that the Commonwealth had severed its "connection with the Northern hive of abolitionists and takes her stand as a sovereign and independent State."[52]

Three other Upper South states soon followed Virginia's lead. Although North Carolina and Tennessee in February had voted against forming secession conventions while an Arkansas convention postponed a popular referendum on secession, Virginia's response to Lincoln's call for troops turned the tide in each state. In Arkansas, wealthy cotton planters in the eastern Arkansas delta led the secessionist charge, and a reconvened convention in early May voted to leave the Union by a vote of 65–5. A secession convention eventually assembled in late May in North Carolina, and it unanimously voted to secede by repealing the state's ratification of the US Constitution. Tennessee seceded last, when in early June the state's voters in a popular referendum approved disunion by a margin of more than two to one.

Despite these moves, substantial Unionist sentiment remained throughout the Upper South. The Virginia convention vote of 88–55 was not overwhelming, with the opponents of secession concentrated in the cities, the Shenandoah Valley, and the northwestern portion of the state (which ultimately would become the state of West Virginia). Inhabitants of Virginia's mountainous areas, where neither slavery nor tobacco had ever been a way of life, shared neither the planters' racial fears nor their political extremism. A similar pattern held in the other Upper South states. Arkansas, Tennessee, and North Carolina all had Unionist strongholds. The Ozark region in northwest Arkansas and the Appalachians in East Tennessee and western North Carolina displayed persistent political sympathy for the Union. The political culture of these "white belts," containing almost no slaves, bore little resemblance to the honor-drenched regions of the Deep South, where slavery, white supremacy, and the economic interests of the planter aristocracy provoked outrage and political separatism.

In none of the border slaveholding states—Missouri, Kentucky, Maryland, or Delaware—did secessionist sentiment ever make headway. Only Missouri ever called a secession convention, and in March 1861, it voted against disunion 89–1. Lincoln's call for troops made little difference, for none of these states assembled to consider disunion in the aftermath of the proclamation. In fact, in congressional and state legislative elections in 1861, Unionists won large majorities in all these states, confirming that states with the closest cultural and economic ties to the North had little sympathy for the Southern Confederacy. Still, the "black belts" within the border states, areas with slave-based economies such as the Kentucky Bluegrass and the Eastern Shore of Maryland, did display sympathy for secession in their raising of men to fight for the Confederacy. Thus, one historian concludes, one of the clear patterns of the secession crisis was as follows: "The more and thicker the black belts, the faster and more enthusiastically a neighborhood massed behind secessionists."[53] Support for secession in the Upper South and border states, in other words, was nowhere nearly as strong as in the slavery-dominated Deep South.

SLAVERY, SOVEREIGNTY, AND THE CAUSES OF THE WAR

Understanding the crisis of 1860–1861 and the outbreak of war ultimately comes down to two questions. Why did eleven Southern states attempt to secede from the United States? And why did the remaining states, the historic federal Union, resist Southern secession by force rather than simply letting them go? If neither of these had occurred, after all, there would have been no war.

The first question is easier to answer than the second. The seven states of the Deep South that led the secession movement clearly sought to preserve and protect the institution of slavery and the ideology of white supremacy that lay behind it. In these states, slavery remained deeply entwined in nearly every aspect of society, economy, and culture. Slave property was an enormous economic investment—worth approximately $3 billion at the time—and was the linchpin of a social structure that sustained whites' notions of supremacy, power, and honor. Rights were also at stake. The Supreme Court insisted in *Dred Scott* that the Constitution protected slaveholders' rights to carry their

Alexander Stephens of Georgia served as vice president of the Confederate States of America. His "Cornerstone Speech," delivered soon after the formation of the Confederacy, claimed that the Southern republic was founded to protect the rights of slaveholders and uphold the principle of white supremacy. Courtesy of the Library of Congress, LC-DIG-cwpbh-04224

property at least into the territories and perhaps even into free states. Slavery played a less significant role in the states of the Upper South, but when forced to either contribute troops to suppress their sister slaveholding states or join them in seceding, the Upper South chose the latter course. After seceding, Southerners protected the right to slaveholding by explicitly writing it into the Confederate Constitution.

In March 1861, just after the drafting of the Confederate Constitution, Alexander Stephens, the newly elected vice president of the Confederacy, concisely summarized the purpose of the new nation. After enumerating the constitution's differences with the US Constitution, Stephens came to the subject of slavery. "The new constitution has put at rest, forever, all the agitating questions relating to our peculiar institution," he stated. "This was the immediate cause of the late rupture and present revolution." Thomas Jefferson and the others of his generation, Stephens continued, were mistaken about slavery, for they believed that it was a social, moral, and political wrong, an evil "they knew not well how to deal with." Such notions, Stephens argued, were wrong. "They rested upon the assumption of the equality of the races. This was an error." Stephens then got to the nub of the matter. "Our new government is founded upon exactly the opposite idea; its foundations are laid, its cornerstone rests, upon the great truth that the Negro is not equal to the white man; that slavery—subordination to the superior race—is his natural and normal condition," he announced. "This, our new government, is the first, in the history of the world, based upon this great physical, philosophical, and moral truth," he proudly concluded.[54] Clearly, according to the Confederate vice president, secession and the formation of the Confederacy rested on the twin pillars of slavery and white supremacy.

If secession represented the culmination of the South's decades-long commitment to slaveholders' rights and proslavery ideology, it also represented the logical outcome of the state sovereignty position. Rooted in the Articles of Confederation, nurtured by the early Jeffersonians, and most forcefully expressed by Calhoun and the nullifiers during the 1830s, the notion of state sovereignty had never been an exclusively Southern idea. Antislavery Northerners discovered the potency of the doctrine in their attempts to undermine the fugitive slave acts, particularly during the 1850s. But it was Southerners—facing an ever-growing Northern population and the possibility of permanent minority status within the American Union—who looked more consistently to this constitutional doctrine of state power. Guided by a persistent strain of Lockeanism that emphasized the rights of property and the right of revolution, the secessionists took the ultimate step to protect what they believed to be their fortunes, their honor, their liberties, and their way of life. Secession, from the South's perspective, protected private rights through constitutional means. Thus, secession and the creation of the Confederacy represented an attempt to finally and conclusively resolve the issues—slavery and sovereignty—that had been left unresolved at the time of the Constitutional Convention of 1787.

The answer to the second question—why the remaining states sought to hold the seceded states in the Union—is less apparent. Lincoln and the Republicans obviously rejected compromising with the South on the extension of slavery. Having won election on a free soil platform, Lincoln saw no reason to negotiate on the issue. His party thus helped to sink the peace conference proposal of February 1861 so that the consequences of the election could play out on the national stage. Still, unwillingness to compromise on the extension of slavery did not mean that Lincoln and the North went to war with the South for the aim of liberating its slaves. While Stephens's "Cornerstone" speech clarified Confederate intentions about slavery, Lincoln and his administration offered no antislavery counterpart, no declaration that the Northern states stood for emancipation and racial equality. Nothing at the outset of the war offered evidence that the incoming administration or the Congress sought to interfere with slavery in the Southern states, and Lincoln even reiterated his commitment not to do so. However great its success in the 1860 election, the Republican Party remained a loose coalition of forces united only around free labor ideology and opposition to the extension of slavery.[55] Despite Southern fears, moreover, only a faction within the Republican Party embraced anything resembling racial equality. The position of antebellum black constitutionalists, such as David Walker and Frederick Douglass, was not—at the time of the outbreak of war—the position of Lincoln and his party. A significant minority of the Northern population, moreover, had not even voted for Lincoln and the Republicans. Most Northern Democrats, even by the spring of 1861, remained sympathetic to the South, sensitive to slaveholders' rights, and supportive of white supremacy. In short, the Northern states did not go to war to liberate enslaved African Americans or to establish racial equality.

Lincoln, his fellow Republicans, and most Northern Democrats supported war because they believed it was necessary to defend and preserve the federal Union. In general, they believed that secession represented an extreme version of state sovereignty that posed a threat to the integrity of the American Union. If the South were allowed to secede, they reasoned, there would be no end to secession and division. If secession stood, any aggrieved section or state could decide voluntarily to depart the Union, and the nation as it had come to be known would cease to exist. A variety of lesser republics might eventually take its place on the North American continent, perhaps to be eventually subject to interference by European powers. Wanting to prevent the disintegration of the United States, in this sense Lincoln's devotion to the Union put him in company with other mid-nineteenth-century nation builders, such as Otto von Bismarck in Germany, in that they sought to unify nascent nations and build them into great powers. In this sense, going to war over secession would thus provide an answer to the lingering question of the nature of American sovereignty. In a conversation with Senator Garret Davis of Kentucky, just days after the bombardment of Fort Sumter, Lincoln reportedly put the conflict in just these terms. According to Davis, Lincoln said, "It must be decided whether our system of federal government was only a league of sovereign and independent States, from which any State could withdraw at pleasure, or whether the Constitution formed a government with strength and powers sufficient to uphold its own authority."[56] Hearkening back to the Hamiltonian tradition of national greatness, Lincoln sought to preserve the future "strength and powers" of the nation by attempting to put down the Southern rebellion.

To Lincoln and many Republicans, moreover, the very idea of secession struck at the heart of American traditions of law, order, and stable government. This is what Lincoln meant when, in his inaugural address, he referred to secession as "the essence of anarchy." To Lincoln the lawyer and constitutionalist, secession was anathema. It represented the triumph of passion over order, of self-interest over the public good, of lawlessness over law. Republican newspapers echoed these beliefs. The *New York Times* put it this way: "The issue is between anarchy and order—between Government and lawlessness—between the authority of the Constitution and the reckless will of those who seek its destruction." One Northern paper described secession as "Lawlessness on a Gigantic Scale," while another argued that had the founders provided for peaceable secession, they "would have organized anarchy."[57] "It is a war to defend the life of our nationality, the sacredness of our Constitution, the permanence of our Union, and the being of our government," another newspaper wrote. As the New England poet and social critic James Russell Lowell succinctly stated, "Our Constitution claims our allegiance because it is law and order."[58] At bottom, if the South were allowed to secede, not only the Union but all the legal and constitutional ideals on which it rested would be in shambles. In contrast to Confederates who viewed secession as a legal mechanism to protect slaveholders' liberties, most Northerners viewed the perpetuation of the Union as necessary to thwart an illegal, treasonous act and ensure the survival of the Constitution.

If the South left the Union primarily to resolve the slavery issue and the North went to war mostly to resolve the sovereignty issue, neither section of the country could predict or prepare for the swift and dramatic changes that lay ahead. A disrupted social order, a fluid political environment, and new constitutional arrangements would suddenly allow the claim of black constitutionalists—that slavery and white supremacy stood opposed to America's founding principles—to move to the forefront. A revolution was on the horizon.

Part II
WAR AND REVOLUTION

4
THE BATTLE JOINED,
1861–1862

A month and a half after directing the Confederate bombardment of Fort Sumter, General P. G. T. Beauregard arrived in northern Virginia to take command. Born on a Louisiana sugar plantation, Beauregard had gone to West Point, served in the Mexican-American War, and spent a dozen years traveling the country shoring up the nation's defenses as an engineer for the US Army. When the Civil War began, Beauregard returned to his native state, and upon the formation of the Confederacy, President Jefferson Davis made him the army's first brigadier general and sent him to Charleston. But with Sumter surrendered, Beauregard settled into his new position in Virginia. Two days after a Union incursion into the western part of the state, on June 5, 1861, Beauregard issued a proclamation to the people of Loudoun, Fairfax, and Prince William counties. "A reckless and unprincipled tyrant has invaded your soil," the announcement began. "Abraham Lincoln, regardless of all moral, legal, and constitutional restraints, has thrown his abolition hosts among you, who are murdering and imprisoning your citizens, confiscating and destroying your property, and committing other acts of violence and outrage too shocking and revolting to humanity to be enumerated." Hoping to stir up local citizens to defend their beleaguered homeland, Beauregard claimed that "all that is dear to man, your honor, and that of your wives and daughters, your fortunes, and your lives, are involved in this momentous contest."[1] Beauregard wasted little time in attempting to destroy Unionist sentiment and to demonize Lincoln and the Northern army. Despite its clear intent, Beauregard's bellicose rhetoric seemed out of place in the summer of 1861. Only a few skirmishes had occurred at that point, and only a handful of men had died. Some still hoped for peace, and few expected a four-year-long war that would result in the loss of hundreds of thousands of lives.

But rather than an anomaly, Beauregard's proclamation served as a powerful statement of the different ways in which Confederate and Union officers understood the coming fight. At that point, few Northern generals would have agreed with such a stark portrayal of the contest. Upon taking command of Union forces in late 1861, for example, General George B. McClellan explained to his commanders in the field that the war was being fought only to restore the authority of the general government and that the rebellion could best be suppressed "by religiously respecting the constitutional rights of all" enemies, including the right to own slaves.[2] This was the difference between the Southern states that seceded to protect slavery and the Northern states that entered the war only to prevent secession. From the start, Southerners perceived the conflict as an assault on their institutions, as a war to preserve all that they held dear. Not until the following summer did the Union's military and political leaders change their conception of the war, and with it their attitude toward Southerners' rights to own slaves. Beauregard's proclamation—with its call to protect property, homes, families, and a way of life—presaged the hard war that was to come.

PREPARING FOR LIMITED WAR

In the aftermath of Sumter, presidents Abraham Lincoln and Jefferson Davis faced the daunting task of preparing for war. In 1860, the entire United States Army consisted of only about 16,000 men, barely enough to staff coastal forts and patrol the frontier. Once hostilities began, a majority of the enlisted men remained loyal to the Union, while about a third of the officer corps defected to the Confederacy. Both the Union and the Confederacy thus needed to raise armies. After the fall of Sumter, Lincoln had called for 75,000 volunteers who would serve three-month terms of service, while Davis had asked for 100,000 volunteers to serve for a year. Both presidents saw almost immediately that these numbers would prove insufficient, and in May, both issued calls for additional enlistments. During the first few months after Sumter, neither side had any difficulty convincing young men to join the ranks, for few imagined that the war would last more than a year. Lincoln and many within his Cabinet still hoped that Southern Unionists would assert themselves and change the political dynamic, while many Confederates convinced themselves that Northern men lacked the will—and the skill—to beat them.

The North possessed considerable advantages with regard to both manpower and resources. On the eve of the war, the states that remained with the Union had a white population of approximately twenty million, while the Confederate states had a white population of about 5.5 million. In addition, the remaining Union states contained about a half million African Americans.

Broken down by optimal age for military service, population totals revealed an even greater Northern advantage. The Union states' total white male population between the ages of fifteen and thirty was more than 2.5 million. By contrast, in the Confederate states the number of white men aged fifteen to thirty was fewer than 800,000. Thus, the Union states had approximately three times the number of white men in this age group available for military service.[3] The North held other advantages as well. It far outpaced the South in overall industrial production, textile production, iron production, coal production, railroad mileage, and—most importantly—firearm production. The North had far more merchant ships and naval ships, and even in the realm of agriculture, the Northern states possessed a striking superiority. The North had more farm acreage, livestock, horses, and pack mules, and it grew more wheat and more corn. Among agricultural commodities relevant to the war effort, cotton production constituted the South's only advantage.

Still, the outlook for the Confederacy was neither dire nor predetermined. President Davis possessed impressive credentials and experience. A graduate of West Point, Davis had commanded a regiment in the Mexican-American War, served as secretary of war under President Franklin Pierce, and chaired the Senate Committee on Military Affairs. Lincoln's limited experience—as a militia captain who saw no action in the Black Hawk War—paled in comparison. Confederates, moreover, theoretically needed only to fight a defensive war, and its huge territory and extensive coastline would make it difficult to conquer. These advantages were significant. The South's military and political leaders knew that any Northern invasion would be a boost to Confederate nationalism, as Southerners would move to defend their communities, homes, and families. History proved, moreover, that nations with smaller populations and fewer resources did not necessarily lose wars to more powerful foes. The American Revolution offered a compelling example of a fledgling nation that had thrown off the yoke of tyranny and achieved its independence from a colossal power, an example to which President Davis referred in his inaugural address. Throughout the war, Confederates cast themselves as the heirs of the patriots of 1776.

If the Confederacy sought to defend its territory, the Union required a plan to conquer the enemy. To formulate a strategy, Lincoln initially turned to Winfield Scott, the first general in chief of the Union Army. A Virginian with a long and illustrious career, Scott had served his country in every war since the War of 1812. Nearing his seventy-fifth birthday, Scott put forth a strategy for Union victory: impose a naval blockade of the Confederate coastline to cut off foreign trade and advance Union forces into the Mississippi River Valley and down the Mississippi River to split the Confederacy in half. As they advanced, the army would secure the key Southern river ports, which would then serve as supply depots for Union forces. Scott's approach, labeled the "Anaconda Plan" by its critics, sought to strangle the South into submission by starving it of foreign foodstuffs and military supplies while taking control of its major transportation and trade routes.

Widely ridiculed and never formally approved, Scott's plan in some respects resembled the strategy that the Union ended up pursuing. Within days of the fall of Sumter, Lincoln announced a naval blockade, and after the secession of the Upper South, he applied the measure to the coastlines of North Carolina and Virginia. Despite Union success in holding Fortress Monroe in Virginia and using it as a base of operations in the Chesapeake Bay region, during the first few months of the war, Union forces failed to make much headway in securing control of the Virginia coast. They lost the first land battle of the war in early June at Big Bethel on the Virginia peninsula, where a large but confused Union force ended up retreating and suffering seventy-nine casualties (the total number of dead, wounded, and missing). Still, the blockade did achieve early success further south, when in August Confederates surrendered garrisons on the North Carolina coast. In early November, the Union navy won a major victory at Port Royal, South Carolina, which gave the Federals a foothold in the Deep South between the key cities of Charleston and Savannah. By seizing such places, the Union became better equipped to enforce the blockade. Eventually Scott's plan to control the Mississippi River proved to be one of the most effective Union strategies of the war, but the river campaign constituted only a single part of a war with a variety of theaters of operation.

WAR ON THE BORDER: MARYLAND, KENTUCKY, AND MISSOURI

In the early months of the conflict, Lincoln navigated a fragile situation in the border states. Although slavery had never been particularly strong in Delaware, Kentucky, Maryland, and Missouri, secessionist elements existed in all of these states except Delaware. With its economic ties to the North and only a handful of slaveholders, Delaware remained firmly attached to the Union. But Lincoln would have to handle the other states with care, silencing pro-Rebel voices while making sure that he did not drive these states into the Confederacy. Davis, in the meantime, combined political overtures to the border states with sporadic military campaigns, in hopes of adding them to the Confederate nation. Both presidents viewed the border states as crucial battlegrounds in which public opinion loomed large.

Maryland was Lincoln's first priority. Because it lay to the north of Washington, DC, and Virginia to the south, the Union had no choice but to secure Maryland in order to keep the nation's capital from being surrounded by enemy territory. Within days of Sumter, prosecessionists raised a Confederate flag on Federal Hill in Baltimore, angering the city's Unionists. When Union troops from Massachusetts detrained in the city on their way to Washington, a mob of pro-Confederate civilians threw bricks and stones at the Union forces. Despite what one witness described as "the extraordinary coolness and forbearance of the troops," they eventually fired on their attackers.[4] Four Union soldiers and at least nine civilians died in the April 19 fracas, arguably the first bloodshed of the war. Because Baltimore possessed the railroad line nearest to Washington, the disturbance cut off the Union capital from the rest of the North, and for several days in April, Lincoln feared an imminent Confederate invasion before more Federal troops finally arrived. At the end of April, the Maryland legislature convened and rejected secession, thus soothing nerves in Washington. Still, tensions between pro-Union and pro-Confederate elements in Maryland continued to simmer. Early in the war, Lincoln suspended the privilege of the writ of habeas corpus in part of the state, which allowed Union troops to arrest and jail Rebel sympathizers without trial, and months later the president attempted to keep pro-Confederate forces at bay by arresting several members of the Maryland legislature. Apart from the questionable constitutionality of such actions, these measures silenced the pro-Rebel leaders and helped keep the state in the Union.

Kentucky presented a challenge to both presidents. The birthplace of both Lincoln and Davis, the state initially attempted to remain neutral and officially refused to send troops to either side. Nevertheless, thousands of Kentuckians, in roughly equal numbers, fought for either the Union or the Confederacy. In early September 1861, with military forces from both sides poised to move into the state, the Confederates invaded first. Fearing that Union troops would take control of key locations, Southern forces under the command of Major General Leonidas Polk entered Kentucky from Tennessee and advanced to Columbus, located at the extreme western end of the state along the Mississippi River. There they built a fort that Polk dubbed the "Gibraltar of the South," complete with a long chain that stretched across the river to prevent enemy ships from passing. Polk's advance into Kentucky, in violation of its supposed neutrality, allowed Federal forces to make their own move. Within a few days of Polk's capture of Columbus, Union soldiers under the command of Brigadier General Ulysses S. Grant seized Paducah, strategically located at the confluence of the Ohio and Tennessee rivers. Politically, Kentucky would maintain two governments throughout the war—one loyal to the Union and one that claimed that the state had joined the Confederacy. In practical terms, for the first year of the war, Kentucky witnessed an intense military struggle for control of the state, and the Confederate state government existed mostly as a shadow organization that traveled with the Rebel army.

Missouri proved to be the most explosive of the border states. Having played such a role during the 1850s in fomenting violence in Kansas, proslavery Missourians eagerly hoped to drive their state out of the Union. But when a popularly elected convention called by prosecessionist governor Claiborne Jackson voted in March to remain with the Union, prosecessionist forces focused their attention on helping the Confederate cause. Initially, this meant taking control of the arsenal at St. Louis, one of the largest stockpiles of weapons in the West. The pro-Confederate state militia assembled at Camp Jackson in St. Louis, where they allegedly plotted to seize the arsenal. In early May, before the Confederates could take any action, a Union home guard unit of roughly 7,000 men surrounded the Confederate camp, and the Rebels surrendered without firing a shot. When the leader of the Union force, the brash Captain Nathaniel Lyon, subsequently marched his prisoners through St. Louis, a riot erupted. In two days of clashes between Federal troops and Confederate sympathizers, at least two dozen people died.

By the summer, full-scale warfare broke out in Missouri. Although controversial within the Lincoln administration for his extreme actions and rhetoric, Lyon—now a brigadier general—moved aggressively against pro-Confederates. Forcing Governor Jackson and his Southern sympathizers into a continual retreat, Lyon took control of the state capital at Jefferson City, installed a pro-Union military governor, and pushed the pro-Confederate militia into the far southwestern corner of the state. Despite being outnumbered nearly two to one, on August 10, the fearless Lyon attacked Confederate forces and the state militia near Springfield. The assault failed miserably, resulting in the death of Lyon and the retreat of Union forces, thus leaving all of southwest Missouri under Confederate control. Casualties at the Battle of Wilson's Creek, as it was known, proved heavy on both sides—1,235 for the Union and 1,095 for the Confederates. With Federal troops out of sight, the pro-Southern governor and legislature—now operating out of tiny Neosho, Missouri—claimed to act as the legitimate government, and in October they approved an ordinance of secession. Like Kentucky, Missouri eventually had stars in the flags of both nations and sent representatives to both congresses, but Missouri's connections to the Confederacy proved mostly symbolic. In reality, more than twice as many Missourians ended up fighting for the Union than for the Confederacy, and Union forces never did surrender control of the state capital. More than anywhere else, the war in

Missouri became a guerilla war, marked by sporadic raids involving soldiers and civilians alike.

Confronted with the reality of pro-Confederate civilians attacking Union forces or obstructing Union military operations, the new Federal commander in Missouri, former Republican presidential candidate John C. Fremont, took a dramatic step. On August 30, 1861, Fremont issued a declaration of martial law throughout the state. The order provided for military trials for all armed civilians caught behind Union lines, the death penalty for all found guilty, and the confiscation of the property of Missourians "who shall take up arms against the United States." Most remarkably, Fremont's proclamation provided that "their slaves, if any they have, are hereby declared freemen."[5] Having never authorized such an order of emancipation, Lincoln was furious. Not wanting to offend border state Unionists, and believing that Fremont's order had no legal basis, Lincoln rescinded the proclamation. Writing to a friend a few weeks later, the president described the order as "purely political, and not within the range of military law or necessity."[6] In spite of Fremont's military success in Missouri, Lincoln soon relieved him of command, and a few months after his dismissal, at the urging of radical Republicans in Congress, Lincoln reassigned him to western Virginia. Clearly, during the summer of 1861, Lincoln neither believed in emancipation as an effective military tool nor embraced it as a Union war aim. Keeping the border states loyal to the Union remained a more important concern.

WAR IN VIRGINIA: THE FIRST BATTLE OF BULL RUN

The situation in Virginia overshadowed developments in the border region, primarily because of the proximity of Richmond to Washington. The two national capitals lay within 100 miles of each other, and for a good portion of the war, the two presidents seemed preoccupied with each other's capital city. Although General Scott counseled against an advance, the Northern public favored quick and decisive action. Union victories in skirmishes in western Virginia in June and early July bolstered the confidence of Northerners and seemed to increase the public's desire for a full-scale advance on the Confederate capital. Lincoln, still feeling his way into the job, understood the importance of public opinion to any endeavor of his administration, and he soon ordered Brigadier General Irvin McDowell to move against the Confederates. McDowell realized that his large, undisciplined volunteer army needed more time to train, and he protested the president's decision. Lincoln and his advisers remained committed to an advance. "You are green, it is true," a reluctant General Scott replied to McDowell, "but they are green also; you are all green alike."[7] So on July 16, McDowell's forces, nearly 30,000 strong, began lumbering south toward Richmond.

The Confederates, meanwhile, had positioned themselves at the major invasion routes. Beauregard and his men stood near Bull Run (a tributary of the Potomac), guarding the railroad just north of Manassas Junction, while Brigadier General Joseph E. Johnston commanded a force stationed at the mouth of the Shenandoah Valley. Beauregard soon learned of the Union advance from a Washington spy, Rose O'Neal Greenhow, and began preparing for battle. McDowell's men, meanwhile, moved at a snail's pace, and their lack of discipline showed. Along the way, some wandered off to pick berries while others consumed their rations, and the need to acquire more provisions—along with poor roads—caused critical delays. By the time Union troops approached Beauregard's forces, some of Johnston's men had already arrived by train and foot as reinforcements.

On July 21 the Battle of Bull Run began. As was the case with many early engagements, chaos proved one of the dominant characteristics of the battle, as the variety of uniforms worn by soldiers and the similar flags flown by the opposing armies made it at times difficult to distinguish friend from foe. Union soldiers initially outnumbered their opponents and at first succeeded in pushing back the Confederates, but by late afternoon, the arrival of Confederate reinforcements turned the tide. With an entire brigade (about 5,000 men) coming by train from the Shenandoah Valley, the battle turned into a rout. Although the two armies were of about equal size, with the Confederates at a slight advantage, Union soldiers became demoralized upon seeing the mass of Rebel reinforcements. As the Confederates charged, many let out a loud, martial cry—the Rebel yell—and frightened Yankees began a hasty retreat, dropping weapons, canteens, and other accouterments along the way. Complicated by the fact that civilian spectators were having picnics on the hillsides, the Union retreat degenerated into chaos. The landscape teemed with both combatants and picnickers, all attempting to flee from danger. Straight from Richmond, President Davis arrived in the field just in time to witness the victory. Exhausted and hindered by a steady rain, the Confederates remained near Manassas, content to celebrate their triumph rather than to pursue their foes. The Union suffered nearly 3,000 casualties, including 460 deaths, while the Confederates had 1,750 casualties, including 387 dead. Not for several months would Union forces attempt another move into Virginia.

The Battle of Bull Run, also known as the Battle of Manassas, changed both sides' perceptions of the war. Lincoln blamed himself for the defeat, but he immediately replaced the suddenly unpopular McDowell with George B. McClellan. Compounding the Union rout was another lopsided Confederate victory three months later along the Potomac River. The Battle of Ball's Bluff, an ill-fated Federal attempt to cross the river and capture the town of Leesburg, Virginia, resulted in more than 900 Union casualties, including hundreds who drowned after being driven over a high bluff into the river. Confronting the fact that a difficult struggle lay ahead, Lincoln began reading military strategy, and he would soon develop his own ideas about what the Union army needed to do to win. In the short run, he favored tightening the naval blockade and securing longer enlistments for soldiers. Meanwhile, President Davis and most Southerners, giddy after their triumph, assured themselves that victory and independence lay within their grasp. One Southern clergyman linked victory at Manassas to divine approval of the Confederate government and its protection of slaveholders' rights. "God has given us of the South to-day a fresh and gold opportunity—and so a most solemn command—to realize that form of government in which the just, constitutional rights of each and all are guaranteed to each and all."[8]

WAR IN THE WEST: THE RISE OF GRANT AND THE BATTLE OF SHILOH

Despite the Union's limited victories in the border states and the Confederacy's momentous win in Virginia, the western theater proved to be the one place of unequivocal Union success early in the war. In a matter of a few short months during early 1862, the Union achieved impressive victories. Federal forces secured the surrender of two Confederate river fortifications, invaded Tennessee and occupied its capital city, and forced Confederates to retreat all the way into northern Mississippi. Each of these accomplishments owed its success in part to Ulysses S. Grant, a native of Ohio and a graduate of West Point. Nothing in Grant's early life seemed to portend his future triumphs. He had failed at nearly everything he attempted, and after service in Mexico, he resigned from the army in 1854 to return to his family. Rumors of excessive drinking plagued him throughout his career. But when the Civil War began, Grant raised a company of infantry volunteers in Illinois, and with the help of a congressman friend, he secured a colonelcy. In wartime, Grant proved a keen strategist and indefatigable fighter. After his capture of Paducah, he received orders to engage the Rebels at Belmont, Missouri, just across the river from the Confederate stronghold at Columbus, Kentucky. Although unsuccessful at dislodging the Confederates, Grant demonstrated at Belmont the leadership qualities that marked his later victories: a willingness to strike the enemy and calmness in the midst of difficult circumstances.

In early 1862, Grant pressed his commander to allow him to attack forts Henry and Donelson, located just south of the Kentucky–Tennessee border on the Tennessee and Cumberland rivers, respectively. The Confederate command had concentrated most of its efforts on securing the Mississippi River, and in doing so, they had left the Tennessee and the Cumberland poorly defended. General Henry Halleck assented to Grant's suggestion, and Grant began mobilizing forces in Paducah, where he joined with a gunboat fleet commanded by Flag Officer Andrew H. Foote, a nearly forty-year veteran of the US Navy. Moving his troops down the Tennessee River, Grant first went after Fort Henry, a poorly located earthen fortification on the river's swampy east bank. As Grant began to surround the fort by landing his men on both sides of the river, the Confederate commander decided to save most of his force of 3,000 by evacuating them via boat to the much safer Fort Donelson. The artillery and a small force stayed behind to defend the fort and slow the Union advance. When Foote's fleet began firing on Fort Henry, the remaining Confederates soon surrendered. The Northern victory, on February 6, opened up the Tennessee River to the Union Navy.

Although his force missed the action at Fort Henry, Grant and his 15,000 men were on their way to Fort Donelson, twelve miles away, where Confederate forces from throughout the region now amassed. After Grant's men took their positions, Union reinforcements arrived. With the fort now surrounded by a large, well-armed Union force, Foote's gunboats began their assault. Fort Donelson's artillery proved remarkably effective, though, and after several hours of fighting, the gunboats withdrew, four of the six badly damaged and Foote wounded in the ankle. After surviving the naval assault, Confederates decided to attack the Federals in the hope of clearing a way to escape, but after a day of combat, the Confederates were in no better position to get away than before. Still surrounded with no way out, Rebel commanders requested terms of surrender. Grant's reply made him famous: "No terms except unconditional and immediate surrender can be accepted," he wrote. "I propose to move immediately upon your works."[9] On February 16, 1862, a Confederate force of approximately 12,000 surrendered to Grant. With the fall of forts Henry and Donelson, the Union achieved a significant victory. Kentucky lay solidly in Union hands, and with control of two major navigation routes in the heart of the South, the Union army made significant inroads into Tennessee. Within ten days, Federal troops under the command of Major General Don Carlos Buell had moved down the Cumberland and occupied Nashville, at which point Tennessee governor Isham Harris fled to behind

Confederate lines. Grant, meanwhile, received orders to proceed south along the Tennessee River to Pittsburgh Landing, a small steamboat wharf just north of the Tennessee–Mississippi border.

General Albert Sidney Johnston faced Union forces deep in Confederate territory. A distinguished soldier and old friend of Jefferson Davis, Johnston was a Texas planter with strong proslavery and antiabolitionist convictions. Before the war, he had expressed his hope that Northerners would "give up their fanatical, idolatrous negro worshipping," so that the country could "go on harmoniously, happily & prosperously."[10] As commander in the West, Johnston led Confederate forces from the Appalachian Mountains to the Mississippi River. His fragile line had initially extended all the way across Kentucky, but after the fall of forts Henry and Donelson, he had given up most of Tennessee and retreated to Mississippi. Now Johnston attempted to concentrate his forces at Corinth, Mississippi, a railroad junction in the northeast corner of the state. Combining his troops with those of General Braxton Bragg, who had been in Alabama, and P. G. T. Beauregard, who had recently arrived from the east, together they planned a major offensive against Grant. Just a day's march south of Pittsburgh Landing, Confederate forces at Corinth numbered approximately 45,000, compared to Grant's 40,000 men. The number of Southern troops at Corinth might have been larger had Confederates not attacked Union soldiers in northwest Arkansas in an unsuccessful attempt to advance back into Missouri. The Battle of Pea Ridge (or Elkhorn Tavern) in early March not only produced a Confederate defeat but also prevented some 20,000 Confederate soldiers from arriving in time to merge with Johnston and Beauregard's attack force. Time was of the essence, because the Confederate command wanted to move against Grant's men before General Buell in Middle Tennessee could provide reinforcements.

At sunrise on April 6, 1862, the Confederates attacked the unsuspecting Federals at Pittsburgh Landing. Grant, apparently convinced that the Rebels at Corinth were fortifying their position rather than preparing for an attack, had set up headquarters in Savannah, Tennessee, nine miles up the Tennessee River, where he was waiting for Buell. When Grant heard that fighting had begun, he rushed to the site of the battle, which occurred in the thick woods, peach orchards, and open fields near Shiloh Church, a small log-cabin Methodist meetinghouse. The battle involved more troops than any other engagement of the war to that point, and the fighting proved more intense. For many soldiers, Shiloh was their first combat experience. Early in the battle, the Confederates achieved success against their opponents, as Rebel forces drove the Yankees back. Union soldiers made a heroic stand along a sunken road, a place that, because of the extreme nature of the fighting there, became known as the Hornet's Nest. The toughness of these Union forces proved critical, for by the end of the day, the Northern army had fought just long enough to keep from being pushed into the Tennessee River. Without question, the first day of the battle belonged to the Confederates. Only the demise of Johnston, the Confederate commander, cast a pall over the apparent Rebel victory. Shot just above the knee, where the bullet pierced the femoral artery, Johnston suffered a serious wound. Unable to find his personal physician, the general bled to death.

As night fell and the fighting ceased, Beauregard—now in charge—figured that he would finish off the Yankees in the morning. Mistakenly informed by telegram that Buell had changed his course and was headed elsewhere, Beauregard, before going to bed, confidently wired Richmond that the Confederates had won "a complete victory" at Pittsburgh Landing. What Beauregard did not know was that as he slept, Buell's men—20,000 of them—finally arrived. Although the Confederates achieved some success on the battlefield early on the second day, the Union soon thwarted their efforts. With the help of a few gunboats that provided cover, the fresh Union troops eventually pushed the Confederates back and successfully resisted a subsequent Rebel counterattack. Outnumbered and exhausted, Beauregard's forces retreated to Corinth. Within a few months, the Union forces would seize Corinth, which the Rebels later abandoned to move eastward.

The Battle of Shiloh was a Union victory. The Rebels' attempt to destroy the Yankee force at Pittsburgh Landing and move back into Tennessee had proven unsuccessful, and Union forces advanced as far south as northern Mississippi. Grant later put it this way: "The enemy fought bravely, but they had started out to defeat and destroy an army and capture a position," he wrote in his *Memoirs*. "They failed in both, with very heavy loss in killed and wounded, and must have gone back discouraged."[11] In fact, the costs to both sides were enormous. Shiloh witnessed the highest casualties of the war to that point, with 1,754 Union and 1,728 Confederate dead, 8,408 Union and 8,012 Confederate wounded, and 2,885 Union and 959 Confederate missing. Total casualties, in other words, approached 24,000. Makeshift field hospitals, the first of the war, appeared on the battlefield to handle the inordinate number of wounded, and in the aftermath of battle, soldiers placed hundreds of unknown Confederate dead in unmarked burial trenches. The bloodshed shocked the American public, which had never before witnessed death and suffering on such a massive scale. No one had died at Fort Sumter, and Bull Run had resulted in a total of fewer than 900 dead. By comparison, Shiloh was a bloodbath.

A torrent of criticism soon rained on both commanders. Northern critics blamed Grant for being caught by surprise, and unfounded rumors circulated that the general had been drunk. For weeks Northern newspapers kept up the criticism, and Lincoln came under enormous pressure to demote him. At first Lincoln sought any information regarding Grant's purported misconduct, but eventually the support of General Halleck helped to vindicate Grant. Halleck probably relied heavily on the reports of Brigadier General William T. Sherman, who stoutly defended Grant. Twice wounded in the battle, Sherman had played an indispensable role in the action, and Grant had singled him out for displaying "great judgment and skill in the management of his men."[12] Loyal to each other, Grant and Sherman began a mutual admiration at Shiloh that lasted for the remainder of the war, and indeed for the rest of their lives. The Confederates' defeat also brought out tensions within the Southern high command, as President Davis—grieving the loss of his friend Johnston—blamed Beauregard for not finishing off the Union forces at the end of the first day of battle. Given the enormity of the sacrifice, the finger-pointing was understandable. Eventually the American public would come to see Shiloh for what it really was: the first of many great and terrible battles.

WAR ON THE RIVER: THE FALL OF NEW ORLEANS AND MEMPHIS

The Union effort to take control of the Mississippi River proved even more successful than Grant's push through Tennessee. At the outset of the war, the US Navy possessed no vessels suited to such a task. Only a small force, the Home Squadron, remained in domestic waters, patrolling the nation's coastlines. Remarkably, of the twelve ships that made up the squadron, not a single one was suited for riverine service. This meant that if securing the Mississippi River remained a strategic goal, a fleet of rivergoing vessels would need to be constructed. James Buchanan Eads, an engineer and entrepreneur, proposed to design and build a fleet of ironclad and tin-clad gunboats to take the Mississippi for the Union. Although no such fleet had ever before existed, Eads possessed unbounded confidence, and after meeting with Lincoln, he quickly began construction of the awkward, ugly vessels that became the Union's "brown water navy." Derisively referred to as "turtles" or "stinkpots," the naval vessels that made up the Mississippi River Squadron played a key role in Union success.

Commanded by Flag Officer Foote, the flotilla had initially proven its worth at Fort Henry, and in March 1862 the gunboats began operations on the Mississippi. Although the original Confederate strategy for defense of the river had involved a series of barrier fortifications, Grant's success forced the Confederates to withdraw from Columbus in order to fortify their position at Corinth. About sixty river miles to the south of Columbus lay Island Number Ten, a two-mile-wide island near the Kentucky–Tennessee line and the only stronghold protecting the lower Mississippi. After Union major general John Pope easily captured the town of New Madrid, Missouri, situated just downriver from the island, he planned to attack the Confederates, both on the island and on the other side of the river. Knowing that he would need help, Pope requested the assistance of Foote's gunboats. Pope believed that if a gunboat could run past the heavily fortified island and provide cover, he could ferry his troops across the river and trap the bulk of the Rebel force. Despite Foote's initial reluctance, two gunboats eventually did manage to skirt past the island, thereby cutting off the Rebels' escape route and making it possible for Pope's forces to cross. On April 8, 1862—the day after Grant's and Buell's forces rallied to victory at Shiloh—the Confederate commanders surrendered Island Number Ten to Foote. Although losses on both sides were minimal, the Union captured approximately 4,500 Confederates. Foote's flotilla then eyed its next target, the Confederate outpost downriver at Fort Pillow, located about forty miles north of Memphis.

Meanwhile, in late January 1862, 400 miles to the south, the blue water navy began an expedition to capture New Orleans, a hub for trade throughout the western hemisphere. With nearly 167,000 residents, New Orleans was the South's largest city and the sixth largest city in America, with one of the busiest ports and slave markets in the world. Capturing New Orleans would strike at the very heart of the Confederacy and—even if not intentionally—at the soul of Southern slavery. While awaiting the start of the mission, Vermont-born general John W. Phelps issued an antislavery proclamation from Ship Island, off the coast of Mississippi. "The Constitution was made for Freemen, not for Slaves," he declared, criticizing slavery for "demand[ing] rights, to the exclusion and annihilation of those rights which are insured to us by the Constitution."[13] Despite Phelps's more revolutionary aims, the actual mission was a military one—to capture the city—and David G. Farragut would lead the effort. Born in Tennessee and residing in Virginia at the time of secession, Farragut moved north after the war began. A retired sixty-year-old veteran of the War of 1812, Farragut had reportedly vowed "to live and die owing allegiance to no flag but that of the Union under which he had served."[14] Possessing just the right combination of experience and determination, Farragut seemed the perfect man for the job. His expedition included a total of eighteen warships, including an assortment of steam frigates, propeller-driven warships, and wooden gunboats. Meeting up with a flotilla of mortar schooners commanded by David Porter, the impressive naval force arrived at the mouth of the Mississippi. There the fleet united with 15,000 army troops, floated in on transport ships and commanded by General Benjamin Butler.

By mid-April 1862, Union forces were in position to begin their attack. Forts Jackson and St. Phillip guarded the mouth of the Mississippi in the Gulf of Mexico, and New Orleans lay about seventy miles upriver. In addition to the star-shaped masonry forts, the Confederates had stationed a handful of ironclad gunboats there. Confident that the forts could resist any attack, President Davis had ordered a bunch of other armed vessels north to defend Memphis and the Memphis-Charleston Railroad line. Because Confederate soldiers in the Gulf region had converged at Corinth for the battle at Shiloh, moreover, Farragut's task was easy to surmise. If the Union Navy could make it past the forts, it would have little trouble capturing the undefended city. Beginning on April 16 and continuing for a solid week, Union mortar boats bombarded forts Jackson and St. Phillip. But as the Confederate guns continued to fire back, Farragut daringly decided to make a run past the forts. On the morning of April 24, Farragut sent his ships toward New Orleans, and the vessels incurred little damage. Eventually, thirteen of seventeen Union warships successfully made it beyond the forts and upriver toward the Crescent City. On April 28, defenseless New Orleans residents surrendered, and Farragut became a Northern hero. President Davis had badly miscalculated. By removing a flotilla of armed steamers from the area, he had made the Union's job considerably easier. When he heard news of the capture of New Orleans, the devastated Davis reportedly "buried his face in his hands."[15]

Within a few weeks, the Union Army and naval forces advanced further upriver and captured the undefended state capital of Baton Rouge and eventually Natchez, Mississippi. These successful Union operations penetrated deep into the region's plantation districts, and enslaved African Americans understood the Federal military presence as a sign of the coming of freedom. By the end of May 1862, more than a hundred runaway slaves had already made their way to Camp Parapet, located just north of New Orleans. Welcomed by General Phelps, who had issued his antislavery proclamation some months before, the camp became a haven for those who fled nearby plantations, even though official Union policy still opposed emancipation. Regardless of the implication for slavery, at this point, with the exception of Mobile Bay, the Union Navy controlled the Gulf of Mexico from Key West all the way to the Mississippi River, effectively ending Confederate hopes of supplying their troops from the Gulf. The dual raids on Island Number Ten and

New Orleans during April 1862 thus revealed the Union strategy of simultaneously attacking Confederate outposts along the Mississippi, making a successful Confederate defense virtually impossible.

While Farragut's flotilla headed north, Foote's gunboats continued their trek southward. Initially, Foote and Pope planned to work jointly, as they had done in Missouri, in attacking Fort Pillow. But when General Halleck ordered Pope and his men to join the advance against Corinth, the assault on the fort was left to the navy. Foote, still nursing his injured ankle and now anxious about his chances of success, decided to surrender his command and take leave. The day after his departure, May 10, the Confederate River Defense Fleet gunboats attacked the Union vessel *Cincinnati* at Plum Point Bend (or Plum Run Bend), four miles upriver from Fort Pillow. The ensuing engagement resulted in the sinking of the *Cincinnati* and heavy damage to another Union vessel, the *Mound City*. A Confederate victory, the Battle of Plum Point Bend stalled the Union advance down the river. As Union commanders plotted another attack on Fort Pillow, General Beauregard ordered its evacuation, and when Union forces arrived there on June 5, they found the fort deserted.

Having secured a new base of operations, the Union's brown water navy at once continued its advance toward Memphis. At dawn on June 6, five Union ironclads and two rams—light, unarmed vessels intended to smash enemy ships—met the remaining eight vessels of the Confederate River Defense Fleet on the river at Memphis. Thousands of locals lined the bluff to cheer on the Rebel ships, the decks of which were stacked high with bales of cotton, rather than iron, for protection. Expecting a repeat of Plum Point Bend, onlookers were soon disappointed. In the hour-and-a-half battle that ensued, Union ships sank or destroyed all but one Confederate vessel. Flag Officer Charles H. Davis, Foote's successor, thereafter demanded the surrender of the city, and Mayor John Park, admitting that it had "no resources of defense," acknowledged to Flag Officer Davis, "the city is in your power."[16] With Memphis captured, the South lost another base of operations, but slaves gained another outpost for freedom. In the following weeks and months, just as had occurred around New Orleans, enslaved African Americans began fleeing toward the Federal-occupied city. The only remaining river stronghold still in Confederate hands was Vicksburg, Mississippi, about equidistant between Memphis and New Orleans. Union operations on the Mississippi River, apart from the minor setback at Plum Point Bend, had been an unqualified success.

WAR IN THE VALLEY AND ON THE PENINSULA:
MCCLELLAN, JACKSON, AND LEE

In the eastern theater, it was an altogether different story. After their victory at Manassas in the summer of 1861, the Confederates fortified their defenses in northern Virginia and over the next several months managed continually to demoralize their Federal opponents. During the first half of 1862, the Union experienced a series of setbacks that highlighted the superiority of Rebel commanders in the East. Union general George B. McClellan proved tentative and ineffective in his attempts to develop a plan for moving on Richmond. His Confederate counterparts, in contrast, demonstrated strategic brilliance and tactical bravery. Generals Thomas "Stonewall" Jackson and Robert E. Lee won a string of victories that kept Confederate hopes high and almost overshadowed the Union's simultaneous springtime victories in the West.

After the Union debacle at Bull Run in 1861, Lincoln had appointed McClellan commander of the Army of the Potomac, the main Union army. Number two in his class at West Point and a veteran of the Mexican-American War during his early twenties, McClellan seemed to have everything going for him. Dashing, ambitious, and supremely confident, McClellan had won a degree of fame during the war's early months after decisive victories in skirmishes in western Virginia. Dubbed "the Napoleon of the Present War" by the *New York Herald*, McClellan had earned the respect of both General Scott and President Lincoln. As the months passed, though, McClellan urged Lincoln to ease the aging general into retirement. When Lincoln obliged, on November 1, 1861, McClellan assumed as well Scott's position as general in chief of the Union Army. Never lacking in self-confidence, McClellan famously stated at that point, "I can do it all."[17] Adored by his men, who referred to him as "Little Mac," McClellan appeared to be the one who would lead the North to victory.

Upon assuming command, McClellan made clear that he viewed the conflict as a limited war, solely for the restoration of the old Union. In letters to commanders in the field in November 1861, McClellan conveyed the simultaneous importance of the Union's political and military goals. "You will please constantly to bear in mind the precise issue for which we are fighting: that issue is the preservation of the Union and the restoration of the full authority of the general government over all portions of our territory," McClellan wrote. In these letters, McClellan used nearly identical phrasing, as he informed officers that only by "religiously respecting the constitutional rights of all" could this aim be accomplished. Just to make certain that one of his commanders understood what he meant, McClellan added in his letter to

Brigadier General Don Carlos Buell that the general should assure the inhabitants of Kentucky that "their domestic institutions will in no manner be interfered with."[18] McClellan's orders reflected Lincoln's will, and McClellan said so. Having just rescinded Fremont's emancipation order in Missouri, at this point Lincoln shared McClellan's view of a war with limited goals.

Much to Lincoln's dismay, McClellan spent most of the fall and winter of 1861–1862 drilling his men and developing a strategy. In late January, Lincoln set a deadline for McClellan to begin his advance. McClellan responded with an alternative plan. He would float his massive army down the Rappahannock River, land at the town of Urbanna, and then advance on Richmond by land. Glad that McClellan finally appeared ready to move, Lincoln agreed to the plan. But by the time McClellan was ready to launch the invasion, the enemy had marched south of the Rappahannock, thus rendering the scheme useless. Forced to revise his strategy, McClellan proposed to sail his fighting force through the Chesapeake Bay, south to Fortress Monroe. From there, his army would advance up the Virginia peninsula that lay between the James and the York rivers, all the way to Richmond.

Before he would carry out this strategy, McClellan insisted on the elimination of a Confederate ironclad ship. Formerly the United States wooden ship *Merrimack* but since heavily armored and renamed *Virginia* by the Rebels, the slow, steam-powered vessel sat in McClellan's way at the mouth of the James River. On March 8, the *Virginia* attacked the Federal fleet of wooden ships stationed in the area, thus beginning the Battle of Hampton Roads. Because no guns at the time could pierce armor, the five Union vessels proved no match for the Confederate ironclad. Two of the Union ships ran aground and played no meaningful role in the battle. The remaining three put up a fight but ultimately fared no better. The *Virginia* rammed and sank the *Cumberland*, ran aground the *Congress*, and heavily damaged and ran aground the *Minnesota*. These events terrified many in Washington, especially Secretary of War Edwin M. Stanton, who feared that the seemingly indestructible *Merrimack*, as Northerners called it, would come up the Potomac and destroy the capital, or sail north to attack New York or Boston.

The Union had constructed its own ironclad ship, the *Monitor*, which arrived from New York the evening of the day the *Virginia* had wreaked havoc. The following morning, the two vessels engaged in an epic naval battle, the first in history between ironclad ships. For more than two hours, the two vessels fired on, rammed, and attempted to outmaneuver each other. Despite heavy firing, neither inflicted much damage to the other, as scores of shells bounced and slid off the sides of the odd-looking vessels. Although historians have debated who won the famous naval engagement, the Battle of

Hampton Roads (often simply labeled the battle between the *Monitor* and the *Merrimack*) is most aptly described as a draw. On the one hand, the two-day naval battle was a tactical success for the South. Union casualties were much higher than those of the Confederates (409 to 24), and the sinking of the *Cumberland* was a loss to the Union Navy. On the other hand, to the North, the battle was a strategic victory. The Confederate ironclad withdrew to Norfolk and never again threatened Union ships or ports, although the *Virginia*'s continued presence on the James River did delay McClellan's invasion a bit longer.

The day after the naval battle, as McClellan continued planning his invasion, Lincoln relieved him of his command as general in chief. Over the months, the president had grown increasingly impatient with McClellan, who thoroughly drilled and prepared his troops for combat but seemed unwilling to actually lead his men into battle. Relying on poor intelligence, McClellan repeatedly overestimated the size of enemy forces, which prompted him on numerous occasions to request more troops and more time. Moreover, with many Republicans in Congress interpreting McClellan's idleness as sympathy for the Rebels, Lincoln felt political pressure to demote him. A Democrat, McClellan made no secret of the fact that he possessed no ill feelings toward slavery at a time when Radicals within the Republican Party were lobbying to turn the war into an abolition crusade. Lincoln allowed McClellan to remain as commander of the Army of the Potomac, but the president did so mainly because he could not find a suitable replacement. Arguing that as McClellan prepared to lead his men in battle he should focus only on his immediate command, Lincoln put McClellan on notice that he would be held accountable for the success of his upcoming offensive. On March 17, almost nine months after he had initially assumed command, McClellan's army finally set sail from Alexandria, Virginia. For twenty days, an assortment of steamers, schooners, and barges transported more than 100,000 men, forty-four artillery batteries, 1,150 wagons, 15,600 horses and mules, and loads of equipment and supplies. The voyage of McClellan's army to the peninsula was, as his biographer put it, "one of the spectacular sights of the Civil War."[19]

Despite months of preparation, McClellan's much-anticipated invasion of Virginia was flawed. In contrast to an overland assault, the plan left Washington exposed to attack. Although the Rebels had no intention of actually advancing on the capital, General Robert E. Lee turned Lincoln's anxiety into a key component of Rebel strategy. Acting as an adviser to President Davis, Lee ordered General Stonewall Jackson to take his 17,000 men in the Shenandoah Valley and attack Union troops around Washington in order to create the impression that he planned to move on the capital. While the Rebels suf-

General Stonewall Jackson earned a reputation as a military genius for his operations in the Shenandoah Valley in spring 1862, when he became the Confederacy's first genuine hero. Courtesy of the Library of Congress, LC-USZ62-17661

fered a tactical defeat at the Battle of Kernstown in late March, the engagement, as Lee intended, provoked Lincoln to redirect Union forces. The president removed one corps of McClellan's army, ordering these forces to stay behind to protect the capital until the situation was deemed safe, at which point Lincoln would release the troops to join McClellan's forces.

Over the next two months, Jackson saw to it that Lincoln never felt comfortable enough to allow these forces to support McClellan. In late April, Lee wrote to Jackson, expressing his hope "in the present divided condition of the enemy's forces, that a successful blow may be dealt them by a rapid combination of our troops before they can be strengthened themselves, either in their position or by re-enforcements."[20] Jackson executed Lee's orders flawlessly, as the ensuing Shenandoah Valley campaign became the stuff of legend. A professor of military strategy at Virginia Military Institute in Lexington, Jackson successfully used his small but nimble fighting force to tie down a combined Union force nearly three times as large. Geographically dispersed and divided into three separate commands, the poorly led Union troops in the valley proved no match for Jackson's intelligence, skill, and daring. Jackson struck quickly, moved swiftly, and left his opponents defeated and confused. Between May 8 and June 9, Jackson and his men marched nearly 400 miles, won six different battles, took thousands of Union prisoners, and captured tons of much-needed ammunition and supplies. Jackson's efforts completely disrupted Union operations in Virginia.

As a result, Jackson became a Confederate hero and the most talked-about soldier of the war to that point. Having already earned a degree of fame for his bravery at the Battle of Manassas, where he had earned his nickname, the valley campaign transformed him into a larger-than-life figure in the Confederacy's young history. Even before the war, Jackson had made known his deep commitment to the Southern way of life—and his willingness to fight for it. If the North, "instead of permitting us to enjoy the rights guaranteed to us by the Constitution of our country, should endeavor to subjugate us, and thus excite our slaves to servile insurrection," he wrote in early 1861, "it becomes us to wage such a war as will bring hostilities to a speedy close."[21] A reserved and deeply religious man, as well as a fierce warrior, Jackson gave God the glory for his stunning victories, thus adding to his mystique. Louisa McCord of South Carolina offered a grimly heroic assessment of the general. "They say he does not care how many are killed," she wrote. "His business is to save the country and not the army. He fights to win—God bless him—and he wins. If they do not want to be killed they can stay at home. . . . They say he wants to hoist the black flag—have a short, sharp, decisive war and end it! Then he is a Christian soldier!"[22] Religious publications, as well as Southern evangelical clergy, contributed to the Jackson legend by providing regular commentary on the general's righteousness and resolve. Jackson's persona as the determined Christian warrior conformed to religious white Southerners' developing sense of the Confederacy as a divinely chosen nation.

McClellan's peninsula campaign did little to dampen Southern enthusiasm. In early April, after landing his army at Fortress Monroe, McClellan unexpectedly encountered Confederates in a defensive position. The Union had the overwhelming advantage—about 60,000 men to the Confederacy's 13,000, stretched along a thin defense line about a dozen miles long. Despite a telegraph from Lincoln urging him to attack and break the line, McClellan again believed that Confederates had more men than they actually did. Consequently, the general brought his forces to a halt, ordered the construction of fortifications, and began the long process of moving heavy artillery into position. What might have been a speedy Union victory that cleared the way to Richmond instead turned into a month-long siege at Yorktown. Nevertheless, the siege was not entirely a lost opportunity. Eventually, seeing the size of McClellan's forces, the Confederates evacuated the region, including the nearby Rebel navy yard at Norfolk, which spelled the demise of the iron-clad *Virginia* (the *Merrimack*). Barely seaworthy, the clumsy Confederate vessel was unable to retreat up the James River, and the Rebels exploded the ironclad to prevent it from falling in Yankee hands. Southern forces commanded by General Joseph E. Johnston then withdrew toward Richmond.

Over the next month or so, as McClellan's massive army crawled up the peninsula, it engaged in a series of battles with the Rebels, most of which yielded relatively low casualties and inconclusive results. By the end of May, Union forces had made it to within six miles of Richmond, where they engaged in a pitched battle with Johnston's Confederates. Although the Confederates attacked and made early gains in the battle, the Federal position later stabilized, and the Yankees successfully repelled further attacks the next day. An inconclusive struggle, in which both sides laid claim to victory, the Battle of Seven Pines of May 31–June 1 (also known as Fair Oaks) resulted in nearly 14,000 total casualties. Among the wounded was General Johnston, whose injury prompted President Davis to appoint Robert E. Lee as the new commander of the Army of Northern Virginia.

Lee's ascension was a boost for the Confederacy. A Virginian with a distinguished pedigree (he was the son of "Lighthorse" Harry Lee of Revolutionary War fame), Lee embodied the Southern aristocratic tradition. A graduate of West Point and a celebrated veteran of the Mexican-American War, he also initially possessed a devotion to the US Constitution and the Union. "The framers of our Constitution never exhausted so much labour, wisdom and forbearance in its formation, and surrounded it with so many guards and securities, if it was intended to be broken by every member of the Confederacy at will," Lee had written in January 1861 to his son. "It is idle to talk of secession; anarchy would [otherwise] have been established, and not a government, by Washington, Hamilton, Jefferson, Madison and all the other patriots of the Revolution."[23] After the secession of the Deep South, Lee had remained conflicted and noncommittal about his allegiances. Although he opposed disunion, during a meeting with General Winfield Scott on April 19, 1861, two days after the secession of his home state, Lee at last had declared his intention to fight for the Southern Confederacy. "General," Lee had reportedly said to Scott, "the property belonging to my children, all they possess, lies in Virginia. They will be ruined if they do not go with their State. I can not raise my hand against my children."[24] Although he was Lincoln's first choice to command the Union armies, Lee chose instead to go with Virginia. In the early stages of the war, his Confederate military service proved unspectacular. He initially commanded forces in western Virginia, but with a large Unionist population there, the Rebel effort appeared doomed from the start. Afterward he led operations on the

General Robert E. Lee, commander of the Army of Northern Virginia, continually frustrated his Union counterparts in the East during the first two years of the war, thereby giving hope to those who believed that the Confederacy could secure its independence. Courtesy of the US National Archives, 111-B-1564

southeastern seaboard and then moved into a position as military adviser to President Davis. More aggressive than Johnston, whom he replaced, Lee made his mark in his showdown with McClellan. What had worked so well in the valley Lee now attempted to carry out on the peninsula—concentrating his forces and taking the initiative against the enemy.

During the last week of June, Confederate and Union forces engaged in a half dozen battles just to the east of Richmond, often referred to as the Seven Days Battles. As Federal forces approached the Confederate capital, according to one study of runaway ads in the *Richmond Daily Dispatch*, the number of slaves who fled their masters saw a sharp increase.[25] Again, despite McClellan's announced commitment to limited war aims and the protection of slaveholders' rights, many African Americans imagined their best hope for freedom in allying themselves with the enemies of their masters. While McClellan hoped to advance far enough to bring the Confederate capital within range of his siege guns, Lee's offensive movements thwarted the Union effort. Lee and his forces, which he dubbed the Army of Northern Virginia, initiated perhaps the largest Confederate attack of the war—57,000 men—at the Battle of Gaines' Mill, the third of these engagements. With a total of 15,500 casualties on both sides, Gaines' Mill was also by far the costliest and most decisive of the Seven Days Battles. Repeatedly charging against a heavily entrenched Union line, the Confederates suffered serious losses but eventually broke through and forced the Union into retreat. After Gaines' Mill, the Union began a withdrawal as it moved down the peninsula.

Despite possessing an overall numerical advantage in the Seven Days Battles, McClellan was sure that inferior numbers had caused his defeat. "They were overwhelmed by vastly superior numbers even after I brought my last reserves into action," he reported to Secretary Stanton. "I have lost this battle because my force was too small. I again repeat that I am not responsible for this." Demoralized and, according to his biographer, in a state of "emotional hysteria," McClellan abandoned his campaign for Richmond.[26] Retreating to Harrison's Landing on the James River, where gunboats sat ready to defend his foot soldiers, McClellan brought the vaunted peninsula campaign to an end.

WAR IN NORTHERN VIRGINIA AND MARYLAND: NEW STRATEGIES, SECOND BULL RUN, AND ANTIETAM

Victory in the Seven Days Battles gave the Rebels fresh hope, as Southerners put faith in their new hero, Lee. Developments in the western theater during the first half of 1862, after all, had given Confederates little reason to cheer. Much of the Mississippi River, all of Kentucky, most of Tennessee, and a large swath of Louisiana lay under Union control. Nevertheless, the pluck and success of the Army of Northern Virginia, as well as the dispersal of Union forces in the West, prompted Confederate leaders to plan a series of counteroffensives in the second half of 1862. If successful, they believed, the strategy could encourage Northern opposition to the war or draw a European power into the war on the side of the Confederacy. As he had already demonstrated both in his orders to Jackson in the valley campaign and in his leadership during the Seven Days Battles, Lee believed in taking the offensive. The longer the war lasted, he reasoned, the greater the Union's chances of victory, as the North's overwhelming numbers would eventually give it a distinct advantage. Only if the Confederates could strike quickly and defeat Union forces could the war be won. President Davis fully supported Lee's approach.

Meanwhile, frustrated with the inability to win, Lincoln reorganized Federal forces in the eastern theater. In late June, while McClellan was fighting the Seven Days Battles, Lincoln issued orders combining all Union troops in the vicinity of Washington, DC, except those in the Army of the Potomac, into a single department. The purpose of the new Army of Virginia was to protect Washington and reinforce McClellan. Lincoln appointed John Pope, the celebrated captor of Island Number Ten, as its commander. A close friend and Republican political ally of Lincoln's, Pope understood the need for a new strategy in the East and immediately proved adept at the politics of generalship. Summoned by Lincoln to Washington on June 19, within days he gave a rousing speech to Congress about the need to take the war to the enemy, received his formal appointment a few days later, and then delivered more tough talk in testimony before the Joint Committee on the Conduct of the War. Lincoln then named Henry Halleck as general in chief, a position that had been vacant since March when the president had stripped McClellan of the title. Nicknamed Old Brains, Halleck had a reputation as an intelligent strategist who had orchestrated Union victories in the West. The new chief ordered the obstinate McClellan to withdraw completely from the peninsula.

Pope's appointment signaled a sea change in Union strategy. Determined not to continue to be on the defensive, Lincoln believed that Northern forces in Virginia needed to be as aggressive as their Southern counterparts. In the midst of the Seven Days Battles, a desperate Lincoln had pledged to do whatever necessary to win the war and save the Union. "I expect to maintain this contest until successful, or till I die, or am conquered, or my term expires, or Congress or the country forsakes me," he wrote to Secretary of State Seward.[27] Pope, the president believed, could provide the leadership necessary to win. With Lincoln's approval, during July and August Pope issued a series of general orders that reflected the new strategy. Pope's General Order No. 5 announced that, to the extent possible, his troops "will subsist upon the country in which their operations are carried on."[28] This meant that the Army of Virginia would have a free hand to seize supplies from civilians, although a month later Pope tempered the order somewhat when Union troops abused the power. General Order No. 7 held civilians responsible for the frequent guerilla attacks on Union supply lines and troops in Virginia. "If a soldier or legitimate follower of the army be fired upon from any house, the house shall be razed to the ground and the inhabitants sent prisoners to the headquarters of this army," the order read. "Any persons detected in such outrages, either during the act or at any time afterward, shall be shot, without awaiting civil process."[29] General Order No. 11 provided that Southern civilians who refused to swear allegiance to the Union would be turned out of their homes and sent south. Pope's orders initiated a policy of "hard war," which at times blurred the lines between military forces and hostile civilians.

McClellan resented Pope and the new strategy, and rather than partners, the two became bitter rivals. McClellan believed that Pope's orders violated centuries-old Christian doctrine and the most fundamental principles of civilized warfare. In a meeting with Lincoln in the field in July 1862, McClellan brazenly presented Lincoln with a letter in which he lectured the president on how the war needed to be conducted. "It should not be a War looking to the subjugation of the people of a state. . . . It should not be, at all, a War upon population; but against armed forces and political organizations," he wrote. "Neither confiscation of property, political executions of persons, territorial organizations of state or forcible abolition of slavery should be contemplated for a moment." Three weeks later, in a letter to General Halleck, McClellan reiterated, "The people of the South should understand that we are not making war upon the institution of slavery, but that if they submit to the Constitution and Laws of the Union they will be protected in their constitutional rights of every nature."[30] McClellan even issued his own orders to the Army of the Potomac, which were exactly the opposite of what Pope had decreed, noting in a letter to his wife that he would "not permit this army to degenerate into a mob of thieves."[31] Pope's other pronouncements, meanwhile, only stoked McClellan's anger. Addressing the Army of Virginia, the new commander vowed to bring the western can-do spirit to demoralized eastern forces. "I have come to you from the West, where we have always seen the backs of our enemies," Pope wrote. "I desire you to dismiss from your minds certain phrases, which I am sorry to find so much in vogue amongst you. I hear constantly of 'taking strong positions and holding them,' of 'lines of

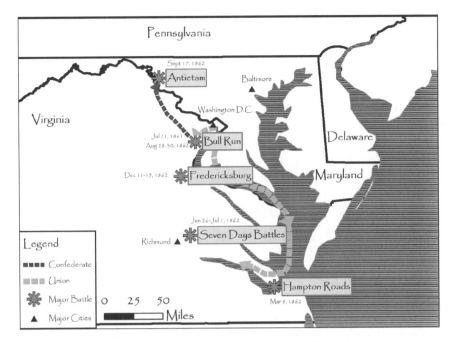

Major offensives in the eastern theater, 1861–1862. Map by Andrew Tait

retreat,' and of 'bases of supplies.' Let us discard such ideas."[32] A not-so-subtle criticism of McClellan, Pope's rhetorical bravado further alienated the newly appointed general from his supposed collaborator.

The Confederates, meanwhile, continued to display the unity of purpose and strategic creativity necessary to win battles in the East. After McClellan's withdrawal from the peninsula, Lincoln ordered him to join up with Pope's forces for another assault on Richmond. Anticipating this move, Lee used an unorthodox strategy: he divided his army, with half commanded by Jackson and half commanded by Major General James Longstreet. Already outnumbered, Lee took a risk in doing this, as he exposed each half of his army to defeat. On Lee's orders, Jackson's men then marched fifty miles in two days around Pope's right flank and succeeded in capturing and looting the Union's supply depot at Manassas, twenty miles to the rear of Pope. When Pope's forces attempted to come after Jackson and his men, the Rebels stealthily disappeared into the landscape. For the next few days, the confused Pope attempted to find Jackson's corps, which concealed itself in and along the woods and hills of the old Bull Run battlefield.

On August 28, Jackson and his troops reemerged and attacked a Union column at Brawner's Farm, the first engagement of the Second Battle of Bull Run. Fighting to a stalemate after several hours, Pope decided to concentrate his army against Jackson's much smaller force in the hope of wiping them out. The next day, confident of victory and certain that Lee and Longstreet were nowhere in the vicinity, Pope's men continued their assaults, but with little success. That afternoon, without Pope realizing it, Longstreet's forces arrived and took their positions on the Union's left flank. Knowing that Pope was unaware of his presence, Longstreet waited for the right moment to attack. The following day, August 30, Pope renewed his assaults and, incorrectly perceiving that the Rebels were in retreat, ordered his army to pursue. Instead, the Federals met a barrage of artillery, after which Longstreet's wing of 28,000 men engaged in a full assault on the already weak Union left. The Second Battle of Bull Run—Second Manassas, as the Rebels called it—resulted in the near annihilation of Pope's army.

Northern defeat at Second Manassas laid bare the ugly divisions with the Union command and led to another reorganization of forces. A large part of the reason for Pope's failure had been McClellan's unwillingness to assist. Despite a series of telegrams from Halleck to McClellan ordering him to send forces to Manassas, each time McClellan replied with excuses and delay. After eventually instructing one corps to march toward the site of the battle, on August 29 McClellan halted the troops six miles away—and within earshot of the fighting—in defiance of Halleck's direct order. Even though McClellan had repeatedly been instructed to join Pope, that same day McClellan suggested to Lincoln another course of action: "To leave Pope to get out of his scrape & at once use all of our means to make the Capital perfectly safe."[33] Dismayed at McClellan's apparent desire for Pope's defeat, Lincoln found himself in a nearly impossible position. The president felt great affection for Pope, and most of the Cabinet thought McClellan deserved dismissal or court-martial. But the soldiers favored Little Mac. Bowing to the reality that an army led by Pope would have a hard time winning, Lincoln dissolved the Army of Virginia and combined all Union forces in the region into the Army of the Potomac under the command of McClellan. Lincoln then sent the defeated Pope back out West.

Fresh from another victory, meanwhile, the Confederates resolved to build on their momentum by initiating a series of counteroffensives. The major thrust was to be into Maryland, and if their efforts succeeded, the Rebels planned to move into Pennsylvania. Less than a week after Second Manassas, Lee began crossing the Potomac River. Again, Lee and Davis were in perfect accord on strategy, and Davis, in fact, initially hoped to meet up with Lee and his army in Maryland. Acutely aware of the important relationship between military and political events, Davis departed Richmond with Enoch Lowe, a former Maryland governor whom Davis hoped would help coordinate pro-Confederate efforts in the state. Realizing the danger and difficulty of the journey, though, the two men returned to the capital before they had gotten very far. Nevertheless, Davis gave Lee specific instructions to issue proclamations condemning Union aggression and urging those in the state to join the Confederacy.

Lee's audacious move into Maryland ultimately proved a costly mistake. The campaign initially met with success, as Lee easily moved through the western part of the state. When he learned that the Federals had not yet abandoned Harper's Ferry in western Virginia, Lee ordered Jackson to surround and capture the garrison, and Jackson took more than 12,000 Union prisoners. He then marched north to join up with Lee, who took up positions along Antietam Creek near the town of Sharpsburg. Meanwhile, in one of the biggest strokes of luck of the entire war, on September 13, two Union soldiers in Frederick, Maryland, found a paper wrapped around a few cigars. The paper, it was soon discovered, contained Lee's orders for the Maryland campaign, and it was immediately conveyed to McClellan. Now knowing that Lee's army was divided, McClellan began to move, although not as quickly as he might have, and on September 16, he arrived at Antietam Creek, opposite Lee's forces. Instead of attacking immediately, McClellan delayed, which allowed time for Jackson's corps to arrive and take its positions.

The following morning, a Union corps led by Joseph Hooker began the assault, and for the rest of the day, intense fighting occurred. Because McClellan poorly communicated his attack plan to his subordinates, the battle ended up being fought almost as three separate battles—a Union assault on Lee's left, followed by an attack in the center, followed by a Union attack on Lee's right. These successive strikes allowed the Confederates, outnumbered almost two to one, to react without ever having to face the full force of the massive Army of the Potomac. In fact, while Lee used his entire force, even by the end of the battle McClellan had only utilized about three-quarters of his army of 80,000. Although the two armies fought to a standstill, the next day Lee retreated to Virginia and the Union claimed victory. Total casualties numbered above 23,000—comparable to Shiloh and Second Manassas—and included more than 2,100 Union killed and perhaps as many as 2,700 Confederate dead. At least another 2,000 would die of their wounds. Union victory at the Battle of Antietam, also known as Sharpsburg, halted Lee's incursion into Maryland and squelched Davis's hope of bringing the state into the Confederacy.

The consequences of Union victory stretched well beyond the battlefield.

The Battle of Antietam marked the bloodiest single day of the war, with more than 23,000 casualties. This photograph by Alexander Gardner shows some of the Confederate dead. Courtesy of the Library of Congress, LC-DIG-ds-05168

For months, Lincoln had considered making a move against slavery. Even though he had rescinded Fremont's emancipation order in 1861, during the spring of 1862, Lincoln, working in concert with Republicans in Congress, began to see emancipation as a way to weaken the Confederacy. Some enslaved African Americans had already signaled their willingness to abandon their masters and head toward Federal military lines, and Northern black leaders were calling for the enlistment of black troops. Despite the momentum in favor of a change in Federal policy toward slavery, Secretary of State Seward had wisely urged Lincoln to wait for a Union victory on the battlefield before issuing any sort of emancipation proclamation. With the closest thing to a victory the Union had ever achieved in the eastern theater, a week after Antietam, Lincoln made his announcement. He issued the Preliminary Emancipation Proclamation, which declared that slaves in those areas of the South still in rebellion and not yet occupied by Federal forces would become free on January 1, 1863. McClellan, who represented a different conception of the war, could see the handwriting on the wall. "It is very doubtful whether I shall remain in the service after the rebels have left this vicinity," he wrote to his wife at the end of September. "The Presdt's late Proclamation, the continuation of

Stanton & Halleck in office render it almost impossible for me to retain my commission & self respect at the same time. I cannot make up my mind to fight for such an accursed doctrine as that of a servile insurrection—it is too infamous."[34] McClellan correctly sensed that the Union's new military and political strategy would require new leadership.

WAR IN THE HEARTLAND: CONFEDERATE COUNTEROFFENSIVES

At the same time that Lee crossed the Potomac, the Confederacy initiated two other counteroffensives, one aimed at recapturing Corinth, Mississippi, and the other designed to claim Kentucky. Corinth remained critical to Confederate operations. Once Memphis fell into Union hands, the western portion of the Confederacy relied on a single railway extending from Vicksburg, Mississippi, as its lifeline to supplies and troops in the East. An advance on Corinth, the Rebels hoped, would divert Union attention from Vicksburg and reclaim a vital link in the Southern supply chain. Confederate leaders hoped that an invasion of Kentucky, meanwhile, would draw Federal forces out of the Deep South as well as help rally popular support and secure the state for the Confederacy.

By early fall, Confederate forces under the command of Major General Sterling Price positioned themselves to recapture Corinth. Joining up with Major General Earl Van Dorn's forces, these Confederates in northern Mississippi numbered about 22,000, roughly equal to the number of Union troops located in the area. After several months of holding the town, Union soldiers had erected extensive fortifications to protect the rail junction. Despite the strength of the Union's position, on October 3, Rebel soldiers successfully pushed the Yankees back in initial fighting, and the Rebels subsequently pressed all the way to the inner line of fortifications. As the sun set, though, the confident Van Dorn ceased the Rebel advance. The scorching heat of the day and the fatigue of battle had taken a toll, and he planned to resume action the next day. Given time to regroup, the next morning, Union general William Rosecrans successfully repelled the Confederate attack with artillery, and despite incurring serious losses, Van Dorn continued to order his men to charge against the Union's heavily fortified position, to no avail. Unable to defeat the Union troops, and having suffered great losses, Van Dorn withdrew. Southern casualties were more than double those of Northern forces (4,800 compared to 2,350), and Van Dorn received withering criticism for ordering frontal assaults in the face of heavy losses. The most significant result of Confederate defeat in the Battle of Corinth was that the Confederates failed to regain the railroad line. This left them in a vulnerable position when it came to transporting soldiers and supplies throughout the region, and it meant that Memphis and West Tennessee would remain in Union hands. Defeat in northern Mississippi, moreover, put pressure on Confederate forces engaged in the invasion of Kentucky.

The advance into Kentucky constituted the final part of the Rebels' counteroffensive strategy. This initiative involved two armies under the respective commands of General Braxton Bragg and General Kirby Smith. A North Carolina native and West Point graduate, Bragg had served in the Mexican-American War, but frustration with his military career had prompted him in 1855 to resign his commission and purchase a large plantation in Louisiana. When war came, he had helped organize troops in Louisiana and had seen action at Shiloh. Smith, a Florida native and also a West Point graduate, had distinguished himself in the Mexican War, returned to West Point to teach, and later ended up pursuing bands of Comanche Indians in Texas. Although initially conflicted over secession, Smith accepted a Confederate commission and spent the early part of the war in Virginia before ending up in Tennessee.

President Davis's goals for the campaign were lofty. He had instructed Bragg and Smith, once they combined forces, "to crush Buell's column and advance to the recovery of Tennessee and the occupation of Kentucky."[35] The two devised a plan to carry out this strategy: Smith would attack Union forces in the Cumberland Gap, Bragg would advance on Buell's forces around Nashville, and both armies would eventually cross into Kentucky. The aggressive Smith, however, could not suppress his desire to liberate the Bluegrass State and achieve military glory. Jettisoning the agreed-upon plan and immediately setting his sights on Lexington and Louisville, Smith moved directly northward toward Cincinnati. On August 30, Smith's men defeated Union troops at Richmond, Kentucky (about twenty-five miles south of Lexington), and within a few days his troops occupied Lexington. Although outranking Smith and skeptical of this bold advance, Bragg reluctantly followed Smith's lead and moved his larger force along a more westerly route. In mid-September, Bragg captured the Union garrison at Munfordville, Kentucky, but in the process, he unwisely dispersed his troops into defensive positions throughout the region, thus permitting Buell's pursuing Federals to make it to Louisville.

Both Bragg and Smith agreed that popular support constituted an essential component of the offensive, and on October 4, the two men attended the inauguration of a new Confederate governor of Kentucky. An established government operating out of the recently captured capital of Frankfurt, they reasoned, would surely help generate public support for the Rebel cause and spur

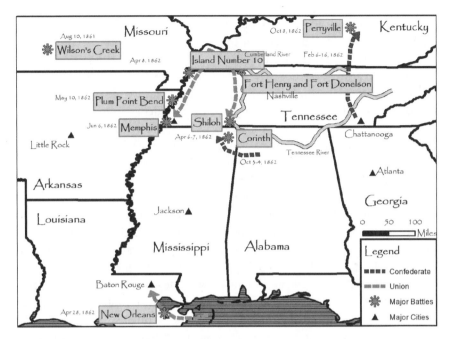

Major offensives in the western theater, 1861–1862. Map by Andrew Tait

enlistments. In an ominous moment for the Confederacy, however, a Union offensive interrupted the ceremonies. As an aide to Bragg later wrote, "The inaugural was being read when the booming of cannon, shortly followed by dispatches from our cavalry outposts, announced the near presence of the enemy."[36] The gray-clad military men who filled the hall quickly dispersed, the new governor cut short his address, and the evening's inaugural ball was canceled. Before long, the Confederate government of Kentucky, heretofore an appendage of the Rebel army, reverted to its previous shadowy status.

The opening moments of the governor's inauguration proved to be the high-water mark of the Confederate incursion into Kentucky. Within a few days, an engagement occurred near the town of Perryville, in the rolling hills around Doctor's Fork Creek, where Rebel forces had come seeking water. What began with skirmishing on October 7 evolved the next day into a hard-fought battle. About 15,000 Confederate troops—about a third of Bragg's army—attacked the smallest and least experienced of Buell's three divisions. Although Buell's total forces far outnumbered the Confederates, poor communication prevented Buell from learning about the fighting, and not until the end of the day did the Union commander become aware that a battle had raged nearby. Because his entire force never actually joined the fight, about an equal number of Rebels and Yankees engaged each other at the Battle of Perryville, and the Southerners got the better of their opponents. Nevertheless, once Buell and his remaining forces were mobilized, Bragg's exhausted and depleted army—still not close enough to Smith's forces to receive proper support—withdrew, thus rendering the battle a victory for the Union. The human costs to both sides were high. The Confederacy suffered more than 3,000 casualties there, while the Union lost more than 4,000. Within days of the fight, the pessimistic Bragg gave up altogether on the idea of regaining Kentucky and began a withdrawal. Smith, as well as many of Bragg's men, disagreed with the decision to retreat from ground that they had so recently won, and Bragg came under heavy criticism.

The Confederate counteroffensive in Kentucky failed. The two commanders had wasted valuable time arranging for the installation of a new governor, and regardless of their efforts, popular support never materialized. Coupled with the South's resounding defeat at Corinth during the same week, the inability of the Confederate commanders to defeat Buell's army and retake the Bluegrass State struck a severe blow to Southern morale. The campaign proved nearly as frustrating to the Union. Despite Buell's success in halting the Rebel advance, Lincoln pressed his commander to pursue and attack. Buell demurred, arguing that his army needed to rest and reorganize. Halleck, the general in chief, delivered a stern telegram in response. "I am directed by the President to say to you that your army must enter East Tennessee this fall," he wired to Buell on October 19. "[The president] does not understand why we cannot march as the enemy marches, live as he lives, and fight as he fights, unless we admit the inferiority of our troops and of our generals."[37] Ignoring the order, Buell returned to the safety of Nashville rather than advancing. Like McClellan, Buell frustrated Lincoln. An Ohio native who shared McClellan's strict interpretation of the Constitution and his belief in limited war aims, Buell had moved too slowly—or not all—at critical moments. Within a few days, on October 24, Lincoln relieved him of his command, replacing him with Rosecrans, the victor of Corinth. Although a strategic success for the Union, the Kentucky campaign had satisfied the larger war aims of neither side.

PREPARING FOR HARD WAR: FREDERICKSBURG AND THE CLOSING MONTHS OF 1862

During the last few months of 1862, presidents Lincoln and Davis contemplated what was to come. The Union still held much of the West in its grasp, and Federal forces had halted Confederate offensives in Maryland, Mississippi, and Kentucky. The Union seemed to be in a stronger position strategically than it had all year. Nevertheless, Lincoln remained frustrated with his generals' apparent inability to attack the enemy. Contrary to the president's wishes, McClellan had not pursued after Antietam, and many Republicans in Washington speculated that the Democratic general could not be counted on as an ally in what had become a war for emancipation. In early October, Lincoln spent several days camped out with McClellan in the field, visiting hospitals, reviewing the troops, and planning strategy. Lincoln counted 88,095 men in the Army of the Potomac, which he jokingly referred to as "General McClellan's bodyguard." At the end of the month, after continued prodding by the president, McClellan finally crossed the Potomac into Virginia, but in the ensuing days, the notoriously sluggish general continued to delay. Having lost all patience, on November 5, Lincoln fired McClellan. The president replaced him with Ambrose Burnside, who had led a successful amphibious campaign along the North Carolina coast, while McClellan went home to New Jersey. He never received another military assignment.

If Lincoln remained frustrated, Davis surely faced greater challenges. Disappointed in Confederate failures on the battlefield over the previous few months, Davis seemed even more distraught over the Union's new emancipation policy. While it confirmed, in Southerners' minds, that the Republicans were indeed abolitionists bent on violating the South's constitutional rights and destroying its social system, it made Davis's hope of attaining foreign support for the Rebel war effort nearly impossible. In late October, the Confederate president began to draw up tentative plans to combine the remaining Rebel forces in the West in an attempt to retake Helena, Arkansas, and Memphis on the Mississippi River and then move eastward toward Nashville. But troop shortages posed a problem in planning any fresh offensive. By November, Davis found his fledging nation on the defensive on three fronts—with Union armies simultaneously poised to attack on the Mississippi River at Vicksburg, in the Confederate heartland in Middle Tennessee, and in the eastern theater in the vicinity of Richmond.

In December, the Rebels regained some of their optimism as Confederate forces won a resounding victory in the East. On November 14, the newly appointed General Burnside began the Union offensive into Virginia by occupying Falmouth, located along the Rappahannock on the opposite side of the river from Fredericksburg. Burnside intended to cross the river using pontoon bridges and then advance quickly on Richmond. Logistical problems, though, prevented the bridges from arriving on time, and Burnside and his men unwisely decided to wait for the bridges and proceed with the plan. The delay allowed Lee and his 75,000 men to arrive and take their positions on the high ground overlooking Fredericksburg. Led by Longstreet, Jackson, and Major General J. E. B. Stuart, a cavalry commander, the experienced Confederate soldiers ended up winning one of the most lopsided victories of the war. On December 11, Union engineers, under fire, finally began to lay the bridges, and over the next two days, the Union army crossed the river and began a doomed series of assaults on the Confederates. Safe in their well-defended positions overlooking the town, the Rebel army repeatedly repulsed the Union advances and inflicted heavy casualties. By the time it was over and the Yankees had recrossed the river on December 15, the Union had suffered more than 13,000 casualties, compared to only about 4,500 Confederates. Burnside's initial attempt to attack Lee's army had failed miserably. The decisive Battle of Fredericksburg again displayed the apparent futility of the Union military effort in the eastern theater.

By the end of 1862, despite its huge advantages in resources and manpower, the Union had not been able to subdue the Confederacy and restore the Union. During the second half of the year, Lincoln had taken crucial steps toward initiating a new war strategy—one that moved away from the concept of limited war and embraced the idea of a hard war. This clearly was not the total warfare of the twentieth century—war without rules, in which no lines existed between soldiers and civilians, between combatants and noncombatants. But Lincoln's belief in conciliation, based on the existence of a large Unionist population in the Confederate states did give way to a more severe struggle, in which Southern civilians would feel the effects of war. Combining severity with restraint, new policies changed how the war would be fought. In July and August, General Pope's series of general orders had revealed that civilians would pay a price for guerilla activities against Union soldiers. The announcement of the Preliminary Emancipation Proclamation in September confirmed that Lincoln believed that making war on Southern society—including slavery—would help win the war. Finally, the dismissals of dithering Democratic generals Buell and McClellan indicated that a new style of aggressive fighting loomed on the horizon. These efforts to destroy civilian morale, interfere with slavery, exhaust Southern resources, and attack the Confederates lay at the heart of a new Northern conception of the war, one that embraced revolutionary change and a potential redefinition of the Constitution. McClellan had articulated a belief in the Constitution and the Union as it had been in 1861—a Union that protected slaveholders' rights, among other forms of civilian property. But by the end of 1862, hard war increasingly converged with the goal of a new constitutional order, one based on the emancipation of the enslaved.

5
THE WAR TRANSFORMED, 1863–1864

On August 30, 1863, less than a year after the announcement of the Preliminary Emancipation Proclamation and less than two months after capturing the Confederate stronghold at Vicksburg, General Ulysses S. Grant penned a letter to his longtime friend and political patron, Congressman Elihu B. Washburne. "The people of the North need not quarrel over the institution of slavery," the general wrote from Vicksburg. "What Vice President Stephens acknowledges the cornerstone of the Confederacy is already knocked out. Slavery is already dead and cannot be resurrected. It would take a standing Army to maintain slavery in the South if we were to make peace to-day guaranteeing to the South all their former constitutional privileges." Grant continued with candor. "I never was an abolitionest, [n]ot even what could be called anti-slavery, but I try to judge farely & honestly and it become patent to my mind early in the rebellion that the North & South could never live at peace with each other except as one nation, and that without Slavery. As anxious as I am to see peace reestablished I would not therefore be willing to see any settlement[s] until this question is forever settled."[1]

Grant's letter came at a critical junction in the war, at a time when key Union military victories reinforced both Republican political goals and African American aspirations. That summer, the Union won major battles at Vicksburg and Gettysburg, and later that fall it would again triumph at Chattanooga. Although these victories gave Union forces a distinct advantage, they did not yet ensure Northern victory, as General Robert E. Lee's Army of Northern Virginia remained a formidable fighting force and the embodiment of the Confederate cause. In early 1864, President Abraham Lincoln called his most successful general east to face Lee, while General William T. Sherman initiated operations against Confederate forces in Georgia. Grant and Sherman would emerge as the architects of Union military victory. Under their leadership, it would be a harder, more relentless war—one in which the stakes were clear for all to see. The fate of slavery in the federal Union hung in the balance.

ROSECRANS HOLDS TENNESSEE: THE BATTLE OF STONES RIVER

In the early months of 1863, Union military operations involved three armies, which would need to work in concert to maximize pressure on Confederate forces with far inferior numbers. The Army of the Potomac, despite the humiliating loss at Fredericksburg, still aspired to defeat Lee's Army of Northern Virginia. Grant's Army of the Tennessee (named for the Tennessee River) hoped to continue its push southward along the Mississippi River with the aim of capturing Vicksburg and linking up with Union forces who occupied much of Louisiana. And the Army of the Cumberland, after repelling the Rebel offensive in Kentucky the previous year, needed to press further south from its base in Nashville in order to capture the key railway junction of Chattanooga and liberate the Unionist population in East Tennessee.

At the end of October 1862, in response to General Don Carlos Buell's insufficiently aggressive operations, President Lincoln had named General William Rosecrans the new commander of the Army of the Cumberland. An Ohioan known for his excitable temperament and devout Catholicism, Rosecrans spent two months resupplying and training his men, and on the day after Christmas 1862, he departed Nashville with 43,000 soldiers and moved against the Confederates, who since July had occupied the town of Murfreesboro, about thirty miles to the southeast. General Braxton Bragg had concentrated his forces on the edge of town, along the Nashville and Chattanooga Railroad and on both sides of Stones River. On December 31, Bragg's army clashed with Rosecrans's Union forces on a frozen field. Hoping to surprise the Federals, Bragg's men attacked in the early dawn hours, and by late that morning the Confederates had successfully driven their opponents back. In intense fighting, Rosecrans sustained the Union position along the railroad and the Nashville Pike—critical supply lines—after a series of Confederate assaults. Both armies remained in position the next day.

Although Bragg expected Rosecrans to retreat, the plucky new Union commander held his ground and planned his next move. The following day, January 2, the battle resumed. With a small number of Union forces having positioned themselves on a strategically important hill overlooking Stones River, Bragg determined to go after them. He ordered Major General John C. Breckinridge (the former presidential candidate) to take his five brigades and seize the hill. After his men succeeded in doing so and started flooding into the open plain on the other side of the heights, they were met by a barrage of Union artillery. Some forty-five Union cannon started firing. "We had gotten only fairly started, when the great jaws of the trap on the bluff from the opposite side of the river were sprung," wrote one Confederate soldier, "and bursting shells that completely drowned the voice of man were plunging and tearing through our columns."[2] In an hour and a half, Union guns killed or wounded nearly 1,800 Confederates, more than a third of the 4,500 troops who had begun the assault. With his forces seriously depleted, Bragg retreated. Having recaptured Murfreesboro and driven back the Rebels, Rosecrans claimed victory. The cost of the Union's success was high. Total casualties at the Battle of Stones River (also known as the Battle of Murfreesboro) were more than 23,000, the highest percentage casualties (32 percent of the total number of soldiers) of any battle of the entire war.

The Union victory brought to an end the Confederates' six-month-long counteroffensive in the heartland. Lincoln was thrilled that he had found a competent replacement for Buell. Several months later, he wrote to Rosecrans, "I can never forget . . . you gave us a hard earned victory which, had there been a defeat instead, the nation could scarcely have lived over."[3] Union victory moreover meant that enslaved people increasingly saw federally occupied Middle Tennessee as a haven, much to the chagrin of the region's pro-Rebel slaveholders. A few months after the victory at Murfreesboro, the Nashville chief of police reported to Rosecrans that slaveholders were attempting to kidnap and reclaim their escaped slaves, large numbers of whom had made it to the city. "Very General efforts is being made by owners & drivers to Run them South and Large Numbers Have been Taken from the City," the chief wrote.[4] By early 1863, it was clear that where Union forces found success on the battlefield, enslaved African Americans would seek freedom.

LEE AND JACKSON TRIUMPH: THE BATTLE OF CHANCELLORSVILLE

Despite Rosecrans's success in Tennessee, the level of Union frustration in the east only seemed to rise. Robert E. Lee and Stonewall Jackson had outsmarted and outmaneuvered the Federals for much of 1862, and their victories proved crucial in the creation of Confederate nationalism. The Union defeat at Fredericksburg, in contrast, had been particularly devastating for Northern morale, and General Burnside, McClellan's replacement, had done nothing yet to earn the respect of his men or his president. In order to attack General Lee's well-fortified position at Fredericksburg, Burnside proposed to cross the Rappa-hannock River north of Fredericksburg and then attack Lee's lines of com-munication and supply from the rear. The ill-fated expedition never even made it to the crossing point. A hard, unrelenting rain turned the primitive road along the river into a morass of mud and slime, and Burnside's men—along with their supply wagons, heavy artillery, horses, and mules—became helpless and stuck. Despite Burnside's best efforts, the weather won the battle that day. Unable to continue, the exhausted, demoralized, and drenched North-ern troops abandoned their mission and managed to return to camp. The embarrassing Mud March, as it came to be known, abruptly ended Burnside's brief career as commander. Within days, on January 25, 1863, Lincoln relieved him and named Joseph Hooker as his replacement. While the strife-torn Army of the Potomac welcomed its latest leader, Confederates placed their total trust in Lee and Jackson, who by the spring of 1863 had achieved mythic status for their leadership of the Army of Northern Virginia.

Still ensconced at Fredericksburg, Lee knew that Hooker would have to make the next move. Having served under McClellan and Pope, Hooker had proven himself at Antietam and earned a reputation as a fighter. Claiming that he had assembled "the finest army on the planet," Hooker drew up what he thought was a perfect plan of attack.[5] He would fix Lee's position at Freder-icksburg by attacking with a portion of his army while sending the bulk of his forces across the river above Fredericksburg to strike at the Confederate lines of communications in the rear. Facing Union forces that vastly outnumbered his own, Lee would be forced to either fight in the open or retreat to Rich-mond. Hooker was confident of success, and the first few days of the cam-paign, which began on April 27, went well for the Federals. After crossing the Rappahannock and putting himself in a good position to continue the advance, Hooker lost his nerve. Perhaps he believed reports that he was about to face overwhelming numbers of Confederates, or maybe he was stunned that things had gone so well. For whatever reason, rather than continuing to advance, Hooker ordered his men to create defensive positions around Chan-cellorsville, about ten miles west of Fredericksburg.

Learning of Hooker's defensive approach, Lee and Jackson began to strate-gize, as they had before, about exactly how to divide and utilize their smaller, nimbler fighting force. Discovering further that Hooker's right flank was in the open and unprotected, the Confederate generals again displayed their strategic and tactical brilliance. After a late-night discussion, Lee decided to divide his army, sending Jackson's whole corps to attack the flank while Lee and his remaining men stayed behind to face Hooker's much larger force that at any time could advance. On May 2, Jackson's men carried out the assault on the Union forces in three distinct waves. Surprised that the Confederates were hitting them with so large a force, Federal soldiers retreated down a turnpike and past Hooker's headquarters at Chancellorsville. The aggressiveness of the Rebel attack nearly severed the Union lines, but the Federals rallied and staved off annihilation. Darkness, exhaustion, and disorganization brought an end to the fighting. That evening, as Jackson and a small party of Confederates returned to Rebel lines, Jackson suffered three bullet wounds at the hands of his own men. (The accidental shooting resulted in the amputation of his left arm, then pneumonia, and on May 10 Jackson's death.) Hearing of the wounding of Jackson, Lee placed cavalryman J. E. B. Stuart in command of his corps. The Rebels continued the offensive the next day, as they successfully gained Hazel's Grove, a bit of high ground abandoned by the Federals. There the Confederates consolidated their forces and amassed their artillery for an attack. The full-fledged Rebel assault finally broke the Union line, and an injury to Hooker—a Confederate cannonball struck a porch post that hit him in the head—further damaged Union morale. Before long Hooker's forces began retreating and on May 5 recrossed the Rappahannock. The Rebels had scored another victory.

The Battle of Chancellorsville, Lee's greatest triumph, seemed to confirm the invincibility of the Army of Northern Virginia, and it marked yet another frustrating defeat for the larger and better-equipped Army of the Potomac. The battle resulted in horrible losses on both sides, with total casualties roughly on par with Shiloh, Second Manassas, Antietam, and Stones River. For the Confederates, of course, the greatest loss was that of Stonewall Jackson. Not only did Lee lose his closest advisor but the entire Confederacy grieved the passing of its Calvinistic Christian warrior, a loss that created a veritable "spiritual crisis" in the South.[6] Not only did Jackson's death spur soul-searching among the faithful, but also the general's absence would be keenly felt in the campaigns to follow. In the meantime, the Confederacy took comfort in again repulsing an attempted Union offensive in Virginia.

GRANT SECURES THE MISSISSIPPI:
THE VICKSBURG CAMPAIGN

At the end of 1862, General Ulysses S. Grant set his sights farther south. Charged with maintaining control of a 12,000-square-mile district in Western Tennessee and Mississippi, Grant focused his attention on defeating the Confederate stronghold at Vicksburg, a railroad junction located halfway between Memphis and New Orleans on the Mississippi River. Perched high

General Ulysses S. Grant, already known for his successes in Tennessee, especially earned national fame for his successful campaign against the Confederate stronghold at Vicksburg. Grant's strategic brilliance and tactical aggressiveness made him the Union's greatest military leader. Courtesy of the US National Archives, 111-B-2481

on a bluff over a hairpin turn in the river, the town of 4,500 residents on the east bank would be especially difficult to seize. A maze of waterways, marshes, and bayous made it hard to approach, and Grant realized that taking it would involve a series of maneuvers just to seize the ground from which to initiate an actual offensive. Nevertheless, its strategic value was unquestioned. General Halleck, writing from Washington, described taking control of Vicksburg as "the most important operation of the war" and of more significance "than the capture of forty Richmonds."[7]

Assisted by General William T. Sherman and General John A. McClernand of Illinois, Grant focused on establishing an invasion route to Vicksburg. Realizing that swampy ground to the north of the city and its strong defensive fortifications on the high ground would make it nearly impossible to attack from the north, Grant favored an advance from the south and east, where the ground was firm and the roads passable. Still, the city's defenses made it difficult to imagine navigating downstream in order to plan such an assault. In the meantime, Port Hudson, Louisiana—another well-fortified Confederate outpost on the east bank of the river, about 100 miles to the south—prevented the Union from attempting a river assault from that direction. With few good options, Grant and his men spent the winter attempting to find or construct a more favorable route for invasion. This involved repeated efforts to dig canals, blow up levees, and navigate through various lakes, bayous, cutoffs, and streams—none of which succeeded.

Never one to give up, Grant eventually set into motion a bold plan that he had been considering for some time. He would march the army down the west side of the Mississippi, cross the river south of Vicksburg, and attack from the south and east. In order for the plan to work, Porter's fleet would have to sneak past Vickburg's batteries, so as to move sufficient gunboats and transport ships south of the city. It was a risky move, for it would expose the Union fleet to possible destruction while requiring the movement of Union forces across the mile-wide river to the rear of a Rebel force of unknown size and strength. Sherman disapproved. "I feel in its success less confidence than in any similar undertaking of the war," he confided at the time in a letter to his brother.[8] At the end of March, Grant ordered McClernand's men to begin building bridges and makeshift roads through the swampy terrain on the west side of the river below Vicksburg. Within three weeks, they had constructed a rough road that stretched along the river from the staging area for the operation to the south about seventy miles.

Grant proceeded to order Union forces down the west bank, and on April 16, Porter's boats made a dramatic run past the city's imposing defenses. A flotilla of ten—seven ironclads and three transport boats—attempted to pass the Confederate defenses, and despite a ferocious flurry of cannon fire, all but one of the Union vessels, a transport boat, survived intact. Remarkably, the Union suffered no loss of life and only minimal damage to the fleet. Confederate leaders apparently failed to grasp the significance of Porter's run. Even Robert E. Lee naively assured President Davis that the Union could "derive no material benefit" from having passed the city's defenses.[9] Writing in her diary in Columbia, South Carolina, Mary Chesnut perhaps had a better sense of the import of what had occurred. "Bad news. Gunboats pass Vicksburg," she wrote. "The Yankees are spreading themselves over our fair Southern land, like red ants."[10]

Once Vicksburg had been passed, Grant planned to move his army across the river, but first he attempted to divert the Confederates' attention by ordering cavalry under the command of Benjamin Grierson to head south from Tennessee and into the middle of Mississippi. A daring advance through 600 miles of hostile territory, Grierson's raid destroyed property, struck fear in the local population, and caused confusion within the Confederate command. Shortly after Grierson's forces starting moving, Grant ordered Sherman and his men to create another diversion by attacking Confederate units on the bluffs just north of Vicksburg. Meanwhile, Grant ordered a second group of vessels past Confederate defenses on the river at Vicksburg, again with little resulting damage. By early May, Grant's bold plan and its near-flawless execution allowed him to move approximately 20,000 Union men across the river at Bruinsburg Landing and into the heart of Mississippi, just south of Vicksburg. Grant later wrote in his *Memoirs*, "All the campaigns, labors, hardships, and exposures, from the month of December previous to this time that had been made and endured, were for the accomplishment of this one object."[11]

With his army in Mississippi, Grant planned to move east toward Jackson, with the intention of striking at Confederate forces before turning around to advance on Vicksburg. With a beachhead established, Grant's forces speedily moved toward Jackson, a railroad junction and supply depot. Although he had a long and tenuous supply line stretching back to the river and up to Memphis, for the most part Grant lived off the land in enemy territory. Having consolidated his forces and met up with Sherman, Grant's men at this point numbered about 33,000. The Confederates had a total force of nearly 60,000 in the area, but they were spread out at various sites of strategic importance, with the majority of these forces occupying Vicksburg.[12] Advancing toward Jackson, Grant engaged Confederate forces outside the city before gaining control of the railroad line, thus isolating the garrison at Vicksburg and forcing the relatively small Confederate force in Jackson to evacuate after hardly a fight. Grant's army moved in, burned part of the town, and destroyed factories. With the surrender of Jackson on May 14, another Confederate capital—Nashville and Baton Rouge were already occupied—fell into Union hands.

A combination of inexperience and dissension within the Confederate command worked in the Union's favor throughout the campaign. President Davis had placed John C. Pemberton, a native of Pennsylvania who had cast his lot with the Confederacy, in charge of the defense of Vicksburg, and he proved a poor match for Grant. Even worse, as it turned out, Davis had placed Joseph Johnston in command of the entire western theater of war. Convinced of the hopelessness of the Confederate cause in Mississippi, Johnston also proved ineffective. He engaged in weeks of pointless correspondence with the Confederate president over the precise scope of his authority, and his dispatches to Davis focused repeatedly on his inferior numbers.

Deeply concerned about the course of events in Mississippi, his home state, President Davis had ordered Johnston there immediately after Grant's army had crossed the river. But Johnston did not arrive until Grant stood poised to invade Jackson. While Johnston subsequently ordered Pemberton to move away from Vicksburg—which he had naively been guarding, thus allowing Grant to move about freely—Johnston never mounted a serious attack against

Union forces. Confusion about where Johnston's and Pemberton's troops were to consolidate caused Pemberton to stumble onto Grant's ever-expanding army on May 16, and heavy fighting ensued in the Battle of Champion Hill. Suffering a major defeat, Pemberton retreated to Vicksburg. Although Johnston urged Pemberton to escape with his army and sacrifice the city, Pemberton resolved to defend the Confederate stronghold. After Grant initiated two unsuccessful assaults on the city, the second with significant losses, Union forces—at this point some 75,000 strong—settled in for a siege. For almost the next seven weeks, Union troops shelled and starved Vicksburg into submission. Restless for freedom, slaves in the surrounding region began meeting openly in large groups, stopped working, or joined the Union Army. Some recruits saw action almost immediately, when in early June they defended a Union supply depot just north of Vicksburg at Milliken's Bend.

On July 4, 1863, the Confederates surrendered Vicksburg. Rather than unconditional surrender—Grant apparently did not want to have to deal with transporting more than 37,000 Rebels to Union prison camps—the Union general offered parole to the half-starved Confederates.[13] Believing them too sick and weak to fight again, he hoped that other Rebels, military and civilian, would see the utter helplessness of the soldiers and realize the futility of the cause. The Confederates' defeat in the Vicksburg Campaign was all-encompassing and demoralizing, as it cost an entire army and nearly 60,000 small arms. On July 7, in a sign of Union dominance, Federal troops burned President Davis's plantation at Brierfield, about twenty miles south of Vicksburg. A bit further downriver and a few days later, Rebels at Port Hudson surrendered to Union forces under the command of Nathaniel Banks after a siege. Banks's men included newly recruited black troops, mostly former slaves who had walked off Louisiana plantations and had joined the Union Army after the Emancipation Proclamation. With not a single Confederate outpost remaining on the Mississippi River, North America's greatest waterway was entirely under Union control.

The Vicksburg Campaign proved critical to the outcome of the war. When it was over, Davis blamed Johnston for the defeat, and said so in a fifteen-page personal letter charging the general with dereliction of duty. The city's capture opened up the river to navigation and trade, put the state of Mississippi almost entirely under Federal control, and cut off the trans-Mississippi West from the rest of the Confederacy. Arkansas succumbed to Union forces in early September, when the Federals added Little Rock to their collection of conquered capitals. After Union general in chief Henry Halleck read Grant's final report on the Vicksburg Campaign, he replied to Grant with stirring words of praise and appreciation. "You and your army have well deserved the gratitude of your country, and it will be the boast of your children that their fathers were the heroic army which reopened the Mississippi River."[14] Grant became a Northern hero and soon gained promotion to major general, the highest rank in the Union Army.

LEE INVADES PENNSYLVANIA: THE GETTYSBURG CAMPAIGN

On May 14, the same day that Jackson, Mississippi, fell to Grant, General Robert E. Lee arrived in Richmond to consult with President Davis. Fresh from his brilliant victory at Chancellorsville and aware of the dire situation of the Confederates in the West, a confident Lee hoped to persuade the president to allow him to begin a new offensive into Pennsylvania. Such a bold proposal immediately provoked criticism, as Secretary of War James Seddon and others believed that the Confederacy needed to redeploy men in order help the beleaguered Mississippians. Davis was inclined to agree. Still, Lee made a compelling case for another move into the North: his poorly supplied army could procure provisions from Pennsylvania's abundant countryside, the presence of his men in a Northern state would strike fear in the hearts of local residents, and the offensive would force the Union to redeploy troops from Tennessee and Mississippi, thus helping the Confederates there. A Southern victory on Northern soil, Lee argued, would boost the Northern antiwar movement, put political pressure on President Lincoln, and perhaps even reopen the question of European recognition. There was much to be gained, in other words, from making an aggressive and unexpected move rather than fortifying the Confederates' increasingly tenuous defensive position out West. Lee's string of successes had bred a collective sense of pride and confidence that Lee no doubt both believed and exuded. After extensive discussions within the Confederate Cabinet, Davis agreed to Lee's plan. In preparation for the campaign and in response to the death of Stonewall Jackson, Lee reorganized his army into three corps under the leadership of lieutenant generals James Longstreet, Richard S. Ewell, and Ambrose Powell Hill.

In early June, the Confederates broke camp around Fredericksburg and began marching first to the west, over the Blue Ridge, and then north through the Shenandoah Valley. Cavalry under the command of J. E. B. Stuart took part in the first engagement of the campaign on June 9, when, after departing from their headquarters at Brandy Station, Virginia, they fell under attack by 7,000 Union horsemen with another 4,000 Federal infantrymen following close behind. Convinced that the Confederates were about to stage a massive cavalry invasion of the North, General Hooker had ordered the surprise attack. Stuart responded with his full force of 10,000 men, and the resulting battle proved the largest cavalry engagement of the war. For a whole day, Confederate and Union cavalry slashed and stabbed at each other, while Federal bullets whizzed through the air. At the end of the day, the Union had lost more men and had not succeeded in disrupting Lee's northward movement.

Confederate forces advanced rapidly through the Shenandoah Valley and across the Mason-Dixon Line. They captured 4,000 Union soldiers, artillery, and extensive supplies at the Federal arsenal at Winchester, Virginia, as well as additional guns and supplies at Martinsburg, just to the north. By the last week of June, Lee's entire army was marching through Pennsylvania, where they lived off the land, intimidated local civilians, and indiscriminately began arresting African Americans—many of them freeborn—to be sent into slavery in Virginia. One historian estimates that "perhaps as many as several hundred Pennsylvanians of African descent" suffered this fate, including some 250 African Americans in Chambersburg, Pennsylvania.[15] While plundering their way toward the capital at Harrisburg, Ewell received a message from Lee to reverse direction and prepare to join up with the other two corps to face the Federals. Still, Lee had poor reconnaissance and did not know the precise location of his enemy. After the engagement at Brandy Station, J. E. B. Stuart had failed to communicate with his superior about the position of the Union army. The eventual convergence of Union and Confederate forces happened by accident, just north of the Maryland border.

On June 27, in the midst of the Confederate offensive, Lincoln once again appointed a new commander of the Army of the Potomac. Still reeling from the defeat at Chancellorsville and subsequently frustrated with Hooker's ineffective response to the invasion of Pennsylvania, the president turned to George G. Meade, an experienced corps commander with a distinguished record. Lee and Meade had served together on General Winfield Scott's staff in Mexico, so they were well known to each other. But at the end of June, they were equally unaware of each other's intentions. On June 29, two days after assuming command, Meade positioned his men just south of the Pennsylvania state line at Pipe Creek, where he established a defensive position and hoped to do battle. The following day, Union cavalry under the command of John Buford headed on a reconnaissance mission north toward Gettysburg, a small crossroads town that was home to a college, a Lutheran seminary, and a recently opened railroad station.

The events of July 1 altered Meade's initial plan and made Gettysburg, rather than Pipe Creek, the site of battle. When Lee learned of the Union army's northward movement, he quickly attempted to consolidate his forces in anticipation of a major engagement. Although the Union cavalry had initially claimed the high ground along two ridges just to the west of Gettysburg, the arriving Confederates began to attack their position. The besieged Buford called for reinforcements, and the lead corps of Meade's army advanced to engage the Confederates. By the middle of the afternoon, two Union corps were attempting to hold the high ground against a Rebel assault from portions of Hill's corps and Ewell's corps. By late in the day, the Confederates succeeded in driving the Union forces back through town to Cemetery Hill and along Cemetery Ridge, the last pieces of high ground in the area. Although at first unsure about the strategic advantage of a Confederate assault at Gettysburg, Lee decided to seize the opportunity before more of Meade's massive army arrived.

General Longstreet, the corps commander chosen by Lee to lead the assault, disagreed with the decision to go on the offensive. The only non-Virginian among the leaders of the Army of Northern Virginia, Longstreet from the start had opposed the idea of invading the North. A trusted associate of Lee and a key player in Southern victories at Second Bull Run and Fredericksburg, Longstreet tried to persuade his commander to avoid a battle at Gettysburg, move south to secure a strong defensive position, and then force the enemy to attack. But Lee had made up his mind. With the enemy in front of him, he wanted to stay and fight. Late the next morning, Lee gave the formal attack order, and with some delay, Longstreet executed the circuitous five-mile march of his men necessary to get in position for the assault. Historians have long debated the extent to which Longstreet waited and the difference that such a delay might have made on the battlefield. By the time he launched the attack at 4 P.M., reinforcements had arrived on both sides, which made the Battle of Gettysburg the largest and bloodiest of the war. More than 83,000 Union troops and more than 75,000 Confederates ended up taking part. Although the Confederates did not realize it until after Lee had issued his order, Union forces were not where the Confederates had supposed. Reconnaissance had failed to detect a corps of Union soldiers that had positioned themselves almost a mile in front of the rest of the Union line in a peach orchard and dispersed within a cluster of boulders, nicknamed Devil's Den.

Despite not realizing the position of the enemy until the afternoon of July 2—part of the reason for Longstreet's delay—the Confederate attack was largely successful. Whatever reservations he had about Lee's decision did not hinder Longstreet's ability to fight. Longstreet and his men nearly annihilated Union forces in the peach orchard and Devil's Den, and only a heroic bayonet charge by Union soldiers on a rock formation known as Little Round Top, at the end of the Federal line, prevented the Confederates from breaking through and achieving victory. Another corps of Confederates, led by Hill, stationed at the other end of the Union line closer to town, achieved less success. At the end of the second day of fighting, the Union line along Cemetery Ridge, although somewhat weakened, remained intact. Rather than quit, which Longstreet again recommended, Lee decided to renew the assault the following day. On July 3, Longstreet's corps again attacked the Federal position from one side while Ewell attacked from the other. Union reinforcements, as well as lack of coordination among Confederate corps commanders, allowed Union troops to gain the upper hand. Rebel gains made the previous day were lost.

Lee was undaunted. On the afternoon of July 3, the Confederates attempted the most infamous assault in American military history. After bombarding Union troops with artillery fire for nearly two hours—albeit to little effect—Lee ordered the reluctant Longstreet and his corps to advance across an open field toward the center of the Union line along Cemetery Ridge. Figuring that a day and a half of attacks at the ends of the line had left Yankee forces weakened in the center, Lee ordered Major General George Pickett and his fresh division to lead the charge. Meade seemed to know that it was coming. "If Lee attacks tomorrow," he had reportedly confided to an associate the night before, "it will be in your front. He has made attacks on both our flanks and failed and if he concludes to try it again, it will be on our center."[16] The flamboyant Pickett enthusiastically urged his men on before leading the fateful march of nearly 13,000 Confederate soldiers. But no amount of Rebel passion could make up for the fact that the men were marching three-quarters of a mile across a vast unprotected piece of ground, and "Pickett's Charge" proved disastrous. A barrage of Yankee artillery, as well as repeated fire from well-positioned infantry, cut down the advancing Rebels in droves. Although a handful of Confederates managed to cross the body-strewn expanse to a low stone wall that served as part of the Union defenses, the Rebels were soon repulsed and forced into full retreat. The Battle of Gettysburg was a devastating defeat for the Confederates. Afterward, upon riding up to meet with Pickett and surviving members of his decimated division, Lee reportedly said, "Your men have done all that men could do; the fault is entirely my own."[17] Although Lee's army remained in place on July 4, in expectation of a Union attack, Meade and his exhausted men failed to finish off the enemy. Even after the Rebels retreated and floods delayed their crossing of the Potomac for a week, Meade infuriated Lincoln by delaying and pursuing only half-heartedly. By the time Meade's men made it to the river, Lee and his army had already crossed.

Despite Lincoln's frustration, the Union victory at Gettysburg successfully halted the Confederate incursion into Pennsylvania. Like the Yankee triumphs that had ended the three Rebel counteroffensives in the early fall of 1862, Gettysburg crushed Confederate hopes of forcing Northern leaders to the negotiating table and ensured that the military struggle would continue. In fact, President Davis had sent Vice President Alexander Stephens under a flag of truce to Union lines at Norfolk, hoping that Stephens would arrive at the same time as news of a Rebel victory and thereby gain a meeting to negotiate peace with Lincoln. Instead, the administration learned of the Union's success and summarily dismissed Stephens's request. Of course, both sides suffered horribly during the three days of battle, and the casualty figures were the worst of the entire war: approximately 23,000 on the Union side and 28,000 Confederates. Gettysburg considerably weakened Lee's vaunted Army of Northern Virginia, whose fighting force had been reduced by a third.

The summer of 1863 had not been kind to Lee and the Confederacy. With the devastating loss of Vicksburg, an ongoing Union naval bombardment of Charleston Harbor, and uncertain prospects in the Confederate heartland, whatever Southern hopes remained would rest on Lee's shoulders. Deeply committed to his home state and deeply enmeshed in the South's slaveholding aristocracy, Lee believed that "the people of the North" were "seeking to wrest from the South dearest rights," the right to property in slaves.[18] But defeat at Gettysburg laid bare the weaknesses of the venerable Virginian. Perhaps afflicted with a bit of hubris, Lee had exercised poor judgment in believing that his men, marching across open terrain, could dislodge and defeat a larger army positioned on higher ground. Apparently convinced of the superior skill and spirit of his forces, in addition to the rightness of his cause, Lee had ordered a frontal assault that appeared to many to be doomed. Confederate soldier William D. Lyon, writing home to his brother a few days after the battle, perhaps put it most succinctly: "Gen. Lee made a great mistake in storming the heights."[19] Distraught over the failure of the Rebel invasion, a month after the battle, Lee tendered his resignation, which Davis refused to accept. Nevertheless, Lee had lost his aura of invincibility and perhaps some of his confidence.

THE UNION TAKES THE HEARTLAND: THE CHATTANOOGA CAMPAIGN

In late June, 1863, at the same time that Lee began his move into Pennsylvania, William Rosecrans at long last began to advance southward. After nearly six months of inactivity following his victory at Stones River, Rosecrans began the campaigns to capture Chattanooga. An important rail hub in the foot of the Cumberland Mountains and on the south bank of the Tennessee River, Chattanooga was as strategically significant as Vicksburg. Securing the city would cut off supply lines in all directions, ensure Union dominance in Tennessee, and provide a base of operations in the Deep South. By the time the campaign began, Rosecrans seemed to hold increasingly radical opinions about the war. Arguing in an open letter that spring that the rebellion could only be overthrown on the basis of "national unity and equal justice to all," Rosecrans labeled Northern advocates of peace on any other terms as "traitors," banned two Democratic newspapers from the army, and imposed harsh punishments on a group of colonels who had made public antiwar statements.[20] His Confederate counterpart, General Braxton Bragg, meanwhile, became more outspoken about his own beliefs, telling an interviewer "that the only mode of making the black race work, was to hold them in a condition of involuntary servitude."[21] Rosecrans could back up his convictions with military might. He had 82,000 men to Bragg's 54,000—some of Bragg's troops had been transferred to Mississippi—and benefited from the able assistance of Major General George H. Thomas, a former Virginia slaveholder who had stayed loyal to the Union.

Surprising the Confederates, Rosecrans quickly moved his troops against Bragg's forces, who were entrenched at Tullahoma, about halfway between Murfreesboro and Chattanooga. Confusing his opponent, who seemed to never grasp where he was, Rosecrans sent a small force to Bragg's left, forcing the Confederate commander to turn his army. This move left the gaps in the Cumberland Mountains lightly defended, and Rosecrans drove the rest of his troops through the gaps, to Bragg's right, until they slipped behind the Rebels and forced them to retreat to Chattanooga. Although several skirmishes occurred, the result of the brief Tullahoma Campaign was an astonishingly rapid and successful Union advance with minimal casualties. Not even heavy rainstorms could slow the Union march, and by early July, Federal forces stood on the outskirts of Chattanooga. Despite being strongly urged by Lincoln to continue into the city, Rosecrans paused to make preparations. Known for his caution and precision, Rosecrans ordered repairs of the railroad to his rear in order to ensure his supply line and waited until August to continue southward.

Rosecrans's advance, by this time, coincided with that of General Ambrose Burnside. Moved out of Virginia after January's disastrous Mud March, Burnside was leading a force of approximately 24,000 Union soldiers toward Knoxville, a Unionist-populated city to the northeast of Chattanooga held by a much smaller Confederate force. Meanwhile, Rosecrans ordered a brigade to march to a location northeast of Chattanooga, where the Rebels expected an attack, and to begin shelling the city from across the Tennessee River. Continued periodically over a two-week period, the artillery bombardment distracted the Confederates and allowed the bulk of Rosecrans's army to cross the river to the south and west of the city, where they moved into northern Alabama and Georgia. Caught completely unaware by the maneuver and wanting to avoid a trap, Bragg retreated again. On September 2, Burnside's men entered Knoxville with little resistance, and a week later, Rosecrans's army entered Chattanooga. Union operations in East Tennessee during the late summer had been a smashing success.

Incompetence and dissension within the Confederate command had harmed the Rebels' fortunes. Bragg was notoriously difficult to get along with. Grant, who knew him from the Mexican-American War, described him as "possessed of an irascible temper" and "naturally disputatious," and Bragg's Confederate colleagues no doubt agreed.[22] Constant finger pointing between Bragg and his corps commanders, particularly General Leonidas Polk, plagued the Rebels nearly a year after their failed operations in Kentucky, and Rosecrans's ability easily to outmaneuver Bragg in Tennessee led to even more infighting. Since the previous fall, Bragg's record had consisted of a series of failures. Still, he somehow managed to retain the respect of Davis, who desperately wanted him to succeed, and instead of dismissing him, Davis reinforced him. The president ordered troops from Mississippi, where they were no longer needed, and from Lee's Army of Northern Virginia in the aftermath of Gettysburg, to join with Bragg to defend the Confederate heartland.

His army strengthened, Bragg went on the attack to reclaim Chattanooga. Marching north on September 18, the Confederates positioned themselves on the west bank of Chickamauga Creek in northern Georgia just south of the Tennessee state line. There they met Rosecrans's slightly smaller Union force, located on the opposite side of the creek. Through thick brush and timber—the poor visibility made worse by smoke and carnage—some of the most intense fighting of the war ensued. On September 19, battle began in earnest as the Confederates concentrated on attacking the left side of the Union line, and the Rebels made significant progress in pushing the Yankees back. The next day proved decisive, when Rosecrans made "a grave and almost inexplicable mistake."[23] Taking the word of one of his field commanders that a gap existed in the Union line (without confirming this for himself), Rosecrans ordered one of his division commanders to fill the supposed hole. In reality, there was no gap, but Rosecrans's order created a real gap—and tremendous havoc—within the Union ranks. The Confederates, led by the recently arrived General Longstreet, smashed through the hole in the Union line and routed the Federals. A third of the Union army, led by a stunned Rosecrans, engaged in a full retreat toward Chattanooga. General Thomas rallied what remained of the Union army by forming a new line on high ground, which he bravely defended against repeated Confederate assaults. Earning the nickname the "Rock of Chickamauga," Thomas prevented the Confederate victory from turning into a complete disaster for the Union. Bragg not only failed to reinforce Longstreet's attacks but also neglected to pursue the retreating Federals, much to the dismay of his army. Thus, the Battle of Chickamauga was a Rebel victory but mostly a hollow one. It came at the cost of more than 18,000 Confederate casualties to the Union's 16,000 (roughly a quarter of each army), and the Federals continued to hold Chattanooga.

The defeat precipitated changes in the Union command structure. The demoralized Rosecrans, who had abandoned the field to lead a thirteen-mile retreat, seemed unable to recover from the trauma. Despite receiving repeated assurances from Lincoln during the days that followed, Rosecrans seemed dazed for weeks on end—in Lincoln's words, "like a duck hit on the head."[24] Although for political reasons they hesitated to dismiss Rosecrans—he was a War Democrat whose success paid political dividends for the administration—Lincoln and Secretary of War Edwin Stanton eventually agreed that he needed replacing. With Vicksburg and the Mississippi secured, in mid-October they discharged Rosecrans and created a new Military Division of the Mississippi—which included the armies previously led by Rosecrans, Burnside, and Grant—with Grant in command. Ordering Thomas, now in charge at Chattanooga, to hold the city at all costs, the hero of Vicksburg thus rushed east to save Chattanooga.

Remarkably, Bragg held onto his command. Despite the Rebel victory at Chickamauga, Bragg remained unpopular both with enlisted men and his fellow officers, particularly Polk and Longstreet, who roundly criticized him for failing to pursue. The intensity of the backbiting within the Rebel command prompted President Davis to intervene personally, and in early October he traveled to Georgia to meet with the involved parties. After listening to all sides for five days, the weary Davis made a plea for harmony, left Bragg in charge, transferred his severest critic (Polk), and returned to Richmond. "As commander in chief," Davis's biographer writes, "this was arguably the worst and most damaging decision Davis made during the war."[25] Finally, in an apparent attempt to remove another of Bragg's detractors, Davis sent Longstreet with 15,000 soldiers and another 5,000 cavalrymen on an ill-fated mission to take Knoxville, thus unwisely reducing the size of the Rebel force surrounding Chattanooga.[26]

Grant's appointment and Bragg's retention meant that the Union's most effective general now faced one of the Confederacy's least effective generals. After Federal forces retreated into the city, the Rebels had occupied the surrounding heights and had severed all of the supply lines except for a single mountain road that proved nearly impossible to travel. With his army short of rations, Grant immediately launched an aggressive operation at Brown's Ferry, on the opposite bank of the Tennessee River, in order to open a new supply line to a Union base of operations in north Alabama. After attacking a Rebel force and laying a pontoon bridge, within a few days, food and supplies again flowed into the city. Their stomachs full and spirits high, Grant's men received reinforcements from Virginia and Mississippi, and in late November, they launched an attack on the Rebel strongholds surrounding the city, which by this time included a formidable combination of trenches and rifle pits.

Grant decided that his men would attack both ends of the Confederate line, which extended along Missionary Ridge to the southeast of Chattanooga. The Virginia forces (now commanded by Joseph Hooker) would attack one side, while Sherman's men from Mississippi would attack the other. Grant assigned a secondary role to Thomas's Army of the Cumberland, ordering them to secure a hill to the west of Missionary Ridge before engaging in a feint at the center of the Confederate line. On November 24, Hooker attacked aggressively, as planned, and successfully dislodged a Confederate division located high atop Lookout Mountain, southwest of the city. Then, the following day, Hooker and his men pushed ahead to the Confederates' left side on Missionary Ridge, while Sherman and his men advanced across the Tennessee River and against a Rebel stronghold on the right side of the Confederate line. Contrary to Grant's plan, the primary action on the second and decisive day of the battle came in the center. Watching from Orchard Knob, the hill captured by Thomas and his men, Grant stood incredulously as the Army of the Cumberland—the same army that had been embarrassed at Chickamauga—scaled the heights in the center of Missionary Ridge and relentlessly attacked the Rebels in their secure positions. In what seemed like Pickett's Charge in reverse, with the Union now making the seemingly suicidal frontal assault, the determined Federal troops began sweeping across Confederate trenches, defeating and intimidating their opponents, and rapidly scaling the heights of Missionary Ridge. All watched in amazement—including Grant and Thomas—as the Union troops continued their steep upward climb until the Rebels fled, first in shock and then in despair. His men thoroughly whipped, Bragg retreated thirty miles to Atlanta.

The decisive Battles of Lookout Mountain and Missionary Ridge, the culmination of the Chattanooga Campaign, concluded a string of Union successes during the second half of 1863—including Vicksburg and Gettysburg—that greatly strengthened the Union's military position. In securing Tennessee for the Union, Grant finished the job that Rosecrans had begun nearly a year before at Stones River. To cap off the success of Union operations, within days after Bragg's retreat, Longstreet's forces abandoned their attempt to recapture Knoxville and fled into Virginia. Bragg finally submitted his resignation, which President Davis promptly accepted.

FORREST DISRUPTS UNION OPERATIONS: HARD WAR IN THE WEST

After winter began and Confederate leaders consolidated their forces and debated their next move, General Nathan Bedford Forrest attempted to keep Southern hope alive in the West with his intrepid raids in Union-held territory. Born into poverty in rural Tennessee, Forrest had risen rapidly after his move to Memphis, and by 1860 his investments in real estate and cotton in Mississippi—as well as his slave trading business in Memphis—made him one of the city's wealthiest citizens. From the start viewing the Civil War as "a war upon slavery," Forrest understood what was at stake. In July 1861 Forrest had received authorization from Tennessee's governor to raise his own battalion of cavalry, and he soon earned a reputation as a hard fighter.[27] He had broken his troops away at Fort Donelson where the rest of the garrison surrendered, attacked a Federal camp at Murfreesboro in the summer of 1862 and seized 1,200 prisoners, and captured another 3,500 Federals during raids on Union camps in middle Tennessee in the spring of 1863. After serving under Bragg at Chickamauga and brazenly criticizing his commanding officer for his unwillingness to pursue, in early November Forrest gained approval from President Davis to move into north Mississippi, where he was to "raise and organize as many troops for the Confederate States service as he finds practicable."[28] Cut off from the remaining Confederate armies in north Georgia and in Virginia, Forrest never amassed enough of an army to pose a serious threat to Union dominance. Still, his fierce brand of fighting and his impressive military successes made him a hero to Confederates in Mississippi and Tennessee.

General Sherman acknowledged the threat that Forrest posed. Having won the West in a series of important victories, the Union had left garrisons throughout the region to maintain control in places of strategic significance. New Orleans, Vicksburg, Memphis, and Corinth all continued to have a strong Federal military presence, and Sherman hoped to reduce the size of these garrisons and concentrate his forces in a campaign against Meridian,

Mississippi, located due east of Jackson. By moving his army across the state—from Vicksburg to Meridian—Sherman planned to tear up the railroads and "paralyze" Rebel forces in the region. Doing so would allow him to eventually remove 20,000 soldiers from Mississippi so that they could be used in the coming advance on Atlanta. The Meridian Campaign had a second purpose. "I wanted to destroy General Forrest," Sherman admitted, "who, with an irregular force of cavalry, was constantly threatening Memphis and the river above, as well as our routes of supply in Middle Tennessee."[29]

In the early months of 1864, Forrest wreaked havoc in the West. Establishing his headquarters at Jackson, Tennessee, some eighty miles northeast of Memphis, Forrest began recruiting men and building a command. When Union forces in the surrounding area threatened to converge on the Confederates, the Rebels moved into Mississippi, where Forrest continued recruiting and established a base at Starkville. From there, Forrest's men skirmished with and pursued Federal cavalrymen who were supposed to join Sherman's Meridian Campaign. These engagements in February 1864 might best be described as running fights, with Forrest's cavalry relentlessly slashing and attacking. Using their rifles at long range and their sabers up close, Forrest's men eventually drove a column of Yankee cavalry into a full retreat to Memphis. Although Sherman accomplished his march to Meridian without the defeated cavalry, Forrest's attacks had reduced the size of his force. A month later, Forrest set out from Mississippi with nearly 3,000 men and moved through Tennessee into western Kentucky. After a raid on Union City, Tennessee, Forrest's cavalry rode into Paducah, Kentucky, on the Ohio River, where they ransacked the town, terrorized civilians, and seized animals and supplies. Hard war was taking its toll.

In early April, Forrest moved back into West Tennessee to attack the garrison at Fort Pillow, upriver from Memphis. By early 1864, the fort possessed little strategic significance, and only a small force remained there. Believing that Forrest had little reason to attack the fort, Union commanders had given little thought to its defense. But the local pro-Confederate population viewed it as an affront, for the garrison represented the Federal occupation and served as a haven for local Unionists and runaway slaves. Even more offensive to Confederates, over half of the approximately 600 soldiers stationed there were African Americans, the vast majority of them formerly enslaved. Black soldiers had served the previous year in the Vicksburg Campaign, and many remained at Union garrisons throughout the West. On April 12, 1864, Forrest and a force of 1,500 attacked Fort Pillow, killed its commanding officer, and demanded its unconditional surrender. When the acting commander refused to capitulate, Forrest's cavalry overran the fort and drove the surviving Federals down the river bluff as a Union gunboat ineffectively attempted to defend the retreating forces. The fierce Battle of Fort Pillow resulted in nearly half of the Federal soldiers being killed in battle, and Forrest reported the results with brutal candor: "The river was dyed with the blood of the slaughtered for 200 yards."[30] Soldiers of the United States Colored Troops suffered a stunning death rate of 63 percent, nearly double that of their white counterparts. It was hard to escape the conclusion that raging Confederates, blinded by racial hatred, had deliberately massacred black soldiers as they were attempting to surrender.[31] Despite the bloodbath, the Confederates did not try to hold the fort, and their vengeful victory did little to undermine Union strength in the region.

In early June, Forrest resolved to destroy the critical rail link between Nashville and Chattanooga, which would serve as the supply line for the coming Union assault against Atlanta. Setting out from Tupelo, Mississippi, Forrest moved into northern Alabama with 3,500 men. Knowing that he would have to contend with Forrest, Sherman ordered Brigadier General Samuel Sturgis to take a column of Federal soldiers from Memphis and advance into northern Mississippi in order to draw Forrest back to defend the Magnolia State. Forrest indeed halted his advance, and his cavalry confronted Sturgis's much larger force of more than 8,000 at Brice's Crossroads, just south of Corinth. In another fierce battle, Forrest's repeated, aggressive attacks won the day, despite the Rebels' inferior numbers, as the Yankees retreated in panic across a creek. Hoping to avenge the massacre at Fort Pillow, Colonel Edward Bouton's Fifty-Ninth Colored Infantry battled valiantly. "My men, gathering around me," Bouton later reported, "fought with terrible desperation. Some of them, having broken up their guns in hand-to-hand conflict, unyielding, died at my feet, without a thing in their hands for defense."[32] The entire Union force ended up fleeing all the way back to Memphis, with Forrest's men in periodic pursuit. The Battle of Brice's Crossroads was an unequivocal Confederate victory.

Frustrated with the Union cavalry's inability to neutralize Forrest, Sherman again gave the orders to go on the offensive. Directing two divisions fresh from an ill-fated expedition in the Red River Valley to pursue and defeat the Confederate cavalryman, the Union finally accomplished its aim at the Battle of Tupelo in mid-July, as the Rebels suffered more than twice the number of casualties as their opponents. Although wounded, Forrest was neither captured nor killed, and he continued his raids, with a reduced force, until the end of the war. Still, Union victory at Tupelo prevented the Rebels from interfering with Sherman's operations, and Forrest never again posed as serious a threat as he did in the first half of 1864.

GRANT PURSUES LEE: FROM THE WILDERNESS TO PETERSBURG

In the early months of 1864, after Federal victories at Gettysburg and Chattanooga and before Forrest's raids had begun, Union leaders considered their next move. However much territory the Rebels had surrendered in the West, two large Confederate armies still stood in the way of Union victory. The Army of Tennessee remained in north Georgia opposite Federal troops in Chattanooga, while the Army of Northern Virginia camped on the south bank of the Rapidan River (a tributary of the Rappahannock), arrayed against its long-standing rival, the Army of the Potomac. For months Grant had advocated taking troops from Chattanooga in order to initiate a major operation against Mobile, Alabama, the primary port for Confederate blockade runners. But Lincoln disagreed with this strategy. As commander in chief, he confronted a new challenge that made the situation more complex. France had recently installed a puppet governor, Ferdinand Maximilian, in Mexico, and in January the president ordered an offensive from New Orleans and into Texas—the Red River Campaign—as a show of American strength on the border. The necessary diversion of troops to Texas made an assault on Mobile impractical, Lincoln believed, because it would require even more men to be moved away from Chattanooga. Concentrating forces in Chattanooga would solidify Lincoln's political goal of holding East Tennessee, allow the Union to launch a major offensive into Georgia, and ensure the safety of Union supply lines back to Nashville. At the same time, Lincoln favored an advance in the eastern theater against Lee's army, which had established defensive positions after Gettysburg. Only by initiating two simultaneous advances—in both Georgia and Virginia—could the Union take advantage of its superior numbers.

In early March 1864, Lincoln directed Grant to come east to oversee the campaign in Virginia. In a brief ceremony at the White House, Grant received the rank of lieutenant general, which no one had held since George Washington, in effect making Grant the general in chief of all Union forces. Lincoln offered words of praise for the military leader he had so longed to find. "General Grant," Lincoln stated, as the Cabinet and handful of military dignitaries and visitors looked on, "the nation's appreciation of what you have done, and its reliance upon you for what remains to do in the existing great struggle, are now presented, with this commission constituting you lieutenant-general in the Army of the United States."[33] The following day, the new lieutenant general visited the Army of the Potomac, where he acknowledged the victory at Gettysburg by graciously leaving General Meade in command. Nev-

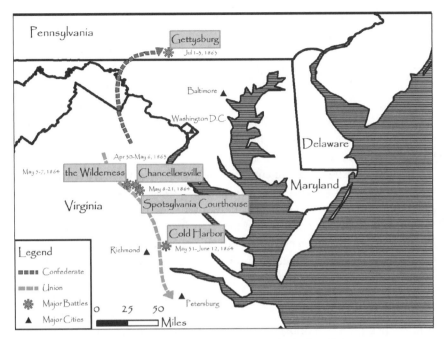

Major offensives in the eastern theater, 1863–1864. Map by Andrew Tait

ertheless, Grant kept his headquarters in the field, gave orders to Meade, and thus for all practical purposes served as commander. After all of the blood that had been shed in the east during the previous three years, the Union army that Grant now led remained just a few miles south of where it had camped when the war began. Grant's singular aim was to attack and destroy Lee's army. Capturing Richmond would be a secondary goal.

Early on May 4, the Army of the Potomac, more than 100,000 strong, crossed the Rapidan to meet the enemy. General Burnside's corps joined them with nearly another 20,000 men, making the total Union force approximately 120,000 troops. Marching through a thick patch of trees and isolated farmhouses—an area nicknamed "the Wilderness"—Grant desired to face off against Lee's 65,000 men on open ground. But Lee quickly surmised Grant's moves and plans. Hoping to lessen the impact of the Federal advantage, the following day Lee ordered an attack. For the next two days, Union and Confederate soldiers confronted each other through the trees, brush, and thickets, not far from where the Rebels had defeated the Yankees in the Battle of Chancellorsville the previous spring. The intense battle in the woods devolved into a blind fight through thick smoke and searing fire. Some burned to death.

The occasional appearance of skeletons unearthed from Chancellorsville made it seem to some less like a military engagement and more like a hellish nightmare of flames, screams, and corpses. When the Battle of the Wilderness had ended, the Union had suffered more than 18,000 casualties, compared to 11,400 for the Confederates. It was a gruesome two days with no clear victor. But rather than retreat, rest, and reorganize to plan the next offensive—as all of Grant's predecessors had done—the new commander continued pursuing Lee's army. Upon hearing the news, Lincoln praised Grant's "dogged pertinacity."[34]

The day after fighting had ended in the Wilderness, Grant headed about a dozen miles south toward Spotsylvania Court House, a crossroads that would allow him to control access to Richmond, located another sixty miles south. Lee, again predicting Grant's next move, arrived at Spotsylvania first, where he immediately began to establish defensive positions. When Grant arrived, a nearly two-week battle ensued—a series of skirmishes and engagements that often resembled trench warfare. Lee established a strong defensive line just north of one of the roads leading to Spotsylvania, and the terrain and vegetation created a large protrusion in the Confederate line. Lee placed his artillery here, but he removed it on May 11 when—on a day when Grant did not attack—Lee assumed that his opponent was preparing to move out. Grant did not move. Instead, he assaulted the opening in the Confederate line, where the artillery had been removed, and came close to cutting the Confederate army in two. The Southerners counterattacked, and this severe fight at the "bloody angle" on May 12 proved deadly for both sides. Casualties totaled nearly 12,000 on that day alone. Fighting continued sporadically for the next several days until Grant disengaged and continued to advance toward Richmond. The casualties were mounting. The thirteen-day Battle of Spotsylvania resulted in approximately the same numbers of dead, missing, and wounded on both sides as had the Battle of the Wilderness. Clearly, Grant was waging a war of attrition.

Throughout Grant's "Overland Campaign" against Lee in spring 1864, Union cavalry under the command of General Philip Sheridan provided support. A stocky Ohioan who started out as a bookkeeper, Sheridan became a soldier and rose through the ranks of the Union cavalry after an astonishing 1862 victory in Mississippi over a much larger Confederate force. A veteran of Union triumphs at Perryville, Stones River, and Chattanooga, Sheridan came east at the request of Grant to serve as chief of cavalry for the Army of the Potomac. Finding the Union cavalry in Virginia in poor shape and underutilized, Sheridan continuously debated General Meade about the proper role of his mounted force. Rather than conveying messages, escorting officers, and patrolling enemy territory, Sheridan believed that cavalry should fight battles, and Grant intervened in the dispute by authorizing Sheridan to do just that. While Grant headed out of the Wilderness toward Spotsylvania, Sheridan took 10,000 men toward Richmond in the hope of attacking J. E. B. Stuart's Confederate cavalry. After doing extensive damage to railroad and supply depots, Sheridan's forces and the Rebels faced off near an abandoned inn known as Yellow Tavern, just six miles from the Confederate capital. The larger, better-armed Union force won the day against the Confederates, dispersing the Rebels and mortally wounding the legendary Stuart. Sheridan's victory thus deprived the Confederacy of one of its tactical geniuses and symbolic leaders. The next day President Davis visited Stuart on his deathbed in Richmond, while Lee lamented the loss of his cavalry commander. Sheridan's offensive had dealt a significant blow to the Confederates.

After Spotsylvania and Yellow Tavern, Grant continued southward and, after a few skirmishes along the North Anna River, advanced toward the crossroads at Cold Harbor, about fifteen miles northeast of Richmond. Out in front of the main army, Sheridan and his men arrived there before the Confederates and succeeded in holding off the small Rebel force that attacked them. Confederate reinforcements, followed by the Union army's arrival, turned the engagement into a major battle. Two diversionary campaigns that Grant had previously ordered to coincide with his overland advance failed to achieve their goal of tying up additional Rebel troops, which allowed the Confederates to send about 10,000 more reinforcements to Cold Harbor than Grant had originally anticipated. By June 2, both armies had taken entrenched positions that stretched for seven miles. Knowing that Richmond lay just beyond the Confederate lines, Grant optimistically believed that repeated charges could rout the Rebel army and allow his men to seize the Confederate capital. Knowing that Grant would send them rushing against the Confederate earthworks the next day, some Union soldiers fatalistically believed that their fate had already been determined. Early the next morning, Grant indeed ordered a series of assaults, with horrific results, as the Union suffered approximately 6,000 casualties in one day. "I have always regretted that the last assault at Cold Harbor was ever made," Grant later admitted in his *Memoirs*. "No advantage whatever was gained to compensate for the heavy losses we sustained."[35] Continuing with sporadic fighting over the next several days, the Battle of Cold Harbor proved to be a terrible Union defeat. In a twelve-day period, the Yankees suffered a total of 13,000 casualties, compared to the Rebels' 2,500. In the short term, Cold Harbor damaged Grant's reputation and drained optimism from the campaign. It was hard war at its hardest.

Defeat did not deter Grant. Immediately after the disaster, he decided to implement a two-pronged strategy that, if successful, would curtail the flow of supplies and communications to and from Richmond and eventually cripple Lee's army. He sent Sheridan north, back toward Spotsylvania at the southern end of the Shenandoah Valley, to tear up the railroads leading south into Richmond and cut off the food supply of the Army of Northern Virginia. In the meantime, Grant stealthily moved the bulk of the army east and south—in an arc away from Richmond and toward Petersburg, located twenty-five miles due south of the Confederate capital. Securing control of Petersburg, Virginia's second largest city and a major railway hub, would shut off access to Richmond from below. Sheridan's forces met resistance at Trevilian Station, where Confederate cavalry fought them to a standstill, but Grant's movement proved an unqualified success. Described by one historian as "an almost unprecedented achievement of combat engineering," Union army engineers constructed a 2,100-foot-long pontoon bridge across the James River, and on June 14 the massive Army of the Potomac inched across, eventually positioning themselves just outside Petersburg.[36] While Grant crossed the James, Lee only learned of his enemies' whereabouts once it was too late. Trying an old trick that had worked well before, he had ordered a cavalry raid to the north to threaten Washington and draw away Union troops. Jubal Early's cavalry assault did put a scare into President Lincoln, who literally watched from a Union fort as the Rebels came to within five miles of the White House, but the move did nothing to help Lee. In the final analysis, the Confederates had failed to prevent the Federals from arriving on the doorstep of Petersburg.

Despite the tactical brilliance of their arrival, the Union forces bungled their attack. Grant had delegated the assault on Petersburg to William F. "Baldy" Smith, who arrived there first and was to strike early on June 15, as Grant continued to supervise the crossing at the James. Over the next three days, a combination of timid leadership, confused orders, and exhausted Federal troops resulted in a missed opportunity to take the city and, perhaps, end the war. The Confederates had previously dug a long line of trenches and built heavy earthworks to defend Petersburg. Intimidated by the impressive-looking defenses and haunted by the memories of Cold Harbor, Smith delayed. But behind the massive earthworks, fewer than 3,000 men under the command of P. G. T. Beauregard stood between Smith's army of 16,000 and the capture of the city. Even the Union's swift success in advancing across the first line of Rebel defenses did little to boost their confidence, as officers and soldiers alike proved reluctant to move against such well-fortified positions. The arrival of reinforcements on both sides changed the equation, and when a frustrated Meade gave direct orders to his hesitant corps commanders to strike on June 18, heavy Union losses prompted Meade and Grant to call off the attack. Having missed their chance to overrun the Confederate defenses, the Union troops settled in for a siege that would last into 1865.

Lincoln's decision to bring Grant east had been an important one, for the Overland Campaign had transformed the war in Virginia. Before Grant took over, the armies fought a battle and then went into camp. Months had separated the battles of Antietam and Fredericksburg, Fredericksburg and Chancellorsville, and Chancellorsville and Gettysburg. And each of these battles had lasted only a few days. But between the firing of the first shots in the Wilderness on May 5 to the silencing of Union guns at Petersburg on June 18, Grant's and Lee's armies remained in contact with each other every day. Grant relentlessly marched, attacked, and pursued, just as Lincoln had hoped, and as the Battle of the Wilderness raged, the president hailed the general for having "the grit of a bull-dog."[37] Of course, Grant's bull-doggedness exhausted his men and sent a great number of them to their graves. From the start of the campaign till its end, Union operations in Virginia resulted in 73,000 casualties, compared to approximately 44,500 Confederate losses. While Union casualties constituted a smaller ratio of the original strength of their army than that of the Confederates, such strategic considerations mattered little to the average soldier or to the Northern public. Not since being caught unaware at Shiloh had Grant encountered the level of criticism that came during the summer of 1864. Although hailed just weeks before as a national hero, the carnage in Virginia caused critics both military and civilian to decry Grant as a "butcher" who had little regard for the lives of his soldiers. "I am disgusted with the generalship displayed," wrote Colonel Emory Upton at Cold Harbor. "Our men have, in many instances, been foolishly and wantonly sacrificed. Assault after assault has been ordered upon the enemy's entrenchments, when they knew nothing about the strength or position of the enemy. Thousands of lives might have been spared by the exercise of a little skill; but, as it is, the courage of the poor men is expected to obviate all difficulties."[38] Through six intensive weeks of marching and fighting, Grant's Overland Campaign had inflicted heavy damage on the Army of Northern Virginia and threatened to strangle Petersburg. It had been a hard and costly success.

SHERMAN TAKES ATLANTA AND MARCHES TO SAVANNAH

On May 7, 1864, two days after Grant launched his campaign in Virginia, General William T. Sherman began his operations in Georgia. This would be

General William T. Sherman, Grant's collaborator and friend, embodied the Union's hard war strategy. His 300-mile march through Georgia in fall 1864 all but sealed the fate of the Confederacy. Courtesy of the US National Archives, 111-B-1769

his moment. A native of Ohio and a graduate of West Point, Sherman had served in the Seminole War and the Mexican-American War, but he had left the army during the early 1850s to pursue other interests. He went into banking in California, tried his hand at real estate in Kansas, spent two years at a military academy in Louisiana, and moved to St. Louis when secession came. Throughout these years, he experienced financial troubles and bouts of depression. But when the war broke out, Sherman returned to the army and rose quickly. At Shiloh he and Grant had forged a bond, and when it came time for the Atlanta Campaign two years later, Grant could have imagined no one else leading the offensive. Sherman took about 100,000 men, leaving another 80,000 or so behind to maintain garrisons and protect supply lines.[39] The Confederates had about 60,000 soldiers and a solid defensive position north of Atlanta.

With Bragg's dismissal months before, General Joseph Johnston now commanded the Confederate forces. Still on poor terms with President Davis, who blamed him for the fall of Vicksburg, Johnston had his work cut out for him. With inferior numbers and orders to protect Atlanta, another rail hub, Johnston maintained a defensive posture. As was the case with Grant, Sherman's primary aim was to defeat the enemy army. Knowing that Grant's simultaneous operation in Virginia would deny Johnston reinforcements, Sherman decided to fight a war of maneuver. From the beginning of May until the middle of July, he carried out a series of flanking movements, as he continually turned his army toward the left side of the Confederate line. Each time Sherman did this, Johnston repositioned his men southward in order to remain between Atlanta and Sherman's army. By doing so, Johnston reasoned, he drew Union forces deeper into enemy territory, lengthened their tenuous supply lines, and made inevitable a Union frontal attack on Confederate defenses. In the process of making these southward movements, of course, Johnston surrendered a bit of ground each time, and after a series of minor engagements as Sherman drove Johnston closer to Atlanta, President Davis grew impatient. The Confederacy did win a victory at the Battle of Kennesaw Mountain on June 27, when Sherman ordered an assault on Rebel defenses and suffered significant losses, but even this victory prompted another Rebel withdrawal and made Atlanta more vulnerable. All the while, Davis wanted Johnston to go on the offensive, and Johnston appeared unwilling to do so. On July 17, Davis finally replaced him with John Bell Hood. With relatively little blood shed by his own men and plenty of dissension in the ranks of the enemy, Sherman was winning.

Hood's appointment changed the dynamic of the campaign. A tall, aggressive Texan whose wartime service had already resulted in a wounded arm and an amputated leg, Hood was eager to go on the attack. Sherman welcomed the change in the enemy's command. "Notice of this important change was at once sent to all parts of the army, and every division commander was cautioned to be always prepared for battle in any shape," Sherman later wrote in his *Memoirs*. "This was just what we wanted, viz., to fight in open ground, on any thing like equal terms, instead of being forced to run up against prepared intrenchments."[40] Fulfilling everyone's expectations, in late July Hood carried out three attacks within eight days. None of the offensives succeeded, and the battles resulted in more than 18,000 Rebel casualties (more than three times that suffered by the Union), which the Confederacy could ill afford. After the last of these failed offensives, the Battle of Ezra Church, Hood ceased attacking. His hard-hitting offensive strategy had proven even less effective than Johnston's reactive, defensive one.

For the next month, Sherman essentially maneuvered around and surrounded Atlanta, and he repeatedly attempted to use cavalry forces to sever the railroad lines. Hood seemed to face the inevitability of a siege and carefully guarded the city's earthworks. In a final engagement at Jonesboro in late August, Hood ordered an attack to prevent Sherman's seizure of the last railroad line in and out of Atlanta, the Macon line to the south. Facing superior numbers with a bedraggled army, Hood lost control of the railroad and vacated the city. Rather than pursue Hood's army, Sherman settled for Atlanta. With a keen sense of the political importance of his victory for the reelection campaign of President Lincoln, on September 2 Sherman wired the triumphant news to Washington: "Atlanta is ours and fairly won."[41] A relieved Lincoln lauded Sherman's "distinguished ability and perseverance," while proclaiming that Union operations in Georgia "must render [the campaign] famous in the annals of war."[42] Coming less than a month after a Union naval victory at Mobile Bay, which set the stage for later land operations there, the victory in Atlanta seemed to indicate a significant change in Union fortunes. Largely as a result of these sudden successes, Lincoln won reelection.

With Atlanta captured, Sherman proposed to make an unconventional move. Throughout the campaign, Sherman and his opponents had always clung to the railroad between Chattanooga and Atlanta, the lifeline of their armies. Immediately after the capture of Atlanta, Sherman initially used a portion of his army to chase after Hood, who had begun to move north along the railroad. But rather than defending his supply line and following Hood around Georgia, Sherman had another idea. He asked Grant if instead he could destroy the railroad he had been guarding to his rear—from Atlanta all the way back to Chattanooga—and then move his army south, through Georgia, toward the sea. Inspired by his success in the Meridian Campaign in Feb-

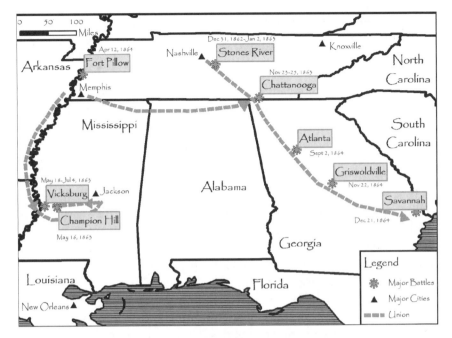

Major offensives in the western theater, 1863–1864. Map by Andrew Tait

ruary, when he had demolished over 100 miles of railroad track, dozens of bridges, and vast amounts of supplies in northern Mississippi, Sherman wanted to carry out a similar operation through the heart of Georgia. Going after the sources of supply, transportation, and communication that supported the Rebel army, Sherman would aim his operation at the destruction of infrastructure and property rather than the loss of life. In the process, he would deal a huge psychological blow to the civilian population. Sherman was offering a variation on the hard war strategy that he and Grant had been pursuing for some time, and "mak[ing] Georgia howl," as Sherman described his plan, was a far cry from McClellan's 1861 order to "religiously respect the constitutional rights of all" enemies.[43] A skeptical Grant, who maintained that Hood's army remained the goal, feared that a southward march would allow Hood to advance unchecked into Tennessee, putting a scare into the local Unionists and damaging Northern morale. Sherman responded that General Thomas and the 55,000 men that he could assemble would repel any attack. After convincing a dubious Lincoln, Grant wired to Sherman on November 2, "Go as you propose."[44]

Go he did. Rather than leave behind a garrison in Atlanta, Sherman burned everything of military value in the city and early on November 15 set out on a 300-mile-long march toward Savannah. Sherman took 62,000 of his best and healthiest foot soldiers, along with 5,000 cavalrymen, 2,500 wagons, 16,000 horses and mules, and sixty-five artillery pieces. He established two wings of infantry and used his cavalry as scouts on either side of his marching force, where they would fend off any armed resistance. Sherman spread his forces between thirty and sixty miles wide, following four roughly parallel roads in a generally southeasterly direction, with messengers constantly galloping among the four columns as they advanced. He ordered his corps commanders to organize along the way "able-bodied" blacks who could be of service, particularly as part of a "pioneer battalion" to clear roads and repair bridges, but he instructed his commanders not to accept black refugees that the army could not feed. Most important, Sherman instructed his men to pack lightly and to live off the land. "The army will forage liberally on the country during the march," he ordered.[45] Designated foraging parties led the way in seizing the massive amount of food and supplies that lay in the path of the army. Having studied maps and census reports, Sherman knew that the Georgia countryside was rich in foodstuffs. "We found abundance of corn, molasses, meal, bacon, and sweet-potatoes. We also took a good many cows and oxen, and a large number of mules," Sherman wrote. "As a rule, we destroyed none, but kept our wagons full, and fed our teams bountifully."[46]

Of course, the purposes of the march were to damage property and kill the Rebel spirit. Sherman succeeded on both counts. Moving at a pace of between ten and fifteen miles each day, the invading army systematically ruined the railroads by pulling up the wooden cross ties and the iron rails. Soldiers burned the wood and then heated the rails until they could be bent and made unusable by wrapping them around trees or telegraph poles. Nicknamed "Sherman's Neckties" or "Sherman's Bowties," these twisted rails became visible signs of the destructive presence of the Union army. Although Sherman had issued specific orders forbidding trespassing into private homes, his forces inevitably engaged in some pillaging, which Sherman later justified by arguing that, because the Rebels had brought on the war, they "deserved all they got and worse."[47] The movement of such a massive force through the countryside spurred unintended consequences as well, for a multitude of black refugees and Rebel deserters followed the troops and contributed to the plundering. Not wanting Sherman to seize or destroy their property, Georgians engaged in destruction as well.

Sherman's marching columns encountered little opposition along the way. Not knowing Sherman's destination, the confused Confederates could not figure out where to amass forces or which towns to defend. When a contingent of Georgia state militia struck on November 22 at Griswoldville, the Yan-

Sherman's march through Georgia damaged property and killed the Rebel spirit. In this photograph, Sherman's men famously destroyed the railroads. Courtesy of the Library of Congress, LC-DIG-cwpb-03391

kees' repeating rifles devastated the attackers and perpetrated more than 500 casualties. The Union commander avoided a heavily defended munitions factory in Augusta because he wanted to dodge a concentrated Rebel force and instead marched to Milledgeville, the Georgia state capital. As the governor and legislators fled in panic, Sherman's men inflicted heavy damage on an arsenal and other public buildings after holding a mock legislative session in the capitol. Throughout the five-week march, Sherman's presence struck fear in Rebel hearts and inspired black Georgians to celebrate their freedom. By the time Sherman arrived at Savannah a week before Christmas—and six weeks after Lincoln's reelection—Grant congratulated his friend on the "splendid results" of the campaign.[48] Although in the decades after Sherman's March through Georgia civilians told larger-than-life stories of wanton destruction and indiscriminate burning of everything in his path, Sherman's army simply did not engage in such activity. Despite plundering on the part of some, Sherman aimed at purposeful destruction of those resources most useful to the

Confederacy—a form of psychological warfare that he hoped would bring a speedy end to the conflict.

THE END OF 1864 AND THE CUSP OF UNION VICTORY

By the final few weeks of 1864, the Union stood on the cusp of victory. After the Rebels evacuated Savannah, Sherman and his men moved into the city and destroyed the navy yard, war ships, and ammunition stores, and on December 22, Sherman sent a famous telegraph to Lincoln: "I beg to present you, as a Christmas gift, the city of Savannah, with 150 heavy guns and plenty of ammunition, and also about 2,500 bales of cotton."[49] After resupplying his army, Sherman prepared for the next campaign. Initially, Grant had indicated that he needed him to bring his army north by sea to assist in operations against Lee, but Grant quickly changed his mind and decided to allow Sherman to continue his march north toward Columbia, South Carolina. "I do sincerely believe that the whole United States, North and South, would rejoice to have this army turned loose on South Carolina to devastate that State, in the manner we have done in Georgia," Sherman wrote to Grant, "and it would have a direct and immediate bearing on your campaign in Virginia."[50] As the cradle of nullification, secession, and slaveholders' rights, South Carolina had symbolic importance, and both men realized that a strike at Columbia, another rail hub, would further cripple the Confederacy's capacity to make war. Sherman would move toward Virginia by land rather than by sea.

Meanwhile, as expected, Sherman's march to the south had prompted General Hood to make a mad dash to the north. President Davis fully approved of the plan to take what remained of the Army of Tennessee and head as far into enemy territory as possible, perhaps even to the Ohio River. Marching past Chattanooga on his way to Nashville, Hood's forces—only about 20,000 strong—engaged in a number of frontal assaults on entrenched Union troops at Franklin with disastrous results, particularly in the leadership ranks. On a bloody day of fighting on November 30, the Confederacy lost a number of generals and dozens of regimental commanders in a battle that resulted in more than 6,000 overall Southern losses. Rather than retreating, Hood attempted another offensive further north, when his remaining force made it to Nashville. General Thomas's forces attacked, and the Rebels suffered another crushing defeat, resulting in an additional 4,462 casualties. Key to the Union victory had been black troops, who by their bravery in battle convinced the skeptical Thomas, a Virginian and former slaveholder, that African Americans could and would fight. Soundly beaten by superior Union numbers, the exhausted and nearly starved Army of Tennessee retreated with fewer than half the men with which it had begun. Thomas and his men performed brilliantly, and news of their success delighted Lincoln. Davis subsequently dismissed Hood, whose defeat marked the end of Confederate operations in Tennessee.

In the east, Grant remained outside of Petersburg, where the situation was relatively unchanged since summer. In late July, Grant had suffered a defeat when, against his better judgment, he allowed explosive experts to attempt to blow up a mine beneath the Rebel fortifications. When the explosion occurred, hundreds of Union soldiers, including a large number of black troops, rushed in to fill the huge hole in the ground that resulted, which prompted the Rebels to begin taking aim and shooting. The so-called Battle of the Crater demoralized Union forces for weeks afterward, but in the long run the Federals made progress in their attempts to disrupt railroad operations out of the city while shelling the residents of Petersburg into submission. General Sheridan, meanwhile, continued his heroic leadership of Union cavalry during the fall, when he successfully repelled a series of Rebel cavalry attacks in the Shenandoah Valley. In doing so, Sheridan went after the remaining sources of supply of Lee's army, burning the barns and mills while confiscating the livestock. In short, by year's end, Lee's Army of Northern Virginia— surrounded by a line of Union trenches that stretched from the outskirts of Richmond to Petersburg—found itself in a perilous position.

Hard fighting had marked the last two years of the war. The Union's fortunes had risen considerably during 1863, when it won impressive victories in the campaigns to take Vicksburg, defeat the Rebel offensive at Gettysburg, and seize Chattanooga. But none of those victories, however important, crippled the Army of Tennessee or the Army of Northern Virginia. Not until late spring 1864 did Union persistence and perseverance under the leadership of generals Sheridan, Sherman, and Grant begin to cause the gradual disintegration of the Rebel armies that opposed them, and by the end of 1864, only Lee's poorly fed Army of Northern Virginia remained a viable fighting force.

It would be up to Grant, of course, to lead the final campaign for Union victory. His impressive early victories in the West, his successful offensive in the heartland, and his relentless attacking in the east had conspired to make him a man of destiny. More than a strategic and tactical military genius, Grant held a political and constitutional conception of the war that condemned both secession and slaveholding. Both during the war in his August 1863 letter to Washburne and later in his *Memoirs*, Grant presented the conflict as fundamentally between those who sought to preserve slavery and those who hoped to end it. "The South claimed the sovereignty of States, but claimed the right to coerce into their confederation such States as they wanted, that is, all the States where slavery existed," he wrote in his *Memoirs*. "They did not seem to think this course inconsistent. The fact is, the Southern slave-owners believed that, in some way, the ownership of slaves conferred a sort of patent of nobility—a right to govern independent of the interest or wishes of those who did not hold such property. They convinced themselves, first, of the divine origin of the institution and, next, that that particular institution was not safe in the hands of any body of legislators but themselves."[51] It was a conception of the war that perfectly mirrored the evolving priorities and policies of the Lincoln administration.

6
POLITICS AND CONSTITUTIONALISM IN THE WARTIME UNION, 1861–1864

On Saturday afternoon, June 29, 1861, after leading a Cabinet meeting on military strategy, President Abraham Lincoln strode out of the south portico of the White House. Joined by his wife as well as an assortment of generals, Cabinet members, and a "cluster of ladies in hoopskirts and blossoming bonnets," the president greeted friends and associates before making his way to the flagpole on the south lawn. A large crowd had gathered there to see the new president and to hear the marine band play a concert. As the band struck up the "Star-Spangled Banner," soldiers stood at attention and civilians doffed their hats. All focused their gaze on Lincoln and the flag. "When the president pulled the cord, it stuck," Julia Taft Bayne wrote later. "He pulled harder, and suddenly the upper corner of the union tore off and hung down." Horrified at the symbolism of a torn flag, a gasp went up from the dignitaries who surrounded the president. At once, a quick-thinking staff officer asked the ladies for pins, and several women, including Mrs. Lincoln, readily supplied them from their dresses and collars. "The officer swiftly and efficiently pinned the corner, and the flag was raised," Bayne reported.[1] Most of the onlookers—too far away to have seen what actually occurred—noticed only a delay in the raising of the banner. Many of those who did witness the episode kept the ominous occurrence to themselves, so as not to alarm the superstitious.

The ripping of the American flag that day on the White House lawn was an apt metaphor, for the new president confronted a country that had been torn in two. During the next four years, Lincoln labored tirelessly to mend the Union. Doing so involved taking a series of extraordinary steps. In addition to directing the US military to suppress the rebellion, Lincoln exercised unprecedented executive power, worked with Congress to build the apparatus of a powerful national state, and used the rhetorical power of the presidency to give meaning and purpose to the war effort. But more than simply stitching together the pieces of the fragmented Union, Lincoln both shaped and responded to a series of political pressures—from white and black abolitionists, as well as enslaved African Americans seeking their freedom—to bring about the abolition of slavery. Throughout the war, the Republican president aroused fierce opposition from Democrats, as well as from many within his own party, but he never wavered and eventually won reelection to a second term. By the end of 1864, Lincoln seemed close to realizing his goal of establishing "a new nation, conceived in liberty and dedicated to the proposition that all men are created equal."

LINCOLN, HABEAS CORPUS, AND THE SHOWDOWN WITH TANEY

A young and untried executive with little experience in Washington, Lincoln faced a number of challenges when coming into office. The first involved selecting his Cabinet. The new president needed to draw on the wisdom of more experienced hands while also placating the disparate factions within his party and assembling a geographically diverse group. After consulting with vice president–elect Hannibal Hamlin in Chicago a few days after the election of 1860—the first time the two men had ever met—the incoming president turned to his rivals for the Republican nomination. The leading figure within Republican circles, New Yorker William H. Seward, had served twelve years in the Senate and four years as a governor. Deeply disappointed that he had not received the nomination and the presidency, Seward still desired a seat in the Cabinet, primarily because he hoped to be able to dominate the new president and his administration. Lincoln offered him the post of secretary of state, which Seward accepted. Not until after Seward had agreed to serve did Lincoln approach his second chief rival, Salmon P. Chase of Ohio. A former Democrat, the Ohioan had made his name as an antislavery lawyer in the 1840s, and in subsequent years he helped found the Republican Party in his home state, served as governor, and took a seat in the US Senate in 1860. Ambitious and sanctimonious, Chase did not get along well with others, and he had a particularly contentious relationship with Seward. Chase accepted the invitation to become secretary of the treasury. A third rival for the nomination, Edward Bates of Missouri, was Lincoln's choice for attorney general, an appointment that satisfied a number of important constituencies. Bates was a conservative antislavery former Whig and Know-Nothing from a border state. Other Cabinet appointments also reflected the necessity of achieving both political and geographical balance. Lincoln's nomination of such a strong cast displayed the weak political position in which he found himself, as well as his own personal self-confidence. With the exception of Secretary of War Simon Cameron, whom Lincoln dismissed after less than a year for corruption, this so-called team of rivals served the president well.[2]

In the weeks after the outbreak of war, in consultation with Cabinet members and generals, Lincoln took several steps to meet the crisis at hand. On the day after the fall of Fort Sumter, he issued a proclamation that included three orders: calling Congress into session on July 4, 1861, commanding the Rebels "to disperse, and retire peaceably," and calling forth "the militia of the several States of the Union to the aggregate number of seventy-five thousand."[3] The latter constituted a request to the states to send 75,000 militia volunteers, who would then be federalized for the maximum amount of time under law at the time, ninety days. On April 19, he ordered a naval blockade of the ports of the seceded states, and in early May he called for more than 40,000 three-year volunteers while also increasing the size of the regular army and navy. Congress was not in session, and the president implemented all of these emergency measures on his own authority. Although Ohio congressman Clement Vallandigham expressed outrage at these "high-handed usurpations of power," neither a court challenge nor much political fallout ensued.[4]

Lincoln's decision to suspend the privilege of the writ of habeas corpus, in contrast, provoked substantial criticism. Events in the state of Maryland, which had never been hospitable to Lincoln, precipitated the decision. The state had gone for Breckinridge in the 1860 election, and well before the outbreak of the war, in February 1861, fears of assassination at the hands of pro-Confederate elements had forced the president-elect to pass through Baltimore on a night train in disguise. On April 19, a fracas between Union soldiers and Confederate sympathizers in Baltimore had resulted in several deaths, and that night pro-Confederate forces burned key railroad bridges, allegedly out of fear that other Federal soldiers would invade the city in retaliation. Rumors of secession and violence were rife. The day after the Baltimore riots, the president asked Attorney General Edward Bates to look into the legality of suspending the privilege of the writ of habeas corpus in parts of Maryland, primarily to ensure that adequate troops could be transported to the national capital and that telegraph lines would remain intact.

No precedent existed in American history for a president to suspend the privilege of the writ. Originating in English common law centuries before, habeas corpus literally means "you have the body," and the writ served as a legal order to bring a person before a court. In practical terms, the writ ensured that no one could be detained without cause. Suspension of the writ meant that one would not have protection against detention. Because of the fundamental nature of this right, the American founders had exalted habeas corpus by placing it in Article I, Section 9 of the Constitution, in the list of restrictions on the powers of Congress. In essence, it was one of the few rights written into the original Constitution, before the addition of the Bill of Rights. "The Privilege of the Writ of Habeas Corpus shall not be suspended," the text reads, "unless in Cases of Rebellion or Invasion the public Safety may require it." Only under specific circumstances, rebellion or invasion, could Congress take such a step, and at the time that Lincoln asked his attorney general to look into the matter, Congress had never before done so. A president had certainly never done so. The leading constitutional scholar of the early nineteenth century, Justice Joseph Story, had concluded that only Congress possessed any power relative to suspension of the writ. In sum, habeas corpus possessed a distinguished constitutional pedigree, only Congress appeared to have any power to suspend the writ (in specific circumstances), and Congress had never exercised this power.

During the few days after Lincoln asked Bates to look into suspension, the situation in Maryland became particularly perilous. The president waited anxiously in the White House for more troops to arrive, guarded only by several shaken companies of the Sixth Massachusetts regiment, the troops who had been attacked in Baltimore. According to his secretaries, John Hay and John Nicolay, the new president lived during these days in a "state of nervous tension," wondering when more troops would arrive.[5] In the midst of widespread fear of an invasion of the national capital, and just after the Maryland legislature refused to consider a secession ordinance, a determined bunch of federal troops arrived in Washington. Led by Brigadier General Benjamin Butler, the soldiers had commandeered a steamboat to cross the Chesapeake Bay and then repaired railroad tracks running out of Annapolis before arriving triumphantly in the nation's capital. Within days, thousands of troops began pouring into the city.

With the crisis averted, on April 27, 1861, Lincoln authorized the suspension of the privilege of the writ of habeas corpus. In an unpublicized letter to General Winfield Scott, Lincoln instructed the general to take action to protect the capital: "If at any point on or in the vicinity of any military line, which is now or which shall be used between the City of Philadelphia and the City of Washington, . . . you find resistance which renders it necessary to suspend the writ of Habeas Corpus for the public safety, you, personally or through the officer in command at the point where the resistance occurs, are authorized to suspend that writ."[6] Maryland having officially cast its lot with the Union, Lincoln acted not to shut down the secessionist movement but to prevent further interference with the transportation of Union troops into the city.

Two weeks later, the president issued a public proclamation that similarly authorized the Union commander to suspend the privilege of the writ in Florida, where the islands of Key West, the Tortugas, and Santa Rosa remained in Union hands. Subsequent orders expanded the scope of the suspension to other areas.

Within a month of the order to Scott, a legal challenge came to Chief Justice Taney. Despite his overt sympathy for the Confederate cause, after the outbreak of war, the aging chief justice remained on the bench, and he heard this case in his capacity as a federal circuit judge in Maryland.[7] John Merryman, a Baltimore County farmer, had allegedly burned bridges and cut telegraph wires in the aftermath of the riots. Arrested at his home in the middle of the night and taken to Fort McHenry by Federal forces on May 25, Merryman petitioned for a writ of habeas corpus, whereupon Taney ordered that such a writ be issued. When the writ was served, Brevet Brigadier General George Cadwalader, who oversaw Merryman's detention, refused to "produce the body" of Merryman and instead informed the chief justice that he had been duly authorized to suspend the writ. The following day, Taney directed the clerk of the court to transmit a copy of his opinion on the matter to the president.

Taney's twenty-page opinion blasted Lincoln's suspension of the writ. Drawing on history, precedent, common law, and the constitutional text, Taney argued that the president lacked the authority to take such action. Only Congress had the power to do so, he contended, and any person arrested by a military officer should be turned over to civil authorities rather than be subject to military trial. In general, the chief justice claimed, the powers of the president were narrow and restricted. Serving "the brief term of four years" (Taney at that point had been chief justice for twenty-four years), the president, under the Constitution, acted mostly as an administrator. Although deemed "commander in chief of the army and navy," he relied on Congress to raise an army and allocate funds. Although he could negotiate a treaty, he needed the Senate to ratify it. And, in Taney's words, he "is not empowered to arrest anyone charged with an offence against the United States, and whom he may, from the evidence before him, believe to be guilty; nor can he authorize any office, civil or military, to exercise this power."[8] In the chief justice's view, the president possessed the power neither to suspend the writ nor to authorize arrests.

If presidential power was limited, individual liberty was paramount. The Fifth Amendment, according to Taney, offered protection to Merryman and anyone else who might be arrested by federal authorities. "The fifth article of the amendments to the Constitution expressly provides that no person 'shall be deprived of life, liberty, or property, without due process of law'—that is, judicial process," Taney wrote.[9] Such protections originated in English common law and, through judicial precedent and legal treatises, had become deeply entrenched in American constitutionalism. Emphasizing individual liberty, Taney mentioned the Fifth Amendment four times in the opinion, nearly as often as he did the portion of the constitutional text that specifically dealt with habeas corpus. With confidence in the soundness of the decision, Taney enjoined the president to fulfill his obligation "to take care that the laws be faithfully executed" and to "cause the civil process of the United States to be respected and enforced."[10] Merryman was not the only civilian incarcerated at Fort McHenry under Lincoln's order. Frank Key Howard, grandson of Francis Scott Key, also ended up in the Baltimore fortress—made famous, ironically, as the very place during the War of 1812 where his grandfather had witnessed the flying of the American flag that had inspired him to write "The Star-Spangled Banner."

The president ignored Taney's opinion in the short term, but a little more than a month later, in a July 4 written message to Congress, Lincoln offered a brief response. While Taney had viewed the suspension of the writ as a rights issue, Lincoln framed the debate in a different way—as a matter of national survival. Underscoring the fact of a large-scale rebellion against the government of the United States, Lincoln offered a rationale for his actions. "The whole of the laws which were required to be faithfully executed, were being resisted, and failing of execution, in nearly one-third of the States," he argued. "Are all the laws but one [habeas corpus] to go unexecuted, and the government itself go to pieces, lest that one be violated?" Lincoln believed that the suspension served the greater purpose of preserving the Union, and in the same message he described the Union cause as synonymous with the larger cause of liberty. "On the side of the Union," he argued "it is a struggle for maintaining in the world that form and substance of government whose leading object is to elevate the condition of men—to lift artificial weights from all shoulders—to clear the paths of laudable pursuit for all—to afford all an unfettered start and a fair chance in the race of life."[11] Long a devotee of the ideals of free labor, which he saw as embodied in the Declaration of Independence, Lincoln attempted to link the principles of freedom to the survival of the government of the United States.

The showdown between Lincoln and Taney presented in stark terms the constitutional questions created by the war. In a sense, the dispute captured a long-standing tension in American constitutional history over the relationship between liberty and power. Heir to the late eighteenth-century republican perspective that viewed concentrated power as the enemy of liberty, Chief

Justice Taney attempted to protect individual rights from the exercise of executive power. At the same time, confronted with a massive rebellion in eleven states, Lincoln attempted to preserve the republic and, he believed, advance the larger cause of liberty. Despite this high-profile constitutional contest, two months after being taken into custody, Merryman was released. Although indicted for treason, the case never went to trial, and the charges against him were eventually dropped.

CONGRESS AND THE REPUBLICAN AGENDA

On July 4, 1861, the eighty-fifth birthday of the United States, the unfinished Capitol dome beckoned members of the 37th Congress to a special session. Although it had been only half a year since they had gathered for the start of the previous session in December, the new Congress looked very different than before. Gone was one of the giants. Stephen Douglas, who first took a seat in the House of Representatives in 1843, had died on June 3. After Lincoln's election, Douglas had firmly supported the new president, and between the presidential election and the evacuation of Sumter, Lincoln had conferred with his old rival on four different occasions. After Douglas's death, Lincoln ordered that all government offices close on the day of his funeral and that the White House be draped in mourning for thirty days. Gone too were the Southerners, who had begun leaving their seats as their respective states seceded. The South Carolinians had withdrawn from Congress first, just days after Lincoln's election, not even showing up for the start of the session in December. During the first few months of 1861, one by one their Southern brethren in both the Senate and the House joined them in departing. Senator Andrew Johnson, the stubborn Unionist from East Tennessee, was the only member of Congress from a seceded state who remained. With the Confederates having left, Republicans were ascendant. Orville Browning, a Republican friend of Lincoln's, took Douglas's old Senate seat from Illinois. Two senators and a single representative from the new state of Kansas took their seats for the first time, all of them Republicans. And a host of other Republicans, either elected for the first time or reelected to their positions, joined them as the session got underway. Republicans held 108 of the 183 seats in the House of Representatives and 31 of 50 Senate seats. Others were quasi-Republicans: three senators called themselves Unionists, while another thirty-one representatives either claimed the Unionist or Independent Democrat label. With such majorities, Republicans would dominate the 37th Congress.

Initially, it seemed, legislators of all political persuasions were united by a belief in limited war aims. On July 25, 1861, three weeks into the session and four days after the disastrous defeat at Bull Run, Congress passed almost unanimously the Crittenden-Johnson Resolutions. Sponsored by Senator John Crittenden of Kentucky and Senator Johnson of Tennessee, both from slaveholding states, the resolutions announced support for a limited war—one fought not for the purpose "of overthrowing or interfering with the rights or established institutions of these states," but only to "defend and maintain the supremacy of the Constitution and all laws made in pursuance thereof and to preserve the Union."[12] Approved early in the war, at the time when the Lincoln administration viewed the loyalty of the border states as the key to a surge of Southern Unionism, the resolutions reflected both military intentions and political goals.

Despite the conservative tone of the resolutions, a broader free labor agenda was never far from the minds of many Republicans. In 1859, while positioning to run for president, Lincoln had outlined a vision for the nation that stood in stark contrast to the view of Southern planters that every society required a "mudsill" to perform mundane labor. Most Americans, Lincoln noted, were neither masters nor slaves, neither hirers nor hirelings. Instead, most were independent farmers and laborers who desired upward mobility. Even the status of those who occupied the lowest rungs of society was not "fatally fixed for life," Lincoln argued.[13] Providing land and education to laborers, along with dignity and freedom, would eventually produce a free and productive society. Reflecting the influence of former Whigs, Republicans held a deep belief in social harmony and possessed tremendous faith in Americans' common progress. The party's platform in 1860 echoed these themes and included a number of ideas that, once in power, Lincoln and his congressional allies hoped to implement: a higher tariff to promote domestic economic growth, a homestead act to offer cheap land to Western settlers, internal improvements to promote national commerce, and a transcontinental rail route to settle the West.

Slavery figured prominently in the free labor equation, and the radical wing of the Republican Party pushed the issue to the top of the national agenda at a relatively early stage in the war. Despite the conservatism of the Crittenden-Johnson Resolutions, during the first few months of the conflict a quiet revolution appeared to be brewing on the slavery question. While in command of Union forces at Fortress Monroe, in late May Union general Benjamin Butler had faced the absurd spectacle of a Virginia planter requesting that three of his escaped slaves, who had fled to the fort, be returned to him under the Fugitive Slave Act. Noting that Virginia claimed it was no longer part of the

United States, General Butler offered to return the slaves only if the planter swore an oath of loyalty to the Union. When the Virginian refused, Butler, a lawyer, claimed the slaves as "contraband of war." The idea stuck. In the ensuing weeks, escaping slaves streamed into US forts and camps, and in July the administration seemed to express support for this contraband policy. On July 4, Secretary of the Treasury Chase sent a report to Congress recommending, in general terms, the seizure and sale of "the property of those engaged in insurrection."[14] Referred to the Senate Judiciary Committee for study, Chase's report fell into the hands of Lyman Trumbull, one of only five senators who opposed the Crittenden-Johnson Resolutions. Over the next few weeks, Trumbull and his colleagues crafted legislation that gave statutory structure and authority to Butler's initial order. By this time, according to one historian, nearly a thousand slaves had already made their way to Union lines.[15]

The proposed Confiscation Act provided that any slaves being used by the Confederate military were liable to federal seizure, just like vessels on the high seas. In essence, Congress attempted to apply the principles of international law—law between two separate, warring nations—to America's civil war. It was a potentially problematic legal strategy and an even more volatile political one. A contentious debate ensued in Congress, in which border state senators and representatives warned that such a measure signaled that a general emancipation lay in the future, but the bill ultimately passed in both houses. Lincoln doubted both the constitutional and political soundness of the legislation, particularly in light of the Union's inglorious defeat at Bull Run. But with strong pressure from the radical wing of his party, the president signed the bill into law. Enacted August 6, the Confiscation Act was the most significant legislative act of 1861 and the first piece of federal legislation ever to regulate or interfere with slave property in the Southern states. When Congress reassembled for its second session in December, Radicals such as Representative Thaddeus Stevens succeeded in tabling an attempt to renew the Crittenden-Johnson Resolutions. In the months and years ahead, Stevens and other like-minded members of Congress would continue to push for federal action against the South's peculiar institution.

Democrats, meanwhile, found themselves on the outside looking in for the first time in their history. Ever since the party's rise to power in the days of Andrew Jackson, Democrats had dominated national politics. Between 1829 and 1861, Democratic presidents occupied the White House for all but four years, and the party controlled Congress during all but eight of these years. With the South seceded and Lincoln elected, however, the Democrats who remained in Congress constituted a small and inexperienced minority. Many of the party's leaders had been Southerners—Jefferson Davis, Alexander Stephens, and John C. Breckinridge, for example—and with Douglas and Buchanan having passed from the scene, few experienced lawmakers remained. At the opening of the 37th Congress, three-quarters of the Democrats in the House were serving their first terms in office, while eight of the eleven Democrats in the Senate were doing so. However inexperienced, congressional Democrats clung to the ideals that had long defined their party: limited government, low tariffs, individual liberty, slaveholders' rights, and white supremacy. As Lincoln and the Republicans sought to preserve the Union by promoting a Republican agenda, three Democratic factions eventually emerged. War Democrats responded to Lincoln's attempts to promote patriotism over partisanship and generally backed the president's policies. At the state level, they often formed Union coalitions with Republicans. Regular Democrats, the largest group, supported the idea of a war for the Union but often disagreed with the president's prosecution of the war, particularly his interference with civil liberties, his policy of emancipation, and his treatment of Democratic generals. Peace Democrats, a small but vocal faction, opposed the war outright, called for negotiations with the Confederacy, and railed against the gradual accretion of federal power.

ECONOMIC POLICY

Economic policy resulted from both the practical needs of a wartime state and the ideology of Republicans. Raising revenue to pay for the Union war effort was the government's most immediate concern. When Lincoln came into office, he inherited a disastrous budget situation, for the Buchanan administration "had created the largest debt ever accumulated by an administration without engaging in war."[16] At the time, the government's reach and resources were limited. Before 1861, the federal government had raised revenue from two main sources—the collection of the tariff and the sale of public lands. Financing a massive military mobilization to suppress a rebellion in a third of the country would require more extensive and creative steps.

Secretary of the Treasury Chase initially believed the government would need about $320 million in the first year to wage a war, and he advocated a number of measures to achieve this goal. First, he pushed for increases in the tariff. Republicans had already raised tariff rates through the Morrill Tariff Act in March, signed into law in the last days of the Buchanan administration as a way of dealing with the fiscal crisis. Chase asked Congress to increase rates again in the hopes of securing about $80 million. Second, he asked for new excise taxes. Such duties had not existed since the early days of the Republic, when Alexander Hamilton had taxed distilled whiskey, but Chase hoped to raise about $20 million through taxing various enterprises associated with the domestic manufacture and distribution of goods. Third, the secretary asked Congress to approve issuing $200 million in bonds, so as to tap the patriotic spirit of the people. Finally, Congress planned to raise another $20 million through imposing an income tax. Signed into law by Lincoln on August 2, 1861, the income tax actually did not go into effect until further adjustments and amendments to the policy were enacted nearly a year later.

Despite these measures, Northerners witnessed considerable economic uncertainty during the early months of the war, some of which stemmed from government policies. It soon became clear that initial efforts to fund the war would prove insufficient, as federal expenditures rose more rapidly than expected. At the outset of the war, the entire federal budget stood at just under $67 million, but within six months, the government was spending nearly $2 million per day to feed, clothe, and equip the Union Army and Navy. Chase's estimate had proven low, in other words, and the government needed more revenue. A potentially explosive diplomatic incident between the United States and Great Britain only exacerbated financial uncertainty. In November 1861, the Union Navy intercepted a British vessel, *Trent*, and seized two Confederate diplomats who were on the way to Britain and France to seek recognition of the Confederacy. Although the Lincoln administration ultimately released the prisoners and resolved the situation, for several weeks, the threat of war with the world's greatest economic power spooked investors. Because specie—gold or silver—backed the notes issued by both the US government and the banks, the so-called Trent Affair, combined with the government's shaky finances, led to the hoarding of gold. A lack of gold in the treasury, quite simply, prevented the government from meeting its obligations. At the end of 1861, the Northern economy stood poised to fall off a metaphorical cliff.

As the situation worsened, many in Congress suggested paying the government's bills in paper money, backed not by gold but by the people's faith in their government. Opponents of this idea were legion. Chase himself had long been a hard money advocate, and only the exigencies of the moment caused him to reconsider his position. Some critics feared that excessive inflation and further uncertainty would result from such a drastic step, while others decried the growing influence of the national government in making financial policy. A certain segment of Congress and the public simply believed that such fiat money was immoral. In both houses of Congress, Democrats led the opposition, joined by a handful of Republicans with strong ties to the banking industry. After a contentious debate, Congress passed and the president signed, in February1862, the Legal Tender Act. The law provided for issuing $150 million in banknotes, which would enter circulation as the government met its obligations, to military contractors and soldiers, for example. Printed in distinctive green ink, these greenbacks served as legal tender for all private and public debts (with the exception of tariff, which had to be paid in specie), and greenbacks soon began circulating throughout the country. When fears of hyperinflation proved unfounded, Congress authorized issuing two more installments of greenbacks, first in 1862 and again in 1863. Ultimately, almost $450 million in such notes entered circulation.

The war also brought about changes in the tax structure. After Chase's initial efforts proved inadequate, Congress went to work on a comprehensive package of tax increases that resulted in the Revenue Act of 1862. The act created the office of Commissioner of Internal Revenue, who would oversee a new bureaucracy of collectors and deputy collectors, as well as a web of taxes and regulations that touched nearly every type of transaction within the North's vast and complex economy. The new tax system led to higher prices for consumers, but it generated hundreds of millions of dollars in revenue. The Revenue Act also revised the income tax that had been passed the previous year but never implemented. The law imposed a 3 percent tax on those with incomes between $600 and $10,000 and a 5 percent tax on those whose incomes exceeded $10,000. Changes to the act, passed in 1864, created additional tax brackets. Under the Revenue Act, every American was "to make return in the list or schedule, as provided in this act, to the proper officer of internal revenue, of the amount of his or her income, . . . and in case of neglect or refusal to make such return, the assessor or assistant assessor shall assess the amount of his or her income and proceed thereafter to collect the duty."[17] Also administered by the Office of Internal Revenue, the nation's first income tax proved popular among Americans because it spread the burden of war financing throughout the population rather than favoring or harming specific classes of people.

Perhaps the most revolutionary change in economic policy came with the establishment of a national banking system. The existing financial structure in 1861 proved ill-suited to the demands of war. In addition to the greenbacks in circulation, about 1,600 different banks throughout the country issued their own notes—a recipe for corruption, counterfeiting, and financial chaos. Many of the circulating notes came from bogus banks or institutions that had gone out of business, while the value of other notes hinged on the reputations of the banks that issued them. At the end of 1862, in a rare public statement on economic policy, Lincoln strongly endorsed a system of government-chartered banks, in which, in exchange for purchasing government bonds, banks would be able to issue national banknotes. These notes would provide what the nation lacked—a "uniform circulating medium," as Lincoln put it.[18] Ultimately, nationalism and patriotism carried the day. In a notable speech to his colleagues, Senator John Sherman of Ohio argued that supporting the bank bill would promote a harmony of interests among "stockholders of banks, the people, and the Government." He even speculated that such institutionalized economic nationalism could have prevented the war in the first place. "If this system had been spread all over this country, and these banks had been established as agencies upon the basis of national credit," Sherman opined, "I believe they would have done very much indeed to maintain the Federal Government and to prevent the great crime of secession."[19] The House and Senate passed the measure by razor-thin votes, with voting along party lines. On February 25, 1863, Lincoln signed it into law.

The National Banking Act provided that five or more individuals could request a charter for a national bank, so long as they had at least $50,000 in capital stock and invested at least a third of it in government bonds. In effect, the law invited state banks to become national banks. In exchange for purchasing these bonds, the newly created Bureau of Currency in the Department of the Treasury would issue national banknotes to the bank in the amount of 90 percent of the value of the bonds. These notes would then circulate throughout the economy, alongside greenbacks and state banknotes. The law limited the value of these new notes to be issued to $300 million and required national banks to keep reserves on hand of 25 percent. Congress later made adjustments to the act, and the most important of these, passed in March 1865, placed a tax of 10 percent on all state banknotes, thereby driving these nonnational banks out of existence and reducing the inflation created by the excessive variety of notes still in circulation. In the final analysis, the purpose of the act was to stimulate the purchase of bonds, to regulate the supply of money so as to prevent inflation, and to cement the alliance between the financial class and the Union cause. The act proved one of the most innovative and useful pieces of legislation of the entire war.

Congress, moreover, through the Homestead Act of 1862, distributed Western lands to individual settlers. Reformers had long questioned the wisdom of federal land policy set during the 1780s, which resulted in the sale of large parcels to wealthy speculators, who in turn split up the land into individual plots to sell at a profit. Critics lambasted these "land sharks" and argued for a new policy that would make free Western lands available to individual cultivators. Republicans particularly took up the cause, for the idea of offering land to individuals conformed to their belief in free soil and free labor. Such legislation also promised to break speculators' monopoly on ownership and increase the national prosperity by creating more productive, tax-paying citizens. Democrats depicted homestead legislation as an unconstitutional exercise of congressional power and as poor fiscal policy. Although Congress had approved homestead legislation in 1859, President Buchanan vetoed it, and not until three years later, with Republicans in control, did a homestead bill pass. Under the Homestead Act of 1862, the government offered any head of family, male or female, up to 160 acres of unappropriated public land in exchange for living on the land for five years and paying a modest fee of $10. Not only did it offer an unprecedented opportunity for women to gain land, but the law also provided that immigrants who had declared their intention to become citizens were eligible, provided they had "never borne arms against the United States Government or given aid and comfort to its enemies."[20] The law also stated that these lands were not subject to any debts—meaning that the granting of a homestead promised an individual a fresh start. Despite its popularity—26,500 settlers claimed homesteads under the law—the Homestead Act was an imperfect policy. Only those who could afford to migrate could claim the land, and not all of the 160-acre plots distributed to settlers were sufficiently drought-free to ensure a productive living for their owners.

Another major piece of legislation, the Pacific Railway Act, provided for the expansion of railroads. Enacted a few months after the Homestead Act, the law aimed to spur the construction of a transcontinental railroad and telegraph line. Although members of Congress bickered over the exact terminus of the line, they agreed that a transcontinental railroad would aid the prosecution of the war, encourage economic integration of the East and West, and spur production for both domestic and foreign markets. In keeping with the pattern of antebellum railroad development, rather than build the line itself, Congress authorized private companies to carry out the task. The act incorporated the Union Pacific Railroad, which would construct a westward route from Nebraska, while the existing Central Pacific Railroad would build eastward from California. Under the law, Congress granted the right of way to the railroad companies and gave millions of acres in public lands and millions of dollars of loans—in the form of subsidized bonds—to the railroad companies in exchange for the construction of track from Omaha to Sacramento. When the sale of bonds to support the railroads lagged, Congress made the already generous terms of the law even more favorable to the industry. In an amendment to the act, passed in 1864, lawmakers increased the amount of the grants, added the rights to minerals found on these lands, and changed the financing requirements both by setting up a more lenient repayment plan and by making it easier for the railroads to raise their own capital from investors. Railroads thus received huge benefits from the legislation, while Native Americans lost another portion of their ever-vanishing domain and homesteaders complained that the railroad companies took control of the best lands. Nevertheless, both the administration and Congress viewed the extension of the nation's rail lines as an urgent matter, largely because they believed that the extraction of the West's vast mineral resources—including gold—would help the cause of the Union.

Taken together, the Union government's wartime economic policies provided revenue to sustain the Northern war effort, embodied the ideology of the Republican Party, and dramatically increased the role of the national government in the economy. Greenback currency ensured that money would circulate throughout the economy, taxation provided the assurance of future government revenues, and national banks brought stability to the financial system—all of which created an environment that boosted investor confidence. Aided by a propaganda campaign, bond sales proceeded at a steady pace and provided the bulk of war financing. In the end, $447 million in greenbacks, $667 million in tax revenue, and approximately $2.5 billion in bonds fueled the Union war machine. Homesteads and railroads, meanwhile, reflected the Republican vision of a populated, productive, and prosperous West. Rather than simply sell federal lands to acquire revenue for the treasury, Republicans hoped to create a free labor frontier, a republic of stable and prosperous settlements, connected to the East by railroad tracks and telegraph wires. Politically, all of these measures had been difficult to enact. In addition to igniting Democratic opposition to national power, they sometimes brought out divisions among Republicans, particularly between Eastern interests favorable to bankers and industrialists and Midwestern agriculturalists who were politically and culturally suspicious of concentrated capital. Unforeseen at the start of the conflict, Republican economic policies redefined federal power and reshaped the economy for years to come.

THE FEDERAL COURTS

During the war, Lincoln and the Congress remade both the staff and structure of the federal courts, beginning with the Supreme Court. Within a few months of taking office, Lincoln confronted three vacancies on the nation's highest court. One existed before he ever took office, another resulted from the death of Justice John McLean in March 1861, and a third seat opened up after the April resignation of Justice John A. Campbell, who returned to his home state of Alabama. Four years after *Dred Scott*, the infamous decision still rankled Republicans, and Taney's ruling in the habeas corpus case only served to remind many Northerners of why they held such animosity toward the Court. With five members of the seven-justice majority in *Dred Scott* still on the bench, Republicans sensed an extraordinary opportunity to remake the most powerful court in the land.

Proposals for judicial reform abounded. Horace Greeley's *New York Tribune* favored a plan to increase the number of Supreme Court justices from nine to thirteen. Taking the idea of Court packing a step further, in December 1861, Senator John P. Hale of New Hampshire introduced a resolution proposing that the Supreme Court be abolished altogether and that another Supreme Court, presumably made up entirely of Republican appointees, be created in its place. Hale questioned the very legitimacy of the Taney Court, which he regarded as a bastion of Democratic partisanship. "The Supreme Court of the United States, as at present established, has utterly failed," Hale asserted. "It is bankrupt in everything that was intended by the creation of such a tribunal. It has lost public confidence; it does not enjoy public respect; and it ought not." Although the constitutionality of the proposal was dubious at best, Hale justified his plan by engaging in an extremely loose reading of Article III, Section 1 of the Constitution. That section states that "the judicial power of the United States shall be vested in one Supreme Court and in such inferior courts as the Congress, may, from time to time, ordain and establish." Hale interpreted the phrase as allowing Congress to "ordain and establish" a Supreme Court whenever it chose to do so. "My idea is that the time has come," Hale argued. "That this is one of the very times the framers of the Constitution contemplated."[21]

While Hale's resolution received some support, most congressional Republicans viewed a reorganization of the federal circuits as a more prudent course. Lincoln had previously urged action on this issue and hesitated to make appointments to the Supreme Court until Congress had made changes. Because members of the Supreme Court also served as federal circuit court judges, any rearrangement of the circuits would affect the makeup of the Court. Twenty-five years had passed since Congress had last taken up the matter, and the states that had entered the Union since that time were not included in any circuit. Proposals to redraw circuit lines focused on redistributing the nation's population into nine relatively equal circuits based on the results of the 1860 census. Such a plan would also, not coincidentally, increase the number of Northern circuits and reduce the number in the South. Under the 1837 legislation, the slave states were spread among five circuits. Because one Supreme Court justice was appointed from each, Southerners usually had held a majority of seats on the Supreme Court. Under reorganization, the

Southern states would most likely be consolidated into three circuits. As debate dragged on about the exact groupings of the states, Lincoln proceeded to nominate his first justice. On January 22, 1862, Lincoln appointed Noah H. Swayne of Ohio to take the seat that had been held by the deceased McLean, another Ohio native. Swayne won quick confirmation in the Senate.

Over the next several months, as Congress continued to wrangle over the rearranging of circuits, the question of who would fill the remaining two seats on the Court became closely connected to how circuit lines would be drawn. Iowans in particular wanted to place their state in a different circuit from neighboring Illinois. Because Iowans hoped for the nomination of Samuel F. Miller, a respected lawyer and Republican leader in the state, they wanted to avoid being connected to Illinois, the home state of David Davis, a close Lincoln associate and another much-discussed possible nominee. Such disputes among various states containing aspirants for Supreme Court seats caused the debate over circuit reorganization to continue for more than seven months.

On July 15, 1862, Congress enacted legislation settling the matter. Under the new law, the first three circuits, covering New England and the Mid-Atlantic states, remained the same as before. The other six circuits, however, looked vastly different, with all of the slaveholding states consolidated into the Fourth, Fifth, and Sixth Circuits. Iowa was added to the Ninth Circuit, along with Missouri, Kansas, and Minnesota. This paved the way for the appointment of Miller. For months, Miller's Iowa friends and allies had not only played a critical role in the debate over circuit reorganization but had also flooded the White House with letters recommending their favorite son. The massive campaign paid off. On July 16, 1862, the day after circuit organization passed, Lincoln appointed Miller, who was unanimously confirmed the same day. Rearranging the circuits had allowed the president to fill the seat of Justice Peter V. Daniel, a Virginian, with an Iowan. After Miller's appointment, Lincoln appointed David Davis, judge of the Illinois circuit court, for the second position. Davis had known the president for many years and had worked tirelessly on his behalf both during his 1858 Senate race and during the presidential campaign. With this appointment, the Supreme Court again was composed of nine justices, three of whom owed their seats to Lincoln.

Congress took one more step to ensure Lincoln's imprint on the Court. During debate about the circuits, lawmakers generally assumed that the Western states, California and Oregon, would continue to be served by a circuit judge who did not sit on the US Supreme Court. Since 1855, an independent federal circuit judge had served California, but by the end of 1862, concerns arose about whether that judge was performing his duties, and

Republicans realized that elevating the Western circuit to a status equal to that of the others offered an opportunity for Lincoln to appoint an extra justice to the Supreme Court. With important cases regarding the prosecution of the war looming on the docket, Republicans knew that adding another seat would help solidify their party's grip on the Court. It made sense, moreover, to add a justice who was familiar with the complicated cases involving land titles that were coming from California to the Supreme Court at the time. During the month of February 1863, at the same time that the Court began considering the *Prize Cases*, a series of disputes involving the constitutionality of the blockade of the Confederacy, Congress initiated the process of adding a tenth justice to the Court. The action reminded the justices that Congress, under the Constitution, controlled the size of the Court and signaled that lawmakers were prepared to take such steps to ensure the successful prosecution of the war. Congress passed the measure creating the Tenth Circuit on March 3, 1863, and Lincoln signed the bill into law the same day. Immediately thereafter, the president appointed Stephen J. Field, a leading California jurist, to fill the new seat. A week later, Congress confirmed the nomination of a tenth justice of the Supreme Court.

These acts relating to the federal courts proved as important as the pathbreaking legislation pertaining to Union finances and Western lands. In the short term, these laws constituted a robust attempt by Congress to exert its constitutional authority over the structure of the courts. In the long term, they allowed Lincoln to appoint more Supreme Court justices than any other nineteenth-century president and severely limited Southern influence on the nation's highest tribunal.

LINCOLN'S EMANCIPATION PROCLAMATION

Despite the flurry of legislation relating to war finances, public lands, and federal courts, emancipation remained the most compelling and controversial issue on the national agenda. Lincoln's views on the subject were not exactly clear. Years before becoming president, Lincoln had expressed strong personal opposition to slavery in some of his private correspondence. Still, his public statements lacked the moral fervor of abolitionists, and during the 1850s his official position constituted no more than opposition to the spread of slavery into the territories. Lincoln thought long and hard about the issue, though, and the Declaration of Independence and the Constitution—and the relationship between the two—figured prominently in his thinking. In his debates with Stephen Douglas, Lincoln had frequently cited the Declaration's claim that "all men were created equal" as the basis for his contention that no person had a right to enslave another, that all were entitled to the fruits of their own toil. In December 1860, he took this idea a step further. In a note that he scribbled to himself while corresponding with Alexander Stephens, Lincoln described the Declaration as an "apple of gold" and the Union and Constitution as "the picture of silver, subsequently framed around it." He wrote, "The picture was made for the apple—not the apple for the picture. So let us act, that neither the picture, or apple, shall ever be blurred, or bruised or broken." In other words, the whole reason for the existence of the Constitution and the Union was to preserve the principle articulated in the Declaration, which Lincoln described as "liberty for all."[22]

As a lawyer and politician, Lincoln tempered his personal feelings about slavery with concern for the legality of any emancipation measure, as well as a keen political sense of the timing required for success. The president had rescinded General John C. Fremont's emancipation order in Missouri in 1861 on just such grounds, and he only grudgingly signed the Confiscation Act into law later that year. Congress obviously had its own agenda and timetable, and Radical Republicans continually pressed Lincoln on the subject. African Americans too forced the issue, mostly by continuing to leave plantations and head toward Federal military lines. But Lincoln, always careful in formulating his antislavery position, often spoke of colonization and compensation as conditions for the abolition of slavery. If the president and Congress quarreled over the specifics of emancipation policy, they ultimately agreed on the larger aim of moving against slavery, step by step, in order both to hinder the cause of the Confederacy and to advance the cause of liberty.

Major strides toward emancipation occurred in the first half of 1862, when military successes in the West coincided with legislation abolishing slavery in the nation's capital and in federal territories. The District of Columbia was the one area of the country over which Congress had unquestioned legal authority over slavery. A few weeks into the second session of the 37th Congress, Senator Henry Wilson of Massachusetts introduced a DC emancipation bill, and after an amendment that would have mandated colonization was narrowly voted down, the measure passed. The House approved it soon thereafter. In its final form, the law compensated loyal DC slave owners up to $300 for each slave and also set aside funds for those freed slaves who voluntarily wished to emigrate. On April 16, 1862, Lincoln signed the legislation, which incorporated the two principles—compensation and colonization—that he believed necessary for any successful scheme of emancipation. A few months later, Congress passed and Lincoln signed a law banning slavery in all existing federal territories and any that might be acquired in the future. The law liberated, without compensation, the handful of enslaved blacks who resided in Nebraska, New Mexico, and Utah. By enacting this law, Congress and the president for the first time directly challenged the Supreme Court's ruling in *Dred Scott*, which had upheld slaveholders' rights and denied to Congress power to prohibit slavery in the territories.

While Lincoln and his fellow Republicans agreed that they possessed legal authority over slavery in the District of Columbia and the territories, they did not see eye to eye on the issue of confiscating slaves held by Confederates. The intraparty dispute had originated when Lincoln rescinded Fremont's order. At the time, Radical Ohio senator Benjamin Wade condescendingly described Lincoln's decision as one that only a president "born of 'poor white trash' and educated in a slave state" could have taken.[23] In May 1862, General David Hunter had tried the president's patience when he too issued an emancipation order, this one pertaining to slaves held in South Carolina, Georgia, and Florida. Lincoln rescinded that order as well, prompting another round of criticism from the Radicals. Despite Lincoln's constitutional and political reservations about emancipating the slaves of Confederates, other Union military commanders—even some conservatives—were coming to the conclusion that Rebels had forfeited the rights to hold slaves. Writing in summer 1862 from Memphis, where he supervised a Union occupying force, General William T. Sherman reasoned that the act of secession nullified all Southern claims to the rights of property. In a letter to a former West Point classmate who sought the return of his slaves who had taken refuge in the city, Sherman explained why he would not cooperate. "We who contend for the old existing law," Sherman wrote, "contend that you by your own act take away your own title to all property save what is restricted by *our* constitution, your slaves included."[24] Sherman, though he harbored no antislavery sentiments, thought the Union needed to use all of the resources available to it— including black laborers—to win the war.

In July 1862, Radical Republicans led by Lyman Trumbull goaded Lincoln by passing the Second Confiscation Act. The act held that all slaves held by Confederates and their supporters—whether having escaped to Union lines or found in newly occupied Union territory—"shall be deemed captives of war, and shall be forever free of their servitude and not again held as slaves."[25] It also explicitly repealed the Fugitive Slave Law for all slave owners engaged in rebellion against the United States and authorized the president to use black troops to suppress the rebellion. These were significant steps, to be sure, and although Lincoln agreed with the spirit behind the legislation, he questioned its constitutionality and feared that it would not survive a challenge before Taney's Supreme Court. Ever the legalist, Lincoln believed that the president, rather than Congress, possessed the most constitutional authority to take action against slavery, as commander in chief of the armed forces in wartime. In the end, the president signed the Second Confiscation Act into law, but only reluctantly.

Lincoln became increasingly convinced that only a presidential proclamation could legally liberate slaves in the Confederacy. Just a few days before affixing his signature to the Second Confiscation Act, on July 13, Lincoln had told Secretary of State Seward and Secretary of the Navy Gideon Welles of his plans to issue just such a proclamation. "[Lincoln] had given it much thought," Welles later wrote in his diary, "and had come to the conclusion that it was a military necessity absolutely essential for the salvation of the Union, that we must free the slaves or be ourselves subdued."[26] Several days later, Lincoln presented the idea to the full Cabinet. Although Cabinet members gave the idea mixed reviews, the president was determined to move ahead. He did heed Seward's advice on the matter, which pertained to timing. Warning that an emancipation order would appear to be an act of desperation, Seward urged the president to delay until the Union had achieved a military victory.

In the meantime, Lincoln laid the political groundwork for a proclamation. In mid-August, he invited a delegation of African Americans to the White House—the first president ever to do so—in order to discuss the possibility of voluntary colonization of freed blacks. The invitation itself boldly proclaimed that Lincoln believed in some form of racial equality, while at the same time the subject of the meeting perhaps alleviated concerns in the border states and in the North that emancipation posed a threat to whites. A more important attempt to prepare the public for emancipation came in response to a Greeley editorial in the *New York Tribune*, where the influential editor had advocated decisive action on the slavery issue. Lincoln famously responded that whatever course he pursued "on slavery and the colored race," he would do for the sake of preserving the Union. "If I could save the Union without freeing *any* slave I would do it, and if I could save it by freeing *all* the slaves I would do it; and if I could save it by freeing some and leaving others alone I would also do that." At the end of his response to Greeley, published in the *Tribune* and throughout the land, Lincoln perhaps revealed a bit more of his hand. "I have here stated my purpose according to my view of *official* duty; and I intend no modification of my oft-expressed *personal* wish that all men every where could be free."[27] A careful lawyer and a skillful politician, Lincoln knew that only by connecting emancipation to the cause of preserving the Union could the proclamation win the support that it would need from the Northern public. Within days of military victory in the Battle of Antietam, the first Union success in the eastern theater, Lincoln made his announcement.[28]

On September 22, 1862, the president issued a Preliminary Emancipation Proclamation. Lincoln had begun composing it in early summer and had continued to labor over the text in the ensuing weeks at the Soldier's Home (a presidential retreat for Lincoln) and at the White House. Legalistic in tone, the language was clear and direct. The document began by asserting Lincoln's constitutional authority as commander in chief of the army and navy. Then it stated Lincoln's intention to recommend a "practical measure" to Congress that would encourage the seceded states to implement gradual emancipation measures, including voluntary colonization. Most important, Lincoln proclaimed freedom 100 days hence for enslaved African Americans: "That on the first day of January [1863] . . . all persons held as slaves within any state, or designated part of a state, the people whereof shall be in rebellion against the United States shall be then, thenceforward, and forever free." In contrast to the Confiscation acts, which he cited in the proclamation, Lincoln opted to use the term "persons held as slaves," rather than the word "slaves." In Lincoln's mind, the choice of words reflected the language of the Constitution, which referred to slavery only obliquely—and always by using the term "persons." Perhaps the most striking passage of the proclamation, though, was the pledge to use military power to "recognize and maintain the freedom of such persons" and to "do no act or acts to repress such persons, or any of them, in any efforts they may make for their actual freedom."[29] In essence, this provision signaled to enslaved African Americans—who had already anticipated these events—that the military would support any attempt that they themselves made to throw off the yoke of slavery.

The Northern reaction proved swift and, for the most part, predictable. Lincoln's Republican allies voiced strong approval. Radicals in Congress, such as Senator Charles Sumner, exulted over the president's action. "The skies are brighter and the air is purer, now that slavery has been handed over to judgment," Sumner stated in a speech in Boston.[30] Frederick Douglass expressed a dissenting view by lamenting the presidential proclamation's preference for legalistic jargon over moral fervor. The proclamation, in Douglass's words, contained no "expression of sound moral feeling against Slavery" and not "one word of regret and shame that this accursed system had remained so long the disgrace and scandal of the Republic."[31] True, the proclamation reflected Lincoln's lawyerly approach, particularly his concern that any move against slavery in the Confederacy stand on a sound legal basis. But opponents took no comfort in legalism. Northern Democrats saw the measure as a brazen attempt to turn what had begun as a war to preserve the Union into a dan-

Lincoln's signing of the Preliminary Emancipation Proclamation in July 1862, depicted here, shifted the emphasis of the war from preserving the Union to liberating enslaved African Americans. Courtesy of the Library of Congress, LC-USZ62-2070

gerous crusade to liberate slaves. Their outrage combined constitutional conservatism, overt racism, and fear of a black uprising and social revolution. Horatio Seymour, the Democratic candidate for governor of New York in 1862, described emancipation as "a proposal for the butchery of women and children, for scenes of lust and rapine, of arson and murder, unparalleled in the history of the world."[32] Some War Democrats, who largely supported the president's agenda, questioned whether such a bold step was really necessary to save the republic.

Because the political impact of the proclamation proved ambiguous, the Lincoln administration continued to press its agenda. That fall, election results at both the federal and state levels showed signs of a Democratic resurgence, as Democrats won governorships in New York and New Jersey and gained control of the state legislatures in Indiana, New Jersey, and Illinois. In the US House of Representatives, Democrats went from holding 44 of 183 seats to 72 of 184 seats. At the same time, Republicans retained control of both houses of Congress, and the party of Lincoln even gained a number of seats in the US Senate. The increase in Democratic seats in the House, moreover, proved to be among the smallest of any minority party in an off-year election in American history to that point. Thus, despite its controversial emancipation policy, the administration seemed to enjoy broad public support in the North.

If the Preliminary Emancipation Proclamation sought to undermine slavery, a November 1862 opinion by Attorney General Bates took subtle aim at an even more entrenched foe—white supremacy. Bates's opinion came in response to a query from Secretary of the Treasury Chase about "whether colored men can be citizens of the United States." The legal inquiry originated when a federal revenue cutter detained a coastal trading vessel because it was commanded by an African American. The captain of the revenue cutter asked Chase to clarify whether blacks were citizens, "and therefore competent to command American vessels."[33] In a carefully reasoned discussion, Bates claimed that all people born in the United States possessed American citizenship. Relying heavily on European precedents stretching back to ancient Rome, as well as the US Constitution's reference to "natural born" citizens, Bates argued for birthright citizenship. Sidestepping the issue of slaves born in the United States, Bates concentrated on free blacks—those referred to in Chase's query—and concluded that no person born in the United States could be denied citizenship solely on the basis of their race or color. Bates dismissed the portion of the *Dred Scott* decision that pertained to citizenship as irrelevant, arguing that the ruling applied only to Scott's specific plea and possessed "no authority as a judicial decision."[34] Bates's opinion constituted an important part of the Lincoln administration's gradual assault on *Dred Scott*.

The decisive move against slavery came in the final Emancipation Proclamation, issued January 1, 1863. The document reaffirmed the president's constitutional authority as commander in chief and described the proclamation as a "fit and necessary war measure." Then, as indicated in the preliminary proclamation, the final version listed all of the areas still in rebellion against the United States and announced that, in these places, slaves were "henceforth and forever free." The four slaveholding border states that had remained loyal to the Union were exempt. All of the parishes surrounding New Orleans that were under federal occupation, as well as the entire state of Tennessee—which was mostly under Union control on January 1—were also exempt. This fact led many at the time to charge that Lincoln had freed only those slaves over whom he had no direct control. Again, though, in legal terms, Lincoln conceived of the situation in precisely the opposite way: he believed he only had authority over those slaves in areas still in rebellion, meaning controlled by the Rebels. Moreover, just because these areas were exempted from the proclamation did not mean that slavery remained undisturbed there, for slavery had already begun disintegrating in these areas at the first sign of Union military incursion.

Lincoln's Proclamation put the Confederacy on notice that the Union army would act as a liberating force, as it repeated the Preliminary Proclamation's promise "to recognize and maintain the freedom" of all enslaved persons in the Confederate states. From this point on, the Union military adopted the policy of "enticement"—the idea that Union troops could deliberately entice enslaved African Americans to Union lines in order to emancipate them.[35] The final Proclamation also provided for the use of black soldiers in the United States Army and Navy. This too proved a revolutionary step, as it signaled to Southern slaves that leaving their masters could result in a direct opportunity to engage in the fight against slavery. Finally, in a phrase recommended by Secretary Chase and perhaps in response to Douglass's criticism, the final Emancipation Proclamation concluded with a moral flourish: "And upon this act, sincerely believed to be an act of justice, warranted by the Constitution, upon military necessity, I invoke the considerate judgment of mankind, and the gracious favor of Almighty God."[36] Signing the final proclamation on New Year's Day, 1863, while Union soldiers were winning a crucial victory at Stones River, Lincoln reportedly proclaimed, "I never, in my life, felt more certain that I was doing right, than I do in signing this paper."[37]

The Emancipation Proclamation profoundly changed the political dynamic of the Civil War. However legalistic in tone, the Proclamation in practice transformed the war effort into a moral crusade to liberate slaves, initiated the enlistment of black soldiers into the Northern army, and helped win the support of wavering antislavery European powers, thus preventing their intervention on behalf of the Confederacy. In a broader sense, moreover, the Emancipation Proclamation undermined the Supreme Court's proslavery jurisprudence, thus transforming the decades-old debate over slavery. Although Lincoln expressed continued concern about a constitutional challenge to the Proclamation and wondered whether the measure could apply in peacetime, the boldness of the Proclamation—combined with Union victories on the battlefield—meant, over time, that forces appeared to be moving inexorably toward total abolition. Enslaved African Americans certainly thought so. By April 1863, fugitives were arriving at a "contraband camp" in Lake Providence, Louisiana, at a rate of 100 per day, while another camp in Grand Junction, Tennessee, reportedly already had a population of 1,700. Because the final Emancipation Proclamation mentioned neither compensation nor colonization, the debate no longer focused on conditions for black freedom. Rather, the only question seemed to be when ultimate Union victory and total emancipation would be achieved.

PRESIDENTIAL POWER AND CIVIL LIBERTIES

Emancipation only exacerbated existing fears about the unwarranted amalgamation of executive power. Ever since his initial orders suspending the writ of habeas corpus, Lincoln had taken a string of unprecedented actions. In September 1861, on the basis of intelligence about an impending secessionist riot and declaration of secession by the state of Maryland, the president had arrested and jailed at least twenty-seven Maryland state legislators, as well as a host of other state officials. In October, he had written to General Scott, granting him authority to suspend the writ of habeas corpus along a military line from Washington, DC, all the way to Bangor, Maine, even though no threat to the operation of the military existed there.

The next year Lincoln went further. In July 1862, Congress passed the Militia Act, which authorized the secretary of war to draft into military service members of state militias. A draft had no precedent in American history, and no one could have imagined such an act when the war began, when thousands eagerly enlisted to put down the rebellion. But the need for more troops was pressing. The draft of militia went into effect in early August 1862, along with a series of orders issued by Secretary of War Edwin Stanton that attempted to prevent individuals from avoiding military service. One of these orders—personally read and approved by Lincoln—suspended the writ of habeas corpus throughout the United States for those who evaded or opposed the draft, while another order imposed military trials for such persons, the first use of US military trials for civilians. Over the next month, according to one historian, the War Department arrested and imprisoned at least 354 Northern civilians under these orders.[38] Although another military order ended these arrests after a month, and although most arrests did in fact pertain to draft evaders, these measures placed extraordinary power in the hands of federal officials.

The sum of these actions, from the perspective of many Democrats, amounted to nothing less than tyranny. Energized by gains in the elections during the fall of 1862, Democratic opponents of the president stepped up their criticism. During the spring of 1863, political meetings, newspaper editorials, and legislative debates all reflected increasingly partisan rhetoric. Democrats generally charged that Lincoln and his allies in Congress had committed a litany of outrages that undermined the fundamental guarantees of constitutional liberty. Peace Democrats in particular called for an end to hostilities and the restoration of the status quo antebellum, while Union losses on the battlefield caused even some war-supporting Democrats to waver in the commitment to the cause, particularly since Lincoln had made emancipation a Union war aim. Republicans countered by deriding Peace Democrats as "Copperheads"—venomous snakes—whose criticism of the administration only helped the traitorous Confederates.

While the political rhetoric reached a fever pitch, the Supreme Court considered the constitutionality of one of Lincoln's first presidential acts, the blockade of Confederate ports. After the outbreak of hostilities, Lincoln had made the decision to blockade the major ports of the seceded states, a move later affirmed by Congress. Under the order, a variety of suits involving naval seizures of contraband came before the Supreme Court. Collectively known as the *Prize Cases*, the disputes raised the issue of the relative powers of the president and Congress during wartime, as well as the nature of the conflict between the Union and the Confederacy. Because these matters were very much intertwined, the *Prize Cases* posed a potential political minefield for the president. The existing rules of international and prize law implied that Lincoln's authority to wage war as commander in chief of the nation's armed forces depended on the sovereignty of the Confederacy, which the Lincoln administration refused to recognize. Conversely, a ruling that the war constituted a mere domestic insurrection threatened the president's power under law to blockade Southern ports.

On March 10, 1863, the Supreme Court upheld the blockade in a 5–4 decision. Justice Robert C. Grier, who penned the majority opinion, held that the existence of war constituted a matter of fact rather than law. "As a civil war is never publicly proclaimed, *eo nomine* [by that name] against insurgents," he wrote, "its actual existence is a fact in our domestic history which the court is bound to notice and to know."[39] The Union's refusal to recognize the sovereignty and independence of the Confederacy had no bearing on whether a state of war existed between them. Ironically, the justice buttressed his pro-Lincoln decision by citing England's neutrality proclamation. How could the owners of the seized vessels, who had brought suit in these cases, Grier wondered, "ask a court to affect a technical ignorance of the existence of a war, which all the world acknowledges to be the greatest civil war known in the history of the human race?"[40] This essential fact of war gave tremendous latitude to the president when it came to exercising his powers. As commander in chief, the president could legitimately exercise those powers in the face of a crisis like the one that the nation confronted after the attack on Fort Sumter. Although acknowledging that only Congress could declare war, Grier concluded that a president had no choice in such a situation but to take measures such as those taken by Lincoln. The president had power to institute a blockade of Confederate ports prior to obtaining the approval of Congress.

The dissenters, including Chief Justice Taney, argued that the fact of war meant nothing under the law, and by taking into account such matters, the majority of the justices were asking the wrong questions. Only congressional action, they contended, could formally and legally initiate a war. Once Congress did enact legislation that authorized Lincoln to interdict trade with the South—on July 13, 1861, after the president's blockade proclamation—the blockade became lawful. Congress could not, however, make its declaration apply retroactively, which it had attempted to do in order to legitimize Lincoln's actions. Because the dissenters admitted that the war assumed lawful status after the act of July 13, the justices' decisions proved to be less contentious than the political rhetoric leading up to the case. The decision in the *Prize Cases* in the spring of 1863 constituted an important constitutional victory for Lincoln and a pivotal ruling in the development of presidential war powers. By granting the executive wide authority to act as commander in chief and by refusing to acknowledge the sovereignty of the Confederacy, the outcome could not have been more favorable for the Lincoln administration.

Perhaps more than any other step taken by Congress and the president during wartime, conscription appeared to pose the greatest direct threat to individual liberty. Congress and the president had taken initial steps toward a draft in the Militia Act, but by 1863 the numbers of casualties and Union military failures in the eastern theater prompted Republicans to go further. "The needs of the nation demand that we should rely not upon volunteering, nor upon calling forth the militia," argued Senator Wilson of Massachusetts, in advocating a draft law, "but that we should fill the regiments now in the field, worn and wasted by disease and death, by enrolling and drafting the population of the country under the constitutional authority to 'raise and support armies.'"[41] Enacted in March 1863, the Enrollment Act made all men between the ages of twenty and forty-five years old subject to military service and established a bureaucratic structure to oversee the drafting and enrolling of soldiers (by lottery) in each congressional district, as the president believed they were needed. In effect, the act nationalized the enlistment of soldiers by avoiding the use of state militias. The law included an exception that allowed those actually drafted into service to "furnish an acceptable substitute to take his place in the draft" or to pay $300 to the War Department to avoid service.[42] Antiwar Democrats opposed the passage of the law and continued their criticism after its enactment. Anticipating a legal challenge that never came, both President Lincoln and Chief Justice Taney wrote out their thoughts on the constitutionality of the act.

The most prominent Copperhead, the two-term Ohio congressman Clement Vallandigham, assailed the law as well as Lincoln's high-handed assertions of power. In a series of speeches in early 1863, Vallandigham pressed his case to the point of arrest. On May 5, 1863, General Ambrose Burnside, acting on his own authority, detained and imprisoned the antiwar crusader in Dayton for "publically expressing . . . his sympathies for those in arms against the Government of the United States, declaring disloyal sentiments and opinions, with the object and purpose of weakening the power of the Government in its efforts to suppress an unlawful rebellion."[43] Tried and convicted before a military commission the following day in Cincinnati, Vallandigham was sentenced to military prison for the remainder of the war. His arrest made him a hero to the antiwar community and a headache to the Lincoln administration. Faced with the political conundrum of having used the military to detain an antiwar activist, Lincoln decided to exile the troublemaker to the Confederacy. Vallandigham remained in Dixie for less than a month before jumping a ship to Canada. A symbol for self-proclaimed liberty-loving Democrats, Vallandigham gained the unanimous nomination of the Ohio Democratic Party for governor.

That summer, Lincoln attempted to quell what was turning into a minor uprising in the North. Congressman Erastus Corning, a prominent War Democrat and president of the New York Central Railroad, organized a meeting in Albany that announced support for the war but opposed Lincoln's unprecedented actions. New York War Democrats were an important constituency, one that Lincoln had to cultivate in order to prevent the antiwar movement from gaining momentum. In a widely published June 12 letter to Corning and his associates, Lincoln responded to their criticism. Appealing to their desire to maintain the Union, Lincoln defended his actions by emphasizing that as president he faced "a clear, flagrant, and gigantic case of rebellion."[44] Lincoln strenuously argued that the existence of a rebellion allowed a president to take actions that would be neither justified nor necessary in ordinary times. "The Constitution is not in its application in all respects the same, in cases of rebellion or invasion involving public safety, as it is in times of profound peace and public security," he asserted. Pointing to the language allowing for the suspension of the writ of habeas corpus "in cases of rebellion or invasion," Lincoln held that "The Constitution itself makes the distinction."[45] Unconvinced that the war constitutionally augmented presidential power, Corning remained critical of Lincoln.

A month later, despite Union victories at Vicksburg and Gettysburg, the debate over presidential power and federal conscription spilled onto the streets. Violent opposition to the draft broke out in New York City, and for five days in mid-July 1863, antidraft rioters wreaked havoc. Venting their frustration, mobs composed mostly of young, working-class Irishmen attacked the offices of federal officials, the homes of the state's Republican elite, and the city's free black population. At least 100 people died. The riot put a violent political face on long-simmering local economic grievances and ethnic tensions, which the Emancipation Proclamation and the Enrollment Act had exacerbated. The more articulate protesters railed against the unfairness of the substitute and commutation provisions of the Enrollment Act, as well as against the prospect that emancipated blacks would flood north to steal jobs or drive down wages. Racial fear and hatred surely motivated many of the rioters, who burned New York's Colored Orphans Asylum and proclaimed their unwillingness to fight to liberate slaves. Minor antidraft disturbances broke out in other places, including Boston, and it took Union troops being ordered back to New York from duty at Gettysburg to restore order. Although some Republicans urged the president to declare martial law and come down hard on the insurgents, Lincoln thought it better to tread cautiously, and he appointed a local Democrat with ties to the city's political machine to take command of Union forces in New York.

That fall, still reeling from a summer of unrest, Lincoln and the Republicans fought hard to keep antiwar Democrats from making gains in state elections. In addition to Vallandigham's running for governor of Ohio, other Peace Democrats mounted challenges to prowar gubernatorial candidates in Pennsylvania, Minnesota, Wisconsin, California, New Hampshire, Rhode Island, Vermont, and Connecticut. The administration particularly singled out Vallandigham, who waged his campaign from Canada, and used the full muscle of the Republican Party and the government to prevent his election. Lincoln sent Ohio-born federal workers home on a two-week furlough to campaign, joined by Secretary of the Treasury Chase, an Ohio native. Vigorous politicking also ensued among Ohioans in the Union army, who voted in the field. These efforts succeeded. On October 13, 1863, Vallandigham lost by a large margin, and despite relative increases in voting for antiwar candidates in some states, all of the peace candidates nominated for governor went down to defeat. The antiwar movement had suffered a setback.

THE GETTYSBURG ADDRESS

On November 18, 1863, amid lingering Northern doubts about whether war was worth the cost, President Lincoln boarded a train to Gettysburg to help dedicate a cemetery. In October, Pennsylvania's Republican governor, Andrew Curtin, had won reelection by a slim margin over a Peace Democrat, and a week before Lincoln's arrival, the state supreme court had declared the federal conscription law unconstitutional. War pessimism still hung over the state.

Months after the Rebel invasion of Pennsylvania had resulted in the bloodiest battle in American history, some of the bodies at Gettysburg remained inadequately buried, a grim reminder of the war's high price. To confront the carnage and honor the dead, local leaders had formed a commission to develop a national cemetery near the site of the battle. They hired a rural architect to develop the plans, and they worked with Governor Curtin and the War Department to reorganize, identify, and rebury thousands of Union men who lost their lives in the three-day struggle. (Confederate dead were not included in the national cemetery.) With the extensive reburial process not yet completed, Lincoln agreed to close the ceremony with a few remarks. Using the opportunity to explain the meaning of the war, both to Pennsylvania and the nation, the president delivered his first prepared speech since his inauguration.

The Gettysburg Address, although a tight 272 words, touched on broad themes. "Four score and seven years ago," he began, "our fathers brought forth on this continent, a new nation, conceived in liberty, and dedicated to the proposition that all men are created equal."[46] By making reference to the founding of the country eighty-seven years before, Lincoln placed the battle within the larger arc of American history, thus connecting the work of Union soldiers at Gettysburg to the work of the Union's founders at Philadelphia. The date was significant. Lincoln marked the creation of the republic not with the ratification of the Constitution in 1787 but instead with the signing of the Declaration of Independence in 1776. Thomas Jefferson's Declaration supplied the founding principle that "all men were created equal," the principle for which, according to Lincoln, the war was now being waged.

Having nearly a year before issued the Emancipation Proclamation, a legalistic document, Lincoln now painted in bolder strokes. In a sense, he returned—as he had often expressed in his debates with Stephen Douglas—to his deep devotion to the Declaration of Independence and his assertion that equality among men meant that no person could be held as a slave. But speaking these words in the midst of a profound revolution, as African Americans walked off Southern plantations and into the United States Army, Lincoln seemed to be pushing the country toward an even loftier ideal. The president called for Americans to dedicate themselves to "the unfinished work" of those who had fought at Gettysburg, and he called for "a new birth of freedom" in the land. In doing so, he hoped to join America's founding ideal of equality with African Americans' aspirations for liberty. The speech, moreover, made much of the sacrificial nature of the Union deaths, for Lincoln noted that the "brave men" who struggled there had already "consecrated" the ground, "far above our poor power to add or detract." In August he had

Lincoln's delivery of the Gettysburg Address, shown in this detail of a photograph, represented the high point of Union wartime idealism, as Lincoln deftly attempted to resolve the sovereignty and slavery issues in a 272-word speech. Lincoln appears hatless, facing the crowd almost directly below the bare tree in the background. Courtesy of the Library of Congress, LC-DIG-ds-03106

taken note of black sacrifice in other battles when, in a letter to critics of emancipation, he had observed, "You say you will not fight to free negroes. Some of them seem willing to fight for you."[47] In trumpeting the ideals of the Declaration at a critical moment of black liberty and sacrifice, Lincoln at Gettysburg set out a new vision for the meaning of American freedom, the broadest definition of freedom the country had ever known. Less than four months later, Lincoln would suggest to the wartime governor of Louisiana that some African Americans should even have the right to vote. In short, if the Emancipation Proclamation had struck a blow against slavery, the Gettysburg Address took subtle aim at white supremacy.

Lincoln also attempted to define the meaning of American nationhood. The Constitution had not once referred to the United States as a "nation" and had consistently used the term "Union" instead. The major political speeches of the antebellum era, delivered by the country's most revered states-men, moreover, had almost always preferred the word "Union" to "nation." In his speech on the Compromise of 1850, in fact, Calhoun had mocked those who referred to the United States as a "nation." In his first inaugural address of 1861, Lincoln conformed to this antebellum rhetoric of Union, referring to "the Union" twenty times. Always using the term "Union" in the speech, Lincoln had not once referred to "the nation." Similarly, in his letter to Horace Greeley in 1862, just before issuing the Preliminary Emancipation Proclamation, Lincoln had repeatedly referred to his efforts to "save the Union." But by the end of 1863, Lincoln's rhetoric changed significantly. Although at his inauguration he had described the Union as having originated in the Articles of Confederation, matured under the Declaration, and been made "more perfect" with the Constitution, Lincoln at Gettysburg sketched out a very different history of America. Lincoln referred to the founders of 1776 as having "brought forth on this continent a new nation." The war had changed Lincoln's perspective. Wartime exigencies had vastly expanded the federal government, which Lincoln viewed, in a Hamiltonian sense, as a pow-erful means of unifying the people and promoting liberty. Only a united nation with a strong central government, he believed, could end slavery and promote freedom. Not once at Gettysburg did Lincoln refer to "the Union," a term that implied the existence—if not the assent—of the states. Instead, referring to "the nation" five times in a two-minute speech, Lincoln advocated a vig-orous national state based on popular sovereignty. Drawing on the Constitu-tion's preamble, Lincoln envisioned a government "of the people, by the people, for the people" that would bring about "a new birth of freedom" in America.[48] The speech succinctly captured Lincoln's beliefs, his shifting emphasis from the Constitution and "the Union" to the Declaration of Inde-pendence and "the nation." In a single eloquent oration, Lincoln offered his solution to the problems of slavery and sovereignty that had plagued the republic from the beginning.

THE SUMMER OF NORTHERN DISCONTENT

Northern support for the war effort tracked Union fortunes on the battle-field. Within a week of the Gettysburg Address, the Federals won a key vic-tory at Chattanooga, and the Lincoln administration went into winter confident that it was winning the war for public opinion. General Ulysses S. Grant's bloody Overland Campaign of 1864 changed all that. Within a mat-ter of months—from his being named a lieutenant general in March 1864 to the arrival of Union forces outside Petersburg in June—the general's stock plummeted as critics blamed him for the staggering losses in the field. The rapid rise in casualties at a time when many Northerners hoped for and expected a quick end to the conflict proved politically harmful to Lincoln. During the summer months of 1864, with Grant's army stalled outside of Petersburg and General William T. Sherman's forces stuck outside of Atlanta, criticism of the administration came from all sides.

Radicals within Lincoln's own Republican Party, who had never quite trusted the president, lashed out. Viewing the war as an opportunity to push an abolitionist agenda, they had never had much patience for Lincoln's legalistic, methodical attempts to free the slaves. By 1864, they especially worried about what would happen when the war ended. They favored a revolution in Southern society and the punishment of Confederate traitors. Concerned that Lincoln intended to implement a lenient reconstruction policy that would welcome the Rebels back into the Union and allow them to reorganize autonomous state governments, Radicals saw an opportunity to capitalize on Lincoln's declining political fortunes. With widespread opposition to the president's direction of the war, Radicals considered thwarting Lincoln's renomination and flirted with a number of potential candidates. Secretary of the Treasury Chase, who believed he had deserved the nomination in 1860, remained a favorite to many, as did the former general, John C. Fremont, whose 1861 emancipation order still made Radical hearts flutter. In July, Radical dissatisfaction with Lincoln culminated with a dispute over a congressional proposal for reconstruction known as the Wade-Davis Bill. When Lincoln pocket vetoed the measure, explaining that he favored flexibility in dealing with such matters, the Radicals howled. In early August, Senator Benjamin Wade and Representative Henry Winter Davis issued the Wade-Davis Manifesto in response, in which they accused Lincoln of dictatorship in attempting to formulate his own postwar reconstruction plans. "A more studied outrage on the legislative authority of the people has never been perpetrated," they wrote.[49] Black leaders were split in their opinion of the president. Lincoln had welcomed a delegation of African American leaders—most of them formerly enslaved—to the White House in April and had listened respectfully to their political demands and aspirations. Many such activists found Lincoln personally appealing but remained critical of what they saw as his hesitant and halting moves against slavery.

While Radicals hit the president from one flank, Peace Democrats assailed him from the other. Lincoln suffered particularly withering attacks at the hands of Democratic editors, such as Charles Chauncey Burr of the *Old Guard*, a New York monthly magazine. "In the name of liberty, the people have been arrested contrary to all law, and immured in military bastilles. In the name of the Constitution, the Constitution has been stricken down," Burr wrote in June 1864. "In the name of laws, the laws have been violated. In the name of freedom, the habeas corpus has been destroyed. In the name of humanity, a grand scheme of robbing and murdering the people of the South has been urged by the Abolitionists."[50] Slavery and racial issues in particular moved to the forefront of the Copperheads' criticism of Lincoln, as they condemned Lincoln's drift toward a more radical stance on abolition and black rights. Peace Democrats claimed that only the president's insistence on emancipation prevented an end to the war, and as proof, they pointed to a letter from Lincoln, written that summer, that said as much. They railed against what they saw as the needless sacrifice of white lives for the sake of black rights and frequently warned that abolition would lead to the promotion of "negro equality" and racial intermarriage. Playing on white fears about the consequences of black freedom, one Democratic editor nicknamed the Emancipation Proclamation the "Miscegenation Proclamation," while another claimed that the Republican Party aimed to change the name of the United States to "New Africa."[51]

Despite the overheated rhetoric on both sides that summer, neither end of the political spectrum wholly triumphed in the party conventions. The Democrats nominated George B. McClellan, the former Union general whose countless delays had stalled the Army of the Potomac during much of 1862. After having been dismissed by Lincoln at the end of that year, Little Mac had gone home to New Jersey, but by 1864 Democrats of all stripes saw the general in exile as a strong candidate to unite the party and unseat the president. Although McClellan was a War Democrat, the peace wing dominated the party convention. Vallandigham, who had slipped across the border and back into Ohio, wrote most of the platform, and Peace Democrats succeeded in nominating their choice for vice president, George Pendleton of Ohio. When McClellan released a statement in early September, reaffirming his support for the war, the political winds had shifted. Sherman had taken Atlanta, and General Philip Sheridan's successful operations in the Shenandoah Valley showed that the tide had turned. Favorable news from the front suddenly bolstered Lincoln's reelection chances.

Although a renegade group of Radicals had previously met to nominate Fremont as their candidate for president, Lincoln built a strong coalition of Republicans and War Democrats, who nominated him as the candidate of the Union Party, a wartime stand-in for the Republican Party. Governor Andrew Johnson of Tennessee, a War Democrat, won the vice presidential nomination, thus replacing Hannibal Hamlin. The combination of Union success on the battlefield and McClellan's nomination by the Democrats caused Radicals to close ranks behind the president. Black leaders, who held a convention of their own in Syracuse, New York, during the first week of October, acknowledged Lincoln's efforts on their behalf, roundly condemned Democratic racism, and called for further action in the future to ensure black freedom, progress, and enfranchisement. By fall, Lincoln was in a much stronger political position than he had been since the previous winter.

THE DEATH OF TANEY AND THE REELECTION OF LINCOLN

During the final three months of 1864, two momentous events converged within weeks of each other to signify the coming of a new political and constitutional order: Chief Justice Roger B. Taney died, and President Abraham Lincoln won a second term as president. The first event marked the symbolic end of a long period of Democratic control of the Supreme Court and the final passing of the proslavery jurisprudence that had been the hallmark of the Court's recent history. The second ensured that the war would continue until Grant and Sherman had defeated the enemy, and it confirmed that the abolition of slavery would result from Northern victory.

Eighty-seven years old and in failing health, Taney died on October 12, 1864. Three days later, Lincoln joined Secretary Seward and Attorney General Bates, along with the postmaster general, in attending a simple ceremony at the deceased chief justice's rented home in Washington before accompanying the casket to a nearby train station. From there, a special train transported the chief justice's body back to Frederick, Maryland, where he had spent his early career. Taney had served as chief justice since 1836, making him one of the longest-serving justices in American history to that point. Although he had believed in secession and viewed the war as a needless assault on Southerners, Taney held onto his position as chief justice of the United States, presumably to do all that he could to thwart Lincoln's agenda. He was the only member of the old *Dred Scott* majority who remained on the Court and sympathized with the Confederacy. During his tenure, with the appointment of four justices by Lincoln between 1862 and 1863, the Court became increasingly pro-Union and antislavery. The death of Taney marked the symbolic passing of the *Dred Scott* decision, and Radicals believed the chief justice's demise reinforced the revolution that was occurring before their eyes. "Providence has given us a victory in the death of Chief Justice Taney," wrote Senator Charles Sumner in a letter to Lincoln. "It is a victory for Liberty and the Constitution." A few days later, the *New York Times* identified Taney with the Confederate cause, arguing that the South's "Montgomery Constitution . . . does not contain a syllable in the interest of Slavery which is not found precisely in this Dred Scott Decision of Chief Justice Taney."[52] A few months later, acting upon the advice of Sumner and others, Lincoln appointed former secretary of the treasury Salmon P. Chase, a veteran of the abolition movement, as the new chief justice.

If Taney's passing marked a shift in the history of the Court and Constitution, Lincoln's reelection proved even more consequential. On November 8, Lincoln received 55 percent of the popular votes cast and 212 of 233 electoral votes, making him the first president to win reelection since Jackson more than three decades before. Of the twenty-five states participating in the election (excluding the eleven Confederate states), Lincoln won all but three and received at least 55 percent of the vote in fifteen of the twenty-five states he carried. In Kansas, where a decade before a bloody struggle over slavery had grimly presaged the violence of the war, Lincoln won nearly 80 percent of the vote. As president, Lincoln had utilized all of the powers of his office to help secure a second term. A week before the election, he and Congress speeded Nevada to statehood, thus allowing the president to gain its two electoral votes, and the administration had gone to great lengths to ensure that soldiers in the field would be able to participate in the voting. The president ended up receiving more than three-fourths of the ballots cast by men in arms. Despite his attempts to consolidate electoral support, Lincoln never considered postponing the election, and the fact that the voting went on in the midst of a civil war stands as a testament to Lincoln's faith in the people and the Constitution. The election certainly mitigates charges, then and now, that Lincoln simply set the Constitution aside and governed as a dictator. Overall, the results of the election of 1864 confirmed the war policy of the administration. Sherman's army would continue its march through Georgia on the way to Savannah, while Grant's army would persist in the siege of Petersburg. There would be no peace without victory, and no victory without abolition. Frederick Douglass viewed the election results as a "full and complete" endorsement of Lincoln's policies, "looking to the final extirpation of slavery from our land."[53] In effect, the electorate had ratified Lincoln's once-controversial strategy of attacking and pursuing the enemy while liberating and empowering enslaved African Americans.

By the end of 1864, Lincoln had guided the country through a terrible civil war, almost to its conclusion. Using the powers of his office, Lincoln had both shaped and responded to events. His unwavering commitment to his presidential oath gave him a clear-eyed determination to suppress the rebellion, and in order to do so, the president was willing to suspend the writ of habeas corpus, push bold financial legislation, and implement a controversial military draft. At the same time, Lincoln pursued the larger goals of the Republican Party, including enacting legislation to promote new uses of federal lands, transforming the federal courts, and issuing an Emancipation Proclamation to liberate slaves. War accelerated these changes, as the long and bloody conflict unleashed political and social forces unforeseen at the outset. Thousands of African Americans fled to military lines and put on the uniform of the Union army, thus exerting pressure on the president and the entire political system. Rather than simply stitch back together the fragments of a tattered Union, Lincoln had helped bring about a "new birth of freedom."

POLITICS AND CONSTITUTIONALISM IN THE WARTIME CONFEDERACY, 1861–1864

On January 12, 1863, in his office in Richmond, President Jefferson Davis put the finishing touches on a message to the Confederate Congress. The written report, submitted by Davis at the opening of the Congress's third session and officially received by lawmakers two days later, dealt with a variety of important matters, including military campaigns, foreign affairs, and government finances. Despite these pressing concerns, President Davis could not help but refer briefly to another matter—one which, the more he thought about it, perhaps grew in importance in his mind. Some days before, newspapers had reported that his Union counterpart had signed the Emancipation Proclamation, and the Confederate president could not allow the measure to go unmentioned. Davis denounced the proclamation, which, in his words, encouraged "several millions of human beings of an inferior race, peaceful and contented laborers in their sphere" to engage in "a general assassination of their masters." Those slaves who responded in such a way, in Davis's words, were "doomed to extermination." The Confederate president could hardly conceal his fury. Describing the proclamation as "the most execrable measure" in the history of humankind, Davis outlined a policy whereby Union officers who carried out the emancipation order would be treated as having instigated slave revolts. Abraham Lincoln's attempt to free slaves in the Confederacy, Davis continued, only confirmed what Southerners had long suspected—that declaring abolition and fomenting insurrection constituted the true agenda of Lincoln and the Republicans. Given Lincoln's actions, Davis lauded the wisdom and foresight of secession, whereby the Southern people had demonstrated "vigilance in resisting the stealthy progress of approaching despotism." With the issues at stake in the war clarified once and for all, President Davis offered a final observation to Confederate lawmakers: "This proclamation will have another salutary effect in calming the fears of those who have constantly evinced the apprehension that this war might end by some reconstruction of the old Union or some renewal of close political relations with the United States."[1]

Davis's reaction to Lincoln's Emancipation Proclamation revealed both the thinking of the Confederate president and the stakes in America's bloodiest war. Not only did Davis display his commitment to slavery and white supremacy but he also made clear that secession had originated in Southern attempts to protect the rights of slaveholders from potential interference by the North. It had been for this very reason—the possibility of an overbearing, abolitionist federal government—that the South had seceded in the first place. More significantly, Davis's message revealed that he was beginning to recognize the revolutionary ramifications of Lincoln's move against slavery. Like Lincoln, who saw in emancipation the possibility of "a new nation," and like African American Federal soldiers who rejected the idea of fighting for the "old Union," Davis recognized that the Emancipation Proclamation made the restoration of the antebellum Union impossible. Either the South would gain its independence, or a new Union, without slavery, would emerge. As president of the Confederacy during its entire four-year existence, Davis tried mightily to create a unified Southern nation that could achieve military victory, gain political independence, and preserve black slavery and white supremacy. But by the end of 1864, military defeats and political controversies combined to lay bare the tensions within Confederate nationalism.

DAVIS AND THE CONFEDERACY

Despite the challenges that lay ahead, there was not a hint of pessimism in February 1861 in the days after Jefferson Davis and Alexander Stephens took their oaths to lead the newly formed Confederacy. The two had been elected in secret session as provisional president and vice president by the provisional Congress of the Confederacy, and they apparently enjoyed broad popular support. Even many of those who had vigorously argued that the best way to preserve Southern interests was to remain in the Union now embraced secession, as well as the Confederacy's new leaders. A festive mood pervaded Montgomery, a small crossroads on the Alabama River, which had become the capital of the Confederate republic for no other reason than the fact that it was the home of prominent secessionist William Lowndes Yancey. On the night of their inauguration, hundreds of well-wishers crammed into a local recep-

Although not a secessionist firebrand before the war, Jefferson Davis assumed the presidency of the Confederate republic in early 1861 amidst enormous enthusiasm about the prospects for Southern independence. Courtesy of the Library of Congress, LC-DIG-ppmsca-23852

tion hall to greet the newly anointed leaders. Adoring women reportedly showered the Confederate president with kisses, and the joyful crowd even included the two sisters of Mary Todd Lincoln, who had journeyed from Kentucky. (They made a point of telling the Confederate president that they were related to Mary Todd rather than her husband.) Optimism and goodwill marked the festivities, and many in Montgomery believed that they were witnessing an epochal moment in the history of American liberty.

The overwhelming support for Davis sprung in part from an antiparty spirit. Jaded by the inability of parties to protect Southern interests and horrified at the rise of the purely sectional Republicans, the Southerners of 1861 imagined a republic in which a commitment to the public good would overcome the factious spirit of partisan division. The Confederate founders believed that providing for a single-term president would help eliminate the spirit of partisanship. Invoking the name of George Washington, the Confederate founders hoped to return to a purer era in American history—before the rise of factions—when the traditional eighteenth-century republican notion of public-spiritedness ruled the day. During the first year or so of the Confederacy, this antiparty way of thinking, grounded in the Constitution, seemed to hold sway. Davis became a symbol for this "revolution against politics." He was to be a "second Washington," who would lead the republic toward independence and serve as a model of public virtue.[2] When the Confederacy conducted its formal election for president and vice president in fall 1861, there was no opposition and so no campaign. There were no rallies, no conventions, no politicking. The election thus bore no resemblance to the presidential elections that had occurred in the United States during the previous three decades. For the first year of the Confederacy's existence, this antiparty ideology helped contribute to a spirit of national unity.

During that first year, Davis would work with a provisional Congress, an assemblage that began with delegations from six states but that expanded over time as other states seceded. National elections for Congress would take place in fall 1861, and not until early 1862 would a separate Confederate House of Representatives and Senate exist. In the meantime, this original unicameral legislature began the task of working with the president to create a government. Its members included a handful of fire-eaters, including Robert Barnwell Rhett of South Carolina and Louis Wigfall of Texas, but for the most part, legislators exemplified moderation and pragmatism. A mix of planters and lawyers, including a cadre of distinguished Southern state supreme court judges, members of the provisional Congress brought a wealth of experience in politics at both the state and national levels. They also brought enormous wealth, as the vast majority of them were slaveholders.[3]

The provisional Congress immediately created a number of executive departments, and Davis believed that in filling these Cabinet positions every state should be represented. His most important choices were Georgia's Robert Toombs for secretary of state, South Carolina's Christopher Memminger as secretary of the treasury, and Louisiana's Judah Benjamin for attorney general. A longtime member of the US Senate and part of a triumvirate of leading Georgia politicians that included Stephens and Howell Cobb, Toombs immediately succeeded in convincing European powers to grant the Confederacy belligerent status, but he resigned later in 1861 to accept a brigadier generalship in the Confederate Army. Memminger, a lawyer, received appointment upon the recommendation of his state's delegation to the Montgomery convention, but he possessed little experience in financial matters. His would be a stormy tenure as secretary of the treasury as the Confederacy struggled to pay for the war. Benjamin did an able job as attorney general, and Davis moved him to the Department of War in fall 1861 after Alabamian Leroy Pope Walker proved to be incompetent. By the end of the war, six different men would head the War Department, and a total of seventeen different men would hold the six positions in the Confederate Cabinet. This considerable turnover owed partly to the mediocre cast and partly to Davis's notorious attention to detail and inability to delegate.

The provisional Congress also created a supreme court, but its actual life span proved to be even shorter than that of the typical Confederate Cabinet member. The Confederate Constitution duplicated the provisions of the US Constitution with regard to the judiciary, and the provisional Congress established a supreme court and a federal court system by statute in March 1861. The law provided for a single district court in each state, and these district judges, sitting together, would constitute the Confederate supreme court. Controversy over the power of the court relative to state courts, in addition to the impracticality of a high court composed solely of judges who would hear their own cases on appeal, prompted Congress in July 1861 to suspend the sitting of the supreme court until early 1862, after the formal election of the president and vice president. Subsequent political disputes would prevent a supreme court from ever being created.

During the early months of the Confederacy, Davis and his Cabinet devoted much of their attention to the crisis over Fort Sumter and the consolidation of the new government. Overzealous South Carolinians complicated matters, for some considered the possibility of attacking the Federal fort on their own, without any authorization from the government in Montgomery. Confronted with challenges to its authority both from Washington, DC, and Charleston, Davis walked a tightrope. Surprised that the incoming Lincoln administration rebuffed its offers to negotiate over Sumter, Davis took a hard line when Lincoln decided to supply the Union garrison. Having already formed the foundations of an army, on April 12, Confederate guns—on Davis's authority—began shelling the fort as the new nation sought to secure its independence with fire and blood.

The Union's speedy surrender at Sumter not only provided Davis with the first triumph of his presidency but also created a surge of nationalism that enveloped the Upper South and prompted Virginia, Arkansas, North Carolina, and Tennessee to secede. After the secession of Virginia and at the urging of that state's secession convention, the provisional Congress voted to move the national capital from Montgomery to Richmond, a much larger city that contained the Tredegar ironworks, an essential industrial resource. Moving to Richmond also allowed the government to attempt to quell the popular opposition to the Confederacy in Virginia's western counties, which had overwhelmingly rejected secession. At the end of May, Davis led the migration of the young government, which by then included a thousand employees, to its new capital city, located along the James River a scant hundred miles from Washington, DC. Two weeks after the government established itself in Richmond, President Davis issued a proclamation declaring a national day of fasting for the Confederacy.

The move of the capital to Virginia solidified the Confederacy's symbolic connection with the American founders, thus serving an ideological as well as practical purpose. The Old Dominion's place at the head of the Confederacy offered confirmation of Davis's inaugural claim that the Southern states acted in the tradition of George Washington, Thomas Jefferson, and other venerable Virginians in exercising their right to throw off the yoke of a tyrannical government. In the months and years to follow, Confederate symbolism made much of the connection. The new nation eventually created a national seal that depicted George Washington on horseback, above the Latin motto *Deo Vindice*, "God will vindicate." After Davis's formal election as president in fall 1861, the Confederacy established Washington's birthday, February 22, as the date of the president's 1862 inauguration, at which time he took the inaugural oath beneath the grand equestrian statue of Washington on the grounds of the Virginia state capitol. And in speech after speech, the Confederate president invoked the spirit of the eighteenth-century American founders in describing and justifying the Rebels' cause to Southerners and to the world.

Such rhetoric intentionally captured the nature and purpose of the Confederacy. To be sure, secession was a revolutionary movement, a radical act. Few had gone so far as to advocate it a decade before, but the ranks of potential secessionists grew substantially during 1860, and Lincoln's election and eventual call for troops after Sumter moved secessionism, even within the Upper South, from the margins to the mainstream. Despite the drastic nature of severing ties with the United States, Confederates believed they did so for conservative purposes—to preserve the true Constitution of 1787 that they believed had been trampled by Northern "Black Republicans," abolitionists, and other radical Northern reformers. One of Georgia's most ardent secessionists, the Southern lawyer and treatise writer on slavery Thomas Reade Roots Cobb, portrayed the ascendant Republicans as possessing not a shred of decency—as a motley assortment of radicals bent on destroying the republic of the founders: "Look at its leaders and see the heroes who deify John Brown; the mad preachers like [George Barrell] Cheever and [Henry Ward]

The Confederate seal evoked the American founding by portraying George Washington on horseback. Deo Vindice, "God Will Vindicate," was the Confederacy's motto. Courtesy of the Library of Congress, LC-DIG-pga-01405

Beecher . . . the Sewards and Sumners, and Hales, and Fred Douglass. . . . Search in vain among them for one gentleman . . . one sound conservative . . . one noble patriot." The secessionists of 1861, in other words, viewed themselves as the true conservators of the American constitutional tradition. The formation of the Confederacy was, as many scholars have noted, a "conservative revolution."[4]

Southerners had long revered the Constitution of 1787, so when they created their own founding document, they mostly preserved the original text. But the parts of the US Constitution that they did change revealed a great deal about the type of republic the Southern founders of 1861 envisioned. In addition to overtly protecting the institution of black slavery, Southerners prohibited a protective tariff and internal improvements, recognized the sovereignty of the individual states, and invoked "the favor of Almighty God." Arguably, they thus imagined a slaveholding, agricultural, decentralized, Christian republic—a nation in which white liberty, especially the right to hold slaves, would be preserved under the loose authority of a central government.

But if the American founders of 1787 had failed to resolve the sovereignty question, the Southern founders of 1861 produced an equally murky document with regard to the precise relationship between the state governments and Confederate government. On the one hand, the Confederate Constitution exhibited more than a trace of nationalism. Its founders retained many of the provisions of the US Constitution that had contributed to the centralization of authority, which they surely knew would be useful in mobilizing the country to fight a war of independence. The US Constitution's clause referring to federal laws and treaties as the "supreme law of the land" remained, even though it had historically been used to overrule state court decisions, as did the "necessary and proper clause" that had tended to augment congressional power. The Confederate president, moreover, possessed a "line-item veto" and served a single six-year term, provisions intended to augment executive power and diminish partisan factionalism. Thus, the Confederate Constitution respected the practical need for national unity. On the other hand, the document explicitly announced that each state acted "in its sovereign and independent character," and some delegates even argued, unsuccessfully, that the right of secession ought to be included in the text. Despite the constitutional clauses that contributed to national authority, the provision disallowing national internal improvements would surely hinder the effort to wage a war for independence. A fierce commitment to decentralized power remained a guiding light among some of the Confederacy's founders and among some state governors, a strain of thought that would manifest itself the moment the Davis administration or Congress carried out some unpopular policy. Protective of their liberties, some white Southerners continued to view their primary loyalties as being to their own seceded states and saw a threat of tyranny in the enactment of Confederate legislation designed to mobilize for war. Notions of state sovereignty and individual liberty thus combined to create a potent oppositionist ideology, one that posed a potential barrier to any attempt at national consolidation.

The task of creating and sustaining a Confederate nation, then, would be a formidable one. After establishing a centralized government where there had been none, Davis and the Confederate Congress would need to put the new government on a war footing, wage a military struggle for independence, engage in a diplomatic campaign for foreign recognition and assistance, and in the process of doing all these things solidify a sense of national patriotism and purpose in order to unify the Southern people.

THE CONSCRIPTION CONTROVERSY

Given the built-in disadvantage in the Confederacy's smaller population, President Davis would spend a great deal of time during the first year of the war attempting to create a sufficient fighting force. Southerners met with enthusiasm his initial call for 100,000 men for a year's enlistment, and the Confederacy's July 1861 victory at the Battle of Manassas (Bull Run) had raised Southern hopes for a smooth and speedy road to independence. Nevertheless, Davis speculated that more men for a longer term of service would be necessary. As in the United States, to secure the service of citizen soldiers, Davis needed to go through the states to enroll members of state militias in the Confederacy's fighting force. Congress authorized and set the terms of enlistments, the president called for troops, and the governors supplied them.

In the process of raising an army, Davis confronted head-on the issue of state sovereignty, as some governors jealously guarded their powers and eagerly sought to protect the interests of their own states. In January 1862, for example, the governors of South Carolina, North Carolina, Florida, and Georgia all clamored for the return of state-owned arms, and Georgia's governor, Joseph Brown, in particular attempted to thwart the president's efforts to raise troops. Such division and obstruction, from Davis's perspective, simply could not be tolerated. Faced with waning enthusiasm for enlistment in early 1862, the Confederacy would not be able to sustain the fight for long if it could not secure sufficient numbers of munitions and men. The impending expiration of the initial year-long enlistments and the Confederacy's surrender of thousands of prisoners at Tennessee's Fort Donelson made the situation especially urgent.

In early 1862, Davis and Congress took important steps to consolidate Confederate authority and defend the country. Political activity on the part of Southern Unionists, victories by Federal forces in the western theater, and the surrender of some coastal areas to Union control all demonstrated the need for the Confederate government to tighten its grip. In order to keep a lid on disloyalty and dissent that might hinder enlistments and aid the enemy, in February the Confederate Congress authorized the president to suspend the writ of habeas corpus. The law granted the president the authority to do so "in such towns, cities, and military districts as shall in his judgment be in such danger of attack by the enemy as to require the declaration of martial law for their effective defence."[5] The law seemed to confuse the suspension of the writ, which allowed the military to arrest and imprison on suspicion of disloyalty, and the imposition of martial law, which meant the closing of civil courts and the imposition of military justice. Nevertheless, Davis wasted no time in exercising all of the authority he had been given. During the next two months, he issued proclamations that both suspended the writ and declared martial law in and around all of the major cities of Virginia, in several counties in western Virginia, in all of East Tennessee, and in portions of the South Carolina coast most vulnerable to naval attack. These orders established military control and suspended the normal operation of civil courts. The legal authorization to suspend the writ lasted for a year.

Meanwhile, to deal directly with the enlistment crisis, in April 1862 the Confederate Congress passed a conscription act. Listed in the statute book simply as "An Act to Further Provide for the Public Defense," the law was the first of its kind ever passed in North America. The need for additional forces was clear: lawmakers enacted the legislation within days after the Confederacy suffered nearly 11,000 casualties at Shiloh and as General George B. McClellan's massive 100,000-man army lumbered up the peninsula toward Richmond. The statute authorized the president to "call out and place in the military service of the Confederate States, for three years, unless the war shall have been sooner ended, all white men who are residents of the Confederate States, between the ages of eighteen and thirty-five years at the time the call or calls may be made, who are not legally exempted from military service."[6] The law, moreover, extended the terms of enlistment of those already serving to three years from the date of their original enlistments. Under the law, one subject to the draft could procure a substitute—someone who was not subject to enrollment under the law—to take his place. Within a week of the passage of the act, Congress enacted further legislation establishing various classes of men who would be exempt from the draft. These included those who worked in areas that the Confederate government deemed essential to the war effort: government, the railroads, education, the ministry, nursing, and industry. That fall, Congress adjusted the law to raise the maximum age to forty-five years of age, and more importantly, they provided for an exemption for "one person, as agent, owner or overseer, on each plantation of twenty negroes, and on which there is no white male adult not liable to military service."[7] In order to implement and enforce this far-reaching legislation, the Congress created a new agency known as the Conscript Bureau.

The Confederacy's conscription act, which predated the Union's conscription law by nearly a year, proved as controversial as it was comprehensive. The *Daily Journal* of Wilmington, North Carolina, described the law at the time as, "beyond question, the most important measure that has ever passed the Confederate Congress."[8] Given the extent of the disputes that ensued, this was an apt description. Critics complained that the law took the enlistment process out of the hands of state governments and put it into the hands of Confederate authorities. Under the Constitution, states possessed the power to appoint officers of the militia, but the conscription act seemed to abolish militias, along with state control over appointments. Proponents of state sovereignty, led by Georgia's Governor Brown, howled over the interference with state prerogative. Writing to the Confederate president, Governor Brown complained to Davis that the law violated the Confederate Constitution, imposed extraordinary hardships for his state, and subverted the principles on which the Confederacy had been founded. "I cannot consent to commit the state to a policy that is in my judgment subversive of her sovereignty, and at war with all the principles for the support of which Georgia entered into this revolution," Brown wrote.[9]

A lengthy exchange of letters followed, in which Davis and Brown debated the meaning of Congress's constitutional power to "raise and support armies." It was a highly legalistic debate, as each sought to put forth his own interpretation of the meaning of this power. Davis argued that Congress could decide the means of carrying out its own war powers and that a national army—a Confederate army—lay within the scope of congressional power under the Constitution. Brown, in contrast, maintained the power to "raise and support armies" could only be understood in the context of other clauses within the Constitution that referred to the existence of the militia. Such clauses, according to Brown, meant that states were first to raise militia companies and appoint military officers, which could then be deployed on behalf of the Confederate government. "If this is done, the army is raised as directed by the Constitution, and the reserved rights of the states are respected," he wrote. "But if the officers of the militia, when called forth, are appointed by the President, the army composed of the militia is not raised as directed by the Constitution, and the reserved rights of the States are disregarded."[10] To Brown, whether an army went through the states or bypassed the states was a critical distinction, for it constituted the difference between maintaining state sovereignty and submitting to national consolidation. Brown's letters did nothing to change the president's mind or his policies, and an attorney general's opinion that fall reiterated the administration's position that the Confederate Congress had the power to determine the means of raising an army. Still, Brown began his own form of protest by increasing the number of exempted men through expanding the scope of his state's government workforce, a practice that he continued throughout much of the war.

Other critics took aim at the legitimacy and fairness of the exemptions in the conscription act. As these exceptions were written into the law, it did not take much time for savvy young men to figure out ways of securing them. Finding work as a government clerk or factory employee kept one out of the army, as did finding a physician willing to attest to one's physical infirmities. Personal favoritism and class bias gradually took root. The provision allowing for the securing of substitutes clearly benefited the rich, as they were the only ones who could afford to pay others to take their places, and this exemption became the subject of political discussion. As early as August 1862, Secretary of War George Randolph alerted President Davis to the fact that "great abuses" existed in the substitute system. "The procuration of substitutes has become a regular business," Randolph wrote. "Men thus obtained are usually unfit for service and frequently desert."[11] The "twenty-negro" exemption, moreover, also worked to the advantage of the wealthy and to the disadvantage of the poor. This provision allowed an exemption for those who owned or supervised at least twenty slaves, with one exemption for every twenty slaves owned. Although designed to ensure order and security on Southern plantations in wartime, the provision immediately provoked charges of favoritism. Such elements of the conscription act only stoked nonslaveholding whites' suspicions that the war served primarily the interest of the planter elite.

Neither the constitutional nor the fairness critique of conscription prompted an immediate revision of the legislation. The Confederate Congress later attempted to reform the twenty-negro provision, first by requiring those exempted to have actually been overseers before the passage of the original legislation and later by reducing the exemption to fifteen slaves. It finally abolished the practice of substitution in early 1864. But Davis defended the law initially in all of its features and only later favored the ending of substitution. As president, Davis believed strongly that conscription was necessary to raise a sufficient fighting force. Although he had advocated state sovereignty principles throughout his political career, Davis had always made an exception for cases of national defense, and surely in his mind this constituted one of those instances that required a national policy. In spite of Brown's attempts to limit the conscription law's effect in Georgia—an effort that won some sympathy in South Carolina—most governors and state governments understood, as Davis did, that sacrificing some individual liberties and state prerogatives would be necessary for the sake of achieving military victory and national independence.

STATE COURTS AND CONFEDERATE LIBERTY

When legal challenges to Confederate legislation arose, they came to state courts rather than a Confederate supreme court. In February 1862, the newly inaugurated Davis had reminded the first permanent Congress of its duty to create a supreme court for the Confederacy, and members introduced bills to create a court in both houses of the new Congress. These proposals sparked extensive debate, mostly over the issue of whether it ought to have the power to review state court decisions. The Congress of the United States had enacted legislation in 1789 that allowed certain cases to be transferred out of the state courts and to the US Supreme Court, in effect giving the US Supreme Court appellate jurisdiction over state courts. The 1861 act establishing the Confederate judiciary adopted similar language. But because some members of Congress believed that these provisions undermined state sovereignty and threatened individual liberty, they advocated striking these lines from the law in order to create a less powerful supreme court. Tempers flared during these debates, as those with a more nationalistic view clashed with those who advocated a pure form of state sovereignty. In the end, not only did the Confederacy fail to establish a supreme court, but the absence of such a high court made the federal district court system largely irrelevant and empowered the state courts to serve as the real arbiters of disputes pertaining to federal law.

When confronted with questions of Confederate authority, however, state courts usually deferred to congressional power. Even the most controversial legislation won the legal approval of Southern state supreme courts. Despite popular dissatisfaction with the Confederacy's policy of impressment, whereby the military could seize private property (usually foodstuffs) in order to supply the army, in 1863 the Georgia supreme court upheld the law and took issue only with the Confederacy's inadequate compensation of property holders. Conscription also passed constitutional muster. In nearly every state where conscription came to the state's highest court—Alabama, Mississippi, Texas, Virginia, South Carolina, Florida, and even Governor Brown's own state of Georgia—judges upheld the power of the Confederate Congress to enact a conscription law. Alabama's Judge George W. Stone, for example, although he paid lip service to the importance of state sovereignty, nevertheless sided with Davis in describing Congress in *Ex parte Hill, in re. Willis v. Confederate States* (1863) as the "sole arbiter" of the means of executing its war powers.[12] In upholding the conscription law against the charges that Congress had exceeded its constitutional authority, moreover, Southern judges found themselves unabashedly—and ironically—relying on some of the US Supreme Court's most nationalistic early nineteenth-century decisions and adopting some of the very same constitutional arguments that Southerners had long opposed. Judge Reuben A. Reeves of the Texas supreme court in *Ex parte Mayer* (1864), for example, quickly dismissed the claim that state sovereignty trumped the power of Congress to enact conscription, and in doing so adopted Chief Justice John

Marshall's early nineteenth-century formulation of popular sovereignty as the basis of national power. "The government of the Confederate States, like the government of a state, is derived from the same source, the people, and founded on their authority," Reeves wrote. "That the constitution and laws of the Confederate States are the supreme law of the land, and not in any sense dependent on the constitution of a state for their authority."[13] Unwilling to restrict the war powers of the Confederate Congress for the sake of adhering to state sovereignty, state courts granted wide authority to the Confederacy to raise a national army in the way that it saw fit.

Only the North Carolina supreme court ever challenged the Confederacy's power to conscript. In a series of decisions in 1863, after the presidential suspension of habeas corpus had expired, Judge Richmond M. Pearson claimed that his court had original jurisdiction in habeas corpus cases involving draftees and deserters. In these cases, Pearson consistently held in favor of those claiming exemptions from conscription and ruled against home guard units that attempted to detain deserters. Although Pearson never declared the Confederate conscription act unconstitutional and only challenged it in a limited way by granting habeas corpus petitions, his opinions nevertheless caught the attention of the Davis administration. Seeking the uniform approval of state courts on the matter, Davis in response sought to again suspend the writ.

TAXATION AND FINANCE

Funding the Confederate war effort proved every bit as difficult, both politically and practically, as raising an army. Constitutional concerns about state sovereignty and individual liberty again emerged, exacerbated by economic questions that brought out class tensions. Most Southerners hated taxation, especially when it came from a centralized authority, and the disparity between the rich and poor in Southern society, coupled with the fact that most of the Confederacy's wealth remained concentrated in slaves, land, and cotton, meant that any national economic policy would likely disrupt decades of established values and practices. No war financing scheme, in other words, would be popular. While Davis mostly took a hands-on approach to the matter of conscription, the president left the question of paying for the war largely to Secretary of the Treasury Memminger.

Memminger's background offered some early clues that he would not be especially suited to the position. A South Carolina lawyer with no particular expertise in finance, Memminger became an advocate of secession in 1860 and served as a delegate from his state to the Montgomery convention in

1861. There he seemed more interested in enshrining Southern political orthodoxy in the Confederate Constitution than in considering the realities of waging war. Memminger attempted to ensure that Congress would not abuse the power to enact tariffs, and he successfully amended a draft of the Confederate Constitution to ensure that Congress could not use the tariff "to appropriate money for any internal improvement intended to facilitate commerce."[14] Given that railroads, roads, and navigable rivers and harbors would all be necessary to move men and matériel in wartime, his focus at the convention might have indicated a limited vision when it came to mobilizing for a war for independence. To his credit, once he assumed the position as secretary of treasury, Memminger realized that a combination of taxing, borrowing (mostly through the issuing of government bonds), and the printing of treasury notes (currency not backed up by specie) would be required to pay for the war. In some ways, tax revenue would have to be the foundation for any war finance plan, because a reliable revenue stream would be required to pay interest to bondholders and to demonstrate to future investors the political stability and financial sustainability of the government.

Even though he realized the importance of taxes, Memminger lacked the political skill to push for legislation that would provide sufficient revenue. When the war began, Memminger ironically—given his stance at the convention—placed too much emphasis on tariffs. He overestimated the amount of revenue that could be generated from the tariff, and he underestimated the expenses of running the new government and prosecuting the war. After the transfer of former US customhouses to Confederate control, these revenues came into the treasury for the first few months of the new nation's existence, but the Union blockade gradually choked off international trade and restricted the amount of revenue collected in Southern ports. Instead of the $25 million that Memminger had estimated, actual receipts turned out to be less than $1.3 million for the first year—a paltry figure that declined each subsequent year as the blockade tightened. A self-imposed embargo of cotton to Europe, moreover, further slowed international commerce, thus severely shrinking any possible revenue from taxes on either imports or exports.

Other forms of revenue would need to be found. In August 1861, Memminger and Congress enacted a "war tax" to be paid during the following year on slaves, real estate, and other forms of property, at a rate of fifty cents per $100 of assessed value, but collection of the tax proceeded unevenly. Unwilling to create a force of assessors and collectors on the scale that was required, the Confederacy left the collection of the tax to the states, who either paid the federal tax in state banknotes or bowed to popular opposition and simply refused to collect what their people owed. With revenues lagging, inactivity and denial ensued. The Confederate government refused to renew the war tax after the first year and neglected to address the tax question again until spring 1863.

Subsequent tax measures not only failed to raise revenue but also proved unfair in their assessment and implementation. In April 1863, the Confederate Congress enacted three types of new taxes: a direct tax on income, a variety of excise taxes and license duties on professions and businesses, and a tax in kind on agricultural products. This time, the income tax exempted any assessment of real estate, slaves, and livestock, because some lawmakers argued that such taxes were "direct taxes" on property that, under the Confederate Constitution, had to be apportioned among the states on the basis of population. The war tax of 1861 had been enacted under the provisional Constitution, which had not included such a clause. Because the war made it nearly impossible to conduct a census for this purpose, the law excluded these valuable forms of wealth, which meant that planters largely escaped paying the tax. The excise taxes and license fees raised some revenue, but they left bankers, brokers, distillers, innkeepers, doctors, lawyers, and others resentfully wondering how planters had managed to neglect paying their share into the Confederate treasury. Finally, the tax in kind came down most heavily on the region's nonslaveholding yeomen. Already suffering from the military practice of impressment, whereby the Confederate army could impress, or confiscate, any forms of property—livestock, crops, household items—that it needed from farmers and landholders in the vicinity, yeoman farmers now faced the systematic seizure of a portion of their crops. In order to acquire these foodstuffs to feed the Confederate army, the government did what it had not been willing to do in 1861 for the war tax: it created an entire bureaucracy of thousands of assessors and collectors to move throughout the South to collect crops from even the most humble farmstead. The tax in kind might have been the only tax that the Confederacy ever collected with any degree of seriousness or success. With complaints that the war had turned into a "rich man's war and a poor man's fight," and at the urging of Davis, the Confederacy again revised its tax laws in early 1864, but a new 5 percent tax on land and slaves, which ignored the constitutional requirement of apportionment among the states, came too late to have any real effect on the treasury. In the final analysis, the Confederacy never raised sufficient revenue to support the war. Wealthy antitax slaveholders who held most of the seats in Congress for the most part proved unwilling to look beyond their own interests, while Davis and Memminger moved hesitantly and half-heartedly on the issue. In the end, revenue from taxes amounted to about $218 million, which covered only about 8 percent of the total cost of the war.

Borrowing turned out to be a more important source of revenue for the

Confederacy. The state of Alabama provided an initial loan to get the Confederate government going, but Memminger and Congress soon provided for the issuing of bonds. During 1861, the Confederacy successfully secured $15 million in bond purchases from states, businesses, and individuals, but a subsequent attempt in 1861 to raise another $50 million created more problems than it solved. Because the South lacked specie, this second bond issue allowed planters and farmers to pledge the income from yet-to-be-harvested crops as security for the bonds. This "produce loan," as it came to be called, raised the ire of the planters. Implemented by the South's eminent economist James D. B. DeBow, the plan called for treasury agents to canvass the countryside asking planters to subscribe the future profits on a portion of their crop. But planters were already seeing their personal fortunes shrink. Depressed cotton prices, owing both to the Union blockade and the Confederacy's attempts to secure foreign recognition by withholding cotton, made most planters reluctant to pledge their much-needed income toward the Confederate cause. Many balked at the financing scheme and instead wanted the Confederate government to buy their crops directly—at what planters considered a fair price—and then sell them abroad. The Davis administration never embraced the idea, and the disagreement over how to handle the South's cotton crop led to ongoing tensions between the government and its most important supporters. Remarkably, the Confederacy never made a serious attempt to sell bonds, cotton, or bonds backed by cotton to international creditors, a decision that severely hindered wartime financing. With the exception of a single modestly successful foreign loan, virtually all bond sales occurred within the Confederacy. In total, sales of government bonds yielded about $867 million, about 34 percent of the total revenue the Confederacy spent on the war.

Printing treasury notes proved in the short term a more popular way to pay for the war, but in the longer term the practice simply produced out-of-control inflation. The Confederacy issued treasury notes from the first days of the government. A small portion of these notes, like bonds, actually represented small loans made by individuals to the government and bore modest rates of interest, but more common were non-interest-bearing notes. Printed by the Confederate treasury in denominations ranging up to $500 in order for the government to pay its bills, these notes, when passed from individual to individual, in effect served as the Confederacy's only nationally circulating medium of exchange. State banks continued to issue their own notes, though, and unlike the Union government during wartime, the Confederate Congress made no attempt to create a national banking system to eliminate state notes. The large number in circulation decreased the value of the notes, and, coupled with endemic commodity shortages caused by the war, prompted prices to skyrocket. Widespread counterfeiting of Confederate treasury notes, carried out by both Southerners and Northerners, only added to inflation. Estimates vary, but economic historians generally believe that by the end of the war the inflation rate in parts of the South reached nearly 9,000 percent. Memminger and Congress vainly attempted to regulate the amount of currency in circulation by, for example, enacting legislation in March 1863 that allowed people to use their non-interest-bearing notes to purchase interest-bearing government bonds.

But it proved nearly impossible to halt the disastrous financial spiral in which the Confederacy found itself. Many people believed that future inflation would decrease the value of the interest to be paid on the bonds, so they opted to hold onto their treasury notes, which, for the moment, still held a known value. The fact that some bonds were sold for paper treasury notes, moreover, did nothing to solve the larger problem of the Confederate debt. Memminger and Congress often found it easier simply to approve another infusion of treasury notes into the economy than to make difficult political and constitutional decisions regarding the nation's finances. In summary, the issuing of treasury notes provided the South with a circulating medium, but excessive reliance on such fiat money exacerbated the hardships of war and shook public confidence in the government. In total, the issuing of treasury notes accounted for more than $1.5 billion of Confederate spending, meaning that the Confederacy paid for about 59 percent of the cost of the war simply by printing money.

In contrast to the operation of the Union government, the Confederacy clearly mismanaged its public finances. Davis did achieve some successes, including convincing Congress to allocate money for the extension of railroad lines, which, despite a constitutional prohibition on internal improvement, Davis justified under congressional war powers. But for the most part, Confederate economic policies failed. In simplest terms, the Confederacy neglected to collect enough tax revenue to carry on the war, and its overreliance on treasury notes created a vicious inflationary spiral from which it could not escape. Amidst the crisis, Memminger resigned his position in June 1864, but his replacement, George A. Trenholm, fared no better. Many reasons accounted for the Confederacy's troubles in this area. Memminger lacked both financial acumen and political experience, while Davis offered little assistance in promoting political solutions to these problems. Most members of the Confederate Congress spent more time considering their self-interest as slaveholders than the needs of the Confederacy as a whole, as many had convinced themselves that it would be a short war that the South could finance easily through borrowing. Finally, constitutional issues figured prominently. Popular constitutionalism held that direct taxation violated sacred liberties, while savvy planter-lawmakers used the constitutional requirement that taxes be apportioned by state population to exempt most of their own valuable property. Given the level of opposition to taxation, especially when considered in the light of the heated debate over conscription, it is easy to see why the Confederate government moved cautiously to impose the requisite taxes on its citizens. Still, the end results were an empty treasury, little investor confidence in the government, and rampant price inflation. Though Confederates may have kept their liberties intact, they never acquired the financial resources to fight a war.

"KING COTTON DIPLOMACY"

The attempt to secure European allies was equally elusive. Davis knew that like the revolutionary patriots, Confederates would achieve success only if they secured foreign assistance. Just as the Americans had relied on French support against the British during the Revolutionary War, so would the Confederates need help to overcome the more populous and more powerful Union. European governments could provide assistance—money, munitions, even men, perhaps—that would sustain the Southern cause, prolong the war, and wear down the Union. Because of its industrial muscle and its naval power, Great Britain became the chief target of Confederate diplomatic efforts.

Cotton would be the key to enlisting British assistance. Because the South grew so much of it and Britain relied so heavily on it, Southerners reasoned, they could easily persuade the British to offer diplomatic recognition and then to provide concrete assistance. In fact, up to 85 percent of the cotton that Great Britain imported came from the American South, and five million workers employed in the British textile industry relied on the crop for their livelihoods. Even before the war began, Texan Louis Wigfall echoed others in proclaiming cotton to be "king," adding that "he waves his scepter not only over these thirty-three states, but over the island of Great Britain and over continental Europe."[15] The need for cotton, Southerners believed, would shape British policy toward America's civil war, despite whatever doubts the British harbored about aiding a slaveholding republic. "Old prejudices against our misunderstood domestic institution of African servitude (it is the word 'slavery' that has blinded their eyes)," Southern planter Henry Ravenal observed in April 1861, "are giving way before the urgent calls of Self Interest & we only need that they should become more intimately acquainted with it, to dissipate their mistaken notions." Increases in the tariff imposed by the

United States, moreover, provided another reason why a strong relationship with the Confederacy would benefit the English. "We furnish what is absolutely essential to their commercial & and manufacturing prosperity, & we alone—We offer them a market for their goods on better terms than heretofore," Ravenal confidently opined.[16] Thus, with the same bravado that had prompted thousands of Southern soldiers initially to enlist and some Confederate leaders to hold to a short-war mentality, the Davis administration pursued this "King Cotton diplomacy." Congress rejected the imposition of an actual legal embargo, not wanting to antagonize the British, but the Davis administration implemented an informal policy of refraining from cotton sales until the British recognized the Confederacy.

Despite Confederate self-assurance, during the first year of the war, Southern hopes for recognition rose and fell as economic, diplomatic, and military realities unfolded. First was an economic reality: Britain would have no pressing need for cotton during 1861. The previous few years had yielded bumper cotton crops in the American South, and Britain had purchased stockpiles of the stuff before the Civil War began. Despite whatever policies the Confederate government enacted, the need for cotton would not dictate immediately Britain's decision regarding recognition. More important would be the quality of the initial delegation sent to the British Isles—a diplomatic reality. Here Davis made a mistake. Wanting to send the hot-headed Yancey out of the country simply to get him out of the way, Davis appointed him, along with two other less distinguished men, to serve as the first emissaries to Great Britain. The British were not impressed with the delegation, which the *London Times* described as a group of "American fanatics."[17] It would take some changes in personnel before Anglo-Confederate diplomacy could proceed. Finally, the military reality was that Britain would only recognize the Confederacy as a nation if it proved that it was actually close to achieving nationhood. This meant that the Southerners would need to win some critical victories on the field of battle to show the British that they were indeed waging a viable movement for independence. The only two positive developments for the Confederacy during the first year arose from Union actions, rather than Confederate ones. First, Lincoln's announcement of the blockade of Southern ports in April prompted the British to grant belligerent status to the Confederacy and to announce neutrality in the conflict. Second, a diplomatic brouhaha in November 1861—involving the Union seizure of two Confederate emissaries on a British mail packet, the *Trent*, on its way to Europe—temporarily soured relations between the Union government and Great Britain. Neither of these events, though, paved the way for diplomatic recognition of the Confederacy.

During 1862, the Confederacy came as close as it ever did to securing any outside assistance, as a succession of events seemed to create momentum in favor of the South. Once James Mason, the Confederate commissioner, arrived in Britain after the *Trent* affair, he organized a group of British sympathizers in Parliament into the "Confederate lobby," which pressed the Southern cause within Britain's corridors of power. Working with these and other supporters, Mason helped to secure modest financial assistance through the public sale of bonds. In the meantime, Confederate propagandist Henry Hotze attempted to influence public opinion. A native of Switzerland who had settled in Alabama and become an American citizen, Hotze departed for Britain at the end of 1861 at the urging of Secretary of War Judah Benjamin and Secretary of State Robert M. T. Hunter with official instructions to monitor the British press, convince the British public of the viability and desirability of Southern independence, and "keep constantly before the public view in Great Britain the tyranny of the Lincoln government."[18] In spring 1862, Hotz began publishing a newspaper in London, the *Index*, in which he focused on the British need for Southern cotton, the damage done by US tariffs, and the constitutional principles relating to the right of secession and self-government. That summer, the Confederacy signed contracts with British shipbuilders for the manufacture of warships, and in doing so skirted a British law prohibiting the building of warships by not arming them until they were at sea. In Parliament, meanwhile, Confederate supporters introduced a resolution calling for the British to cooperate with the French in mediating the war. Many in the British government—increasingly horrified at the carnage on the battlefields of America—believed that mediation could bring about a cease-fire and the peaceful separation of the Confederacy from the United States.

Despite the momentum in favor of Southern independence, the Confederates never did achieve their goal. The failure of Confederate military offensives in September 1862, culminating in the defeat in the eastern theater at the Battle of Sharpsburg (Antietam), again led the British to hesitate, for they did not want needlessly to antagonize the Union government and risk war, which the Lincoln administration threatened if the British interfered. Although in 1863 the French hoped to take the lead in mediating the American conflict in order to pursue their own interest in establishing a foothold in Mexico, Union victories on the battlefield put the United States in a position to stand down such French adventurism while Confederate dreams of foreign assistance grew increasingly dim. Lincoln's Emancipation Proclamation, moreover, decisively altered the dynamics of foreign policy, as the Confederates found it increasingly difficult to persuade the British of the viability and desirability of Southern independence.

UNIONIST DISSENT AND THE HABEAS CORPUS CONTROVERSY

If the Davis administration found it difficult to make friends abroad, so did it struggle to contain its enemies at home. The existence of Unionism persistently hindered the development of Confederate nationalism. From the beginning, the border states and Upper South states possessed stronger ties to the North and demonstrated less enthusiasm for secession than did the Deep South. In the slaveholding border states of Kentucky, Maryland, Delaware, and Missouri, secessionism made little headway, and Davis failed to bring these states into the Confederate orbit. Kentucky, the most likely candidate to join the Confederacy, in 1861 drifted into the Union column after Confederate forces violated its stated neutrality, and the Rebel military offensive into the state the following year failed in large part because popular support for the cause never materialized. The Upper South states of Arkansas, Virginia, North Carolina, and Tennessee had acceded to disunion after Lincoln's call for troops following the surrender of Fort Sumter. But even after the secession of the Upper South, pro-Union sentiment continued to thrive in the mountainous areas of these states, where slavery hardly existed. A Unionist rim stretched from the Ozarks to the Appalachians and included thousands of nonslaveholding whites in the states of the Upper South. Many of these folk, isolated and unbothered by the political issues that animated the fire-eaters, maintained either an outward devotion to the old Union or a silent indifference to the Confederacy.

Social and economic realities went a long way toward explaining this lack of enthusiasm for disunion. Nearly all-white, nonslaveholding areas proved to be the least committed to the Confederate experiment, and both before and during the war, planter elites in the seceded states held onto lingering fears that nonslaveholders would upend elites' political power and eventually fall under the spell of abolitionism. In some states, secession conventions had even considered changes intended to limit suffrage or otherwise muffle the popular voice in politics. Georgia drafted a new constitution in 1861 precisely because planters feared that nonslaveholders might one day ignore appeals to white solidarity and decide instead to challenge planter dominance. Its new constitution barred any legislation interfering with slavery, reduced the number of senators in the state legislature, and ended the popular election of judges. Virginia attempted to go even further in limiting popular government, as some delegates recommended limiting the franchise to property-holding taxpayers and significantly reducing the number of state elective offices. Although the Virginia measures never passed, they showed the extent to which elite forces in the state saw the need to consolidate their power in order to protect slaveholders' rights and interests. Southern Unionism, rooted in these geographical and class divisions, plagued Davis and the Confederate government throughout the war.

Eventually, Confederate military losses resulted in the erosion of Confederate and state authority over both Unionist-leaning and pro-Confederate areas. The western portion of Virginia had opposed secession, and in summer 1861, Unionists gathered in Wheeling to denounce the rebellion and repudiate Virginia's Confederate government as illegitimate. When Union forces invaded the area in summer 1861, Confederates failed to dislodge them, despite repeated raids. Unionists formed what they termed the "Restored Government of Virginia." Claiming to be the legitimate government for all of Virginia, the Restored Government authorized the creation of a new state from fifty counties in northwestern Virginia that had largely opposed secession. Although Lincoln possessed doubts about the constitutional legitimacy of the new state of West Virginia and Davis denounced it as a "monstrous usurpation," Lincoln ultimately signed the enabling legislation, and in 1863 West Virginia adopted a new state constitution and joined the Union.[19] In effect, the Unionist elements in Virginia had seceded from the rest of the state. The Confederacy also lost control of a large portion of Tennessee, although not initially in the Unionist-dominated part of the state. After a string of Federal victories in the state in the spring of 1862, nearly the entire pro-Rebel portion of Tennessee fell under Union control. Governor Isham Harris's state government left Nashville and settled briefly in Memphis before retreating to safety behind Confederate lines in Mississippi for much of the war. The Tennessee supreme court did not meet at all for three years, from April 1862 until the war ended, and at least one of its members took to the field of battle. The demise of state authority and the presence of Union troops meant that Federal authority, in all of its forms, displayed itself relatively early in the war. Although a band of local citizens had met Unionist US Supreme Court justice and Tennessee native John Catron outside of Nashville in 1861, warning that if he attempted to hold Federal circuit court in the state his safety could not be guaranteed, Catron triumphantly returned in spring 1862 after Union forces had secured control of the state's capital city. Catron held Federal court, much to the dismay of the local Rebels. Ironically, it was heavily Unionist East Tennessee that remained under Confederate control for the longest period of time, until the successful Union campaigns in the fall of 1863.

Even in those areas of the Confederacy under firm Confederate control, Davis took drastic steps to stifle dissent and protect internal security. Davis's 1862 suspension of the privilege of the writ of habeas corpus and the declarations of martial law that followed had empowered local military authorities in the affected areas to impose all sorts of regulations. In Richmond, for example, Brigadier General John H. Winder instituted a strict regime, and residents quickly learned what it meant to have their liberties curtailed. Winder banned the sale of liquor, seized personal firearms, posted armed guards, and instituted a passport system to regulate those who came in and out of the city. Winder's measures set an example for other military commanders, who instituted similar regulations in many parts of the South for much of the duration of the war. The passport system became especially widespread. Although never enacted into law by Congress, the system gradually emerged from the orders of local military commanders, with the approval of the War Department, and meant that travelers on a variety of roads and railroads—particularly those close to military operations or Unionist activity—would have to show a passport each time they wished to travel. Southerners immediately and indignantly noted the similarity to slavery. In 1861, William G. Brownlow, an East Tennessee Unionist, decried the system. "Every little upstart of an officer in command at a village or crossroads would proclaim martial law," he wrote, "and require all going beyond, or coming within, his lines to show a pass, like some negro slave."[20] Although Congress attempted to draw some limits around the suspension of the writ—including legislation justifying suspension only for offenses against the Confederate government—it is not clear that military officials ceased using their own discretion in dealing with local circumstances.

In February 1863, when the authorization of presidential power to suspend the writ of habeas corpus expired, Congress seemed in no hurry to renew it. Talk of an overbearing government and the excesses of martial law filled the corridors of Congress, and legislators took no action on the matter. Davis took a different view. Unionist activity, Federal invasion, and black insurrection, the president believed, all constituted imminent threats to Confederate forces as well as to the very existence of the fledgling nation. The problem of raising and maintaining an army, moreover, remained a top priority for the Confederate government, and Davis and the War Department quickly realized in 1863 the intimate connection between the enforcement of the conscription act and the suspension of the writ. For those seeking to avoid military service, habeas corpus was the legal weapon of choice. North Carolina supreme court judge Pearson and Virginia Confederate district judge James D. Halyburton earned reputations for their willingness to approve habeas corpus petitions, thereby freeing individuals from Confederate military service. These decisions flummoxed Confederate officials, who believed that only another suspension could thwart such unhelpful judicial rulings.

The emergence of an active peace movement in North Carolina in 1863, moreover, made the need for suspension all the more apparent to Davis. Led by William W. Holden, editor of the Raleigh, North Carolina, *Standard*, the movement began holding open meetings in summer 1863 and threatened to divide the state. These peace advocates were not antislavery. Most simply wanted to end the death, suffering, and disruption caused by the war and hoped that the antebellum order could be restored. "We favor peace," Holden wrote in July 1863, "because we believe that peace now would save slavery, while we very much fear that a prolongation of the war will obliterate the last vestige of it."[21] But this brazen attempt to break with Richmond aroused the indignation of many who had faithfully supported the Confederate cause. The aging Thomas Ruffin, retired chief justice of the North Carolina supreme court, although an opponent of secession in 1861, saw no good coming from the movement. "Is peace to be gained by divisions among ourselves," he wrote to a friend in August 1863. "We are all Secessionists now."[22] Later that year, Governor Zebulon Vance, skillfully attempting to satisfy the peace movement's demands while keeping the state loyal to the Confederacy, recommended to Davis that he make peace overtures. "If fair terms are rejected," Governor Vance argued, "it will tend greatly to strengthen and intensify the war feeling, and will rally all classes to a more cordial support of the government."[23] Davis dismissed the idea, thanked Vance for his loyalty, and urged him to "rally around" him "all that is best and noblest" in the state in order to defeat the movement.[24]

Largely in response to developments in North Carolina, President Davis delivered a forceful message to Congress on February 3, 1864, on the question of the suspension of habeas corpus. Painting a bleak picture in which war weariness and traitorous activity would produce roaming bands of plundering deserters, Davis implored lawmakers to act. "Must these evils be endured? Must the independence for which we are contending, the safety of the defenseless families of the men who have fallen in battle and of those who still confront the invader, be put in peril for the sake of conformity to the technicalities of the law of treason?" he asked. "Having thus presented some of the threatening evils which exist, it remains to suggest the remedy. And in my judgment that is to be found only in the suspension of the privilege of the writ of habeas corpus." Believing that congressional inaction would only aid those who sought to undermine the Confederacy, Davis put the task before lawmakers in blunt terms. "To temporize with disloyalty in the midst of war is but to quicken it to the growth of treason."[25] After extensive debate, Congress responded favorably to Davis's request and passed legislation on February 15 authorizing suspension of the writ for the next five months, although the act attempted to prevent discretionary action on the part of local commanders. Repudiating its earlier legislation on the subject, this time Congress claimed that only the legislative branch possessed the power to suspend the writ, although the president still determined where it could be suspended based on local circumstances.

In response, a wave of opposition to the suspension of the writ arose from the states. The Mississippi legislature urged the law's repeal on the grounds that suspension violated state sovereignty and threatened individual liberties, while Governor Vance of North Carolina—still battling the peace forces—advised Davis to use the power lightly for fear of further antagonizing the Confederacy's opponents. Georgia went the farthest in its opposition. On this issue, Governor Brown found an ally in Vice President Alexander Stephens. The vice president had always been a curious case. Looked on with suspicion from the start because of his strong Unionist views at the time of Georgia's secession, Stephens nevertheless accepted the vice presidency and for the first several months acted as a trusted adviser to Davis. But by winter 1861–1862, Davis had stopped consulting him, and Stephens left Richmond to return to his home in Crawfordville, Georgia. There he emerged as a sometime critic of the Davis administration, as he supported taxation rather than loans and argued for an impressment policy that provided fairer compensation to property holders. Stephens especially found his voice on the habeas corpus issue. Joining forces with Brown, Vice President Stephens and his brother, Judge Linton Stephens, organized the opposition to the suspension law and decided that a formal set of resolutions from the legislature would best demonstrate the depth of opposition in his state. Rallying support for the resolutions, Vice President Stephens delivered the most impassioned speech of his career, in which he described the suspension as "unwise, impolitic, unconstitutional, and dangerous to public liberty."[26] The resolutions, as passed, reflected Stephens's view that the constitutional power to suspend was merely implied and that it could only be understood in light of the constitutional guarantee to preserve due process of law. "The said act is a dangerous assault upon the constitutional power of the courts, and upon the liberty of the people, and beyond the power of any possible necessity to justify it," one of the resolutions read.[27] Davis had gotten what he wanted, as he usually did, but this time he paid a severe political price.

The habeas corpus controversy in many ways proved as damaging to the Davis administration, if not more so, than the conscription controversy. The persistence of Unionism, continuing military setbacks, and a growing Southern peace movement all converged with the debate over habeas corpus. To Davis, these simultaneous developments were reasons to suspend the writ, in order to crack down on dissent and reinforce Confederate control. Despite the limited time during which habeas corpus was actually suspended—a total of fifteen months—the discretion of local military commanders often continued to hold sway, regardless of whether the writ had been suspended. According to one historian, the Confederate military arrested and detained more than 4,000 individuals in wartime, whose fate remained in the hands of capricious habeas corpus commissioners.[28] Such abuses angered the critics of suspension, who saw little reason to sacrifice more liberties to a government that seemed as oppressive as the one they were fighting. When the suspension law expired on August 1, 1864, Congress did not renew the authorization, despite Davis's continued pleas.

THE RESPONSE TO EMANCIPATION

Nothing seemed to offend or threaten the Confederacy more than the Emancipation Proclamation. The *Richmond Examiner*, referring to it as "the most startling political crime, the most stupid political blunder, yet known to American history," observed, "It is difficult to decide whether wickedness or folly predominates in this extraordinary document."[29] President Davis immediately characterized the proclamation as an invitation to savage insurrection in violation of the most cherished principles of civilization. As Davis understood, the proclamation raised the stakes—it established that Lincoln would no longer simply seek to restore the status quo antebellum. The *Macon Telegraph*, a leading Georgia newspaper, echoed this realization in decrying the attempt by Lincoln and "Radical Abolitionism" to create a new Union without slavery. "They murdered the Union and have buried it, and are now seeking to construct a new one, better fitted to their tastes than the old one," the paper scornfully noted.[30]

Davis knew that this attempt to bring about a social revolution in the South made the Confederacy's path to victory more difficult. First, it meant that even if Southern blacks did not act out the deepest fears of whites by raping and murdering their masters, many of them would at the very least take freedom into their own hands and, as the Union army advanced, rebel against their owners. Second, it meant that Southern black men in particular would attempt to make it to Federal lines in order to join the Union army, thus augmenting the size of the already superior Union forces. Third, given a generally antislavery climate in Britain and France (despite their reliance on Southern cotton), the Confederacy would need to work harder to secure diplomatic recognition or actual assistance. At the same time, acknowledging these possibilities flew in the face of the Southern proslavery argument—the story that white Southerners had told themselves about slavery for at least the past thirty years. If the South's enslaved population did abandon plantations and set out in search of freedom, if they did rush to Federal lines to fight, if the South did stand against world opinion in its embrace of slavery, then the whole idea of a paternalistic Southern slave system in which benevolent masters cared for improvident slaves did not hold together. As if to assure fellow Southerners that none of these horrors was possible, the *Richmond Dispatch* simply dismissed the Emancipation Proclamation by asserting, "No proclamation which the Yankees have issued or may issue will have the slightest effect upon the slave population of the South."[31]

Because of the proclamation's potential consequences, Davis and Congress—initially convinced of the rightness of their cause—enacted retaliatory legislation. Describing any Union attempt to undermine slavery as "inconsistent with the spirit of those usages which in modern warfare prevail among civilized nations," the Confederate Congress authorized the president in May 1863 to engage in "full and ample retaliation" against the Union for any actions that it took against slavery. In particular, lawmakers provided for a death sentence or other punishment for any Union officer commanding a black regiment or engaging in the training, organizing, or preparing of such troops. Military courts would handle such cases. Moreover, under the law, all "negroes or mulattoes who shall be engaged in war, or be taken in arms against the Confederate States" would be delivered to state authorities, presumably to be enslaved.[32] In response, US secretary of war Edwin M. Stanton suspended prisoner exchanges, and although Lincoln issued an order to retaliate for the execution of any officers by doing the same, the order was never enforced. Still, the conflict over the treatment of black regiments and the white officers who commanded them did end prisoner exchanges between the Confederacy and the Union. Retaliatory legislation thus deepened the divide between the sides, as Union and Confederate war aims came to represent starkly antislavery and proslavery positions.

Just as important as this domestic legislative reaction to the Emancipation Proclamation was the response from the Confederacy's chief propagandist in Britain. The editor Hotze unabashedly attempted to defend slavery and white supremacy to a nation that had abolished the institution throughout its empire thirty years before. "The emancipation scheme of the North," Hotze wrote in the *Index*, "is condemned by the interests of mankind and of civilization, since it aims at converting into a barren waste one of the most fertile and productive regions of the inhabited globe. It is condemned by the law of God and man, since it is in open violation of that Constitution for which the North professes to wage war, and since it incites and employs servile insurrection, with the attendant horrors of rapine and murder." Attempting to convince the British of the ill-advisedness of Lincoln's move, Hotze fell back on familiar Southern arguments about black slavery and white supremacy. Citing the natural increase in the slave population and the growth of Christianity among the enslaved, Hotze painted an idyllic portrait of slavery as guided by the steady, benevolent influence of whites. "The hand can surely not have been an unfriendly one which has thus raised the negro from the turpitudes of the African savage," he wrote, "thus, in a half century has the fierce sanguinary African become a Christian laborer, contented with his lot, industrious, under a moral guidance rather than a system of rigorous coercion, and looking upon the white man as his friend, teacher, and protector."[33] Not only did Hotze's essays reveal the deep contradictions in Southern thought—the fear of black violence along with the assurance of white benevolence—but they also showed the South's willingness to dig in its heels in defense of its way of life. Although Hotze's writings initially won some sympathy, British opinion increasingly turned away from the Confederacy during 1863.

More than a year after the proclamation, official Confederate efforts to condemn the measure continued. Defeats at Vicksburg, Gettysburg, and Chattanooga during the second half of 1863 had greatly demoralized the Confederate populace, and in February 1864, Congress, in an "Address to the People of the Confederacy," attempted to rally and unify white Southerners by describing the ominous future that lay ahead if the Union and abolition ultimately triumphed. Describing the Emancipation Proclamation as a violation of international law and American constitutional traditions, the address raised the specter of the Haitian revolution and portrayed Lincoln as the heir of Britain's Lord Dunmore who, during the American Revolution, had promised freedom to slaves who rose up against their owners. "President Lincoln has sought to convert the South into a Santo Domingo, by appealing to the cupidity, lusts, ambition, and the ferocity of the slave," it stated. "Abraham Lincoln is but the lineal descendant of Dunmore, and the impotent malice of each was foiled by the fidelity of those who, by the meanness of the conspirators, would only, if successful, have been seduced into idleness, filth, vice, beggary, and death." Asserting that history would consign such emancipationist instigators to "immortal infamy," the address went on to warn Southerners of a dark future of degradation, submission, and humiliation that would result from defeat. "Subjugation involves everything that the torturing malice and devilish ingenuity of our foes can suggest—the destruction of our nationality, the equalization of blacks and whites, the obliteration of state lines, degradation to colonial vassalage, and the reduction of many of our citizens to dreary, hopeless, remediless bondage." The Congress further warned of the impending threat to white liberty in the stark language of white supremacy. "Sinking us into a lower abyss of degradation, we would be made the slaves of our slaves, hewers of wood and drawers of water for those upon whom God has stamped indelibly the marks of physical and intellectual inferiority."[34]

Such desperate and defensive rhetoric revealed that the Confederacy did not really know how to respond to emancipation. Even though Southerners had been warning of the possibility for years, they seemed shocked and unprepared when the moment actually arrived. Offering retaliatory policies and ominous warnings about life under black rule, the Confederate government failed at every turn. It could not contain black aspirations, could not sway British public opinion to its side, and could not rally white Southerners in disaffected areas of the slaveholding states to embrace an all-out defense of white supremacy. Nothing that Confederate officials did or said seemed able to halt the relentless momentum of events. The issuing of the Emancipation Proclamation arguably marked the beginning of the decline of the Confederacy.

THE AUTUMN OF SOUTHERN DESPERATION

By fall 1864, Davis's job as president of the Confederacy had become increasingly difficult. Reeling from continued defeats on the battlefield while confronted with declining numbers of men in arms, Davis struggled to prevent military defeat, political dysfunction, and popular despair. In the face of these challenges, Davis calmly attempted to maintain a viable Confederate military force, keep the government functioning, and rally the Southern people.

The military situation was obviously deteriorating. General Ulysses S. Grant, having completed the Wilderness Campaign, remained in position outside Petersburg, where he was attempting to starve the Confederates into submission. General William T. Sherman, meanwhile, took Atlanta and began marching his massive army through Georgia on a quest to conquer the spirit of rebellion. General Philip A. Sheridan routed Confederate forces in Virginia's Shenandoah Valley. Aggressive warfare by Union forces, the scourge of disease, and the end of prisoner exchanges had seriously depleted Southern forces. In early September, General Robert E. Lee wrote to Davis to express the urgent need for more fighting men. "A considerable number could be placed in the ranks by relieving all able bodied white men employed as teamsters, cooks, mechanics, and laborers, and supplying their places with negroes," Lee wrote. "I think measures should be taken at once to substitute negroes for whites in every place in the army or connected with it when the

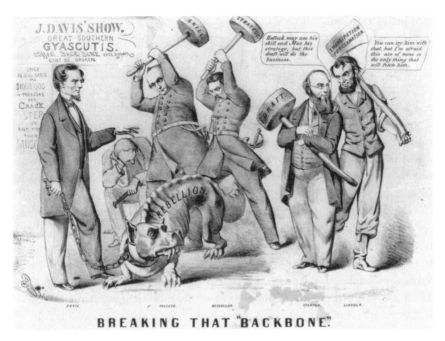

BREAKING THAT "BACKBONE."

The Confederate nation faced considerable difficulties by the time this lithograph appeared in late 1862 or 1863, as the combination of "skill," "strategy," the "draft," and emancipation all began to contribute to "breaking that backbone" of the Confederacy. President Davis is represented on the left, while President Lincoln, on the far right, wields the Emancipation Proclamation in the form of an ax. Courtesy of the Library of Congress, LC-USZ62-42560

former can be used. It seems to me that we must choose between employing negroes ourselves and having them employed against us."[35] Realizing that African American laborers could take the place of whites in noncombat positions in the Confederate army, Davis agreed with Lee. But both men knew that these adjustments would offer only temporary support.

If the military situation appeared bleak, the political outlook was no better. For months, Confederate officials had observed President Lincoln's political fortunes in the hope that he would lose his reelection bid to George B. McClellan, the former Union general and Democratic nominee for president. From the start, Lincoln had proven unwilling to compromise and negotiate, so McClellan was the candidate of choice in the Confederacy. Because McClellan waited until September before declaring his support for the war, peace-seeking Confederates for months had longed for a Democratic victory, thinking that such an outcome would produce a negotiated settlement, Confederate independence, and the preservation of slavery. Lincoln's reelection trampled Confederate hopes and served as a collective reminder of the ongoing struggle. "Lincoln has been re-elected President of the United States by overwhelming majorities," Confederate ordnance chief Josiah Gorgas wrote in his journal. "There is no use in disguising the fact that our subjugation is popular at the North, & that the war must go on until this hope is crushed out and replaced by desire for peace at any cost."³⁶ A second Lincoln term, from the Confederate perspective, meant that the fight would have to continue.

If the fight were to continue, slavery would be affected. Given the deteriorating condition of Confederate forces, Davis came to believe that the Confederacy would have to consider the employment of black troops in combat. As revolutionary as the prospect was, it merely reflected the rapidly changing realities of the war. Although Confederate general Patrick Cleburne had initially suggested the idea in January 1864, not until that fall did Davis warm to the proposal. In his November 1864 message to Congress, Davis prepared lawmakers for the notion of black Confederates, noting that "should the alternative ever be presented of subjugation or the employment of the slave as a soldier, there seems no reason to doubt what should then be our decision."³⁷ For more than a year, slavery had been slowly disintegrating before their eyes, as a phalanx of black troops abandoned their masters to serve in the Union army that had liberated them. This tide of black activism laid bare the contradictions in Southern proslavery thought and led to a thoroughgoing reevaluation of the South's peculiar institution. A movement to reform slavery emerged in the South during 1864, as religious and political leaders alike looked for ways to humanize the institution in order to save it. In response to the events happening around them, reformers advocated legalizing slave marriages, ending restrictions on teaching slaves to read and write, and enacting laws that would protect slaves from inhumane treatment at the hands of harsh masters. In October 1864 in Maryland—a slaveholding state that had remained loyal to the Union—voters approved a new constitution abolishing slavery altogether. Davis could see the handwriting on the wall. To many Confederates, of course, the idea of using slaves as soldiers and offering limited emancipation seemed to undermine the very notion of protecting slavery and white supremacy. The proposal, once made formal, would prompt a divisive debate over slavery and the purpose of the Confederacy.

If slavery were to be changed or reformed in some way, Davis reasoned, perhaps European intervention remained a possibility. At the end of December 1864, Davis thus made a final desperate overture to Britain and France through a diplomatic mission carried out by Duncan Kenner, a wealthy Louisiana sugar planter and member of Congress. Through Kenner, Davis offered gradual emancipation in exchange for recognition and assistance, but by then—with the Confederates still facing the armies of Grant and Sherman, as well as a reelected Lincoln—neither Britain nor France put any faith in the future of the Confederacy.

CONFEDERATE NATIONALISM AND ITS LIMITS

The Confederate national identity that emerged in wartime remained as riddled with contradictions as it had been at the start of the conflict. Confederate constitutional principles allowed for both national unity and state sovereignty, while the South's political culture lent itself both to public-spiritedness and partisan sniping. The ideological commitment to slavery, meanwhile, brought out class divisions within society that at times also manifested themselves in heated political debate. These tensions played themselves out over the life of the Confederacy.

To die-hard Confederates, the constitutional causes of the conflict and the dire consequences of defeat required ongoing devotion to the cause. In late summer 1863, more than a month after the surrender of Vicksburg and the defeat at Gettysburg, Judge Ruffin of North Carolina, himself a latecomer to secession, remained steadfast in his commitment to the Confederacy. Echoing the Lockean notion of the right of revolution, Ruffin forcefully argued that the South had been justified in secession and needed to remain united in war. "By the law of Nature and the rights of civilized man, we had a right and power to overthrow that Government *as far as it was our Government*, when it became intolerably oppressive," he reflected in a letter to a friend. "Therefore, I think we are engaged in a Great and Righteous *Revolution*; in which, from the beginning, I felt, that we put everything to stake, and for which state I feel that I and everyone else, who deserves the name of Freeman ought to fight to the bitter end." Defeat, in Ruffin's mind, promised nothing but the enemy's "bitterest hatred."[38] Because the consequences of losing the war seemed too terrible to contemplate, Southerners needed to rally around the cause.

Throughout the war, President Davis assiduously cultivated the idea of setting aside partisanship and states' rights for the sake of Southern independence. In his messages to lawmakers, his addresses to the armies in the field, and his public speeches throughout the South, Davis repeatedly sounded the theme of national unity, a practical nationalism that called for short-term hardship and sacrifice for the sake of long-term success. Davis justified each of his major policies—conscription, taxation, suspension of habeas corpus—on just these grounds. Over the course of the war, many followed Davis's lead in embracing this vision. Florida's Governor John Milton probably best exemplified this realistic brand of patriotism in his 1864 reply to Georgia's Governor Brown, who had asked him to join in protesting a Davis administration proposal for the regulation of shipping. Milton refused. Instead, the Florida governor offered a concise and compelling statement of his views of the Confederacy's wartime constitutional authority. "The safety of the people and preservation of their rights under the Government of free, sovereign, and independent States, confederated for mutual protection, demand the utmost confidence and generous support of the State governments to the maintenance of the Confederate Government in the execution of sacred trusts which have been confided to it," Milton wrote. "It is best, therefore, where it can be honorably done, to avoid all conflicts and competition between the State and Confederate authorities for political power, or commercial privileges, at all events during the existing war. When the independence of the Confederate States shall have been achieved and recognized by other powers and the din of war shall have ceased, the rights of the States will be adjusted."[39] Milton and other like-minded Confederates placed national unity and public-spiritedness above state power.

At the same time, many others sounded a loudly discordant note. Beginning with the conscription controversy, critics emerged across the Confederacy—on the battlefield, in the statehouses, in Congress, and eventually even within the administration—with each detractor offering a specific criticism of a policy that violated state sovereignty or ran counter to his own interests. Some of this distrust had originated in the debates over secession. Fervent disunionists sometimes doubted latecomers to secession—"eleventh hour men," the wife of one prominent fire-eater called them—and remained suspicious throughout the war that such leaders would attempt to strike a deal to end the fighting and restore the Union.[40] Another reason for the political cacophony in late 1863 and 1864 was the persistence of the culture of honor, a prickly sensitivity to insult that fed the region's deep-dyed devotion to white liberty. Honor not only worked against the antiparty ideology of Confederate leaders but also exacerbated the tensions that arose from the absence of political parties. This lack of parties created what one historian calls an "unorganized" form of politics in the Confederacy.[41] Committee chairs within Congress refrained from attempting to mobilize voting blocs or coalitions on key issues, while Davis, not wanting to appear as if he was creating a proadministration party, acted in the same disinterested manner. With no secure base from which to launch policy initiatives and no established opposition in Congress, Davis downplayed his own role in the lawmaking process. Lawmakers simply voted independently as each issue arose, as new coalitions formed on the basis of the differing sides of each legislative proposal. Unorganized politics also led to an unorganized opposition, which quickly grew into a strident collection of critics, each decrying some supposed insult, abuse of power, or failed policy. Criticism of Davis stemmed from personal slights as much as from constitutional principle. Robert Toombs of Georgia, who never got over the fact that Davis had been elected to lead the Confederacy rather than he, referred to the Confederate president as a "false and hypocritical wretch."[42] Texas senator Louis Wigfall became one of Davis's loudest detractors, mostly because of the strained relationship that developed between the president and General Joseph Johnston, one of Wigfall's close friends. The same might be said for Vice President Stephens, who, upset that the president began ignoring him, eventually turned against Davis and many of his policies. By the end of 1864, honor's individualistic voice nearly drowned out the antiparty spirit of national harmony.

If contradictions characterized the constitutional principles of the Confederacy, tensions also grew out of Confederate policy toward slavery. From the start, proslavery ideology and planter interests dictated government policy on a whole range of matters. Controlling the black population on the home front required the "twenty-negro" exemption to the conscription law. Preserving planter wealth lay behind an economic policy that shunned taxation and favored borrowing and printing money. Overestimating the value of the cotton produced by slaves drove Confederate diplomatic policy. But the reality was that none of these policies could claim much success, as each fell hardest on the yeomanry and aroused domestic opposition. Governor Brown of Georgia proved especially adept at achieving political success in his state while channeling the popular passions of nonslaveholders into his public speeches and official letters. Historians disagree about the extent to which divisions between slaveholders and nonslaveholders undermined Confederate nationalism or contributed to the South's defeat, but the fact remains that nonslaveholders' opposition did not prove so great as to prevent the yeomanry from doing most of the fighting for the Confederacy. The Confederate commitment to slavery, in other words, did not always unify, but neither did it cause the South to lose the war.

If any single policy did contribute to defeating the Confederacy and undermining Southern nationalism, it was Lincoln's issuing of the Emancipation Proclamation. Reflecting on the matter in the quiet of his Richmond office in the early days of 1863, Davis perhaps came to realize that the South was doomed. In labeling the Emancipation Proclamation "the most execrable measure" in human history, the Confederate president might have foreseen the consequences of Lincoln's policy: mass abandonment of plantations, black enlistment in the Union army, no foreign help, and Confederate desperation within two years' time. With slavery disintegrating before his eyes by the end of 1864, Davis would soon respond to events by putting forth his own last-ditch plan for emancipation, proposing to use the South's remaining enslaved population in defense of the Confederacy. To Davis, it seemed the Confederacy's last, best hope of achieving its independence and preserving its constitutional principles. To many other Rebels, the proposal promised to undermine the foundation of white supremacy and black subordination on which the Southern nation had been founded. Such were the tensions inherent within Confederate nationalism.

8

SOLDIERS, CIVILIANS, AND REVOLUTIONARY CONSTITUTIONALISM

In spring 1863, white abolitionist Edward Kinsley, a New England native, arrived in New Bern, North Carolina, to recruit black soldiers for the US Army. Traveling as an emissary of the governor of Massachusetts with hand-written orders from President Abraham Lincoln and Secretary of War Edwin Stanton, Kinsley scoured for recruits the small coastal town that had just come under Union control. Although a few months earlier local slaves had peti-tioned to join the Union Army, Kinsley noticed that something was wrong—few were interested in enlisting. All directed him to Abraham Galloway, a fugitive slave who had traveled to the North and then to Haiti before return-ing to his native North Carolina. "So great was his influence among the col-ored people," Kinsley later wrote, "that all matters of importance concerning them were left to his decision."[1] When Kinsley, Galloway, and other African Americans subsequently met in an attic room in the home of Mary Ann Starkey, another local black leader, Kinsley suddenly found himself in the most intense negotiating session of his life. The tall, charismatic Galloway claimed that he could quickly raise an entire regiment of black soldiers, but only if Kinsley could assure him that they would truly be fighting for the abolition of slavery rather than merely the restoration of the Union. Galloway boldly laid out a list of demands: equal pay for black soldiers, provisions for their fam-ilies, and schooling for their children. In addition, Galloway insisted that the Union require the Confederacy to treat captured blacks as prisoners of war rather than reenslave or execute them. At the end of the all-night meeting, Galloway and an associate put revolvers to Kinsley's head, forcing him to pledge that the Union army would deliver what they had just negotiated. Dur-ing the next few days, Galloway lived up to his end of the deal, as more than 5,000 African Americas joined together to form the 35th, 36th, and 37th Regiments, United States Colored Troops, also known as the African Brigade.

Stunned by the leadership, organization, and aspirations within New Bern's African American community, Kinsley never forgot what occurred that night.

That 1863 meeting between a white abolitionist and a cadre of freedom-loving African Americans captured the revolutionary tenor of what was occurring all over America in wartime. The war dramatically transformed the lives of Northerners and Southerners—white and black, rich and poor, men and women—and led to unforeseen changes in American society. While it confirmed existing notions of courage and honor among white men, the war also prompted black men to claim their own understanding of manhood and women to take on new roles that challenged existing conventions. While it initially appeared to be a struggle over the definition of white liberty and the future of the Union, the war unleashed African Americans' deep desires for freedom and allowed black men to serve in the Federal Army. While it at first affirmed the convictions of religious people, the war eventually caused Americans to rethink theological assumptions, as they witnessed the destruction of slavery and the depths of suffering. All whose communities were invaded, occupied, or destroyed felt the hard hand of war, and the large numbers of soldiers who were sickened, maimed, or killed as a result changed even those places that never heard the crack of gunfire or the roar of cannon. In short, the turmoil of war pointed to a different future for America.

COURAGE, CAMP, AND COMBAT

The notion of courage loomed large in the minds of young white men in both the North and the South. In the spring of 1861, the ideal of courage spurred enlistments, as men from cities, towns, and villages rushed to enroll in their respective armies. The overwhelming majority of the three million men who ended up fighting in the Civil War were volunteer citizen-soldiers—neither professionals nor draftees. More precisely, about 93 percent of the 2.2 million men who fought for the Union and about 77 percent of the approximately 800,000 who fought for the Confederacy enlisted of their own accord.[2] A quarter of the soldiers who fought in the Union army were foreign born, mostly of German or Irish extraction. Despite their different backgrounds, almost universally, nineteenth-century men believed in courage as an essential trait of masculine identity. Viewing war as an honorable affair and combat as an adventurous undertaking, young recruits held to a naive notion of what they were about to experience. Supremely confident, many believed that the imminent war would be over within a year, perhaps even a few months. With enthusiasm and bravado, these young men held fast to traditional

Confederate private Sampson Altman Jr. of Georgia was one of the hundreds of thousands of young men who volunteered on both sides in the war. Altman saw action at the Battle of Shiloh and died of disease about a year later, in April 1863. Courtesy of the Library of Congress, LC-B8184-10518

notions of manhood that emphasized the gallantry and glory associated with military service. War, in their minds, was a way to prove one's bravery and virtue, a means of making an impression on young women and earning the respect of their male peers.

War heightened men's sense of honor, creating a hypermasculinized environment that fostered a sense of duty to enlist and fight. Not only was this a duty to one another but it was also a duty to those at home—to families and neighbors, to wives and sweethearts. Civil War soldiers frequently mentioned defending "home," "hearth," or "hearthstone" as the reason they were fighting, and this connection between military service and civilian life proved a powerful one. Parents urged their sons to enlist in order to uphold the family reputation. Young women often refused to become engaged to young men until they had proven themselves on the battlefield, and women aggressively advocated courage and duty while heaping opprobrium on cowardice and desertion. The community would come down hard on those who neglected to do their manly duty.

Before soldiers could prove how courageous they were, they first had to confront the utter monotony of camp life. Once enlisted, soldiers came to realize that they would not immediately be displaying their bravery, defeating the enemy, and heading home. Instead, they learned, the process of building an army would take months and involve a great deal of drilling and waiting. In fact, the vast majority of soldiers during the first year after the bombardment of Fort Sumter spent most of their time in camp. There they found out how to organize themselves: companies of a hundred men were combined into regiments, a collection of regiments became a brigade, a handful of brigades composed a division, and three divisions constituted a corps. An army was composed of at least two corps. Once in camp, soldiers learned how to march in formation and how to properly load, fire, and maintain their weapons. When not learning rudimentary lessons in the art of war, soldiers passed the time telling tales, playing cards, reading newspapers, and engaging in horseplay. They wrote letters, read books, sang songs, attended worship services, and played musical instruments. They often complained about the food, usually a small ration of pork and a healthy dose of hardtack (square, hard flour biscuits). They dealt with the constant discomforts of camp life, including flies, mosquitoes, lice, and ticks, not to mention the horrible hygiene. As the war continued, it was easy to become demoralized from the misery of it all. "Starvation, rags, dirt, and vermin may be borne for a time by the neatest of gentlemen," North Carolinian Randolph Shotwell wrote, "but when he has become habituated to them, he is no longer a gentleman."[3] In many instances soldiers fell victim to the diseases that accompanied long-term exposure, poor diet, and primitive sanitation. Medical care in camp left much to be desired, even by the standards of the day. When orders came from their commanding officers, soldiers packed up the tents, blankets, and supplies and began to move—either on foot, by rail, or by steamboat. If on foot, they marched for dozens of miles at a time, often without knowing exactly where they were going or why. Each time they broke camp and began moving, enlisted men soon found the monotony crowded out by anxiety as they wondered if this would be their time, their opportunity to confront the enemy.

Combat, when faced for the first time, posed the ultimate test of courage. Euphemistically referred to as "the big show" or "seeing the elephant," combat brought out all of men's deepest anxieties and insecurities. As men rushed to war in 1861, they viewed the battlefield as the site of a supreme trial where they would receive an unalterable verdict: either one would stay and fight, thus demonstrating bravery in the face of danger, or one would shirk one's duty and run, thus demonstrating fear and cowardice. The stakes were high. Fighting earned the respect of peers and recognition by superiors and civilians, whereas fleeing brought shame and scorn. The shock of battle, however, caused even the men who seemed most certain they would fight suddenly to decide otherwise. Sam Watkins, a Confederate private who took part in his first major engagement at Shiloh, noted the sheer chaos of battle. "Men were lying in every conceivable position; the dead lying with their eyes wide open, the wounded begging piteously for help, and some waving their hats and shouting to us to go forward. It all seemed to me a dream; I seemed to be in a sort of haze, when siz, siz, siz, the Minnie balls from the Yankee line began to whistle around our ears," he later wrote. Amidst the smoke and flash of guns, enlisted men did their best to fight on and follow orders, although some ran away, looked for cover, or, as Watkins noted of one of the men in his unit, shot "his finger off to keep out of the fight."[4] Such men often saved their lives but damaged their reputations.

Desertion represented the antithesis of displaying courage. The most extreme form of shirking one's duty, desertion usually occurred when the news from home proved particularly distressing. Hearing of the death of a loved one, the destruction of one's home, or destitution among one's family members could cause a soldier to abandon camp and risk the consequences. The Confederate experience proved distinctive in this regard, as Yankee incursions into the Southern homeland especially prompted Rebels to abandon camp. One study of the Army of Northern Virginia showed that deserters tended to be poorer, older, less connected to slavery, and more likely to have children than those who did not desert. Whatever their motives, not many made it all the way home without incident, and even if they did, they faced not only criticism within their communities (particularly from the families of those who had not deserted) but also consequences from the authorities. Both the Union and Confederate armies looked askance at deserters and inflicted severe punishments—sometimes even death—as commanders were quick to make examples of those who absconded. Overall, the Confederate army probably experienced a higher rate of desertion than the Union army, largely because conditions in the army and on the home front steadily declined over the course of the war. Still, desertion did not follow a linear pattern among Confederates. It peaked in 1862—probably out of anger that the conscription law had extended men's service beyond what they had volunteered for—and did not hit similarly high levels until the end of the war. Evidence suggests that some deserters even rejoined the army.[5]

Of course, the vast majority of men on both sides continued to fight rather than flee, and in light of their deteriorating circumstances, courage-minded Confederate soldiers persisted to a remarkable degree. Despite its declining fortunes and disappearing rations, for example, the Army of Northern Virginia remained a viable fighting force and a popular symbol for Confederate nationalism throughout the war. The South's particular cultural emphasis on proving masculine prowess not only contributed to Confederates' tenacity but also affected military strategy and tactics. Some historians have argued that "Southern pride" or "Confederate invincibility" fostered a deep belief in Southern superiority on the battlefield, while other scholars have claimed that the Southern emphasis on the code of honor caused Confederate commanders to order unnecessary frontal assaults and their men eagerly to follow orders. Eschewing a purely defensive strategy, "the South simply bled itself to death in the first three years of the war by taking the tactical offensive in nearly 70 percent of the major actions," these historians charge.[6] Courage and honor had a powerful hold, especially over Southern warriors.

PATRIOTISM AND PRINCIPLES

Despite the potent force of courage, Civil War soldiers did not just enlist and fight because their comrades and communities demanded it. Deeply held ideological convictions often propelled men into the army and kept them there, as patriotic and political principles proved to be significant motivating forces. The armies that went to war in 1861 were overwhelmingly literate and openly political.[7] They had just come through the most contentious decade in American history, in which debate over the extension of slavery and the return of fugitives, the rights of slaveholders and the rights of states had dominated politics at both the national and state levels. They lived at a time when countless newspapers covered the political goings-on, each with a specific party loyalty or partisan slant. With the waiting often associated with camp life, soldiers read all the newspapers they could get their hands on and then passed them along to others. Not only did enlisted men consume the news but they also debated the events that were swirling around them. During less active times, some units even went so far as to form debating societies, which argued formal resolutions about the constitutional and political questions of the war. Many soldiers held strong views about liberty, slavery, and the Union and about Lincoln and Davis, and many expressed these political and patriotic sentiments in diaries and letters home. Because of these sources, historians know a great deal about what soldiers thought about the causes for which they were fighting. For the most part, soldiers on both sides emphasized the protection and preservation of liberty, but they held very different interpretations of the concept.

To Northern soldiers, fighting for liberty meant preserving the Union, the Constitution, and what they viewed as the great American experiment in republican government. Seeing themselves as the heirs of the patriots of 1776, Yankee soldiers exalted the work of the American founders and vowed to preserve their handiwork by rejecting secession and subduing the rebellion. Their letters often echoed the rhetoric of Abraham Lincoln's first inaugural address, in which the president described secession as "the essence of anarchy." Samuel

Evens, an Ohio private who had been a blacksmith and miller in peacetime, offered a sophisticated and compelling analysis of this constitutional position. "Admit the right of the seceding states to break up the Union at pleasure . . . and how long will it be before the new confederacies created by the first disruption shall be resolved into still smaller fragments and the continent become a vast theater of civil war, military license, anarchy, and despotism?" The Ohioan offered a sure solution and justification for the fighting: "Better settle it at whatever cost and settle it forever."[8] Rather than accept secession and allow the Union to dissolve into a multitude of warring states, many Federal soldiers believed that the future of republican government hinged on their success and thus sought to preserve the United States as a beacon of liberty to the rest of the world.

Again taking the American founders as the point of reference, Union soldiers glorified the patriotic work of their forebears, and many who fought knew that they might have to make the supreme sacrifice for the sake of the country and for the advancement of liberty. New Yorker John Worrell Northrop perhaps best articulated this patriotic devotion. After enlisting as a private in 1863 and being captured by the Confederates during Grant's Overland Campaign in spring 1864, Northrop kept a diary while being held prisoner and eventually ended up at the notorious Confederate prison at Andersonville, Georgia. On July 4, 1864, writing from Andersonville, Northrop marked Independence Day in his diary. "Eighty-eight years this day since our fathers gave to the world that important document setting forth the immortal truth that all men are born free with equal rights to life, liberty, and the pursuit of happiness, and declaring the independence of these states from foreign domination." Northrop continued, extolling American liberty and describing the enormity of Northern sacrifice. "On these great truths they founded a Republic. Today their posterity are in mourning for the loss of sons. In painful expectation, in earnest hope and fear, their eyes are turned toward two mighty armies contending on the same soil—one for those principles and that Republic, the other battling to maintain a dying rebellion inaugurated to overthrow the work of their hands, and to found a government on principles the reverse." Observing the thousands of suffering prisoners before his eyes, Northrop hoped that their "living sacrifice" would allow the republic soon to be free of slavery, "the contaminating influence that has stained our fair emblem" of liberty.[9] Northrop's powerful words amidst horrible suffering attested to the cultural force of constitutionalism among Northern soldiers. In short, most Union troops saw themselves as engaged in a great struggle to preserve the Union—the uniquely American experiment in constitutional liberty that stood as an example to the world.

Southern soldiers expressed their own commitment to liberty, country, and cause. Confederates saw themselves as fighting for their ability to govern themselves and to prevent the imposition of Northern tyranny. In this way, their words echoed the decades-old rhetoric of antebellum Southern politics as well as the passionate secessionist arguments of 1860–1861. As in the North, soldiers' letters in the South often repeated the rhetoric of their political leaders. In his inaugural address in February 1861, Jefferson Davis emphasized the Lockean right of revolution and secession, and soldiers too expressed their belief in the right to break away from what they viewed as an oppressive central government. Confederate soldiers made much of the parallel to the American Revolution, as they cast themselves as the patriots of 1776 seeking to throw off oppression and establish independence. They repeatedly used the words "subjugation" and "enslavement" when referring to the fate that would have overtaken them if they neglected to fight against the Union. Like Northerners, therefore, they believed that it might be necessary to give their lives for this cause. "It is awful to think of the countless numbers of good men, who have been sacrificed in this terrible war, and the large number who are yet to go, but we had better all go the same way, and leave the women and children free, than suffer the wretches who are trying to enslave us, to accomplish their ends," wrote Joseph C. Webb, a North Carolina soldier. "I prefer death to Yankee rule."[10] Because they feared that Northern victory would lead to their enslavement, to the destruction of their liberties, many took pride in describing themselves as Rebels. Washington, Jefferson, and the rest of their revolutionary forebears, they reasoned, surely defined themselves in the same way. For Confederates who viewed their land as imperiled by an invading army, the defense of liberty often seemed inseparable from the defense of community and family.

Relative to these broader notions of patriotism and liberty, Union and Confederate soldiers devoted less specific attention in their wartime letters and diaries to the slavery issue. Some Northern soldiers surely embraced the Union government's purposeful shift toward emancipation in 1863, but the majority of Union soldiers committed themselves more to fighting a "Union war" than a war to liberate African Americans. Nowhere did this tension between the Union's political leadership and its foot soldiers come into sharper relief than among Kentucky's slaveholding Unionists. One Union commander from the Bluegrass State wrote to President Lincoln in November 1862, criticizing him for "trampl[ing] upon the Constitutional rights of a loyal people in a loyal state," and later condemned the Union Army for abandoning the high principle of preserving the Union and degenerating into "a mere negro freeing machine."[11] Southern soldiers fought for slavery but mentioned it far fewer times in their writings than they did "liberty." Instead, slaveholding was implied among the rights and liberties that Southerners continually espoused, particularly given the political and constitutional debates leading up to the war. If Southerners made any assumptions about the type of society they wanted to preserve, it was the type of society in which they lived—one in which whiteness carried with it both pride and privilege. In other words, for Northern soldiers, the slavery issue served as a subordinate reason for fighting, while for Southern men, it remained an assumed—and often unspoken—element of their ideology.

Deep political convictions even moved some to break with their states or otherwise to defy convention. Some Southerners, because of their Unionist principles, followed their beliefs to their logical conclusion by enlisting in the Federal army. From the start, the United States War Department sent military officers on special missions to Unionist-leaning areas of the Confederacy to enlist soldiers. Although recruiting and arming men in enemy territory involved extensive planning and stealthy operations, the War Department succeeded early in the war in enlisting thousands in East Tennessee and in the western counties of Virginia (before the formation of the state of West Virginia). Imbued with a devotion to the Union of their fathers and the flag of the United States, Southern Unionists displayed great courage in defying their communities and casting their lots with the Yankees. For many, adherence to conviction meant that they had no choice. "I loved my country too well to stand edley by, and see it insulted without linding my ade in its support," wrote one Georgia Unionist, who, upon threat of arrest for disloyalty in 1862, left his home state for Union lines.[12] As Northern troops advanced further into the Confederacy, Unionists of fighting age actively sought refuge behind Federal lines and joined the army. An estimated 100,000 from the Confederacy—including men from every Rebel state—ended up in the Union ranks.[13] A much smaller cohort of men from Northern states, mostly transplanted Southerners who lived in the southern part of Illinois, took up arms for the Confederacy. Patriotic principles and political conviction even prompted some women to transgress the norms of the day and to disguise themselves as men in order to join the fighting, often to be with a beloved brother or husband. Although they were often discovered—particularly if wounded—one study finds evidence that a total of approximately 250 women soldiers actually fought in the Civil War.[14]

To be sure, not all Union or Confederate soldiers immediately enlisted and fought, either for the sake of courage or politics. Some men postponed joining to attend to other obligations, some waited until the draft required them to serve, and some hired substitutes or paid commutation fees in order to stay home. Others signed up to fight but spent more time running away, hiding out, or looking for ways to save their necks rather than their country. A small number held religious convictions that disallowed them from fighting, some took noncombat positions, and others avoided the conflict altogether. Not all, in other words, adhered to the dictates of courage or believed that their political convictions compelled them to take up arms. Nevertheless, for an overwhelming majority of the men who did the actual fighting, the war held great meaning and purpose, reflective of the larger political debates of the era.

CHRISTIAN SOLDIERS AND CHRISTIAN CIVILIANS

Religious ideals also gave meaning to the conflict, in the eyes of both soldiers and civilians. When the war began, Americans in large numbers adhered to the Christian religion, the Protestant version of Christianity, and the evangelical strain within Protestantism. One scholar estimates that by midcentury, 40 percent of the American population identified strongly with evangelicalism.[15] Theirs was an individualistic, personal faith, forged on the frontier and marked by an emphasis on the authority of the Bible and a belief that God intervened in human affairs. Although the three great evangelical denominations of the nineteenth century—the Methodists, Baptists, and Presbyterians—shared common theological assumptions, they had largely fractured along sectional lines during the 1840s and 1850s over the issue of slavery. By the time of the outbreak of war, men and women on both sides of the Mason-Dixon Line believed with equal certainty that God took their side in the great struggle that was unfolding.

From the start, Christian faith influenced the beliefs and actions of soldiers in a number of ways. First, religious belief provided a foundation for moral absolutism that swept aside doubts about whether their cause was just or whether the fight was worthwhile. Yankee warriors knew that they were fighting for "the best government on God's footstool," while Rebel fighters held with equal confidence a belief that the God of Battles took their side in the struggle.[16] While many soldiers certainly abhorred killing, this sense of the rightness and justness of their cause went a long way toward alleviating any doubts about whether such mayhem was justified. Violence and destruction, they believed, were sometimes necessary for the sake of accomplishing a greater good. Second, religion offered a sense of comfort for those who lay sick or suffering—on the battlefield, in hospitals, or in prison camps. Faith provided assurance that God would take care of them in their misery or, if they were to die, that their deaths were a part of God's larger will and plan.

Much of this thinking had the air of predestination or fatalism about it: it was all in God's hands. But for soldiers, this spiritual confidence offered solace and peace amidst misery and mortality. Third, and perhaps most important, religious faith gave a specific framework for coping with the possibility of imminent death. Most Christian soldiers believed in a literal heaven, a lovely paradise to which they would be immediately transported when they died. This confidence in life beyond death often alleviated their fears and gave them strength to face repeatedly the perils of combat. Believing that they fought for a righteous cause and holding an assurance that God would take care of them on this earth or beyond, the soldiers who fought in the Civil War were the most religious in American history.

On the home front, zealous ministers and pious women offered spiritual and material support. Among the religious faithful of the North, prewar evangelistic and social reform efforts gave way to harsh condemnation of the Confederacy and a militant commitment to the Union. Ministers preached sermons and religious newspapers published essays advocating war and trumpeting Northern values as a confident Christian nationalism took shape. Pastors who seemed lukewarm in their denunciation of the rebellion risked their pulpits, and the most popular sermons became those that used biblical illustrations to cement Christian theology to Union policy. Martial themes became common, and many went so far as to advocate destruction and carnage in order to purge the nation's sins. The Methodists, the largest of the Northern Protestant denominations, became some of the Union government's staunchest allies. President Lincoln reportedly told a group of White House visitors in 1864, "We never would have gotten through this crusade without the steady influence of the Methodist Episcopal Church."[17] Even those like the evangelical abolitionist William Lloyd Garrison, who had long railed against the corrupting influence of politics, fell in line. Hoping that the conflict would become an abolition crusade, Garrison abandoned his critiques of American constitutional and political institutions and offered fervent support to the cause of Union, Lincoln, and the Republicans. But it was not all sermonizing and politicking. Women rushed to contribute to the effort in more tangible ways through a vast network of wartime philanthropic organizations, such as the Christian Commission and the Sanitary Commission. Guided by Christian charity and professional efficiency, these and other institutions devoted themselves to meeting the spiritual and physical needs of Union soldiers in the field and in the hospital. They distributed Bibles, as well as religious books, tracts, and newspapers, while also providing care and comfort to the afflicted. Religious Northerners' solid support for the cause demonstrated their sincere belief that Union victory would represent the triumph of righteousness. In May 1861, a Presbyterian publication captured the Northern religious mood. "This movement of the churches as such is something quite new, this raising of funds and providing of material equipment on the Sabbath for the war is significant," it read, "and must certainly be taken as indicating their feeling, that this is a religious war."[18]

Southern evangelicals too saw the conflict in religious terms, and clergymen consistently portrayed the Confederacy as a new Zion. On the eve of secession, Benjamin Morgan Palmer, pastor of First Presbyterian Church of New Orleans, had declared that the South possessed a "providential trust" to "conserve and to perpetuate the institution of domestic slavery."[19] Only separation from the Union, he believed, would allow the Southern states to embody this special calling. Palmer's portrayal of Dixie as the righteous remnant resonated across the region. In an 1861 sermon, Reverend Edward Reed praised the Confederacy's constitutional framers for not following the example of their predecessors of 1787. "Whether through inadvertence, or, as is unfortunately more probable, from infidel practices imbibed in France by some members of the Convention, which framed the original Constitution, it contained no recognition of God. Our present Constitution opens with a confession of the existence and providence of the Almighty."[20] Throughout the war, clergymen prayed for Confederate victory, expelled members of their congregations for defying government directives, and exhorted both the South's people and its politicians to have faith in the purposes of the Almighty, however mysterious His ways. In 1863 Palmer and Bishop George Foster Pierce of the Methodist Episcopal Church South, in a pair of sermons preached to the Georgia legislature, assured their hearers that even in the midst of military setbacks, the Lord favored the Confederacy. Pierce proudly noted that "the Southern people . . . have never corrupted the gospel of Christ," while Palmer similarly proclaimed, "Our cause is pre-eminently the cause of God himself, and every blow struck by us is in defense of His supremacy."[21] Defeats on the battlefield sorely tested Southerners' faith, but they did not destroy it. Increasingly, evangelical men and women came to believe that the hardships of war provided evidence that God was chastening the Southern people rather than abandoning them. Preachers often cited lack of faith, moral laxity, and the abusive behavior of some slave masters—but not the existence of slavery itself—as lying at the root of the Lord's censure. By the fall of 1864, Georgia's Ebeneezer Baptist Association insisted that "while the chastising rod of God has been visited upon us, a wicked people, we still believe we are on the side of truth and justice."[22]

Religious revivals in the ranks, particularly Confederate forces, provided further evidence to the faithful that God was moving in history. Beginning in fall 1862 in Lee's Army of Northern Virginia, Confederate soldiers experienced a fresh infusion of the Spirit and a renewed commitment to Christ. In the aftermath of failed offensives in Maryland, Kentucky, and northern Mississippi, thousands of Rebel soldiers turned their attention increasingly to the Christian faith. Confederate defeat at Gettysburg and increasing deprivation within the ranks spurred further expressions of religiosity, and the revivals spread to the Army of Tennessee and to trans-Mississippi forces. Particularly in late fall 1863 and continuing until the end of the war, Confederate enlisted men by the thousands began attending the multiple daily services led by army chaplains or civilian preachers held in hastily constructed chapels. Many men were baptized for the first time, started attending prayer groups, and took part in the singing of hymns in camp. The proliferation of Bibles, as well as religious tracts, pamphlets, and newspapers, supported and sustained the faith of the men, and the collective experience of Christian brotherhood fostered group cohesion and solidarity in the ranks. With deep assurance of the religious nature of their cause, soldiers became better fighters who were less likely to evade their duty in combat or abandon the army altogether. Some historians speculate that had it not been for the revivals, Confederate forces would not have continued to fight as long as they did. The Union side experienced sporadic outbursts of religious intensity as well, but it witnessed nothing like the fervor that practically turned Confederate camps into camp meetings. Like courage and patriotism, religion stirred soldiers and sustained armies.

Religion during the Civil War did not always satisfy the spiritual hunger of soldiers or civilians. Amidst disease in camp and death on the battlefield, soldiers experienced plenty of trauma, and civilians heard enough bad news to sow the seeds of doubt, anxiety, and despair even within the most devout. Faith, hope, and love, in other words, did not always triumph in the hearts of men and women during wartime. Indeed, the social changes brought about by the war would eventually force many religious Americans—particularly Southerners—to rethink some of their theological assumptions and to consider how to reorder their religious lives.

EMANCIPATION AND BLACK ENLISTMENT

To enslaved African Americans, war represented a pathway to freedom. Armed conflict, they correctly reasoned, could not have broken out after years of political debate over the slavery issue without affecting their status, and once the fighting did start, it became even clearer to African Americans that their fate hung in the balance. Eventually, freedom for the enslaved came about in different times and in different ways, but it always resulted from a combination of black initiative, Union military operations, and Federal policy.

Emancipation was an uneven process dictated by local circumstances. In those areas firmly under Confederate control or remote areas well beyond combat operations, slavery remained entrenched throughout the war. But the presence of the Union military almost always initiated the unraveling of the institution of slavery. Only seven months after Fort Sumter, in November 1861, the Union attacked the Sea Islands off the coast of South Carolina, in the hope of establishing a coaling and supplying station for Union blockade vessels. After pounding Confederate defenses, Union landing parties secured control of the Port Royal area, thus prompting local masters to flee to the mainland and local slaves to experience autonomy for the first time in their lives. Some 11,000 enslaved people, by refusing to flee with their masters, entered Union lines by simply remaining where they were. Freed by circumstances and liberated under the terms of the First Confiscation Act, the federal government began an experiment in free labor, as the formerly enslaved began growing cotton for wages. Over the next several months, the existence of a Union foothold on the Atlantic coast, between Charleston and Savannah, caught the attention of slaves throughout the region. By August 1862, planters in Liberty County, Georgia, located to the south of Savannah, reported to the region's Confederate commander that they had lost "20,000 [slaves] & their value from $12 to $15 millions of Dollars." The masters reported that some even fled "out to the vessels of the enemy seaward."[23]

By the end of 1862, the announcement of President Lincoln's Preliminary Emancipation Proclamation inspired increasing numbers of slaves to seek Federal protection. As other areas of the Confederacy fell under Union control, slaves viewed military lines as the threshold of freedom and initiated a gradual exodus from plantations and small farms. Often the mere rumor of Union troops in the vicinity set these migrations in motion. As John Eaton, the freedman's superintendent for Tennessee, noted in a report to President Lincoln, "All the testimony goes to show that the slaves had almost universally a strong desire to be free, and a vague idea that fleeing to the enemies of their masters would make them free."[24] At first mostly men made the decision to flee, but in time whole families, extended families, and large groups began to claim their freedom. Federally occupied cities such as Nashville and New Orleans became havens for enslaved people seeking refuge and opportunity. In Memphis, which fell under Union control in June 1862, the army estimated that the black population increased fourfold between 1860 and 1865, as blacks from nearby Mississippi Delta plantations flooded into the city. Military installations, such as Fortress Monroe in Virginia, also became havens for self-emancipating slaves. In May 1863, Union captain Charles B. Wilder estimated in testimony before a War Department commission that 10,000 formerly enslaved people had arrived at the fort. "This is the rendezvous," he testified. "They come here from all about, from Richmond and from 200 miles off in North Carolina. . . . I have questioned a great many of them and they do not feel much afraid; and there are a great many courageous fellows who have come from long distances in rebeldom. Some men who came here from North Carolina knew all about the [Emancipation] Proclamation and they started on the belief in it; but they had heard these stories and they wanted to know how it was."[25] In places where Federal authority was secure, blacks petitioned provost marshals asking for their "free papers," provided legal testimony against their former owners, and sought legal recognition of their marriages. Some women attempted to claim pensions as widows of war veterans. Such assertions of black agency often flummoxed Union officers, who struggled to formulate rules regarding the newly freed population.

Apart from major cities and Union forts, "contraband camps" sprang up at military outposts in the Mississippi Valley and Tennessee, as well as in parts of Northern Virginia and in coastal towns that came under Union control. The name came from Union general Benjamin Butler's 1861 designation of slaves as contraband, enemy property seized in wartime. The camps initially served as informal assembly points for the newly freed, but they eventually took on a more formal existence under the authority of the Union military. Contraband camps varied widely. Some were simply depots of neglect and disease, while others proved to be exemplars of interracial cooperation and black advancement. Irony abounded in the locations of these new black communities. At Davis Bend, Mississippi, where Confederate president Jefferson Davis and his brother had owned plantations before the war, black settlers succeeded in electing their own sheriffs and judges while also producing a profitable cotton crop. Perhaps the most famous camp emerged just across the Potomac River from the District of Columbia on the confiscated estate of Confederate general Robert E. Lee. In 1863, thousands of African Americans fleeing bondage in Virginia and Maryland began converging at Arlington, where a "Freedman's Village" quickly arose, complete with schools, a hospital, a chapel, and dozens of two-family homes. In these camps, Federal authorities, Northern missionaries, and African Americans struggled to provide for the basic needs of increasing numbers of people while also attempting to define the parameters of freedom. Because these were temporary havens often governed by no set laws, formerly enslaved people sometimes found themselves subject to Union military abuses as well as Confederate raids.

The desire for freedom and rights, rooted in black constitutional ideals, drove and sustained the exodus from plantations. In contrast to Union soldiers who often had little affinity for their government's post–Emancipation Proclamation policy of liberation, African Americans had always viewed the conflict as a war to end slavery. A month after Fort Sumter, in May 1861, a meeting of African American activists in Boston described the conflict as "a contest between liberty and despotism" and offered, quoting the Declaration of Independence, to "defend the Government as the equals of its white defenders—to do so with 'our lives, our fortunes, and our sacred honor' for the sake of freedom." Religious ideals deeply informed blacks' notion of freedom, as black Christians shared with white evangelicals a providential sense that God was working out His purposes through the war. Slaves' theology of deliverance, which cited the parallels between their experience and that of the ancient Israelites, confirmed that the time had come for liberation. Henry McNeal Turner, a free-born black man and pastor of an African Methodist Episcopal church in Washington, DC, assured his congregation in August 1863 that "God will surely speak peace when His work, which this affliction is designed to produce, is accomplished."[26] Such sentiments inspired thousands of African American men and women to view Union forces as liberators.

The gradual, uneven arrival of freedom prompted calls for black military service, which became a subject of national debate. Although blacks had served in the navy for decades and although small numbers of blacks had fought in America's previous wars, that black men would don uniforms in the United States Army was by no means a foregone conclusion in 1861. Some advocated black military service at the outset of the conflict because they believed that doing so would contribute to the cause of emancipation and citizenship. Immediately seizing on the potentially revolutionary consequences of the Southern rebellion, just weeks after Fort Sumter, Frederick Douglass urged the arming of black men. "*Let the slaves and free colored people be called into service, and formed into a liberating army*, to march into the South and raise the banner of Emancipation among the slaves," Douglass thundered in his monthly newspaper.[27] In late 1861, informal units composed of Northern free blacks began drilling and offering their services, but wary of the political and constitutional implications of such a policy, the Lincoln administration demurred. In May 1862, General David Hunter attempted to raise a black regiment by issuing an emancipation order from Hilton Head, South Carolina, but the president immediately rescinded it.

Some African Americans and white abolitionists continued to take matters into their own hands. In May 1862, Robert Smalls, a South Carolina slave, commandeered a Confederate transport vessel, navigated it through heavily guarded Charleston harbor, and sailed toward Union blockade ships in open waters, where he showed a flag of truce and surrendered the vessel to the Union Navy. Hailed as a hero in the North, Smalls became a powerful advocate for black participation in the military. In the meantime, abolitionist US senator James Henry Lane began organizing black volunteers in Kansas on his own authority. His First Kansas Colored Volunteers—composed mostly of formerly enslaved Missourians—saw combat action that fall at the Battle of Island Mound in Missouri, where black troops suffered their first casualties of the war.

Congress took the first official steps toward black military service in summer 1862 by enacting the Second Confiscation Act and the Militia Act. The former provided for the confiscation of slave property owned by Rebels and the latter for the use of blacks in the military. As a result of this legislation, in August Secretary of War Edwin Stanton formally authorized the raising of 5,000 troops in South Carolina, and a few months later Secretary of the Navy Gideon Welles dramatically expanded the number of black sailors. Lincoln's Emancipation Proclamation of January 1863 culminated Union policy on black military service, stating that "such persons of suitable condition, will be received into the armed service of the United States to garrison forts, positions, stations, and other places, and to man vessels of all sorts in said service."[28] In early 1863, the War Department created a Bureau of Colored Troops and began actively recruiting and raising black regiments on a grand scale in those parts of the South that had already come under Union control, particularly in portions of Louisiana, Mississippi, and Tennessee. Once Northern leaders realized that black soldiers both helped the Union and harmed the Confederacy, Federal policy converged with black aspirations.

Still, not all African American leaders rushed to support enlistment. Some within the black community cautioned against it from the beginning by arguing—like Abraham Galloway in New Bern—that blacks needed to make sure that the conferring of rights and privileges would accompany black service. John Rock, a free-born black man from New Jersey who had become a leading lawyer and activist, insisted that the war presented an opportunity for blacks to assert their rights and overcome the Supreme Court's stinging *Dred Scott* decision. "Seventy-five thousand freemen capable of bearing arms, and three-quarters of a million of slaves wild with the enthusiasm caused by the dawn of the glorious opportunity of being able to strike a genuine blow for freedom, will be a power that 'white men will be bound to respect,'" he argued in a January 1862 speech in Boston, in a mocking paraphrase of Chief Justice Taney's infamous opinion. "Let the people of the United States do their duty, and treat us as the people of all other nations treat us—as men; if

The journey of some enslaved African American men, literally from the plantation to the battlefield as Union soldiers, represented one of the most dramatic social revolutions in the history of the United States. This 1863 lithograph captures the transformation. Courtesy of the Library of Congress, LC-DIG-ppmsca-05453

they will do this, our last drop of blood is ready to be sacrificed in defence of the liberty of this country," Rock continued. "But if you continue to deny us our rights, and spurn our offers except as menials, colored men will be worse than fools to take up arms at all."[29] At a particularly contentious public meeting over black enlistment in New York in April 1863, Frederick Douglass admonished a crowd of potential recruits for their lack of enthusiasm. According to one observer, a Mr. Robert Johnson suddenly rose and defended the skeptical attendees, noting that "a proper respect for their own manhood" lay behind the unwillingness to enlist. "If the Government wanted their services, let it guarantee to them all the rights of citizens and soldiers," Johnson argued, to great applause.[30]

From the start, all knew that black service and sacrifice were in some way connected to black manhood and liberty, and just as these concepts suffused the political debate, they also served as motivations for individual black soldiers. Northern units were usually composed of a mix of free blacks and fugitive slaves, while regiments recruited in the South—the vast majority of all black troops—were made up almost exclusively of those who had just emerged out of bondage. They had no doubts about why they were fighting, and it was not to save the old Union. James Caldwell, a free black man in Massachusetts and the grandson of black feminist and abolitionist Sojourner Truth, put the matter bluntly. "Now is our time, Grandmother," he wrote to Truth, "to prove that we are men."[31] Recognition of one's manhood connoted a conception of courage, as well as the basic rights and liberties of individuals. Others made the point in a more explicitly political and patriotic way. "We are fighting for liberty and right, and we intend to follow the old flag while there is a man left to hold it up to the breeze of heaven," exclaimed a black sergeant. "Slavery must and shall pass away."[32] In standing up for themselves as free men possessing rights, African American soldiers rejected the idea of fighting for the Union—the Union that had allowed slavery. Instead, by fighting, they made claim to nascent notions of citizenship, to full participation in the American political community, and to a new Union organized along these lines. Whether long free or recently freed, African Americans joined the fight with a common sense of purpose, to create a Union that ensured liberty for all and that advanced the cause of freedom throughout the world. In a poignant speech in Union-held Alexandria, Virginia, the formerly enslaved famous author of *Incidents in the Life of a Slave Girl*, Harriet Jacobs, urged black soldiers to "take the dear old flag and resolve that it shall be the beacon of liberty for the oppressed of all lands, and of every soldier on American soil."[33]

Despite a deep desire to fight for freedom, most black soldiers performed noncombat support roles as laborers, teamsters, guards, and personal servants.

As more of the Confederacy fell under Union control, black soldiers often garrisoned forts in order to provide a sustained Federal presence while white soldiers engaged in formal military operations. Others performed more specialized tasks as carpenters, cooks, physicians, scouts, and steamboat pilots. A handful served as army chaplains to black soldiers, while a significant cohort of black men and women served as spies who offered crucial intelligence regarding Confederate military operations. The Emancipation Proclamation had referred specifically to some of these supporting roles, but the sheer need for fighting men, along with African Americans' eagerness to see battle, eventually allowed blacks to enter more combat situations.

Supervised by white officers, black regiments saw action in 1863 and 1864 in a series of major engagements. They fought at Milliken's Bend and Port Hudson, Louisiana, both part of the Vicksburg Campaign, after which General Ulysses S. Grant lauded their abilities as soldiers. Perhaps most famously, black troops fought near Charleston, South Carolina, after the Union established a beachhead there in the middle of 1863. Commanded by the young Colonel Robert Gould Shaw, the son of a prominent white Massachusetts abolitionist, the Massachusetts 54th Regiment led a heroic assault on the well-defended Fort Wagner. Incurring heavy losses after hand-to-hand combat, the men of the 54th won national acclaim for their valor. Early the following year, the Massachusetts 54th and other black regiments participated in an ill-fated attempt to invade northern Florida, an operation that culminated in Union defeat at the Battle of Olustee. Later in 1864, black troops fought intensely at the Battle of Nashville and the Battle of the Crater in Petersburg. Black women could not formally join the fight, of course, but some nonetheless served as nurses, spies, and scouts, with Harriet Tubman being the most famous black woman scout. In all, nearly 180,000 black soldiers and an additional 18,000 black sailors served in the Union military during the Civil War—about 10 percent of the approximately two million men who fought on the Union side. Over the course of the war, nearly 40,000 black soldiers died.

In short, enslaved African Americans played a significant role in securing their own freedom and shaping the national debate over their fate. Knowing that Lincoln's election and the outbreak of war created space for black insurgency, some African Americans began abandoning their owners, heading to Union lines, and offering themselves for military service. According to some estimates, nearly 400,000 enslaved people, by the middle of 1864, fled their masters and made it to Federal lines.[34] In taking these steps, blacks put pressure on the Union army, the Lincoln administration, and Congress to strike at slavery and white supremacy. Federal policy both shaped and responded to black initiative, while the advance of the Union armies and the reality of black military sacrifice made it increasingly unlikely, as time went on, that slavery could survive the war. Certainly it was not all jubilation for those seeking freedom. Northern racism persisted, and Union soldiers often proved hostile to slave contrabands and black soldiers alike. Despite their devotion to the cause, moreover, black soldiers fought in segregated units, served under white officers who did not always view them as equals—General William T. Sherman, for example, never embraced the notion of black military service—and faced Confederates who threatened to reenslave or execute them. Not until mid-1864 did Congress agree to pay black soldiers, retroactively, at the same rate as whites. Nevertheless, as the Republican *New York Times* noted after the triumphant departure of black regiments from the city in early 1864, "It is only by such occasions that we can at all realize the prodigious revolution which the public mind everywhere is experiencing. Such developments are infallible tokens of a new epoch."[35]

DESPERATION, OCCUPATION, AND DESTRUCTION

As the Union army battled the Confederates on Southern soil, the region's civilian population felt the effects of hard war. Because most men of fighting age were away serving in the Confederate army, women and children usually bore the brunt of the suffering on the home front. Most women found themselves taking on new tasks to which they were unaccustomed—managing slaves, harvesting a crop, or negotiating contracts—while children experienced the loss of fathers or older brothers and unexpectedly assumed the responsibilities of adulthood at an early age. Whether they lived in the vicinity of the fighting, in an area actually occupied by Federal forces, or in a place subject to Union siege and destruction, civilians confronted the loss of their property, the devastation of the landscape, and a new sense of insecurity in their lives.

In many areas of the South, war created shortages, disruptions, and desperation. Harsh battles sometimes wreaked havoc on farms and fields, while military authorities on both sides usually confiscated foodstuffs from local plantations and farmsteads to feed their men. The Confederacy's tax in kind meant that a certain portion of crops automatically went to the Confederate authorities, who fanned out across the countryside to collect the food for the Rebel army. Union control of ports, roads, and railroad lines prevented available crops from making it to market, thus putting further pressure on food supplies. Meat and the salt to preserve it became especially scarce commodities, particularly after one of the South's two major sources of salt, the Avery Islands in southern Louisiana, fell under Union control. Facing hunger, the poorest families flooded into military lines—both Confederate and Union—as they sought out whomever they thought might be able to provide them with basic rations. Others raided army supply depots to take what they needed or stole what they could from farms or plantations, thus creating patches of lawlessness. Union officers in particular expressed concern about roving bands of unruly poor whites, sometimes including deserters, who stole property and threatened other civilians. In places where both planters and slaves had fled in the face of Union forces, the poor and desperate sometimes moved in as squatters to scavenge what remained, while others moved from place to place in order to seek out safety and sustenance. Some Southerners directed their anger at government officials or military authorities. In communities across the war-torn South, crowds of women instigated riots in attempts to secure food for their families. At one especially large food riot in Richmond in 1863, President Davis himself had to calm the people. Even the wealthiest Southerners—planters and other slaveholders—could not escape the disruptions that war created. Many slaveholders watched helplessly as the Rebel army confiscated slaves as laborers, or, more dramatically, as enslaved people left plantations, refused to work, or began negotiating or imagining a new future where they were. Planters often seemed shocked when long-serving slaves abandoned them, although some did stay out of fear or loyalty. Not immune to the shortages and inflation that increasingly plagued the South, planters altered decades-old agricultural rhythms by switching from cotton to food crops, either at the behest of the Confederate government or out of necessity.

In places subject to military occupation, Southern civilians confronted their Northern enemies on a daily basis. Occupation came about when the Yankees won critical battles at railroad junctions, at river ports, or in cities, and soldiers stayed behind to establish a military presence. By mid-1862, Nashville, New Orleans, and Memphis, for example, had become major headquarters for Union military operations and important supply points in the shaping of Northern strategy. In these and other places, Union soldiers and pro-Confederate civilians coexisted uneasily. Occupying soldiers sought to prevent smuggling and spying, promote loyalty, and foster the rule of law, while pro-Confederate civilians did all in their power to make life difficult for Yankee invaders.

Because women constituted such a large portion of the civilian population, occupation often affected gender relations. By all accounts, Confederate women seemed especially hostile to Union forces and often went out of their way to show disdain for their foes. Shouting insults, holding their noses, turning up their skirts, and in some instances spitting and dumping chamber pots on Union troops earned Rebel women a reputation for rudeness and treach-

General Benjamin Butler of Massachusetts, one of the more colorful and controversial figures of the war, issued his infamous "woman order" in 1862. His headquarters in New Orleans, pictured here, surely symbolized to local residents the affront of Union occupation. Courtesy of the Library of Congress, LC-DIG-ppmsca-32996

ery. In Baton Rouge, the young Sarah Morgan, whose three brothers fought for the Confederacy, became a vociferous critic of the Union forces that arrived in the city in May 1862. After confiding murderous thoughts to her diary, Morgan lamented, "O if I was only a man! Then I could don the breeches, and slay them with a will! If some few Southern women were in the ranks, they could set the men an example they would not blush to follow."[36] Morgan's desire to become a man and show Confederate soldiers how to get the job done revealed the frustration that many upper-class Southern women experienced as their feelings of anger and aggression clashed with prewar notions of female piety and submissiveness.

In occupied New Orleans, the combination of women's rebelliousness and the Union commander's strictness led to a confrontation between soldiers and civilians. Exasperated with the constant hostility of the women of the city, on May 15, 1862, a month after the Union established control there, General Benjamin Butler issued an order that provoked widespread outrage. "As the officers and soldiers of the United States have been subject to repeated insults from the women (calling themselves ladies) of New Orleans in return for the most scrupulous non-interference and courtesy on our part," he wrote, "it is ordered that hereafter when any female shall by word, gesture, or movement insult or show contempt for any officer or soldier of the United States she shall be regarded and held liable to be treated as a woman of the town plying her avocation."[37] Butler's order gave license to Union soldiers to openly disrespect local women who proved insolent by giving men permission to disregard the gender conventions of gentility and consideration. Treating local women like prostitutes was a public insult, a symbolic denigration of Confederate pretensions to civility. If the ladies of New Orleans did not behave as ladies, Butler reasoned, they would not be treated as such. The controversy over the "woman order" reverberated throughout the Confederacy, the Union, and the world. Southern governors issued proclamations condemning it, President Jefferson Davis officially declared Butler "a felon, deserving of capital punishment," and European leaders wondered aloud how the North could allow such an order to stand.[38] Butler later ordered the execution of a male civilian for tearing down a US flag from a government building, and New Orleans residents howled in protest and began calling the general "Beast Butler." Union occupation only seemed to stir enmity and controversy.

Such confrontations contributed to the Union's adoption of a strategy of hard war. Butler was not the only Union commander who found Rebel civilians to be entirely too rebellious. General William T. Sherman, who spent the second half of 1862 commanding a Union occupying force in Memphis, witnessed firsthand the stubborn resistance of local residents. Confronting smugglers and spies within the city while battling guerillas and raiders in outlying areas, Sherman ordered the burning of Randolph, a small town thirty miles upriver from Memphis, after a guerilla raid on a Union ship, and he became pessimistic about the prospects of ever convincing Confederates to return to the Union fold. Although early in the war Sherman had hoped for minimal destruction and quick conciliation with the South, his hopes for a limited war soon vanished. Writing from Memphis to his brother in August 1862, Sherman confided his belief that the North would need to "colonize" the South by having Northerners move in to take over Southern lands. "Enemies must be killed or transported to some other country," he wrote.[39] Although Sherman's Memphis thoughts never became military policy, his Memphis experience undoubtedly shaped his belief in taking the war more directly to the civilian population.

Confederate resistance strengthened Union resolve, thus creating a cycle that led to further destruction and despair. In 1863, General Ulysses S. Grant unflinchingly starved Vicksburg into submission as civilians ate rats and lived in caves, and the following year, during the siege of Petersburg, civilians created dug-out shelters covered with logs in order to ride out the shelling that destroyed their homes, businesses, and churches. Petersburg residents convinced themselves that Grant's willingness to bombard noncombatants constituted outrageous, uncivilized behavior. Likewise, when Sherman made his march through Georgia in late 1864, destroying infrastructure and targeting the trappings of secessionism—he burned the plantation of Confederate leader Howell Cobb, for example—civilians howled against the destructiveness and violation. Confederate women reacted in especially strong terms to the intrusion of Sherman's men into private homes, including women's domestic spaces such as bedrooms, parlors, and kitchens. But relatively small numbers of civilians actually lost their lives in these campaigns, in which property damage and psychological submission were the ultimate aims. Historians still debate the extent of the destruction, as well as the morality of Union tactics, but the intransigence of die-hard Rebel civilians all over the South had surely helped contribute to the new brand of destructive warfare.

GUERILLA FIGHTERS AND THE LAWS OF WAR

The destructiveness and disorder of war proved most evident in guerilla fighting. Also known as irregular warfare, guerilla fighting encompassed all of the violent activity carried out by armed men who operated outside of the Union and Confederate armies. Although guerilla activity occurred on both sides, the majority of guerillas were pro-Confederates who fought aggressively against Union operations in the South. Most Southern civilians never came into direct contact with the regular armies that faced each other on the battlefield, but guerillas could be found at one time or another in most areas of the South, particularly those in which neither Union nor Confederate forces were operating. Guerillas abided by no rules of engagement, and they moved about freely and rapidly. Their fearsome fighting style resembled that of General Nathan Bedford Forrest, and their operations often served a similar purpose of keeping alive the spirit of Southern independence. But guerillas acted on their own authority, outside of the bounds of accepted military conventions. In 1862, the Confederacy passed the Partisan Ranger Act, which attempted to use irregulars to its advantage by commissioning them. Whether independent guerillas or commissioned partisans, irregulars engaged in the same behavior. They ambushed or "bushwhacked" supply depots, trains, wagons, and steamboats, as well as contraband camps and Unionist enclaves. More extreme—and more deadly—forms of guerilla warfare also emerged, driven more by issues of community control, family feuds, and blood vengeance than by a genuine desire to aid the success of the Union or the Confederacy. The war generated violence and created chaos.

Guerilla activity was most prevalent in the Upper South and border states, where Unionist sentiment remained strong. In fact, much of this violence could be described as part of a civil war within the South—a series of strikes and counterstrikes waged by pro-Confederate and pro-Union guerillas against each other, which often involved regular troops as well. In the state of Arkansas, for example, Confederate general Thomas C. Hindman turned to the raising of independent guerilla companies, not subject to the Confederate draft, as a way of defending the state against Union forces. The formation of these partisan units prompted Federal authorities, in turn, to recruit Arkansas Unionists for counterguerilla operations. In East Tennessee, a heavily Unionist area that for much of the war remained under Confederate control, local guerillas waged a lengthy campaign of sabotage and harassment against regular Confederate forces, tactics that dramatically limited Confederate operations there. By cutting telegraph lines, burning bridges, raiding supply stores, and firing on Rebel units, Unionist irregulars made their presence known. In Shelton Laurel, a remote valley in the Appalachian Mountains in the western part of North Carolina, local pro-Confederate guerillas recruited Confederate officers to shoot and kill thirteen men in supposed retaliation for a Unionist raid on a salt store. Although promised a military trial, all of them were shot in the head and buried in a shallow mass grave. The youngest of these victims was only thirteen years old. Guerilla warfare often yielded murderous results.

The most infamous example of the excesses of guerilla warfare occurred on the border between Missouri and Kansas. A state with a long history of internal division over slavery and secession, Missouri became a bloody battleground in wartime. Pro-Confederates constituted a sizable minority of Missouri's population, and guerilla groups there destroyed property, ambushed Federal troops, drove people from their homes, and murdered civilians. William C. Quantrill proved the most notorious of these fighters. A native of Ohio, before the war Quantrill had moved to Kansas and joined the Jayhawkers, a fierce band of antislavery guerillas based in Lawrence. He later betrayed the Kansans and, after the war began, formed a group of pro-Confederates in Missouri. On August 21, 1863, supposedly in retaliation for a Union raid on Osceola, Missouri, Quantrill led approximately 400 outlaws in a raid on Lawrence, Kansas, long the center of antislavery activity in the region. Charging into town, Quantrill and his gang destroyed the business district and murdered

150 men and boys—nearly every man he could find—in the worst guerilla atrocity of the war. A few months later, Quantrill and his group massacred some 100 Federal soldiers at Baxter Springs, Kansas. Such activities outraged even Confederate leaders, who attempted to capture Quantrill, but the outlaw hid out in Missouri for much of 1864 before finally being seized by Union guerillas in Kentucky in May 1865.

Guerilla activity surely spawned desolation, fear, and death wherever and whenever it flared up, but its effects should not be exaggerated. Irregular forces did not significantly alter the course of the war. Despite the wide extent of guerilla activity in Missouri, the single most important result of the violence there was an attempt to codify the rules of war. In 1862, General Henry Halleck, who had previously commanded Union forces in the state, asked Professor Francis Lieber to produce a set of guidelines for use by the Union Army, particularly regarding the distinctions between legitimate enemy combatants and unlawful guerilla fighters. Lieber, a native of Prussia, veteran of the Napoleonic wars, and professor at New York's Columbia University, produced a pamphlet, *Guerrilla Parties Considered with Reference to the Laws and Usages of War*, which Halleck ordered reproduced and distributed to all Union generals.

Impressed with the work, Halleck then ordered Lieber to create a comprehensive code of the laws of war, and he eventually drafted what came to be known as General Orders No. 100, a code of 157 specific rules that governed the military treatment of, for example, partisans, prisoners, and private property. The Lieber Code, officially authorized by President Lincoln in April 1863, attempted both to restrain the regular army and to announce to irregulars that they would not be treated as prisoners of war. Although the code considered many of the men commissioned under the Partisan Ranger Act as legitimate soldiers, those who fought "without commission, without being part and portion of the organized hostile army, and without sharing continuously in the war" were to be treated as "highway robbers or pirates" rather than as enemy combatants.[40] The code was the first of its kind in American history, and the Confederacy never drafted anything comparable. Guerilla fighting had not undermined all notions of legalism and restraint.

PRISONERS AND PRISONS

Like guerillas, prisoners of war raised a host of issues for the Union and Confederate governments. Initially, prisoners posed few problems. Only a small number resulted from the fighting in 1861, and governments adequately housed them in old forts, warehouses, or jails. Occasionally armies engaged in informal exchanges of prisoners, particularly the sick and wounded. But General Grant's Tennessee River campaign produced huge numbers of prisoners at the battles of Fort Henry, Fort Donelson, and Shiloh, while General McClellan's operations in the Seven Days Campaign, Second Bull Run, and Antietam proved just as costly in terms of men captured by the opposing army. Although Union authorities initially hesitated to negotiate on the matter because it implicitly recognized the Confederacy as a belligerent under the international laws of war, by summer of 1862, both sides desired a formalized agreement for the return of prisoners. In July, the Union and Confederate governments agreed on a formula for the swapping of prisoners based on rank. Officers of the same rank were equal to one another, while each officer was equal to a certain number of privates. This system also provided for the paroling of soldiers. On the basis of an honor system, parole allowed a captured prisoner to go free so long as he promised not to take up arms against the enemy until he had been notified that he had been officially exchanged for another prisoner, either in a holding camp or on parole. The paroled soldier, in the meantime, would either return home or, in the case of those from states that had passed laws forbidding the return of parolees, to a detention camp maintained by his own side. This system of prisoner exchange worked through the remainder of 1862, but two major controversies soon led to its deterioration and eventual abandonment.

The first controversy pertained to the Union's use of black soldiers. Once the Union army began enlisting black men, the Confederacy announced its refusal to exchange any black prisoners. Continuing to view slaves turned soldiers as property rather than men, the Confederate government refused to yield an inch on the issue. Confederates officially held that all captured black soldiers would be treated as fugitive slaves and returned to bondage and their white officers convicted of instigating slave rebellions, a capital offense in the South. In response, the Union government ceased engaging in prisoner exchanges with the Rebel government. The Lieber Code affirmed the Union position. The code specifically included a color-blind clause with regard to prisoners, for it stated that "the law of nations knows of no distinction of color" and held that "no belligerent has a right to declare that enemies of a certain class, color, or condition, when properly organized as soldiers, will not be treated" as prisoners of war.[41] This remarkable language, combined with Lincoln's Emancipation Proclamation and a November 1862 opinion by Attorney General Edward Bates announcing the citizenship of free blacks, served as another weapon in the legal assault on slavery and white supremacy. Union policy affirming the status of black soldiers as men directly contradicted the Confederate position. Conceiving of black soldiers as fugitive slaves affirmed the Confederates' continued emphasis on slaveholders' rights, while viewing the formerly enslaved as men with rights of their own epitomized the revolutionary changes occurring in the Union.

The second controversy over prisoners proved more a practical matter than an idealistic one. In July 1863, Grant had captured some 37,000 prisoners from General Pemberton's army at the surrender of Vicksburg, and instead of having to transport and take responsibility for so many men, Grant had paroled them. But rather than holding these men for proper exchange, Confederate authorities illegitimately allowed thousands of these soldiers to return to combat within a few weeks. Some months later, Grant faced at Chattanooga many of the same men he had captured and paroled after Vicksburg. Stung by the experience, Grant's views hardened on the subject. He came to believe that exchanging prisoners simply allowed men back into the ranks, and he knew that the Confederacy needed its prisoners to be returned more than the Union did.

When prisoner exchanges came to a halt in 1863, both the Union and Confederacy began expanding the holding pens they had created for prisoners before they were swapped, in effect turning these temporary camps into prisons. More than 150 of them sprang into existence during wartime, and one scholar has identified five different types of prison structures: coastal fortifications, enclosed barracks, old converted buildings, groups of tents surrounded by a high fence, and, most notoriously, barren stockades that provided no shelter to prisoners. None of these makeshift compounds—Union or Confederate—provided much in the way of comfort, and all suffered from grim sanitary conditions. Often the soldiers who arrived in prisons were already sick, and if they were not, they soon became so. Prison hospitals typically failed to meet the most basic standards of the day for medical care, and huge numbers of men lingered in these compounds before dying. Approximately 408,000 men spent time as prisoners during the war, and more than 56,000 of these died while incarcerated.[42]

By far the most atrocious conditions in any Civil War prison existed at the Confederacy's Camp Sumter, more commonly known as Andersonville, the name of the closest village. Built in Sumter County in southwest Georgia by slave labor, Andersonville prison was a huge stockade formed by the construction of walls made up of hundreds of vertically positioned twenty-two-foot logs, placed five feet in the ground and seventeen feet above ground in the middle of an open field. The prison opened in February 1864 under the command of Captain Henry Wirz, a Swiss immigrant who had settled in Louisiana. Originally designed to hold 10,000 men, Camp Sumter quickly filled up during the bloody months of the spring and summer, the height of Grant's Wilder-

This August 1864 photograph of Andersonville, officially known as Camp Sumter, offers a glimpse of the horribly crowded conditions at the Confederacy's most notorious prison camp. Courtesy of the Library of Congress, LC-DIG-ppmsca-33768

ness Campaign. By the time the sweltering heat of August arrived, 32,000 prisoners crowded into the barren stockade. Although originally intended to have wood barracks, Camp Sumter contained no buildings or structures of any sort, and the captured Union men who lived there had to construct their own makeshift shelters from clay bricks, blankets, sticks, and assorted pieces of clothing collected from the dead. Its only water supply came from a narrow stream that ran through the middle of the compound, and the cookhouse and bakery located outside the stockade and just upstream contaminated the water, which the prisoners used for drinking and bathing. It offered little in the way of rations to the men, as it operated in an isolated area of the South during the hardest year in the life of the Confederacy, a time when ordinary civilians often lacked basic necessities. The extreme overcrowding meant that each man literally had only about twenty-five square feet of space, about enough room to lie down, so sickness became rampant. A mostly lawless environment developed within the stockade, where gangs of raiders robbed, beat, and sometimes killed others for the sake of food and shelter. In only fourteen months of operation, nearly 13,000 men died at Andersonville. "I have counted twenty-six dead in one day who lay in the sun festering until an hour before sundown," wrote Union private Robert Knox Sneden. "Here they are loaded up in the ration wagon like cordwood and carried to [the] graveyard."[43] Most experienced the slow, agonizing deaths of those suffering from malnutrition, dysentery, or diarrhea. It is hard to imagine a worse fate for a Civil War soldier than to have ended up at Andersonville.

Reports of the conditions at Andersonville and other Confederate prison camps provoked outrage in the North. Not surprisingly given the declining fortunes of the Confederacy, the situation in Rebel prisons generally proved worse than in Yankee compounds, and Northern newspapers filled up with horrific accounts of the miseries endured by the imprisoned. The issue became a political one. Since the very existence of prisons resulted from the breakdown of the exchange system, Northern critics blamed the suffering on Lincoln and Grant's devotion to the idea of exchanging prisoners only on the basis of racial equality. Some of these criticisms revealed the depths of Northern racism, as they wrote frankly and disparagingly of the administration's willingness to allow thousands of white prisoners to suffer for the sake of protecting black soldiers. In the meantime, blacks who had been captured by the Confederacy—that is, those who did not perish in massacres such as the one that occurred at Fort Pillow in 1864—suffered execution or reenslavement. Robert Ould, who supervised prisoner exchanges for the Confederacy, believed that executions performed on the spot without fanfare offered the best solution to the dilemma of black prisoners, while some Southern governors implemented plans to return captured black soldiers to their owners and, if they could not be located, sell them for the benefit of the state. The Confederacy, in other words, refused to change its policy. The Lincoln administration responded with threats of retaliation—of implementing a policy of killing one Confederate soldier for every Union soldier who had suffered that fate—but such threats never became reality.

Despite the controversy, the Union held to its policy of nonexchange unless Confederates agreed to do so on a color-blind basis. In August 1864, a year after the exchange system had ground to a halt, only a small number of prisoner exchanges continued—wounded men, surgeons, and other noncombatants, for example—and Grant defended the Union policy with candor, noting the long-term military advantages. "It is hard on our men held in Southern prisons not to exchange them, but it is humanity to those left in our ranks to fight our battles," Grant wrote. "Every man we hold, when released on parole or otherwise, becomes an active soldier against us at once either directly or indirectly. If we commence a system of exchange which liberates all prisoners taken, we will have to fight on until the whole South is exterminated."[44] Prisoner policies clearly had humanitarian, political, and military implications.

THE SICK AND THE DEAD

The Civil War brought sickness, suffering, and death to the forefront of the American consciousness. Losses were minimal during the first several months of the war, but the Battle of Shiloh in spring 1862 witnessed more than 23,000 casualties (nearly 3,500 killed) and as a result dramatically transformed public perception of the war. Overnight, with massive armies situated in Virginia and in the Tennessee River Valley, Americans awakened to the fact that the carnage would continue and the numbers of losses would escalate.

Estimating the number of total deaths in the Civil War is difficult. At the start of the war, no bureaucracy existed to identify and count the dead, to notify the next of kin, or to bury the bodies. Records were simply incomplete. For years, historians mostly agreed on a figure of approximately 620,000 deaths—360,000 on the Union side and 260,000 on the Confederate side. But one recent study has argued that this figure severely undercounts the number of Confederate dead. On the basis of a rigorous analysis of census data, the author argues that a significant number of "excess deaths" occurred between the end of the war and the tallying of the 1870 census. These include soldiers who died from wounds, diseases, and infections contracted during wartime, as well as noncombatants who suffered at the hands of guerillas. This new estimate puts the total number of dead at 752,000, an increase of 20 percent from the previous figure.[45] The precise number will never be known, as mass unmarked graves and the destruction of records, particularly on the Confederate side, have hindered historians and demographers. If we acknowledge 620,000 dead as a minimum, the losses were still enormous, for they accounted for about 2 percent of the total population of the United States at the time. A comparable proportion today would be six million deaths.

Using the 620,000 figure as a baseline, Civil War deaths can be divided into various categories. About 425,000—two-thirds—resulted from sickness and disease. Poor diet, sanitation, and personal hygiene contributed a great deal to the unhealthy atmosphere, as did the primitive practices in hospitals and surgical tents. Thousands lost their lives to typhoid, malaria, dysentery, diarrhea, and pneumonia, as army camps became virtual breeding grounds for sickness and death. Far fewer men—about 160,000—died on the field of battle, while at least another 80,000 died later from wounds. Battlefield deaths resulted from a variety of factors having to do with military commanders, weapons technology, and common soldiers. First, the aggressive, hard war strategy used by Union military leaders during the second half of the war contributed to the human toll. The final two years of the war belonged to men such as Grant, Sherman, and Sheridan, all of whom used a more aggressive, attacking style than had marked the first two years of the conflict. Second, military technology advanced at a rapid pace. At the outset, most soldiers fought with smooth-bore muskets that were accurate only at about a hundred yards. But as the war progressed, more and more soldiers began to carry Springfield rifles that could kill at a range of 300 yards, and the later introduction of breech-loading rifles on the Union side made loading and shooting faster and easier. Strategic considerations simply did not keep pace with changes in weapons technology, as commanders continued to order frontal assaults even as weapons became more deadly. Finally, soldiers exhibited an enthusiasm for their respective causes, as well as a lack of experience. This proved a potentially lethal combination. Motivated by courage, patriotism, and faith, soldiers persisted at a remarkable rate. At the same time, the lack of experience and training of the fighting men on both sides—the fact that the vast majority were ordinary citizens rather than professional soldiers—contributed to the chaos in battle. Failure to understand or execute military orders surely contributed to many deaths, as did tactical mistakes and poor judgment. Perhaps evidence of this fact, an estimated 40,000 soldiers perished in accidents.[46] For all of these reasons, the war proved a bloody affair.

Whether sick or wounded, Civil War soldiers found themselves in the makeshift hospitals that began to appear. Homes, churches, schools, and government buildings were often transformed into places of care and respite in wartime, depending on the need and the proximity to the fighting. Wagons, steamboats, and trains all transported wounded soldiers to hospitals, but at times hospital boats or tent hospitals also served the afflicted. In the immediate aftermath of battle, physicians did all that they could to extract bullets from the wounded, prevent men from bleeding to death, and alleviate pain and suffering. But medical advances, like strategy, failed to keep pace with weapons technology, and even by the end of the conflict little progress had been made. Doctors knew nothing of germs and so did little to prevent their spread. Some practices clearly made the situation worse, such as the repeated use of the same surgical tools without cleaning. When a badly damaged arm or leg could not be repaired or treated, physicians did not hesitate to amputate, and witnesses frequently mentioned the piles of limbs that accumulated outside of hospitals. In the midst of such gruesome scenes, soldiers attempted to muster up enough courage to endure the suffering. Despite whatever pain one experienced from an injury, soldiers believed that they needed to face distress with manly strength and dignified stoicism. Openly expressing one's pain, many believed, revealed weakness of character. All nineteenth-century men, moreover, whether Northern or Southern, knew what it meant to die an honorable death: to fight without flinching and to confront one's fate with bravery. Wounded and dying soldiers often made a point of asking physicians and nurses to make certain that their loved ones back home knew that they had done their duty, for their reputations—in life or death—depended on it. Notions of courage, in other words, influenced a soldier's behavior from start to finish, from the decision to enlist to the moment of death.

Nurses attended to the sick and the dying in hospitals. An exclusively male profession at the outset of the war, nursing underwent significant changes during wartime. The sheer number of patients created a demand for medical assistants of every sort, and although men still held the majority of nursing positions, women eagerly joined the ranks. The advent of women nurses did not come without controversy, for women's mere presence threatened to challenge antebellum notions that women should tend only to the domestic sphere of family and child rearing. Many objected to women serving in this all-male environment—dressing wounds and bathing soldiers while being exposed to all sorts of sights and sounds to which they were assumed to be unaccustomed. Others imagined that women nurses would become too assertive and would interfere with the proper work of surgeons and physicians. The debate held particular significance in the South, which had far fewer woman nurses than the North. Southern women who did volunteer, deeply moved by scenes of suffering and by the meaningful work they were doing, sometimes responded to their critics. One Southern nurse wrote mockingly of those who took issue with her calling: "Are the women of the South going into the hospitals? I am afraid candor will compel me to say they are not! It is not respectable and requires too constant attention, and a hospital has none of the comforts of home!" She concluded dryly, "A lady's respectability must be at a low ebb when it can be endangered by going into a hospital."[47] In the North, the Christian Commission and the Sanitary Commission played a significant role in mobilizing women for the nursing profession, as they used the vast resources of their organizations to promote the spiritual and physical health of Union soldiers. Many women responded out of Christian faith and commitment, and in doing so they ameliorated concerns about the transgression of gender roles by portraying their work as firmly within traditional bounds—as an expression of Christian charity and womanly nurture. The war had opened a new profession to women, and for many, such wartime experiences affected them for the rest of their lives.

If the war produced innovation in the care of the wounded, it also transformed the burying of the dead. Before the war, soldiers were buried informally at the site of death, at a nearby military post, or at a spot chosen by the family. The number of deaths during the Civil War, though, prompted the US

Congress to formulate a national policy on the subject. On July 17, 1862, Congress passed legislation empowering President Lincoln "to purchase cemetery grounds and cause them to be securely enclosed to be used as a national cemetery for the soldiers who shall die in the service of the country."[48] During the next six months, the Federal government created fourteen national cemeteries spread across the Union from Cypress Hills in Brooklyn to Fort Leavenworth in Kansas. With neither a budget nor guidelines, the government in most instances simply designated space for Union soldiers in existing cemeteries located near military outposts or hospitals. Keokuk, Iowa, for example, the home of five army hospitals that cared for the thousands of soldiers transported by steamboat up the Mississippi River from Southern battlefields, became the site of one of these first national cemeteries. The government added others over the course of the war, particularly at places such as Antietam and Gettysburg, where large numbers of soldiers had lost their lives. In 1864, the War Department established the most famous and controversial of all national cemeteries when it purchased the confiscated estate of Confederate general Robert E. Lee in a Treasury Department auction. Believing that converting Lee's lands into a Union cemetery would serve as a grim reminder to the Rebels of the harm done by Lee's decision to join the Confederacy, Quartermaster General Montgomery C. Meigs personally supervised the burials of dozens of Union soldiers in Mary Lee's rose garden. Reactive and improvised, congressional action on burials and cemeteries reflected the exigencies of war. More formal legislation—accompanied by an appropriation of funds—would follow the surrender of the Confederacy. Nevertheless, the establishment of national cemeteries symbolized the vast expansion of government power and enshrined the notion of patriotic sacrifice in the Northern consciousness. Thousands of reburials, gravestones, ceremonies, and speeches would hail the heroes of the Union.

Beset by Union victories, Federal incursion on its soil, and limited resources, the Confederate government engaged in no systematic effort to bury the dead in wartime. Many deceased Rebel soldiers ended up in Hollywood Cemetery and Oakwood Cemetery in Richmond, the latter located conveniently near to the South's largest wartime military hospital. But the Union victors interred countless others in mass graves, such as those at Shiloh, and some remained unburied. Not until after the war did the work of locating and identifying Confederate corpses really begin. In contrast to what occurred in the North, where burying became "the work—and expense—of the Quartermaster Corps, the US Army, and the Federal government," in the South burial or reburial became the work of the people—as one scholar describes it, "a grass-roots undertaking that mobilized the white South in ways that extended well beyond the immediate purposes of bereavement and commemoration."[49]

Sickness and death yielded a grim harvest in both the North and South. Mounting losses and persisting grief caused many Christians to express wonder and doubt about how a loving God could allow such carnage. On the one hand, such doubts held the potential to alter the entire intellectual landscape, as American Christians simultaneously came to grips with midcentury European scientific discoveries and scholarly research that questioned commonly held assumptions about the Genesis account of creation, as well as the origins and authorship of the biblical text itself. On the other hand, massive death potentially reaffirmed faith, albeit in an altered form. For some American Christians, the war provoked a reconceptualization of the notion of afterlife and heaven, as an outgrowth of popular literature on the subject portrayed heaven in intimate, personal terms as a place where family and friends were joyfully reunited. Death's effects were both social and spiritual.

HARD WAR AND REVOLUTIONARY CONSTITUTIONALISM

By the outset of 1863, the American Civil War had become a hard war, a war of unrelenting struggle and harsh consequences. Generals Ulysses Grant and William Sherman fought a different style of warfare than the Union had imagined at the outset. The war brought desperation, occupation, and destruction to communities all over the South, creating food shortages, altering gender relationships, and laying waste to property and livelihoods. In the Upper South and border states, it produced guerilla fighting that threatened social chaos and civilian casualties. The war created thousands of captured soldiers in both the North and South, who languished for many months in makeshift prison camps under deplorable conditions. And it spawned disease and death on both sides on a massive scale, which allowed women to fill a nursing shortage and led to Federal legislation regarding the interment of corpses. In four years, the war's consequences were enormous. Amidst the turmoil, civilians and soldiers viewed these experiences through the lenses of courage, patriotism, and faith, ways of seeing that also helped them to make sense of the revolutions occurring around them.

The most profound change took place in the lives of African Americans, particularly black Southerners making the transition from slavery to freedom. The young men who went from being enslaved field hands one day to cross-

This 1865 print, titled "The True Defenders of the Constitution," portrays two dead white and two dead black Union soldiers on a battlefield of the war. Courtesy of the Library of Congress, LC-USZ62-138362

ing Union lines the next and, potentially within weeks, putting on the uniform of the United States Army lived as dramatic a transformation as anyone could have imagined during their day. Surely it was both exhilarating and empowering, as they saw themselves living out a great event made possible only by the providence of God. Linking military service to aspirational notions of citizenship and political participation, African Americans expected that their loyalty and patriotism would yield dividends. But fierce resistance proved the most immediate response to assertions of black manhood in the South, as Confederates engaged in an intentional military campaign to intimidate, kill, or reenslave any who dared wear the Union blue. After the April 1864 massacre of the black soldiers who garrisoned Fort Pillow in Tennessee, followed by a similar incident less than a week later at Poison Spring in Arkansas, African American servicemen gained a sobering awareness of the meaning of hard war.

But neither Confederate rage nor Union hesitancy could stem the tide of black activism that had already begun to spread throughout America. In addition to enlisting, black Americans continued to organize and mobilize, as they had been doing for three decades, in order to bring about political and constitutional change. Their methods were as important as the substance of their demands. One of the most arresting features of the Civil War era is not just what happened but what did not happen. Despite the fact that Confederates often referred to the Emancipation Proclamation as the "insurrection proclamation," there was no massive violent rebellion on the part of the slave population. There was no race war, no widespread murdering of masters, no gangs of formerly enslaved guerilla warriors engaging in acts of indiscriminate violence. That is, none of the worst nightmares of white Southerners came true. For the most part, African Americans in the South remained true to the prewar black constitutional tradition by heading to Union lines or contraband camps, enlisting in the Union army, petitioning their government, and organizing themselves to advocate for freedom and rights. Even in the aftermath of horrific acts of violence perpetrated against black soldiers—against those fighting for their liberty—black leaders noticeably eschewed random retributive violence. In the days after the Fort Pillow massacre became known, for example, black and white officers at Fort Pickering in nearby Memphis met, discussed, drafted, and voted on a set of written resolutions, in which they vowed that "as officers commanding colored troops in the service of the Union, we now know our doom if we are captured by our enemies, but that so far from being intimidated thereby, we accept the issue, and adopt as our significant motto, 'Victory or death.'"[50] Such patriotic expressions through constitutional means—in the face of the threat of brutal violence—certainly stood as a testament to the deep belief in American liberty and constitutionalism among those African Americans serving in the Union army. It might have been one of the greatest ironies of a hard war that it did not beget a sudden, chaotic, violent revolt on the part of four million enslaved African Americans.[51]

Instead, black leaders began laying the groundwork for thoroughgoing political and constitutional change. On April 29, 1864, in the aftermath of the massacres of black soldiers in Tennessee and Arkansas, Abraham Galloway, the fugitive slave who had raised 5,000 Union soldiers in New Bern the year before, led a delegation of African Americans to meet with President Lincoln at the Executive Mansion. Others joined Galloway in the meeting, including "a brick mason, two barbers (one also a carpenter), a farmer, a baker, and a preacher."[52] It was an astonishing assemblage—one certainly not typical of those that gained an audience with the president. Although Lincoln had conferred with Northern black leaders in 1862, this appears to be the first time the president met with black leaders from the South, four of them former slaves. Displaying extraordinary hospitality and respect for his guests, the president listened as the delegation made its views known. Remarkably, after thanking Lincoln for issuing the Emancipation Proclamation, Galloway and his colleagues recited the words of the Declaration of Independence to the president—that "all men are created equal"—and pressed their case for black rights, including suffrage. In this act of boldness, the six African American men embodied the black constitutional tradition, the blending of the aspirational language of the Declaration with the orderly framework for government set out in the Constitution. Moreover, they brought to the highest level of the government the revolutionary spirit of freedom that was sweeping the Southern states, the spirit that animated those who had made their way to contraband camps and had joined the Union Army.

In the days and months that followed, Galloway and other African American leaders took their campaign for black freedom and equality to the Northern public, and in October, 144 black delegates from seventeen states (some from the South) and the District of Columbia assembled in convention in Syracuse, New York. Just as they had done since first meeting in Philadelphia in 1830, black leaders met to claim their share of America's heritage of constitutional liberty. All the nation's most famous and accomplished black leaders were present, and the delegates included intellectuals, ministers, and political activists of every sort. For four days, the National Convention of Colored Men of the United States discussed and debated the past, present, and future of black people in the United States. Ultimately, they drafted the "Declaration of Wrongs and Rights," a formal statement modeled on the American Declaration of Independence, that listed the historical grievances of African Americans while also lauding black military service. Most importantly, the declaration laid out a program for the future. Dismissing any notion of black colonization or emigration, the delegates made their own claim to American citizenship. "Here were we born," they wrote, casting their lot with the country that had mistreated those of their race for nearly two and a half centuries. "For this country our fathers and our brothers have fought, and here we hope to remain in the full enjoyment of enfranchised manhood and its dignities." Asserting their rights "as citizens of the Republic," the delegates defined these rights as "a portion of what we deem to be our rights as men, as patriots, as citizens, and as children of the common Father."[53] Although it would be more than a year before the Constitution would be amended to end slavery, the institution was already dead or dying in many parts of the South, and already African Americans were creating a new discourse of rights—one that focused not on the rights of slaveholders, but on the rights of the formerly enslaved.

Such wartime expressions of black constitutionalism—rooted in courage, patriotism, and faith—affected politics and government in both the Union and the Confederacy. In essence, neither the Union nor Confederate governments could ignore the chorus of black voices demanding constitutional equality. At the outset of war, Lincoln had pledged not to interfere with slavery in the South and to return fugitives who had escaped to the North, while the Union Congress had declared in the Crittenden-Johnson Resolutions that the war would not upset the South's peculiar institution. Yet by 1862, black agency and activism had nudged the president and the Congress into action, transforming the conflict into a war to end slavery and remake the Union. Lincoln issued a proclamation freeing slaves in the Confederacy and aspired to establish a new nation based on the principles of the Declaration of Independence. Even Jefferson Davis acknowledged that Southerners would have to reform or rethink the future of slavery in light of the gradual disintegration of the institution and the declining military fortunes of the Confederacy. Thus, the actions of African Americans on the ground both shaped and responded to constitutional and political change. In continuing to claim freedom—as well as the rights that they believed came with freedom—African Americans helped to bring about a constitutional revolution.

Part III
LIBERTY AND UNION

9
THE END AND THE BEGINNING
1865–1866

In the early days of 1865, the perpetually agitated South Carolinian Robert Barnwell Rhett had never been angrier. Some weeks before, it had become clear that President Jefferson Davis's hint that it might be necessary to use slaves as soldiers was moving forward. In December 1864, Secretary of War Judah Benjamin had publicly discussed the possibility of enrolling slaves in the Confederate Army in exchange for granting them limited freedoms. By confiscating slaves, putting them under arms, and granting them some form of emancipation, the Davis administration hoped that the Confederacy could yet secure its independence and sway European opinion. The irate Rhett would have none of it. On January 13, in the pages of his *Charleston Mercury*, the fire-eating editor unleashed his fury. "It was on account of encroachments upon the institution of slavery by the sectional majority of the old Union, that South Carolina seceded from that Union," the *Mercury* stated. "It is not at this late date, after the loss of thirty thousand of her best and bravest men in battle, that she will suffer it to be bartered away; or ground between the upper and nether mill stones, by the madness of Congress, or the counsels of shallow men elsewhere." Even though General Robert E. Lee had publicly endorsed the idea, Rhett's *Mercury* attempted to make clear to all the obvious contradiction in Confederates giving up slavery as they knew it in order to win independence for the South. "Neither Congress, nor certain make-shift men in Virginia, can force upon [South Carolina] their mad schemes of weakness and surrender. She stands upon her institutions—and there she will fall in their defence. *We want no Confederate Government without our institutions.* And we will have none. Sink or swim, live or die, we stand by them, and we are fighting for them this day."[1]

Despite Rhett's passion to preserve slavery in the Confederacy, within four months' time, all Rebel armies had surrendered and Southerners pondered an uncertain future. Union victory and Confederate defeat ushered in a turbulent postwar period, during which slavery was abolished by constitutional amendment. As newly freed African Americans sought additional legal rights, and as the president and Congress clashed over how far the postwar revolution would go, white Southerners did all that they could—in the spirit of Rhett—to preserve control over black labor and to resist the changes occurring around them. Southern defiance manifested itself in repressive legislation and in extralegal violence, and during much of 1865 and 1866, Northerners considered the appropriate response to the South's intransigence. The end of the war thus marked the beginning of intense debate over the meaning of a new Union under an antislavery Constitution.

THE FATE OF SLAVERY

During the early months of 1865, Americans North and South debated the future of slavery. Considered in the light of recent history, these debates constituted a remarkable development. Just eight years before, Chief Justice Roger B. Taney had thought that he brought to an end all quarreling on the subject when he held, in *Dred Scott v. Sandford*, that the Constitution protected the rights of slaveholders in federal territories. At the time, it was almost universally accepted that slavery, since it was governed by state law, remained legally safe and secure everywhere that it already existed. Taney's ruling had given Southern slaveholders an extra measure of protection by guaranteeing that they could take their slave property into new lands. By early 1865, though, Taney's opinion seemed like a relic from a bygone era. Taney was dead, as was the proslavery Supreme Court that he had presided over for nearly three decades. More important, African Americans and President Abraham Lincoln had moved boldly against the institution in the Southern states—African Americans by walking off plantations and Lincoln by announcing his Emancipation Proclamation. War had rendered the *Dred Scott* decision practically irrelevant.

With the war's end in sight, in the first few weeks of 1865 members of the United States House of Representatives debated a constitutional amendment to abolish slavery. Such a measure was in no way a foregone conclusion. Only two amendments had been added to the Constitution since the original Bill of Rights had been ratified in 1791, so Americans lacked a tradition of resolving issues in this way. But changing the Constitution promised to end the matter in a way that a federal statute would not, and some even doubted whether Congress possessed the constitutional authority to enact a statute abolishing slavery. In early 1864, abolitionist organizations thus began petitioning Congress to devise an amendment, and in February 1864, the Senate Judiciary Committee drafted a proposed thirteenth amendment to the Constitution. A few months later, the Senate passed it by a vote of 38–6, but the proposal went down to defeat in the House. Many Republicans, including Lincoln, believed that an abolition amendment was absolutely necessary. The Emancipation Proclamation, the president reasoned, might not apply after the war ended. He had justified it as a war measure under his authority as commander in chief in areas in rebellion against the government, and once the war had concluded, Lincoln could not be certain of its legal authority. Even if the Proclamation continued in force, it had exempted areas already under Union occupation and had excluded the loyal border states. In fall 1864, Maryland had abolished slavery by legislative enactment, and on January 11, 1865, Missouri's governor announced the end of slavery in that state by executive proclamation. But at the time, slavery survived in areas previously occupied by Union forces, as well as in Delaware, Kentucky, and Tennessee, and Lincoln did not want there to be any doubt about the legal status of slavery in the rest of the Southern states.

Succinctly written and patterned after the Northwest Ordinance of 1787 that had banned slavery north of the Ohio River, the wording of the proposed amendment held profound implications. The first section read as follows: "Neither slavery nor involuntary servitude, except as a punishment for crime whereof the party shall have been duly convicted, shall exist in the United States, or any place subject to their jurisdiction." The second section added an enforcement clause: "Congress shall have power to enforce this article by appropriate legislation." This stemmed from the fact that Article I, Section 8, which enumerated all of the powers of Congress, had not included any power for Congress to regulate slavery. The absence of such power had made possible Taney's claim that Congress could not prohibit slavery in the territories, and it had also prompted Lincoln to question the constitutionality of the First and Second Confiscation acts. By adding an enforcement clause, in effect, the Constitution for the first time added a new enumerated power to those possessed by Congress.

The precise scope of this enforcement power was unclear. On the one hand, some advocates—and opponents—believed that the clause granted far-reaching powers to Congress to eliminate all vestiges of slavery. On the other hand, some either supported or opposed the amendment because it only emancipated slaves. According to this conservative interpretation, additional amendments would be required to accomplish anything other than abolition. In short, while everyone was certain that passage of the amendment would eliminate the peculiar institution—the text even used the word "slavery," which the original Constitution had not—disagreement existed over whether the amendment might provide additional guarantees to African Americans.

Despite this uncertainty, after extensive discussion, the House of Representatives passed the Thirteenth Amendment. In the final few weeks before the House vote, Lincoln had assumed a key role by personally lobbying some representatives, and on January 31, 1865, by a margin of 119 to 56 (with eight members absent), the amendment secured the necessary two-thirds majority by just 2 votes. A delighted Lincoln hailed it as "a King's cure for all the evils," and upon news of its passage, celebrations erupted across the North as well as in black communities across the South.[2] William Lloyd Garrison, the abolitionist who had made his name by describing the Constitution as a "covenant with death," now celebrated "a radical change" in the document. "For more than seventy years," Garrison told a Boston audience, "it served as a mighty bulwark for the slave system, giving it national sanction and security, now it forbids human slavery in every part of the republic!"[3] The *New Orleans Tribune*, a black newspaper, attached global significance to the event, noting that "our rejoicings will be echoed and responded to by millions in the Old World" and that the event attested to "the enduring vitality and assured integrity of the republic."[4] Although ratification by three-fourths of the states would still be necessary, the real battle over the amendment had been won. Despite Lincoln's occasional talk of compensation and colonization as accompanying black freedom, the Thirteenth Amendment would end slavery with neither conditions nor qualifications.

Days after the House vote, on February 3, representatives of the governments of the United States and the Confederacy met aboard a steamboat on the James River at Hampton Roads, Virginia, to discuss the possibility of peace. It was a curious meeting, one that provoked controversy at the time and since. Both Lincoln and Davis acceded to the idea for political reasons. Lincoln hoped to mollify elements within the North (including his own party) who were calling for peace negotiations, while Davis thought that such a meeting would prove to his own political opponents that the North's conditions for peace would be unacceptable. Davis sent three representatives, including Vice President Alexander Stephens. For the Union, Lincoln and Secretary of State William Seward attended. The participants agreed that no written transcript or notes would be kept. According to Stephens's account of the meeting, Seward indicated that Southern states could block ratification of the amendment, and Lincoln stated that Georgia could ratify the amendment "prospectively, so as to take effect—say in five years."[5] At least one historian has seized on such claims, in order to cast doubt on Lincoln and Seward's commitment to immediate emancipation.[6]

Regardless of what might have been said at Hampton Roads, Lincoln's actions during the previous four months had demonstrated a firm commitment to abolition. He had placed the abolitionist Salmon P. Chase in the chief justiceship, had won reelection on a platform favoring an abolition amendment, and had worked assiduously for the amendment's passage throughout the month of January. Lincoln did believe, unlike Radical elements within his own party, that the former Confederate states would take part in the ratification process, but at the time of Hampton Roads, there were already twenty-three free states (including Maryland, Missouri, and West Virginia, which abolished slavery on February 3, the day of the conference), all of which Lincoln presumed would ratify the amendment, and thus only four slaveholding states would be required to meet the three-fourths threshold required for ratification. Federally supported Unionist governments were already in place in Arkansas, Louisiana, Tennessee, and Virginia, and Lincoln had every reason to believe that these states too would ratify the amendment, making the "King's cure" the law of the land. Even if ratification did not succeed, Lincoln surely knew that the Republican-dominated Supreme Court would protect federal and state antislavery legislation, as well as the Emancipation Proclamation, from legal challenges. For good measure, the onward march of Sherman's soldiers from Savannah into South Carolina continued to attract thousands of African Americans seeking freedom, and in mid-January Sherman had even issued a special order redistributing land to newly freed blacks. The cork was already out of the bottle. Whatever discussions took place at Hampton Roads, the reality of slavery's demise seemed more apparent each day, and Lincoln's commitment to both Union and liberty remained steadfast.

Perhaps further evidence that the fate of slavery had been sealed by this time was the Confederacy's own much-debated proposal to free and arm enslaved African Americans. A year before, in January 1864, Major General Patrick Cleburne had first suggested the idea of using slaves as soldiers in exchange for emancipation. Davis initially suppressed the idea, but several months later, deteriorating military circumstances prompted the president to hint at just such a plan in his November 1864 message to Congress. Sensitive to public reaction, he made few remarks on the subject. But the support he expressed in private letters, as well as that shown by Secretary Benjamin in December 1864 and General Lee in January 1865, made it apparent that the administration favored such a proposal. The plan emerged neither from a dislike of slavery nor an underestimation of its importance. Rather, the proposal resulted from a realistic assessment of the Confederacy's chances in early 1865. That winter, with only 60,000 cold and hungry Confederates defending

Petersburg against Grant's much larger, well-provisioned forces, it seemed only a matter of time before the Union siege of the city succeeded and Grant's men moved on to Richmond. Davis and Lee desperately needed extra men to fight in the Confederate Army. They saw how the Union had used former slaves against them as soldiers and thought that the Confederacy had to either use black soldiers or continue to have them used against them. Blacks' history under slavery would make them orderly and obedient soldiers, proponents of the plan believed. Moreover, with Davis already floating the idea of a general emancipation through Duncan Kenner's mission to Great Britain, a plan to link black military service to black freedom fit with the Confederate president's thinking in early 1865.

Southern critics blasted the idea. The most optimistic opponents asserted that the military situation did not require additional troops. Realists contended that the use of black soldiers would damage the morale of whites, who would never abide fighting side by side with slaves. The most fearful charged that armed black soldiers would desert the army and incite widespread insurrection. But the fiercest objections arose out of the question of slaveholders' rights and the very purpose of the Confederacy. Because the Confederate Constitution had specifically prohibited any law "denying or impairing the right of property in negro slaves," critics asserted that any such proposal would violate the Constitution. Davis's longtime nemesis, Governor Joseph Brown of Georgia, protested, "If we admit the right of the Government to impress and pay for slaves to free them, we concede its power to abolish slavery, and change our domestic institutions at its pleasure."[7] Davis's longtime friend, Senator David Yulee of Florida, reminded his old Senate colleague that "whenever the Confederate government treats slaves in the States otherwise than as *property* a social revolution is begun in the South, the end of which may not be foreseen."[8] Others protested that the idea of black troops undermined the very purpose of the Southern nation. Like Rhett, these critics believed that the South had seceded to protect slavery and slaveholders, and they could not fathom any proposal to undermine the institution. Former secretary of state Howell Cobb described the plan as "the most pernicious idea that has been suggested since the war began." To Cobb, the very notion of black soldiers contradicted all that white Southerners believed. "The day you make soldiers of them is the beginning of the end of the revolution," he stated. "If slaves will make good soldiers our whole theory of slavery is wrong—but they won't make good soldiers. As a class they are wanting in every qualification of a soldier."[9] If the South were to take Lee's advice and allow slave soldiers to gain their freedom, plantation mistress Catherine Edmondston believed, Southerners would destroy the essence of their society and abandon all of their principles. "Our Country is ruined if we adopt his suggestions," she wrote in her diary.[10] Many Southerners, in other words, saw any proposal linking slaves' military service to emancipation as unimaginable.

After extensive debate and in a close vote, on March 13 the Confederate Congress enacted legislation allowing the use of slaves as soldiers. The law placed in the hands of the president the power to "ask for and accept" from slave owners the service of such a number of slaves for military service as the president deemed necessary, but the act did not provide emancipation for such soldiers. Instead, the law explicitly stated that the Confederate states had enacted the law in order "to preserve their institutions" and left the issue of emancipation to slave owners and to the states.[11] Davis tried to get around this part of the law by securing pledges from masters on the front end that service by their slaves would win them their freedom. Although Congress and Davis seemed to hold differing views on whether freedom would accompany military service, both lawmakers and the president believed that using slaves as soldiers might allow the Confederacy to salvage victory, in which case Confederates—rather than the hated Yankees—would have the power to dictate the terms of black freedom. In other words, no one in the Confederacy favored a general and immediate abolition, as the South faced in the form of the Union's Thirteenth Amendment. Confronting defeat and freedom on the Union's terms as the alternative, Confederates thus made a final effort to secure their independence and define the conditions of emancipation—a last-ditch attempt to preserve what remained of slaveholders' rights. Each day, it seemed, slavery moved closer to extinction.

LINCOLN'S SECOND INAUGURAL AND THE END OF THE WAR

On March 4, 1865, a month after the Hampton Roads meeting and a little more than a week before the Confederate Congress enacted legislation allowing black troops, President Lincoln swore the oath of office to begin a second term. In several respects, this second inauguration day differed from Lincoln's first. In contrast to the tense atmosphere in 1861, for the first time in the nation's history, Inauguration Day had taken on the feel of a national holiday. Across the North, bank closings, church services, fireworks displays, and grand celebrations would mark the start of the president's new term. With victory in sight, Northerners seemed in a mood to celebrate. Large crowds descended on the nation's capital, including huge numbers of African Americans, many of them just liberated from bondage.

Part of the celebration stemmed from the feeling that a revolutionary era was dawning. A few weeks before, John S. Rock of Massachusetts had become the first African American to gain admission to the bar of the United States Supreme Court, where previously, as the *New Orleans Tribune* observed, "the infamous Taney sat enthroned, decreeing that a colored man has no rights that a white man is bound to respect."[12] A new chief justice, Salmon P. Chase, who had spent much of his legal career fighting for the freedom of African Americans and who had welcomed Rock to the bar, would administer the oath of office to Lincoln. And the swearing in of a new vice president, the Unionist from Tennessee Andrew Johnson, added a hopeful sense that reconciliation between the North and South was at hand. Many who witnessed the inauguration remarked that just as Lincoln rose to speak at the east front of the Capitol, the clouds that had hung over the gathering for hours suddenly parted, and rays of sunshine shone over the newly completed Capitol dome.

Lincoln delivered his only prepared address since the cemetery dedication at Gettysburg, and like that speech, this one became known as a sweeping yet concise attempt to capture the significance of the war. Although the president began by noting that all depended on "the progress of our arms," he avoided any prediction as to what would happen next or when the war would end. Rather than boasting of the achievements of generals or armies, Lincoln chose instead to focus much of the first part of the speech on the origins of the conflict. He emphasized the role that slavery played in bringing about the war, observing that slavery "constituted a peculiar and powerful interest." "All knew," he noted, "that this interest was, somehow, the cause of the war." Yet, he continued, no one anticipated such a long and bloody struggle, for "neither anticipated that the cause of the conflict might cease with, or even before, the conflict itself should cease."[13]

With victory and abolition on the horizon, Lincoln framed the great drama that had played out over the past four years in religious terms. In comparison to all of the previous inaugural addresses delivered by presidents, Lincoln's referred far more frequently to God, to prayer, and to biblical texts. Emphasizing that which the North and South held in common, the president noted that those on each side "read the same Bible, and pray to the same God" but that neither section had its prayers fully answered. Instead, Lincoln emphasized the pain and suffering that both sections of the country had experienced because of their mutual complicity in the "offence" of slavery. In fact, Lincoln referred to it as "American slavery"—not Southern slavery—so as to emphasize this national, collective sense of accountability. The most arresting portion of the speech came when, sounding more like a Hebrew prophet of old than a modern American president, Lincoln promised that the war would continue, as long as necessary, in order to cleanse the nation of the sin of slavery. "If God wills that it continue, until all the wealth piled by the bondsman's two hundred and fifty years of unrequited toil shall be sunk, and until every drop of blood drawn with the lash, shall be paid by another drawn with the sword . . . so still it must be said 'the judgments of the Lord, are true and righteous altogether.'" Lincoln then shifted from judgment to mercy. In the most memorable lines of the address, the president closed on a gentle note— "with malice toward none, with charity for all"—thus hinting at a speedy and generous reconstruction.[14]

Lincoln's tone and emphasis had changed considerably from the first inaugural to the second. In contrast to Lincoln the constitutionalist who had emphasized his oath sworn to uphold the Union and to protect slavery where it existed, the reelected Lincoln gave a sober yet piercing assessment of the great and terrible events that had transpired. The war president offered in the second inaugural a reflective address with an overtly religious interpretation of recent events. Although Lincoln's theological views were and remain somewhat of a mystery, the address displayed the sense of Calvinistic fatalism that seemed to run consistently throughout Lincoln's thinking. The entire oration demonstrated his belief that a providential purpose had been worked out through America's suffering and bloodshed. Standing on abolitionist principle while humbly extending a hand of reconciliation, Lincoln both summarized recent events and offered a glimpse of the future.

Meanwhile, military events moved swiftly toward an end to the war. In February, Sherman began his northward advance into South Carolina with the goal of meeting up with Grant in Virginia. This was a more difficult operation than the previous fall's March to the Sea. While the Georgia campaign had occurred in good weather with little opposition, Sherman's army moved into the already swampy low country of South Carolina during the rainy season. Nevertheless, the enthusiastic and experienced soldiers carried out more destruction in South Carolina, the cradle of secession, than they had in Georgia, again with the aim of demoralizing the local population. In contrast to the Georgia campaign, Union forces encountered regular Confederate troops at various points, most of whom had been released from duties along the coast or detached from other units. Sherman's fighting force won victories in each of these engagements, despite the treacherous terrain and growing size of the forces that opposed them. The fiercest opposition came from Rebel cavalry under the command of General Wade Hampton, who instituted a policy of killing Union foragers who fell into Confederate hands. In mid-February, Sherman's men arrived in Columbia, South Carolina, and zealous Yankee soldiers, cotton-burning Rebels, and recently freed African Americans all probably contributed to setting the fires that eventually engulfed the city. In early March, Union soldiers crossed into North Carolina, and the final, decisive battle of the campaign occurred on March 19–21 near Bentonville, in the eastern part of the state. There, entrenched Confederates under the command of Joseph Johnston—mostly the remnants of General John Hood's Army of Tennessee—made a last attempt at thwarting Sherman's advance. After three days of fighting, the Rebels retreated toward Raleigh.

In the meantime, in Virginia, Grant finally made a breakthrough in his operations against Petersburg. Ever since the previous summer, Grant and his men had attempted to force the surrender of Confederate troops in the "Cockade City," the key supply base for Richmond, knowing that Petersburg's fall would precipitate the surrender of the Confederate capital. At the conclusion of the Overland Campaign, Grant had ordered frontal assaults against the massive Confederate earthworks and had even assented to a plan to blow up a mine under the Rebel defenses that resulted in the disastrous Battle of the Crater. When these tactics failed, Grant plotted a more deliberate strategy of capturing, one by one, each of the roads and railroads that led into Petersburg, thus choking off supplies. Eventually, with only two roads open, Grant again went on the offensive. On April 1, the first day of a remarkable month, Union forces won a victory about fifteen miles outside of the city at Five Forks, at the far right flank of the Confederate line of defense. Hours later Grant ordered an all-out, predawn frontal assault. With a force of approximately 60,000 men, some three times the size of the Confederate forces, at 4:40 A.M. on April 2, the Union began the attack. In one of the great military achievements of the war, the Union Sixth Corps broke through the Confederate defenses. Once General Robert E. Lee's lines had broken, the Confederates fell back and formed new lines before ultimately withdrawing from the city later in the day. With Petersburg having fallen, Lee ordered the remnants of the once-vaunted Army of Northern Virginia to begin moving west in the hope of joining up with Johnston's forces. Meanwhile, when President Davis received news of the defeat at Petersburg, he and the rest of the government began evacuating Richmond and heading toward nearby Danville, directly to the west. Before they departed, Confederate military officials set fire to the city's tobacco warehouses, and winds fanned the flames. Black and white rioters subsequently took control and looted whatever food and supplies remained. On April 3, Union forces entered the Confederate capital and began extinguishing the fires that ended up destroying much of the city's business district. Long the object of Union designs, Richmond was finally in the hands of the Federals.

On April 4, 1865, the two war presidents made dramatic moves. Lincoln, the leader of the victorious Union forces, decided to visit Richmond, while Davis, after fleeing the capital city, issued what turned out to be his last proclamation to the Confederate people. Lincoln's decision to come to Richmond was a bold one. Stepping off a Union steamboat at the James River landing, the president, guarded by a small contingent of sailors, began to walk through the still smoldering city. Immediately recognized by local slaves, who the day before had exulted in their new freedom when Union forces marched through the city, Lincoln found himself in the middle of a swarming crowd of joyous African Americans, who hailed him as their liberator and savior. Lincoln was stunned. Some of the formerly enslaved people literally bowed at the president's feet, and Lincoln struggled to make it through the adoring masses and up to the capitol, which overnight had become a Union military command post. Eventually arriving at the "Confederate White House," Lincoln sat at the desk where, just forty hours before, the Confederate president had been. Meanwhile, after arriving in Danville, Davis issued a proclamation that seemed to indicate his desire to turn the war into a guerilla effort. "We have now entered upon a new phase of a struggle," he wrote. "Relieved from the necessity of guarding cities and particular points, important but not vital to our defense, with our army free to move from point to point, and strike in detail the detachments and garrisons of the enemy, operating in the interior of our own country . . . nothing is now needed to render our triumph certain but the exhibition of our own unquenchable resolve." More defiant than ever, Davis urged the Southern people to fight on "with unconquered and unconquerable hearts."[15]

At this point, General Lee confronted a crucial decision. On the run, his army was diminished, as defeat and desertion had taken a toll. With no rations left, his men were starving, having been almost entirely without food since they had left Petersburg a week before. While Lee had begun with approximately 60,000 men who had occupied the trenches around Petersburg and Richmond, by April 7, he had no more than 10,000, including infantry and cavalry, under his command. On that date, Lee received a note from Grant asking for the surrender of the Army of Northern Virginia, and Lee crafted a careful response in which he inquired of the terms. More notes passed between the men the following day before the Confederates hoped to mount a final attack on April 9. When Lee realized that his small force was surrounded, he raised a flag of truce to continue his communication with Grant. It was time to surrender.

That afternoon, at a private home in the village of Appomattox Court House, Lee and Grant met. After exchanging pleasantries and memories of the Mexican-American War, Grant presented Lee with generous terms. Lee's men would give up their "arms, artillery, and public property" but would be allowed to keep their own sidearms, horses, and baggage. "This done," the document read, "each officer and man will be allowed to return to their homes not to be disturbed by United States authority so long as they observe their paroles and the laws in force where they may reside."[16] After their meeting, Grant ordered that Lee's men receive rations, and the following day, April 10, Lee's headquarters issued the Southern commander's final orders, which stated that the Army of Northern Virginia had been "compelled to yield to overwhelming numbers and resources."[17] Lee, the leader of the South's most successful and victorious army—in many ways the embodiment of the Confederate cause—had conceded defeat. Grant, meanwhile, lauded the soldiers of the armies of the United States for having "maintained the supremacy of the Union and Constitution" and "overthrown all armed opposition to the enforcement of the laws and the proclamations forever abolishing slavery."[18] A few weeks later, Johnston surrendered what remained of his army, and in the weeks to follow, all Confederate forces, including Nathan Bedford Forrest's cavalry in Alabama and Kirby Smith's trans-Mississippi army, would follow suit. There would be no official guerilla campaign as Davis had intimated. The cause was lost; the war was over.

The North's celebrations soon turned into mourning. Just five days after Lee's surrender, on April 14, President Lincoln suffered a mortal wound after being shot in the head while attending a play with his wife at Ford's Theater in Washington. The murderer, a famous young stage actor, John Wilkes Booth of Maryland, had been conspiring to kidnap or kill Lincoln for some time. Working with a motley crew of Confederate sympathizers in Washington and Maryland, Booth despised Lincoln, the Republicans, and the revolutionary changes that were occurring before his eyes. Convinced that Americans would thank him for delivering them from tyranny, Booth viewed his actions as heroic and imagined himself an American Brutus. Booth had coordinated the murder with his co-conspirators, who were simultaneously to attack both Vice President Johnson and Secretary of State Seward. Johnson's assailant got cold feet, while Seward's attacker seriously injured the secretary by stabbing him numerous times. Once the reports of Lincoln's assassination and the attempt on Seward's life swept the country, fear, rage, and sorrow quickly ensued. After Johnson was sworn in as president on April 15, Secretary of War Stanton organized a massive manhunt for the conspirators, and eleven days later, the chase ended when a cavalry detachment found, shot, and killed Booth in Bowling Green, Virginia. The next day, nearly 1,800 newly released Union prisoners died when the overloaded steamboat that was taking them north caught fire and sank to the bottom of the muddy Mississippi River, just north of Mem-

WASHINGTON MADE   UNDER PROVIDENCE   LINCOLN SAVED
AND

OUR COUNTRY

BEHOLD OH AMERICA, YOUR SONS. The greatest among men.

Lincoln's assassination in 1865 immediately elevated him to the status of one of the greatest men in the history of the young republic. Here the martyred president is pictured, holding the Emancipation Proclamation, alongside Washington, who is holding the Constitution. Courtesy of the Library of Congress, LC-USZ62-13959

phis. The sinking of the *Sultana*, the nation's worst ever maritime disaster, marked the tragic close of a mournful month.

The fortunes of the two wartime presidents, Lincoln and Davis, were intertwined till the end. Abraham Lincoln, who had sworn an oath as president to preserve the Union in 1861, had sacrificed his own life to save it. Booth shot Lincoln on Good Friday, and the North's Christian clergy could not resist drawing parallels between the martyred president and the crucified Christ. Others, such as the poet Walt Whitman, wrote movingly of Lincoln as America's great "Captain," who had safely steered the "ship" of the Union to shore before being found on the deck, "Fallen cold and dead," in the words of a soon-to-be famous poem. Imagery after the assassination portrayed the martyred Lincoln alongside George Washington, drawing a parallel between Washington as the father and Lincoln as the savior of the country. The president's body set out on a 1,700-mile trip through the North, with stops in Philadelphia, New York City, Buffalo, Cleveland, and Chicago, before ending in the president's hometown of Springfield, Illinois. After an outpouring of grief

A PROPER FAMILY RE-UNION.

If Lincoln earned an exalted position beside Washington, Jefferson Davis, in this cartoon, found his place in hell, with the devil and Benedict Arnold, the infamous traitor of the American Revolution. Here the devil expresses pride in his "American sons, Benedict and Jeff." Courtesy of the Library of Congress, LC-USZ62-40505

across the North, Lincoln was finally laid to rest on May 4. Less than a week later, the Confederate president turned fugitive Jefferson Davis fell into the hands of the Union military. In early April, soon after he had fled Richmond for Danville, the Rebel leader had moved further south with a small group of close advisors. For several days after Lee's surrender, Davis had continued to lead what remained of the Confederate government, meeting with the Cabinet, issuing military orders, and overseeing the treasury while evading his pursuers. He apparently hoped to make it to Texas. In early May, Davis and his entourage arrived in Georgia, where he was reunited with his wife, Varina, and their children. Secretary Stanton, convinced that Davis had been involved in the plot to kill Lincoln, had ordered army units to hunt down the absconding Rebel leader. On May 10, in Irwinville, Georgia, Federal cavalry units found and seized Davis, and they subsequently transported him to Fortress Monroe for imprisonment.

ANDREW JOHNSON AND THE BEGINNING
OF RECONSTRUCTION

In the wake of these tumultuous events, leadership of the country fell to Lincoln's vice president, Andrew Johnson. Born into poverty in 1808 in Raleigh, North Carolina, Johnson had lost his father at a young age and become a tailor's apprentice. He never went to school, but after he moved to East Tennessee in 1826, he became successful in the tailoring business, attained basic literacy, and a few years later won election as an alderman in the town of Greeneville. There he purchased some land and a small number of slaves, a sign of his wealth and standing in the community. Largely because of his abilities as an extemporaneous speaker, Johnson rose in local and state politics as a Jacksonian Democrat, methodically climbing each rung of the political ladder, from small-town mayor to US senator. The only member of the Senate from a seceded state to remain in his seat, Johnson delivered a notable pro-Union speech during the secession crisis, in which he cited the words of Washington, Madison, Jefferson, and other members of the founding generation. "Let us stand by the Constitution; and in preserving the Constitution we shall save the Union; and in saving the Union, we save this, the greatest Government on earth," Johnson proclaimed. Such loyalty impressed Lincoln. In 1862, describing Johnson as "a true and a valuable man—indispensable to us in Tennessee," Lincoln appointed him military governor, and the following year, Johnson embraced the Emancipation Proclamation and liberated his five slaves.[19] The apparent transformation of the lifelong Southern Democrat caught the attention of Republican leaders, and in 1864 the Tennessean earned the vice presidential slot on the National Union ticket with Lincoln.

With the war's end and Lincoln's death, Johnson suddenly confronted three big issues, all of them with constitutional implications. First, what would be the fate of former Rebels? Many in Congress believed that the Rebels needed to be punished. But who exactly was a Rebel—did that mean all who fought for and supported the Confederacy? Or should just the Confederacy's military officers and political leaders suffer punishment? Would amnesty and reconciliation prove the most effective way to reunify the country? Lincoln and his Cabinet had already begun discussing these questions, and they were preparing a proclamation of amnesty before Lincoln's death. Second, how would the former Confederate states be reincorporated into the Union? Lincoln and the Republicans had long asserted the illegality of secession—that states could not actually leave the Union. Still, the fact was that the seceded states had formed the Confederate government, seized US government forts and arsenals, and made war on the United States. Their relationship with the

President Andrew Johnson of Tennessee, who succeeded to the presidency after Lincoln's death, proved to be a man ill-suited for the moment. Courtesy of the US National Archives, 111-B-2914

federal government had somehow been altered, and it remained unclear how they would be readmitted. Lincoln had favored lenient terms, based primarily on building new governments led by a small cadre of Unionists. This had been the model established in Lincoln's Ten Percent Plan of 1863, when he had held out the possibility that if 10 percent of the voting population in 1860 swore an oath of loyalty, that state could begin forming a government under Federal military supervision. But would military government continue in the South, or was the reestablishment of civil government the goal? Did the South remain "in the grasp of war," as some insisted, and thus subject to further reform at the hands of the national government, or was the speedy restoration of self-government in the states the ultimate aim of reconstruction? Third, what would be the status of formerly enslaved African Americans? Would they gain additional legal rights? If so, what would those be? And would the conferral of such rights be a precondition for a state's readmission to the Union?

Johnson initially gave the impression that he might get along better with congressional Radicals than Lincoln. Deeply insecure about his humble roots and poor education, Johnson displayed a virulent hatred for the South's wealthy planters who had initiated the secession movement. During his short tenure as vice president, Johnson had delivered a fiery speech to a crowd in the nation's capital in which he denounced the leaders of the rebellion. "Treason is the highest crime known in the catalogue of crimes. . . . My notion is that treason must be made odious and traitors must be punished and impoverished," he had said in early April.[20] Once president, Johnson took a tough stance on Lincoln's assassination conspirators, authorizing a military tribunal and the speedy executions of the four convicted of involvement in the plot. More significantly, he worked with General Grant to change the excessively lenient surrender terms that General Sherman had offered to Confederate general Johnston in North Carolina, ordering Grant to renegotiate the terms along the lines of those worked out at Appomattox. During the early weeks of his administration, moreover, Johnson met with several delegations of African Americans, and he heard them discuss their fears for their safety in the South as well as their pleading for presidential leadership in support of black suffrage. During his first month and a half in office, in short, Johnson seemed determined to take a hard line with the Rebels and appeared open-minded on matters involving black rights. Radicals had long feared that Lincoln would be too conciliatory toward the South, so many now saw Johnson's ascension as a victory for their cause.

With Congress out of session until December, Johnson had nearly eight months and a free hand to establish his own policy of reconstruction. Building on Lincoln's expansion of executive power in wartime, Johnson acted unilaterally to set forth his plans. He claimed to act under the authority of the Constitution's Guarantee Clause, Article IV, Section 4, which states, "The United States shall guarantee to every State in this Union a Republican Form of Government." Johnson viewed the clause as, in effect, an open-ended grant of authority to the federal government to ensure the continuance of republican institutions. On May 29, 1865, with the unanimous support of the Cabinet, the president issued two reconstruction proclamations.

Johnson's first proclamation offered amnesty to Rebels. It required that all former Confederates take an oath of allegiance to the government of the United States, which would in effect restore all of that person's civil and political rights. At the same time, the proclamation contained fourteen categories of exceptions, excluding thousands who would have to apply individually for pardons. These included those who had held high positions in the Confederate government and military, those who graduated from the US military or naval academy and served as Confederate officers, those who had served in the US Congress before aiding the rebellion, and all who participated in the rebellion and whose taxable property was estimated to be at least $20,000. The amnesty proclamation reflected both Johnson's background and the Cabinet's previous discussions. The provision pertaining to wealthy Southerners emerged from Johnson's distrust of the plantation aristocracy, while the overall idea of a general amnesty grew out of deliberations during the last weeks of the Lincoln administration. For his part, Johnson thought that this measure struck a middle-of-the-road stance between blanket punishment and blanket leniency.

Johnson's second proclamation established a provisional government in North Carolina, thus setting a precedent for how other states would be handled. Because he had already recognized the loyal governments that the Lincoln administration had been nurturing in Arkansas, Tennessee, Louisiana, and Virginia, these proclamations pertained only to the remaining seven Rebel states. Johnson believed that the states of the Confederacy had not and could not actually leave the Union, so he rejected the idea of military rule and foresaw minimal requirements for the states' return. Under the North Carolina proclamation, those who had sworn an oath of loyalty to the Union under the amnesty proclamation and had met the qualifications for voting before the state's ordinance of secession could participate in voting for delegates to a new state constitutional convention. This meant that the vast majority of North Carolinians who had exercised the franchise before the war—with the exception of those excluded from the amnesty proclamation—would continue to do so. Newly freed African Americans would not vote in these elections. The proclamation also named a provisional governor, William W. Holden, the former leader of the Unionist peace movement in that state. All of the other provisional governors whom Johnson appointed possessed Unionist credentials, although they had exhibited varying degrees of loyalty, and several seemed to be chosen more for their broad appeal than their strict Unionism.

Over time, the administration's plans for reconstruction came into focus. Provisional governors would call for elections for constitutional conventions, and the new constitutions would need to repeal secession ordinances, cancel wartime debts, and abolish slavery. Johnson also urged the states to ratify the Thirteenth Amendment. During the summer and fall of 1865, almost all of the states carried out these steps. When a few states failed to comply—South Carolina did not nullify its secession ordinance, and Mississippi did not ratify the Thirteenth Amendment—the president did nothing to coerce them. He did continue to make suggestions to Southern leaders, even recommending at one point, following Lincoln's example, that Louisiana and Mississippi extend the right of suffrage to educated and propertied African Americans, a prompting to which neither state responded. Perhaps because of his constitutional views or maybe for political reasons, Johnson never forced the defeated Rebel states to meet his conditions for readmission. In Johnson's mind, once new constitutions were written and new governors and legislatures elected under their provisions, the state would be considered readmitted and their representatives and senators seated in Congress. An experienced politician, Johnson seemed intent on building up a broad base of support in the South while creating a governing coalition in Washington. Given the great divergence of opinions in Congress—a spectrum that ranged from conservative Democrats to Radical Republicans—Johnson believed his reconstruction plan to be moderate, sensible, and consistent with the policies of the slain president.

JOHNSON, THE FREEDMAN'S BUREAU, AND THE BLACK CODES

If Johnson quickly made known his plans for dealing with former Rebels and reincorporating the ex-Confederate states into the Union, his views regarding the rights of African Americans were not immediately evident. During the summer and fall, two disputes—the first over the powers of the Freedman's Bureau and the second over the South's enactment of black codes—offered insights into the president's thinking. Both showed that Johnson's lenient policies with regard to individual Rebels and Confederate states would have a significant impact on the future status of African Americans, as well as the relationship between the national government and the states. And both showed that when forced to choose between expanding national power to protect the rights of newly freed blacks and preserving state power in order to promote the interests of recently defeated Southern whites, Johnson would side with the latter.

Before Johnson had formulated any policies regarding the freedpeople, the Freedman's Bureau had already been helping the formerly enslaved adjust to their new condition. Created by an act of Congress in March 1865 and formally known as the Bureau of Refugees, Freedmen, and Abandoned Lands, the Bureau seemed to possess great powers. Under the law, it took responsibility for "the supervision and management of all abandoned lands, and the control of all subjects relating to refugees and freedmen from rebel states, or from any district of country within the territory embraced in the operations of the army."[21] By summer of 1865, the Bureau controlled 800,000 acres previously held by Confederate supporters. Building on experiments in black landownership in the South Carolina Sea Islands, as well as Sherman's order granting lands to freedpeople along the southeast Atlantic coast, the law authorized the commissioner of the Bureau to "set apart, for the use of loyal refugees and freedmen, such tracts of land within the insurrectionary states as shall have been abandoned, or to which the United States shall have acquired title."[22] These plots would not exceed forty acres and would initially be rented before the occupant would have the right to purchase. These rents would serve as the primary source of revenue for the new agency. In addition to overseeing this process, the Bureau would also distribute provisions, clothing, and fuel to meet the immediate needs of freedpeople, refugees, and their families. Envisioned as a temporary agency, the Bureau was to last a year from the end of the war.

A dispute quickly emerged over the Bureau's powers over Rebel lands. During spring 1865, Bureau officials had begun consolidating abandoned or confiscated Rebel lands under its authority, but Johnson's amnesty proclamation provided for the "restoration of all rights of property, except as to slaves," a fact that some Bureau officials interpreted as a direct threat both to its revenue and its purpose. If former Rebels were to be restored all rights of property, they feared, freedpeople would have these lands taken from them. After asking for an opinion on the matter from the attorney general and receiving an ambiguous response, Bureau commissioner Oliver O. Howard took the initiative. In late July, he started actually distributing and renting the lands that the Bureau had acquired, and he declared that "the pardon of the president will not be understood to extend to the surrender of abandoned or confiscated property, which by law has been set apart for refugees and freedmen."[23] Howard's bold move eventually prompted a challenge in Tennessee, where a pardoned Rebel sought to reclaim his land after its redistribution by the Bureau. In an unequivocal fashion, Johnson ordered that the Bureau relinquish the property to the former Rebel, a policy that, according to the president, applied "in all similar cases."[24] In a single, sweeping order, Johnson asserted that his pardon power had superseded the statute granting the Freedman's Bureau its powers over land distribution. During the next few months, while Howard vainly attempted to devise a way for freedpeople to hold onto lands while still following Johnson's orders, African Americans protested. Rural blacks in particular, who had spent their entire lives working the land, possessed a deep belief that land ownership was part and parcel of emancipation. Their religious conception of the ultimate triumph of justice taught them that their labors would be rewarded in a biblical day of jubilee, while reason assured them that they deserved the land for their fidelity to the Union. A committee of black leaders in Edisto, South Carolina, where blacks had acquired land under Sherman's field order, argued that they "were the only true and loyal people that were found in possession of these Lands."[25] Despite such patriotic appeals, Johnson's order remained in place. Unwilling to expand federal military authority in the South through the Freedman's Bureau, in this the first dispute over postwar reconstruction policy, the president cast his lot with the interests of Southern whites.

While Johnson worked to thwart the Freedman's Bureau, African Americans actively sought legal rights from the national government. Black leaders had long insisted that rights accompany abolition, and even before the ratification of the Thirteenth Amendment, African Americans organized a series of conventions to press their case. In meetings throughout the ex-Confederate states, blacks repeatedly invoked the spirit of the American founders and sounded familiar themes: their loyalty to the Union, their service and sacrifice as soldiers during the war, and their shared constitutional inheritance as Americans. The Reverend James D. Lynch of Nashville perhaps best captured the spirit of these assemblages when he announced to delegates of his state's freedman's convention, "We have met here to impress upon the white men of Tennessee, of the United States, and of the world that we are part and parcel of the American Republic."[26] These state conventions during the summer and fall of 1865—held by African Americans who had been denied the right to vote under Johnson's North Carolina Proclamation—served as a visible alternative to the Johnson-organized state constitutional conventions. African Americans also organized at the national level. In September, black leaders formed the National Equal Rights League, a successor to pre-emancipation-era national conventions. Gathering in Cleveland, delegates openly criticized Johnson's policies for leaving the freedpeople in the hands of their former masters and called for the nation "to guarantee us the full enjoyment of our liberties, protection to our persons throughout the land, complete enfranchisement . . . until all are equal as American citizens before the law." Noting that "the United States shall guaranty to every State in the Union, a republican form of government," the forty-one delegates from ten states (including a handful of delegates from the South) called on Congress to take swift action. The delegates ambitiously advocated a constitutional amendment that prohibited any legislation "against any civilized portion of the inhabitants, native-born or naturalized, on account of race or color."[27]

Although he took no interest in a civil rights amendment to the Constitution, Johnson did encourage the newly elected Southern legislatures to enact legislation to protect African Americans. Because few high Confederate officials and wealthy planters had received pardons by the fall, prewar Whig office-holders who had opposed secession made up the majority of those who assumed power in these legislative bodies, and Johnson believed that this fresh cadre of leaders would take the postwar South in a new direction. In correspondence with provisional governors, he encouraged state governments not only to abolish slavery but also to enact legislation "for the protection of freedmen in person and property, as justice and equity demand."[28] Most of the ensuing legal codes did provide basic rights to African Americans, including the right to acquire and sell property, sue and be sued, testify in court, and marry. These constituted significant gains.

But Southern legislatures also enacted laws that severely restricted blacks' economic opportunities. These "black codes," as they were disparagingly deemed by the Northern press, constituted an overt attempt to cling to the old order. Most egregious was the black code of Mississippi. It included a strict vagrancy law that singled out "all freedmen, free negroes, and mulattoes . . . with no lawful employment or business, or found unlawfully assembling themselves together."[29] Requiring written evidence of "a lawful home or employment" for blacks, the code provided that labor contracts be established between blacks and their white employers. It forbade blacks to quit before the expiration of their contracts and prohibited others from luring them away to other employment. Worse still, the state established an apprenticeship system for blacks under eighteen years of age who were orphans or "whose parent or parents have not the means or who refuse to provide for and support" them. Under the law, local white officials possessed the power to apprentice such a minor, with the former owner of the apprentice having first preference. This supervisor had a legal right to inflict punishment and even a right to "pursue and recapture said apprentice" in the event that the apprentice attempted to leave.[30] It is hard to imagine a law that more resembled the old slave regime. Although no other state went as far as Mississippi, during the winter of 1865–1866, all of the Southern states enacted laws that controlled black labor, and many states also imposed restrictions on blacks renting land, assembling in groups, and possessing firearms. Because Johnson had already removed black federal troops and allowed Southern states to form their own militias, an entire white legal apparatus began to take shape in some states to enforce the codes.

Although dismayed by the black codes, Johnson remained overly sensitive to the white Southern belief that black labor required white direction and coercion. When he refused to use executive power to undermine the codes, Radicals began arguing that the passage of the codes proved that Johnson's reconstruction plans had failed and that the restoration of civilian power in the Southern states had proceeded too quickly. The Radicals were not the first to notice that more vigorous federal oversight of the former Rebel states might have yielded a different result. Barely a month after the issuing of Johnson's reconstruction proclamations, one group of African American leaders had surmised that "the golden moment to secure justice . . . was not taken."[31]

COMPETING VISIONS FOR RECONSTRUCTION

In spite of these controversies, by late 1865 Johnson remained the head of the Republican Party and still enjoyed a fair degree of goodwill in Congress and from the Northern public. But over the next several months, a sequence of events initiated a sharp break between Johnson and most Republicans. Emerging from a volatile mix of intense personality conflicts, sharply divergent views of Southern race relations, and deep divisions over constitutional interpretation, the rupture between the president and Congress split the Cabinet, kept sectional tensions alive, and eventually culminated in Johnson's impeachment.

The rift began in early December. In the aftermath of a heated argument over reconstruction policy between Johnson and Senator Charles Sumner at the White House on December 2, each side—the administration and the Radicals—saw the other as exemplifying extremism, and each side came to believe that it could reap political benefits from confrontation rather than compromise. At the opening of the first session of the 39th Congress, on December 4, the House of Representatives made the first move. Acting under its authority to judge the qualifications of its members, the House initiated proceedings by omitting the ex-Confederate states from the roll, thus refusing to recognize representatives from the state governments that Johnson had organized. Almost immediately, House members approved a resolution offered by Radical Thaddeus Stevens of Pennsylvania to create a fifteen-member Joint Committee on Reconstruction, which would examine the question of the seating of Southern members. Thus, the House, soon joined by the Senate, signaled that it did not accept the legitimacy of Johnson's reconstruction proclamations.

Deep philosophical differences soon became apparent. In his first annual message to Congress that same month, Johnson defended the policies he had already implemented. Outlining his views on the relationship between the national government and the states, Johnson hailed the preservation of the Union and repudiated "the sovereignty of the states," but he also made clear that a strong Union did not require the subjugation of the states. Quite to the contrary, he claimed, in language reminiscent of his political mentor, Andrew Jackson, the whole and parts were mutually beneficial. "So long as the Constitution of the United States endures, the States will endure; the destruction of the one is the destruction of the other; the preservation of the one is the preservation of the other."[32] Johnson thus explained to Congress how he had sought to restore "the rightful energy of the General Government and of the States." In his view, these things went hand in hand—the reopening of the post office and the federal courts in the South accompanied the extension of the pardon and the establishment of state legislatures. Acknowledging the risk in such a policy, Johnson argued that the restoration of state power was connected to "the clearest recognition of the binding force of the laws of the United States."[33] The "binding force" came in the form of the Thirteenth Amendment, while the restoration of state power required that states alone would decide the question of black suffrage. For months, Johnson had vacillated on this volatile issue, but by year's end, he had concluded that federal action would be neither constitutionally permissible nor politically practical. The Constitution had conferred no power on the federal government to deal with voting, which, in Johnson's mind, meant that the issue was reserved to the states. Apart from the constitutional question, Johnson understood the political perils of pushing forward on suffrage, particularly because several Northern states still excluded African Americans from the ballot box. Thus, justifying his position as rooted in tradition and moderation, Johnson concluded that each state could decide whether black voting was "to be adopted at once and absolutely, or introduced gradually and with conditions."[34]

Having left most matters to the states, Johnson proclaimed the Thirteenth Amendment the centerpiece of reconstruction. At the time Johnson assumed office, twenty-one states had already ratified it, just six short of the twenty-seven states required under the Constitution. Two Northern states passed it that summer, and—at Johnson's repeated urging—four ex-Confederate states with provisional governments followed suit during fall and winter. Days after Johnson sent his message to Congress, Georgia became the twenty-seventh state to ratify. Johnson gloried in this impending triumph. "The adoption of the amendment reunites us beyond all power of disruption. It heals the wound that is still imperfectly closed: it removes slavery, the element which has so long perplexed and divided the country; it makes of us once more a united people, renewed and strengthened, bound more than ever to mutual affection and support."[35] For the Tennessean, it represented a remarkable personal and political journey, and Southerners' acceptance of the end of slavery marked a sharp break with their past. Surely, Johnson believed, the nation had witnessed a revolution—and one for which he could justifiably take some credit. "It is one of the greatest acts on record," he exulted, "to have brought four millions of people into freedom."[36] By the end of 1865, in short, Johnson's reconstruction plan amounted to securing the abolition of slavery through the Thirteenth Amendment and restoring self-government to the states.

Republicans in Congress, for the most part, held a different vision. With majorities of 75 percent in both houses, Republicans dominated the legislative branch like no party in recent history. Yet they remained an amalgam of factions—from Radicals with strong ties to African American activists to old-line conservatives ensconced in the border states—unified only by their enthusiasm at having defeated the rebellion and by their attachment to the notion of free labor. During the summer and fall of 1865, some Republicans had feared that Johnson's amnesty proclamation would ensconce the antebellum Southern political order and that his North Carolina proclamation had made it too easy for Rebel states to rejoin the Union. Johnson's reliance on these new governments to protect black rights, moreover, it now seemed clear, had proven naive. Radicals were particularly alarmed. In order to break up the Slave Power and reform the South, they believed, a more limited amnesty, a more onerous readmission process, and a more expansive civil rights agenda would be required. In a December 18 speech on the floor of the House, widely viewed as the Radical response to Johnson's message, Stevens described the Southern states as "dead carcasses" and argued that only congressional action could resuscitate them.[37] Because Stevens and other Radicals refused to recognize the Johnson governments, they argued that ratification of the Thirteenth Amendment by these states meant nothing—that ratification had occurred long before, when three quarters of the loyal states had accepted the amendment.

Regardless of when it had been ratified, Radicals saw the Thirteenth Amendment as only the beginning of the revolution, not the end. Having been in the vanguard of the political antislavery movement for years, men such as Stevens in the House and Sumner and Benjamin Wade in the Senate viewed the issue of black rights as an extension of the slavery issue. In their minds, Union victory offered a singular opportunity to transform the nation. Like black activists, they viewed Christian principle and the Declaration of Independence as essential components of a reformed postwar American constitutionalism that would enshrine liberty and equality under the law—that would complete the unfinished work of the founders. Moreover, Radicals agreed with what most African American leaders had been urging since early in the war— that civil and political rights should accompany black liberty. In their minds, both principles and practicalities necessitated black suffrage. From a principled standpoint, voting constituted the next step on the progression of liberty, the ultimate manifestation of fulfilling one's God-given rights and one's responsibilities as a free citizen. Practically speaking, voting rights for former slaves would consolidate the revolution by strengthening Republicans, for black voters would presumably align with the political party most responsible for their liberation. This was important. Because abolition had rendered the Constitution's Three-Fifths Clause moot, once the former Rebel states did in fact gain admission to Congress, Southern representation would increase, based on counting the whole number of black people, rather than three-fifths. The granting of black suffrage promised to act as a Republican buffer against any Democratic attempt to undo the changes brought about by the war. The black suffrage issue divided the Republicans, for moderates and conservatives generally opposed giving African Americans the vote. Still, even conservatives could see the practical advantages, and the political momentum was gradually moving toward the Radical position.

While Johnson and the Radicals had staked out opposite positions on suffrage, continuing disputes over the Freedman's Bureau and the black codes pushed the issue of civil rights to the forefront. Johnson had again expressed displeasure with the black codes in his message to Congress, and he did nothing to interfere when in early 1866 Freedman's Bureau officials suspended or nullified the codes of Mississippi and South Carolina. Believing they had presidential support, in February 1866 Republicans affirmed this military solution to the problem by enacting a comprehensive bill to empower and extend the life of the Bureau. Justified under the enforcement clause of the Thirteenth Amendment, the bill increased the number of Bureau agents, set aside land for freedpeople and loyal whites, and authorized the establishment of Bureau-run schools and courts. Such an expansion of the Bureau promised to thwart the enforcement of the remaining codes, or at least offer a heavy federal counterweight to the Johnson-formed state governments. Broadening the powers of the War Department–run Bureau beyond those in the legislation that had created it, the proposal codified some practices—the operation of Bureau courts—that were already underway, and the bill earned unanimous Republican support.

Despite his own misgivings about the black codes, Johnson vetoed the Freedman's Bureau bill. Angry over Congress's refusal to seat Southern representatives, Johnson portrayed the measure as unnecessary and challenged the legitimacy of any legislation enacted without all states represented in peacetime. After an attempt to override the veto failed, the president believed he stood at the head of a new moderate governing coalition, one that would restore constitutional government to the South with neither military rule nor black suffrage. In the days and weeks to follow, though, Johnson overplayed his hand while displaying his tendency toward a defensive inflexibility. In an impromptu, rambling speech in late February, he lashed out at his opponents as enemies of the government and the Constitution. Comparing Radicals in Congress to Rebels in the South, Johnson described the Joint Committee on Reconstruction as a "central directory" that had assumed "nearly all the powers of Congress." Pushing the French Revolution analogy further, Johnson even implied that the Joint Committee sought to send him to the guillotine.[38] Although such statements hurt him in the Northern press, Johnson had already set his mind on taking on the Radicals.

Having lost to Johnson on the Freedman's Bureau, in March Congress pushed back by enacting a civil rights bill. The first proposed civil rights legislation in American history, the bill provided that all persons born in the United States were citizens. During the antebellum era, the notion of citizenship connoted privileges and obligations to the community and seemed to belong only to those who supposedly proved themselves deserving. In the *Dred Scott* case, the Supreme Court had held that blacks, whether free or enslaved, could not be citizens. The drafters of the civil rights bill upended the antebellum notion of citizenship and overturned *Dred Scott* by articulating a list of rights associated with citizenship that the federal government would protect. In enumerating these rights, the drafters of the legislation proceeded with caution. In their minds, they attempted to interpret what the Constitution already supposedly guaranteed when it referred to the "privileges and immunities of citizens in the several states" in Article IV, Section 2. The proposed legislation provided that all citizens possessed the right "to make and enforce contracts, to sue, be parties, and give evidence, to inherit, purchase, lease, sell, hold, and convey real and personal property, and to full and equal benefit of all laws and proceedings for the security of person and property, as is enjoyed by white citizens."[39] The bill also provided that the federal courts would have jurisdiction in cases involving any offenses under the act. Making no mention of what nineteenth-century Americans often referred to as "political rights," including the right to serve on juries, vote, and hold office, the proposed legislation overrode the black codes and vastly expanded federal authority. Justified on the basis of congressional power under Section 2 of the Thirteenth Amendment, the bill passed with overwhelming majorities in both houses of Congress.

Against the advice of most of the Cabinet, Johnson vetoed the bill. In a document that defined his presidency, on March 27, 1866, Johnson laid out his constitutional views on the issues presented in the legislation. First, the president disparaged the attempt to grant citizenship to all American-born former slaves. After again questioning the legitimacy of any legislation enacted with the Southern states still unrepresented, Johnson portrayed African Americans as ill-prepared for and undeserving of new rights and responsibilities. "Four millions of them have just emerged from slavery into freedom. Can it be reasonably supposed that they possess the requisite qualifications to entitle them to all the privileges and immunities of citizens of the United States?" Arguing that the legislation discriminated against "large numbers of intelligent, worthy, and patriotic foreigners" who had to prove themselves worthy of citizenship during a probationary period, Johnson inveighed against the sudden attempt to grant citizenship status to the formerly enslaved. Second, Johnson expressed his belief that under the Constitution, states possessed almost complete power over their own affairs. Deep-seated customs, he argued, were woven into laws against interracial marriage, for example, and traditional constitutional interpretation had always held that states alone governed matters such as landholding and contracts. If Congress possessed authority over such areas, he argued, imagining the far-reaching consequences, "then Congress can by law also declare who, without regard to color or race, shall have the right to sit as a juror or as a judge, to hold any office, and, finally, to vote 'in every State and Territory of the United States.'"[40] In other words, Johnson feared that the civil rights bill marked the first step toward congressional efforts to nationalize these more closely guarded political rights. Finally, Johnson argued that the proposed civil rights law interfered with the postwar relations between "capital and labor."[41] Overly sensitive to the complaints of white Southerners about freed blacks' supposed unwillingness to work and completely deaf to the cries of white Radicals and African American leaders about the necessity of protecting black liberty and opportunity, Johnson defined the issues in terms of race and labor. In Johnson's conception of the postwar South, it was becoming clear, white landholders would continue to hold sway, while black laborers would remain in a subordinate position. In Johnson's view, the bill interfered with these established traditional economic—and racial—relationships. Despite the president's objections, in April Congress overrode the veto with the requisite two-thirds vote in both houses.

Once the Civil Rights Act of 1866 became the law of the land, Johnson's presidency careened toward a state of near-perpetual conflict with the legislative branch. Though he repeatedly claimed to act in the spirit of his "lamented predecessor," Johnson soon lost nearly all his allies within the Republican Party. To be sure, both sides bore some of the blame. Congressional Radicals, self-righteous and zealous for power, simply hated watching as Johnson set in motion his own plan for the South's postwar future, and once Congress assembled, the leadership's inflammatory rhetoric made reasoned dialogue and compromise nearly impossible. Johnson, of course, proved just as bullheaded, and despite his supposed political savvy, he utterly failed to persuade

This 1867 print by Thomas Nast, "Slavery Is Dead?," attempted to capture the ongoing struggle of African Americans to achieve their rights. Even after the passage of the Thirteenth Amendment and the Civil Rights Act of 1866, white supremacy retained a hold on the South. The image depicts a slave, on the left, being sold and a freedman, on the right, being whipped. Courtesy of the Library of Congress, LC-USZ62-108003

or engage the Radicals. Lincoln had also habitually feuded with the progressive wing of his party, but it had always seemed more like a family quarrel than a real fight. Although Lincoln privately acknowledged that the Radicals were "the unhandiest devils in the world to deal with," he believed that "their faces [were] set Zionwards."[42] Johnson clearly lacked Lincoln's flexibility and forbearance with the Radicals. The Tennessean never forgave their unwillingness to admit Southern members to Congress, and he felt personally slighted by the fact that congressmen from his own state—which as governor he had worked so hard to reform—had been turned away. Even worse for his political fortunes, he spurned moderates by vetoing measures that enjoyed broad Republican support. Despite reports warning that a significant number of Southerners remained unrepentant and hostile to federal authority, Johnson pressed ahead with policies that appeared to be based more on preserving Southern white power than on protecting black liberty. The combination of his stubborn temperament, racial prejudice, and Jacksonian constitutional views made Johnson ill-suited to the moment.

SOUTHERN DEFEAT AND SOUTHERN VIOLENCE

While the president and Congress spent most of 1865 and early 1866 debating the future of the vanquished South, Southerners themselves were realizing the full impact of their defeat. Having lost perhaps as many as 300,000 lives in a struggle for independence, the sense of grief and loss was overwhelming. Those men who did return home were reunited with family members who had borne the brunt of the war's harsh effects on their lives and landscape. Virginia and Tennessee had experienced most of the fighting and devastation, but Grant's campaigns in Mississippi and Sherman's marches through Georgia and the Carolinas had inflicted considerable destruction as well. Farms, fields, and homesteads lay in ruins. Western cities that had experienced Union occupation early in the war emerged relatively unscathed, but urban centers along the eastern seaboard where the fighting intensified during the last two years of the conflict—Atlanta, Charleston, Columbia, Petersburg, and Richmond—suffered the most. Losses in crops, livestock, personal property, and cash left Southerners with little from which to rebuild their lives. For former planters, of course, the war had also resulted in the uncompensated loss of their slave property—nearly $3 billion in total at the time—which suddenly cast the region's former elite into despair, if not destitution.[43]

Some of the most ardent Confederates, perhaps fearing retribution, simply could not abide the prospect of a Yankee-dominated Union. Some 10,000 former Rebels left the United States altogether. A sizable contingent fled to Mexico and Brazil, while smaller numbers scattered themselves throughout other parts of Latin America. Former Confederate generals John C. Breckinridge, Robert Toombs, and Kirby Smith were among those who left. Former governor Isham Harris of Tennessee, who headed to Mexico, later described it as "far better, for me that I should have lost position, fortune and home and stand here today a penniless exile than to have violated principle and forfeited self-respect."[44] Edmund Ruffin, a leader among the fire-eating secessionists who had lit the first canon for the attack on Fort Sumter, expressed more vitriolic feelings, as well as more tragic means of escape. "I here declare my unmitigated hatred to Yankee rule—to all political, social and business connections with the Yankees and to the Yankee race," Ruffin wrote. "Would that I could impress these sentiments, in their full force, on every living Southerner and bequeath them to every one yet to be born!"[45] With that, Ruffin took his own life.

For those who remained to confront the consequences of reunion, evangelicalism and honor set the mental parameters of their response. Most religious Southerners retained a sense of certainty immediately after the war that

In some Southern cities, such as Charleston, the result of hard war was destruction and ruins. Courtesy of the US National Archives, 111-B-744

their cause had been just, and they continued to defend the righteousness of both Southern slavery and secession. Viewing both as moral issues, most evangelicals remained confident that the Bible sanctioned slavery and that, as the *Southern Presbyterian* maintained, "those views of States' Rights for which [Southern men] battled so stoutly . . . were the views of the framers of the Constitution." Some religious Southerners still believed that through the chastising effects of defeat, God was in some way preparing them for future victory and vindication. Writing a few weeks after Lee's surrender, Tennessean Eliza Fain seemed assured of the South's righteousness. "Every prayer, every moment, every view I take of our country's cause, every thing I hear in regards to our slaves but serves to impress me more certainly of our final triumph. Whether it is to be independence or not I cannot know but I do believe the honor and character of the South will be maintained before the nations of the earth."[46] The desire to retain honor simply reinforced this Christian sense of certainty. Because humiliation and defeat stood as the polar opposites of honor and victory, white Southerners more often than not held audacious attitudes toward the Northern victors. Submission and resignation implied weakness, and in the weeks after Confederate surrender, white Southerners displayed determined defiance. Traveling through the South during May 1865 in an attempt to promote the cause of black suffrage, a surprised Chief Justice Chase reported to President Johnson "how little [Southerners] seem to realize that any change in personal or political relations has been wrought by the war."[47] The combination of piety and pride produced more than a small number of die-hard Rebels.

Some Southerners turned to violence. Although poverty, migration, and guerilla activity produced a fair degree of ordinary lawlessness and criminality, more serious violent outbreaks issued from the fear and disruption associated with changing race relations. The continued presence of black troops, the emergence of the Freedman's Bureau as a force in Southern affairs, and a new assertiveness on the part of some African Americans combined to alarm and frighten whites. Across the South, bands of white "regulators" or "scouts" attempted to reassume the power of the antebellum slave patrols, policing the countryside and disarming African Americans. Outbreaks of violence against blacks—and at times white Unionists and Radicals—became a regular feature of postwar Southern life, even as federal troops remained. A massacre in Memphis was the most horrific example of white terror. During wartime, Memphis had drawn thousands of formerly enslaved African Americans, who fled nearby Mississippi Delta plantations for the safety of the Union-occupied city. But after the war, the city's Democratic newspapers, in a brazen propaganda campaign against the mass of black newcomers, intoned repeated warnings about black brutality and the looming specter of "social equality." The fact that black troops remained at a local garrison especially offended local whites, and a confrontation between black troops and white police officers in early May prompted a three-day-long rampage against the black community. When the mayhem had subsided, at least forty-six African Americans had lost their lives, and another seventy to eighty had sustained wounds. Other blacks were robbed and raped, while more than 100 buildings—homes, business, churches, and schools—burned down. Outraged congressional leaders dispatched a three-man committee to investigate.

THE FOURTEENTH AMENDMENT AND THE POLITICAL AFTERMATH

By summer 1866, Republicans saw a new amendment to the Constitution as the best long-term solution to the problems in the South. Johnson's speedy reestablishment of civilian governments had yielded repressive legislation and horrific violence, a fact that only served to increase Radical influence and rally

Republicans of all stripes to push for further federal oversight of Southern affairs. In addition to a revised version of the Freedman's Bureau bill that Johnson had previously vetoed, Republicans favored a constitutional amendment, which would reform the South by disabling the Slave Power and protecting black civil rights, changes that would not be easily repealed by future Democratic majorities in Congress. The Senate had first agreed on language for a proposed amendment in April, and Southern atrocities—Stevens referred to "the screams and groans of the dying victims at Memphis"—played into the hands of the measure's proponents in the House.[48] On June 13, 1866, on a strictly party-line vote—all 120 Republicans in favor and all 32 Democrats against—the Fourteenth Amendment secured passage in the House of Representatives. Written to gain maximum Republican support so as to ensure its passage, the final language combined a variety of issues into a single amendment with five sections.

The first section of the amendment stood out as the most revolutionary. Echoing both Attorney General Edward Bates's opinion of 1862 and the first section of the Civil Rights Act of 1866, the amendment provided for birthright citizenship, writing into the Constitution the principle that all born on American soil are "citizens of the United States and of the state wherein they reside." Just as much as the abolition of slavery, the conferral of citizenship on African Americans by an amendment to the Constitution represented the realization of a long-standing aspiration. Legal precedents, such as the fact of black citizenship in some Northern states at the time of the founding (cited in the *Dred Scott* dissents), and political arguments, such as black loyalty and military sacrifice during wartime, surely contributed to the idea that blacks deserved status as full partakers in the American republic. But more important—at least in the minds of Radicals—were the fixed principles upon which black activists had long stood. From the early decades of the republic, anti-slavery black constitutionalists had forged a notion of equality and citizenship based on Christian principle and Jefferson's Declaration of Independence. Recognizing that blacks' status as citizens—and the citizenship of all Americans—emerged from the simple fact of being born on US soil constituted a profound shift in thinking about what it meant to belong to the American republic. No longer to be earned or deserved, citizenship under the Fourteenth Amendment bestowed inherent rights.

The precise nature of these rights was unclear. The rest of the first section held that "no state shall make or enforce any law which shall abridge the privileges or immunities of citizens of the United States; nor shall any state deprive any person of life, liberty, or property without due process of law; nor deny to any person within its jurisdiction the equal protection of the laws." This was not wholly new language. In fact, the framers of the Fourteenth Amendment fashioned most of Section 1 from existing materials—from Article I, Section 10's limitation on state power, from the "privileges and immunities" that drafters of the Civil Rights Act had attempted to define, and from the Fifth Amendment's Due Process Clause. The other phrase—"equal protection"—arguably originated in the assertion of the Declaration of Independence that "all men were created equal," words that had resonated powerfully through antebellum political thought. All of these phrases carried ambiguous meanings, and congressional debates included discussion of the vast potential implications of these clauses for all Americans. Representative John Bingham of Ohio, one of the drafters of the amendment, argued that "privileges and immunities" included all of the guarantees of the Bill of Rights, a much more expansive interpretation of rights than the drafters of the Civil Rights Act had enumerated. In making this argument, Bingham in effect hoped to overturn an 1833 Supreme Court decision that had held that the guarantees of the Bill of Rights did not apply to the states.[49] Regardless of whether most in Congress agreed with Bingham, by creating the Fourteenth Amendment from existing materials rather than from whole cloth, the architects of reconstruction left tremendous power in the hands of the Supreme Court and the president to interpret and enforce the amendment as they understood it. However these rights would be defined, the key to the Fourteenth Amendment was that it aimed to protect rights against infringement by the states. In dealing a blow to state power, the amendment thus also changed the relationship between the national government and states.

The other sections dealt more specifically with reconstruction. Section 2 overturned the Three-Fifths Clause, providing that representation in the House would be based on "the whole number of persons in each state, excluding Indians not taxed." To ensure that the Southern states would not simply continue to elect Democrats as they gained seats in Congress, the amendment provided that representation would be reduced in proportion to the population of male citizens who were denied the right to vote. In other words, this section indirectly ordered states—in both the South and North—to allow black men of age to vote. If the states did not do so, their numbers of representatives would be reduced proportionally. Section 3 regulated officeholding. It banned those who had held office "under the United States or any state" before the war and who had then supported the rebellion from again holding any such office, though it did provide that Congress could "remove such disability" with a two-thirds vote in each house. Radicals had originally supported language that would have imposed a short-term ban on Rebel voting rather than officeholding, but moderates thought disfranchisement too severe and too politically unpopular. The ban on officeholding thus replaced disfranchisement in the final version. Section 4, after holding that the validity of the public debt of the United States "shall not be questioned," provided that no debts incurred in support of the rebellion would be paid and that "no claim for the loss or emancipation of any slave" would be recognized. Finally, Section 5 gave Congress the power of enforcement, a provision that many deemed the key to the entire process of reconstruction. None of these provisions proved particularly controversial with Republicans, for they revealed the consensus within the party on such questions by that summer. Black suffrage would prevent Southern states from reverting to rebellion, a ban on Confederate officeholding would ensure the election of Unionists to state governments, cancellation of Confederate debts would mean that no Rebel reaped rewards from having financed treason, and the enforcement of these provisions ensured their success.

In approving the Fourteenth Amendment, Congress implicitly signaled to the ex-Confederate states that their ratification of the amendment would be required for readmission to the Union. Although the president possessed no formal role in the process of amending the Constitution, Johnson went out of his way to express his opposition, even sending a special message to that effect. Johnson's stance encouraged the Southern states to ignore the amendment, which they did. But when Tennessee's legislature, under the strong arm of its Radical governor William Brownlow, an old rival of Johnson's, immediately ratified the amendment in late July, Congress responded in the most effective manner possible: by seating the congressmen from Tennessee, including senator-elect David Patterson, Johnson's son-in-law, a gesture that lent clarity and credibility to congressional reconstruction efforts. Despite unanimous Republican support, the Fourteenth Amendment proved disappointing to black activists, who wondered publicly how the Constitution could affirm black citizenship without directly conferring the right to vote, while women's rights activists expressed even greater dismay that the Constitution now referred to "male" voters, thus damaging the cause of woman suffrage. Nevertheless, congressional passage of the Fourteenth Amendment marked a milestone in American history. Republicans had gone beyond abolishing slavery to writing birthright citizenship and civil rights into the text of the Constitution, and only if Southern states ratified the amendment would they be readmitted to the Union.

Subsequent events affirmed the Republicans' stance and belied Johnson's claims that abolition and the restoration of civilian government proved sufficient to restore union and peace. On July 30, 1866, just days after the readmission of Tennessee, New Orleans erupted in violence. This time the bloodshed resulted when a mob of ex-Confederates attempted to prevent a convention organized by the state's governor, James Madison Wells. A Unionist appointed under Lincoln's Ten Percent Plan, Wells had advocated reconvening the Union constitutional convention, which had first assembled in 1864, in order to enfranchise blacks and disfranchise former rebels. Warned that the mere act of assembling would provoke violent opposition, the governor and other leaders came under the false impression that the president would use federal troops to protect the gathering. But when the white delegates and their black supporters began to assemble, former Confederates went on a rampage. When order was finally restored, 34 African Americans and 3 white Radicals had been killed, while more than 100 others sustained injuries.

In the months following the massacre in New Orleans, Johnson's political position deteriorated rapidly. Earlier in the summer, the president and his closest supporters had decided to hold a National Union Convention in order to rally support among pro-Johnson conservatives, both Republicans and Democrats, Northerners and Southerners. The ultimate goal was to build a national political movement in opposition to congressional reconstruction policies, particularly the Fourteenth Amendment. Secretary Seward took the lead in organizing the convention, and when Johnson asked for the support of the rest of his Cabinet, in July three members—Attorney General James Speed, Postmaster General William Dennison, and Secretary of the Interior James Harlan—tendered their resignations. All announced that their support for the amendment was determinative of their decisions to resign. Meanwhile, problems plagued the National Union Convention from the start. Elections for delegates produced an overabundance of Democrats, most of whom had opposed both the war and the abolition of slavery. Most of the Southerners were former Confederates. Only last-minute maneuverings prevented the notorious Copperhead Clement Vallandigham of Ohio from taking the seat to which he had been elected, and former Confederate vice president Alexander Stephens, himself elected as a delegate, neglected to participate only because of illness. Historians disagree about how much the convention hurt Johnson politically, but none argue that it helped him.

With congressional elections just a few months away and Congress and the president arrayed on opposite sides of a constitutional amendment, Johnson took his case directly to the people. At the end of August, the president embarked on an unprecedented campaign tour, what he called "the swing around the circle," which included stops in cities throughout the Northeast and Midwest. Bringing Admiral David Farragut and General Grant along for political effect, Johnson attempted to rally public support against his congressional opponents. Johnson's extemporaneous speaking style had served him well on the stump in Tennessee, but when the president encountered hecklers in various cities along the way, matters quickly got out of hand. The president engaged in increasingly bitter exchanges with members of the crowd and made a series of outlandish claims. In Cleveland, Johnson implied that Providence had brought about the death of Lincoln in order to make Johnson president. In St. Louis, he laid blame for the New Orleans massacre at the feet of "the radical Congress." In Indianapolis and Pittsburgh, the jeering of the crowds practically prevented Johnson from being heard. The spectacle of a president engaging in such undignified behavior prompted Grant to quit the tour, and Johnson's political ineptness helped unify Republicans. In the fall congressional elections, Johnson's reconstruction policies—particularly his opposition to the Fourteenth Amendment—suffered a resounding defeat. The election of even more Republicans gave Johnson's opponents an apparent veto-proof majority in both houses of Congress, a result that ensured that the revolution would continue.

BLACK RIGHTS, STATE POWER, AND RECONSTRUCTION

The critical years 1865–1866 were arguably the most eventful of the entire Civil War and reconstruction era. During a span of fewer than twenty-four months, the US Congress passed an amendment to the Constitution abolishing slavery, Robert E. Lee's Army of Northern Virginia surrendered to Union general Ulysses S. Grant, President Abraham Lincoln suffered death at the hands of an assassin, President Andrew Johnson initiated a policy of pardoning Rebels and restoring civilian rule in the Southern states, and Republicans in Congress reacted against Johnson's plans and enacted a series of measures, including another constitutional amendment, designed to expand the rights of African Americans. At the time, no one doubted that these dramatic events constituted a true revolution in American life.

The first great revolutionary consequence of the war was obviously the abolition of slavery. Despite slavery's hold on North America for nearly two and a half centuries, the Thirteenth Amendment brought legal slavery to an end. During the antebellum period, the debate over slavery had torn apart America's churches, fragmented and realigned its political parties, and ultimately severed the South from the rest of the Union. But by the summer of 1865, the consensus in favor of the abolition of slavery was overwhelming. Among Republicans and Democrats, in free states and in border slave states, support for abolition became an accepted fact in American political life. Republicans hailed an event that many of them had strived toward for their entire careers, while President Johnson attempted to claim all the credit he could for slavery's demise. Even postwar Southern state legislatures—with the exception of Mississippi—quietly assented to the end of slavery.

But the more complex issue of the legal rights of formerly enslaved people remained. Although political leaders had uniformly embraced the idea of abolition, the notion of conferring black rights produced a wide range of political opinions. At one end of the spectrum stood white Southerners, who even in the aftermath of abolition largely remained convinced of slavery's morality and utility. Ever defiant, they sought to do all they could to define black freedom narrowly, in order to preserve whatever elements of the old regime they could in the postwar environment. At the other end of the spectrum were black activists, some of them formerly enslaved, who sought the entire panoply of rights they believed were inherent in their humanity and nationality— including civil rights, political rights (jury service, voting, and officeholding), and social rights (the right to interact freely in society with whites). Blending Christian principle and American constitutionalism, African American leaders committed themselves to dismantling white supremacy and promoting black equality under law. Between these opposing poles were a variety of positions represented by the nation's policy makers. President Johnson, who stood closest to the white Southern point of view, had championed abolition but opposed federally imposed civil rights. Moderate and conservative Republicans embraced civil rights, but they accepted political rights more for expediency than for principle. Radicals, who hewed closely to the positions articulated by African American activists, held a deep devotion to civil and political rights but some seemed hesitant on matters of "social equality." Although no immediate consensus existed, by the end of 1866, the boisterous back-and-forth of national politics had prompted Congress to pass the Fourteenth Amendment, which, if ratified, would establish that citizenship and civil rights followed emancipation. In short, within a half decade, the political debate had shifted from the Crittenden-Johnson Resolutions' conservative call for noninterference with Southern institutions and slaveholders' rights in 1861 to congressional approval of birthright citizenship and civil rights for all Americans in 1866. Not only had the Constitution been amended but the entire political debate had undergone a dramatic transformation.

The second great revolutionary consequence of the war was the delegitimizing of secession. Despite frequent references during the antebellum era to the idea of withdrawing from the federal compact, the constitutional idea of secession and the general notion of disunion died on the battlefields of the war. Realizing that the military contest had been lost, Southerners who had embraced secession in 1861, as well as some who had opposed it, made fervent appeals for pardons to President Johnson in 1865 and 1866, and these statements—self-interestedness aside—included countless attestations of devotion to the American Union.

But the more complicated question of the relationship of the national government to the states remained. If all Americans agreed on the illegitimacy of secession as a political act against the national authorities, Southerners did not concede the supremacy of the national government. Instead, former Rebels took heart from Johnson's opposition to Republicans, viewing his stance as a hopeful sign of the restoration of traditional constitutional principles, as well as license to oppose further change. The Richmond journalist Edward A. Pollard, who completed a massive history of the war in the midst of the dispute between Johnson and the Republicans, urged Southerners to hold fast to their ways with regard to race relations and state power. In the final paragraphs of his 752-page magnum opus, which he titled *The Lost Cause*, Pollard argued that the South would submit only to "what the war has properly *decided*." In his view, the war settled only "the restoration of the Union and the excision of slavery," nothing more. Apparently taking his cues from the president, Pollard clearly linked the future of Southern race relations to the reassertion of state power. "The war did not decide negro equality; it did not decide negro suffrage; it did not decide State Rights, although it might have exploded their abuse; it did not decide the orthodoxy of the Democratic party; it did not decide the right of a people to show dignity in misfortune, and to maintain self-respect in the face of adversity," Pollard wrote. "And these things which the war did not decide, the Southern people will still cling to, still claim, and still assert in them their rights and views."[50]

If slavery and secession died in 1865, then the interconnected questions of black rights and the scope of state power persisted. If African Americans were to enjoy the rights of citizenship outlined in the Fourteenth Amendment, a stronger national government would need to enforce those rights. And if the Republicans were to continue to act as "the party of revolution," as they had during the past half decade, they would have to contend with a variety of counterrevolutionary forces in the postwar era: the desire for sectional peace, the hope for restored civilian government, and—most important—the belief in preserving state power within the American constitutional order.[51] Acknowledging Americans' deep belief in state control of local affairs in an 1866 article in *Atlantic Monthly*, Frederick Douglass argued that changing "the character of the government at this point is neither possible nor desirable." Instead, in an essay advocating black suffrage, he offered optimistically, "All that is necessary to be done is to make the government consistent with itself, and render the rights of the States compatible with the sacred rights of human nature."[52]

Realizing the worst fears of Robert Barnwell Rhett during the debate over Confederate emancipation, the South had not been able to preserve the institution of slavery. Nevertheless, by continuing to argue for the traditional powers of states within the federal Union, white Southerners could at least hope to slow the pace of the revolution.

10
POLITICS AND THE RECONSTRUCTED CONSTITUTIONAL ORDER, 1867–1876

On March 30, 1870, a little more than a year after assuming office, President Ulysses S. Grant had reason to be proud. Having learned that the requisite three-quarters of the states had ratified the Fifteenth Amendment, which protected the right of black men to vote, Grant drafted a special message to Congress. The president took note of the revolutionary nature of the event, particularly the contrast with the *Dred Scott* ruling thirteen years before. "A measure which makes at once Four Millions of people, heretofore declared by the highest tribunal in the land not citizens of the United States nor eligible to become so, voters in every part of the land . . . is indeed a measure of grander importance than any other one act of the kind from the foundation of our free government to the present day," the president announced. Two days later, in a brief speech, a delighted Grant called the amendment "the realization of the Declaration of Independence."[1]

The ratification of the Fifteenth Amendment culminated a period of intense partisan debate over postwar reconstruction policy. President Andrew Johnson and Republicans in Congress spent much of 1867 and 1868 locked in a bitter struggle over the role of the military in reconstructing the South—a contest that climaxed with the ratification of the Fourteenth Amendment—and Grant's rise to the presidency represented, for a time, a consensus among Republicans. That consensus centered on restoring the former Confederate states to the Union and protecting the civil and political rights of African Americans. Still, violent resistance continued to spread across the South during the early 1870s, and as time went on, it became increasingly difficult for the federal government to use its legal and military might to enforce the rights of blacks. The Republican vision of a revolutionary reconstruction thus peaked in 1870 with the ratification of the Fifteenth Amendment, a vision that merged the power of the national government with the aspirations enunciated in the Declaration of Independence. Thereafter, countervailing forces—indiscriminate violence by white Southerners as well as serious divisions among Republicans—blunted the effects of the constitutional revolution.

THE BEGINNING OF 1867: CONGRESS, THE PRESIDENT, AND THE SUPREME COURT

After their victory in the elections of 1866, Republicans in the 39th Congress returned for the final session knowing that they controlled the future of reconstruction. With confidence, Republicans thus enacted a series of laws that embodied their postwar agenda. In January 1867, Congress passed landmark legislation granting African American men the right to vote in Washington, DC, a small step toward what Radicals envisioned for the entire South. In early March, Congress passed a Tenure of Office Act that made it difficult for the president to remove government officials, enacted a Military Appropriations Act that provided that all presidential instructions regarding military operations "be issued through the General of the army" (Ulysses S. Grant), and passed the Military Reconstruction Act.[2] Assured that their ranks would expand when new members took their seats and unwilling to leave Washington for fear that President Johnson would attempt to subvert their plans, Republicans began the first session of the 40th Congress on March 4, 1867, immediately after the adjournment of the previous one. Although the Republicans remained an amalgam of factions, their opposition to Johnson produced a renewed sense of unity, and the new session generated the first signs of a movement to impeach him. Stung by Johnson's eagerness to use executive power in support of his own vision of reconstruction—he had already removed hundreds of local postmasters for political reasons and issued orders that effectively eviscerated the Freedman's Bureau—Radicals in particular began to believe that impeachment constituted a plausible course of action. The Constitution was not clear about the grounds for impeachment. Article II, Section 4 states that a president may be "removed from Office on Impeachment for, and Conviction of, Treason, Bribery, or other high Crimes and Misdemeanors." Taking a broad view of the clause, many Radicals believed that Johnson's obstructionism constituted a form of malfeasance in office, and during the early months of 1867, the House Judiciary Committee initiated investigations of Johnson's behavior.

For his part, Johnson remained as obstinate as ever. "I have, during all of my political life," he remarked at the end of 1866, "been guided by certain fixed political principles. I am guided by them still. They are the principles of the early founders of the Republic, and I cannot certainly go far wrong if I adhere to them, as I intend to."[3] Confident of the correctness of his position, Johnson seemed content to allow congressional leaders to enact a radical agenda, which he believed would eventually cause their downfall. Johnson's assessment of the political situation grew out of his ideological convictions and racial beliefs, and he held firm in his opposition to the Fourteenth Amendment. Having already vetoed eight bills during 1866 (one fewer than the record nine vetoes of Franklin Pierce's entire presidency), Johnson began the new year by vetoing the DC black suffrage bill. Citing the founders' conception of presidential power as constituting "a check upon unconstitutional, hasty, and improvident legislation," Johnson's actions made clear that the election had not had a chastening effect.[4]

With confident Republicans in control on Capitol Hill and an obdurate president in the White House, the Supreme Court loomed in the background. Composed of five Lincoln appointees—all but one a Republican—the postwar Court looked dramatically different from the Southern and Democratic Court that had decided the *Dred Scott* case. After the death of Justice John Catron of Tennessee in May 1865, the number of justices had dropped from ten to nine, including only three who had participated in the now-embarrassing proslavery decision. In summer 1866, Congress had enacted new legislation redrawing federal judicial circuits, a further attempt to augment the power and influence of the North and the Republicans. The act also reduced the size of the Supreme Court by attrition, thus preventing Johnson from appointing any justices. Chief Justice Salmon P. Chase, hoping to restore the Court's reputation, wished to steer clear of political controversies. But at the end of 1866, despite Chase's best efforts, the justices had issued a decision that immediately affected the political environment. In *Ex parte Milligan*, a case dealing with an antiwar activist in Indiana, the Court had held that civilians could not be tried in military courts where civil courts remained open, outside of the theater of war. The decision appeared to support a presidential proclamation from the previous spring, declaring a formal end to the rebellion and, by implication, the end of military tribunals. Although the opinion never referred to the South, congressional Republicans worried that the decision threatened some of the enforcement provisions of the Freedman's Bureau and the Civil Rights acts. And they openly fretted about whether the Military Reconstruction Act—or any law imposing military justice on the South— would withstand the scrutiny of the justices. Despite being composed of Republicans who at first glance seemed sympathetic to the congressional agenda, the Court appeared destined to have its say about the future of reconstruction.

MILITARY RECONSTRUCTION

The Military Reconstruction Act arose from Republican attempts to wrest control of reconstruction from Johnson and ensure ratification of the Fourteenth Amendment. During the fall and winter of 1866–1867, a succession of Northern states had endorsed the amendment, but with the exception of Tennessee, no Southern state had done so. One by one, former slaveholding states took up the amendment and rejected it. By March 1867, the battle lines were drawn: nineteen Northern states, one Southern state (Tennessee), and one former slaveholding border state (Missouri) had ratified the amendment, while ten former Confederate states plus former slaveholding border states Kentucky, Maryland, and Delaware had rejected it. With the admission of Nebraska to statehood on March 1, there were thirty-seven states in the Union. This meant that it would take twenty-eight states to meet the three-fourths threshold required under the Constitution. With twenty-one states having already approved the amendment, seven more would need to do so. Congressional Republicans, of course, wanted all Southern states to approve it, for by this time all Republicans believed that ratification of the Fourteenth Amendment was necessary for readmission.

Republicans remained divided on the question of whether more than ratification of the amendment was required. Tennessee had already been readmitted solely on the basis of ratifying, but Republican victories in the 1866 elections had altered the political landscape. Moderates led by Representative John Bingham of Ohio continued to view the Fourteenth Amendment as the centerpiece of reconstruction and believed that Southern states should be fully restored once they ratified the amendment. Radicals led by Representative Thaddeus Stevens, in contrast, favored further steps, including a total reorganization of Southern state governments. Under his proposed plan, states could return to the Union through individual enabling acts passed by Congress, and only after state constitutional conventions had been elected on the basis of universal suffrage and Rebel disfranchisement for a period of five years. After a contentious debate, moderate House leaders succeeded in referring Stevens's proposed bill to committee, where a compromise emerged. The committee combined the moderate idea of restoration upon ratification, the radical notion of black suffrage, and a separate Senate proposal for military supervision of the Southern states into a single bill.

The product of this intra-Republican compromise, the Military Reconstruction Act, laid out the new terms of reconstruction. The first part attempted to combat Southern violence and protect black rights. It divided the former Rebel states (excluding Tennessee) into five military districts and required the commanding officer in each district "to protect all persons in their rights of person and property, to suppress insurrection, disorder and violence, and to punish, or cause to be punished, all disturbers of the public peace and criminals." The military authorities could use the civil courts to maintain order or, at their discretion, could establish "military commissions or tribunals" for this purpose.[5] The second portion of the law established a framework for the formation of new state governments and the readmission of states. States were required to hold elections for delegates to constitutional conventions, based on male suffrage for all at least twenty-one years of age "of whatever race, color, or previous condition," excluding those prohibited from holding office under the proposed Fourteenth Amendment.[6] These new constitutions were subject to approval by a majority of the state's voters (again using the same suffrage requirements) and Congress. Once the state's new legislature, elected under its new constitution, approved the amendment and when it "shall have become a part of the Constitution," the state would regain its representation in Congress.[7] At that point, the state would no longer be subject to military rule. In essence, the act attempted to establish a new legal regime in the South in order to ensure the ratification of the amendment.

Predictably, Johnson vetoed the bill. The proposal for the establishment of military districts particularly drew Johnson's ire. This arrangement, he argued, gave the commanding officer in each district the powers of "an absolute monarch," which he charged would lead to cronyism, corruption, and despotism of every sort. The law imposed, in his view, a form of servitude far worse than what African Americans had experienced. "No master ever had a control so absolute over the slaves as this bill gives to the military officers over both white and colored persons," Johnson asserted.[8] What made the law so despotic, in Johnson's mind, was the fact that Congress enacted it in a time of peace, after the Southern states had nullified their secession ordinances. Quoting at length from *Ex parte Milligan*, Johnson argued that martial law could only exist when wartime conditions closed the civil courts—conditions that certainly did not exist in the postwar South. The real purpose of the law, he claimed, was not to protect life and property but to compel the states "by force to the adoption of organic laws and regulations which they are unwilling to accept if left to themselves."[9] Increasingly identifying himself as the champion of white Southerners, Johnson's rhetoric echoed the lamentations that arose across the South in the aftermath of the act's passage. General

Ulysses S. Grant, to whom many Republicans were looking for leadership, bluntly described Johnson's veto message as "one of the most ridiculous that ever emanated from any president."[10]

Johnson's veto marked a further deterioration in his relations with Congress. Although he still hoped to build a broad-based, antiradical coalition, Johnson's own political position became increasingly conservative. While in 1865 and 1866 he had nudged Southern states to enact legislation protecting black civil rights and had even suggested (like Lincoln) that states consider black suffrage, by early 1867 Johnson outlandishly claimed that African Americans had "not asked for the privilege of voting" and openly disparaged the Reconstruction Act for "Africanizing the southern part of our territory."[11] The change in Johnson's attitude appeared even more telling when compared to his previous comments regarding the end of slavery. At the end of 1865, Johnson had celebrated emancipation as the chief accomplishment of the war. In 1867, in contrast, Johnson referred back to the Crittenden-Johnson Resolutions of 1861 as the touchstone for reconstruction. Those resolutions, Johnson noted, declared that the war would leave "the constitutional rights of the states and of individuals unimpaired."[12] It was an odd document for Johnson to cite—even if he had cosponsored it—given the fact that the resolutions had originally intended to protect slavery where it existed. In reaction to Republican attempts to propel the revolution forward, Johnson began to turn backward.

By the spring of 1867, Congress undoubtedly controlled reconstruction policy, ably assisted in the field by General Grant. Both houses quickly overrode Johnson's veto, and in grudging compliance with the law, the president appointed commanders for the five military districts. In filling these positions, Johnson followed Grant's recommendations. With an unblemished reputation for courage and leadership, Grant emerged in early 1867 as a political figure in his own right, and some Republicans saw him as a potential presidential candidate. For the most part, Johnson attempted to maintain cordial relations with the general in chief in the hope that it might bolster his own political position. Still, rendered increasingly powerless, Johnson could not help but strike a defiant pose. In late March, the president vetoed the Second Military Reconstruction Act, which authorized the district commanders to begin registering voters in order to set the new governments in motion, and Congress again overrode the veto. In June, Johnson's attorney general attempted to narrow the powers of the district commanders in an official legal opinion, but Congress responded by overturning it in a Third Military Reconstruction Act. This law authorized the commanders to remove and appoint state officials, to create voter registration boards that could deny the right to vote to individuals who perjured themselves about their prior allegiances, and bestowed upon Grant the power to oversee military affairs in the former Confederate states. In a July 19 veto message, Johnson protested the measure, excoriating the act for conferring upon commanders the power to enforce the laws at the expense of the constitutional authority granted to the president. Congress again overrode the veto.

When Congress adjourned later that summer, Johnson went on the offensive. Having long been at variance with his secretary of war, the president moved against Secretary Stanton, a Lincoln appointee with a radical bent who had held his post since early 1862. Johnson first asked for Stanton's resignation, but when Stanton refused, Johnson "suspended" him in conformity with the terms of the Tenure of Office Act.[13] Then, in a savvy political stroke, Johnson appointed Grant to take Stanton's place. Although the president and the general were clearly at odds over reconstruction, Johnson hoped that appointing Grant would put the general off balance, unnerve the Republicans, and strengthen his own hand. Placed in an awkward position, Grant ended up accepting the post on an interim basis until the Senate confirmed a successor, in keeping with terms of the Tenure of Office Act. The president then turned to the one power that he retained under the reconstruction acts—the power to remove district commanders. He dismissed General Phillip Sheridan, the commander of Texas and Louisiana, who had attempted to counteract a rash of violence by removing the civilian governors of Texas and Louisiana as well as a slew of city officials in New Orleans. At the same time, Johnson terminated General Daniel Sickles, commander of North Carolina and South Carolina, for what Johnson viewed as high-handedness in exercising his authority. The fact that all three firings occurred in August, while Congress was out of session, seemed a brazen assertion of executive power.

Johnson's behavior laid bare the divisions among Republicans. That fall, Johnson's most radical opponents, including Stevens and James Ashley in the House and Charles Sumner and Benjamin F. Wade in the Senate, pushed hard for impeachment, which they thought would ensure a more radical course of reconstruction, one that included black suffrage, public education, and land reform. Having a Radical in the White House was critical to advancing this agenda. Were Johnson removed, Wade, as president pro tempore of the Senate, would assume the presidency. Somewhat distrustful of Grant because he had accepted a position in Johnson's Cabinet, Radicals hoped that removing Johnson would give Wade time to build support and head off a potential Grant candidacy. Non-Radical Republicans, meanwhile, wanted to proceed with caution. Republicans suffered defeats in several Northern states in the fall 1867 elections, and in three Northern states—Kansas, Minnesota, and

Ohio—voters rejected proposals to institute black suffrage. With Johnson's position bolstered at the polls, non-Radicals such as senators William Pitt Fessenden of Maine and Lyman Trumbull of Illinois urged restraint. When Radicals introduced an impeachment resolution on December 7, it failed even to gain the support of a majority of Republicans.

While Congress and the president battled over military reconstruction, the actual process of implementing the reconstruction acts moved steadily forward. In accordance with the law, during the summer and fall of 1867, district commanders had directed the registration of voters, including African American men but excluding Confederate officeholders. Across the South, for the first time in their lives, hundreds of thousands of black men cast ballots, and the convention delegates they elected formed the first racially integrated official assemblies in the history of the United States. States that had high concentrations of African Americans and that had experienced lengthy Union occupations elected the highest proportion of black delegates to their conventions. In Louisiana and South Carolina, African American delegates constituted a majority, but in most conventions the percentage of black delegates was far lower, proportionally, than that of the black population. When taken together, white Southern Republicans who had remained loyal to the Union constituted the majority of all convention delegates, while white Northerners—most of whom had fought in the Union army—made up about one-sixth of the overall membership of the conventions.

As state conventions began assembling during the final months of 1867 and the first part of 1868, ex-Confederates were outraged. They referred to Southern Republicans as "scalawags" and Northern Republicans who had come South as "carpetbaggers," two epithets intended to cast doubt on the legitimacy of the proceedings. Most white Southerners expressed particular indignation at the sight of black political participation. Chief among them, President Johnson believed African Americans were simply incapable of participating in political affairs. In his third annual message delivered on December 3—while some of the conventions in the South were in session—the president offered a candid assessment. "It must be acknowledged that in the progress of nations negroes have shown less capacity for government than any other race of people," Johnson stated. "No independent government of any form has ever been successful in their hands. On the contrary, wherever they have been left to their own devices they have shown a constant tendency to relapse into barbarism."[14] White violence marred some of the voter registration and election proceedings, but in an attempt to delegitimize the entire process, boycotting proved a more common white response.

While not wholly radical in character, the constitutions of 1868 represented in many respects a break from the past. Replacing the state constitutions of 1864 and 1865, which had simply abolished slavery, these new documents went much further in promoting constitutional equality and political democracy—in embodying the spirit of black constitutionalism. In addition to banning slavery, all of the constitutions explicitly affirmed the principle of human equality under the law, usually by quoting or paraphrasing the "all men are created equal" language of the Declaration of Independence. Moreover, they uniformly extended suffrage rights to all men over twenty-one years of age, and some constitutions included provisions designed to prevent the imposition of property qualifications or other restrictions on voting and officeholding. A handful provided for the popular election of state judges. Most of the conventions took up the question of disfranchising former Rebels, but few went beyond the restrictions already imposed in the Military Reconstruction Act. All of the constitutions provided for the establishment of free public education, though the question of whether schools would be segregated was left to future debate. None of the constitutions instituted land reform, a fact that reflected the probusiness Whig backgrounds of many white Southern Republicans. The constitutional conventions of 1868, in short, instituted moderate to radical reforms that mirrored the diverse interests of their members.

By the spring, military reconstruction had fulfilled the hopes of many Republicans for establishing biracial governments in the South. Once drafted, the new constitutions would be submitted to popular ratification within the states and transmitted to Congress for approval. And once new legislatures had assembled under the constitutions, they could take up the Fourteenth Amendment. Each day, despite the actions of Johnson—he had dismissed two more district commanders at the end of 1867—military reconstruction came closer to becoming an accomplished fact.

IMPEACHING THE PRESIDENT, LIMITING THE COURT, AND RATIFYING THE FOURTEENTH AMENDMENT

As the conventions completed their work in early 1868, the greatest threat to the fulfillment of reconstruction and the ratification of the Fourteenth Amendment was not President Johnson; it was the Supreme Court. Some congressional Republicans had long feared that the Court might, in a sense, come to the rescue of Johnson and his white Southern constituency. With the *Milligan* decision lurking in the background, conservative Democratic lawyers allied with the president instigated a court challenge to the Military Reconstruction acts. The litigation was made possible by an 1867 statute that had expanded the jurisdiction of the Supreme Court by specifically granting the right of appeal in habeas corpus cases. William McCardle, a Mississippi editor who had been arrested by military authorities for his criticisms of reconstruction, sought a writ of habeas corpus on the grounds that the First Military Reconstruction Act under which he was arrested violated the Constitution. Sensing trouble, in January, House Republicans passed a bill that would have required a two-thirds vote on the Supreme Court in order to invalidate an act of Congress. When the measure died in the Senate, many Republicans feared that after nearly a year of fighting with Johnson over the implementation of military rule, they stood poised to lose the battle before the justices.

In the meantime, the impeachment movement continued unabated. In January 1868, the Senate committee that had been investigating Stanton's removal concluded that Johnson's suspension of Stanton the previous August had been unjustified, and on January 13, the full Senate voted to refuse to consent to Stanton's dismissal. In response, Grant immediately surrendered his office to Stanton. A month later, on February 21, Johnson dismissed Stanton, this time replacing him with General Lorenzo Thomas, and in response Stanton barricaded himself in his office, refusing to relinquish his position. By again firing Stanton, Johnson had essentially dared Congress to impeach him for violating the Tenure of Office Act, which prohibited such a removal without Senate consent. Three days later, the House approved an impeachment resolution, 126–47. This time every Republican present voted in favor.

In early March, a little more than a week after the passage of the impeachment resolution, lawyers argued McCardle's case before the Supreme Court. Having been arrested and held prior to trial before a military commission, McCardle's attorneys made his case: that his arrest for writing editorials violated the freedom of press, that trial by commission violated his right to trial by jury, and that the entire Military Reconstruction Act violated the Constitution. Their worst fears playing out before them, Republicans in Congress took a bold step. On March 12, three days after oral arguments had concluded in the case, Congress enacted legislation repealing the 1867 habeas corpus statute under which McCardle had brought his case, in effect stripping the Supreme Court of its jurisdiction to hear the matter. Johnson promptly vetoed the bill, which both houses quickly overrode. Chief Justice Chase, again attempting to steer clear of controversy, persuaded a majority of his colleagues to hold the case over till the next term, thus delaying a decision on the merits of the dispute, as well as on Congress's adjustment of the Court's jurisdiction. The Court thus stayed out of the partisan fray.

Greatly relieved, congressional Republicans pushed forward with impeachment. When the trial began on March 30, Johnson faced eleven articles of impeachment, the first nine of which pertained to the firing of Stanton and the appointment of Thomas in violation of the Tenure of Office Act. The remaining two articles were more political in nature. The tenth charged that the president had attempted "to bring into disgrace, ridicule, hatred, contempt, and reproach the Congress of the United States," while the eleventh summarized Johnson's various attempts to circumvent the measures enacted by Congress during the past year.[15] In a newspaper interview, Johnson scoffed at the impeachers, whom he viewed as mere partisans who showed no respect for the Constitution, and he made a politically astute point about his own situation, relative to that of the former Confederate president, who by this time had been released from prison on bail and still awaited trial for treason. "Jefferson Davis, the head and front of the rebellion, is not brought to trial," Johnson observed. "Yet Congress proposes to try the President at once, for what kind of offence, compared with that of Mr. Davis, the country and the Senate may perhaps justly decide."[16]

Johnson's trial indeed sparked nationwide debate. Newspaper editors and political cartoonists devoted enormous energy to covering the spectacle of a president on trial, and the proceedings became a vehicle for the expression of all of the partisan feelings of the previous two years, with Northern Democrats and former Confederates on one side, and African Americans and most Republicans on the other. Johnson's allies portrayed him as the defender of the Constitution against an out-of-control Congress. The *Macon (Georgia) Telegraph* referred to the entire notion of impeaching Johnson as a "farce," and instead, tongue in cheek, proposed a bill of impeachment against the Radicals. "Their attempts to take away the constitutional powers of the Executive Department; their efforts to upset the Judicial Department or to reduce it to a mere party machine; their negro supremacy policy of Southern Reconstruction; their financial follies, extravagances, spoliations, and corruptions will all be in the bill," the *Telegraph* read.[17] The president's opponents took a different view. The *Elevator*, a black newspaper published in San Francisco, formulated its own list of charges against the president, which, the paper argued, were grounds for impeachment. "He has broken his most solemn promises to extend equal justice to all loyal citizens, irrespective of caste or color; he has set the Constitution of his country at naught, and trampled under foot the laws he had sworn [to] respect and administer with justice and impartiality," the paper wrote. "Instead of making treason odious, and punishing traitors for their crimes, he has absolved the most malignant traitors, and made evidence of treason a sure passport to Executive favor . . . [and] he has endeavored to get the army to support him in his nefarious purposes."[18]

From the start, it was clear that Johnson's fate would be decided more for

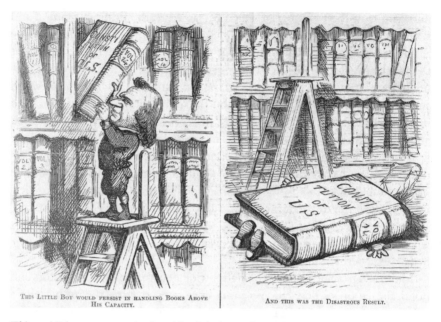

THIS LITTLE BOY WOULD PERSIST IN HANDLING BOOKS ABOVE
HIS CAPACITY.

AND THIS WAS THE DISASTROUS RESULT.

This anti-Johnson cartoon, in the midst of the impeachment saga, portrayed the president as immature and unable to understand constitutional matters, which were, in the words of the cartoon, "above his capacity." Courtesy of the Library of Congress, LC-USZ62-131563

political reasons than legal ones. Non-Radical Republicans were the key. It would take a two-thirds vote in the Senate to remove the president, meaning that nearly all Republicans would need to vote against Johnson for him to be forced out of office. Despite the impassioned pleas of many moderates to convict, the more cautious among them worried about the political ramifications. Some felt more comfortable with Johnson than Wade, while others feared that impeachment would only hurt the party's fortunes in the 1868 presidential elections. The trial itself, part legal proceeding and part political theater, offered the opportunity for both sides to present their arguments. Most of the testimony against Johnson pertained to the details of Stanton's dismissal, while other witnesses testified about various speeches the president had made, mostly during his infamous 1866 "swing around the circle." Johnson's counsel offered a thorough defense of the president, arguing, most importantly, that the Tenure of Office Act violated the Constitution in that it undermined the prerogative of the executive.

On May 16, 1868, when senators voted on whether Johnson was guilty of the charges spelled out in the eleventh article of impeachment, seven Republicans went against the majority of their colleagues and voted no, one vote short of the necessary two-thirds vote required for removal. After the vote, the Senate adjourned temporarily so that many could attend the Republican national convention in Chicago, where the party promptly nominated Grant for president on the first ballot. When the senators returned and the trial resumed on May 26, they acquitted Johnson on two other articles of impeachment (by the same one-vote margin), and the trial ended. In a surprising coda to the entire affair, upon learning of the verdict, Secretary Stanton resigned his position.

Johnson's own behavior during the trial probably contributed to the outcome. Two presidential decisions in particular seemed to indicate a more cooperative demeanor on the part of the president, and both involved extensive back-channel negotiations, through which Johnson received assurances that his actions would secure votes on his behalf. First, he nominated as secretary of war General John Schofield, a widely respected veteran of Sherman's Atlanta Campaign and district commander of Virginia under the Military Reconstruction Act. Although Stanton remained holed up in his office throughout the impeachment proceedings, Johnson's gesture seemed to indicate that a postimpeachment presidency with a new secretary of war would strike a more conciliatory tone. Second, the president sent to the Senate for its approval the new constitutions of Arkansas and South Carolina, which had been drafted by the constitutional conventions and duly ratified by voters. (Under the Second Military Reconstruction Act, state conventions were to send their new constitutions to the president, "who shall forthwith transmit the same to Congress.")[19] These were largely symbolic gestures, for Johnson at this point presented no threat to the continued implementation of military reconstruction. His controversial dismissal of district commanders had occurred too late to have halted the reconstruction process, and Congress had already demonstrated a willingness to alter the rules if things did not go as planned. On March 11, for example, in response to white Southerners' attempts to sabotage the state constitutional approval process by boycotting elections, Congress simply changed the proportion of votes required from a majority of registered voters to a majority of votes cast. In other words, little that the president did or did not do during April or May 1868 could affect the course of military reconstruction. But the symbolism of an apparently compliant president surely helped to swing some, if not all, of the seven Republicans to the president's side.

The culmination of military reconstruction—indeed, the whole purpose of military reconstruction—was the ratification of the Fourteenth Amendment. In that sense, the impeachment drama offered a sideshow to the more significant constitutional story that unfolded before and after the trial. Since the passage of the First Military Reconstruction Act in March 1867, two more states—Nebraska and Iowa—had ratified the amendment, bringing the total number of states that had ratified to twenty-three. Five more states were needed. After the transmittal of the new constitutions from the state (through the president) to the Congress, and after Congress had approved of the constitutions, state legislatures began assembling in the late spring of 1868. Arkansas acted first, ratifying the Fourteenth Amendment on April 6, a week after Johnson's impeachment trial had begun. Congress responded by passing legislation admitting Arkansas to the Union on June 20, and rather than waiting on the other states, Congress followed up five days later with a law providing for the readmission of six additional states—Alabama, Florida, Georgia, Louisiana, North Carolina, and South Carolina, all of which had had their constitutions approved—immediately upon their ratification of the amendment. With incentive to act, by mid-July, all but Georgia did so. With twenty-nine states having approved, on July 21 Congress adopted a concurrent resolution announcing that the Fourteenth Amendment had been ratified (Georgia ratified that day), and a week later, Secretary of State Seward issued a proclamation to the same effect.[20] The great power struggle between Congress and the president had ended.

By this time, with Republicans having accomplished what they set out to do, Johnson was forgotten but not gone. True to form, the president vetoed both the Arkansas statehood bill and the bill providing for the admission of the six other Southern states. These veto messages presented the ironic and absurd spectacle of Johnson negating measures to restore the ex-Confederate states to the Union, the very thing that Johnson had so desired from the beginning! Of course, for Johnson it was all a matter of constitutional principle. Signing the laws would have meant accepting that the states had left the Union in the first place and recognizing the legitimacy of the Military Reconstruction acts. Johnson could stomach neither idea, and Congress quickly overrode both vetoes. Johnson did issue a major amnesty proclamation on July 4, which granted pardon to all rebels except those "under presentment or indictment in any court of the United States" (meaning Jefferson Davis), but the proclamation did not have the desired effect of securing for Johnson the nomination of the Democratic Party for president.[21] His political ambitions thwarted, Johnson spent the rest of his term largely irrelevant to national affairs. In the end, the Republican Congress had gotten its way. Between early 1867 and the middle of 1868, Congress had successfully implemented the Military Reconstruction acts, ratified the Fourteenth Amendment, and restored most of the former Confederate states to the Union. In the process, congressional Republicans had fended off a challenge in the Supreme Court and impeached the president. The Republican revolution—though not a radical revolution—continued.

THE ELECTION OF 1868

As Johnson faded from view, Grant moved to the forefront. The general's nomination for the presidency culminated his uneven ascent. Grant's renown had originated six years before with his celebrated victories at forts Henry and Donelson, ebbed after it appeared he had been caught off guard at Shiloh, and then rose again after the brilliant Vicksburg campaign. Admired by Lincoln for his willingness to attack and revered by Sherman for his leadership qualities, Grant had suffered the worst blows to his reputation during the bloody Overland Campaign of 1864. But victory at Appomattox made the horrors of Spotsylvania and Cold Harbor recede into the background, and by the summer of 1865, no man in America could claim the respect that Grant had earned. So great was their admiration for his accomplishments that many Americans were comparing him to George Washington. Although Grant professed no great interest in politics, the general had escaped the postwar partisan fighting relatively unscathed, and by the time of his nomination, he clearly represented the Republican Party's best hope of claiming the White House and seeing military reconstruction through to completion. Grant's statement at the time, "Let us have peace," perhaps because it lent itself to a variety of interpretations, resonated with a large portion of the electorate in both the North and South.[22]

Grant ran on a Republican platform that, despite the party's divisions, blended pride in past accomplishments with lofty future aspirations. The platform hailed the bravery of Union soldiers, saluted the success of congressional policy in restoring the Union, and called for further reconstruction "upon the basis of impartial justice and equal rights." Not surprisingly, given its drafting during the impeachment trial, the platform reserved its lengthiest section for a description of Johnson's "treacherous" behavior in office. It also encouraged foreign immigration—a striking stance, given the party's historic connection to nativism—and declared sympathy "with all the oppressed people which are struggling for their rights." The Republican Party platform of 1868 concluded with these words: "We recognize the great principles laid down in the immortal Declaration of Independence as the true foundation of Democratic Government; and we hail with gladness every effort toward making these principles a living reality on every inch of American soil."[23]

Despite their successes in the elections of 1867, the Democrats struggled

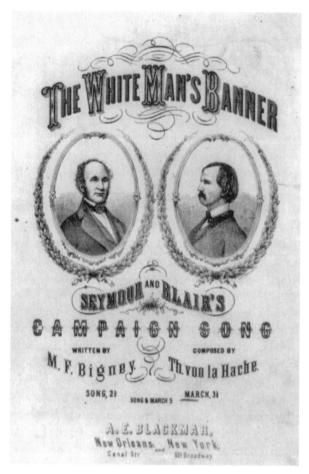

Leaving no doubt about where the Democratic candidates, Seymour and Blair, stood on the question of the rights of African Americans, this 1868 campaign sheet music was for a song called, "The White Man's Banner." Courtesy of the Library of Congress, LC-USZ62-89310

to find compelling candidates for the national ticket in 1868. At a contentious convention in which former Confederate generals Wade Hampton and Nathan Bedford Forrest played prominent roles, the party settled on Horatio Seymour, ex-governor of New York, as its presidential nominee and Francis Blair Jr. of Missouri as his running mate. Both men seemed susceptible to the Republican caricature of the Democratic Party—that it was beholden to the Slave Power before the war, in sympathy with the Confederacy during the war, and devoted to white supremacy after the war. In the midst of the New York City draft riots of 1863, Seymour had addressed a group of rioters as "my friends," words that Republicans were quick to use against him. Worse still, in a public letter, Blair offered his candid assessment of what a newly elected Democratic president should do: "Declare these [reconstruction] acts null

Table 10.1. Presidential Election of 1868

Candidate	Party	Electoral Votes	Percent of Popular Vote
Ulysses S. Grant	Republican	214	52.7
Horatio Seymour	Democratic	80	47.3

and void, compel the army to undo its usurpations at the South, disperse the carpet bag State governments, allow the white people to re-organize their own governments and elect Senators and Representatives."[24] For an electorate weary of the continued debates over reconstruction, the prospect of a Democratic administration seemed only to promise more turmoil.

The Democratic Party platform picked up on President Johnson's assertions that wartime policy under the Republicans had produced a radical revolution in American life, contrary to what Congress had originally promised. Referring obliquely to the Crittenden-Johnson Resolutions of 1861, the platform argued that the Republican-dominated Congress had "instead of restoring the Union, . . . so far as in its power, dissolved it, and subjected ten States, in time of profound peace, to military despotism and negro supremacy." After listing a litany of Republican outrages—including undermining habeas corpus, establishing military tribunals in peacetime, and curtailing the jurisdiction of the Supreme Court—the document concluded that if another Republican president were elected, "we will meet, as a subjected and conquered people, amid the ruins of liberty and the scattered fragments of the Constitution."[25] If the Republican platform viewed the national government as the vehicle for implementing the aspirations enunciated in the Declaration of Independence, the Democratic platform portrayed the national government under Republican control as a profound threat to the sovereignty of states and the constitutional liberties of white people. In essence, the Democrats called for a reversal of the revolutionary changes that had occurred and a return to the Constitution of 1861. Perhaps never before in American history had a presidential election presented such sharply contrasting visions of the future.

When the results were in, Grant achieved a resounding victory in the Electoral College, but the popular vote totals revealed that Americans remained divided. At age forty-six, the youngest president ever elected at that time, Grant won twenty-six states and 214 electoral votes to Seymour's eight states and 80 electoral votes. (Because they had not yet ratified the Fourteenth Amendment, Mississippi, Texas, and Virginia did not participate in the election.) Grant received more than three million votes (almost 53 percent of the popular vote), and Seymour just over 2.7 million. In addition to winning populous Republican strongholds in the Midwest and Northeast, Grant carried most of the newly reconstructed states of the former Confederacy. But nationwide Grant failed to win a majority of the white vote, and his slim margins of victory in a handful of states revealed the tenuousness of the Republican triumph. The general also failed to claim the 33 electoral votes of New York—Seymour's home state, to be sure, but a striking loss, given that the state had gone for John C. Fremont in 1856 and twice for Lincoln.

The most disturbing outcome for Republicans was what occurred in the South. Throughout the region, violence plagued the campaign season as reactionary whites terrorized blacks who attempted to cast their ballots for the first time in a federal election. The Ku Klux Klan, founded in Tennessee in 1866, emerged as the best known of a variety of formal and informal organizations that attempted to terrify and intimidate African Americans and their white allies. Georgia, one of the two reconstructed states that Grant lost, witnessed the killing of at least thirty-one African Americans at the hands of whites between August and October, including a shootout in the town of Camilla, where ruffians dispersed a black political meeting and hunted down the potential voters. This occurred a few weeks after the state legislature had expelled its black members. Arkansas experienced 200 murders in the three months before the election, including the assassination of Congressman James Hinds, a white Northern-born Republican who had come to the state with the Union army in 1865. Louisiana, the other reconstructed state that Grant lost, was worst of all. A congressional investigation concluded that between April and November, 1,081 African Americans were killed, 135 shot, and more than 500 were "otherwise outraged" in the state.[26] While Grant undoubtedly won the votes of African Americans who succeeded in safely exercising the franchise, the recurrent violence in the South portended problems that would plague his presidency.

THE FIFTEENTH AMENDMENT

Trouble in the fall election provided further impetus to those who had been calling for a constitutional amendment to protect black suffrage. From the black conventions that had assembled in the antebellum North to Frederick Douglass's 1865 admonition that "slavery is not abolished until the black man has the ballot," African Americans had long argued for full political rights, and they continued to agitate on the question during the postwar period, as a host of state and national black conventions adopted resolutions in support of a suffrage amendment.[27] Of course, the question of black voting had woven its way throughout congressional debates over reconstruction, and all Republicans eventually came to support the idea—but only for the South. The Fourteenth Amendment prodded the Southern states into enfranchising blacks by threatening to reduce the states' representation in Congress, and the Military Reconstruction Act directly enfranchised black voters in elections for state constitutional conventions. Still, in the absence of an affirmative amendment guaranteeing black voting, many Republicans feared that, free of military supervision, the newly reconstructed states might implement suffrage restrictions. Voting had always been considered a state matter, and once the requirements of military reconstruction had been fulfilled, nothing seemed to stand in the way of states exerting their traditional powers over the franchise.

If the situation in the South prompted Republicans to consider a suffrage amendment, politics in the North gave them pause. To put it simply, white Northerners were in no hurry to enfranchise African Americans. At the outset of the war, only five states—all of them in New England—allowed black voting on the same basis as whites, while a sixth state, New York, enfranchised blacks who met specific property requirements. Despite black claims to the ballot based on Union military service, no other Northern states extended suffrage rights to African Americans during or after the war. In fact, between Appomattox and Grant's election, nearly every state or territory that had held a referendum on black suffrage rejected it. Colorado, Connecticut, Wisconsin, and Minnesota did so in 1865, and Nebraska, Kansas, Ohio, Michigan, and Missouri did the same during the next few years. In fall 1868, Iowans did approve black suffrage by popular referendum, as did Minnesotans (a reversal of their previous vote), but Democrats charged that the ballot in Minnesota had disguised the issue by not clearly labeling it. Although a majority of Northern Republicans supported black suffrage, they remained keenly aware of the political challenge and thus had not forced the issue. Despite its lofty commitment to the Declaration of Independence, the Republican Party platform of 1868 had simply stated that the question of black voting in the North ought to be reserved to the states. In the aftermath of Grant's election, a mix of principled and pragmatic concerns propelled the issue forward. The Republicans' double standard for the South and the North rang hypocritical; some speculated that the party's halfway stance on black suffrage had even hurt it at the polls. Democrats had canvassed for some African American votes in the South, and many Republicans believed that only a suffrage amendment could cement the loyalty of black Southern voters. Petitions from African Americans in both Northern and Southern states, meanwhile, poured into Congress in support of some form of suffrage amendment.

Throughout this period, members of Congress argued over whether voting was a right or a privilege, as well as whether it was primarily a state or federal matter. If a right, Congress would enact as far-reaching an amendment as possible, one that would affirmatively state that a right to vote existed and would be protected by the national government. If a privilege, states would retain power to prescribe who voted. Four versions of a fifteenth amendment to the Constitution eventually emerged. One proposal would prohibit both the state and the federal governments from interfering with the right to vote based on race, color, or previous condition of servitude, while a second would prohibit only the states from doing so. A third proposal, in addition to prohibiting state interference with voting based on race, color, or previous condition of servitude, added literacy, nativity, and property qualification to the list of restrictions on the state. Finally, the most radical proposal simply affirmed the right to vote of all men who were twenty-one years of age. (Although distressing to women's rights activists, who had largely put their own aspirations on hold during the war, Congress never gave serious consideration to extending the vote to women at this time.) Particularly because Republicans on the East and West coasts wanted to allow states to continue to limit the voting rights of groups such as the Irish and the Chinese, the most far-reaching proposal—the affirmatively worded version—was doomed from the start. While Radicals expressed dismay that the right to hold political office was not included in the language of the amendment, moderates controlled the process from beginning to end, and they drafted the final version: "The right of citizens of the United States to vote shall not be denied or abridged by the United States or by any State on account of race, color, or previous condition of servitude." A second section repeated word for word the enforcement clauses that had been included in the Thirteenth and Fourteenth amendments.

As the debate over the amendment wound down, the appearance of black Mississippian Hiram Revels in the US Senate chamber in February 1869 reminded lawmakers of the revolution in their midst. Duly elected by the reconstructed legislature of his state, Revels arrived to claim his seat. Senate Democrats howled. The Constitution specifies that no person may be a senator who has not been a citizen of the United States for at least nine years, and because the *Dred Scott* decision had been in force until overruled by the Fourteenth Amendment in 1868, Democrats contended, Revels had not held citizenship long enough. Republicans attacked this position, arguing that because *Dred Scott* betrayed fundamental American principles it should never have been considered as valid in the first place. After three days of debate before packed galleries, all forty-eight of the chamber's Republicans voted in favor of admitting Revels, while all eight Democrats voted against. Revels took his oath of office and his seat, after which the Senate immediately adjourned and "a great crowd of both sexes, who wanted to shake hands with the new senator" swarmed onto the Senate floor.[28] It was a historic moment. The black preacher, Union veteran, and Mississippi state legislator became the first African American member of the US Congress and the first Mississippian to serve in the Senate since Jefferson Davis had resigned. As lawmakers debated the Fifteenth Amendment, they knew what was at stake—that if they expanded the black electorate, other African American members of Congress would follow. Two days after admitting Revels, after securing the necessary votes in both houses, on February 27, Congress passed a joint resolution sending the amendment to the states.

President Grant offered strong support for ratification of the Fifteenth Amendment. In his brief inaugural address on March 4, 1869, the new president called for sectional peace, but he also made clear that he favored protecting black voting rights throughout the country. "The question of suffrage is one which is likely to agitate the public so long as a portion of the citizens of the nation are excluded from its privileges in any State," he stated. "It seems to me very desirable that the question should be settled now, and I entertain the hope and express the desire that it may be by the ratification of the fifteenth article of amendment to the Constitution."[29] Heeding Grant's advice, a dozen state legislatures—those already in session and dominated by Republicans—ratified the amendment within a month. Grant's election changed the dynamic of reconstruction politics. For the first time since Lincoln's death, Congress and the president worked together to advance the rights of African Americans.

TEXAS V. WHITE, THE STATUS OF THE STATES, AND THE CONSTITUTIONALITY OF RECONSTRUCTION

A little more than a month after Grant's inauguration, the Supreme Court tackled the last of a series of cases that challenged the constitutionality of military reconstruction. While the Court had upheld the power of Congress to alter its jurisdiction in *Ex parte McCardle* and had similarly dismissed other challenges to reconstruction on technical grounds, the Court squarely confronted the issues in *Texas v. White*. After the war, Texas had filed suit against a group of bondholders whom the state claimed had never provided payment for the bonds. As a state, Texas could invoke the Court's original jurisdiction to hear the case—but only if it was, in fact, a state. Having not ratified the Fourteenth Amendment and still under military rule, Texas' status embodied the constitutional conundrum that lay at the heart of congressional reconstruction. Had the seceded states ever actually left the Union? On the one hand, if the ex-Confederate states had left, their ratification of the Fourteenth Amendment would have been meaningless. They remained outside of the Union and could not engage in the ratification process. On the other hand, if the states had never left the Union, they remained sovereign entities, subject to neither federal oversight nor military rule.

The murky constitutional status of the states had been an underlying theme throughout the debates over reconstruction. Because he believed that states had never really left the Union, President Johnson required of them as little as possible to regain their seats in Congress and argued that if Congress had recognized them as states for the purpose of ratifying the Thirteenth Amendment, they were—by virtue of having exercised the power to ratify an amendment—fully restored to the Union at that point. The Republican Congress, in contrast, seemed to take a more inconsistent approach—recognizing states for the purpose of accepting their ratification of the Thirteenth Amendment but denying their existence in order to impose military rule to ensure ratification of the Fourteenth Amendment, which the states had proved unwilling to do on their own.

In *Texas v. White*, the Court attempted to resolve this quandary. Writing for a 5–3 majority, Chief Justice Chase held that the Court possessed jurisdiction in the case—that Texas was in fact a state and that it had never left the Union. At the same time, Chase maintained that during the war Texas did not have a valid state government and that at the conclusion of the rebellion, Congress needed to provide one for the state, which it had done through the process of reconstruction. In order to thread this constitutional needle—simultaneously holding that the states had not actually left the Union but that Congress could nevertheless impose military rule—Chase drew a distinction "between a state and the government of a State."[30] This distinction, he believed, was evident in the Guarantee Clause, Article IV, Section 4 of the Constitution: "The United States shall guarantee to every State in this Union a Republican Form of Government." This clause, Chase maintained, described a duty and "a legislative power" held by Congress, and Congress had exercised this duty and power by "reestablishing the broken relations of the State with the Union" through the Military Reconstruction acts.[31] In the most memorable passage of the opinion, Chase made the argument for a perpetual Union of states. "The Constitution, in all its provisions, looks to an indestructible Union composed of indestructible States," he wrote. "When, therefore, Texas became one of the United States, she entered into an indissoluble relation. All the obligations of perpetual union, and all the guaranties of republican government in the Union, attached at once to the State. The act which consummated her admission into the Union was something more than a compact; it was the incorporation of a new member into the political body. And it was final."[32] Writing in the tradition of Alexander Hamilton, John Marshall, and Abraham Lincoln, Chase offered a compelling defense of the notion of a durable national union.

Chase's majority opinion was a constitutional and political tour de force. It affirmed congressional power over reconstruction without delving into the messy details of the Military Reconstruction acts, recognized the "indestructible" nature of the states without affirming the theory of state sovereignty, and appeared to lay to rest, especially with a Republican president in office, challenges to the legitimacy of reconstruction. In broadest and simplest terms, the decision in *Texas v. White* meant that secession was unconstitutional and that the existence of the states posed no barrier to federal enforcement of the civil and political rights of African Americans. It was everything the Republicans at the time could have wanted.

RATIFYING AND ENFORCING THE FIFTEENTH AMENDMENT

Throughout the rest of 1869, the process of ratifying the Fifteenth Amendment moved steadily forward. In addition to the dozen states that ratified in the early part of the year, others did so as their legislatures convened. Ratification came easily in the reconstructed South, where Republicans dominated state governments. North Carolina, Louisiana, Arkansas, South Carolina, Florida, and Alabama all ratified the amendment by wide margins. Black suffrage was already an accomplished fact in these states, and overall a higher percentage of Southern legislators voted for the amendment than non-Southern legislators.[33] The strongest opposition came from the former slaveholding border states of Delaware, Kentucky, and Maryland, as well as the Democratic-controlled legislatures of California and Oregon. Tennessee also voted against ratification. Because it had gained readmission to the Union after its ratification of the Fourteenth Amendment, Tennessee never experienced military rule, and reconstruction in the state had depended on the leadership of Governor William Brownlow. When Brownlow left to take a seat in the US Senate, his successor, Dewitt Senter, a conservative Unionist, reached out to the state's Democrats for political support, in effect setting aside the state's disfranchisement of former Confederates and paving the way for Democratic domination of the legislature. That legislature rejected the Fifteenth Amendment.

This print commemorating the ratification of the Fifteenth Amendment incorporates a pantheon of heroes, including Frederick Douglass and Hiram Revels, along with Lincoln and others. A scene of the Baltimore celebration of the amendment dominates in the center, framed by portrayals of the advancement of education and science. Courtesy of the Library of Congress, LC-USZ62-22396

With the Northeast and South assenting to the amendment and the border states and Northwest opposing it, the fate of ratification seemed to hinge on the Midwest. The contentious nature of the debate there provoked concern over whether the amendment would pass, and in April 1869, Senator Oliver P. Morton of Indiana, a Radical leader, introduced legislation requiring the still unreconstructed states of Virginia, Texas, and Mississippi to ratify the amendment in order to rejoin the Union. Despite an outcry by some moderates that Congress had in effect changed the rules for readmission of these ex-Confederate states, the legislation passed. Georgia was a unique case. After expelling the African American members of its legislature in September 1868, the state again fell under military rule, and in December 1869 Congress required that Georgia also ratify the amendment in order to regain representation in Congress. In the end, all of these states—and a narrow victory for the amendment in Ohio—proved crucial to ratification. With Georgia's approval in February 1870, every one of the former Rebel states had been readmitted to the Union, and Iowa's approval that same month marked ratification by the requisite twenty-eight states. On March 30, 1870, Secretary of State Hamilton Fish formally certified the amendment.

Despite the limitations of its language and the contentious debate over its ratification, African American leaders celebrated the Fifteenth Amendment as the apogee of a mighty revolution. At gatherings around the country, jubilant blacks celebrated by participating in parades, watching fireworks, and listening to speeches. In Baltimore, 10,000 African Americans marched through the streets, and the procession included a wagon holding a printing press that produced sheets containing the text of the amendment. In Macon, Georgia, Henry McNeal Turner referred to ratification as "one of the grandest events and inestimable blessing that ever crowned a nation's brow or marked the term of a generation." A former Union army chaplain and delegate to the Georgia constitutional convention of 1868, Turner viewed the amendment in providential and patriotic terms. "The ratification of the Fifteenth Amendment to the Constitution, all will concede, is the finish of our national fabric," he proclaimed. "It is the headstone of the world's asylum; the crowning event of the nineteenth century; the brightest glare of glory that ever hung over land or sea."[34] In Cincinnati, a gathering of African Americans heard a letter read from Chief Justice Chase, who predicted that black suffrage would soon become such a universally accepted part of the nation's political life that "it will be impossible to find a man who will avow himself in favor of denying or abridging" black voting rights.[35] In Albany, New York, the usually circumspect Frederick Douglass admitted his pleasant surprise at the rapid advance in the rights of African Americans. "One of the most remarkable features of this grand revolution is its thoroughness. Never was revolution more complete," he announced. "Nothing has been left for time. . . . The most exacting could not ask more than we have got; the most urgent could not have demanded it more promptly. We have all we asked, and more than we expected."[36] Black constitutionalists, Douglass included, had long held that America's founding promises were deep and broad enough to include all of the nation's inhabitants, and the passage of the amendment appeared to bear out such long-standing aspirations.

Beyond the celebrations, white and black Republicans knew that it would take more to make the reconstruction amendments a living reality. Despite having reestablished civilian rule in the former Confederate states, readmitted their representatives to Congress, and ratified an amendment to protect the voting rights of blacks, violence continued to haunt the South, as the Ku

Klux Klan and other white supremacists engaged in campaigns of terror and intimidation. Reconstructed state governments organized militias, composed mostly of African Americans, to protect black voters, but the presence of armed black men only seemed to further incite the white population, and Southern Republican governors appealed for help from Washington. In a firm show of resolve, Congress and Grant acted. At the end of May 1870, the president signed the Enforcement Act of 1870. Its most important provisions established punishments for those who obstructed qualified voters by "force, bribery, threats, intimidation, or other unlawful means" as well as those who conspired to "injure, oppress, threaten, or intimidate" any citizen attempting to exercise the right to vote.[37] Not only did the law thus establish categories of federal crimes where heretofore none had existed but it also provided that the entire existing federal legal apparatus—district courts, district attorneys, marshals, deputy marshals, and commissioners—would be used for enforcement. In addition, the law authorized the president to use "the land or naval forces of the United States, or of the militia."[38] To aid in enforcement, in June lawmakers created the US Department of Justice, transforming the role of the attorney general from that of a mere legal advisor to the head of an agency of attorneys permanently employed by the federal government.

The following spring, at Grant's urging, Congress expanded the Justice Department's legal arsenal when it passed the Enforcement Act of 1871, also known as the Ku Klux Klan Act. Designed to combat violence against African Americans, the law aimed to enforce the guarantees of the Fourteenth Amendment in all cases of "insurrection, domestic violence, unlawful combinations, or conspiracies in any State." To do so, the law specifically deemed a state's inability or failure to protect citizens' rights under the Fourteenth Amendment as "a denial by such State of the equal protection of the laws," and thus a violation of the amendment.[39] Taken as a whole, the enforcement legislation of 1870–1871 represented an unprecedented attempt to expand national power to meet the challenge of Southern violence. Twenty years before, the full force of the federal government had been used to implement the Fugitive Slave Law of 1850. With the passage of the Enforcement acts, the tables were completely turned: an expanded federal legal apparatus would be used to protect the rights of formerly enslaved people rather than the rights of slaveholders. Never in American legal history had there been a more stunning reversal.

Knowing the stakes, ex-Confederates and black activists offered distinct interpretations of the new legislation. Former Confederate vice president Alexander Stephens, who had spent five months in a Boston prison after the war, devoted the immediate postwar years to writing a constitutional treatise justifying the South's attempt to secede. Published in two volumes, Stephens's book drew criticism from Grant's newly appointed attorney general, Amos Akerman, who denounced the work for promoting "pernicious doctrines." Stephens responded in kind. In an open letter to the attorney general in fall 1870 (just before the passage of the second Enforcement Act), Stephens argued that Akerman and the administration were leading the country down the road to tyranny, by attempting to erect "a Centralized Empire over the ruins of the principles of that wonderful Federal Union."[40] African Americans, meanwhile, had a different view of the aggregation of national power. "The cry raised against . . . centralization," Massachusetts black leader George Ruffin later noted, "is against the interests of the colored people; it means that the power of protecting us against the midnight raids of armed bodies of men, and defending us at the ballot-box, should be taken away from the Federal Government and we and all our dear and blood-bought rights should be left to the tender mercies of the Kuklux." Ruffin continued, "No centralization of power is harmful where the purpose of it is for the public good."[41] Even though Stephens and other Confederate apologists wanted to portray their opposition to enforcement legislation as a matter of constitutional principle, the reality of white violence and black suffering made such appeals mostly ring hollow to Northern ears. Both Enforcement acts passed with overwhelming Republican support.

Armed with the Fourteenth and Fifteenth amendments, as well as two robust enforcement statutes, Congress, the president, and the Department of Justice began the difficult work of cracking down on white offenders. On the same day that it passed the Enforcement Act of 1871, a joint committee in Congress began hearings on Klan outrages in the former Confederacy. Beginning in April, over a period of several weeks, members heard firsthand stories from the perpetrators and victims of Southern violence. With plenty of evidence of past wrongs and continued reports of atrocities, the federal government began to round up suspects, secure indictments, and bring cases to trial. Usually this involved federal troops. Only about 8,000 soldiers remained in the South at this time, so small detachments of men typically accompanied civil authorities to make arrests. During 1871, the federal courts handled 314 criminal cases brought by the Department of Justice under the Enforcement acts, with 128 resulting in convictions.

The trying and convicting of individual defendants was surely important, but the constitutional doctrine that developed from these early cases would decide what Congress had left unanswered: what precisely were the rights protected by the Fourteenth Amendment? The first such case, *United States v. Hall*, an 1871 federal circuit court case in Alabama, involved two whites indicted under the Enforcement Act of 1871 for breaking up a black political meeting. Charged with interfering with blacks' freedom of speech and right of assembly, the defendants argued that these were not federally protected rights—that they were not included in the "privileges and immunities" protected by the Fourteenth Amendment. The court ruled otherwise. The opinion, issued in May 1871 by Judge William B. Woods, held that "the right of freedom of speech, and the other rights enumerated in the first eight articles of the amendment to the Constitution of the United States, are the privileges and immunities of citizens of the United States, that they are secured by the Constitution."[42] A native Ohioan appointed by Grant, Judge Woods provided a broad interpretation of the rights protected by the federal government. Subsequent decisions proved less expansive. Informed in fall 1871 of the existence of a climate of lawlessness in a portion of South Carolina, President Grant issued a proclamation that suspended the writ of habeas corpus in a nine-county area, and over a period of several months, federal marshals and cavalry rounded up hundreds of suspects. In these trials, Judge Hugh Lennox Bond, another Grant appointee, offered a more cramped view of the reconstruction amendments. In quashing a portion of an indictment, Bond ruled that the Fifteenth Amendment did not grant an affirmative right to vote and that the Fourteenth Amendment did not apply the Bill of Rights to the states. Bond held, in other words, that the Fourteenth and Fifteenth amendments were not as revolutionary as federal prosecutors had claimed.

Despite the uncertainty of these decisions, in the short term, the Grant administration continued its enforcement efforts. In addition to the large-scale operations in South Carolina, in 1872 the War Department reported 160 temporary detachments of troops in the Southern states for the purpose of escorting and aiding civilian authorities, state and federal, in carrying out their duties.[43] The Justice Department, meanwhile, brought 856 criminal cases under the Enforcement acts into federal court, 456 of which resulted in convictions. In South Carolina, the trials of Ku Klux Klansmen resulted in a highly publicized round of prosecutions, even if they did not include the organization's ringleaders, who mostly escaped capture. In the vast majority of federal enforcement cases, blacks sat on juries, thus helping to bring to justice the white men who had terrorized their communities. The combination of military force, an expanded federal law enforcement structure, and an empowered black populace helped curb the violence that had been carried out with impunity by white supremacist organizations since 1866. At the same time, the Republican administration and Congress offered amnesty to many former Confederates. The General Amnesty Act of 1872 removed the restriction on officeholding imposed by Section 3 of the Fourteenth Amendment, in effect

Table 10.2. Total Criminal Prosecutions under Enforcement Acts, 1871–1873

	1871	1872	1873
No. of cases	314	856	1,304
No. of convictions	128	456	469
Conviction rate	40.8%	53.3%	36.0%

Source: Xi Wang, *The Trial of Democracy: Black Suffrage and Northern Republicans, 1860–1910* (Athens: University of Georgia Press, 1997), appendix 7, 300–301.

meaning that Congress would no longer have to deal with individual appeals to remove the disability.

Grant's policies seemed to be working. With the Klan on the defensive, the 1872 national elections were largely free of violence, and most voters rallied behind the president. After winning renomination by the Republicans and earning high praise from African American leaders for his efforts, President Grant won a resounding victory over his opponent, the eccentric newspaper editor Horace Greeley, who had been nominated by both the Democratic Party and an offshoot of anti-Grant Republicans who styled themselves "Liberal Republicans." Although considered a Radical during the war, Greeley had grown disillusioned with the Grant administration's enforcement policies and had become a vocal advocate of a more conciliatory stance toward the former Rebels. But Greeley's message failed to resonate with most Americans. With a free and fair ballot throughout the country—and with the administration's treatment of the South as the main issue of the campaign—Grant garnered 56 percent of the vote and 600,000 more votes than he had in 1868. In contrast to some of his narrow margins of victory in individual states in 1868, Grant won twelve states with at least 60 percent of the vote, including four states (Nebraska, Rhode Island, South Carolina, and Vermont) where his vote tally exceeded 70 percent. By the end of 1872, the American electorate largely approved of Grant's vigorous policy of protecting blacks' rights.

While enforcement continued, the US Supreme Court prepared to hear its first cases pertaining to the Fourteenth Amendment. Congress had denied Andrew Johnson the opportunity to appoint any justices to the Court, but the Judiciary Act of 1869 had added a seat to the Court (fixing its size at nine), thus allowing Grant a chance to nominate a justice during his first year. Unfortunately for Grant, his first nominee failed to secure Senate confirmation, while his second choice for the position (former secretary of war Edwin Stanton) died before he could take his seat. Grant chose Joseph P. Bradley of New Jersey for the new seat. At around the same time, Grant filled another vacancy when he appointed William Strong of Pennsylvania to take the place of the retiring Robert Cooper Grier. Two years later, when Justice Samuel Nelson retired, Grant replaced him with New Yorker Ward Hunt. Both Grier and Nelson had been part of the old majority in *Dred Scott*, and Grant's first-term appointees thus completed the transformation of the Supreme Court that had begun under Lincoln. By 1872, with the exception of a single Buchanan appointee, all of the justices owed their seats to Republicans Lincoln and Grant. Not a single member of the Court that had decided *Dred Scott* remained.

The first Supreme Court cases involving the Fourteenth Amendment, heard in early 1873, pertained to reconstruction in only a tangential way. Brought by a group of disgruntled white butchers from Louisiana, the suits challenged a law passed by the reconstructed legislature that granted an exclusive franchise to a private slaughterhouse company in New Orleans. The law attempted to clean up a filthy industry by confining its operation to a single facility in a designated district, thus depriving some butchers of their livelihoods. Justice Samuel Miller, a Lincoln appointee, wrote for a five-justice majority in the series of cases known as the *Slaughterhouse Cases*, upholding the statute as a valid exercise of the state's police powers, a legitimate attempt to protect public health. Because attorneys for these butchers, including the former Confederate assistant secretary of war John A. Campbell, charged that their rights under the Thirteenth and Fourteenth amendments had been violated, the Court for the first time offered an interpretation of these postwar amendments. Confronted with the spectacle of an ex-Rebel claiming rights for white clients by attempting to overturn an act of the reconstructed, biracial legislature of Louisiana, Miller and his colleagues concluded that the "pervading purpose" of the amendments had been "the freedom of the slave race, the security and firm establishment of that freedom, and the protection of the newly made freeman and citizen from the oppressions of those who had formerly exercised unlimited dominion over him."[44] Miller thus dismissed out of hand the claim that the butchers' plight could be compared to the "involuntary servitude" banned by the Thirteenth Amendment. More important, Miller ruled that the butchers' right to practice a trade was not among the privileges and immunities protected by the federal government.

At the time, the *Slaughterhouse* decision seemed to present no barrier to the federal government's continued enforcement of blacks' civil and political rights. In fact, in his majority opinion, Miller indicated strong support for the rights of African Americans. In addition to arguing that the safeguarding of these rights was the very reason for the passage of the amendments, Miller implicitly affirmed that the Southern state constitutions of 1868 offered adequate protection of blacks' civil rights. At this time, with the exception of Tennessee, Virginia, and Georgia, the governments of all of the states of the

Justice Samuel F. Miller wrote the majority opinion in the Slaughterhouse Cases, *a collection of cases in which the US Supreme Court for the first time interpreted the scope and meaning of the Fourteenth Amendment. Courtesy of the Library of Congress, LC-DIG-cwpbh-03988*

former Confederacy remained in the hands of Republicans. But in case state civil rights protections proved inadequate, Miller defined black voting as among the "privileges and immunities" under the protection of the federal government, and he affirmed that in cases of "state oppression, by denial of equal justice in its courts," the Equal Protection Clause offered a clear remedy to black clients.[45] For decades, historians have vilified the *Slaughterhouse* decision for failing to offer an expansive interpretation of the Privileges and Immunities Clause, thus leaving too much power with the states. But with Republicans' success in implementing the Enforcement acts, Miller and his colleagues had every reason to believe that reconstructed state governments, backed by federal action, could sufficiently protect the rights of blacks.

By spring of 1873, the Enforcement acts and the Grant administration's vigorous efforts to enforce them appeared to be a success. With a Republican Congress and a reelected Republican president working in concert, black suffrage had become a reality throughout the country. Both reunion and revolution—two goals at times perceived to be at odds with one another—seemed to have been simultaneously achieved. The decision in *Slaughterhouse*, in essence, captured the spirit of the times. Republicans—who held the White House, the Congress, and the Court—mostly hoped to protect the rights of African Americans while also respecting the main features of the American system of federalism. By early 1873, they had good reason to believe that they had succeeded.

VIOLENCE, DEPRESSION, AND DEMOCRATIC RESURGENCE

The justices did not know it yet, but the day before the Supreme Court delivered its opinion in *Slaughterhouse*, the small town of Colfax, Louisiana, witnessed the most violent episode of the era. On April 13, 1873, Easter Sunday, a group of armed whites assailed an all-black Republican militia, resulting in the death of perhaps as many as 150 African Americans.[46] The massacre grew out of the tense and often violent relationship between blacks and whites in postwar Louisiana. Not only had a major riot occurred in New Orleans in 1866 but also continued outrages had earned Louisiana a reputation as the most openly hostile to federal law of all of the ex-Confederate states. The statewide elections of 1872 had resulted in Republicans and Democrats both having claimed the governorship, and when a federal judge resolved the dispute in favor of the Republican, Grant had sent in troops to enforce the ruling. Resistant to federal authority, white Louisianans formed a rival government backed by the White League, a paramilitary group that wreaked havoc across the state and captured control of a number of rural parishes. In Colfax, where a black militia assembled outside the county courthouse in an attempt to protect the local Republican government, the White League attacked. Armed with rifles and cannon, the White Leaguers fought a pitched battle for two hours with their outmatched opponents, who mostly ended up retreating into the courthouse, only to be burned to death once the White Leaguers torched the building. "The unfortunate colored men," the *New York Times* reported, "were literally roasted alive in the sight of their enemies."[47] Others were shot in the head while surrendering.

The massacre occurred at a critical moment in the history of federal enforcement. Despite the successes of Grant's Southern policy, enforcement of the rights of African Americans was difficult, expensive work. It was hard to find juries who would convict, and cases took precious time and resources. By early 1873, approximately 7,500 federal troops remained stationed at forty-six different military posts scattered across the states of the former Confederacy.[48] In most instances, detachments of troops were required to arrest suspects, protect witnesses and jurors, and sustain the operation of the federal courts. Because of the rural nature of the South, this work frequently involved the use of cavalry. In addition to supporting the men and horses required for military operations, the federal government paid the salaries of federal judges, attorneys, marshals, and commissioners, as well as provided witnesses with meal allowances and travel expenses. The existence of thousands of potential cases under the Enforcement acts prompted the Justice Department to become, by necessity, selective in prosecutions, and in many instances, beginning in 1873, the department merely threatened prosecution rather than pursuing it. The costs of enforcement not only prompted Democrats to assert that the federal government was spending too much but also made Republicans susceptible to charges that enforcement merely served as a form of patronage, or worse, corruption.

By early 1873, the financial and political challenges associated with enforcement exacerbated the strains and divisions within the Republican coalition. After more than a dozen years in power, the Republican Party struggled to sustain the revolutionary fervor that had originated during wartime and that had driven the party forward. At the national level, Grant's clumsy handling of an attempt to annex Santo Domingo in 1869 and scandals within the administration, particularly the treasury and interior departments, had contributed to the rise of anti-Grant forces within party ranks. Although Grant had soundly defeated these Liberal Republicans in 1872, further revelations of corruption after Grant's reelection—that top Republicans in Congress and the administration had taken bribes from a leading railroad company—only heightened tensions within the national party. Critics of Grant's enforcement policy, including some within the administration itself, contended that a more conciliatory stance toward the South would prove more beneficial to the party's Southern fortunes in the long run. In the Southern states, meanwhile, the potential for factionalism and strife was even greater. Southern-born scalawags at times resented Northern-born carpetbaggers, while both groups of white Republicans often quarreled with blacks. Moderates in some states favored a more conciliatory brand of politics that included broadening the franchise and allying with Democrats in order to sustain the legitimacy of reconstructed governments, while Radicals (including most African American officeholders) wanted vigorous enforcement of civil rights and voting rights. Although all Republicans in the South relied on the promise of the federal government's willingness to uphold the law in the Southern states, those who sought alliances with Democrats supported a lighter federal presence, so as to not engender further opposition from Democrats.

News of the Colfax massacre thus came at a time when the Grant administration, as well as many Republicans, would have preferred to pull back a bit. But the horror of Colfax was too great to ignore. Although many of the ringleaders had already fled, the federal government began making arrests, gathering evidence, and preparing indictments. In May, Grant declared parts of the state to be in insurrection and suspended habeas corpus, and in June a federal grand jury indicted ninety-eight defendants, charging each with violating the Enforcement Act of 1870.

In the months that followed, as the government moved ahead with its case against the Colfax defendants, a financial panic hit the country. The collapse in the railroad building business—which had dramatically expanded during and immediately after the war—triggered the downturn. After the war, European and American investors had poured huge sums of money into the expansion of American railroads. Completion of a transcontinental line in 1869 had only contributed to the railroad-building euphoria, which resulted in railroads becoming the nation's largest nonagricultural employer. In September 1873, Jay Cooke and Company, a large banking firm that was heavily invested in rail construction, went out of business. Cooke's firm had overextended itself, and its collapse led to a stock market crash. For ten days in late September, in order to alleviate the sense of panic, the New York Stock Exchange ceased all operations. Although many Americans initially viewed the crisis as a Wall Street affair, they soon saw otherwise. Over the next several months, thousands of businesses and banks failed, including approximately one quarter of the nation's railroads, all of which prompted a steady, steep rise in unemployment. Under political pressure to stimulate the economy, in spring 1874, Congress passed a bill that would have created $100 million in greenback currency, but Grant resisted. The president vetoed the proposed "inflation bill," as it was known at the time, believing that the long-term costs would far outweigh whatever short-term benefits might have ensued. The president's decision won the applause of bankers but earned him no friends among Northern workers, who wondered why the president seemed more interested in helping Southern blacks than Northern whites. Panic created political hardships for Southern Republicans as well. The sudden decline of the railroad industry undermined fragile coalitions between probusiness elements within the two parties in the South, thus leaving Southern Republicans out on a limb. While the nation fell deeper into depression, in a federal courtroom in Louisiana, a division between the two trial judges over the interpretation of the Enforcement Act of 1870 meant that the case of the Colfax defendants would eventually go to the Supreme Court.

Amidst political challenges and legal uncertainties, the Grant administration attempted to engage in more selective enforcement in 1874, but the president's policy took on an air of inconsistency rather than prudence. Caught between his sincere desire to uphold the Constitution and the law in the South and the political costs of doing so, Grant seemed to treat every state differently. Early in the year, the president refused to intervene in an electoral dispute in Texas, and although he tried to pursue a similar course in Arkansas in the spring, he ended up sending troops to resolve a gubernatorial dispute there, declaring the Republican the winner. During summer, despite rampant violence against black voters in Mississippi and frequent calls for assistance from Republican governor Adelbert Ames, the administration did little to intervene. But in early September, Grant seemed to draw a line in the sand. After describing Southern atrocities as showing "a disregard for law, civil rights and personal protection that ought not to be tolerated in any civilized government," Grant ordered his secretary of war to follow whatever orders might be given by the attorney general for the deployment of federal troops.[49] A few weeks later, when White Leaguers went on the offensive in New Orleans, routing the combined black state militia and metropolitan police force, federal troops moved in swiftly. In the face of federal power, the White League withdrew, and Grant's aggressive intervention raised the charge of military despotism, of using excessive force to prop up a corrupt Republican government for purely partisan purposes. It did not help that the Louisiana faction that Grant supported included the president's brother-in-law.[50]

In fall 1874, in one of the most stunning turnarounds in American electoral history, voters handed Democrats control of the House of Representatives for the first time since before the Civil War. A depressed economy, concerns over corruption, and doubts about continued federal intervention in Southern affairs combined to turn voters against the Republicans. The numbers reveal the extent of the losses. Two years before, in the congressional elections of 1872, Republicans had won 199 of 292 seats in the House and 47 of 74 seats in the Senate. (Liberal Republicans held 7 seats in the Senate at the time). But in 1874, the Republicans lost 96 of those seats in the House, putting them at 103 seats to the Democrats' 182. In the Senate, Republicans retained control and lost 1 seat.[51] Several Southern House delegations—Alabama, Arkansas, Louisiana, Mississippi, Tennessee, and Virginia—went from being majority Republican to majority Democratic, as did those of electorally important Northern states Massachusetts, New York, Ohio, and Pennsylvania. Even Lincoln and Grant's home state of Illinois suddenly found itself with fewer Republican representatives than Democratic. Republicans, moreover, suffered gubernatorial defeats in Illinois, Indiana, Massachusetts, New York, Ohio, and Pennsylvania. Nationwide, Democrats had every reason to celebrate the election results. After a decade and a half, the electoral dominance of "the party of revolution" had come to an end.

Grant struggled to adapt to the new political reality, and in the short term, his party's surprising defeat only seemed to stiffen his resolve. In his December 1874 message to Congress, the president condemned violence and assured Congress that he would continue to enforce federal law in the former Confederate states. While acknowledging white Southerners' "prostrate condition," Grant appealed for peace, justice, and honesty in the South. "Violence has been rampant in some localities and has either been justified or denied by those who could have prevented," he wrote. "Let there be fairness in the discussion of Southern questions, the advocates of both, or all, political parties giving honest, truthful reports of occurrences, condemning the wrong and upholding the right, and soon all will be well." The president continued, "Treat the Negro as a citizen and a voter—as he is, and must remain—and soon parties will be divided, *not on the color line*, but on principle."[52] A few weeks later, clearly indicating that he did not intend to abandon black Southerners, Grant ordered Lieutenant General Philip Sheridan to New Orleans to investigate the unrest in Louisiana and Mississippi. Sheridan's report, delivered a few weeks later, affirmed the need for a robust federal response and described the White League opponents of Louisiana governor William P. Kellogg as "banditti." On January 13, 1875, Grant followed up with a lengthy message to the Senate. Reviewing the history of lawlessness and documenting the outrages that had occurred throughout the South, Grant offered a full-throated defense of his Southern policy and the need for the federal government to protect the rights of all of its citizens. He particularly focused his attention on Louisiana. "To say that the murder of a negro or a white republican is not considered a crime in Louisiana would probably be unjust to a great part of the people; but it is true that a great number of such murders have been committed, and no one has been punished therefor[e], and manifestly, as to them, the spirit of hatred and violence is stronger than law."[53]

If Grant's words in early 1875 indicated a determined course, it was not to be. Over the next several months, events in the nation's capital and in Mississippi portended a grim future. In Washington, DC, Democratic Mississippi senator Lucius Quintus Cincinnatus (L. Q. C.) Lamar, a savvy former Confederate who had suddenly acquired a reputation as a statesman after he delivered an eloquent eulogy for Charles Sumner in spring 1874, succeeded in working with Republican House speaker James G. Blaine of Maine in killing a new enforcement act. The proposed strict enforcement law would have prohibited violence designed to "subvert" or "usurp" state governments, extended the reach of federal authority over elections in rural areas, and

Table 10.3. Total Criminal Prosecutions under Enforcement Acts, 1874–1876

	1874	1875	1876
No. of cases	966	234	152
No. of convictions	102	18	3
Conviction rate	10.6%	7.7%	2.0%

Source: Xi Wang, *The Trial of Democracy: Black Suffrage and Northern Republicans, 1860–1910* (Athens: University of Georgia Press, 1997), appendix 7, 300–301.

imposed the death penalty for murder while engaged in crimes specified in the bill.[54] But during this lame-duck session, before the new Democratic majority assembled, the best the outgoing Republicans could muster was the Civil Rights acts of 1875. Passed in memory of Sumner, the law banned racial discrimination in most public accommodations—in other words, it attempted to protect blacks' "social rights"—but lacked the vigorous enforcement provisions that Sumner had proposed. In Mississippi, meanwhile, the shifting political winds emboldened white Southern Democrats, who engaged in violence against a series of local Republican-controlled governments in the state, thus daring the administration to intervene. Republicans in the state, black and white, appealed for presidential intervention. Writing in haste in September 1875, E. C. Walker Jr., a black resident of Macon, Mississippi, begged Grant to send troops to uphold the Constitution. "I know you Have it in To your Powder To Stop White Peopels from Killing Black Peopels . . . now Pres I will ask To your Hon Doant the 13 & 14 & 15 Demenments Gives the (Cold) Peopels the Same Rights and the voice to the Balord Box as it Do the Whites?"[55] Grant vacillated. Sensitive to the political consequences of again sending in troops in the face of an important impending congressional election in Ohio, the president decided not to intervene, thus leaving Mississippi Republicans to fend for themselves. During the last three years of Grant's presidency, both the number of cases brought under the Enforcement acts and the conviction rate steadily declined.

UNITED STATES V. CRUIKSHANK, UNITED STATES V. REESE, AND THE FUTURE OF ENFORCEMENT

Some months later, in March 1876, the Supreme Court issued decisions in two cases involving the rights of African Americans. One was that of the Colfax defendants. After initially indicting ninety-eight men involved in the massacre, the Justice Department had focused its efforts on nine men, whose cases were taken to trial. When the first case ended in a mistrial, a second trial ensued, and a jury composed of eleven white men and one black man acquitted all but three of the accused, who promptly appealed their convictions to the Supreme Court. At the same time, the Court decided the fate of three municipal election inspectors indicted in Kentucky, for allegedly refusing to accept the vote of an African American man in Lexington on account of his race. Together the cases represented the first time that the Supreme Court would interpret the Enforcement Act of 1870. By the time the Court heard arguments in the cases, Chief Justice Chase had died, and Grant had replaced him with Morrison Waite, a relatively unknown Ohio lawyer. The Court, still composed of eight Republicans and the Democratic justice Stephen Field, would have an opportunity to clarify any constitutional and legal uncertainties growing out of the Grant administration's enforcement efforts.

In both cases, the Supreme Court issued relatively narrow decisions. Attorneys in both instances had raised questions about the constitutionality of the Enforcement Act, particularly with regard to whether the law pertained to the rights protected by the federal government under the Fourteenth and Fifteenth amendments. In *United States v. Cruikshank* (1876), the Colfax case, Chief Justice Waite's opinion for a unanimous Court dealt with this question only indirectly.[56] "To bring this case under the operation of the statute . . . it must appear that the right, the enjoyment of which the conspirators intended to hinder or prevent, was one granted or secured by the Constitution or laws of the United States," Waite began. "If it does not so appear, the criminal matter charged has not been made indictable by any act of Congress." Waite reiterated the Court's holding in the *Slaughterhouse Cases* that the only rights protected by the federal government were, in Waite's words, those rights "acquired under the Constitution or laws of the United States." But rather than examine the Enforcement Act to decide whether it protected such rights, Waite focused instead on whether the indictments had been properly written, a technical matter having to do with whether the prosecution had used the appropriate wording in charging the defendants. The Court held that the indictments had mentioned rights under the First, Second, Fourteenth, and Fifteenth amendments of the Constitution, but that in each instance the charges had failed to specify the precise federally protected right that had been violated. In the case of the Fifteenth Amendment, for example, the indictment had not stated that the victims of the violence at Colfax had been prevented from exercising their right to vote on account of their race. "We may suspect that race was the cause of the hostility," Waite wrote, "but it is not so averred."[57] The Court neglected to rule on the constitutionality of the Enforcement Act, but because of the flaws in the indictments, the three Colfax defendants went free. In *United States v. Reese*, decided on the same day, the Court issued a similarly narrow ruling.[58] In this case, the Court—again with Waite writing for the majority—restricted its analysis to two sections of the Enforcement Act. In an 8–1 decision, the Court held that Sections 3 and 4 of the law were not "appropriate legislation" under the Fifteenth Amendment. Arguing that "the Fifteenth Amendment does not confer the right of suffrage on anyone," Waite explained that the amendment had only established "exemption from discrimination in the exercise of the elective franchise on account of race, color, or previous condition of servitude." Sections 3 and 4 of the Enforcement acts, however, were overly broad in their wording and did not specify violations on account of race. Although Waite acknowledged that this could be implied, particularly because previous sections of the statute did specify racial motivation, Waite concluded that such "radical" changes in the role of the federal government required "explicit" statutes. "Nothing should be left to construction if it can be avoided," he wrote.[59] Deeming the sections too broad, Waite held that they did not constitute "appropriate legislation." Because the sections were the ones under which the defendants had been indicted, the defendants, as in *Cruikshank*, went free.

The decisions in *Cruikshank* and *Reese* did little to clarify the scope and definition of the rights protected by the federal government. In a legal sense, *Cruikshank* had merely attempted to define what a sufficient indictment would entail. From now on, it seemed, successful indictments for violent acts perpetrated by whites against black voters would need to specify racial motivation, in accordance with the language of the Fifteenth Amendment. Although it had engaged in highly formalistic reasoning in the decisions, the Court had not condoned violence, and the justices had even provided guidance to the Department of Justice about how future indictments needed to be drawn. Still, allowing the defendants in both cases to go free surely proved frustrating to the Grant administration.[60]

The formalistic interpretations of the reconstruction constitution in *Cruikshank* and *Reese*, while not necessarily defeats for the cause of enforcement, did present a stark contrast to how the Court had interpreted the antebellum Constitution. The distinction was not lost on Justice Ward Hunt, the lone dissenter in *Reese*. After arguing in favor of the constitutionality of all sections of the Enforcement Act, as well as the sufficiency of the indictments, Justice Hunt's dissent pointed out that the Waite Court proved much stingier in its protection of the rights of African Americans than had the Taney Court in its protection of the rights of slaveholders. Reviewing the Court's decisions in *Prigg v. Pennsylvania* (1845) and *Ableman v. Booth* (1860), Justice Hunt drew a contrast between how the Court had read the Fugitive Slave Clause, compared to the Fifteenth Amendment. "In connection with the [Fugitive Slave Clause], there was not found, as here, an express authority in Congress to enforce it by appropriate legislation, and yet the Court decided not only that Congress had power to enforce its provisions by fine and imprisonment, but that the right to legislate on the subject belongs to Congress exclusively," Hunt wrote. "Courts should be ready, now and here, to apply these sound and just principles of the Constitution."[61] As Hunt pointed out, the Court had seemed more willing to protect slaveholders' rights than the rights of the formerly enslaved.

By 1876, six years after the ratification of the Fifteenth Amendment, federal enforcement of the rights of African Americans faced an uncertain future. In the aftermath of *Cruikshank* and *Reese*, it remained to be seen whether the political order would support a sustained attempt to protect blacks' civil and political rights from white violence, as well as whether the Court would uphold future enforcement efforts. The revolution had peaked in 1870, when a unified Republican Party and a popular Republican president had achieved the ratification of the Fifteenth Amendment. Despite a vigorous enforcement effort in the early 1870s, the cause of ensuring the rights of African Americans lost a great deal of momentum a few years later, as a financial panic, divisions among Republicans, and relentless Southern resistance slowed enforcement efforts. By the time his second term ended, Grant had gone through five attorneys general. The desire among Northerners and Southerners to preserve the existing relationship between the national government and the states meant that federal enforcement efforts could only go so far.

If the force of change no longer emanated from Washington, it might yet be felt in the lives of Northerners, Southerners, and African Americans. For despite disagreement and uncertainty about the rights of African Americans, the fact of freedom remained.

11
FREEDOM, THE SOUTH, AND THE NORTH

On June 14, 1876, Frederick Douglass rose to speak to the delegates at the national convention of the Republican Party in Cincinnati, Ohio. By that point, the fifty-eight-year-old activist, born a slave, had spent more than three decades on the national stage, during which he had witnessed great changes in the life of the republic. Celebrated for his compelling autobiography and his powerful oratory during the antebellum era, Douglass had helped push for emancipation and black military service during the war and afterward had figured prominently in advocating equal rights for African Americans. But by the summer of 1876, with the recent acquittal of the Colfax defendants and a presidential election just over the horizon, Douglass attempted to remind his fellow Republicans of the ideals for which they had long fought. Describing them as "the principles involved in the contest which carried your sons and brothers to the battlefield," Douglass argued that those values "ought to be dearer to the American people, in the great political struggle now upon them, than any other principles we have." Not mincing words, Douglass spelled out those principles while also confronting his hearers. "The question now is, Do you mean to make good to us the promises in your constitution? . . . Tell me, if your heart be as my heart, that the liberty which you have asserted for the black man in this country will be maintained?"[1]

Douglass's pointed questions about the Republicans' commitment to the reconstruction amendments came at a critical juncture, more than a decade after the end of the Civil War and the abolition of slavery. The advent of freedom in 1865 had transformed America, cutting a dividing line between an old regime and a new. The antebellum era of Southern planters and slaveholders' rights, sustained by the Democratic Party and the Supreme Court, had given way to a new epoch. For white Southerners in a postemancipation environment, an almost exclusively agricultural society dominated by plantations and slaves transformed into a more economically diverse order, in which textile mills, growing cities, and new railroad lines took hold. For newly freed African Americans, life suddenly held new possibilities, long denied under bondage: freedom of movement, stable families, religious autonomy, educational opportunity, economic gains, political rights. The achievement of any one of these would have marked a break from the days of slavery, but the sudden and almost simultaneous arrival of all of these advances brought enormous joy and meaning to the lives of formerly enslaved people. For Northerners, the consequences of war were less obvious but still important—rapid industrial growth and tensions between social classes. Douglass's questions, then, came as the Northern-led Republican Party had to decide whether the revolutionary gains implemented on top of emancipation—in particular, the political rights for African Americans—would survive the unrelenting violent resistance of Southern whites.

CONSTITUTIONALISM AND SOCIAL CHANGE IN THE POSTWAR SOUTH

From the start, while most white Southerners accepted the fact of emancipation, they regarded Congress' reconstruction policy as illegitimate and of no force. White Southern Unionists and Northern transplants who settled in the South, of course, held important positions in reconstructed state governments, but these Republicans and their supporters constituted a relatively small portion of the population. They were, in essence, the agents of congressional reconstruction, political aliens in the midst of a hostile population. Most white Southerners despised them and the constitutional and legal structure that allowed them to assume power. Adhering to the convenient belief that the Southern states had never really left the Union, most white Southerners during the postwar era acknowledged that the Thirteenth Amendment held constitutional validity, because the Southern states—reconstructed under President Andrew Johnson—participated voluntarily in the ratification process. But the Fourteenth and Fifteenth amendments, they believed, were the products of vicious and vindictive Radical Republicans, enemies of the republic, who forced ratification of the amendments through military control of the South. Faced with no choice but submission, most white Southerners suddenly found themselves under Republican rule—that is, governed by an alliance of Northern carpetbaggers, Southern scalawags, and newly freed African Americans.

In the same way that Johnson had attempted to delegitimize the work of the 1868 state constitutional conventions, former Confederate leaders attempted to challenge the entire congressionally imposed constitutional and legal regime. Linton Stephens, brother of the former Confederate vice president Alexander Stephens, for example, bitterly fought Georgia's reconstruction government. In the state election of 1870, Stephens had attempted to prevent blacks from voting, for which he was arrested under the Enforcement Act of 1870. Stephens used his arrest as an opportunity to make a lengthy speech at his trial, which he later had published, proclaiming to the world that the forces of tyranny had overtaken the South. "I am accused under the Enforcement Act of Congress," he began. "My first proposition is that this whole act is not a law but a mere legal nullity. It was passed with the professed object of carrying into effect what are called the XIVth and XVth amendments of the Constitution of the United States, and depends on their validity for its own," he argued. "These so-called amendments are . . . not *true* amendments of the Constitution, and do not form any part of that sacred instrument. They are nothing but usurpations and nullities, having no validity themselves, and therefore incapable of imparting any to the Enforcement act, or to any other act whatsoever."[2] Stephens's view represented that of most former Confederates, particularly those who, like his brother, had been disfranchised for their involvement in the rebellion and felt powerless in the face of their former enemies.

For his own part, former vice president Alexander Stephens made it his life's goal to justify the Confederate cause and undo congressional action on reconstruction. Although in 1866 he had initially urged fellow Southerners to take a conciliatory attitude toward the North and accept black citizenship, Stephens later opposed the Fourteenth Amendment and devoted himself to reviving the theory of state sovereignty. Going well beyond the efforts of his brother, Alexander Stephens produced a massive constitutional history of the war, *A Constitutional View of the War Between the States*, published in two volumes in 1868 and 1870, in which he articulated the constitutional stance of ex-Confederates. Dismissing the idea that the South had seceded to preserve slavery, a notion that he had previously championed in his "Cornerstone Speech" of 1861, Stephens now argued that the war "grew out of different and directly opposite views as to the nature of the Government of the United States, and where, under our system, ultimate Sovereign power or Paramount authority properly resides."[3] Describing the Constitution as "strictly Federal in its character" and as a "compact between sovereign states," Stephens reasserted the antebellum state sovereignty position of John C. Calhoun. "There never was any political union between the people of the several states in the United States," Stephens contended, "except such as resulted indirectly from the terms of agreement or Compact entered into by separate and distinct political bodies."[4] Stephens's elaboration of the theory of state sovereignty served a twofold purpose: to justify secession as having been based on principles that, he argued, lay within the mainstream of American constitutional history and, more important, to challenge the validity of the revolutionary reconstruction policies of the day. Two years after completing his work, in 1872, Stephens returned to the US House of Representatives, where he would have a broader platform from which to advance his opinions.

While Confederate apologists attempted to defend the tradition of local control and oppose changes in the constitutional status of African Americans, the society around them was already transforming in dramatic ways. Emancipation had already made a difference. Gone was the three-tier social structure, based on slaveholding, which had marked antebellum Southern society. Each of the prewar white South's distinct classes—planters, small slaveholders, and nonslaveholders—lived through significant changes during reconstruction that affected their social status, occupation, or way of life.

The antebellum planter elite, although retaining its high status compared to others, experienced a significant decline in its overall wealth and power. Old planters kept their lands for the most part, but since they had held the majority of their wealth in slaves rather than land, they had lost the nearly $3 billion in capital that their slaves represented. Just as important, emancipation ended their ability to command labor, which meant that the system of slave labor organized into tightly supervised gangs had vanished. As they coped with this "loss of mastery," Southern planters took on an air of hopelessness as they negotiated labor contracts with their former slaves.[5] Having long convinced themselves that blacks would not work unless coerced, and therefore that emancipation spelled the destruction of their society, many planters viewed any new labor agreements as temporary, the forerunner of a collapse of the social and economic order.

After a few years of economic chaos and political struggle that included the rise and fall of the black codes, planters eventually responded to postwar developments in one of two ways. Dependent on black labor, some broke up their great plantations into small parcels of land, which they rented to African Americans (and some whites) under new types of contracts, the most common of which involved sharecropping. Under this arrangement, small farmers rented land from the landowner and paid the rent in the form of a share, or percentage—usually half—of the crop. Landowners also typically provided housing, stock animals, feed for the stock, farming implements, and seed. In this way, postwar planters assumed the role of a rentier class, and the South gradually took on the character of a tenant-farming agricultural economy, a system that represented a sharp break with the past. When freedpeople responded to emancipation by "withdrawing their labor" from the marketplace—that is, reducing the amount of their work time, so as to bring it in line with that of nonenslaved workers—they not only confirmed white attitudes but also created a labor shortage.[6] This only caused further frustration and disruption in the lives of planters, who had grown accustomed to working slaves to the limits of their capacity to produce. The labor shortage led to a decline in tilled acreage, which in turn led to an oversupply of land and a depression in land prices. Planters who broke up their lands in this way contributed to the development of a Southern economy even more reliant on cotton than during the antebellum era, as cotton seemed to be, immediately after the war, the only crop that promised to earn much-needed cash for both landowners and sharecroppers. Other former planters, in contrast, took a different path. They invested in new economic opportunities—such as manufacturing, banking, retailing, or transportation—thus helping the South gradually take on a more industrial and commercial character. The owners of cotton mills, for example, the most important new industry to develop, frequently hailed from the antebellum planter class. Whether they became landlords or entrepreneurs—and despite their loss of wealth compared to the antebellum era—members of the old planter elite mostly remained atop Southern society.

The antebellum class of small slaveholders, including both small farmers and town-dwelling professionals, also experienced significant changes in their lives. Stripped of their slave property, the source of their status, small farmers suddenly became part of the postwar small landowning class. With insufficient lands to become a rentier class and insufficient cash or education to enter the ranks of industrialists or professionals, these ambitious former slaveholders suddenly found themselves within the large undifferentiated mass of relatively poor rural whites. Antebellum professionals usually fared better. Although lawyers, physicians, and merchants all found their lives more difficult because of the macroeconomic situation in the South, their relatively high levels of education and accumulated property, as well as their specialized skills, meant that they usually continued to practice their professions. Steady urban growth, moreover, stemming largely from the expansion of railroads and manufacturing firms, provided new clients for professionals while also spurring the development of a new white-collar middle class, composed mostly of clerks and managers.

Whites who had made up the antebellum nonslaveholding yeomanry also confronted new circumstances. Although they had lost no slaves, they had borne the brunt of the fighting and the dying during the war, and afterward they confronted enormous economic pressures. Cash was scarce and the future uncertain. Finding themselves increasingly dependent on merchants for credit, most yeoman farmers turned from subsistence farming to cash crops—usually cotton—in order to pay their debts and accumulate much-needed capital. While growing cotton helped them meet their immediate needs, it also subjected them for the first time to larger external forces, and over time, postwar yeomen looked with suspicion on the country stores, railroads, and banks that now played such a role in their lives—forces that drew them, for better or worse, further into a national and even international market economy. When cotton prices fell during the Panic of 1873, many of these small landowners sold or mortgaged some or all of their lands. As a consequence, some entered into sharecropping or renting contracts with large landholders, while others allowed merchants to place liens on their crops, thus giving up the ability to escape from what gradually became a cycle of poverty and indebtedness. These new postwar arrangements flew in the face of the sense of communal cooperation and personal independence that had so marked the lives of yeomen during the antebellum era. Remaining at the bottom of white Southern society, they felt a powerlessness that had been unknown to them during prewar times.

Given these changes, the protests of postwar Southern constitutionalists only went so far. War had settled the slavery question, and things had already changed too much by 1868, after the demise of the black codes, for white Southerners to impose formal control over black labor. Any informal attempts at labor coercion emerged in an uneven and unorganized fashion, usually provoking stiff resistance from African Americans committed to maintaining a degree of autonomy. With the social structure of the white South already transformed by emancipation, Southern constitutionalists attempted not so much to deny black freedom as to control the contours of it—in other words, to restrict the scope and definition of black rights. White Southerners particularly took offense at the exercise of blacks' political rights: the rights to vote, serve on juries, and hold political office. Social rights—the opportunity to intermingle freely with whites—were even more to be dreaded. These expressions of black political and social equality embodied the great inversion that so repulsed white Southerners after emancipation. Thus, Southern constitutionalists specifically and purposefully attacked the basis for these rights—the Fourteenth and Fifteenth amendments—hoping to influence a Northern public that, during the 1870s, remained mostly uncertain about the efficacy of federal enforcement.

BLACK FREEDOM

Emancipation brought immediate and significant improvements in the lives of African Americans. From the first efforts at self-emancipation, beginning with a trickle in 1861 and turning into a flood by 1863, mobility marked the advent of black freedom. Migration allowed for the reuniting and solidifying of black families and kin groups, which in turn led to the consolidation of black churches and schools, while economic gains and access to courts soon followed. Although historians have made much of the role of black agency in bringing about emancipation during the war, they have downplayed the success of blacks' postwar efforts to create and sustain new lives for themselves beyond the gaze of their former masters. Nevertheless, blacks' activism and aspirations stretched well beyond Lee's surrender and proved crucial in the decades after the war.

Mobility was the most obvious and immediate consequence of freedom. Enslaved people in urban areas had always possessed some freedom of movement, but for the 75 percent of slaves who worked the land, the ability to move about became a sudden and significant sign of liberty. As Booker T. Washington later put it, "Most of the coloured people left the old plantation for a short while at least, so as to be sure, it seemed, that they could leave and try their freedom on to see how it felt."[7] Many former slaves, if they had not already done so during wartime, migrated from the country to the city. Between 1860 and 1870, the black populations of several Southern cities doubled or tripled, while a handful experienced even greater gains. The numbers of African Americans in Chattanooga, Memphis, and Vicksburg roughly quadrupled, for example, while Atlanta and Little Rock witnessed fivefold gains. Cities offered new opportunities and hope for a better life beyond the fields. Those who did not migrate to cities took to country roads—some traveling great distances—to reunite with family members, friends, or relatives on other farms or plantations. Despite occasional struggles to maintain their autonomy, it was mobility—the basic right of African Americans to pick up and move—more than any other consequence of emancipation that made freedom real. While small numbers chose to migrate to the North or West (or to Africa) during the decade or so after the war, countless blacks routinely moved within the South to seek out the best opportunities in the labor market. Far from being bound to postbellum landowners, rural African Americans exhibited a freedom of movement that contrasted starkly with their previous experiences under slavery.[8]

The opportunity to consolidate families was another critical component of freedom. Of course, family had played a crucial role in their lives under slavery, offering nurture and support to individuals upon whom unrelenting labor and daily degradation took a heavy toll. But slave marriages lacked legal standing, and slave families suffered under the strain of possible sale and separation. Freedom, in contrast, solidified the structure of the family. Slave marriages received recognition in a haphazard fashion, beginning in some contraband camps in 1864 and later through the efforts of the Freedman's Bureau and Southern state legislatures. In 1866, explaining to his troops the meaning of legal marriage, a black corporal in the US Colored Troops in Alexandria, Virginia, put it this way: "The Marriage Covenant is at the foundation of all our rights. In slavery we could not have *legalised* marriage: *now* we have it. Let us conduct ourselves worthy of such a blessing—and all the people will respect us—God will bless us, and we shall be established as a people."[9] By 1867, the former slave states uniformly recognized black marriage, and state laws typically declared, as an Alabama statute did, "that all marriages between freedmen and freedwomen, whether in a state of slavery, or since their emancipation . . . are hereby ratified and made valid."[10] Marriage offered institutional support to families, as well as new legal rights—involving property and inheritance, for example—to male heads of families. Within black households as well, relationships changed, as women and men attempted to redefine gender roles, often along traditional lines. In most instances after the war, women spent less time working in the fields and more time raising children, while men assumed the role of family head, negotiating agreements with landholders. Whether in rural or urban areas, moreover, black women shunned working in white homes as domestics, choosing instead to devote time to their own households. Once reunited, families often banded together into large kin groups, composed of extended family members and friends, as they worked out living arrangements and labor agreements. These kin groups often labored together in the fields, forming work squads that replaced the plantation gangs of the antebellum era and offered protection against hostile whites. Black family life thus experienced a significant transformation after the war as new domestic arrangements and labor patterns took shape.

Like the reconstituting of families, the formation of autonomous black churches emerged after emancipation. From the time of the Second Great Awakening, religious practice and belief had woven itself throughout the lives of enslaved African Americans, providing hope for this life and the next. Because slaves typically attended white churches, slaveholders had exerted a degree of control over the religious lives of their slaves. But freedom brought change. Although white-led biracial churches remained intact through 1865, emancipation precipitated a mass exodus of blacks out of these churches during the years 1866 to 1870. One study has shown that the number of black members in the Methodist Georgia Annual Conference, for example, fell from more than 27,000 in 1860 to just 1,504 by 1870, while the number of black Methodists in the Tennessee Conference dropped from more than 12,000 in 1860 to just 320 by 1870. White-led Baptist and Presbyterian churches witnessed similar declines in black membership. Having left these churches— often to the chagrin of whites, who attempted to retain as much control as possible over blacks' religious lives—African Americans formed their own congregations and denominational structures. This involved writing charters, acquiring land and erecting new houses of worship, and providing for the education and licensing of ministers. They usually did these things with the help and support of Northern missionaries, Freedman's Bureau agents, and, in some instances, members of the white churches that they had departed. During the late 1860s and early 1870s, a host of denominations took hold among the black faithful in the South. The Northern African Methodist Episcopal (AME) Church, formed in Philadelphia in 1816, proved the most successful in attracting Southern members. Other denominations—such as the African Methodist Episcopal Zion Church, founded in the North in 1821, and the Christian Methodist Episcopal (CME) Church, founded in Tennessee in 1870—also drew freedpeople to their congregations. In addition to swelling the ranks of new and established denominations, the overall numbers of black church members also increased. Between 1860 and 1877, the number of black Baptists in Georgia, for example, rose by three and a half times.[11] Autonomous black churches not only served the spiritual needs of their members but also emerged as the lifeblood of the black community by connecting a variety of institutions—fraternal societies, debating clubs, and political organizations, for example—through the bonds of kinship and faith.

Opportunities to build schools and enhance black education also flowed from freedom. Under slavery, few blacks possessed a chance to acquire even the most rudimentary education. State laws prohibiting the teaching of slaves to read, as well as widespread opposition to the idea among slaveholders, meant that only a tiny portion of the enslaved population attained literacy. During the war, as the process of emancipation unfolded, blacks started schools as soon as they could. In fall 1861, Mary Smith Peake, the daughter of a free black mother and English father, started teaching a group of blacks in Hampton, Virginia, at a contraband camp near Union-held Fortress Monroe, the origins of the first formal school for African Americans. Over the next few years, the Union army and the American Missionary Association began to educate freed slaves on a more systematic basis, and the Freedman's Bureau took on this responsibility after 1865. Although most blacks hungered for education and especially longed to read the Bible, the development of new schools, like churches, usually required white support. Lacking buildings, freedpeople and their white allies established schools wherever they could—often in churches—while Bureau officials, Northern missionaries, and black community leaders served as teachers. At the peak of its influence in 1869, the Freed-

African American children and adults gained new educational opportunities at freedmen's schools, such as this one at Edisto Island, South Carolina. Courtesy of the Library of Congress, LC-DIG-ppmsca-11194

man's Bureau reported the existence of 4,000 schools in the South (about 3,000 of them run directly by the Bureau), enrolling more than 250,000 students, including adults and children. Most were located in cities and towns. Even after reconstructed state governments established new taxes to create the first free public school systems in the Southern states, rural residents still had fewer educational opportunities than their counterparts in towns and cities. Nevertheless, available statistics show that by 1880, more than half of the black children in Mississippi were enrolled in school, while more than a third of children were enrolled in Georgia, Alabama, and South Carolina. Educational gains proceeded steadily. By 1880, in five states of the Deep South, the literacy rate for black children between the ages of ten and fourteen went from almost zero under slavery to nearly 26 percent. Viewed in this way, these were important advancements.[12]

The ability of African Americans to engage in an expanded range of economic opportunities proved another key consequence of freedom. In cities, particularly places such as Baltimore, Washington, Louisville, and St. Louis— places in the border states that emerged unscathed from the war—new jobs were plentiful. Enslaved and free black men and women in urban areas before the war had worked mostly as day laborers, dockhands, and laundresses, and many continued to do so, but a growing number of African Americans acquired new skills and took on new trades—as blacksmiths, brick masons, carpenters, coopers, mechanics, shoemakers, and small shopkeepers. A handful entered the professional class. Between the Civil War and 1877, forty-eight African Americans gained admission to the bar in South Carolina alone. Because whites who lived in cities and towns were much more likely than rural whites to sell real estate to blacks, African Americans in urban areas made significant gains in property ownership over a relatively short period of time. In the cities and towns of the Upper South and border states, total realty holdings by blacks nearly quadrupled between 1860 and 1870. And in the Deep South, during the same period, ownership of realty by blacks who lived in cities increased at a rate three and a half times that of rural blacks.[13] But even for those African Americans who resided in the countryside, emancipation brought expanded horizons and choices impossible under slavery. Taking advantage of their newfound mobility, blacks sought out the best labor and employment opportunities available to them. Sharecropping usually emerged as the best option that blacks could negotiate. A sort of compromise between the races, the system allowed white landowners to continue to control what crops would be grown while giving black laborers a sense of autonomy that they had never possessed. Given the choice between receiving wages for working in a large gang reminiscent of the days of slavery or cultivating a plot of land with one's own family and friends in exchange for half the crop, freedpeople almost always chose the latter. Not only did sharecropping give blacks the freedom to set the pace and schedule of their work but it also promised increased benefits depending on the size and quality of the crop produced. To most formerly enslaved people, who perhaps had never been allowed to reap the gains of their labor on anything more than a simple garden plot, sharecropping represented an increase in quality of life.

Blacks did not become wealthy, but they did experience a dramatic rise in wealth accumulation during the years after the war. Between 1860 and 1880, emancipation resulted in a 29 percent increase in the material income of blacks in the Deep South. Expanding fortunes manifested themselves in new consumption patterns, as most rural blacks made decisions about what to consume for the first times in their lives. In addition to constructing new or enlarged dwellings and buying new items of clothing, African Americans mostly purchased pieces of personal property that helped them carry out their work (horses, mules, wagons, plows, tools), as well as occasional luxury items (watches, jewelry, hams, cheese, candy). Over time, some rural blacks, as one scholar puts it, "by hard work, thrift, and good luck," even succeeded in accumulating land. By 1880, about one-fifth of black farmers owned their own farms.[14] To be sure, the political failure of land reform at the national level meant that no formal redistribution of land ever took place in the postwar South. Still, while the former slaveholding states did not transition to a completely free labor society in the way that some congressional Republicans might have hoped or envisioned—levels of indebtedness for blacks remained high—the South's postwar economic order did allow for gains and choices unknown under slavery.

Not only did blacks experience economic progress and opportunity but they also often succeeded in securing and protecting their contractual rights—their civil rights—in court. During the years after emancipation, African American litigants brought hundreds of civil cases into local courts. By hiring attorneys and testifying before juries, they demonstrated both their determination to assert their rights and their faith in the court system. Appealing to legal precedent, African American litigants often earned the support of white judges, witnesses, and jurors. In fact, in cases on appeal to Southern state supreme courts involving everyday economic concerns—contracts, wills, transactions, and personal injuries—African Americans usually won their claims. Between 1865 and 1877, in civil cases between white and black litigants in state supreme courts, blacks were victorious in 69 of 108 cases, a success rate of 64 percent.[15] This remarkable transformation in the status of African Americans played itself out in lives and legal disputes all over the former slave states. In Kentucky, for example, freedman Stephen Jackson relied on the Civil Rights Act of 1866 to sue for wages that his employer had refused to pay him after emancipation for nearly a year of labor, planting corn and raising hogs. The jury found for Jackson, ruling that his employer had to pay the promised wages, plus damages. This change in status, from owned property to empowered citizen, proved transformative in the lives of African Americans all over the South.

All of these manifestations of black freedom—mobility, family life, religious expression, educational pursuits, economic gains, contractual rights—took hold by 1868, and none relied explicitly on the Fourteenth or Fifteenth amendments for its existence or protection. These fundamental yet far-reaching rights had issued from the simple reality of emancipation, supported by the presence of federal troops, Freedman's Bureau officials, Northern missionaries—and, on some level, a widespread, grudging acknowledgment among white Southerners that they had lost the war and that those whom they had previously held as slaves had attained the status of free people in a new federal Union. Only the right to enter into contracts, which was specifically guaranteed under the Civil Rights Act of 1866, existed on paper. The other rights associated with black freedom might be considered to have issued from the fact of no longer being held as slaves—rights that, if they held any formal basis in American law or tradition, came from the Thirteenth Amendment or perhaps from the Declaration of Independence, as Abraham Lincoln and other Republicans had understood it. In other words, regardless of the protests of white Southerners about the illegitimacy of the Fourteenth and Fifteenth amendments and apart from whether the federal government continued to enforce these amendments, a profound revolution had already taken place on the ground in the South—a revolution in the lived experience of African Americans. Black civil rights, as opposed to black political rights, already seemed secure.

BLACK POLITICS

In another transformative realm of black life after emancipation—the realm of black politics—gains were less stable. Under slavery, Southern black political life appeared nonexistent and manifested itself mostly beneath the surface—in subtle resistance, stealth missions, and secret whispers. But war and emancipation unleashed the pent-up political aspirations of formerly enslaved African Americans, and public petitions, speeches, and conventions during and immediately after the war paved the way for the fruits of congressional reconstruction: voting, jury service, and officeholding. As blacks engaged in formal political activity, they worked hard to implement the vision that black constitutionalists had described from the beginnings of the republic—full equality under the law.

The Union League (or Loyal League) played the most important role in organizing black political participation during the years after emancipation. Growing out of a network of Northern organizations formed during the war to rally support for the Lincoln administration, the Union League gradually spread across the Southern landscape, first attracting white Unionists in federally held portions of the South and then, after the enactment of the Military Reconstruction acts, drawing African Americans into the fold. Union military veterans, Northern political activists, die-hard Southern Unionists, and black ministers all carried out the work of organizing individual chapters of the League—work that, depending on the demographic makeup and political sympathies of the local population, could be dangerous. In some areas, where blacks accounted for an especially small or large portion of the population, the Union League usually operated in the open with little difficulty. But in most of the South, where the number of blacks hovered somewhere between one-third and two-thirds of the population and thus stood on a relatively equal footing with whites, the Union League operated in secret, its members relying on word of mouth to announce meetings and gathering at night in inconspicuous places. Restricting its membership to men twenty-one years of age or older, the Union League mobilized massive numbers of blacks across the South to vote for Republican Party candidates for local and national office.

More than mobilizing voters, the Union League sought to educate newly enfranchised blacks in their civic duties and political rights. Rallying around a number of symbols, including the flag of the United States, the Declaration of Independence, and the Constitution, the League devoted its meetings to teaching black men about recent American political history, the amendments and federal laws enacted during reconstruction, and the basics of the process of voting. Civic education blended seamlessly with partisan appeal, as the League always conveyed the message that only Republicans cared to protect the precious liberties of the American constitutional heritage. One of the particularly widespread and effective methods of the Union League's efforts involved a scripted dialogue between "a newly enfranchised freedman and a sound Radical Republican." In the dialogue, read throughout the South in 1867 and 1868—often by two leaders playing the respective parts—African Americans learned, for example, that a Democrat was "a member of that party which before the rebellion sustained every legislative act demanded by the slaveholders, such as the Fugitive Slave Law." The dialogue also advised African American voters who faced economic reprisals from whites to vote regardless of any threats against them. "Had you not rather suffer, or even starve to death," the sound Radical Republican advised, "than to aid a party to re-enslave you?"[16] Henry McNeal Turner, the wartime Union chaplain and postwar African Methodist Episcopal Church leader, lauded the power of the dialogue when he read it with fellow black political organizer Tunis Campbell in Georgia in 1867. "You ought to have seen the effect which it produced," Turner later reported to Republican officials. "When Campbell would read some of those pointed replies, the whole house would ring with shouts, and shake with the spasmodic motions and peculiar gestures of the audience."[17]

Voting, the most important expression of black political activity, embodied the revolutionary nature of reconstruction-era politics. Because casting ballots during the nineteenth century was a public act, susceptible to intimidation and fraud, organizational and educational efforts played a key role in the voting process. At the time, party organizers printed and distributed their own tickets, which served as ballots. The tickets, usually colored in a way to make them easily identifiable to illiterate voters, listed all of the names of the

This chromolithograph from 1883 depicts "Heroes of the Colored Race," including Frederick Douglass in the center, flanked by Mississippi's two black senators during reconstruction, Blanche K. Bruce (left) and Hiram Revels. Voting and officeholding remained the most visible signs of black progress during the 1870s and 1880s. Courtesy of the Library of Congress, LC-DIG-pga-01619

candidates affiliated with a particular party. With a finite number of printed tickets, distributors attempted to keep control of the distribution process and prevent tickets from ending up in the hands of their opponents. After distributing tickets and mobilizing voters, party organizers offered instructions on proper procedures, after which the group typically marched or paraded together to the polling place, often with banners aloft and in military-style formation. Polling places located at black institutions, such as AME churches or schoolhouses, offered a safe space for the practice of black politics, but those in more isolated areas, such as plantation houses or country stores, could prove less welcoming. After voting—by placing the party ticket in the ballot box—men would often remain at the polling place for the rest of the day, to drink, cajole, and harass each other, celebrating the election holiday as well as the expression of democracy. Voting together offered safety and support while also helping to enforce party discipline. Although Democrats made a serious play for black votes in some areas, the overwhelming majority of African

Americans voted the Republican ticket. Formally excluded from voting, women often took a supporting role in the process. Across the postwar South, determined black women marched with their husbands to the polls and threatened to leave them if they failed to vote for the Republicans. "It was only through the Republican party and the principles of that party," J. Henri Burch, a freeborn black Louisianan later explained in testimony before the Senate, "that [black women] could secure homes for themselves and educational advantages for their children, and protection in all rights accorded to them by the Constitution of the nation."[18]

Jury service was another expression of black political power. A prized responsibility with a deep history in the Anglo-American constitutional tradition, jury service, for African Americans, emerged in an uneven fashion in the former Confederacy. In 1867, a series of military orders issued by district commanders prohibited racial discrimination in the juror selection process, and when reconstructed governments formed, a handful of Southern states quickly moved to enshrine the principle of nondiscrimination. In 1868 and 1869, Tennessee, Louisiana, and South Carolina's legislatures all passed laws explicitly prohibiting discrimination in jury selection, and Congress enacted similar legislation for Washington, DC. Other states included blacks in jury pools without ever legislating on the matter. During the early 1870s, African Americans served on hundreds of juries in Southern states in federal cases involving the Enforcement acts, helping to indict and convict white offenders, but not until the Civil Rights Act of 1875 did the principle of nondiscrimination in jury selection enter federal law.[19] Blacks viewed the right to serve on a jury as the only way to ensure the fair administration of justice and to protect their liberties against those who, in the words of a group of Tennessee blacks, "have been taught from the cradle to the jury box, that the negro is naturally inferior to them."[20] Because of its close connection to voting—juror pools frequently came from voting lists—African Americans considered jury service an important civic obligation and a significant expression of political power.

Officeholding by African Americans represented the pinnacle of black politics. Although guaranteed as a right neither in federal law nor in the reconstruction amendments, blacks held political positions in every state of the former Confederacy plus Missouri. While it is impossible to know a precise number, one scholar estimates that between 1865 and 1877, some 2,000 African Americans held elective or appointive office in the South. About 99 percent were Republicans. Roughly half of all officeholders probably came from the ranks of the freeborn, and for those for whom information can be verified, nearly 83 percent of officeholders were literate. The most common occupation was farmer, but large numbers of ministers, carpenters, laborers, teachers, and storekeepers also held office. Many started their political careers in the constitutional conventions of 1868. Relatively few, of course, attained high offices: Mississippi sent two African Americans to the US Senate (Hiram Revels and Blanche Bruce), another fourteen black men won election to the US House of Representatives, and one African American (P. B. S. Pinchback) served for about a month as acting governor of Louisiana. Scores of blacks held some sort of office with statewide authority—ranging from land commission member to lieutenant governor—while one African American served as a member of a state supreme court.[21] Hundreds of others served in state legislatures.

State legislators and local officials perhaps held the greatest potential to champion the interests of African Americans. Working with fellow Republicans, black members of reconstructed state legislatures helped enact important legislation establishing public education systems (provided for in most of the 1868 constitutions), as well as relief for the poor and disadvantaged, including funding for hospitals, reform-minded penitentiaries, and orphan and insane asylums. While African American legislators generally viewed government in positive terms—as a way to curtail some of the power and advantage held by white landowning elites—black lawmakers neither voted as a bloc on every issue nor held a uniform outlook on how to solve society's problems. Divisions between freeborn blacks and less educated freedmen often came to the surface. Religious beliefs, middle-class aspirations, and connections to white patrons, moreover, often served to restrain black radicalism, as did the need for compromise and conciliation in the lawmaking and political process. Local officials at times proved more effective at bringing about change, at least in their own communities. In McIntosh County, Georgia, for example, Tunis Campbell, a charismatic, New Jersey–born African American, used his position as justice of the peace during the 1870s to build a political machine that consistently afflicted the powerful and uplifted the lowly.

Outside of the formal arena of law and politics, grassroots protest constituted a unique form of black political expression. Beginning with the advent of military reconstruction in 1867, African Americans instigated a host of everyday challenges to the status quo, particularly the custom of racial exclusion or segregation on Southern streetcars, railroads, and steamboats. In March 1867, for example, a large group of African Americans who had just left a political meeting crowded onto streetcars in Charleston, demanding service. When the drivers and conductors refused to operate the cars, protesters responded by "placing stones on the track" and threatening violence, although police and federal soldiers defused the crisis.[22] In New Orleans, black residents succeeded in ending the practice of segregation on the city's streetcar system after their repeated protests prompted General Philip Sheridan in May 1867 to issue a military order to that effect. Similar campaigns in Richmond, Mobile, and Nashville resulted in at least partial success in ending segregation in street-cars. In Washington, DC, in February 1868, the case of Kate Brown, a black woman employed at the US Capitol, became a cause célèbre after local author-ities in Alexandria, Virginia, assaulted and forcibly removed her from a white railroad car. Outraged senators convened a formal committee investigation into the matter, and the injured Brown successfully sued the railroad company for $1,500, a judgment later upheld by the US Supreme Court. Such politi-cal challenges to white supremacy led some state legislatures to debate laws forbidding racial discrimination in public accommodations. Only a handful of states—Texas, Mississippi, Louisiana, Florida, and South Carolina—actually did so, for discussion over such legislation proved divisive among Republi-cans. One white South Carolina legislator summed up the problem. If such legislation passed, "I am no long with the party," he declared. "I am willing to give the Negro political and civil rights, but social equality, never."[23] Black protests against the status quo in social life, in other words, crossed a bound-ary that few white Republicans were willing to accept.

Political activity during the reconstruction era represented the pinnacle of black constitutionalism. From the early days of the republic, black antislavery activists had championed their own version of the meaning of the American founding. Uniformly idealist, they had combined the principle of equality inherent in the Declaration of Independence, the notion that the Constitu-tion referred to slaves as "persons" rather than property, and the ideal of Christian brotherhood under the fatherhood of God into a powerful, com-prehensive critique of both slavery and white supremacy. During the recon-struction era, this notion reached its fullest expression, as emancipation and the Thirteenth Amendment flowed into the Fourteenth and Fifteenth amend-ments. For African Americans, this was precisely what they had always hoped for. In their minds, the end of slavery was part and parcel of the breaking down of all legal barriers to equality and the advancement of all forms of rights—civil, political, and social. Thus, during the reconstruction era, black freedom and black politics intersected and sustained each other. Without the concomitants of black freedom—particularly the solidification of families and churches—there could not have been black political activity, and without black political activity, certain aspects of black freedom, such as economic advance-ment and access to courts, could not have flourished.

Still, while some historians define nearly every aspect of black life during this period as holding political meaning, it is useful to make a distinction between black freedom and black politics because of the different ideas they evoked in the minds of white Southerners. On the nineteenth-century continuum of rights, civil rights seemed the most basic to human experience. These were the first actions taken by blacks and the first fruits of freedom; they were the easiest, relatively speaking, for Southern whites to accept, as they seemingly had the least effect on the lives of whites. Black politics, though, rested on a different set of assumptions. Voting, serving on a jury, holding political office, or engaging in political protest placed blacks on a level of equality with whites in the public sphere and made possible an inversion in everyday life—the possibility that blacks could exercise direct formal power over whites—that few white Southerners could swallow. The expression of black political rights, moreover, seemed to flow inevitably and dangerously toward social rights and social equality, an even more frightful prospect, even among white Republicans. In short, African Americans defined freedom from bondage as opening up to them the entire panoply of rights—civil, political, and social. White Southerners, though resigning themselves to the first, would consistently—and brutally—contest the latter two.

WHITE RESISTANCE

While ex-Confederate elites such as former vice president Stephens devoted their attention to writing constitutional treatises against the reconstruction amendments, other white Southerners engaged in a protracted campaign of violent resistance. Between 1867 and 1877, more than 3,000 African Americans and white Southern Republicans died at the hands of those who engaged in political terrorism throughout the states of the former Confederacy. Although in 1865 Confederates had agreed on the need to lay down their arms and rejoin the Union, an informal resistance, composed mostly of ex-Rebel soldiers, engaged in relentless violence in the years after the passage of the Military Reconstruction Act. They aimed not to restart the war, reignite the secession movement, or even reimpose slavery. Rather, white Southerners engaged in these horrific acts of violence in order to thwart black political participation, undermine reconstructed governments, and prevent the imposition of social equality. The notion of a "white man's government" had not only served for decades as an article of faith among the nation's Democrats but also had sunk deeply into the consciousness of white Southerners. To be sure, whites also resisted expressions of black freedom, or black civil rights. Some burned black churches and schools, hindered black economic advancement, or testified against blacks in court. But it was black voting, jury service, and office-holding that provoked the most intense and widespread response—and that

"HALT"

Violence remained a fact of life in parts of the South during the early 1870s, especially Louisiana, the subject of this 1874 Thomas Nast cartoon. The drawing shows a member of the White League trampling a wounded black man while a female figure of Justice wielding the sword of federal enforcement fights back. Courtesy of the Library of Congress, LC-USZ62-55605 lay behind the vast majority of the acts of terror carried out by whites during the decade or so after the war. In engaging in or supporting such acts, most white Southerners during reconstruction abandoned the habits and culture of American constitutionalism and instead embraced violence.

A number of different organizations engaged in acts of terror. The Ku Klux Klan, founded by six young Confederate veterans in Pulaski, Tennessee, in 1866, began as a fraternal society, but within a year or so it had evolved into an organization to intimidate and harass African Americans in Tennessee during the governorship of Republican William Brownlow. By the election season of 1868, the Klan and its methods spread haphazardly to other states as reconstructed governments took shape. Small bands of disguised men gathered at night, perhaps set out an informal plan of action, and then rode to the homes of those whom they decided to target. Beatings, pistol whippings, and sometimes murder soon followed. Although their secretive practices make it difficult to know precisely who joined, one study of Alabama Klansmen identifies members as the "downwardly mobile sons of middling slaveholders," those who had lost relatively large sums of property—slave property—after emancipation.[24] Over time, a host of vigilante organizations formed, and, depending on the circumstances, frequently operated in the open. The Knights of the White Camellia and White Leagues terrorized blacks in Louisiana, while in Mississippi it was the White Liners and in the South Carolina the Red Shirts. Other groups in other places—known as Democratic clubs, Rifle clubs, and the like—shared the same general purpose: to wreak havoc in the lives of African Americans, particularly black voters and political organizers, so as to restore Democratic Party control. Areas of greatest Union League activity witnessed the most outrages, and black officeholders were frequent targets. Relative to the entire population, only a small segment of white Southerners actually participated in vigilante activity, but even if some Southerners frowned upon the methods used by such groups, they did little, if anything, to stop the violence. In most parts of the South, for example, federal authorities had a hard time finding white jurors who would indict or convict white Southerners accused of perpetrating violence. This reality, among other factors, hindered federal enforcement efforts.

In most instances, the general population of white Southerners willingly aided and abetted the perpetrators of violent acts because they shared the same white supremacist assumptions. Some elites spoke of peaceful resistance while at the same time tipping their hands enough to show that violent night riders had their tacit support. "We do not mean to threaten resistance by arms. But the white people of our State will never quietly submit to negro rule. We may have to pass under the yoke you have authorized, but . . . by every peaceful means left us, we will keep up this contest until we have regained the heritage of political control handed down to us by an honored ancestry," proclaimed a group of respected white South Carolinians in 1868 in response to that state's constitutional convention. "This is a duty we owe to the land that is ours, to the graves that it contains, and to the race of which you and we are alike members—the proud Caucasian race, whose sovereignty on earth God has ordained." The ideology of white supremacy, so thoroughly developed during the antebellum era through the writings of proslavery theorists, remained the central tenet of the defeated South. Even if blacks were now free, they did not, in the eyes of whites, possess the capabilities of voting and governing. The same group of South Carolinians made this very distinction, arguing that emancipation gave blacks "all that the American Declaration of Independence and the English *Magna Charta* claim for man as his inalienable rights," but that these rights did not include suffrage. "This is not a political right nor a civil one for man, either white or black," they argued, offering their own definition of voting, "but it is a *trust*, a delicate trust, to be conferred by the State upon the people thereof."[25] For some Southern elites, who had even opposed universal white suffrage during the antebellum era, black voting was simply too much to bear.

Violent white supremacists, as well as the majority of Southerners who supported them, moreover, linked the ballot box to the bedroom. Most Southern whites possessed a fanatical fear that black political rights would lead inevitably to social equality—the idea that blacks and whites would interact freely in public spaces and that blacks would gain access to the private spaces of domestic life. Social equality meant racial "amalgamation" or "comingling," terms that white Southerners used to refer to miscegenation, or interracial sexual relationships. The black codes of 1865 had all included antimiscegenation provisions, and when the constitutional conventions of 1868 convened, conservative delegates in several states made the argument that voting would be but the first step down a dangerous path. The Arkansas Constitutional Convention of 1868, for example, spent more than two days engaged in a debate over miscegenation as conservative delegates expressed their fears in no uncertain terms. "In enfranchising the negro, you make him your political and social equal. It is to invite him into your house, and make him the companion of your social hours. . . . If he should be enfranchised, he would be taken into the parlors of all that vote for him—to marry their daughters, and, if necessary, hug their wives!"[26] Although Arkansas delegates finally agreed not to include an antimiscegenation provision in the 1868 constitution, the frightful connections between black politics and black sexuality remained present in the minds of most white Southerners throughout the reconstruction era. While most blacks argued for no more than seats on street-cars and trains, most whites seemed convinced that black motivations actually went well beyond equality on common carriers.

Motivated by these tenets of white supremacy, violence against African Americans shaped the contours of Southern politics during the 1870s. Because of the constant threats and the fear they produced among voters and office-holders, Republican-led Southern state governments relied on state militias (composed mostly of blacks) and federal intervention to remain in power, a fact that further damaged their legitimacy in the eyes of white Southerners, who became increasingly and overwhelmingly united over time under the ban-ner of the Democratic Party. Increased factionalism among Republicans only aided the Democrats' strategy of drawing the color line between the parties. As the Grant administration became paralyzed over how to deal with the Southern question, particularly after 1873, Democrats gradually regained power in states that had been subject to military reconstruction, in several states winning control of the governorship and both houses of the legislature: Georgia in 1871, followed by Texas and Virginia in 1873, Alabama and Arkansas in 1874, and Mississippi in 1875. Throughout the South, terror cam-paigns worked hand in hand with political campaigns as white Southerners engaged in violence, all the while seeking the appearance of stability and legit-imacy through formal elections. Although terror intimidated black voters, in most places it did not prevent them from casting their votes. Increased Demo-cratic votes, owing to white appeals for racial unity in party politics, usually made the difference in elections, while the overall number of Republican votes remained mostly consistent with those in previous elections. In Arkansas and Alabama, once Democrats regained political power, they drafted new consti-tutions to solidify their legitimacy, as well as to roll back some of the reforms of their Republican predecessors. White Democrats referred to this retaking of control of their political destinies as "redemption," a term with religious overtones that conveyed the significance that they attributed to this shift in power. Where Republicans continued to hold power, such as in South Car-olina, violence continued unabated. In July 1876, a fracas in the village of Hamburg, South Carolina, where African Americans controlled local affairs, left six dead and scores wounded. While constitutionalism remained an arti-cle of faith among most African Americans, the majority of whites accepted violence as a political tool.[27]

Some historians have styled white resistance an "insurgency," but it is again important to remember what violence did not aim to accomplish.[28] Vigilantes never intended to rekindle the secession movement. Nor did vigilantes intend to reimpose slavery, the root cause of the secession movement. Violent resistance, rather than aiming to continue the war or its aims, therefore, intended instead to overthrow the political order that the Republican Congress had established in the defeated South—a political order based on the establishment of blacks' political rights and, whites feared, their social rights as well. In other words, Southern violence attempted to overthrow "Negro rule"— the reconstructed governments formed at the state level—and resist the constitutional amendments, at the national level, that followed. In this way, the aims and actions of Southern constitutionalists and Southern vigilantes went hand in hand. The Stephens brothers laid out the doctrinal case against the Fourteenth and Fifteenth amendments, while white vigilantes carried out the bloody work of threats and murder that served the same cause. Both engaged not in an insurgency to carry on the Confederate rebellion but in a counter-revolutionary movement to blunt the war's effects.

SOCIAL CHANGE AND CONSTITUTIONALISM IN THE POSTWAR NORTH

As the South underwent a host of changes during the decade after military reconstruction, the North witnessed its own series of transformations. Economic growth continued as new business corporations and railroad lines stretched across the country, while urbanization and immigration occurred at a rapid pace. Industrial development widened the gap between the poor and the wealthy, thus sharpening identity based on class. All of this contributed to declining political interest in enforcing the rights that Congress and the president had pushed for during the peak of postwar revolutionary reconstruction. Still, the reconstruction amendments were not repealed. And constitutionalism—including a commitment to upholding the rule of law and to the protection of those rights spelled out in these amendments—remained an important part of Northern political culture.

Between 1865 and 1873, war unleashed the forces of economic growth and industrial development. Wartime mobilization had brought about huge growth in the manufacturing of weapons, leather goods, iron, and textiles, while federal policy had produced only moderate gains in inflation. After the war, the rise of business corporations further abetted the growth of industry. In contrast to the individual proprietorships that marked the antebellum era, corporations allowed individuals to limit both their investment and their risk in an economic enterprise, thus facilitating access to capital. The consolidation and growth of the railroads best exemplified this shift to the corporate form, as large public companies, such as the Pennsylvania Railroad, swallowed up smaller operations. Sustained development of railroad lines ensued, symbolized by the historic completion of a transcontinental line. Between the end of the war and the beginning of the Panic of 1873, railroad companies laid a total of 35,000 miles of track, a figure that exceeded the nation's entire railway network in 1860. They did so with the active assistance of the federal government, which offered generous allotments of land to rail companies along the lines that they established. In addition to the growth of railroads, new technology in the production of steel and new inventions during and after the war—such as the rapid-fire Gatling gun, the typewriter, and barbed wire—caused industrial production to increase by 75 percent.

Much of the North's economic development occurred in cities, which expanded at a rapid pace. Between 1860 and 1880, the urban population as a proportion of the total population in the Northeast went from 36 percent to more than 50 percent, while in the Midwest it went from about 14 percent to more than 24 percent. (By comparison, during the same twenty-year period, the South's urban population went from 10 percent to 12 percent.) The established East Coast metropolises of New York, Boston, and Philadelphia remained among the most important cities in the nation, but the rise of other urban areas reflected the country's expanded rail network, burgeoning industries, and westward population shifts. Already a major rail hub before the war, Cincinnati gained new railroads and residents after the war, growing by 56 percent between 1860 and 1880, as the iron and meatpacking industries developed. Cleveland sprang on the scene, nearly quadrupling in population between 1860 and 1880. The iron, steel, and machine tool industries turned the city into a major manufacturing center, making it, by 1880, the tenth largest urban area in the country. More than any other city, Chicago epitomized the North's postwar growth. Despite the great fire that destroyed much of the central business district in 1871, the city went from about 112,000 residents in 1860, the ninth largest in America, to the third largest city by 1880, home to more than 500,000 people and a vital center for manufacturing, trade, and transportation. As had been the case before the war, immigrants fueled a good part of the North's urban growth, as nearly five million people entered the country between 1860 and 1880, a significant plurality of them from Germany and the overwhelming majority from Northern and Western Europe. Most settled in the Mid-Atlantic region or the Midwest.

Northern-style industrialization and urbanization, moreover, also occurred in the trans-Mississippi West as the frontier became a vital part of America's postwar economic order. Wartime policies had initiated Western development. The Homestead Act of 1862 offered incentives for the settlement and improvement of new lands, while the Pacific Railway Act, enacted the same

Table 11.1. Population of the Ten Largest US Cities, 1880

Rank	City	Population
1	New York City, NY[a]	1,772,962
2	Philadelphia, PA	847,170
3	Chicago, IL	503,185
4	Boston, MA	362,839
5	St. Louis, MO	350,518
6	Baltimore, MD	332,313
7	Cincinnati, OH	255,139
8	San Francisco, CA	233,959
9	New Orleans, LA	216,090
10	Cleveland, OH	160,146

[a]Some census information lists New York City and Brooklyn as separate entities, with New York City's population at 1,206,299 and Brooklyn's population at 566,663. Here the two are combined.

Source: US Bureau of the Census (https://www.census.gov/population/www/documentation/twps0027/tab11.txt).

year, granted private companies the right of way to build a transcontinental railroad. Homesteading and railroading thus worked hand in hand, pulling and pushing white settlers further West, as they relied on the federal government to drive away Native Americans, thus allowing for the establishment of farms and towns. In other parts of the West, the mining and timber industries took hold, as Eastern corporations extended their reach in order to secure and extract the raw materials required for industrial production. New technologies led to the expansion of coal, iron, and silver mining operations, while logging camps and sawmills emerged as an important part of the region's economy. Urbanization followed. When completed in 1869, the transcontinental railroad linked San Francisco to Eastern metropolises and markets, spurring a transformation of the antebellum gold rush town into a major city of nearly a quarter million residents by 1880, the eighth most populous city in the country. At the same time, Kansas City and Denver, mere frontier outposts before the war, became thriving cities. Kansas City, with more than 50,000 residents, surpassed more established places such as Syracuse and Charleston, while Denver, with more than 35,000 people, suddenly topped Memphis and Savannah. By 1880, more than 30 percent of Westerners lived in cities. If the South still lagged behind, the West followed the development pattern of the North.

Industrial and urban growth changed how Northerners thought about society, class, and political economy. During the antebellum era, an optimistic free labor ideology held that hard work would allow small producers and day laborers to become autonomous owners and managers, who would steadily climb the ladder of wealth and success. Postwar industrialization, though, brought a new perspective that emphasized conflict and division. Increased mechanization meant that workers needed fewer skills and could be easily replaced. Such workers, employed at low wages, were skeptical of the free labor vision of a harmonious economy in which hard work led to success. As urban industrial workers began conceiving of their interests as distinct from those of owners and managers, a nascent class-consciousness and labor movement emerged. In August 1866, the first congress of the National Labor Union drew 60,000 people, and three years later, a more lasting national coalition of workers, the Knights of Labor, formed. Both groups admitted black members. Workers' conception of the adversarial relations between "labor and capital" affected politics, as Republicans began to split between those who saw the struggle of workingmen as part of the larger movement for equality and those who felt threatened by labor's attempts to organize, strike, and make demands. Economic growth, class antagonism, and fear that African American laborers would ally with white workers to threaten private property all affected the Northern political environment during the mid-1870s, as Grant's reconstruction policy went from aggressive enforcement to selective intervention.

By the mid-1870s, white Northerners clearly held mixed feeling about federal enforcement efforts in the former Confederacy. Northern Democrats and even many Republicans had come to see, by 1876, the problems, perils, and public expense associated with using military force to protect black political rights. Having supported a war to preserve the Union that had turned into a war to end slavery, most Northerners believed that abolition itself constituted an historic triumph. They had largely accepted, moreover, the idea that the protecting black civil rights and political rights advanced American constitutional principles and prevented the spirit of rebellion from rearing its head again in the South. But most Republicans had not accepted the black constitutionalist vision, which combined the belief in a vigorous national government with a commitment to the idea that "all men were created equal." Still, Republicans were not ready to eviscerate the constitutional amendments that many of them had worked so hard to pass. The drafting and ratifying of the Fourteenth and Fifteenth amendments had consumed three years, during which time Northern Republicans at both the national and state levels had nearly unanimously agreed that guaranteeing citizenship, equal protection, due process, and the right to vote were essential elements of a national plan to reconstruct the Union, empower the formerly enslaved, and protect social and economic gains associated with black freedom. They certainly had not abandoned altogether the idea of upholding the nation's law and Constitution. In other words, constitutionalism—perhaps more than the notion of racial equality—remained a compelling concept among Northerners. And although some African American activists expressed frustration with what they viewed, by the mid-1870s, as an inconsistent policy of federal intervention, neither had they given up on their allies in the party of Lincoln.

THE ELECTION OF 1876

The presidential campaign of 1876 occurred against the backdrop of all of these changes: a postwar Southern society that bore witness to the realities of black freedom, a dramatic expansion of the political rights of Southern blacks, a violent resistance to the exercise of that political power among Southern whites, and an increasingly industrial North and West that appeared less willing to support federal intervention in Southern affairs. When President Grant declined to run for a third term, the Republican Party, after a contentious convention, settled on Rutherford B. Hayes as its nominee. A native of Ohio, Hayes had studied at Harvard Law School, defended runaway slaves in antebellum courtrooms, and joined the Republican Party in the late 1850s. Although initially inclined to let the South go when it seceded, the Confederate attack on Fort Sumter infuriated him, and in 1861 he was commissioned in the Ohio Volunteer Infantry and eventually wounded five times (once seriously) in battle. After the war, he won election to Congress, and he fully supported the Radical Republican program for reconstructing the South. At the Republican convention in the summer of 1876, Hayes emerged as a dark horse candidate, known for advocating reform in government. Republicans believed that Hayes's nomination offered the best hope of reuniting the party and defeating the Democrats. On the heels of securing control of the House of Representatives in 1874, the Democratic Party nominated Governor Samuel J. Tilden of New York. A native New Yorker, the young Tilden pursued Democratic politics with a passion while earning wealth and status as a railroad lawyer. During the war, he was a Regular Democrat—he supported the Union war effort but opposed the centralization of government and emancipation of slavery that ensued, while also opposing the antiwar extremism represented by Clement Vallandigham and his ally, New York City mayor Fernando Wood. After the war, Tilden moved onto the national stage when he managed Horace Greeley's presidential campaign in 1868 and subsequently fought New York City's corrupt Tweed Ring. Elected as a reform governor

President Rutherford B. Hayes won the contested presidential election of 1876, in which the South remained a key campaign issue. Courtesy of the Library of Congress, LC-DIG-cwpbh-05109

of New York in 1874, Tilden seemed to offer the Democrats their best chance of winning a presidential election in two decades.

While the parties emphasized different themes, the future of the South remained the most compelling issue on the national agenda, eleven years after the end of the war. Hayes and the Republicans hoped to employ a similar strategy as they had in 1872, "waving the bloody shirt" in order to arouse memories of the war and rally the Republican troops. The Republican Party platform echoed these sentiments, as it denounced the Democratic Party as "being the same in character and spirt as when it sympathized with treason."[29] But apart from political rhetoric intended to mobilize Northern voters, Hayes and the Republicans offered principled support for the protection of the rights of African Americans. In a public letter issued after his nomination, Hayes's stance appeared indistinguishable from Grant's. "All of the parts of the Constitution are sacred and must be sacredly observed—the parts that are new no less than the parts that are old," Hayes wrote. "The moral and national prosperity of the Southern States can be most effectually advanced by a hearty and generous recognition of the rights of all, by all—a recognition without reserve or exception." Still, Hayes offered implicit support for those who criticized reconstructed governments as corrupt and illegitimate, arguing that "an intelligent and honest administration of government" was a necessity in the South.[30] Tilden and the Democrats, meanwhile, emphasized the reform issue. In doing so, they attempted not only to combat the caricature of themselves as belonging to the party of the rebellion but also to link reform to the idea of ending federal intervention in the South. The Democratic Party platform criticized what it called a "corrupt centralism which, after inflicting upon ten States the rapacity of carpet-bag tyrannies, has honeycombed the offices of the Federal Government itself with incapacity, waste and fraud."[31] African Americans, concerned by Republican ambivalence about upholding their political rights in the Southern states but more disturbed by what a Democratic victory might mean, eventually fell in line behind Hayes.

Violence and corruption ultimately drove the election toward dispute and crisis. In October 1876, three weeks before Election Day, violence in South Carolina prompted President Grant to again send troops to keep order to maintain the Republican government of that state. Meanwhile, in the other two ex-Confederate states where Republicans remained in power—Louisiana and Florida—Democratic rifle clubs threatened blacks to deter them from voting. But much more powerful were white appeals to racial solidarity, and in each of these three states, white Democratic turnout increased substantially. Throughout the country as a whole, the election witnessed the largest voter turnout in American history, nearly 82 percent. When the voters were counted on the night of November 7, the results seemed to point to a Tilden victory. The Democrat received a majority of the votes cast, by a margin of more than 255,000 votes. He swept every one of the former slaveholding states that had fallen back into Democratic hands, plus New York, New Jersey, West Virginia, and—somewhat surprisingly—Indiana and Connecticut. Hayes took Republican strongholds in the Midwest, New England, and West, including the three electoral votes of Colorado, which had just been admitted to statehood a few months before. In South Carolina, Louisiana, and Florida, where Republicans still controlled the state government, the results were in dispute. The Republican-run election returning boards in each of the three states decided that Hayes had won all three—and thus the election—but Democrats charged that fraud and corruption had tainted the returns. To be sure, both sides had engaged in fraudulent activity. Democrats had stuffed ballot boxes in South Carolina and stolen black votes in Florida, while Republicans had used the levers of power to discount the returns from certain parishes in order to hold Louisiana. Having won 184 electoral votes, one shy of the necessary 185,

Table 11.2. Presidential Election of 1876

Candidate	Party	Electoral Votes	Percent of Popular Vote
Rutherford B. Hayes	Republican	185	48
Samuel Tilden	Democratic	184	51

Tilden hoped to win one of the disputed states. Hayes would need to hold all three states in order to earn 185.

The Senate needed to certify the returns, but when presidential electors from both parties claimed to represent Florida, Louisiana, South Carolina, and Oregon (where the status of one elector was in doubt), Congress passed legislation forming an electoral commission to resolve the dispute. Composed of fifteen members—five members each from the House, Senate, and US Supreme Court—the commission held the authority to decide what to do with the results that had been received. In each case, the commission had to decide whether to "go behind the returns" to consider other evidence and testimony, such as the affidavits gathered by Democrats alleging fraud. Tilden's advocates argued before the commission that such an investigation was necessary, while Hayes's lawyers claimed that the states possessed the sole power to select presidential electors and that the results should stand. Hearings occurred throughout February 1877, and in each instance, the commission, made up of eight Republicans and seven Democrats, upheld the Republican position and awarded all of the disputed electoral votes to Hayes. The Senate confirmed the decision of the commission on March 2, 1877, just three days before the presidential inauguration.

Despite the record turnout and the disputed returns, Hayes's election was not a decisive event in the history of the United States. Contrary to the claims of some historians, Hayes's inauguration in 1877 did not mark the total abandonment of African Americans in the former Confederate states. The Fourteenth and Fifteenth amendments remained in effect, and Hayes had pledged to uphold them. He had expressed his distaste for the Republican regimes that remained in the South, and he had already sent signals during the campaign that he would remove the small contingent of federal troops that remained outside the statehouses in South Carolina and Louisiana, thus causing the Republican governments that had been supported by the Grant administration to be replaced by rival, shadow governments run by Democrats. But even the removal of troops in these instances—which occurred in April 1877—did not mean that African Americans had lost all of their rights, or that Hayes and his successors could never or would never again enforce those rights. Reflecting the political realities within the industrialized North, as well as his own sense of optimism, Hayes chose conciliation over coercion—a path that Grant had pursued inconsistently after 1873—in the hope that Democratic-dominated governments in the South would respect the rights of African Americans. Black civil rights—the fruits of black freedom—remained intact. Black political rights and social rights rested on a more uncertain foundation. Only the future would tell how hard the federal government would work to protect those rights.

In addressing the delegates at the Republican convention in the summer of 1876, Frederick Douglass had wanted guarantees. The venerable African American activist still hoped that all of the rights of African Americans would be protected by the federal government. But guarantees were not forthcoming. The election of Hayes and the implementation of the new president's Southern policy meant that the struggle of the reconstruction era—how to protect all of the rights of African Americans while drawing limits around federal power—would continue.

Epilogue
LIBERTY, UNION, AND
AMERICAN CONSTITUTIONALISM

In 1876, the same year that the Supreme Court acquitted the Colfax defendants and Hayes and Tilden waged their titanic struggle for the presidency, Americans celebrated the centennial of their independence from Great Britain. Some 30,000 exhibits from nearly every country of the world filled massive exhibition halls in Philadelphia as the United States hosted a six-month-long world's fair to mark the occasion. In many ways, it was a fitting moment to commemorate Thomas Jefferson's Declaration of Independence. Having come through a civil war, ended slavery, reunited the country, and amended its constitution to extend rights to the formerly enslaved, America could make a stronger claim than ever that it was fulfilling the ideal that "all men are created equal." To honor the precious parchment that so embodied the heritage of the nation, Philadelphia's civic leaders had engaged in months of negotiations with the federal government to bring the nation's founding document back to Independence Hall, where a century before the revolutionary patriots had affixed their signatures. African Americans, desiring to join in the patriotic celebration, planned to unveil a monument to Richard Allen, the first bishop of the African Methodist Episcopal Church and the host of the very first black national convention, held at Allen's Bethel AME Church in Philadelphia in 1830.

Yet in other ways the timing for such a celebration of the American ideal of equality could not have been worse. Violent outrages against blacks in South Carolina continued to make headlines, and debate raged within the Republican Party and the halls of Congress about what to do about the mayhem. On July 4, 1876, the only black speaker on the program at the centennial celebration in Philadelphia, Reverend J. W. Jennifer, pastor of an AME church in Pine Bluff, Arkansas, expressed his thoughts on the subject. In a passionate address, Reverend Jennifer, ignoring the centennial's theme of national unity, emphasized the strife that continued to plague the country more than a decade after the end of the war. Referring to Southern violence as "the fruits of wanton prejudice, hatred, and hellish passions," Reverend Jennifer denounced the "Ku Klux Klan and White Leagues" and accused the federal government of "weakness" in yielding to lawless Southern whites.[1] It was this paradox—of America having fulfilled the idealism of its founding while at the same time confronting regular reminders of a spirit of lawlessness—that defined national life for years to come.

THE RIGHTS OF AFRICAN AMERICANS

By the time Americans celebrated the centennial and President Rutherford B. Hayes implemented his Southern policy, the Civil War and the era of reconstruction that followed had already brought about revolutionary changes in the lives of African Americans. Before the war, the nature of the national debate over slavery focused almost entirely on the rights of slaveholders—around questions of the slaveholders' rights to recapture fugitive slaves and to take their slave property into new federal territories. Although white and black abolitionists attempted to focus attention instead on the rights of enslaved people—on their fundamental worth as human beings—most Americans continued to see the debate in terms of the rights of white property owners. When the US Supreme Court held in 1857 that Dred Scott, after being taken to free territory and brought back to Missouri, was still a slave, it captured the essence of the antebellum understanding of slavery. Not only did Chief Justice Roger B. Taney hold that the rights of slaveholders were "distinctly and expressly affirmed in the Constitution," but he also claimed that blacks "had no rights which the white man was bound to respect."[2] Though extreme in its formulation, this juxtaposition of rights in the decision—absolute rights for slaveholders, no rights for slaves (or free blacks)—represented the pre–Civil War political order's framing of the constitutional question. Both the constitutional text and the weight of legal precedent favored slaveholders, while enslaved people and their abolitionist advocates clung tenaciously to the ideals of the Declaration of Independence. Even most Republicans at the time refused to conceive of the slavery issue as a question primarily pertaining to the rights of black people. Abraham Lincoln, the standard-bearer of the anti–*Dred Scott* Republicans, who was personally opposed to slavery, refused to embrace black citizenship in the Lincoln–Douglas debates and believed that fidelity to the Constitution, at least in the short term, required a basic acceptance of slavery's protected status within the Union. While Lincoln certainly did not view the Constitution as a proslavery document, he did concede that the Fugitive Slave Clause guaranteed slave owners certain rights, which in his first inaugural address he pledged to protect.

War and its aftermath transformed the national political debate. The rights of black people suddenly moved to the forefront as the long efforts of black constitutionalists finally bore fruit. Of course, the fact of war was the driving force in bringing about emancipation. But African Americans played a critical role in the process—by fleeing to federal military lines, enlisting in the Union army, making speeches and issuing petitions, and thus through their actions and words continually pushing the debate forward. In doing so, African Americans helped bring about a fundamental shift in American notions of rights—from the rights that Taney had discussed in *Dred Scott*—the rights of slaveholders—to the rights of enslaved persons. Taney had relied on the Fifth Amendment of the Constitution to emphasize the rights of property, but African Americans looked to the Declaration of Independence to champion the rights of all human beings. No longer mere chattel to be bought, sold, and exploited, African Americans in the postemancipation order suddenly enjoyed a number of day-to-day freedoms, including mobility, property ownership, and the right to sue in courts of law. After Congress scuttled President Andrew Johnson's plans for reconstruction and passed the Fourteenth and Fifteenth amendments, blacks gained on paper all the rights for which they hoped—civil, political, and social—and the Grant administration engaged in a sincere and at times successful six-year-long effort to enforce these new constitutional guarantees.

President Hayes's withdrawal of federal troops from the South Carolina and Louisiana statehouses in 1877 did not mean that African Americans suddenly found themselves slipping back into slavery. During the 1880s, black freedom remained a reality in the South. First and foremost, mobility still mattered. Although Democratic-controlled Southern state legislatures enacted a patchwork of laws that attempted to restrict blacks' ability to enter into contracts and move about freely, making those laws work proved another matter entirely. In fact, African Americans throughout the South continued to move any time that violence, oppression, or intimidation threatened their families or livelihoods. So long as landowners needed labor, blacks retained some leverage in the marketplace. In their search for new opportunity, some even left the South entirely. Throughout the late 1870s and early 1880s, a wave of some 25,000 black "Exodusters," often traveling by steamboat, migrated from the former slaveholding states to the West—mostly into Kansas. Throughout the South, meanwhile, levels of black wealth, land ownership, and literacy rose steadily, each contributing to the other. Literacy often aided land acquisition, and owning land almost always led to increased wealth. Family and extended kin groups, churches and community institutions played a vital role in sustaining black advancement and in contributing to increasing levels of achievement and wealth. Beyond the 1880s, according to the leading historian of the subject, blacks continued to make gains "in the portion of those who owned their own land, the relative distribution of their acreage, and their portion of total farm wealth."[3] Thus, even after Hayes's inauguration, the fact of freedom remained.

Most Republicans, black and white, remained hopeful that President Hayes's policy of conciliation would uphold blacks' political rights while also reunifying the country. John Mercer Langston, a leading black Republican, seemed optimistic. Born free in Virginia in 1829, Langston had recruited hundreds of volunteers for the Massachusetts 54th Regiment during the war, won election as president of the National Equal Rights League in 1864, and contributed to the drafting of the Civil Rights Act of 1875. He had witnessed the mighty revolution that had occurred in America, transforming enslaved men into soldiers and citizens. In April 1877, the same month in which Hayes ordered the troops back to their barracks, Langston spoke eloquently about the benefits of "pacific reconstruction" and urged fellow African Americans to show themselves deserving of citizenship. With "political excitement" a thing of the past, Langston urged blacks to build on the foundation of freedom and, in essence, prove themselves worthy—to "cultivate industry more thoroughly and advantageously," so that ultimately they would "become, in this way . . . valuable and influential member[s] of society, respected and honored . . . by [their] neighbors and fellow citizens."[4] Seemingly rejecting the tradition of black activism that stretched back to the early days of the republic, Langston's words initiated a debate among African Americans about the proper role of blacks themselves in securing the guarantees of the Constitution, a debate between demonstrating worthiness and claiming rights—between, in essence, black freedom and black politics—that continued for decades to come. For his part, Hayes toured the nation, including the South, where he reminded whites of their obligations to live up to the reconstruction amendments, while also hopefully touting the bonds of friendship that united all Americans.

But many Republicans, including Hayes, soon realized that they had overestimated the extent to which Northern and Southern Democrats had accepted the legitimacy of congressional reconstruction and black political rights. In the elections of 1878, Democrats took control of the US Senate in addition to the House amid charges of voter intimidation and fraud in the Southern states. Awakened to Southern double-dealing, Hayes not only admitted that his policy had failed but also acquired a new sense of resolve. When Democrats tried repeatedly to pass legislation to remove important federal oversight powers from elections—including prohibiting the deployment of federal troops at polling places—Hayes stood firm, each time issuing a veto. Although he never used troops to protect black voters, he jealously guarded executive power to take such action should he believe it necessary. If he refused to deploy the military, he continued to use the Justice Department. By the time his term ended in early 1881, the Hayes administration had brought nearly 500 cases into the federal courts under the Enforcement acts, winning convictions in approximately a fifth of these. True, this was a far cry from the roughly 2,200 cases brought in 1873 and 1874 alone, at the beginning of President Ulysses Grant's second term, but Hayes did not give up on enforcement of blacks' political rights.

If the Hayes administration kept federal enforcement of black political rights alive, so did the US Supreme Court. Although it had initially avoided the constitutional questions in *United States v. Reese* and *United States v. Cruikshank* (1876), during the 1880s the Court decided a series of important cases dealing with racial discrimination in both jury service and voting. In each instance, the Court established important constitutional doctrines that upheld black political rights. In *Strauder v. West Virginia* (1880), a case brought during the Hayes administration, the Court struck down a state statute banning any black man from serving on a grand or petit jury in the state. In a 7–2 decision, the justices viewed the law as a clear violation of the Equal Protection Clause of the Fourteenth Amendment. In a pair of other cases decided that same year, the Court reaffirmed this ruling. In a Virginia case, the Court upheld the conviction of a county judge under the Civil Rights Act of 1875 for systemically excluding black men from jury lists, and in a Delaware case, the justices held that the actions of state officers denying blacks the opportunity to serve on juries violated the Equal Protection Clause. The Court also took a stand on voting rights. In Maryland, after a local judge stuffed ballot boxes during the 1878 elections, the Hayes administration pursued criminal charges under the Enforcement Act, and the US Supreme Court in *Ex parte Siebold* (1880) upheld the conviction, thereby affirming congressional control over federal elections. In Georgia, meanwhile, the continued harassment of African Americans prompted an aggressive Republican US attorney to bring indictments and secure convictions of a group of white ruffians, a case that culminated in a landmark Supreme Court ruling, *Ex parte Yarbrough* (1884). In that case, the justices not only unanimously affirmed the constitutionality of the Enforcement Act of 1870 but also held that in certain instances the Fifteenth Amendment "does *proprio vigore*, substantially confer on the negro the

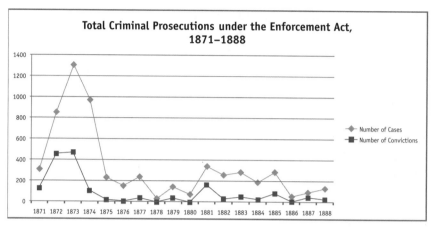

Source: Xi Wang, *The Trial of Democracy: Black Suffrage and Northern Republicans, 1860–1910* (Athens: University of Georgia Press, 1997), appendix 7, 300–301.

right to vote."[5] To be sure, the decisions in these cases did not wholly prevent discrimination, harassment, or intimidation in jury pools or polling places, but black voting continued throughout the South during this period, and the decisions affirmed that federal enforcement efforts, to some extent, would continue as well. In fact, the Justice Department under Republican presidents James Garfield and Chester A. Arthur during the 1880s sought more convictions on average each year under the Enforcement Act than Grant had during the last two years of his presidency.

If black civil rights were mostly secure and black political rights depended on federal enforcement through the courts, black social rights—always the most controversial and least secure—quickly faded. Not only did public accommodations provisions of the Civil Rights Act of 1875 mostly go unenforced, but the Supreme Court in the *Civil Rights Cases* (1883) also overturned the law. Narrowly defining the scope of congressional power under the Enforcement Clause of the Fourteenth Amendment, the justices, in an 8–1 decision, held that Congress did not have the power to prohibit racial discrimination in public accommodations. Under the amendment, according to the justices, Congress possessed only the power to negate discriminatory acts of the states. The first clear and unequivocal defeat for black rights in the Supreme Court, the decision generated considerable protest from African American leaders. Some in the black press likened it to the *Dred Scott* decision, while Frederick Douglass denounced the Court's ruling at a mass meeting. Henry McNeal Turner, the AME bishop, emerged as the most vocal critic. Having felt firsthand the wrath of white Southerners when he was expelled from the Georgia legislature, during the early 1870s Turner gravitated increasingly toward the notion of black emigration and publicly opposed Hayes's Southern policy. The ruling in the *Civil Rights Cases* prompted Turner to all but give up on America. "Those who suppose that the remedy for our ills is to be found in national legislation or supreme court decisions is greatly mistaken," he wrote in 1883. A few months later, Turner went further, arguing that the decision absolved "the Negro's allegiance to the general government" and "makes the American flag to him a rag of contempt."[6] For some black constitutionalists such as Turner, who had long put their faith in American institutions, the Court's blatant unwillingness to protect these rights insulted blacks' loyalty and devotion to the government. Tellingly, most white Republicans offered no more than a whisper of opposition to the ruling. Social equality for African Americans had never been high on the party's agenda, and the Court decision essentially allowed the legal apparatus of racial segregation to take shape.

THE POWER OF STATES

The debate over rights had always been closely connected to the debate over sovereignty and the place of the states in the federal Union. In the antebellum republic, many Americans conceived of state power as protecting the rights and interests of political minorities. By the 1820s, with the population of the free states expanding at a faster rate than that of the slave states, Southern political leaders had feared their section taking on permanent minority status. With this in mind, during the dispute over the protective tariff that began in 1828, South Carolinian John C. Calhoun reasserted the notion of state sovereignty through the doctrine of nullification. Calhoun hoped not only to challenge the trend toward centralization in national life, evident in the decisions of the Marshall Court and the economic policies of Congress, but also to protect the interests of white Southerners. Calhoun's theory, although articulated specifically to challenge increases in the tariff, served just as easily to protect slaveholders from national interference with the South's peculiar institution. Northern antislavery activists at times resorted to assertions of state sovereignty as well, as a means to justify personal liberty laws and protect fugitive slaves from federal attempts to return runaway blacks to their owners. But it was Southerners who took the state sovereignty position to the extreme, beyond nullification to secession. In 1860–1861, when confronting the possibility of Republican domination of the national government, Southerners claimed the power to withdraw from the federal compact and secede from the Union.

War changed the national debate over sovereignty and state power. Although the ideas of disunion and secession had long loomed in the background in ante-bellum American political discourse, Southern secession and the formation of the Confederacy signaled the actualization of what had previously only been an idea. The formation of the Southern republic served as the supreme test of the validity of secession, an experiment in government that, once the North refused to let the South go, became riddled with paradoxes and contradictions. If secession hinged on an extreme understanding of the sovereignty of states, the need to fight a war of independence forced Southern nationalists to the other extreme of having to build a centralized government, raise an army, and develop a sense of national identity. In other words, white Southerners found themselves glorying in their sense of autonomy and independence one day and suffering at the hands of a centralized state the next. Northerners, meanwhile, built a robust central government during wartime, as they extended the reach of national power into a number of areas—from currency and banking to rail-roads and land distribution. Most important, emancipation, announced in the North but implemented and experienced in the South, confirmed in the minds of white Southerners the horrors of centralized authority. Emancipation, in every respect, was a Calhounian's worst nightmare. Imposed by a tyrannical majority on a defenseless minority, in the minds of white Southerners, eman-cipation struck at the very heart of Southerners' constitutional liberties and economic interests. Northerners and Southerners thus took different lessons from the war. Northerners placed more trust than ever in the ability of a cen-tralized state to achieve its aims, as the general government had suppressed the rebellion and stamped out the root cause of the rebellion. White Southerners, in contrast, learned that centralized power in whatever form—Confederate or Union—was oppressive and unjust.

When Republicans brought the lessons of the war into their reconstruction policies, the nation commenced a long debate over the scope of federal power. Acting in the Hamiltonian tradition of nation building and assenting to Lin-coln's assertion of popular sovereignty ("government of the people, by the people, and for the people"), many Republicans sought to bring about a rev-olution in the historic relationship between the national government and the states. Between the passage of the First Military Reconstruction Act in 1867 and the Enforcement Act of 1871, national power expanded in unprecedented ways. Having divided the Southern states into military districts for adminis-trative purposes, Congress enacted a Fourteenth Amendment that gave new powers to Congress and placed specific limits on the powers of states. It passed a Fifteenth Amendment that protected the right to vote from state interfer-ence on the basis of "race, color, and previous condition of servitude" and enacted strong enforcement legislation based on its new powers under the amendment. In doing so, Republicans in essence attempted to transform the relationship between liberty and power, making the national government a powerful agent in the protection of individual liberty. Southerners had a different view. In the face of what they termed the threat of "consolidation," Southern Democrats mounted a vigorous defense of the Calhounian state sovereignty position. In books and magazines throughout the 1870s, Confederate apologists asserted the traditional state sovereignty position and the constitutional right to secede, which became a staple of a larger ideology of the Lost Case that justified and glorified the Southern war effort.

The debate over the nature of sovereignty and federalism continued into the 1880s, well beyond Hayes's administration. None other than Jefferson Davis joined the fray when, in 1881, he published the *Rise and Fall of the Confederate Government*. After spending two years in prison after being charged with treason and another two awaiting trial before the government dropped the case, Davis expressed no regrets about having led the rebellion. After traveling to Canada and Great Britain, he settled in Memphis for a while and made a run at the insurance business. When that failed, the former Confederate president retreated to the Gulf Coast of Mississippi, where he spent years writing his self-justifying history of the Confederacy. Not only did he advocate the legitimacy of state sovereignty and the legality of secession, but he also took particular aim at the government of the United States, describing it as "the aggressor—the Attila of the American Continent," whose action "inflicted a wound on the principles of constitutional liberty."[7] If secession's defenders remained at one end of the spectrum, Northern Republicans by this point had settled on the dual federalism position. Implementing the reconstruction-era amendments and enforcement statutes tested the limits of national authority and diminished some of the most revolutionary of the national supremacist rhetoric of the era, as violence forced Northern political leaders to demonstrate just how much centralization they were willing to accept. Dual federalism, a capacious enough concept to accommodate both the *Slaughterhouse Cases* and *Ex parte Yarbrough*, meant in effect that federal power could and would be used on occasion to uphold political rights, but that much would remain within the purview of the states.

LIBERTY AND UNION

More than a decade after the centennial exposition in Philadelphia commemorating the Declaration of Independence, Americans celebrated another one-hundred-year anniversary in the same city, this time marking the signing of the Constitution. This celebration was different, for it was smaller in scale and more subdued in tone. General Philip Sheridan led a military parade, part of a larger "civic and industrial pageant" in the city that concluded with addresses at Independence Hall on September 17, 1887, by President Grover Cleveland and Supreme Court Justice Samuel Miller. After it was all over, E. L. Godkin, editor of the *Nation*, took the opportunity to reflect. Godkin noted that with all of the celebration, little mention had been made of the flaws in the original Constitution. Godkin noted two. "[The framers'] two great difficulties were the union of slave and free States under a common government, and the merging of State allegiance in national allegiance in the mind of the citizens of the several States." Because the original framers had left these matters unresolved, the Civil War generation had fought and died to remake and repair the Constitution in order to ensure that it would last, ending slavery and defeating a secessionist rebellion. "A very large share of whatever glory is due to its framers," Godkin wrote, "belongs of right to the men of the generation now passing away."[8] As Godkin and millions of Americans plainly knew, they had lived through a significant time of revolutionary change.

Liberty and union were the result. What did liberty mean? Emancipation, the central event of the nineteenth century, had freed four million people who had previously been held as slaves. Liberated from bondage, they lived, worked, moved, bought, sold, sued, testified, gathered, organized, and worshipped more freely than they ever had before. There had been a time—a time still within the memory of most—when they had been talked about and treated mostly as property, a time when they had been bought, sold, traded, shipped, commanded, punished, and exploited with little regard for their humanity and often with no regard for their rights. Those days were gone, and blacks—and whites—knew it. To be sure, they had not gained all of the rights for which they had strived. They had not gained all that they believed the Declaration of Independence, with its ringing claims of equality, had granted them. But their lives were profoundly different than before. And what about union—what did it mean? In simplest terms, it meant that secession had failed and died on the battlefields of the war. But it also meant that, even if national power had been expanded, the Union under the Constitution had been restored—that is, a union in which the idea of federalism would continue to limit and define the contours of national power.

However revolutionary from the perspective of the Civil War generation, liberty and union were not enough. As the end of the century approached, black political rights slowly but steadily eroded. After defeating a Republican-proposed voting rights bill in 1891, Democrats repealed most of the reconstruction-era Enforcement acts in 1894. At the turn of the century, an increasingly conservative Supreme Court, led by Chief Justice Melville Fuller, moreover, offered little hope to those who continued to push for the political and social rights of African Americans. Disfranchisement took hold in many places in the South, while legal segregation became pervasive. But the struggle did continue. The tradition of black constitutionalism that began in the late eighteenth century persisted during the late nineteenth century and beyond, even as African Americans found themselves battling Southern lawlessness and violence in the form of lynching. Because the Constitution had been amended so that it now included a Thirteenth Amendment, a Fourteenth Amendment, and a Fifteenth Amendment, it would be easier—not easy, but easier—for blacks and their white allies to ensure the protection and the advancement of the rights of African Americans. Unlike before, those rights were now specifically stated in the Constitution. Other generations would follow, and they would continue the struggle. But they would not have to fight a war to end slavery. That work was done.

ACKNOWLEDGMENTS

Over the past decade, this book has spanned four academic deans at Rhodes College, five administrative assistants in the college's department of history, dozens of student employees in the department, and hundreds of students who have taken my courses. And it has emerged from scores of conversations with colleagues at conferences and on my own campus. Now, at long last, I have a chance to thank some of these folks by name.

Deans Robert Llewellyn, Charlotte Borst, Michael Drompp, and Milton Moreland provided extraordinary institutional support—including research grants and eventually endowed professorship funds—that allowed frequent travel to libraries, battlefields, and conferences. Administrative assistants Meredith "Murfy" Nix, Heather Walter, Nannette Gills, Esther Kerns, and Patti Fox helped in countless ways, through both their work and their attitude about their work. I am grateful to each of them. A variety of student employees and research assistants contributed at various stages. I acknowledge Claire Carr, Ashley Cundiff, Joseph Doyle, Andrew Howie, Smith Stickney, and Dev Varma. I am also grateful to students in my Civil War classes, who contributed to my thinking about the book over the years: Ebony Archie, Christian Baum, Meredith Bond, John Bordelon, Mia Colson, Ian Engdahl, Elizabeth Henrickson, Mathew Jehl, Nash Keim, Lucy Kellison, Maddie McGrady, Ethan McClelland, and Taylor White. In addition, I thank Charlie Kenney for creating the graph and Andrew Tait for making the military maps. Four student research assistants, finally, are due special mention. David Tyler, Rhodes class of 2006, helped me to start work on this project. By assembling bibliographies, making copies, and tracking down various items at the very beginning, David helped me to see the task ahead. Jordan Redmon, Rhodes class of 2013, played a critical role at a crucial stage. Jordan became a trusted associate while I was on sabbatical, during which time he carried out a number of tasks: checking facts, verifying citations, proofreading chapters, and asking pointed questions. I am still in his debt for the enormous effort that he devoted to the project during that semester. Brooks Lamb, Rhodes class of 2017, checked all of the footnotes in the last third of the book while also helping with proofreading and finding illustrations. His work was excellent. Abbie Hicks, Rhodes class of 2016, finally, came to the rescue at the very end of the process of preparing the book, when she located and secured illustrations. I am grateful to all of these students for their efforts.

Librarians and archivists, of course, helped by answering questions, tracking down materials, and offering plenty of smiles and good cheer. I am grateful to Darlene Brooks, Amanda Ford, Elizabeth Gates, Kenan Padgett, and Bill Short at the Barret Library at Rhodes College, as well as to the staffs of the Memphis Public Library and Information Center and the University of Memphis Library. I am particularly grateful to Wayne Dowdy at the Memphis Public Library, Ed Frank at the University of Memphis Library, and Ryan Jones at the National Civil Rights Museum for inviting me to present some of the ideas in this book in public lectures at their respective institutions.

Colleagues and friends provided enormous support. I am grateful to Michael Boezi for initially convincing me to take on this project, and I am especially thankful for Michael Briggs, Peter Hoffer, and Charles Myers, who placed their faith in the book at a crucial moment. Readers Orville Vernon Burton, Allen Guelzo, Daniel Hamilton, and Jon Lurie offered constructive criticism along the way, which proved enormously helpful in improving the book. Over the years, I have benefited from numerous conversations with fellow historians, including Michael Les Benedict, Clare Cushman, Paul Finkelman, Sally Hadden, Thomas Mackey, Kate Masur, Patti Minter, Cynthia Nicoletti, Susan O'Donovan, Darden A. Pyron, Michael Ross, Melvin Urofsky, Peter Wallenstein, Christopher Waldrep, Gavin Wright, and the late Bertram Wyatt-Brown. On my own campus, I have been fortunate enough to have had a number of conversation partners, who, over time, have provided much-needed moral and intellectual support. Geoff Bakewell, Marshall Boswell, Dee Garceau, Patrick Gray, Stephen Haynes, Charles Hughes, Jeffrey Jackson, Jonathan Judaken, Tait Keller, David McCarthy, Charles McKinney, Gail Murray, John Murray, Michael Nelson, Scott Newstok, Alex Novikoff, Robert Saxe, William Skoog, James Vest, and Lynn Zastoupil have proven especially sympathetic and encouraging. Dee Garceau, Stephen Haynes, John Murray, and Michael Nelson—because they read portions of the manuscript at different stages—are due special thanks. Each provided useful feedback and suggestions. At various points, I relied on the wisdom of friends Daniel Amsler, John Leach, and Donald Park. I like to think of them as the three wise men. The Readers and Eaters book group—Dan, Judy, Haley, and Donna—offered ongoing friendship and support, as did the Friday morning Bible study group. Daniel Stowell, a friend for more than two and a half decades, listened and offered to help at just the right moment. With great respect, I thank him.

My family, of course, lived with this project, and my children have never known me *not* to be working on it. I thank my daughter, Sloan, and son, Charlie, for their willingness to share their father and put up with my obsession. My wife, Kristin, experienced the various stages of the writing of each chapter: the struggle of getting started, the joy of discovering the way forward, the frustration of the roadblock, and then the final epiphany, accompanied by a push to get it done. I cannot thank her enough for all of her love and support, despite all of the challenges during these years. I dedicate the book, finally, to my parents, with enormous love and gratitude. I am daily reminded that one of their greatest gifts was allowing me to be me—letting me pursue my studies in history without ever questioning why. I hope I will do the same for my own children.

With thanks to all who have helped in so many ways, I take full responsibility for any mistakes that remain.

NOTES

PREFACE

1. David Goldfield, *America Aflame: How the Civil War Created a Nation* (New York, 2012), 1; Harry Stout, *Upon the Altar of the Nation: A Moral History of the Civil War* (New York, 2005), xv, 189. Both seem unduly influenced by present political concerns. Goldfield argues that "there may have been other means to achieve [abolition]" and criticizes zealous evangelicals—in the nineteenth century and the twenty-first— for their unbending commitment to principle, while Stout, writing against the backdrop of the American wars in Afghanistan and Iraq, implicitly criticizes religious conservatives for their support of war.

2. See, e.g., Larry Kramer, *The People Themselves: Popular Constitutionalism and Judicial Review* (New York, 2005); Gary D. Rowe, "Constitutionalism in the Streets," *Southern California Law Review* 78 (2005): 401–456.

3. James McPherson, *What They Fought For, 1861–1865* (New York, 1994), 13.

4. See, e.g., David Cecelski, *The Fire of Freedom: Abraham Galloway and the Slaves' Civil War* (Chapel Hill, NC, 2012); David Williams, *I Freed Myself: African American Self-Emancipation in the Civil War Era* (New York, 2014); Steven Hahn, "Did We Miss the Greatest Slave Rebellion in Modern History?" in *The Political Worlds of Slavery and Freedom* (Cambridge, MA, 2009), 55–115.

PROLOGUE: SLAVERY, SOVEREIGNTY, AND AMERICAN CONSTITUTIONALISM

1. James K. Polk, "Inaugural Address," in *A Compilation of the Messages and Papers of the Presidents* (New York, 1897), 5:2224.

2. Ibid., 5:2225.

3. Ibid., 5:2226, 2227.

4. Jonathan Elliot, ed., *The Debates in the Several State Conventions, on the Adoption of the Federal Constitution as Recommended by the General Convention at Philadelphia in 1787* (Washington, DC, 1836), 2:301.

5. Isaac Kramnick, "The 'Great National Discussion': The Discourse of Politics in 1787," *William and Mary Quarterly*, 3rd ser., 45 (1988): 24.

6. "Ten," in Alexander Hamilton, James Madison, and John Jay, *The Federalist*, ed. J. R. Pole (Indianapolis, 2005), 54.

7. Thomas Jefferson, *The Writings of Thomas Jefferson: Memorial Edition*, vol. 1, ed. Andrew Lipscomb (Washington, DC, 1903), 34.

8. David Waldstreicher explains it this way: "Africans and their descendants were not being defined as three-fifths of a person, as is sometimes said, for that would have implied that the men among them deserved three-fifths of a vote, when they had none, or had three-fifths of a person's rights before the law, when they had much less than that, usually. Rather, their presence was being acknowledged as a source of power and of wealth, *for their owners.*" *Slavery's Constitution: From Revolution to Ratification* (New York, 2009), 4–5.

9. Elliot, *Debates*, 4:286.

10. Ibid., 4:478. For the story of this debate, see Sean Wilentz, "Antislavery, Slavery, and the Federal Constitution," paper presented at The Antislavery Bulwark: The Antislavery Origins of the Civil War, Graduate Center of the City of New York, October, 2014, revised for Shelby Cullom Davis Center's Works-in-Progress Series, Princeton University, November 2014.

11. "Thirty-Nine," *Federalist*, 208.

12. Max Farrand, ed., *The Records of the Federal Convention of 1787* (New Haven, CT, 1911), 1:468.

13. "Thirty-Nine," *Federalist*, 210.

14. John C. Calhoun, "Address on the Relation with the States and the General Government Bear to Each Other," in *Reports and Public Letters of John C. Calhoun*, ed. Richard K. Cralle (New York, 1855), 69.

15. *Speech of Mr. Webster in the Senate in Reply to Mr. Calhoun's Speech on the Bill, "Further to Provide for the Collection of Duties on Imports"* (Washington, DC, 1833), 17.

16. "Ordinance of Nullification of South Carolina, November 24, 1832," in *State Documents on Federal Relations: The States and the United States*, ed. Herman V. Ames (New York, 1970), 171.

17. "President Jackson's Proclamation of the 10th December, 1833," Elliot, *Debates*, 4:585.

18. Thomas Paine, *The Political Works of Thomas Paine* (London, 1857), 1:27.

19. Joseph Story, *The Miscellaneous Writings: Literary, Critical, Juridical, and Political* (Boston, 1835), 473.

20. As quoted in Michael Kammen, *A Machine That Would Go of Itself: The Constitution in American Culture* (New York, 1986), 80.

21. Polk, "Inaugural Address," 2230.

22. David Potter, *The Impending Crisis, 1846–1861* (New York, 1976), 1.

CHAPTER 1. SLAVERY, THE SOUTH, AND THE NORTH

1. *Report of the Proceedings of the Colored National Convention, Held at Cleveland, Ohio, on Wednesday, September 6, 1848* (Rochester, NY, 1848), 13, 16, 18.

2. Former slave Denmark Vesey reportedly plotted a revolt in Charleston in 1822. Like Gabriel before him, Vesey and several of his cohorts went swiftly to the gallows. Historians debate where there was an actual conspiracy. See Michael P. Johnson, "Denmark Vesey and His Co-Conspirators," *William and Mary Quarterly*, 3rd ser., 58 (2001), 915–976, who argues that Vesey was the victim of trumped up charges rather than an actual rebel, and, e.g., Douglas R. Egerton, *He Shall Go Out Free: The Lives of Denmark Vesey* (Madison, WI, 1999), who claims that a conspiracy actually existed.

3. Thomas Jefferson, *Notes on the State of Virginia* (London, 1787), 272.

4. David Martin, ed., *Trial of the Rev. Jacob Gruber, Minister in the Methodist Episcopal Church, at the March Term, 1819, in the Frederick County Court, for a Misdemeanor* (Fredericktown, MD, 1819), 43. On Taney and slavery during this period, see Timothy S. Huebner, "Roger Taney and the Slavery Issue: Looking Beyond—and Before—Dred Scott," *Journal of American History* 97 (2010): 39–62.

5. "Speech, On the Reception of Abolition Petitions, Delivered in the Senate, February 6th, 1837," in *The Works of John C. Calhoun*, vol. 2, *Speeches of John C. Calhoun, Delivered in the House of Representatives and the Senate of the United States* (New York, 1883), 631.

6. L. C. Matlack, "Our Past and Present Relations to Slavery," *Methodist Quarterly Review* 50 (April 1868): 254.

7. William Lloyd Garrison to Elihu Burritt, July 16, 1845, in *The Letters of William Lloyd Garrison*, ed. Walter M. Merrill (Cambridge, MA, 1973), 3:300.

8. Garrison to Rev. Samuel J. May, July 17, 1845, in Garrison, *Letters*, 3:301. These phrases come from Isaiah 28:18.

9. "A Petition of Absalom Jones and Others, December 30, 1799," in *Landmark Documents on the US Congress*, ed. Raymond Smock (Washington, DC, 1999), 93.

10. James Forten, "Series of Letters by a Man of Colour," in *Pamphlets of Protest: An Anthology of Early African American Protest Literature, 1790–1860*, ed. Richard Newman, Patrick Rael, and Phillip Lapsansky (New York, 2001), 67.

11. David Walker, *Walker's Appeal in Four Articles; Together with a Preamble, to the Coloured Citizens of the World, but in Particular, and Very Expressly, to Those of the United States of America* (Boston, 1830) 84.

12. Ibid., 85.

13. "The First Colored Convention," *Anglo-African Magazine* 1 (1859), reprinted in Howard Holman Bell, ed., *Minutes of the Proceedings of the National Negro Conventions, 1830–1864* (New York, 1969).

14. The term "black constitutionalism" comes from Christopher Waldrep, *African Americans Confront Lynching: Strategies of Resistance from the Civil War to the Civil Rights Era* (Lanham, MD, 2009), 13–38, although I employ a more expansive definition here.

CHAPTER 2. POLITICS AND THE PROSLAVERY CONSTITUTIONAL
ORDER, 1846–1857

1. Gerrit Smith, *Gerrit Smith's Constitutional Argument* (Peterboro, MA, 1844), 4.
2. *Somerset v. Stewart*, 98 Eng. Rep. 499, 510 (1772).
3. Chase to J. F. Morse, December 12, 1850, Chase Papers, Library of Congress, as quoted in Eric Foner, *Free Soil, Free Labor, Free Men: The Ideology of the Republican Party Before the Civil War* (New York, 1995), 77.
4. 3 *Annals of Cong.* 1414–1415 (1793).
5. *Prigg v. Pennsylvania*, 41 U.S. 539, 611 (1842).
6. 41 U.S. 539, 613.
7. 41 U.S. 539, 620.
8. 41 U.S. 539, 626.
9. *Cong. Globe*, 29th Cong., 1st Sess., 1217 (1846).
10. Ibid., 2nd Sess. Appendix 317 (1847).
11. The initial vote on Wilmot's amendment was 80–64 in favor. All but three of the 64 negative votes were from slave states. The vote on the final war bill, with Wilmot's amendment attached, was similar. According to Potter, "Seventy-four southerners and four northerners voted to table; ninety-one northerners and three southerners voted against tabling." *Impending Crisis*, 22.
12. "Democratic Platform," in *History of American Presidential Elections*, ed. Arthur M. Schlesinger Jr. (New York, 1971), 4:899–900.
13. "Resolutions Adopted at Whig Ratification Meeting," in Schlesinger, *History of American Presidential Elections*, 4:901.
14. George W. Julian to "Brother Isaac," January 25, 1850, in Giddings-Julian Papers, Library of Congress, as quoted in Thomas E. Schott, *Alexander H. Stephens of Georgia: A Biography* (Baton Rouge, LA, 1988), 102.
15. Zachary Taylor, "Inaugural Address, March 5, 1849," in *Inaugural Addresses of the Presidents of the United States from George Washington 1789 to Richard Milhous Nixon 1969* (Washington, DC, 1969), 100.
16. William H. Seward, "Freedom in the New Territories, March 11, 1850," in *Works of William H. Seward*, ed. George E. Baker (New York, 1853), 74.
17. Millard Fillmore, "First Annual Message, Washington, DC, December 2, 1850," as published in *A Compilation of the Messages and Papers of the Presidents, 1789–1897*, ed. James D. Richardson (Washington, DC, 1897), 5:93.
18. Acts of September 9, 1850, ch. 49, 50, 9 *Stat.* 447, 453.
19. Act of September 18, 1850, ch. 60, 9 *Stat.* 463.
20. "Resolutions by a Committee of Philadelphia Blacks, presented at the Brick Wesley African Methodist Episcopal Church, Philadelphia, Pennsylvania, October 14, 1850," in *The Black Abolitionist Papers*, vol. 5, *The United States, 1847–1858*, ed. C. Peter Ripley (Chapel Hill, NC, 1991), 68–69.
21. "Proceedings of the State Convention of Colored People Held at Albany, New York, on the 22nd, 23rd, and 24th of July, 1851," in *Proceedings of the Black States Con-*

ventions, 1840–1865, ed. Philip S. Foner and George E. Walker (Philadelphia, 1979), 1:73. The exact figure is unknown, but one scholar put the number of American blacks who went to Canada before 1860 at around 20,000. See Michael Wayne, "The Black Population of Canada West on the Eve of the American Civil War: A Reassessment Based on the Manuscript Census of 1861," *Social History* 28 (1995): 465–485.

22. Franklin Pierce, "Inaugural Address, March 4, 1853," in *Inaugural Addresses of the Presidents*, 109.

23. The original source of this famous quotation appears to be a conversation between Douglas and Archibald Dixon, US senator from Kentucky. Susan Bullitt Dixon, *The True History of the Missouri Compromise and Its Repeal* (Cincinnati, 1899), 445.

24. Act of May 30, 1854, ch. 59, 10 *Stat.* 284.

25. Ibid., 10 *Stat.* 283.

26. J. W. Schuckers, *The Life and Public Services of Salmon Portland Chase* (New York, 1874), 141, 143.

27. Edwin Erle Sparks, *Collections of the Illinois State Historical Library*, vol. 3, *Lincoln Series*, vol. 1, *The Lincoln–Douglas Debates of 1858* (Springfield, IL, 1908), 53.

28. Michael F. Holt, "Making and Mobilizing the Republican Party, 1854–1860," in *The Birth of the Grand Old Party: The Republicans' First Generation*, ed. Robert F. Engs and Randall M. Miller (Philadelphia, 2002), 34. The classic work is Foner, *Free Soil*.

29. George Fitzhugh, *Cannibals All! Or, Slaves without Masters* (Richmond, 1857), 98.

30. *Selections from the Letters and Speeches of the Hon. James Henry Hammond of South Carolina* (New York, 1866), 319.

31. Joseph Henry Lumpkin, *An Address Delivered Before the South Carolina Institute at its Second Annual Fair on 19th November 1850* (Charleston, SC, 1851), 13. On Lumpkin's own changing views on slavery, see Timothy S. Huebner, *The Southern Judicial Tradition: State Judges and Sectional Distinctiveness, 1790–1890* (Athens, GA, 1999), 86–95.

32. Thornton Stringfellow, *Scriptural and Statistical Views in Favor of Slavery*, 4th ed. (Richmond, 1856), 37.

33. Samuel A. Cartwright, "Report on the Diseases and Physical Peculiarities of the Negro Race," in *De Bow's Review of the Southern and Western States* 11, n.s., 4 (1851): 66.

34. *Bryan v. Walton*, 14 Ga. 185, 198 (1853).

35. *The Pro-Slavery Argument, as Maintained by the Most Distinguished Writers in the Southern States, Containing the Several Essays, on the Subject, of Chancellor Harper, Governor Hammond, Dr. Simms, and Professor Dew* (Charleston, 1852), 462.

36. Frederick Douglass, "What to the Slave Is the Fourth of July? An Address Delivered in Rochester, New York, on 5 July 1852," *Frederick Douglass Papers*, ser. 1, vol. 2, ed. John Blassingame (New Haven, CT, 1982), 363.

37. Ibid., 371.

38. Ibid., 385.

39. Wendell Phillips Garrison and Francis Jackson Garrison, *William Lloyd Garrison, 1805–1879: The Story of His Life as Told by His Children* (Boston, 1885), 3:412.

40. *Cong. Globe*, 34th Cong., 1st Sess. 530 (1856).

41. "Appellate Jurisdiction of the Federal, Over the State Courts," *American Law Register* 4 (January 1856): 151.

42. R. Kent Newmyer, *The Supreme Court under Marshall and Taney*, 2nd ed. (Wheeling, IL, 2006), 116; George Van Santvoord, *Sketches of the Lives and Judicial Services of the Chief Justices of the Supreme Court of the United States* (New York, 1854), 533. The *Monthly Law Reporter*, which included a review of Van Santvoord's book, agreed with this assessment. See "The Chief Justices of the United States," *Monthly Law Reporter*, November 1854, 370–372.

43. James Buchanan, "Inaugural Address, March 4, 1857," in *Inaugural Addresses of the Presidents*, 112.

44. *Dred Scott v. Sandford*, 60 U.S. 393, 407 (1857).

45. 60 U.S. 393, 411.

46. On this point, see Mark A. Graber, *Dred Scott and the Problem of Constitutional Evil* (Cambridge, 2006), 28–30.

47. 60 US 393, 450.

48. 60 U.S. 393, 450, 451.

49. 60 U.S. 393, 451–452.

50. 60 U.S. 393, 451.

51. See Austin Allen, *Origins of the Dred Scott Case: Jacksonian Jurisprudence and the Supreme Court, 1847–1857* (Athens, GA, 2006).

52. 60 U.S. 393, 490.

53. 60 U.S. 393, 550.

54. *Liberator*, July 10, 1857, 2; "Convention of the Colored Citizens of Massachusetts, August 1, 1858" and "New England Colored Citizens Convention, August 1, 1859," in *Proceedings of the Black States Conventions*, 2:98, 101, 214.

CHAPTER 3. THE PATH TO SECESSION AND THE OUTBREAK
OF WAR, 1858–1861

1. "Republican Platform," in Schlesinger, *History of American Presidential Elections*, 2:1126.

2. *Richmond Enquirer*, March 10, 1857, in Paul Finkelman, *Dred Scott v. Sandford: A Brief History with Documents* (Boston, 1997), 130.

3. The official return, described by the territorial secretary as "a roll of paper, forty or fifty feet long, containing names as thickly as they could be written," included the names of 1,601 voters, all in the same handwriting—and 1,500 of them copied in consecutive order from the Cincinnati city directory. See John G. Hay and John Nicolay, *Abraham Lincoln: A History* (New York, 1890), 2:105.

4. "Constitution of Kansas—1857," in *The Federal and State Constitutions, Colonial*

Charters, and Other Organic Laws of the United States, Part 1, ed. Ben Perley Poore (Washington, 1877), 605.

5. James Buchanan, "Message Transmitting the Constitution of Kansas," February 2, 1858, in Richardson, *Compilation of Messages and Papers of the Presidents*, 7:3010.

6. "Speech at Peoria," October 16, 1854, in *The Collected Works of Abraham Lincoln*, ed. Roy Basler (New Brunswick, NJ, 1953), 2:274, 276.

7. "'A House Divided' Speech at Springfield, Illinois," June 16, 1858, in Lincoln, *Collected Works*, 2:461–462.

8. "'House Divided' Speech," in Lincoln, *Collected Works*, 2:466.

9. "Seventh and Last Debate with Stephen A. Douglas at Alton, Illinois," October 15, 1858, in Lincoln, *Collected Works*, 3:313.

10. "Speech at Chicago, Illinois," July 10, 1858, in Lincoln, *Collected Works*, 2:492.

11. Lincoln first referred to this possibility in his initial debate with Douglas, and he mentioned it again in other speeches. See Lincoln, "First Debate with Stephen A. Douglas at Ottawa, Illinois," August 21, 1858, in Lincoln, *Collected Works*, 3:30. Although he never mentioned it by name, Lincoln surely had in mind *Lemmon v. The People*, involving a Virginia couple who had traveled to New York with their slaves to board a steamship for Texas. After arriving in New York, authorities seized the slaves, and the couple's appeals to the New York Supreme Court in 1857 proved unsuccessful. Were the US Supreme Court to have heard the case, it might have overturned the New York court and declared a right to hold slaves in a free state.

12. "Fourth Debate with Stephen A. Douglas at Charleston, Illinois," in Lincoln, *Collected Works*, 3:146.

13. William H. Seward, "The Irrepressible Conflict. Speech of William H. Seward, Delivered at Rochester, Monday, October 25, 1858," 7, James Birney Collection of Anti-Slavery Pamphlets, Johns Hopkins University Sheridan Libraries.

14. "Southern Commercial Convention; Feeling of the South on the Kansas Question. From the Special Correspondent of the New-York Times. Meeting of the Convention at Montgomery, Alabama—Its Probable Action—Topics to be Discussed," *New York Times*, May 14, 1858.

15. As quoted in Eric H. Walther, *William Lowndes Yancey and the Coming of the Civil War* (Chapel Hill, NC, 2006), 218.

16. The US courts incurred a total expense of $6,872.22, and the federal government paid another $7,293.50 to the city of Boston. Stanley W. Campbell, *The Slave Catchers: Enforcement of the Fugitive Slave Law, 1850–1860* (Chapel Hill, 1970), 136, 207, 130.

17. *Cong. Globe*, 33rd Cong., 2nd Sess., Appendix 222 (1855).

18. *Ableman v. Booth*, 62 U.S. 506, 525 (1859).

19. Peter Wallenstein, "'Incendiaries All': Southern Politics and the Harper's Ferry Raid," in *His Soul Goes Marching On: Responses to John Brown and the Harper's Ferry Raid*, ed. Paul Finkelman (Charlottesville, VA., 1995), 149–173.

20. Horace Greeley to Mrs. R. M. Whipple, April 1860, Horace Greeley Papers, Library of Congress, as quoted in Jeter Allen Isely, *Horace Greeley and the Republican Party, 1853–1861: A Study of the New York Tribune* (Princeton, 1947), 266.

21. Lincoln to Henry L. Pierce and Others, April 6, 1859, in Lincoln, *Collected Works*, 3:376.

22. "Constitutional Union Platform," in Schlesinger, *History of American Presidential Elections*, 2:1127.

23. David R. Barbee and Milledge L. Bonham Jr., "The Montgomery Address of Stephen A. Douglas," *Journal of Southern History* 5 (1939): 551.

24. Abraham Lincoln to Alexander Stephens, December 20, 1860, in Lincoln, *Collected Works*, 4:160.

25. Alexander Stephens, "Speech Before the Legislature of Georgia," in Richard Malcolm Johnston and William Hand Browne, *Life of Alexander H. Stephens* (Philadelphia, 1878), 564, 578, 579.

26. R. B. Rhett, draft of unsigned letter to the editor of the *Charleston Mercury*, in Steven A. Channing, *Crisis of Fear: Secession in South Carolina* (New York, 1970), 249.

27. "South Carolina," in *The American Annual Cyclpaedia and Register of Important Events of the Year 1861* (New York, 1867), 1:648.

28. "Secession Ordinance of South Carolina," in *The Rebellion Record: A Diary of American Events, with Documents, Narratives, Illustrative Incidents, Poetry, etc.*, ed. Frank Moore (New York, 1864), 1:2.

29. "Declaration of Causes which Induced the Secession of South Carolina," in Moore, *Rebellion Record*, 1:3.

30. "Mississippi Justifies Secession," in *State Documents*, 70–73.

31. "Address of William L. Harris, commissioner from Mississippi, to the Georgia General Assembly, December 17, 1860," in Charles B. Dew, *Apostles of Disunion: Southern Secession Commissioners and the Causes of the Civil War* (Charlottesville, VA, 2001), 85.

32. Stephen F. Hale to Gov. Beriah Magoffin, December 27, 1860, in *The War of the Rebellion: A Compilation of the Official Records of the Union and Confederate Armies* (hereafter *OR*) (Washington, DC, 1880–1901), ser. 4, 1:8.

33. E. D. Townsend, *Anecdotes of the Civil War in the United States* (New York, 1884), 2.

34. James Buchanan, "Special Message," January 8, 1861, in Richardson, *Compilation of Messages and Papers of the Presidents*, 8:3187.

35. Lincoln to Lyman Trumbull, December 10, 1860, in Lincoln, *Collected Works*, 4:149.

36. Act of March 2, 1861, res. 13, 12 *Stat.* 251.

37. Constitution of the Confederate States of America, in *Statutes at Large of the Provisional Government of the Confederate States of America*, ed. James M. Matthews (Richmond, 1864), 11.

38. Ibid., 11.

39. Ibid., 15, 21.

40. Edmund Ruffin, *Diary of Edmund Ruffin*, ed. William Kaufman Scarborough (Baton Rouge, LA, 1972), 1:551.

41. *New York Herald Tribune*, February 18, 1861, as quoted in William Cooper Jr., *Jefferson Davis, American* (New York, 2000), 328.

42. Inaugural Address, *Journal of the Congress of the Confederate States of America, 1861–1865* (Washington, DC, 1904), February 19, 1861, 1:66.

43. Allan Nevins, "He Did Hold Lincoln's Hat: Senator Douglas's Act Is Verified, at Last, by First-Hand Testimony," *American Heritage* 10, no. 2 (February 1959), 98.

44. Lincoln, "First Inaugural Address," March 4, 1861, in Lincoln, *Collected Works*, 4:268–269.

45. Ibid., 264, 265, 268.

46. Ibid., 271.

47. A. J. Slemmer to Lieut. Col. L. Thomas, March 1861, in *OR*, ser. 2, 1:750.

48. Lincoln, "First Inaugural Address," 266.

49. John G. Hay and John Nicolay, "Abraham Lincoln: A History—Premier or President," *Century Magazine* 35 (1888): 615–616.

50. Ruffin, *Diary*, 1:588.

51. "Monthly Record of Current Events," *Harper's New Monthly Magazine* 23 (June–November 1861): 120.

52. John Tyler to Julia Gardiner Tyler, April 17, 1861, in Lyon G. Tyler, *The Letters and Times of the Tylers* (Richmond, 1885), 2:641.

53. William W. Freehling, *The Road to Disunion*, vol. 2, *Secessionists Triumphant, 1854–1861* (New York, 2007), 530.

54. Henry Cleveland, *Alexander Stephens in Public and Private, with Letters and Speeches, Before, During, and Since the War* (Philadelphia, 1866), 721.

55. James Oakes, *Freedom National: The Destruction of Slavery in the United States* (New York, 2012), argues that the Republicans were unified from the beginning in adhering to an antislavery agenda. But even Oakes's Republicans never claimed in spring 1861 that they favored a war in order to bring about emancipation. They only believed that emancipation was a possible consequence of war.

56. Garrett Davis to George D. Prentice, *New York Times*, May 1, 1861.

57. "The Issue at the North," *New York Times*, April 6, 1861; "Lawlessness on a Gigantic Scale," *Philadelphia North American and United States Gazette*, February 4, 1861; *Daily Boston Traveller*, November 16, 1860; *Christian Herald*, April 25, 1861, as quoted in Stout, *Upon the Altar*, 40.

58. As quoted in Phillip S. Paludan, "The American Civil War Considered as a Crisis in Law and Order," *American Historical Review* 77 (1972): 1013–1034.

CHAPTER 4. THE BATTLE JOINED, 1861–1862

1. "To the Good People of the Counties of Loudon, Fairfax, and Prince William," in *OR*, ser. 1, 2:907.

2. McClellan to Brig. Gen. Don Carolos Buell, November 7, 1861, in *OR*, ser. 1, vol. 4, chap. 12, 342.

3. All of these totals exclude the deeply divided states of Kentucky and Missouri.

For the most useful summary of these population statistics, see Allan Nevins, *The War for the Union* (New York, 1959), 1:424–425.

4. Frederic Emory, "The Baltimore Riots," in *The Annals of the War, Written by Leading Participants North and South* (Philadelphia, 1879), 785.

5. "Proclamation," in *OR*, ser. 1, vol. 3, 467.

6. Lincoln to Orville H. Browning, September 22, 1861, in Lincoln, *Collected Works*, 4:531.

7. Gen. Irvin McDowell, Testimony to the Committee on the Conduct of the War, *Report of the Joint Committee on the Conduct of the War in Three Parts* (Washington, DC, 1863), 2:38. Many historians incorrectly attribute this statement to Lincoln. His name is nowhere mentioned in McDowell's testimony.

8. William C. Butler, *Sermon* (Richmond, 1861), as quoted in Stout, *Upon the Altar*, 74.

9. U. S. Grant to Gen. S. B. Buckner, in *OR*, ser. 1, 7:161.

10. Albert Sydney Johnston to William Preston Johnston, August 21, 1856, as quoted in Charles Roland, *Albert Sydney Johnston, Soldier of Three Republics* (Austin, TX, 1964), 182.

11. Ulysses Simpson Grant, *The Personal Memoirs of U. S. Grant* (1885; reprint, New York, 1995), 138.

12. *OR*, ser. 1, vol. 10, pt. 1, 110.

13. J. W. Phelps, "Proclamation by the Commander at Ship Island, Mississippi," in *The Destruction of Slavery*, ser. 1, vol. 1 of *Freedom: A Documentary History of Emancipation, 1861–1867*, ed. Ira Berlin et al. (New York, 1985), 200.

14. Gideon Welles, *Diary of Gideon Welles, Secretary of the Navy under Lincoln and Johnson* (Boston, 1909), 2:134.

15. C. Vann Woodward, ed., *Mary Chesnut's Civil War* (New Haven, CT, 1981), 360.

16. *OR*, ser. 1, 23:121.

17. *Lincoln and the Civil War in the Diaries and Letters of John Hay*, ed. Tyler Dennett (New York, 1939), 33.

18. McClellan to Brig. Gen. D. C. Buell, November 7, 1861 and November 12, 1861, in *OR*, ser. 1, vol. 4, chap. 12, 342, 355.

19. Stephen W. Sears, *George B. McClellan: The Young Napoleon* (New York, 1988), 168.

20. Lee to Jackson, April 25, 1862, *OR*, ser. 1, vol. 12, pt. 3, 865.

21. "Letter to Nephew, January 26, 1861," in Thomas Jackson Arnold, *Early Life and Letters of General Thomas J. Jackson* (New York, 1916), 294.

22. McCord, quoted in Woodward, *Mary Chesnut's Civil War*, 361.

23. Henry Alexander White, *Robert E. Lee and the Southern Confederacy, 1807–1870* (New York, 1907), 98–99.

24. Townsend, *Anecdotes*, 31.

25. Edward L. Ayers and Scott Nesbit, "Seeing Emancipation: Scale and Freedom in the American South," *Journal of the Civil War Era* 1 (2011): 5–6.

26. Sears, *George B. McClellan*, 213.

27. Lincoln to Seward, June 28, 1862, in Lincoln, *Collected Works*, 5:292.

28. General Orders No. 5, *OR*, ser. 1, vol. 12, pt. 2, 50.

29. General Orders No. 7, *OR*, ser. 1, vol. 12, chap. 24, pt. 2, 51.

30. McClellan to Lincoln, July 7, 1862, McClellan to Halleck, August 1, 1862, in *The Civil War Papers of George B. McClellan: Selected Correspondence, 1860–1865*, ed. Stephen W. Sears (New York, 1989), 344, 381.

31. McClellan to Mary Ellen McClellan, August 8, 1862, in McClellan, *Civil War Papers*, 388.

32. *OR*, ser. 1, vol. 12, chap., 24, pt. 3, 474.

33. McClellan to Abraham Lincoln, August 29, 1862, in McClellan, *Civil War Papers*, 416.

34. McClellan to Mary Ellen McClellan, September 25, 1862, in McClellan, *Civil War Papers*, 481.

35. Cooper, *Jefferson Davis, American*, 399.

36. David Urquhart, "Bragg's Advance and Retreat," *Battles and Leaders of the Civil War* (New York, 1888), 3:602.

37. Halleck to Buell, October 19, 1862, *OR*, ser. 1, vol. 16, pt. 2, 627.

CHAPTER 5. THE WAR TRANSFORMED, 1863–1864

1. Grant to Elihu B. Washburne, August 30, 1863, in *Papers of Ulysses S. Grant*, ed. John Y. Simon (Carbondale, IL, 1982), 9:218.

2. L. D. Young, *Reminiscences of a Soldier in the Orphan Brigade*, in *The Blue and the Gray: The Story of the Civil War as Told by Participants*, ed. Henry Steele Commager (New York, 1982), 1:372.

3. Lincoln to William S. Rosecrans, August 31, 1863, in Lincoln, *Collected Works*, 6:424.

4. Chief of Police of Nashville to the Commander of the Department of the Cumberland, March 7, 1863, in Berlin et al., *Destruction of Slavery*, 301.

5. Alexander K. McLure, *Recollections of Half a Century* (Salem, MA, 1902), 347.

6. Daniel W. Stowell, "Stonewall Jackson and the Providence of God," in *Religion and the American Civil War*, ed. Randall M. Miller, Harry S. Stout, and Charles Reagan Wilson (New York, 1998), 187.

7. Halleck to Grant, April 9, 1863, *OR*, ser. 1, vol. 24, pt. 1, 28; Halleck to Grant, March 20, 1863, *OR*, ser. 1, vol. 24, pt. 1, 22.

8. William Sherman to John Sherman, April 26, 1863, in *The Sherman Letters: Correspondence between General and Senator Sherman from 1837 to 1891*, ed. Rachel Sherman Thorndike (New York, 1894), 201.

9. Lee to Davis, April 27, 1863, *OR*, ser. 1, vol. 25, pt. 2, 752.

10. Woodward, *Mary Chesnut's Civil War*, 415.

11. Grant, *Personal Memoirs*, 189.

12. Although historians have cited a variety of figures, the numbers here are Grant's own. See Robert Underwood Johnson and Clarence Clough Buel, ed., *Battles and Leaders of the Civil War* (New York, 1884), 3:495.

13. This figure comes from Grant's report. See Grant to Col. J. C. Kelton, Assistant Adjutant-General, July 6, 1863, in *OR*, ser. 1, vol. 24, pt. 1, 58–59.

14. H. W. Halleck to U. S. Grant, August 1, 1863, in *OR*, ser. 1, vol. 24, pt. 1, 63.

15. Steven E. Woodworth, *Beneath a Northern Sky: A Short History of the Gettysburg Campaign*, 2nd ed. (Lanham, MD, 2008), 27.

16. John Gibbon, "The Council of War on the Second Day," in Johnson and Buel, *Battles and Leaders*, 3:314.

17. Charles T. Loehr, *War History of the Old First Virginia Infantry Regiment, Army of Northern Virginia* (Richmond, 1884), 38.

18. *Personal Reminiscences, Anecdotes, and Letters of Robert E. Lee*, ed. J. William Jones (New York, 1875), 196.

19. William D. Lyon to George Lyon, July 18, 1863, William D. Lyon Papers, as quoted in Woodworth, *Beneath a Northern Sky*, 205.

20. *Letters from General Rosecrans! To the Democracy of Indiana; Actions of the Ohio Regiments at Murfreesboro regarding the Copperheads* (Philadelphia, 1863), 2; Larry J. Daniel, *Days of Glory: The Army of the Cumberland, 1861–1865* (Baton Rouge, LA, 2006), 254–255.

21. William Howard Russell, *My Diary North and South* (Boston, 1863) 207.

22. Grant, *Personal Memoirs*, 260.

23. John Keegan, *The American Civil War: A Military History* (New York, 2009), 223.

24. John Hay, *Letters from John Hay and Extracts from Diary* (Washington, 1908), 1:112.

25. William J. Cooper Jr., *Jefferson Davis and the Civil War Era* (Baton Rouge, LA, 2008), 76.

26. The numbers are Grant's. See Grant, "Chattanooga," in Johnson and Buel, *Battles and Leaders*, 3:693.

27. *Testimony Taken by the Joint Select Committee to inquire into the Condition of Affairs in the Late Insurrectionary States*, vol. 13, *Miscellaneous and Florida* (Washington, 1872), 20.

28. Special Orders, No. 245, November 14, 1863, *OR*, ser. 1, vol. 31, pt. 3, 694.

29. William T. Sherman, *Memoirs of General W. T. Sherman* (New York, 2000, orig. pub. 1875), 364.

30. Forrest to Lieut. Colonel Thomas M. Jack, April 15, 1864, *OR*, ser. 1, vol. 32, pt. 1, 610.

31. John Cimprich, *Fort Pillow, a Civil War Massacre, and Public Memory* (Baton Rouge, LA, 2005), 129. Cimprich's book includes a complete table of Union casualty figures, based on military records in the National Archives.

32. "Report of Colonel Edward Bouton, Fifty-Ninth US Colored Infantry, commanding Third Brigade," June 17, 1864, *OR*, ser. 1, vol. 39, pt. 1, 126.

33. "Speech to Ulysses S. Grant," March 9, 1864, in Lincoln, *Collected Works*, 7:234.

34. Hay, *Lincoln and the Civil War*, 180.

35. Grant, *Personal Memoirs*, 344.

36. Keegan, *American Civil War*, 249.

37. J. B. McClure, *Anecdotes of Abraham Lincoln and Lincoln's Stories* (Chicago, 1879), 153.

38. *Life and Letters of Emory Upton, Colonel of the Fourth Regiment of Artillery, and Brevet Major-General, US Army*, ed. Peter S. Michie (New York, 1885), 108.

39. For these figures, see Sherman, *Memoirs*, 387.

40. Sherman, *Memoirs*, 444.

41. Sherman to Maj. Gen. H. W. Halleck, September 3, 1864, *OR*, ser. 1, vol. 38, pt. 5, 777.

42. "Order of Thanks to Gen. William T. Sherman and Others," September 3, 1864, in Lincoln, *Collected Works*, 7:534.

43. *Sherman: A Memorial in Art, Oratory, and Literature, by the Society of the Army of the Tennessee with the Aid of the Congress of the United States of America* (Washington, DC, 1904), 305.

44. Grant to Sherman, November 2, 1864, *OR*, ser. 1, vol. 39, pt. 3, 594.

45. Special Field Orders, No. 120, November 9, 1864, in *OR*, ser. 1, vol. 39, pt. 3, 713.

46. Sherman, *Memoirs*, 546.

47. Sherman to J. B. Fry, September 3, 1884, Letterbook, William T. Sherman Papers, Library of Congress, as quoted in Mark Grimsley, *The Hard Hand of War: Union Military Policy toward Southern Civilians, 1861–1865* (New York, 1995), 193.

48. Grant to Sherman, December 18, 1864, in Sherman, *Memoirs*, 584.

49. Sherman to Lincoln, December 22, 1864, in *Sherman's Civil War: Selected Correspondence of William T. Sherman, 1860–1865*, ed. Brooks D. Simpson and Jean V. Berlin (Chapel Hill, NC, 1999), 772.

50. Sherman to Grant, December 18, 1864, *OR*, ser. 1, vol. 44, 742–743.

51. Grant, *Personal Memoirs*, 226.

CHAPTER 6. POLITICS AND CONSTITUTIONALISM IN THE WARTIME UNION, 1861–1864

1. Julia Taft Bayne, *Tad Lincoln's Father* (1931; reprint, Lincoln, NE, 2001), 50.

2. Doris Kearns Goodwin, *Team of Rivals: The Political Genius of Abraham Lincoln* (New York, 2005).

3. "Proclamation Calling Militia and Convening Congress," in Lincoln, *Collected Works*, 4:332.

4. Clement L. Vallandigham, *Speech of Hon. C. L. Vallandigham, of Ohio, on Executive Usurpation* (Washington, DC, 1861), 4.

5. John G. Nicolay and John Hay, *Abraham Lincoln: A History* (New York, 1886), 4:151.

6. Lincoln to Winfield Scott, April 27, 1861, in Lincoln, *Collected Works*, 4:347.

7. Although there has been some confusion among scholars about whether it was a federal circuit court opinion or a Supreme Court decision written in chambers, Jonathan W. White convincingly concludes that Taney wrote the opinion as a circuit judge but that he attempted to lend more weight to the opinion by indicating that he wrote it as chief justice. *Abraham Lincoln and Treason in the Civil War: The Trials of John Merryman* (Baton Rouge, LA, 2011), 40–42.

8. *Ex parte Merryman*, 17 F. Cas. 144, 149 (1861).

9. 17 F. Cas. 144, 149.

10. 17 F. Cas. 144, 153.

11. "Message to Congress," July 4, 1861, in Lincoln, *Collected Works*, 4:430, 438.

12. US *Senate Journal*, 37th Cong., 1st sess., 25 July 1861. The House version had slightly different wording. See US *House Journal*, 37th Cong., 1st sess., 22 July 1861.

13. "Address before the Wisconsin State Agricultural Society, Milwaukee, Wisconsin," September 30, 1859, in Lincoln, *Collected Works*, 3:478.

14. *Cong. Globe*, 37th Cong., 1st Sess., Appendix 5 (1861).

15. Steven Hahn, *A Nation Under Our Feet: Black Political Struggles in the Rural South from Slavery to the Great Migration* (Cambridge, MA, 2003), 70.

16. Jane Flaherty, "'The Exhausted Condition of the Treasury' on the Eve of the Civil War," *Civil War History* 55 (2009): 245.

17. Act of July 1, 1862, ch. 119, 12 *Stat.* 475.

18. "Annual Message to Congress," December 1, 1862, in Lincoln, *Collected Works*, 5:522.

19. John Sherman, *Selected Speeches and Reports on Finance and Taxation, From 1859 to 1878* (New York, 1879), 70.

20. Act of May 20, 1862, ch. 75, 12 *Stat.* 392.

21. *Cong. Globe*, 37th Cong., 2nd Sess., 26 (1861).

22. "Fragment on the Constitution and the Union," in Lincoln, *Collected Works*, 4:169.

23. Benjamin Wade to Zechariah Chandler, September 23, 1861, Zechariah Chandler Papers, Library of Congress, as quoted in James F. Simon, *Lincoln and Chief Justice Taney: Slavery, Secession, and the President's War Powers* (New York, 2006), 203.

24. William T. Sherman, "Commander of the 5th Division of the Army of the Tennessee to a Tennessee Slaveholder," in Berlin et al., *Destruction of Slavery*, 293.

25. Act of July 17, 1862, ch. 195, 12 *Stat.* 591.

26. Welles, *Diary*, 1:70.

27. Lincoln to Horace Greeley, August 22, 1862, in Lincoln, *Collected Works*, 5:389.

28. Paul Finkelman, "Lincoln, Emancipation, and the Limits of Constitutional Change," *Supreme Court Review* (2008): 349–387, makes the point that Lincoln needed a constitutional framework, political support, and a military victory in order to move ahead with a proclamation. By September 1862, Lincoln had all three.

29. Preliminary Emancipation Proclamation, September 22, 1862, in Lincoln, *Collected Works*, 5:435.

30. *New York Times*, October 7, 1862.

31. "January First, 1863," *Douglass's Monthly* (January 1863), as quoted in Edna Greene Medford, "'Beckoning Them to the Dreamed of Promise of Freedom': African-Americans and Lincoln's Proclamation of Emancipation," in *The Lincoln Forum: Abraham Lincoln, Gettysburg, and the Civil War*, ed. John Y. Simon et al. (Mason City, IA, 1999), 49.

32. "Mr. Seymour at the Democratic State Convention, Albany, September 10, 1862, on Receiving the Nomination of Governor," in *Public Record: Including Speeches, Messages, Proclamations, Official Correspondence, and other Public Utterances of Horatio Seymour; From the Campaign of 1856 to the Present Time*, ed. Thomas M. Cook and Thomas W. Knox (New York, 1868), 54. Seymour reacted to the idea of emancipation, not the actual Preliminary Emancipation Proclamation, which was not issued until twelve days later.

33. Edward Bates, *Opinion of Attorney General Bates on Citizenship* (Washington, DC, 1862), 3.

34. Ibid., 26.

35. Oakes, *Freedom National*, 367–376.

36. Emancipation Proclamation, January 1, 1863, in Lincoln, *Collected Works*, 6:31.

37. Frederick Seward, *Seward at Washington, as Senator and Secretary of State: A Memoir of His Life with Selections from His Letters, 1861–1872* (New York, 1891), 151.

38. Mark E. Neely Jr., *The Fate of Liberty: Abraham Lincoln and Civil Liberties* (New York, 1991), 60.

39. *Prize Cases*, 67 U.S. 635, 637 (1863).

40. 67 U.S. 635, 669.

41. *Cong. Globe*, 37th Cong., 3rd Sess., 976 (1863).

42. Act of March 3, 1863, ch. 75, 12 *Stat.* 733.

43. "Habeas Corpus," in the *American Annual Cyclopedia and Register of Important Events of the Year 1863* (New York, 1864), 3:474.

44. Lincoln to Erastus Corning and Others, June 12, 1863, in Lincoln, *Collected Works*, 6:264.

45. Ibid., Lincoln to Erastus Corning and Others, 6:267.

46. "Address Delivered at the Dedication of the Cemetery at Gettysburg, Second Draft," November 19, 1863, in Lincoln, *Collected Works*, 7:18.

47. Lincoln to James C. Conkling, August 26, 1863, in Lincoln, *Collected Works*, 6:409.

48. "Address Delivered at the Dedication of the Cemetery at Gettysburg, Second Draft," in Lincoln, *Collected Works*, 7:18–19.

49. *New York Tribune*, August 5, 1864, as quoted in Edward McPherson, *Of the United States during the Great Rebellion*, 2nd ed. (Washington, DC, 1864), 332.

50. C. Chauncey Burr, "The Tricks of Tyrants," *The Old Guard: A Monthly Journal Devoted to the Principles of 1776 and 1787* 2 (June 1864): 132–133.

51. *Subgenation: Theory of the Normal Relation of the Races; An Answer to "Miscegenation"* (New York, 1864), 65; "The Lincoln Catechism, Wherein the Eccentricities & Beauties of Despotism are Fully Set Forth. A Guide to the Presidential Election of 1864," in *Union Pamphlets of the Civil War*, ed. Frank Friedel (Cambridge, MA, 1967), 2:1008.

52. Charles Sumner to Abraham Lincoln, October 12, 1864. Available at Abraham Lincoln Papers at the Library of Congress, Manuscript Division (Washington, DC: American Memory Project, 2000–2002), http://memory.loc.gov/ammem/alhtml /malhome.html; "The Death of Roger B. Taney," *New York Times*, October 14, 1864.

53. Douglass, "Representatives of the Future South," *Frederick Douglass Papers*, ser. 1, vol. 4, ed. John W. Blassingame (New Haven, CT, 1991), 36.

CHAPTER 7. POLITICS AND CONSTITUTIONALISM IN THE WARTIME CONFEDERACY, 1861–1864

1. Jefferson Davis, "Messages," January 12, 1863, in *Compilation of Messages and Papers of the Confederacy, Including the Diplomatic Correspondence, 1861–1865*, ed. James D. Richardson (Nashville, 1906), 1:290, 292.

2. Sarah Wadley Diary, July 28, 1861, Southern Historical Collection, as quoted in George Rable, *The Confederate Republic: A Revolution against Politics* (Chapel Hill, NC, 1994), 87.

3. A study of the Confederate Congresses revealed that "at least 84 percent of the 267 men who served . . . owned slaves" and "more than half the congressmen had wealth amounting to 600 percent of the average for individuals in their home county." See Paul Escott, *The Confederacy: The Slaveholders' Failed Venture* (Santa Barbara, CA, 2010), 8.

4. Thomas R. R. Cobb, "In Advocacy of Secession," in Lucian Lamar Knight, *A Standard History of Georgia and Georgians* (Chicago, 1917), 3:1491. On secession as a conservative revolution, see, e.g., Emory Thomas, *The Confederate Nation, 1861–1865* (New York, 1979).

5. James M. Matthews, ed., *Statutes at Large of the Confederate States of America, Commencing with the First Session of the First Congress* (Richmond, 1862), 1.

6. Ibid., 30.

7. James M. Matthews, ed., *Public Laws of the Confederate States of America, Passed at the First Session of the First Congress* (Richmond, 1862), 79.

8. *Daily Journal*, April 17, 1862.

9. Brown to Jefferson Davis, May 9, 1862, in Herbert Fielder, *A Sketch of the Life and Times and Speeches of Joseph E. Brown* (Springfield, MA, 1883), 360.

10. Ibid., Brown to Davis, May 9, 1862, 361–362.

11. George Randolph to Jefferson Davis, August 12, 1862, *OR*, ser. 4, 2:45.

12. *Ex parte Hill, in re. Willis, Johnson and Reynolds v. Confederate States*, 38 Ala. 429, 447 (1863).

13. *Ex parte Mayer*, 27 Tex. 715, 720 (1864).

14. Constitution of the Confederate States of America, Article I, Section 8, in James M. Matthews, ed., *Statutes at Large of the Provisional Government of the Confederate States of America, from the Institution of the Government, February 8, 1861, to Its Termination, February 18, 1862, Inclusive* (Richmond, 1864), 14.

15. Wigfall quoted in Benson J. Lossing, *Pictorial History of the Civil War in the United States of America* (Philadelphia, 1866), 1:82.

16. "Henry Ravenel Expects Foreign Intervention," in Commager, *The Blue and the Gray*, 519.

17. *London Times*, March 20, 1861, as quoted in Howard Jones, *Blue and Gray Diplomacy: A History of Union and Confederate Foreign Relations* (Chapel Hill, NC, 2010), 18.

18. R. M. T. Hunter to Hotze, November 14, 1861, in *Henry Hotze, Confederate Propagandist: Selected Writings on Revolution, Recognition, and Race*, ed. Lonnie A. Burnett (Tuscaloosa, AL, 2008), 111.

19. Jefferson Davis, *The Rise and Fall of the Confederate Government* (1881; reprint, New York, 1958), 2:307.

20. William G. Brownlow, *Sketches of the Rise, Progress, and Decline of Secession, with a Narrative of Personal Adventures among the Rebels* (Philadelphia, 1862), 346.

21. "Peace—When Shall We Have Peace?" (Raleigh, NC) *Weekly Standard*, July 22, 1863.

22. Thomas Ruffin to E. J. Hale, in *Papers of Thomas Ruffin*, ed. J. G. de Roulhac Hamilton (Raleigh, 1920), 3:327–328.

23. Vance to Davis, December 30, 1864, in *Jefferson Davis, Constitutionalist: His Letters, Papers, and Speeches*, ed. Dunbar Rowland (Jackson, MI, 1923), 6:141.

24. Ibid., Davis to Vance, January 8, 1864, 6:146.

25. "Message to Congress, February 3, 1864," in Davis, *Jefferson Davis*, 6:168–169.

26. Alexander Stephens, "Speech on the State of the Confederacy, Delivered before the Georgia Legislature at Milledgeville, Georgia," in Cleveland, *Alexander H. Stephens*, 788.

27. "Resolutions on the Suspension of Habeas Corpus," in *OR*, ser. 4, 3:235.

28. Mark E. Neely Jr., *Southern Rights: Political Prisoners and the Myth of Confederate Constitutionalism* (Charlottesville, VA, 1999), 1.

29. *Richmond Examiner*, January 8, 1863, in Orville J. Victor, *The History, Civil, Political, and Military, of the Southern Rebellion* (New York, 1864), 3:465.

30. *Macon Telegraph*, February 12, 1863, 3.

31. "The Emancipation Proclamation," *Richmond Dispatch*, reprinted in the *New York Tribune*, January 12, 1863.

32. "Joint Resolutions Adopted by the Confederate Congress on the Subject of Retaliation, April 30–May 1, 1863," *OR*, ser. 2, 5:940.

33. "A Word for the Negro," *Index*, February 12, 1863, in Hotze, *Henry Hotze*, 192–193.

34. *Address of Congress to the People of the Confederate States, Joint Resolution in Relation to the War, Adopted on February 16, 1864* (Richmond, 1864), 6.

35. Lee to Davis, September 2, 1864, in Davis, *Jefferson Davis*, 6:327.

36. Entry for November 17, 1864, in *The Journal of Josiah Gorgas, 1857–1879*, ed. Sarah Woolfolk Wiggins (Tuscaloosa, AL, 1995), 139.

37. "Jefferson Davis to the Confederate Congress, November 7, 1864," in Davis, *Jefferson Davis*, 6:396.

38. Ruffin to E. J. Hale, in de Rouhac Hamilton, ed., *Papers of Thomas Ruffin*, 3:328–329.

39. John Milton to Joseph E. Brown, April 14, 1864, in *OR*, ser. 4, 3:304.

40. *A Diary from Dixie, as Written by Mary Boykin Chesnut*, ed. Isabella D. Martin and Myrta Lockett Avary (New York, 1905), 29.

41. Michael Perman, *Pursuit of Unity: A Political History of the American South* (Chapel Hill, NC, 2009), 108.

42. Robert Toombs to Alexander Stephens, March 2, 1863, in "The Correspondence of Robert Toombs, Alexander H. Stephens, and Howell Cobb," ed. Ulrich B. Phillips, *Annual Report of the American Historical Association for the Year 1911* (Washington, DC, 1913), 2:611.

CHAPTER 8. SOLDIERS, CIVILIANS, AND
REVOLUTIONARY CONSTITUTIONALISM

1. Albert W. Mann, *History of the Forty-Fifth Regiment, Massachusetts Volunteer Militia* (Jamaica Plain, MA, 1908), 301. Cecelski tells this powerful story in *Fire of Freedom*.

2. E. B. Long, *The Civil War Day by Day: An Almanac, 1861–1865* (New York, 1971), 705–709.

3. "Three Years in Battle and Three in Federal Prisons," in *The Papers of Randolph Abbott Shotwell*, ed. J. G. de Roulhac Hamilton (Raleigh, NC, 1929), 1:316.

4. Sam Watkins, *Company Aytch, or A Side Show of the Big Show*, ed. M. Thomas Inge (1882; reprint, New York, 1999), 27, 25.

5. Gary Gallagher, *The Confederate War: How Popular Will, Nationalism, and Military Strategy Could Not Stave Off Defeat* (Cambridge, MA, 1997), 31–32. Because of poor records, particularly in the Confederacy, it is difficult to pinpoint the number of deserters. See Mark A. Weitz, *More Damning than Slaughter: Desertion in the Confederate Army* (Lincoln, NE, 2005).

6. Wiley Sword, *Southern Invincibility: A History of the Confederate Heart* (New York, 1999); Jason Phillips, *Diehard Rebels: The Confederate Culture of Invincibility* (Athens, GA, 2007); Grady McWhiney and Perry D. Jamieson, *Attack and Die: Civil War Military Tactics and the Southern Heritage* (Tuscaloosa, AL, 1982), 7.

7. Approximately 90 percent of white Union soldiers could read and write, and about 80 percent of Confederates could do so. James McPherson, *For Cause and Comrades: Why Men Fought in the Civil War* (New York, 1997), 11.

8. Samuel Evans to his father, September 13, 1863, in Evans Family Papers, Ohio Historical Society, as quoted in Mcpherson, *What They Fought For*, 33.

9. John Worrell Northrop, *Chronicles from the Diary of a War Prisoner in Andersonville and Other Military Prisons of the South in 1864: Experiences, Observations, Interviews, and Poems Written in Prison, with Historical Introduction* (Wichita, KS, 1904), 84.

10. Joseph C. Webb to Robina Norwood, September 19, 1863, in *Echoes of Happy Valley: Letters and Diaries Family Life in the South Civil War History*, ed. Thomas Felix Hickerson (Chapel Hill, NC, 1962), 74.

11. Marcellus Mundy, "Commander of Kentucky Regiment to the President," in Berlin et al., *Destruction of Slavery*, 547, 570.

12. James R. Matthews to A. Johnson, June 12, 1865, in Andrew Johnson, *The Papers of Andrew Johnson* (Knoxville, TN, 1967–2000), 8:224.

13. Richard Nelson Current, *Lincoln's Loyalists: Union Soldiers from the Confederacy* (New York, 1992), 146, 218.

14. Deanne Blanton and Lauren M. Cook, *They Fought Like Demons: Women Soldiers in the Civil War* (New York, 2002), 7.

15. Richard J. Carwardine, *Evangelicals and Politics in Antebellum America* (New Haven, CT, 1993), 44.

16. Henry Warren Howe, *Passages from the Life of Henry Warren Howe, Consisting of Diaries and Letters Written during the Civil War, 1861–1865* (Lowell, MA, 1899), 15.

17. *A Life's Retrospect: Autobiography of Rev. Granville Moody*, ed. Sylvester Weeks (Cincinnati, 1890), 447.

18. *Presbyter*, May 19, 1861, as quoted in Stout, *Upon the Altar*, 43.

19. *Life and Letters of Benjamin Morgan Palmer*, ed. Thomas Cary Johnson (Richmond, VA, 1906), 209.

20. Edward Reed, *A People Saved by the Lord: A Sermon Delivered at Flat Rock, July 28, 1861* (Charleston, SC, 1861), 9.

21. George Foster Pierce and Benjamin Morgan Palmer, *Sermons of Bishop Pierce and Rev. B. M. Palmer, D. D., Delivered before the General Assembly at Milledgeville, Ga., on Fast Day, March 27, 1863* (Milledgeville, GA, 1863), 5, 39–40.

22. Ebeneezer Baptist Association, Minutes, 1864, 2, as quoted in Daniel W. Stowell, *Rebuilding Zion: The Religious Reconstruction of the South, 1863–1877* (New York, 1998), 38.

23. "Georgia Slaveholders to the Commander of the 3rd Division of the Confederate District of Georgia," in Berlin et al., *Destruction of Slavery*, 795.

24. Robert Dale Owen to Abraham Lincoln, Wednesday, August 5, 1863 (Sends report of John Eaton concerning freedmen in Tennessee; with abstract of Eaton's report), Abraham Lincoln Papers, Library of Congress, Series 1, General Correspondence, 1833–1916.

25. "Testimony by the Superintendent of Contrabands at Fortress Monroe, Virginia, before the American Freedmen's Inquiry Commission," in Berlin et al., *Destruction of Slavery*, 89–90.

26. "Resolutions of a Negro Mass Meeting," *Liberator*, May 31, 1861, in *A Documentary History of the Negro People in the United States*, ed. Herbert Aptheker (New York, 1951), 1:464–465; *Christian Recorder*, August 29, 1863, as quoted in Stowell, *Rebuilding Zion*, 69.

27. Frederick Douglass, "How to End the War," *Douglass' Monthly*, May 1861, in *Frederick Douglass: Selected Speeches and Writings*, ed. Philip S. Foner (1950; reprint, Chicago, 1999), 448.

28. "Emancipation Proclamation," January 1, 1863, in Lincoln, *Collected Works*, 6:30.

29. John S. Rock, "What If the Slaves Are Emancipated?," in *Lift Every Voice: African American Oratory, 1787–1900*, ed. Philip S. Foner and Robert James Branham (Tuscaloosa, AL, 1998), 367.

30. As quoted in James M. McPherson, *The Negro's Civil War: How American Negroes Felt and Acted during the War for the Union* (New York, 1965), 177.

31. As quoted in Carleton Mabee with Susan Mabee Newhouse, *Sojourner Truth: Slave, Prophet, Legend* (New York, 1993), 117.

32. John W. Pratt to Sir, November 30, 1864, *Christian Recorder*, December 24, 1864, as quoted in Joseph T. Glatthaar, *Forged in Battle: The Civil War Alliance of Black Soldiers and White Officers* (New York, 1990), 79.

33. As quoted in Lewis Perry, "Harriet Jacobs and the 'Dear Old Flag,'" *African American Review* 42 (2008): 596.

34. Ira Berlin et al., eds., *The Wartime Genesis of Free Labor, The Lower South*, ser. 1, vol. 3, of *Freedom: A Documentary History of Emancipation* (New York, 1990), 77–80; Hahn, *Political Worlds*, 61–64.

35. "The Ovation to the Black Regiment," *New York Times*, March 7, 1864.

36. *The Civil War Diary of Sarah Morgan*, ed. Charles East (1913; reprint, Athens, GA, 1991), 65.

37. General Orders Number 28, *OR*, ser. 1, vol. 15, chap. 27, 426.

38. Jefferson Davis, "A Proclamation by the President of the Confederate States," in Benjamin F. Butler, *Autobiography and Personal Reminiscences of Major Gen. Benjamin F. Butler—Butler's Book: A Review of His Legal, Political, and Military Career* (Boston, 1892), 543.

39. W. T. Sherman to John Sherman, August 13, 1862, in *Sherman's Civil War*, 273.

40. General Orders Number 100, sect. 4, pt. 82, in John Fabian Witt, *Lincoln's Code: The Laws of War in American History* (New York, 2012), 385.

41. General Orders, No. 100, sect. 3, pts. 57–58, in Witt, *Lincoln's Code*, 383.

42. James I. Robertson Jr., *Soldiers Blue and Gray* (Columbia, SC, 1998), 194, 190.

43. Robert Knox Sneden, *Eye of the Storm: A Civil War Odyssey*, ed. Charles F. Bryan, Jr. and Nelson D. Lankford (New York, 2000), 229.

44. Grant to Gen. Benjamin Butler, August 18, 1864, *OR*, ser. 2, 7:606–607.

45. J. David Hacker, "A Census-Based Count of the Civil War Dead," *Civil War History*, 57 (2011): 307–348.

46. Daniel E. Sutherland, *The Expansion of Everyday Life, 1860–1876* (New York, 1989), 19.

47. Kate Cumming, *A Journal of Hospital Life in the Confederate Army of Tennessee from the Battle of Shiloh to the End of the War with Sketches of Life and Character, and Brief Notices of Current Events during that Period* (Louisville, 1866), 88.

48. J. S. Poland, ed., *A Digest of the Military Laws of the United States from 1860 to the Second Session of the Fortieth Congress, 1867, Relating to the Army, Volunteers, Militia and the Rebellion and Reconstruction of the Southern States* (Boston, 1868), Section 286, 95.

49. Drew Faust, *This Republic of Suffering: Death and the American Civil War* (New York, 2008), 241.

50. "Further of the Fort Pillow Massacre, Statements by an Eye Witness," *San Francisco Bulletin*, published as *Daily Evening Bulletin*, May 20, 1864, vol. 17, issue 37, 1.

51. Some argue that African American agency in wartime made the Civil War "the greatest slave rebellion in modern history," but such an interpretation surely stretches the definition of slave rebellion well beyond that used for the antebellum era. See Hahn, *Political Worlds*, 55–114; Stephanie McCurry, *Confederate Reckoning: Power and Politics in the Civil War South* (Cambridge, MA, 2010), 218–262.

52. Cecelski, *Fire of Freedom*, 116.

53. "Proceedings of the National Convention of Colored Men, held in the City of Syracuse, NY, October 4, 5, 6, 7, 1864; with the Bill of Wrongs and Rights, and the Address to the American People," 42–43, in Bell, *Minutes of the Proceedings of the National Negro Conventions*.

CHAPTER 9. THE END AND THE BEGINNING, 1865–1866

1. *Charleston Mercury*, January 13, 1865, in Robert F. Durden, *The Confederate Debate on Emancipation* (Baton Rouge, 1972), 232.

2. "Response to a Serenade, February 1, 1865," in Lincoln, *Collected Works*, 8:255.

3. "Freedom Triumphant!," *Liberator*, Boston, MA, February 10, 1865.

4. "From Boston," *New Orleans Tribune*, February 15, 1865, 1.

5. Alexander H. Stephens, *A Constitutional View of the Late War Between the States; Its Causes, Character, Conduct, and Results, Presented in a Series of Colloquies at Liberty Hall* (Philadelphia, 1868–1870), 2:613–614.

6. Paul D. Escott, *"What Shall We Do with the Negro?": Lincoln, White Racism, and Civil War America* (Charlottesville, VA, 2009), 201–225.

7. Gov. Joseph Brown, Message to the Georgia General Assembly, February 15, 1865, in Allen D. Candler, *Confederate Records of the State of Georgia* (Atlanta, 1909), 2:835.

8. David Yulee to Jefferson Davis, October 27, 1864, as quoted in Bruce Levine, *Confederate Emancipation: Southern Plans to Free and Arm Slaves during the Civil War* (New York, 2006), 46.

9. Howell Cobb to Secretary James Seddon, January 8, 1865, in *OR*, ser. 4, 3:1009.

10. *Journal of a Secesh Lady: The Diary of Catherine Ann Devereaux Edmonston, 1860–1866*, ed. Beth Gilbert Crabtree and James W. Patton (Raleigh, 1979), 651.

11. "An Act to Increase the Military Force of the Confederate States," in *OR*, ser. 4, 3:1161–1162.

12. "From Boston," *New Orleans Tribune*, February 15, 1865, 1.

13. "Second Inaugural Address," in Lincoln, *Collected Works*, 8:333–334.

14. Ibid., 8:333.

15. "Jefferson Davis to the People of the Confederate States of America," April 4, 1865, in Davis, *Jefferson Davis*, 6:530–531.

16. *Report of Lieutenant-General U. S. Grant, of the Armies of the United States, 1864–65* (New York, 1866), 73.

17. Lee, *Personal Reminiscences*, 308.

18. Charles A. Phelps, *Life and Public Services of General Ulysses S. Grant, from His Boyhood to the Present Time* (Boston, 1868), 297.

19. Andrew Johnson, "Speech on Secession," December 18–19, 1860, in Johnson, *Papers*, 4:46; Lincoln to Henry Halleck, July 11, 1862, in Lincoln, *Collected Works*, 5:314.

20. Johnson, "Remarks on the Fall of Richmond," April 3, 1865, in Johnson, *Papers*, 7:545.

21. Act of March 3, 1865, ch. 90, 13 *Stat.* 507–508.

22. Act of March 3, 1865, ch. 90, 13 *Stat.* 508.

23. "Circular No. 13," July 28, 1865, in *Documentary History of Reconstruction: Political, Military, Social, Religious, Educational, and Industrial, 1865 to the Present Time*, ed. Walter L. Fleming (Cleveland, 1906), 1:353.

24. "Endorsement re. Berryman B. Leake," August 16, 1865, in Johnson, *Papers*, 8:603.

25. Henry Bram et al. to the President of the United States, as quoted in Hahn, *Nation Under Our Feet*, 144.

26. *Nashville Daily Press and Times*, August 8, 1865, as quoted in Hahn, *Nation Under Our Feet*, 120.

27. "Proceedings of the First Annual Meeting of the National Equal Rights League, Held in Cleveland, Ohio, September 19, 20, and 21, 1865," in *Proceedings of the Black National and State Conventions, 1865–1900*, ed. Philip S. Foner and George E. Walker (Philadelphia, 1986), 1:65.

28. Johnson to Gov. William Sharkey, November 17, 1865, in *Index to Senate Executive Documents for the First Session of the Thirty-Ninth Congress, of the United States of America, 1865–66* (Washington, DC, 1866), 234.

29. "Mississippi Vagrant Law," in Fleming, *Documentary History of Reconstruction*, 284.

30. "Mississippi Apprentice Law," in Fleming, *Documentary History of Reconstruction*, 282.

31. "Celebration by the Colored People's Educational Monument Association in Memory of Abraham Lincoln, on the Fourth of July, 1865 in the Presidential Grounds, Washington, DC," in *Proceedings of the Black National and State Conventions*, 1:25.

32. "Message of the President of the United States to the Two Houses of Congress at the Commencement of the First Session of the Thirty-Ninth Congress," December 4, 1865, in Johnson, *Papers*, 9:469.

33. Ibid., 9:471.

34. Ibid., 9:473–474.

35. Ibid., 9:472.

36. Ibid., 9:474.

37. "Reconstruction," in *Cong. Globe*, 39th Cong., 1st Sess. 72 (1865).

38. Johnson, "Speech of the 22nd February, 1866," in *A Political Manual for 1866, Including a Classified Summary of the Important Executive, Legislative, and Politico-Military Facts of the Period, From President Johnson's Accession, April 15, 1865 to July 4, 1866*, ed. Edward McPherson (Washington, DC, 1866), 60–61. Stevens had first brought beheadings into the discussion when he criticized Johnson's proclamation against a suffrage amendment: "Had it been made to Parliament by a British king, it would have cost him his head." *Cong. Globe*, 39th Cong., 1st Sess. 536 (1866).

39. Act of April 9, 1866, ch. 31, 14 *Stat.* 27.

40. "Veto of Civil Rights Bill," March 27, 1866, in Johnson, *Papers*, 10:313, 314–315.

41. Ibid., 10:319.

42. John Hay and Clara Louise Hay, *Letters of John Hay and Extracts from Diary* (Washington, DC, 1908), 1:112.

43. Roger Ransom, *Conflict and Compromise: The Political Economy of Slavery, Emancipation, and the American Civil War* (New York, 1989), 70; Claudia Dale Goldin, "The Economics of Emancipation," *Journal of Economic History* 33 (1973): 73–74.

44. "Isham G. Harris as Warrior and Fugitive," *Atlanta Constitution*, August 1, 1897, as quoted in Sam Davis Elliott, *Confederate Governor and United States Senator Isham G. Harris of Tennessee* (Baton Rouge, 2010), 188.

45. Edmund Ruffin, diary, as quoted in Avery Craven, *Edmund Ruffin, Southerner: A Study in Secession* (New York, 1932), 259.

46. Eliza Fain, as quoted in Stowell, *Rebuilding Zion*, 42, 44.

47. Chase to Johnson, May 21, 1865, in Brooks D. Simpson, Leroy P. Graf, and John Muldowny, eds., *Advice after Appomattox: Letters to Andrew Johnson, 1865–1866* (Knoxville, TN, 1987), 35.

48. Stevens, "Speech on the Fourteenth Amendment," May 10, 1866, in *Selected Papers of Thaddeus Stevens*, ed. Beverly Wilson Palmer and Holly Byers Ochoa (Pittsburgh, 1998), 2:138.

49. *Barron v. Baltimore*, 32 U.S. 243 (1833).

50. Edward A. Pollard, *The Lost Cause: A New Southern History of the War of the Confederates* (New York, 1867), 751–752.

51. Peyton McCrary, "The Party of Revolution: Republican Ideas about Politics and Social Change, 1862–1867," *Civil War History* 30 (1984): 330–350.

52. Frederick Douglass, "Reconstruction," *Atlantic Monthly*, 18 (1866), 762.

CHAPTER 10. POLITICS AND THE RECONSTRUCTED CONSTITUTIONAL ORDER, 1867–1876

1. "To Congress," March 30, 1870, in Grant, *Papers*, 20:130.

2. Acts of March 2, 1867, ch. 149, 150, 151, 153, 154, 170, 14 *Stat.* 427, 428, 430, 486–487.

3. Notes of William A. Moore, private secretary to President Johnson, Johnson MSS, October 26, 1866, Library of Congress, Washington, DC, as quoted in Michael Les Benedict, *The Impeachment and Trial of Andrew Johnson* (New York, 1973), 5.

4. "District of Columbia Franchise Law Veto Message," January 5, 1867, in Johnson, *Papers*, 11:583.

5. Act of March 2, 1867, ch. 153, 14 *Stat.* 428.

6. The Fourteenth Amendment provided that antebellum political office holders who "shall have engaged in insurrection or rebellion" could no longer hold office. The Military Reconstruction Act went further, in that it banned these same antebellum officeholders from voting for delegates or serving as delegates in the state constitutional conventions.

7. Act of March 2, 1867, ch. 153, 14 *Stat.* 429.

8. Andrew Johnson, "Veto of the First Military Reconstruction Act," March 2, 1867, in Johnson, *Papers*, 12:85.

9. Ibid., 12:90–91.

10. Ulysses S. Grant to Elihu B. Washburne, March 4, 1867, in Grant, *Papers*, 17:76.

11. Johnson, "Veto of the First Military Reconstruction Act," 12:91. In fact, Johnson had hosted a delegation of African Americans in 1866, when they had discussed the question. See "Suffrage and Black Americans—A Delegation of Colored Men at the Executive Mansion. The Interview with President Johnson and His Reply, February 7, 1866," in *Proceedings of the Black National and State Conventions*, 1:213–220.

12. Johnson, "Veto of the First Military Reconstruction Act," 12:92.

13. Under the law, while the Senate was in session, the president could remove an official only upon the confirmation of a successor.

14. "Third Annual Message," December 3, 1867, in Johnson, *Papers*, 13:287.

15. *Proceedings in the Trial of Andrew Johnson, President of the United States, before the United States Senate, on Articles of Impeachment, exhibited by the House of Representatives* (Washington, DC, 1868), 5.

16. "Interview with *New York World* Correspondent," March 8, 1868, in Johnson, *Papers*, 13:638.

17. "The Two Impeachments," *Macon Weekly Telegraph*, March 6, 1868, vol. 3, issue 15, 6.

18. "The State of the Country," *Elevator*, March 13, 1868, vol. 3, issue 50, 2.

19. Act of March 28, 1867, ch. 6, 15 *Stat.* 4.

20. The ratifications of Virginia (1869), Mississippi (1870), and Texas (1870) came later.

21. "Third Amnesty Proclamation," in Johnson, *Papers*, 14:318. The amnesty proclamation relieved the threat of prosecution, but it conferred neither the right to vote nor the right to hold office, which remained subject to the regulations outlined in the Military Reconstruction Act and the Fourteenth Amendment, respectively. On Christmas, 1868, Johnson issued another amnesty proclamation that granted full amnesty to anyone charged with treason, Davis included.

22. "Acceptance Letter of General Ulysses S. Grant, May, 29, 1868," in Schlesinger, *History of American Presidential Elections*, 2:1274.

23. "Republican Platform," in Schlesinger, *History of American Presidential Elections*, 2:1270–1271.

24. "General Blair's Letter to Col. Brodhead," June 30, 1868, in *The Political History of the United States during the Period of Reconstruction*, ed. Edward McPherson (Washington, 1871), 381.

25. "Democratic Platform," in Schlesinger, *History of American Presidential Elections*, 2:1268–1269.

26. Allen W. Trelease, *White Terror: The Ku Klux Klan Conspiracy and Southern Reconstruction* (New York, 1971), 135.

27. Frederick Douglass, "The Need for Continued Anti-Slavery Work, speech at the Thirty-Second Annual Meeting of the American Anti-Slavery Society, May 10, 1865," in *Frederick Douglass: Selected Speeches and Writings*, 578.

28. *New York Tribune*, February 26, 1869.

29. "Inaugural Address," March 4, 1869, in Grant, *Papers*, 19:142.

30. *Texas v. White*, 74 U.S. 700, 721 (1869).

31. 74 U.S. 700, 730, 727.

32. 74 U.S. 700, 725–726.

33. William Gillette, *The Right to Vote: Politics and the Passage of the Fifteenth Amendment* (Baltimore, 1965), 92.

34. "Speech by the Hon. Henry M. Turner on the 'Benefits Accruing from the Ratification of the Fifteenth Amendment,' and Its Incorporation into the United States Constitution. Delivered at the Celebration in Macon, Georgia, April 19, 1870," in *Proceedings of the Black National and State Conventions*, 1:417.

35. *American Missionary* 14 (May 1870): 111.

36. Frederick Douglass, "At Last, At Last, the Black Man Has a Future," in *A Just and Lasting Peace: A Documentary History of Reconstruction*, ed. John David Smith (New York, 2013), 374.

37. Act of May 31, 1870, ch. 114, 16 *Stat.* 141.

38. Act of May 31, 1870, ch. 114, 16 *Stat.* 143.

39. Act of April 20, 1871, ch. 22, 17 *Stat.* 14.

40. Alexander H. Stephens, *Reviewers Reviewed: A Supplement to the War Between the States, etc., with an Appendix in Review of "Reconstruction," So Called* (New York, 1872), 188, 193.

41. "Local Intelligence," *Boston Daily Evening Transcript*, September 5, 1872.

42. *United States v. Hall*, 26 F. Cas. 79 (1871).

43. Figures are from October 1871–October 1872. *Report of the Secretary of War, Being Part of the Messages and Documents being communicated to the Two Houses of Congress, at the Beginning of the Third Session of the Forty-Second Congress* (Washington, DC, 1872), 1:84. For the previous year, October 1870–October 1871, the secretary reported "more than two hundred" such temporary detachments. See *Report of the Secretary of War, Being Part of the Messages and Documents Being Communicated to the Two Houses of Congress, at the Beginning of the Second Session of the Forty-Second Congress* (Washington, DC, 1871), 1:63.

44. *Slaughterhouse Cases*, 83 U.S. 36, 71 (1873).

45. 83 U.S. 36, 81.

46. No one knows for certain how many perished in this episode, and recent studies estimate the death toll somewhere between 62 and 150 African Americans. Three whites also died. See LeAnna Keith, *The Colfax Massacre: The Untold Story of Black Power, White Terror, and the Death of Reconstruction* (New York, 2008); Charles Lane, *The Day Freedom Died: The Colfax Massacre, the Supreme Court, and the Betrayal of Reconstruction* (New York, 2008).

47. *New York Times*, April 16, 1873.

48. James E. Sefton, *The United States Army and Reconstruction, 1865–1877* (Baton Rouge, LA, 1967), 262.

49. Ulysses S. Grant to William W. Belknap, September 2, 1874, in Grant, *Papers*, 25:187.

50. Grant's brother-in-law, James F. Casey, served as collector of the port in New Orleans.

51. "Party Division in the United States Senate, 1789–present" (http://www.senate.gov/pagelayout/history/one_item_and_teasers/partydiv.htm) and "Party Divisions of the House of Representatives" (http://history.house.gov/Institution/Party-Divisions/Party-Divisions/).

52. "Draft Annual Message," December 7, 1874, Grant, *Papers*, 25:281.

53. "To the Senate of the United States, January 13, 1875," in Grant, *Papers*, 26:8.

54. 3 *Cong. Rec.* 1748 (1875).

55. E. C. Walker Jr. to Grant, in Grant, *Papers*, 26:294.

56. *United States v. Cruikshank*, 92 U.S. 542 (1876).

57. 92 U.S. 542, 549, 551, 556.

58. *United States v. Reese*, 92 U.S. 214 (1876).

59. 92 U.S. 214, 217, 218, 219.

60. In a new edition of the *Revised Statutes* issued after the decisions in *Cruikshank* and *Reese*, the sections of the Enforcement Act of 1870 remained on the books,

although enforcement efforts declined. See Xi Wang, *The Trial of Democracy: Black Suffrage and Northern Republicans, 1860–1910* (Athens, GA, 1997), 347n165.

61. 92 U.S. 214, 256.

CHAPTER 11. FREEDOM, THE SOUTH, AND THE NORTH

1. "Speech of Mr. Douglass," in *Proceedings of the Republican National Convention, Held at Cincinnati, Ohio, Wednesday, Thursday, and Friday, June, 14, 15, and 16, 1876* (Concord, NH, 1876), 26–27.

2. "Speech of Hon. Linton Stephens, in Macon, Georgia, on the 'Reconstruction Measures' and the 'Enforcement Act' of 1870, Delivered 23^d of January, 1871," in *Biographical Sketch of Linton Stephens, Late Associate Justice of the Supreme Court of Georgia*, ed. James D. Waddell (Atlanta, GA, 1877), 332.

3. Stephens, *Constitutional View*, 1:29.

4. Ibid., 1:10, 81, 19.

5. James L. Roark, *Masters without Slaves: Southern Planters in the Civil War and Reconstruction* (New York, 1977), 68–108.

6. Roger L. Ransom and Richard Sutch, *One Kind of Freedom: The Economic Consequences of Emancipation*, 2nd ed. (New York, 2001), 46, estimate this withdrawal at "between 28 and 37 percent of the quantity of labor that had been extracted through the coercion of slavery."

7. Booker T. Washington, *Up from Slavery* (1901), in *Three Negro Classics*, ed. John Hope Franklin (New York, 1965), 41.

8. According to historian Gavin Wright, the evidence from plantation records in two states shows "not only that [black] tenants frequently left, but that they were often *more* likely to leave if they were heavily in debt." Wright, *Old South, New South: Revolutions in the Southern Economy since the Civil War* (New York, 1986), 65.

9. "A Freedman's Bureau Superintendent of Marriages, to the Freedmen's Bureau Agent at Alexandria, Virginia," in *The Black Military Experience*, ser. 2 of *Freedom: A Documentary History of Emancipation*, ed. Ira Berlin, Joseph P. Reidy, and Leslie S. Rowland (New York, 1982), 672. See also the excellent essay by Laura F. Edwards, "'The Marriage Covenant Is at the Foundation of All Our Rights': The Politics of Slave Marriages in North Carolina after Emancipation," *Law and History Review* 14 (1996): 81–124.

10. "Marriages of Negroes," in Fleming, *Documentary History of Reconstruction*, 1:273.

11. Stowell, *Rebuilding Zion*, 80–81, 90.

12. Ransom and Sutch, *One Kind of Freedom*, 24, 28–30. Literacy figures are aggregate numbers from South Carolina, Georgia, Alabama, Mississippi, and Louisiana. The 26 percent figure, of course, compared unfavorably to that for white children of the same age (65.5 percent) but compared favorably to blacks older than twenty, who had an 18 percent literacy rate.

13. Loren Schweninger, *Black Property Owners in the South, 1790–1915* (Urbana, IL, 1990), 155, 147.

14. Ransom and Sutch, *One Kind of Freedom*, 4; Schweninger, *Black Property Owners*, 183.

15. Melissa Melewski describes these cases in her pathbreaking article, "From Slave to Litigant: African Americans in Court in the Postwar South, 1865–1920," *Law and History Review* 30 (2012): 723–769.

16. *The Position of the Republican and Democratic Parties: A Dialogue Between a White Republican and a Colored Citizen, Published by the Union Republican Congressional Committee* (Washington, DC, 1868), 1–2, 4.

17. Henry McNeal Turner to Thomas Tullock, July 8, 1867, in Richard H. Abbott, "Black Ministers and the Organization of the Republican Party in the South in 1867: Letters from the Field," *Hayes Historical Journal* 6 (1986), http://www.rbhayes.org.

18. Testimony of J. Henri Burch, US Senate, *Report and Testimony of the Select Committee of the United States Senate to Investigate the Causes and Removal of the Negroes from the Southern States to the Northern States*, 46th Cong., 2nd sess., 1880, S. Rep. 693, pt. 2, 232, as quoted in Justin Behrend, *Reconstructing Democracy: Grassroots Black Politics in the Deep South after the Civil War* (Athens, GA, 2015), 202.

19. In *Edwards v. Elliott*, 88 U.S. 532 (1874), relying on the *Slaughterhouse Cases*, the Supreme Court denied that the Seventh Amendment right to trial by jury constituted a federally protected right under the Fourteenth Amendment.

20. *Nashville Banner*, March 1, 1884, as quoted in Howard Rabinowitz, *Race Relations in the Urban South, 1865–1890* (New York, 1978), 40.

21. Eric Foner, *Freedom's Lawmakers: A Directory of Black Officeholders during Reconstruction* (Baton Rouge, LA, 1996), xi–xxxii.

22. "The Attack on the Streetcars by Freedmen in Charleston, SC," *New York Times*, April 2, 1867.

23. "A Republican Member of the Legislature About to Quit the Party," (Columbia, SC) *Daily Phoenix*, September 18, 1868.

24. Michael W. Fitzgerald, "Ex-Slaveholders and the Ku Klux Klan: Exploring the Motivations of Terrorist Violence," in *After Slavery: Race, Labor, and Citizenship in the Reconstruction South*, ed. Bruce E. Baker and Brian Kelly (Gainesville, FL, 2013), 156.

25. *The Respectful Remonstrance, on Behalf of the White People of South Carolina, against the Constitution of the Late Convention of that State, Now Submitted to Congress for Ratification* (Columbia, SC, 1868), 12–13.

26. *Debates and Proceedings of the Convention which assembled at Little Rock, January 7th, 1868, under the Provisions of the Act of Congress of March 2d, 1867, and the Acts of March 23d and July 19th 1867, Supplementary Thereto, to form a Constitution for the State of Arkansas* (Little Rock, AR, 1868), 637.

27. For the contrast between black constitutionalism and white violence in Warren County, Mississippi, see Christopher Waldrep, "Black Political Leadership: Warren County, Mississippi," in *Local Matters: Race, Crime, and Justice in the Nineteenth-Century South*, ed. Christopher Waldrep and Donald G. Nieman (Athens, GA, 2001), 225–249.

28. See Mark Grimsley, "Wars for the American South: The First and Second Reconstructions Considered as Insurgencies," *Civil War History* 58 (2012): 6–36; Gregory P. Downs, *After Appomattox: Military Occupation and the Ends of War* (Cambridge, MA, 2015).

29. "Republican Platform," in Schlesinger, *History of American Presidential Elections*, 2:1443.

30. "Acceptance Letter of Governor Rutherford B. Hayes," July 8, 1876, in Schlesinger, *History of American Presidential Elections*, 2:1449–1450.

31. "Democratic Platform," in Schlesinger, *History of American Presidential Elections*, 2:1437.

EPILOGUE: LIBERTY, UNION, AND AMERICAN
CONSTITUTIONALISM

1. As quoted in Philip S. Foner, "Black Participation in the Centennial of 1876," *Phylon* 39 (1978): 290.

2. *Dred Scott v. Sandford*, 60 U.S. 393, 451, 407 (1857).

3. Schweninger, *Black Property Owners*, 183.

4. John Mercer Langston, "Pacific Reconstruction: The Other Phase of Reconstruction—Pacification the True Policy," in *Freedom and Citizenship: Selected Lectures and Addresses of Hon. John Mercer Langston, LL.D.* (Washington, DC, 1883), 220.

5. *Ex parte Yarbrough*, 110 U.S. 651, 665 (1884). *Propio vigoro* means "by its own force or vigor."

6. *Christian Recorder*, June 21, November 8, 1883, as quoted in David W. Blight, *Race and Reunion: The Civil War in American Memory* (Cambridge, MA, 2001), 310.

7. Davis, *Rise and Fall*, 2:279. On the postwar discussion of secession, particularly its relationship to American traditions of law and constitutionalism, see Cynthia Nicoletti, "The American Civil War as a Trial by Battle," *Law and History Review* 28 (2010): 71–110.

8. E. L. Godkin, "Some Things Overlooked at the Centennial," *Nation* 45 (September 22, 1887): 226.

BIBLIOGRAPHICAL ESSAY

The literature on the American Civil War era is vast and unrelenting. The number of books on Abraham Lincoln alone (more than 16,000, supposedly) is difficult to fathom. What follows is but a small sampling of scholarship—emphasizing the themes of constitutionalism, war, and black activism—that particularly inform the writing of this book. I have attempted to give preference to recent books and articles, but I have also included some classic works.

For overviews of the Civil War and reconstruction era—works that cover ground similar to that covered in this book—see James M. McPherson, *Battle Cry of Freedom: The Civil War Era* (1988); Allen C. Guelzo, *Fateful Lightning: A New History of the Civil War and Reconstruction* (2012); David Goldfield, *America Aflame: How the Civil War Created a Nation* (2011); and Orville Vernon Burton, *The Age of Lincoln* (2007). Laura Edwards's recent study, *A Legal History of the Civil War and Reconstruction* (2015) analyzes the legal issues in greater depth than I do. The best recent essay collection on the Civil War is Edward Ayers, *What Caused the Civil War: Reflections on the South and Southern History* (2006). Two overviews focusing on African American activism are Steven Hahn, *A Nation under Our Feet: Black Political Struggles in the Rural South, from Slavery to the Great Migration* (2003) and Stephen Kantrowitz, *More Than Freedom: Fighting for Black Citizenship in a White Republic, 1829–1889* (2012). The latter two works do not claim to examine the Civil War in any depth, but both show how the war and its aftermath profoundly shaped the black experience. The notion of constitutionalism receives its most comprehensive treatment in Michael Kammen's *A Machine That Would Go of Itself: The Constitution in American Culture* (1986) and Herman Belz's *A Living Constitution or Fundamental Law? American Constitutionalism in Historical Perspective* (1998), while another excellent work, Alexander Tsesis, *For Liberty and Equality: The Life and Times of the Declaration of Independence* (2012), surveys the place of the Declaration of Independence in national life, particularly struggles for justice and equality. David Bodenhamer's *The Revolutionary Constitution* contains a chapter on "Equality" that offers a compelling overview of notions of political and constitutional equality, beginning with the founding and stretching through the nineteenth century and beyond.

On the American founding itself, one should begin with Gordon Wood, *The Creation of the American Republic, 1776–1787* (1969), and Forrest McDonald, *Novus Ordo*

Seclorum: The Intellectual Origins of the Constitution (1985). More recent discussions offering fresh insight include R. B. Bernstein, *The Founding Fathers Reconsidered* (2009); Woody Holton, *Unruly Americans and the Origins of the Constitution* (2007); and Gordon S. Wood, *The Idea of America: Reflections on the Birth of the United States* (2011). The best studies of the Declaration of Independence are Garry Wills, *Inventing America: Jefferson's Declaration of Independence* (1978), and Pauline Maier, *American Scripture: Making the Declaration of Independence* (1998). Larry Kramer, *The People Themselves: Popular Constitutionalism and Judicial Review* (2005), is the foremost work on the notion of popular constitutionalism.

Many scholars have explored the themes of slavery and the Constitution. One should begin with Arthur Bestor's essays, "The American Civil War as a Constitutional Crisis," *American Historical Review* 69 (1964): 327–352, and "State Sovereignty and Slavery: A Reinterpretation of Pro-Slavery Constitutional Doctrine," *Journal of the Illinois State Historical Society* 54 (1961): 117–180. Other landmark works include William Freehling, "The Founding Fathers and Slavery," *American Historical Review* 77 (1972): 81–93; Paul Finkelman, *Slavery and the Founders: Race and Liberty in the Age of Jefferson* (2001); and Don E. Fehrenbacher, *The Slaveholding Republic: An Account of the United States Government's Relations to Slavery* (2001). More recent studies include David Waldstreicher, *Slavery's Constitution: From Revolution to Ratification* (2009), Gordon S. Brown, *Toussaint's Clause: The Founding Fathers and the Haitian Revolution* (2005), and H. Robert Baker, "The Fugitive Slave Clause and the Antebellum Constitution," *Law and History Review* 30 (2012): 1134–1174.

On the issues of slavery and sovereignty in national politics during the early republic—that is, before the 1850s—see Merton L. Dillon, *Slavery Attacked: Southern Slaves and Their Allies, 1619–1865* (1990); Jonathan Earle, *Jacksonian Antislavery and the Politics of Free Soil, 1824–1854* (2004); Don E. Fehrenbacher, *The South and Three Sectional Crises* (1980); Robert Pierce Forbes, *The Missouri Compromise and Its Aftermath: Slavery and the Meaning of America* (2007); William W. Freehling, *Prelude to Civil War: The Nullification Controversy in South Carolina, 1816–1836* (1965); William W. Freehling, *The Road to Disunion: Secessionists at Bay, 1776–1854* (1990); Christian G. Fritz, *American Sovereigns: The People and America's Constitutional Tradition before the Civil War* (2008); Forrest McDonald, *States Rights and the Union: Imperium in Imperio, 1776–1876*, (2000); Matthew Mason, *Slavery and Politics in the Early American Republic* (2006); George William Van Cleve, *A Slaveholders' Union: Slavery, Politics, and the Constitution in the Early American Republic* (2010); and Harry L. Watson, *Liberty and Power: The Politics of Jacksonian America* (2006).

The differences between the antebellum North and South and the experiences of African Americans under slavery have spurred considerable scholarly debate. The best recent overview is Bruce Levine, *Half Slave and Half Free: The Roots of Civil War* (2005). The following is but a tiny sliver of key works that shed light on these subjects: Sven Beckert, *Empire of Cotton: A Global History* (2014); Ira Berlin, *Generations of Captivity: A History of African-American Slaves* (2003); Ira Berlin, *Slaves without Masters: The Free Negro in the Antebellum South* (1974); John Blassingame, *The Slave Community: Planta-*

tion Life in the Antebellum South (1979); William Cooper, *Liberty and Slavery: Southern Politics to 1860* (2000); Marc Egnal, *The Clash of Extremes: The Economic Origins of the Civil War* (2009); Paul Finkelman, "Prelude to the Fourteenth Amendment: Black Legal Rights in the Antebellum North," *Rutgers Law Journal* 17 (1986): 415–482; Lacy K. Ford, *Deliver Us from Evil: The Slavery Question in the Old South* (2009); Lisa Tendrich Frank and Daniel Kilbride, eds., *Southern Character: Essays in Honor of Bertram Wyatt-Brown* (2011); Eugene D. Genovese, *Roll, Jordan, Roll: The World the Slaves Made* (1972); Elizabeth Fox-Genovese and Eugene D. Genovese, *The Mind of the Master Class: History and Faith in the Southern Slaveholders' Worldview* (2005); Sally Hadden, *Slave Patrols: Law and Violence in Virginia and the Carolinas* (2001); Stephen R. Haynes, *Noah's Curse: The Biblical Justification of American Slavery* (2002); Christine Leigh Heyrman, *Southern Cross: The Beginnings of the Bible Belt* (1997); James Oliver Horton and Louis E. Horton, *In Hope of Liberty: Culture, Community, and Protest Among Northern Free Blacks, 1700–1860* (1997); Walter Johnson, *River of Dark Dreams: Slavery and Empire in the Cotton Kingdom* (2013); Walter Johnson, *Soul by Soul: Life Inside the Antebellum Slave Market* (1999); Whittington B. Johnson, *Black Savannah, 1788–1864* (1996); Peter Kolchin, *American Slavery, 1619–1877* (1993); Leon Litwack, *North of Slavery* (1961); James M. McPherson, "Antebellum Southern Exceptionalism: A New Look at an Old Question," *Civil War History* 29 (1983): 230–244; Christopher Morris, *Becoming South: The Evolution of a Way of Life: Warren County and Vicksburg, Mississippi, 1770–1860* (1999); Christopher Olsen, *Political Culture and Secession in Mississippi: Masculinity, Honor, and the Antiparty Tradition, 1830–1860* (2002); Douglass C. North and Robert Paul Thomas, eds., *The Growth of the American Economy to 1860* (1968); Frank Owsley, *Plain Folk of the Old South* (1949); Albert J. Raboteau, *Slave Religion: The "Invisible Institution" in the Antebellum South* (1978); Patrick Rael, *Black Identity and Black Protest in the Antebellum North* (2002); Charles Sellers, *The Market Revolution: Jacksonian America, 1815–1846* (1991); Mark M. Smith, *Debating Slavery: Economy and Society in the Antebellum American South* (1998); Kenneth Stampp, *The Peculiar Institution: Slavery in the Old South* (1956); Ronald G. Walters, *American Reformers, 1815–1860* (1997); Jonathan Daniel Wells, *The Origins of the Southern Middle Class, 1800–1861* (2004); Bertram Wyatt-Brown, *Southern Honor: Ethics and Behavior in the Old South* (1982). On the complex relationship between honor and religion, see Wyatt-Brown, "God and Honor in the Old South," *Southern Review* (1989): 283–296.

On the themes of slavery, race, and sectionalism in national political debates during the 1850s, one should begin with David Potter, *The Impending Crisis, 1846–1861* (1976). Potter's crisp writing and thorough analysis of the sectional political forces that drove the nation toward disunion still stands out after all these years. Michael F. Holt's succinct study, *The Fate of Their Country: Politicians, Slavery Extension, and the Coming of the Civil War* (2004), is also excellent. Other helpful overviews are Richard H. Sewell, *A House Divided: Sectionalism and Civil War, 1848–1865* (1988); John Niven, *The Coming of the Civil War, 1837–1861* (1990); Elizabeth R. Varon, *Disunion! The Coming of the American Civil War, 1789–1859* (2008); and Eric Walther, *The Shattering of the Union: America in the 1850s* (2004). There are a host of more specialized studies, focusing on different aspects of the period. These include Eugene Berwanger, *The Frontier against Slavery: Western Anti-Negro Prejudice and the Slavery Extension Controversy* (1967); Richard Carwardine, *Evangelicals and Politics in Antebellum America* (1997); Christopher Childers, *The Failure of Popular Sovereignty: Slavery, Manifest Destiny, and the Radicalization of Southern Politics* (2012); Charles B. Dew, *Apostles of Disunion: Southern Secession Commissioners and the Causes of the Civil War* (2001); David H. Donald, *Charles Sumner and the Coming of the Civil War* (1960); Yonatan Eyal, *The Young America Movement and the Transformation of the Democratic Party, 1828–1861* (2007); Don E. Fehrenbacher, *Prelude to Greatness: Lincoln in the 1850s* (1962); Paul Finkelman, *His Soul Goes Marching On: Responses to John Brown and the Harper's Ferry Raid* (1995); Eric Foner, *Free Soil, Free Labor, Free Men: The Ideology of the Republican Party before the Civil War* (1995); William W. Freehling, *The Road to Disunion: Secessionists Triumphant, 1854–1861* (2007); Larry Gara, *The Presidency of Franklin Pierce* (1991); Eddie S. Glaude Jr. *Exodus! Religion, Race, and Nation in Early Nineteenth-Century Black America* (2000); Holman Hamilton, *Prologue to Conflict: The Crisis and Compromise of 1850* (1964); Williamjames Hull Hoffer, *The Caning of Charles Sumner: Honor, Idealism, and the Origins of the Civil War* (2010); Robert E. May, *The Southern Dream of a Caribbean Empire, 1854–1861* (1973); John Mayfield, *Rehearsal for Republicanism: Free Soil and the Politics of Anti-Slavery* (1980); Angela Murphy, *The Jerry Rescue: The Jerry Rescue, the Fugitive Slave Law, Northern Rights, and the American Sectional Crisis* (2016); Rita Roberts, *Evangelicalism and the Politics of Reform in Northern Black Thought, 1776–1863* (2010); Elbert B. Smith, *The Presidency of James Buchanan* (1975); Mitchell Snay, *Gospel of Disunion: Religion and Separatism in the Antebellum South* (1993); Kenneth M. Stampp, *America in 1857: A Nation on the Brink* (1990); and Kenneth M. Stampp, "The Concept of a Perpetual Union," *Journal of American History* 65 (1978): 5–33.

There is a rich literature as well on the law, the Constitution, and the courts during the antebellum era and the Civil War. Harold M. Hyman and William M. Wiecek, *Equal Justice Under Law: Constitutional Development, 1835–1875* (1982), is the classic overview of the subject. Some of the most important works include: H. Robert Baker, *Prigg v. Pennsylvania: Slavery, the Supreme Court, and the Ambivalent Constitution* (2012); H. Robert Baker, "A Better Story in *Prigg v. Pennsylvania,*" *Journal of Supreme Court History* 39 (2014): 169–189; Herman Belz, *Abraham Lincoln, Constitutionalism, and Equal Rights in the Civil War Era* (1998); Herman Belz, *Emancipation and Equal Rights: Politics and Constitution in the Civil War Era* (1978); Richard Brookhiser, *Founders' Son: A Life of Abraham Lincoln* (2014); Stanley W. Campbell, *The Slave Catchers: Enforcement of the Fugitive Slave Law, 1850–1860* (1970); David P. Currie, "Through the Looking-Glass: The Confederate Constitution in Congress, 1861–1865," *Virginia Law Review* 90 (2004): 1257–1399; Arthur T. Downey, "The Conflict between the Chief Justice and the Chief Executive: *Ex parte Merryman,*" *Journal of Supreme Court History* 31 (2006): 262–278; Laura Edwards, *A Legal History of the Civil War and Reconstruction: A Nation of Rights* (2015); Daniel Farber, *Lincoln's Constitution* (2003); Don E. Fehrenbacher, *Constitutions and Constitutionalism in the Slaveholding South* (1989); Don E. Fehrenbacher, *The Dred Scott Case: Its Significance in American Law and Politics*

(1978); Paul Finkelman, *An Imperfect Union: Slavery, Federalism, and Comity* (1981); Paul Finkelman, "Lincoln, Emancipation, and the Limits of Constitutional Change," *Supreme Court Review* (2008): 349–387; Sally Hadden and Patricia Hagler Minter, *Signposts: New Directions in Southern Legal History* (2013); Harold Holzer and Sara Vaughn Gabbard, *Lincoln and Freedom: Slavery, Emancipation, and the Thirteenth Amendment* (2007); Mark Graber, *Dred Scott and the Problem of Constitutional Evil* (2006); Kermit L. Hall and James W. Ely Jr., *An Uncertain Tradition: Constitutionalism and the History of the South* (1989); Harold Hyman, *A More Perfect Union: The Impact of the Civil War and Reconstruction on the Constitution* (1975); Timothy S. Huebner, *The Southern Judicial Tradition: State Judges and Sectional Distinctiveness, 1790–1890* (1999); Timothy S. Huebner, *The Taney Court: Justices, Rulings, and Legacy* (2003); Martha S. Jones, "Hughes v. Jackson: Race and Rights Beyond Dred Scott," *North Carolina Law Review* 91 (2013): 1757–1784; James H. Kettner, *The Development of American Citizenship, 1608–1870* (1978); Earl M. Maltz, *"Dred Scott" and the Politics of Slavery* (2007); Earl M. Maltz, *Slavery and the Supreme Court, 1825–1861* (2009); Brian McGinty, *The Body of John Merryman: Abraham Lincoln and the Suspension of Habeas Corpus* (2011); Brian McGinty, *Lincoln and the Court* (2008); Mark E. Neely Jr., *The Fate of Liberty: Abraham Lincoln and Civil Liberties* (1992); Mark E. Neely Jr., *Lincoln and the Triumph of the Nation: Constitutional Conflict in the American Civil War* (2011); Mark E. Neely Jr., *Southern Rights: Political Prisoners and the Myth of Confederate Constitutionalism* (1999); Stephen C. Neff, *Justice in Blue and Gray: A Legal History of the Civil War* (2010); Mackubin Thomas Owens, "Abraham Lincoln as Practical Constitutional Lawyer," in *Abraham Lincoln, Esq.: The Legal Career of America's Greatest President*, ed. Roger Billings and Frank J. Williams (2010), 205–227; Phillip S. Paludan, "The American Civil War Considered as a Crisis in Law and Order," *American Historical Review* 72 (1984): 1013–1034; John B. Robbins, "The Confederacy and the Writ of Habeas Corpus," *Georgia Historical Quarterly* 55 (1971): 83–101; William M. Robinson, *Justice in Grey: A History of the Judicial System of the Confederate States of America* (1941); James F. Simon, *Lincoln and Chief Justice Taney: Slavery, Secession, and the President's War Powers* (2006); Stuart Streichler, *Justice Curtis in the Civil War Era: At the Crossroads of American Constitutionalism* (2005); Christopher Waldrep, *Roots of Disorder: Race and Criminal Justice in the American South, 1817–1880* (1998); William M. Wiecek, *The Sources of Antislavery Constitutionalism in America, 1760–1848* (1977); Jonathan W. White, *Abraham Lincoln and Treason in the Civil War: The Trials of John Merryman* (2011); and John Fabian Witt, *Lincoln's Code: The Laws of War in American History* (2012). See also James McPherson's trenchant essays on Lincoln, liberty, and the Constitution in *Abraham Lincoln and the Second American Revolution* (1991).

The word "voluminous" does not begin to describe the literature on the military aspects of the Civil War itself, the period from 1861 to 1865. One must begin with the work of James McPherson, whose works have shaped the interpretation of the war for a generation. His original textbook, *Ordeal by Fire: The Civil War and Reconstruction*, now in its fourth edition (2010), and his prizewinning narrative, *Battle Cry of Freedom*, remain some of the finest general military histories of the period. Charles P.

Roland, *An American Iliad: The Story of the Civil War,* 2nd ed. (2004), is another classic overview with a military and political emphasis. If Mcpherson writes from a Northern perspective, Roland writes with a bit of a Southern accent. Steven E. Woodworth, one of this generation's finest military historians, offers a compelling narrative of events on the battlefield in *This Great Struggle: America's Civil War* (2011). Other recent works that emphasize the military aspects of the conflict include John Keegan, *The American Civil War: A Military History* (2009); Harry Stout, *Upon the Altar of the Nation: A Moral History of the Civil War* (2005); and Donald Stoker, *The Grand Design: Strategy and the US Civil War* (2010). Each offers its own distinctive insights.

Specialized biographical and military studies of the war include the following: Gabor S. Boritt, ed., *The Gettysburg Nobody Knows* (1997); John Cimprich, *Fort Pillow, a Civil War Massacre, and Public Memory* (2005); Peter Cozzens, *The Darkest Days of the War: The Battles of Iuka and Corinth* (1997); Larry J. Daniel, *Shiloh: The Battle that Changed the Civil War* (1997); Gary Gallagher, *The Confederate War: How Popular Will, Nationalism, and Military Strategy Could Not Stave Off Defeat* (1997); Gary Gallagher, ed., *The Spotsylvania Campaign* (1998); Joseph T. Glatthaar, *General Lee's Army: From Victory to Collapse* (2008); Gary D. Joiner, *Mr. Lincoln's Brown Water Navy: The Mississippi Squadron* (2007); John F. Marszalek, *Sherman's March to the Sea* (2005); James Lee McDonough, *Stones River: Bloody Winter in Tennessee* (1980); James M. McPherson, *Crossroads of Freedom—Antietam: The Battle That Changed the Course of the Civil War* (2002); James M. McPherson, *Embattled Rebel: Jefferson Davis as Commander in Chief* (2014); James M. McPherson, *Tried by War: Lincoln as Commander in Chief* (2008); James M. McPherson, *War on the Water: The Union and Confederate Navies, 1861–1865* (2012); Ethan S. Rafuse, *McClellan's War: The Failure of Moderation in the Struggle for the Union* (2005); Stephen W. Sears, *George B. McClellan: The Young Napoleon* (1988); Brooks Simpson, *Ulysses S. Grant: Triumph over Adversity, 1822–1865* (2000); Jean Edward Smith, *Grant* (2010); Daniel E. Sutherland, "Abraham Lincoln, John Pope, and the Origins of Total War," *Journal of Military History* 56 (1992): 567–586; Joan Waugh, *U. S. Grant: American Hero, American Myth* (2009); Brian Steel Wills, *A Battle from the Start: The Life of Nathan Bedford Forrest* (1992); Terrence J. Winschel, *Triumph and Defeat: The Vicksburg Campaign* (1999); Steven E. Woodworth, *Beneath a Northern Sky: A Short History of the Gettysburg Campaign* (2008); and Steven E. Woodworth, *Six Armies in Tennessee: The Chickamauga and Chattanooga Campaigns* (1998). A subset of the military history of the war is the social history of soldiers, as well as studies of soldiers' motivations for fighting. On these topics, see Gary W. Gallagher, *The Confederate War: How Popular Will, Nationalism, and Military Strategy Could Not Stave Off Defeat* (1997); Gary Gallagher, *The Union War* (2012); Gerald Linderman, *Embattled Courage: The Experience of Combat in the American Civil War* (1987); and James McPherson, *For Cause and Comrades: Why Men Fought in the Civil War* (1997). McPherson also published a precursor to this study in *What They Fought For, 1861–1865* (1995), a series of three introductory lectures on the subject. See also Chandra Manning, *What This Cruel War Was Over: Soldiers, Slavery, and the Civil War* (2008), and James I. Robertson Jr., *Soldiers Blue and Gray* (1998).

There are a number of studies of black activism and the black military experience. Classic works include John Cimprich, *Slavery's End in Tennessee, 1861–1865* (1985); Dudley Taylor Cornish, *The Sable Arm: Negro Troops in the Union Army, 1861–1865* (1956); Louis Gerteis, *From Contraband to Freedman: Federal Policy toward Southern Black, 1861–1865* (1973); Vincent Harding, *There Is a River: The Black Struggle for Freedom in America* (1981); Waldo Martin, *The Mind of Frederick Douglass* (1985); and James McPherson, *The Negro's Civil War: How American Blacks Felt and Acted during the War for the Union* (1965). More recent books include Stephen V. Ash, *Firebrand of Liberty: The Story of Two Black Regiments that Changed the Course of the Civil War* (2008); David S. Cecelski, *The Fire of Freedom: Abraham Galloway and the Slaves' Civil War* (2012); William A. Dobak, *Freedom by the Sword: The US Colored Troops, 1862–1867* (2011); Joseph T. Glatthaar, *Forged in Battle: The Civil War Alliance of Black Soldiers and White Officers* (1990); Sharon Romeo, *Gender and the Jubilee: Black Freedom and the Reconstruction of Citizenship in Civil War Missouri* (2016); Armstead L. Robinson, *Bitter Fruits of Bondage: The Demise of Slavery and the Collapse of the Confederacy, 1861–1865* (2005); and David Williams, *I Freed Myself: African American Self-Emancipation in the Civil War Era* (2014). Scott Hancock, "Crossing Freedom's Fault Line: The Underground Railroad and Recentering African Americans in Civil War Causality," *Civil War History* 59 (2013): 169–205, and Brian Taylor, "A Politics of Service: Black Northerners' Debates over Enlistment in the American Civil War," *Civil War History* 58 (2012): 451–480, are important recent articles. The classic debate over emancipation began with Barbara J. Fields, "Who Freed the Slaves?," in *The Civil War: An Illustrated History*, ed. Geoffrey C. Ward (1990): 178–181, and the rejoinder by James McPherson, "Who Freed the Slaves," in *Drawn with the Sword* (1997), 192–207. The self-emancipation school, building on the work of the massive Freedmen and Southern Society Project at the University of Maryland, now appears ascendant. See Steven Hahn, "Did We Miss the Greatest Slave Rebellion in Modern History?," in *The Political Worlds of Slavery and Freedom* (2009), 55–115. See also the wonderful digital history project run by the University of Richmond, Visualizing Emancipation (http://dsl.richmond.edu/emancipation/).

The politics and policy of the period, on both the Union and Confederate sides, have generated considerable scholarly interest. For the North, the place to start is Phillip Shaw Paludan's classic *"A People's Contest": The Union and Civil War, 1861–1865* (1988), and for the South, Emory Thomas's *The Confederate Nation, 1861–1865* (1985). Other important, more recent, works include the following: Douglas B. Ball, *Financial Failure and Confederate Defeat* (1991); Gabor Boritt, *The Gettysburg Gospel: The Lincoln Speech Nobody Knows* (2006); William Cheek and Aimee Lee Cheek, *John Mercer Langston and the Fight for Black Freedom, 1829–1865* (1989); William J. Cooper Jr., *Jefferson Davis, American* (2000); William J. Cooper Jr., *Jefferson Davis and the Civil War Era* (2008); LaWanda Cox, *Lincoln and Black Freedom: A Study in Presidential Leadership* (1981); William C. Davis, *"A Government of Our Own": The Making of the Confederacy* (1994); William C. Davis, *Look Away: A History of the Confederate States of America* (2002); Brian Dirck, *Lincoln and Davis: Imagining America, 1809–1865* (2001);

David Herbert Donald, *Lincoln* (1995); Paul D. Escott, *After Secession: Jefferson Davis and the Failure of Confederate Nationalism* (1978); Paul D. Escott, *The Confederacy: The Slaveholders' Failed Venture* (2010); Drew Gilpin Faust, *The Creation of Confederate Nationalism: Ideology and Identity in the Civil War South* (1988); Eric Foner, *The Fiery Trial: Abraham Lincoln and American Slavery* (2010); William E. Gienapp, *Abraham Lincoln and Civil War America: A Biography* (2002); Doris Kearns Goodwin, *Team of Rivals: The Political Genius of Abraham Lincoln* (2005); Allen C. Guelzo, *Lincoln's Emancipation Proclamation and the End of Slavery in America* (2004); Daniel Hamilton, *The Limits of Sovereignty: Property Confiscation in the Union and the Confederacy during the Civil War* (2007); Howard Jones, *Blue and Gray Diplomacy: A History of Union and Confederate Foreign Relations* (2010); Bruce Levine, *Confederate Emancipation: Southern Plans to Free and Army Slaves during the Civil War* (2006); Russell McClintock, *Lincoln and the Decision for War: The Northern Response to Secession* (2008); James M. McPherson, *Abraham Lincoln and the Second American Revolution* (1991); William Marvel, *The Great Task Remaining: The Third Year of Lincoln's War* (2010); Stephanie McCurry, *Confederate Reckoning: Power and Politics in the Civil War South* (2010); James Oakes, *Freedom National: The Destruction of Slavery in the United States, 1861–1865* (2013); Phillip Shaw Paludan, *The Presidency of Abraham Lincoln* (1994); George Rable, *The Confederate Republic: A Revolution against Politics* (1994); Heather Cox Richardson, *The Greatest Nation of the Earth: Republican Economic Policies during the Civil War* (1997); Christian G. Samito, *Becoming American under Fire: Irish Americans, African Americans, and the Politics during the Civil War Era* (2009); Thomas E. Schott, *Alexander H. Stephens of Georgia* (1988); Joel H. Silbey, *A Respectable Minority: The Democratic Party in the Civil War Era, 1860–1868* (1977); Jenny Wahl, "Give Lincoln Credit: How Paying for the Civil War Transformed the United States Financial System," *Albany Government Law Review* 3 (2010): 700–740; Jennifer L. Weber, *Copperheads: The Rise and Fall of Lincoln's Opponents in the North* (2006); Ronald C. White Jr., *Lincoln's Greatest Speech: The Second Inaugural Address* (2002); Garry Wills, *Lincoln at Gettysburg: The Words that Remade America* (1992); and William Buck Yearns, *The Confederate Congress* (1960).

The home front encompasses a variety of topics, including family and gender relations, guerillas, urban life, and religion. A handful of the most important recent works include Stephen V. Ash, *When the Yankees Came: Conflict and Chaos in the Occupied South, 1861–1865* (1999); Dennis K. Boman, *Lincoln and Citizens' Rights in Civil War Missouri: Balancing Freedom and Security* (2011); Richard Nelson Current, *Lincoln's Loyalists: Union Soldiers from the Confederacy* (1992); Joseph W. Danielson, *War's Desolating Scourge: The Union's Occupation of North Alabama* (2012); Drew Gilpin Faust, *This Republic of Suffering: Death and the American Civil War* (2008); Lisa Tendrich Frank, *The Civilian War: Confederate Women and Union Soldiers during Sherman's March* (2015); A. Wilson Greene, *Civil War Petersburg: Confederate City in the Crucible of War* (2006); Mark Grimsley, *The Hard Hand of War: Union Military Policy toward Southern Civilians, 1861–1865* (1997); Chester Hearn, *When the Devil Came Down to Dixie: Ben Butler in New Orleans* (1997); Bruce Levine, *The Fall of the House of Dixie: The Civil War and the Social Revolution that Transformed the South* (2013); Stephanie McCurry,

Confederate Reckoning: Power and Politics in the Civil War South (2010); Mark E. Neely Jr., *The Civil War and the Limits of Destruction* (2007); Mark A. Noll, *The Civil War as a Theological Crisis* (2006); Phillip Shaw Paludan, *Victims: A True Story of the Civil War* (1981); and Daniel W. Stowell, *Rebuilding Zion: The Religious Reconstruction of the South, 1863–1877* (1998).

The reconstruction era, a field of particular historiographical controversy during the mid-twentieth century, has witnessed somewhat of a revival of late. The best synthesis remains Eric Foner's detailed *Reconstruction: America's Unfinished Revolution, 1863–1877* (1988), although the abridged version, *A Short History of Reconstruction* (1990), is more manageable. Recent overviews include Michael Fitzgerald, *Splendid Failure: Post Reconstruction in the American South* (2007), and Douglas R. Egerton, *The Wars of Reconstruction: The Brief, Violent History of America's Most Progressive Era* (2014). Another terrific survey, with particular attention to presidents and policy, is Brooks D. Simpson, *The Reconstruction Presidents* (2009). Michael Les Benedict, *Preserving the Constitution: Essays on Politics and the Constitution in the Reconstruction Era* (2006), and Thomas Brown, ed., *Reconstructions: New Perspectives on the Postbellum United States* (2006), are important recent collection of essays.

Specialized studies of the political and constitutional aspects of the period are numerous. Two themes stand out: the contest between Johnson and the Radicals in Congress and the extent to which reconstruction brought about a constitutional revolution. Important studies include Bruce Ackerman, *We the People: Transformations*, vol. 2 (1998); Paul H. Bergeron, *Andrew Johnson's Civil War and Reconstruction* (2011); Michael Les Benedict, *A Compromise of Principle: Congressional Republicans and Reconstruction, 1863–1869* (1974); Edward J. Blum, *Reforging the White Republic: Race, Religion, and American Nationalism, 1865–1898* (2005); Albert Castel, *The Presidency of Andrew Johnson* (1979); Paul A. Cimbala and Randall M. Miller, eds., *The Freedman's Bureau and Reconstruction: Reconsiderations* (1999); Paul A. Cimbala and Randall M. Miller, eds., *The Great Task Remaining Before Us: Reconstruction as America's Continuing Civil War* (2010); Garrett Epps, *Democracy Reborn: The Fourteenth Amendment and the Fight for Equal Rights in Post–Civil War America* (2006); Mary Farmer-Keiser, *Freedwomen and the Freedmen's Bureau: Race, Gender, and Public Policy in the Age of Emancipation* (2010); William Gillette, *The Right to Vote: Politics and the Passage of the Fifteenth Amendment* (1965); Michael F. Holt, *By One Vote: The Disputed Presidential Election of 1876* (2008); Ari Hoogenboom, *The Presidency of Rutherford B. Hayes* (1988); Joseph B. James, *The Ratification of the Fourteenth Amendment* (1984); Alexander Keyssar, *The Right to Vote: The Contested History of Democracy in the United States* (2000); William S. McFeely, *Yankee Stepfather: General O. O. Howard and the Freedmen* (1968); Gerard N. Magliocca, *American Founding Son: John Bingham and the Invention of the Fourteenth Amendment* (2013); Earl Maltz, *Civil Rights, the Constitution, and Congress, 1863–1869* (1990); Earl Maltz, *The Fourteenth Amendment and the Law of the Constitution* (2003); Kate Masur, *An Example for All the Land: Emancipation and the Struggle over Equality in Washington, DC* (2010); Richard A. Primus, "The Riddle of Hiram Revels," *Harvard Law Review* (2012): 1–52; Leonard L. Richards, *Who Freed the Slaves? The Fight over the*

Thirteenth Amendment (2015); Brooks D. Simpson, *Let Us Have Peace: Ulysses S. Grant and the Politics of War and Reconstruction, 1861–1868* (1991); Mark Wahlgren Summers, *A Dangerous Stir: Fear, Paranoia, and the Making of Reconstruction* (2009); Hans L. Trefousse, *Thaddeus Stevens: Nineteenth-Century Egalitarian* (1997); and Michael Vorenberg, *Final Freedom: The Civil War, the Abolition of Slavery, and the Thirteenth Amendment* (2001). David Kyvig, *Explicit and Authentic Acts: Amending the US Constitution, 1776–1995* (1996), offers a nice overview of the amendment process during the period in the context of larger efforts to amend the Constitution.

Southern violence and the role of the executive in enforcement of African Americans' rights has been the subject of surprisingly little scholarship relative to the political and constitutional debates of the era. On Southern violence, see Stephen V. Ash, *A Massacre in Memphis: The Race Riot that Shook the Nation One Year after the Civil War* (2013); Nicholas Lemann, *Redemption: The Last Battle of the Civil War* (2006); George Rable, *But There Was No Peace: The Role of Violence in the Politics of Reconstruction* (1984); and Hannah Rosen, *Terror in the Heart of Freedom: Citizenship, Sexual Violence, and the Meaning of Race in the Postemancipation South* (2009). Allen W. Trelease, *White Terror: The Ku Klux Klan Conspiracy and Southern Reconstruction* (1971), is the classic study of the topic. Jean Edward Smith, *Grant* (2001), offers a favorable view of Grant and enforcement, while William S. McFeely, *Grant: A Biography* (1982), is more critical. The only comprehensive study of federal enforcement efforts is Xi Wang, *The Trial of Democracy: Black Suffrage and Northern Republicans, 1860–1910* (1997), while a good political history of the "Southern question" and enforcement during the late nineteenth century is Charles W. Calhoun, *Conceiving a New Republic: The Republican Party and the Southern Question, 1869–1900* (2006). Greg Downs, *After Appomattox: Military Occupation and the End of War* (2015), examines the role of the military. Robert Kaczorowski, *The Politics of Judicial Interpretation: The Federal Courts, Department of Justice, and Civil Rights, 1866–1876* (1985); Everett Swinney, "Enforcing the Fifteenth Amendment, 1870–1877," *Journal of Southern History* 28 (1962): 202–218; and Lou Falkner Williams, *The Great South Carolina Ku Klux Klan Trials, 1871–1872* (1996), are essential studies. Timothy S. Huebner, "Emory Speer and Federal Enforcement of the Rights of African Americans, 1880–1910," *American Journal of Legal History* 55 (2015): 34–63, takes the story beyond the traditional boundaries of reconstruction.

The role of the Supreme Court in reconstruction has been a favorite topic among constitutional historians. The starting points are Stanley I. Kutler, *Judicial Power and Reconstruction Politics* (1968), and Michael Les Benedict, "Preserving Federalism: Reconstruction and the Waite Court," *Supreme Court Review* (1978): 39–79. More recently, Pamela Brandwein builds on Benedict's insights in *Rethinking the Judicial Settlement of Reconstruction* (2011). In contrast to those who posit a simple declension narrative—that the Court abandoned African Americans—Brandwein shows that the Court's record was far more nuanced and accommodating of black rights, particularly political and civil rights. A number of other works deal with the biographical and jurisprudential aspects of the Court during this era. See Robert M. Goldman, *Reconstruction and Black Suffrage: Losing the Vote in Reese and Cruikshank* (2001); Paul Kens,

The Supreme Court under Morrison R. Waite, 1874–1888 (2010); Ronald M. Labbe and Jonathan Lurie, *The Slaughterhouse Cases: Regulation, Reconstruction, and the Fourteenth Amendment* (2003); Michael A. Ross, *Justice of Shattered Dreams: Samuel Freeman Miller and the Supreme Court during the Reconstruction Era* (2003); William Van Alstyne, "A Critical Guide to *Ex Parte McCardle*," *Arizona Law Review* 15 (1973): 229–269; Christopher Waldrep, *Jury Discrimination: The Supreme Court, Public Opinion, and a Grassroots Fight for Racial Equality in Mississippi* (2010); Christopher Waldrep, *Vicksburg's Long Shadow: The Civil War Legacy of Race and Remembrance* (2005); and R. Volney Riser, *Defying Disfranchisement: Black Voting Rights Activism in the Jim Crow South, 1890–1908* (2010). Finally, Cynthia Nicoletti, "Strategic Litigation the Death of Reconstruction," in *Signposts: New Directions in Southern Legal History*, ed. Sally E. Hadden and Patricia Hagler Minter (2013), offers a look at Democratic attempts to overthrow reconstruction in the courts.

The social, economic, and political consequences of the war in the Southern and Northern states are explored in the following works: Bruce Baker and Brian Kelly, eds., *After Slavery: Race, Labor, and Citizenship in the Reconstruction South* (2013); Justice Behrend, *Reconstructing Democracy: Grassroots Black Politics in the Deep South after the Civil War* (2014); Russell Duncan, *Freedom's Shore: Tunis Campbell and the Georgia Freedmen* (1986); William Cohen, *At Freedom's Edge: Black Mobility and the Southern Quest for White Racial Control, 1861–1915* (1991); Hugh Davis, *"We Will Be Satisfied with Nothing Less": The African American Struggle for Equal Rights in the North during Reconstruction* (2011); Gregory P. Downs, *Declarations of Dependence: The Long Reconstruction of Popular Politics in the South, 1861–1908* (2011); Edmund Drago, *Black Politicians and Reconstruction in Georgia: A Splendid Failure* (1992); Laura F. Edwards, "'The Marriage Covenant Is at the Foundation of All Our Rights': The Politics of Slave Marriages in North Carolina After Emancipation," *Law and History Review* 14 (1996): 81–124; Steven Hahn, *The Roots of Southern Populism: Yeoman Farmers and the Transformation of the Georgia Upcountry, 1850–1890* (1983); Susan O'Donovan, *Becoming Free in the Cotton South* (2007); Michael Perman, *Emancipation and Reconstruction* (2003); Roger L. Ransom, "Fact and Counterfact: The 'Second American Revolution' Revisited," *Civil War History* 45 (1999): 28–60; Roger L. Ransom and Richard Sutch, *One Kind of Freedom: The Economic Consequences of Emancipation*, 2nd ed. (2001); Heather Cox Richardson, *The Death of Reconstruction: Race, Labor, and Politics in the Post–Civil War North, 1865–1901* (2001); C. Vann Woodward, *The Strange Career of Jim Crow*, 3rd rev. ed. (1974); Gavin Wright, *Old South, New South: Revolutions in the Southern Economy since the Civil War* (1986); and Bertram Wyatt-Brown, *The Shaping of Southern Culture: Honor, Grace, and War, 1760s–1880s* (2001). Martin Ruef, *Between Slavery and Capitalism: The Legacy of Emancipation in the American South* (2014), written from a sociological perspective, provides useful insights, although its use of disciplinary jargon might be off-putting to some historians. James M. McPherson's essay, "The Second American Revolution," in *Abraham Lincoln and the Second American Revolution* (1991), nicely captures the changes that resulted from the war.

INDEX

Ableman, Stephen, 108–109
Ableman v. Booth (1859), 108–109
abolitionism, 48–54, 75, 78, 87, 92,
    108, 212, 235, 244
    and the Constitution, 56–58, 61–63,
      81–84
    anti-Garrisonian, 57–58
    effect of *Uncle Tom's Cabin* on, 72
    and free soil, 63
    Garrisonian, 45, 52, 57, 81, 83
    religion as basis of, 39, 45–46, 235
    southern opposition to, 36–37, 39,
      56, 62, 80, 118, 149
    and support for black soldiers,
      300–301
    and Thirteenth Amendment,
      328–329
    violence as a tactic of, 75–76,
      109–111
    See also black constitutionalism;
      emancipation
Adams, John, 19
"Address to the People of the
    Confederacy," 277–278
African Americans, 22
    in antebellum North, 47–54
    celebrate centennial, 439
    colonization of, 36, 48, 81, 229,
      231–232
    emigration of, 51, 53, 72, 81, 95,
      229

    at Lincoln's second inauguration,
      333
    literacy rates of, 416
    lived experience of freedom,
      412–419
    migration to Africa by, 48
    as officeholders, 399, 422–423
    political rights of in antebellum
      North, 48
    protests Johnson's order regarding
      lands of freedpeople, 346–347
    revolutionary experience of during
      Civil War, 320–321, 324
    as sailors, 300, 304
    serve on juries during reconstruction,
      394
    as soldiers, 183, 208, 276, 285–286,
      300–305
    view of Civil War, 299–305
    view of Johnson's impeachment, 377
    view of Lincoln's election, 115
    view of Lincoln's inauguration, 127
    vote in elections for state
      constitutional convention
      delegates, 374–375
    See also black constitutionalism;
      emancipation; free blacks; slaves
African Methodist Episcopal Church,
    51, 70, 415
African Methodist Episcopal Zion
    Church, 415

Freedman's Bureau, 345–347,
   352–353, 368, 369, 414, 415
Freedom's Journal, 49
free labor
   antebellum North and, 22, 44,
      432–433
   and free soil argument, 63
   Lincoln's antislavery views and, 216
   as unifying ideology of Republican
      Party, 135, 218, 223, 225
Freeport Doctrine, 104
free soil, 21, 55, 63, 87, 95, 134, 223
Free Soil Party, 65–67, 72, 78, 82
free speech, 36, 86
Fremont, John C., 87, 145, 229–230,
   244–245, 384
Fugitive Slave Act of 1793, 48, 59–61,
   88, 134
Fugitive Slave Act of 1850, 69–71, 127,
   134
   contrast with Enforcement Acts, 392
   controversy over enforcement of,
      75–76, 81, 99, 107–109, 218
   passage of, 69–71
   repeal of, 230
Fugitive Slave Clause. *See under*
   Constitution, US
fugitive slave issue, 8–9, 56, 58, 58–61,
   70–72, 81, 84, 95
   Burns case, 75–76
   and federal enforcement efforts,
      107–109
   Lincoln and, 125–126
   in secession crisis, 117, 118, 120
   See also Fugitive Slave Act of 1793;
      Fugitive Slave Act of 1850;
      slaveholders' rights
Fuller, Melville, 449

Gaines Mill, Battle of, 162
Galloway, Abraham, 285, 301, 322–323
Garfield, James, 444
Garnett, Henry Highland, 51, 52

Garrison, William Lloyd, 45, 52, 81, 87
   reacts to congressional passage of
      Thirteenth Amendment, 330
   supports Lincoln, Union, and
      Republicans in wartime, 295
   view of the Constitution, 45, 57,
      83–84
gender relations, 37, 44–45, 224,
   306–308, 318, 414. *See also*
   women
General Amnesty Act, 394
Georgia, 7, 27, 31, 33, 70, 80, 100,
   118, 175, 201, 230
   attempt to reopen slave trade in, 106
   constitutional changes (1861) in,
      270
   law providing for readmission of,
      380
   military operations in, 190–191,
      196, 201–205
   postwar education of African
      Americans in, 416
   reconstruction in, 390–391
   "redemption" of, 429
   role in debate over conscription,
      259–260
   violence against African Americans
      in, 384
Gettysburg, Battle of, 175, 185–188,
   190, 193, 196, 201, 239
   as example of hard war, 209
   impact on Confederate morale, 277
   national cemetery at, 241, 319
   Pickett's Charge, 187, 192
Gettysburg Address, 240–243, 334
Glover, Joshua, 108
Godkin, E. L., 448
Gorgas, Josiah, 280
Grant, Ulysses S., 143, 152, 175, 182,
   196, 199, 246, 278, 368
   African Americans praise, 395
   appointed by Johnson to replace
      Stanton, 373